ADO: ActiveX Data Objects

ADO: ActiveX Data Objects

Jason T. Roff

O'REILLY®

Beijing · Cambridge · Farnham · Köln · Paris · Sebastopol · Taipei · Tokyo

ADO: ActiveX Data Objects
by Jason T. Roff

Copyright © 2001 O'Reilly & Associates, Inc. All rights reserved.
Printed in the United States of America.

Published by O'Reilly & Associates, Inc., 101 Morris Street, Sebastopol, CA 95472.

Editors: Nancy Kotary, John Osborn, and Ron Petrusha

Production Editors: Jeffrey Holcomb and Sarah Jane Shangraw

Cover Designer: Hanna Dyer

Printing History:

June 2001:   First Edition.

Library of Congress Cataloging-in-Publication Data

Roff, Jason T.
     ADO ActiveX data objects / Jason T. Roff.
         p. cm.
     ISBN 1-56592-415-0
     1. Internet programming. 2. ActiveX. 3. Web sites. I. Title.

QA76.625 .R64 2001
005.2'76--dc21   2001033138

[M]

Table of Contents

Preface

This book is about ActiveX Data Objects (ADO), including Version 2.6, the latest release of ADO from Microsoft at the time of publication. In this Preface, I will first briefly introduce ADO and explain how the book is organized.

Introduction and Organization

This book is organized into three parts, as described in the following sections.

Part I: Learning ADO

ADO is Microsoft's advanced universal data-access solution, consisting of an object model–based wrapper around OLE DB, which is a technology that allows data-access functionality to different types of data sources. This allows companies such as Oracle, Microsoft, and Sybase to develop what are called "data providers," to do just that—provide data to the OLE DB technology. OLE DB technology can work with all kinds of data sources, including relational databases such as SQL Server or an email system such as Exchange. OLE DB and ADO can even deal with plain text files and Excel spreadsheets. Chapter 1, *Introduction to ADO*, and Chapter 2, *The ADO Architecture*, provide more information on ADO, related technologies, and the structure of key ADO components.

ADO adds a common programming interface to OLE DB, thus allowing developers to use existing skills with multiple languages. ADO can be used with virtually any development language that supports COM, such as Visual Basic, Visual C++, J++, JScript, and VBScript. Developing with ADO in each of these languages is discussed in Chapter 3, *Accessing ADO with Various Languages*. ADO was designed to encourage DAO and RDO developers to migrate to this new technology, without the burden of the many different objects of DAO and RDO.

ADO is a lightweight, disconnected object model, which means that it has few objects, as compared to DAO or RDO, and that the objects do not necessarily rely on each other. For instance, one of the most common objects of ADO is the Connection object (Chapter 4, *The Connection Object*). This object establishes a physical connection with a data source. But you don't need it: the other objects of ADO, such as the Command object, which issues textual commands to the data source, and the Recordset object (Chapter 5, *The Recordset Object*), which is used to store a result set, can create their Connection objects internally if they need to. Of course they use some default options, and hence the advantage of creating your own Connection—more power and control over your data access.

The Fields Collection object represents, unsurprisingly, a collection of fields contained in every Recordset object. Chapter 6, *Fields*, explains the Fields Collection object, as well as the Field objects.

Another example of ADO disconnected object model is the Command object, covered in Chapter 7, *The Command Object*. The Command object issues commands such as SQL statements. You can actually issue statements through the Connection object if you don't mind using the default values. In this case the Connection object creates its own Command object internally to get the job done.

Asynchronous operations are a very big selling feature with a data-access technology—and ADO definitely does not fall short in this category. With the ability to fire events when asynchronous operations are executing and when they complete, ADO offers much greater control of your data access than did previous data-access technologies such as DAO. In addition to asynchronous operations, events can be fired for transactions, connecting and disconnecting to a data source, as well as moving around a recordset and changing values within it. Events are covered in Chapter 8, *The ADO Event Model*.

One of the unique features of ADO is its ability to use the Data Shaping data provider, which allows you to write code that can store hierarchical data within a single Recordset object. It allows you to shape result sets into parent-child relationships, where a single field value can contain an entire child recordset. Data shaping is covered in Chapter 9, *Data Shaping*.

A newer functionality in ADO is the ability to connect to web resources with not only the Recordset object, which stores result sets, but with the Record object, which stores individual rows, and the Stream object, which represents the actual content of a resource, such as a file or a directory. Chapter 10, *Records and Streams*, explains these topics.

Remote Data Services (RDS) extends ADO functionality to three-tier web applications. Chapter 11, *Remote Data Services*, provides an overview of RDS.

Chapter 12, *The Microsoft .NET Framework and ADO.NET*, offers a glimpse into the next generation of ADO and related technologies, in the form of ADO.NET and the .NET Framework and how they will interact with today's ADO projects.

Part II: Reference Section

Part II consists of Chapter 13, *ADO API Reference*. For this chapter, I have compiled an exhaustive list of every object, method, property, event, and enumeration in an easy-to-use alphabetical reference. See also Appendix E.

Part III: Appendixes

Appendix A, *Introduction to SQL*, provides just that—an introduction to using SQL with the Microsoft Jet Engine SQL language, including record selection, data manipulation, and database modification.

In Appendix B, *The Properties Collection*, I explain the Properties collection, which exists within and provides information about ADO objects. ADO is a flexible framework that exposes the functionality of the data provider. Nothing guarantees what functionality a data provider will actually provide your application, but ADO does dictate the interface used for supported functionality. ADO has what it calls "dynamic properties," which can be used to understand the functionality supported by the data provider and to set data provider specific properties that aren't part of the ADO framework. This flexibility that ADO offers contributes to its longevity.

Appendix C, *ADO Errors*, lists trappable errors and data-provider errors, as well as methods for handling them.

Appendix D, *The ADO Data Control*, explains the ADO Data Control Property Pages and how to create connection strings with the Data Control property, including an example application.

The companion to the Chapter 13 reference is Appendix E, *Enumeration Tables*, which alphabetically lists enumerations used by ADO objects and collections.

About the Book

This book covers ActiveX Data Objects up to Version 2.6. It covers every class, method, property, and enumeration included with this release. This book has three sections; the first is a tutorial that explains how each of these components work, with examples in Visual Basic along the way. The second part of this book is a practical reference guide that allows you to easily look up any component to see every piece of detailed information available for it. The third part of this book contains several appendixes providing related information, as well as reference tables.

Although this book includes small sections on Remote Data Objects (RDO), ADO.NET (from Microsoft's .NET Framework), and SQL, it by no means attempts to cover these subjects to any degree of completeness.

Audience

While this book is intended for any person interested in learning about ADO, it is targeted more specifically to the experienced Visual Basic developer who understands the basic principles behind data access and manipulation. This book provides many introductions to secondary topics, including SQL (Appendix A), RDS (Chapter 11), and others, in order to help the less-experienced reader understand all facets of ADO in context.

This book assumes that you know how to develop in Visual Basic—or you at least understand how to read it. Knowledge of one of Microsoft's early database technologies (DAO or RDO) is helpful, but not necessary.

Conventions Used in This Book

I use the following font conventions in this book:

Italic is used for:

- New terms where they are defined

- Internet addresses, such as domain names and URLs

- Pathnames, filenames, and program names

`Constant width` is used for:

- Code examples for Visual Basic, C++, Java, and other languages

- Specific names and keywords in Visual Basic programs, including method names, property names, variable names, enumeration names, constants, and class names

`Constant width italic` is occasionally used for placeholder items in code, replaceable by a specific item in your code.

Comments and Questions

I have tested and verified the information in this book to the best of my ability, but you may find that features have changed (or even that I have made mistakes!).

Please let me know about any errors you find, as well as your suggestions for future editions, by writing to:

O'Reilly & Associates, Inc.
101 Morris Street
Sebastopol, CA 95472
(800) 998-9938 (in the United States or Canada)
(707) 829-0515 (international/local)
(707) 829-0104 (fax)

There is a web page for this book, which lists errata, any plans for future editions, or any additional information. You can access this page at:

http://www.oreilly.com/catalog/ado/

To comment or ask technical questions about this book, send email to:

bookquestions@oreilly.com

For more information about books, conferences, software, Resource Centers, and the O'Reilly Network, see the O'Reilly web site at:

http://www.oreilly.com

Acknowledgments

The people I need to acknowledge the most are the good folk at O'Reilly & Associates, starting with Ron Petrusha, who put up with me while still insisting on a quality piece of work. John Osborn and Nancy Kotary brought it home. Thank you very much for your expertise, guidance, persistence, and understanding.

I need to thank the technical reviewers who—while they didn't go easy on me— didn't beat me up too bad, either. This includes Bob Beauchemin and Ben Willet's MDAC team over at Microsoft: Steve Hoberecht, Rick Feinauer, and Irene Smith. I'd also like to thank the O'Reilly Production staff. Specifically, thanks to my Production Editors, Jeffrey Holcomb and Sarah Jane Shangraw, and the additional Production staff who worked on this book: Linley Dolby, Matt Hutchinson, and Claire Cloutier.

And last but not least, my wife, who put up with me working on this book, before we were married, after we were married, before she was pregnant, while she was pregnant, and after she gave birth to my son, Zachary—the real reason I finished this book. I love you both.

I

Learning ADO

1

Introduction to ADO

In today's computing environments, data exists in many formats, ranging from Access and SQL Server databases to Word documents, email messages, and many others. ADO, or ActiveX Data Objects, data-access technology simplifies use of data from multiple sources, thus freeing developers from learning data, vendor-specific API calls, and any other coding minutiae for each data format involved. With ADO, almost any data source becomes accessible in a consistent way for developers creating standalone applications, client/server applications, or ASP pages.

In this chapter, I define ADO in the historic and current context of Microsoft's overall data-access strategy and related technologies.

ADO in Context: Universal Data Access

Microsoft's philosophy behind ADO and a series of related technologies is *Universal Data Access* (UDA). UDA isn't a tangible product or technology, but rather a strategy for attacking the problem of data access, whose goal is efficient and powerful data access, regardless of data source or development language. Moreover, this universal access is meant to eliminate the need to convert existing data from one proprietary format to another.

With this lofty goal in view, Microsoft developed a series of technologies, collectively known as *Microsoft Data Access Components* (MDAC), that allow developers to implement UDA. MDAC consists of the following four key pieces:

- ODBC (Open Database Connectivity)
- OLE DB (Object Linking and Embedding Databases)

- ADO (ActiveX Data Objects)

- RDS (Remote Data Service)

These components implement the UDA vision both individually and as a whole. To best understand ADO in context, you should have a basic understanding of each MDAC technology and its relationship to ADO.

ODBC

Open Database Connectivity, or ODBC, provides access to relational databases through a standard API, addressing the problem of native application—and platform-specific APIs and their lack of cross-application compatibility. ODBC's industry-standard architecture offers an interface to any Database Management System (DBMS), such as SQL Server or Oracle, that uses the standard ODBC API. The main drawbacks of ODBC are the amount of work required to develop with it and its restriction to SQL-based data sources.

Two COM components (Component Object Model—see "ADO and COM: Language Independence" later in this chapter) designed to help with ODBC complications are DAO and RDO, described briefly in later sections in this chapter.

Jet/DAO

With the release of Microsoft Access 1.1 in 1993, Microsoft introduced the Jet Database Engine, which worked with Access databases (Microsoft Access Databases, or MDB files), ODBC-supported data sources, and Indexed Sequential Access Method databases (ISAM, which includes Excel, dBase, and a few other databases).

Data Access Objects (DAO) was introduced as a means of interacting with Jet. DAO, through COM, provided an object-oriented interface to Jet and Microsoft Access.

Jet and DAO were successful in their flexibility but added layers to the ODBC API and were therefore more efficient for some databases (Access/MDB and ISAM) than others, including Relational Database Management Systems (RDBMS). DAO is still widely used today, but it is most appropriate for single-user, low-traffic database applications. The problem with DAO, as many soon began to see, was that it was *so* full-featured that it brought with it a profusion of objects. Figure 1-1 shows the DAO object model.

As you will see later in this chapter and in other chapters, ADO was designed to address this and other problems with DAO.

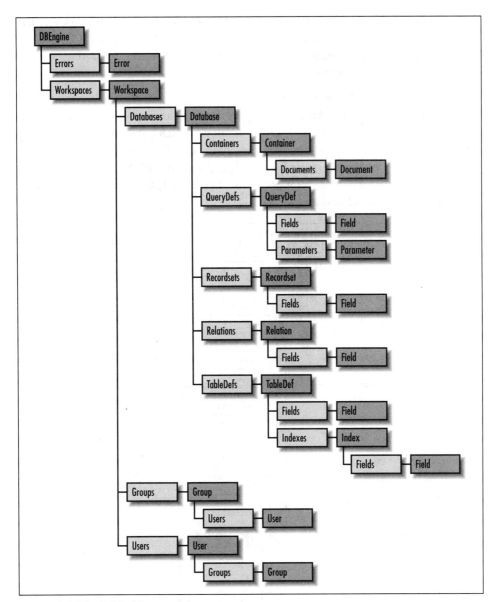

Figure 1-1. The DAO object model

RDO

Microsoft's response to the developer's need for easier access to ODBC data sources came, in 1995, in the form of *Remote Data Objects*, or RDO. RDO provided more direct, and therefore faster, access to the ODBC API, as well as support for RDBMS sources. With RDO, the emphasis moved from data-access methods designed for ISAM databases toward techniques to provide for stored procedures and the results that they returned. RDO lacked some of the power that DAO offered with Jet (for instance, RDO is not designed to access ISAM sources and does not allow the creation of new databases), but it offered more power for newer, more robust enterprise systems.

The problem with RDO is that it is very different from the DAO architecture, which means two things. First, developers had to learn a new interface, and second, converting an existing DAO application to RDO involved a lot of additional development, because almost every piece of RDO differed from DAO, as you can see by comparing Figure 1-1 and Figure 1-2 (the RDO object model). With the introduction of RDO, developers chose between DAO and RDO instead of moving directly to RDO and abandoning DAO.

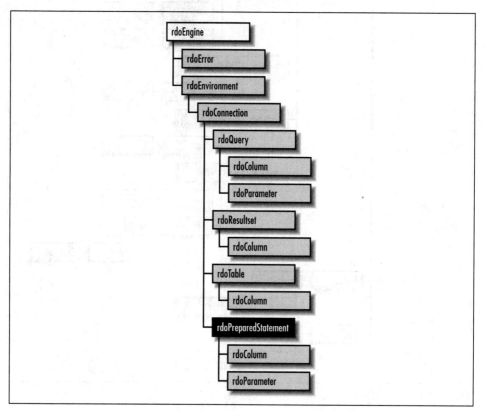

Figure 1-2. The RDO object model

ODBCDirect

ODBCDirect was provided as part of a later release of DAO; to save time, it allows developers to work directly with Access sources without using Jet as the go-between. It is similar to DAO's object model but includes RDO's direct access to remote data sources.

OLE DB

ODBC provides access only to relational databases. Its successor, Object Linking and Embedding Databases (OLE DB), includes all other data sources. OLE DB is the foundation upon which ADO relies.

OLE DB provides the following features:

- Access to data regardless of its format or location (via COM—see "ADO and COM: Language Independence" later in this chapter)
- Full access to ODBC data sources and ODBC drivers
- A specification that Microsoft wants to act as a standard throughout the industry

OLE DB comprises four types of components; Figure 1-3 shows their relationships, which are described here:

Data consumer
> Any application or tool that accesses data from a data source. While the API calls that are available to access the data in your database are considered data providers, the application that uses that data itself is a data consumer, since it requests the data from the data provider.

Data service provider
> The engine that makes OLE DB work; the resource necessary for a data provider to be able to provide data. A data service provider is a modular or add-on component that allows an application to deliver data through OLE DB. Data service providers are usually provided by the vendor for major products such as Oracle, DB2, and Informix. Microsoft promotes the creation of data service providers by either the manufacturer of the data provider or a third-party company.

Business component
> A go-between for a data provider and a data consumer. In today's development environment, it is becoming more and more important not to develop in such a way that every object in your application manipulates your data. With a business component that you call to access your data, which in turn calls your database access component (ADO, RDO, ODBC, OLE DB, or ADO), then you need only modify the code in that business component.

Data provider
> A component (application or database engine, for example) that delivers data from a data source (such as a database, spreadsheet, or email message) in a consistent manner.

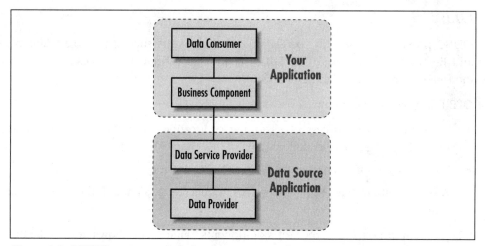

Figure 1-3. OLE DB component relationships

ODBC, as we have just seen, is an excellent technology for accessing SQL-based data. OLE DB incorporates this proven technology with a particular component that allows OLE DB *consumers* to communicate directly with ODBC *providers*. In other words, use OLE DB to access SQL-based data, and you gain the advantage of being able to access both relational and other forms of data with the same code.

As they have done with ODBC, Microsoft is actively encouraging software vendors and tool developers to support the OLE DB standard within their applications and tools. Widespread standardization is an advantage for developers; with OLE DB, we can ensure that our applications become more robust and more powerful as they span the enterprise.

Keep in mind that OLE DB was designed for software vendors who develop data-based applications to expose that data to you, an end-user developer, through a consistent interface. OLE DB is fast, efficient, and powerful. It has everything a developer looks for in a data-access technology. It offers access to any data source known to man (or to Windows, for that matter), and it provides access to these data sources with a consistent interface, regardless of data source. The problem with OLE DB is that, like ODBC, it is inaccessible to Visual Basic and other developers, because it is based on a C-style API. Visual Basic developers, in particular, needed more.

ADO

Enter ActiveX Data Objects (ADO). ADO, an application-level interface to OLE DB, is the latest, greatest piece of Microsoft's UDA strategy. It combines the best features of its predecessors, DAO and RDO, and adds OLE DB accessibility for VBA programmers. ADO provides a consistent, language-independent means to access data from almost any source, including text-based or other legacy data in relational and nonrelational formats. (You can now see why I needed to explain some of the alphabet soup before getting to ADO itself.)

ADO comprises a collection of object libraries in a new, modular object model: in this new model, many objects can exist independently of the others, as you will see in later chapters of this book. The ADO object model is more flexible than the DAO object model, but it's similar, so programmers familiar with DAO will feel at home with ADO. ADO is a smaller version of DAO, generalized to allow easy access to any data source, not just Jet databases or ODBC data sources. The ADO object model simplifies data access more than DAO or RDO did by using fewer objects. See Figure 1-1 and also Chapter 2, *The ADO Architecture*, for more information.

Used with OLE DB, ADO provides fast, simple access to almost any data source. It allows developers to use a single, consistent interface to new and legacy databases and other data sources of all formats, when creating desktop—or web-based—applications.

ADO can also use the OLE DB provider for ODBC. Instead of removing the already proven and tested code for ODBC drivers, ADO allows you to use ODBC through the same interface you would for OLE DB. This may be an option when you have code you are migrating from RDO, which already uses ODBC.

ADO breaks the common characteristics of all data sources into easy-to-use components (which we will look at in Chapter 2). Consistency and language-independence are provided, so that developers can worry more about the content and quality of applications, rather than about the techniques used in delivering data or the type of data being used.

What does language-independent development mean? It is quite simple—one technology, one development interface. You will use the same object, method, and property names with ADO, regardless of the development language that you are using. The difference is almost unnoticeable. Under the covers, ADO, through COM (Component Object Model), worries about the particular language you are developing with, whether it is Visual Basic, Visual C++, or Java. Even scripting languages, such as VBScript and JavaScript in HTML pages are supported. We will look more closely into programming for these different languages in Chapter 3, *Accessing ADO with Various Languages*.

With this feature, you might expect that a lot of specific functionality of data sources would be lost. On the contrary, ADO allows the developer to access any data source–specific commands, methods, properties, and utilities that the vendor has made available through OLE DB. And yes, ADO does this in a well-structured, consistent way. Can you possibly ask for more?

As we will see in chapters to come, an application can be designed to access a simple database, such as Access, and with a little bit of additional code, it can later access more intricate databases, such as SQL Server databases, Word documents, or email files. The only real coding necessary involves altering the connection string used in ADO to read the new data source. This powerful technology will help us move into the future as applications begin to grow across enterprises.

RDS

The final piece of data-access technology in this list of the MDAC components is Remote Data Services (RDS). RDS, based on existing Active Data Connector (ADC) technology integrated into ADO, transports ADO objects via proxy between server and client, thus allowing developers to create web-based applications that can access data on the server in new ways. Some of the advantages of RDS are:

- Client-side caching of data results
- Ability to update data from the client
- Support for data-aware ActiveX components and controls

Client-side caching is something that we will all grow to love. With it, clients (end-users) are able to view data from the server without making numerous round trips. For instance, when you are using a search engine on the Internet, such as Yahoo!, you receive a list of links that relate to your search, usually in groups of tens. If you want to see the next ten sites from the resulting search, your browser must make another request to the server. With client-side caching, all of the data is sent to the client, so that the client can browse this data without incurring time delays that are associated with additional requests. This feature reduces local-area network and Internet traffic and allows the end-user to move freely through data without unnecessary pauses and to perform operations on that data, such as sorting and filtering.

With RDS, web pages can now offer the client the ability to interact with and alter data. This data can be sent back to the server after manipulation. At the server, the data can be verified and then returned to the data source. With this technology, your client/server applications can span the Internet (or your intranet). Clients can now invoke server-side automation objects through HTML, meaning that particular business rules (chosen by the developer) can be accessed via the client.

RDS enables three-tier client/server applications, with the model shown in Figure 1-4.

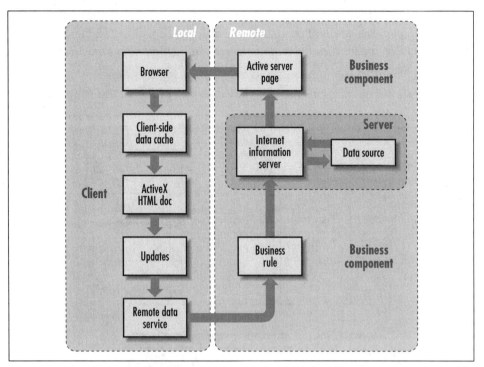

Figure 1-4. The three-tier client/server web-based application model

With automation objects, your application can become an auto-downloaded application. For businesses with a large number of client-side users, you can create, maintain, and update your application on the server alone. When clients run your application, they can use an ActiveX-aware browser (Internet Explorer) to access the application. With auto-download features built into the browser, the client receives an updated version of the application.

RDS also supports data-aware ActiveX controls that can be placed within an HTML page on a client. For instance, if you want to allow the client to view a list of documents that you have stored in your data source on the server, you could link RDS to an ActiveX list box control that is placed in the HTML page and downloaded to the client. The control interacts automatically with RDS, without any additional programming, to download all of the document names.

See Chapter 11, *Remote Data Services*, for a more detailed introduction to RDS.

Putting It All Together

With the addition of RDS to its MDAC family of components, Microsoft has integrated several useful existing technologies into the universal data-access strategy: IE data-access technology for data-bound web pages, remote data capability through RDS, and ASP/IIS-related technologies for better access to data services via the Internet. The result allows applications to work with data offline to reduce network traffic, update data on remote clients, and gather data asynchronously for faster response time.

Figure 1-5 shows the relationships and dependencies of the MDAC components.

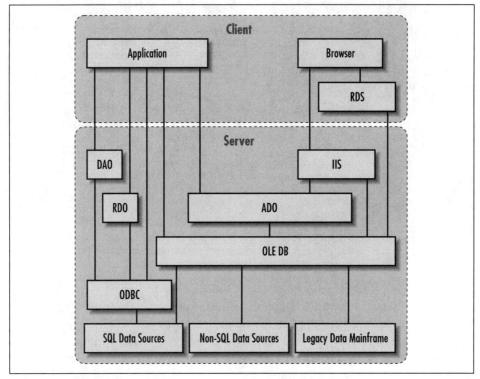

Figure 1-5. MDAC architecture

As you can see from Figure 1-5, your application can use a number of different Microsoft-supplied technologies to access SQL—as well as non-SQL and legacy—data, such as that residing on a mainframe.

Until ADO, we had four choices: DAO, RDO, ODBC, and OLE DB. DAO served its purpose well: it used the power of the underlying (Jet) database engine to access Microsoft and other ISAM data sources. With RDO, things were even better with its easy-to-use interface to ODBC and ability to access almost any SQL data source. Accessing ODBC directly was always a possibility, but it was questionable whether the overwhelming amount of work was worth the extra speed gained in the process. Finally, OLE DB offered everything under the sun. It offered access to ISAM, SQL, non-SQL, and legacy data. However wonderful OLE DB was, it is considered the most difficult interface with which to develop to access data sources. This is where ADO comes into play. ADO reports directly to OLE DB and no one else, meaning that it provides an interface to the whole complicated mess, about which we need to know little or nothing.

ADO provides a consistent development interface to the wonders of OLE DB, and it does so while being language-independent.

ADO and COM: Language Independence

Microsoft's Component Object Model, better known as COM, is a mature technology that offers universal access to components, regardless of the language in which they were programmed. This is the backbone that allows ADO, through OLE DB, to be so versatile. To understand how COM allows ADO to be language-independent, you must first understand what COM is and what it achieves.

COM

COM is technology specification for writing software components that interact through a standard interface. The COM specification is strictly a binary specification. This guarantees that the language in which a COM object is developed has absolutely no importance once the object is compiled, as long as its adheres to the binary specification.

The COM specification sets rules for creating and managing component objects. This specification guarantees that all COM objects are compatible and that they expose a minimal set of interfaces. These interfaces allow COM objects to communicate with each other whether they are on the same machine or supported by networks. Since the COM specification relies on binary compatibility, COM works across heterogeneous networks. In other words, COM objects can run on any machine, even without the Windows operating system.

A particular type of COM implementation is *OLE Automation*, or simply Automation. Automation is a standard way for COM objects to expose their functionality to software products, development languages, and even scripting languages. The use of Automation allows applications to actually manipulate other applications through the exposed features and functionality of the latter's COM objects. Automation allows two applications to communicate with each other.

An example of this type of manipulation is a Visual Basic add-in. Visual Basic exposes an object model through the COM technology to any other component that wishes to interact with it. You can create an add-in for Visual Basic that works seamlessly with the product, through the use of Visual Basic's exposed features. As a matter of fact, many of Microsoft's products expose their features through COM, including the Microsoft Office family of products. Microsoft Word, for example, exposes its functionality through COM and allows itself to be manipulated through scripting with VBA (Visual Basic for Applications).

When a COM object is exposed through OLE Automation, that object is then called an *ActiveX object* or an *ActiveX server.* The application or tool that manipulates the ActiveX object is called an *ActiveX client.*

ADO and COM

As a COM technology, ADO has the ability to communicate with any data source that provides an OLE DB interface. ADO and OLE DB share the same backbone— COM. Figure 1-6 shows COM at work with ADO and OLE DB. When ADO communicates with a data provider at the simplest level, two COM objects are exchanging information, regardless of the connection between them.

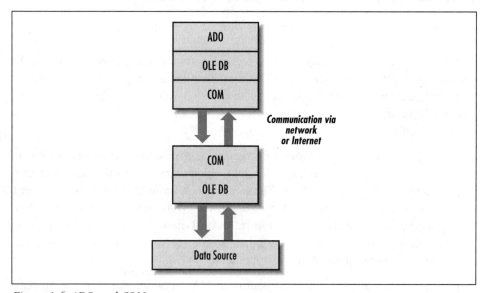

Figure 1-6. ADO and COM

Also, COM has the ability to send events or notifications to other COM objects. This capability is used in ADO, as we will see later on when we execute queries. We have the ability, through ADO, OLE DB, and finally COM, to send a request for a selection of records through SQL and then to be notified when it has completed processing.

What is even better is that COM has been around for a long time, has gained the respect of application and tools developers, has a proven track record, and is supported by Microsoft. COM's architecture does not change between programming languages or operating systems; thus, neither does ADO.

COM objects are easily distributed. They have the ability to communicate across machines and enterprises. This advantage is embraced with ADO through RDS, or Remote Data Service, which I will be talking about in Chapter 11.

As you can see from this very limited introduction to COM, ADO stands upon OLE DB, which relies heavily on COM to communicate with other COM objects. This can do nothing but benefit us as developers, because it enables communication with objects that aren't necessarily written in the same language.*

When to Use ADO

ADO is language-independent, as discussed earlier. This means that no matter which language you are developing with—Visual Basic, VBScript, Visual Basic for Applications (VBA), Visual C++, Visual J++, or JavaScript—the development interface is identical. This allows developers to become familiar with the technology itself, instead of worrying about learning a half-dozen different programming syntaxes for that technology. I suggest that you use ADO whenever your application fits into any or all of the following categories:

- Your application accesses or may later need to access more than one data source.

- Your application accesses or may later need to access data sources other than ISAM or ODBC databases.

- Your application spans or may later span a heterogeneous network.

- Your application uses or may later use multiple languages.

If your application needs to access more than one type of data source, then you should consider integrating ADO technology into your application. For instance, if you were designing an application that had to search Word documents, email messages, and a SQL Server database for keywords and then to show related information based on that query, ADO is the best choice. With ADO, you can create a component to search all three of these data sources using identical code, saving you time in development, as well as in maintenance and upkeep. This choice also provides the option of adding a fourth data source to your application at some later time with little or no additional overhead in development.

If your application may access data sources other than conventional ISAM or ODBC databases, you should use ADO. With ADO, you can search through an Excel worksheet just as if you were searching through email messages. If you use some other technology besides ADO, you must not only code two different

---

* For more information, see *Inside COM* by Dale Rogerson (Microsoft Press, 1997).

components, one for each data source, but you also need to learn that other tech-nology. In this case, you would have to research MAPI API calls, as well as Word document file structures. And then what happens when Word comes out with a new version? Or what about when more APIs are added to MAPI? You could easily ignore these until your application becomes so outdated that it renders itself use-less. With ADO, you simply use the data service providers supplied by Microsoft for both Excel and Word so that the ability to access and manipulate these data sources are exposed identically through ADO.

If your application has or may spread across a heterogeneous network, such as the Internet or your corporate intranet, you should use ADO. For instance, consider an application that is deployed from your company's server to each employee. This application might access data stored on a mainframe containing legacy data. From this point, ADO serves as a driver to access data on this mainframe platform. This alone would save you valuable time and effort, because in order to access the mainframe data source by some other means, you would have to write custom drivers, or even worse, spend a fortune on a third-party tool that might not do everything that you want. Even the client side would benefit from ADO. Suppose you have employees that don't have a Windows machine in front of them, but who need access to the same data that someone running Windows has. Other employees might use a Sun workstation, for instance. As long as they use a browser that supports ActiveX technology, such as Internet Explorer, it is as if they are running the same application. In addition, if your application is prone to updates or fixes, by deploying it over the network using Internet Information Server (IIS) along with Active Server Pages (ASP), you can automatically (and transparently) update the client's version of the application each time it changes.

If your application uses multiple languages, especially if they are in the same tier of an *n*-tier client/server architecture, then ADO is the best choice. If you are the only developer of an application, or even if there are a handful of developers, then by sticking to a language-independent data-access technique, you eliminate the need to know multiple implementations of the same technology. For instance, if your application has business-rule components that update the data source, query the data source, or delete from the data source, it is very likely in today's development environments, that each component could be written in a com-pletely different language. By fully understanding ADO, you can make the best use of the same technology in each of these languages.

On the other hand, there are a few cases in which you shouldn't use ADO. If your application falls into any of the following categories, an alternative method of data access might be preferable:

- Your application is already too far along to redesign and currently does not support business components for data access.

- Your application needs to read in only text data from a flat file, which cannot be broken down into logical rowsets.

- Your application saves data in your own format, and you do not wish to offer others access to your data through OLE DB.

If your application is already under development, it's probably too far along to turn back now. If it does not support business components for data access, you might not have a choice in converting to ADO. If the data-access technology, whether DAO, RDO, or something else, has not been placed within designed business components to handle the data access, you would most likely spend more time rewriting your application to support ADO than is justified.

By using business components in your applications, you can alter a few areas of code to achieve a widespread result. In this case, if your application had a component to read from your data source and a component to write to your data source, your application would call the business components rather than calling DAO, RDO, or even ADO directly. When a new technology such as ADO comes along, you simply change the two components, as opposed to changing every location in your application that now calls the components.

If your application will read in only text data from a flat file, which cannot be broken into logical rowsets of data, you may be better off using the Visual Basic **Open** statement, or the file-access statement equivalent for the language you are developing in. For instance, if your application displays a *readme* text file in a registration screen, can you imagine opening up a database and using the rowset methodology on streamed text? You should use the **Open** statement, if you're using Visual Basic, to read in the *readme* text file yourself. ADO is overkill in a situation like this.

If your application is going to save state information or other data and will not allow others to view this data through OLE DB or any other conventional database technology (DAO, RDO, ODBC API, or ADO), you may not want ADO. To ensure the security of your data, it would be wise for you to write your own functions for storing and retrieving information from an encrypted binary file. This binary file would have a structure that only you, as the developer, would be aware of, as opposed to the structure of an OLE DB–enabled file, which can be read at runtime. Of course, even though nobody knows the structure of your binary file, people are smart—they could figure it out. To ensure that people can't see the data, you must encrypt it. For instance, you might want to write an application that does your taxes for you (and pretend that nobody else ever wrote a program like this before, so that we have a reason to do it now). After a year of entering financial data, the user can automatically print tax reports and forms that can be sent the government. The data that is entered all year long obviously has to be saved somewhere, but the question is where. My suggestion in this case would be to create a binary file in your own data structure, hiding that structure from the outside world. This file will hold personal financial information that you really don't want other people to have access to. With ADO, you would be exposing it to the world, whether you wanted to or not.

Summary

This chapter introduced ActiveX Data Objects, along with the closely related evolution of Microsoft data-access technologies. You also learned when to use ADO, the newest of these technologies. Following is a list of some key items, pointed out in this chapter:

- ADO offers access to virtually any data source on any platform by being a data consumer of OLE DB. OLE DB is an industry standard promoted by Microsoft for exposing data, regardless of its source or format, in a uniform way. With the power of OLE DB, used via ADO, you gain access to any data source that provides an OLE DB interface.

- ADO offers ease of use when writing data access applications. Since ADO was created with a similar design to DAO (Data Access Objects), developers are familiar with the object architecture. And since the development interface is consistent, you can develop for any OLE DB data source with ADO using the same syntax.

- ADO offers language-independence and thus offers developers a choice of languages. With any language, including Visual Basic, VBScript, VBA, Visual C++, Java, and JavaScript, the development interface remains the same, which allows developers to focus on the ADO technology, not the implementation.

Throughout the rest of this book, you will learn how to use ADO with any development language. You will learn every object, collection, property, and method of ADO and how you can use each of them to access the power of OLE DB in your applications.

2

The ADO Architecture

In this chapter, we take a look at the ADO architecture; in the first section, "An Overview of the ADO Architecture," I describe how all of the pieces of ADO fit together to perform all of the functions that are necessary when accessing data sources. The remainder of the chapter is dedicated to the introduction and brief description of each of the key components of the ADO architecture.

An Overview of the ADO Architecture

ADO is built upon layer after layer of solid, proven technologies that allow applications to communicate with data, regardless of where it resides or how it is structured, using any language or scripting language. How can one technology offer techniques to access both relational databases and nonrelational sources such as email?

ADO is the lowest common denominator when it comes to data access. It makes no assumptions when it comes to its data sources. Because ADO cannot assume that the data source being accessed is even a database, it must use objects, methods, and properties that are relevant to all data sources.

With ADO, the data provider (as described in the previous chapter, the connection between the data consumer, or application), not the data consumer, creates the driver for a data source. What this means is that the version of ADO does not dictate the data sources that are available to us; rather, it dictates the functionality that is passed through from the data provider to our software. The burden is on the data provider or vendor to create and distribute the proper resources necessary to develop with their product. ADO is a framework; the behavior of the OLE DB providers can vary widely. ADO does not require that all interfaces and functionality be offered by each provider.

By designing the architecture of ADO as a simple generic interface, ADO is not tied to a specific command type, but is capable of growing with the needs and the abilities of both developers and data sources.

A powerful feature of ADO is its ability to offer the functionality of a particular data source. If your data provider supports stored procedures, for example, then you can use them. In Chapter 4, *The Connection Object*, we take a look at a number of popular providers and their specific functionality.

ADO has already proven to be a very well-thought-out interface for data access, which is worth its weight in gold because it is so very robust and scalable, in addition to being so easy to use.

In the second half of this chapter, I will take a closer look at how each of the major components of the ADO architecture fit together to achieve its desired goal of a generic data-access interface.

ADO Versus DAO and RDO

DAO assumes that it's working with a Jet engine and an Access database. RDO also makes an assumption—specifically, that it is working with an ODBC data source. With DAO, a Database object is used to connect to a particular database. The type of database must be picked from a list that is stored in the version of DAO that you are using to develop your application. If a database is not included in the current list, you are out of luck—you cannot access that database with the version of DAO that you have. ADO has been designed to work with any data source, regardless of version. As long as an OLE DB provider driver is available, you can access that data.

The problem with DAO is that it is too tightly bound to the Microsoft Jet engine. The problem with RDO is that it is too tightly bound to the ODBC API. In contrast, ADO is fitted loosely around the concept of data access and the assumption that all data can be visualized as collections of fields that constitute records. ADO's approach to data-access interfaces allows it to remain up to date with new types of data structures and data-access techniques. If a new type of data query is later invented, as long as a particular OLE DB data provider supports it, ADO can take advantage of it through the use of a Command object.

To summarize, ADO has a smaller object model than DAO because it has been generalized to allow easy access to any data source, not just Jet databases or ODBC data sources. Its architecture is very similar to that of DAO, but it simplifies data access more than DAO or RDO did by using fewer objects. Because the same interface can be used to access any type of data source, ADO is easier to use.

ADO Components

ActiveX Data Objects consists of a generic-style data-access structure that allows you to access any data source, regardless of its structure, with the same programming interface. The individual objects within the ADO object model are used to provide all of the data-storage, manipulation, and retrieval commands needed when writing a data-based application. ADO includes the following objects and collections:

- The Connection object

- The Command object

- The Parameters collection and the Parameter object

- The Recordset object

- The Fields collection and the Field object

- The Record and Stream objects

- The Properties collection and the Property object

- The Errors collection and the Error object

In the next sections, I take a closer look at these objects and collections.

The Connection Object

The *Connection object* is the gateway for all data communications through ActiveX Data Objects. Figure 2-1 illustrates the Connection object's object model.

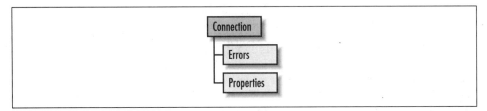

Figure 2-1. The Connection object's object model

In order to access data from any source, a connection for that source must first be established. ADO uses the Connection object to accomplish this. The Connection object uses information that you provide to establish a unique connection to a particular OLE DB data source. The standard information that a Connection object accepts includes filenames, data-provider names, usernames, and passwords. If your particular data provider needs additional information, this information can be passed from the Connection object directly to your data provider. By allowing this form of pass-through of connection specifications, ADO does not make any assumptions or restrict itself to one type of data source. All of the functionality of the chosen data provider is made available through the use of the Connection object.

A Connection object is used to accomplish the following tasks:

- Select a data source and data provider
- Open and close a connection on a selected data source
- Manage transactions on a data source
- Execute queries on a data source

Connection objects can be created explicitly and used later with the Command and Recordset objects, or the Connection object can be created by the Command and Recordset objects implicitly, behind the scenes.

In addition, the Connection object reports errors through an Errors collection and provides ADO version information. The Connection object is examined in greater detail in Chapter 4.

The Command Object

The Command object is used to execute instructions—whether for storing, manipulating, or gathering information—on a specific data source. Figure 2-2 shows the Command object's object model.

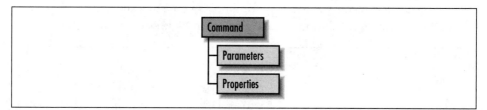

Figure 2-2. The Command object's object model

Once you're connected to a data source, you naturally want to perform some operation on it. One of your options is to use the *Command object*, which executes commands against the associated data source. There are five types of commands that a Command object can execute:

A SQL statement

Probably the most popular type of command, a SQL statement can gather information, manipulate information, or manipulate the structure of the underlying database.

A parameterized query (a query with input and output parameters)
> A parameterized query uses variables that set or return values that are part of a particular query or SQL statement.

A stored procedure from within the current data source
> A stored procedure is a query that resides within the connected data source. By identifying the name of a stored procedure, you can execute, through the data provider, a query that is defined outside of ADO. Stored procedures can also use parameters.

A statement to open a single table
> An open table-type statement does not query data, but instead returns all of the fields in all of the records belonging to the specified table. This is comparable to the DAO OpenTable method.

A string command passed directly to the data provider
> A string command enables the data provider to perform a specific operation that is defined by the provider itself and outside of ADO. Such a command is commonly used, for example, when a particular data provider offers its own version of the SQL language. In such a situation, ADO has no idea how to process a proprietary SQL string for this language, so you tell ADO to forward it directly to the data provider. The data provider, in turn, can take this string and process a result that can be sent back through ADO to your application. The OLE DB provider for Internet Publishing, for instance, allows the passing of a URL statement to identify a data source, within the Command object.

If the Command object is used to retrieve data, then a Recordset object containing the requested records is created and passed back to the application.

The Command object can be associated with a currently open connection, or it can be created independently of any existing Connection objects, in which case the Command object creates its own Connection object but does not share it with you.

The Command object is discussed in Chapter 7, *The Command Object.*

The Parameters collection and the Parameter object

The Parameters collection belongs to the Command object. This collection stores Parameter objects that are used to make parameterized queries or to invoke stored procedures. Every Command object has a Parameters collection created by ADO. You can populate the Parameters collection, or it can be refreshed to retrieve the already defined parameters—for the Command—from the data source.

The Parameters collection and the Parameter object's object model is displayed in Figure 2-3. This collection and object combination defines the characteristics of parameters when referring to a parameterized query or defines the input and output arguments when referring to a stored procedure.

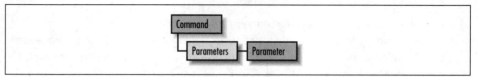

Figure 2-3. The Parameters collection and the Parameter object's object model

With the Parameter object, you can set or read the name, value, and characteristics of a given parameter. If you know this information beforehand for any stored procedure or parameterized query, you can potentially save valuable time by creating Parameter objects yourself that ADO would otherwise spend trying to learn this information.

The Parameters collection and the Parameter object are covered in Chapter 7.

The Recordset Object

A Recordset object is used to access data on a record level. Figure 2-4 illustrates the Recordset object model.

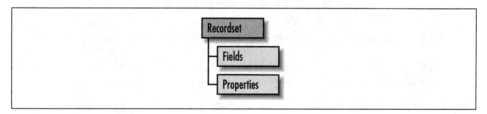

Figure 2-4. The Recordset object model

A Recordset object can be created by the developer to return data itself, or it can be returned from executing a command with a Connection or Command object. This information can be obtained from a table in the underlying data source or from a previous SQL statement, query, or stored procedure executed through the Command object.

The Recordset object consists of a Fields collection of individual Field objects, each with its own properties, characteristics, and values. (The Recordset object may be familiar to you if you have worked with DAO before.)

The Recordset object works well with all types of data because it relies on the ability of all data to be broken into structured records composed of one or more fields. It is easy to see this structure in a database, but what about a data source such as a directory? In this case, each file in the directory may be a record. Each field of this record might be a different attribute of that file, including its name, its size, its creation date, its last modification date, its contents, etc. It is important to realize that all stored data can have a structure that represents records with fields that are located within tables, just as in a more obviously structured database.

With the Recordset object, we can move a virtual record pointer around a list of records, searching for records, placing bookmarks, and editing specific values of designated fields. We can also add and remove records from the recordset. We can view and edit the properties of the fields that make up these records.

Recordset objects, like Command objects, can be created using an existing Connection, or Recordset objects can implicitly create their own Connection object, which is not automatically passed back to your application, unless you request it. Recordsets show you one record at a time. With this view, you can manipulate data any way that you would like through a Fields collection or Field object, which are discussed next. Multiple Recordset objects can access the same data, and, as a matter of fact, Recordset objects can even be cloned using a special method that we will look at in the "Working with Multiple Recordset Objects" section of Chapter 5, *The Recordset Object.*

There are four types of cursors available in ADO. A *cursor* is a way of working within a result set or records. Each provides a different view of the same data, and each has its pros and cons. Not all providers support every type of cursor. The four types of cursors are:

Forward-only cursor

> The forward-only cursor is exactly the same as the static cursor except that you can only move forward through the records in your recordset. Unless you specify otherwise, this is the default view of a recordset, and it offers the best performance of all four recordset types.

Dynamic cursor

> This view of your data source allows you to see dynamically any additions, changes, or deletions made by other users of the data source. The dynamic cursor is the most resource-intensive type of recordset.

Keyset cursor

> This view of your data source only allows you to see modifications made to the data in your recordset by other users. It does not show you records that have been added by other users, and it denies you access to records that have been deleted. The keyset cursor offers slightly better performance than the dynamic cursor.

Static cursor

> The static cursor offers you a snapshot of your data through the Recordset object. The static cursor does not show you any additions, modifications, or deletions of the records in your recordset, regardless of what other users are doing to it. It is generally used for data gathering and reporting in a multi-user environment. The static cursor offers abundant speed advantages over both the keyset and dynamic cursor.

The Recordset object offers two types of data updating: *immediate update mode* and *batch update mode*. In the immediate update mode, changes are made one record at a time. Once you have indicated that you have finished updating a record, the information is immediately transferred to the underlying data source and written. On the other hand, the batch update mode allows the data provider to cache several records in memory to be sent to the data source in a single call, where it is then written as a batch.

The Recordset Object is covered in detail in Chapter 5.

The Fields collection and the Field object

The Fields collection belongs to the Recordset object and the Record object. The Fields collection is a group of Field objects that represent individual columns in a recordset. Figure 2-5 shows the Fields collection and Field object's object model. Every Recordset object and every Record object has a Fields collection that is created by ADO.

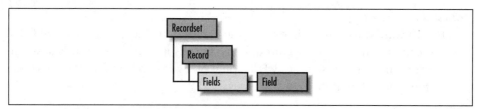

Figure 2-5. The Fields collection and the Field object's object model

The Field object offers the developer complete access to the underlying data of a chosen recordset. The Field object makes available its field's name, value, data size, and attributes. With this information, we can read, alter, and verify field information within the current record of our recordset.

Both the Fields collection and the Field object are discussed in Chapter 5.

The Record Object

The Record object is one of the newest additions to the ADO object model added with Version 2.5. It can represent either a single record within a Recordset object, or it can represent a resource within a hierarchical data source. A Record object can be obtained from a Recorset object (representing a single record of the complete recordset), or it can be created as a standalone object to represent a resource such as a file or a directory. Figure 2-6 shows the Record object's object model.

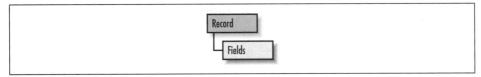

Figure 2-6. The Record object's object model

One of the unique features of the Record object is that it can be used to navigate hierarchical data sources such as a file directory. By using the OLE DB provider for Internet Publishing, the Record object allows the developer to access resources within a web server (files and directories).

The Record object allows for file and directory manipulation, such as copying, moving, and deleting resources. In addition, the Record object can be used to access the actual data belonging to one of these resources through the exposure of a default Stream object.

The Record object is discussed in Chapter 10, *Records and Streams.*

The Stream Object

The Stream object was added at the same time as when the Record object was added to ADO with Version 2.5. The Stream object is used to view and manipulate text and binary data belonging to a resource such as a file or a buffer in memory. A Stream object can be obtained from a Record object or it can be created as a standalone object. Figure 2-7 shows the Stream object's object model.

Figure 2-7. The Stream object's object model

An additional feature of the Stream object is its ability to be created independently of a specified data source. In other words, the Stream object can be created in memory and need not be tied to any predefined data. In this way, the Stream object can be used as a utility object such as a buffer. Added functionality allows the Stream's buffer to be persisted (saved to the datasource) to local files in any directory.

The Stream object is discussed in Chapter 10.

The Properties Collection and the Property Object

The Connection, Command, and Recordset objects each have their own Properties collection. The Properties collection consists of individual Property objects that hold specific information about their associated objects. These collections are supplied automatically by ADO. Figure 2-8 illustrates the Properties collection and Property object's object model.

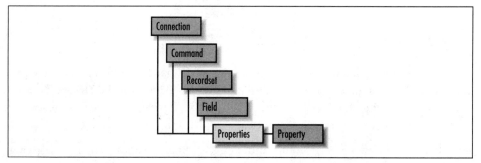

Figure 2-8. The Properties collection and the Property object's object model

In order to fine-tune all of these objects—the Connection, Command, Recordset, and Field objects—ADO offers the Properties collection. This collection contains individual Property objects that allow dynamic characteristics of the data source belonging to the current data provider to be accessed within each object. The Property objects may inform you of special features that are unique to the data source and are not standard ADO functionality. The Property objects may also tell you what standard ADO functions are supported by the current data provider so that you can avoid problems when attempting particular commands. With this ability, we can determine at runtime the capabilities of the data source that we are trying to access. This allows our software to realize the full potential of data-source drivers.

One of the more flexible features of ADO is that it can offer the developer data provider–defined functions that are not part of the standard ADO specification. For instance, the Microsoft Cursor Service for OLE DB offers dynamic properties that are used to specify how often calculated and aggregate columns are calculated within a data-shaping query. Instead of working with only the lowest common denominator in data-access techniques, ADO allows your application to check for and take advantage of functions that are specific to a particular data provider. Each data provider uses the Property objects of the Properties collection differently, but they all use it to expose their special functionality. Consult the documentation of the data provider you are using in your application for more information on how to utilize the Properties collection and the Property object.

The Properties collection and Property object are covered in many chapters throughout this book. For the Connection object, they are covered in Chapter 4. For the Command object, they are covered in Chapter 7. And for the Recordset and Field objects, they are covered in Chapter 5.

The Errors Collection and the Error Object

The Errors collection belongs to the Connection object but services all of ADO. The Errors collection is populated with Error objects whenever an error occurs within a single ADO data-access operation. Figure 2-9 shows the Errors collection and the Error object's object model.

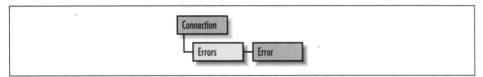

Figure 2-9. The Errors collection and the Error object's object model

The Errors collection contains errors and warnings that are generated both by ADO and by the individual data provider being used. These messages allow us to scan and trap errors that arise when we access data sources. If ADO detects the error, then ADO will throw the error. But if the error is provider-specific, the data provider passes it back to ADO, which will report the error to you. What is nice about ADO's error capabilities is that they can tell you where an error was generated and which object produced the error.

An Error object is added to the Errors collection whenever an error occurs within ADO. The Errors collection is cleared right before a method that can generate an error is called. An Error object provides a description of the error, an error number, the name of the object that generated the error, the capability to access Windows help files based on the particular error, and error information from SQL data sources. An error object can also contain a warning that does not halt the execution of your application.

The Error collection and the Error object model are discussed in detail in Chapter 7.

Summary

This chapter has explained the architecture behind the ActiveX Data Objects technology. The following is a list of some key items pointed out in this chapter:

- ADO offers a generic data-access interface that is used to communicate with a wide range of proprietary data sources and providers.

- With ADO, the burden of creating efficient data access is placed upon the individual data provider, not the data-access technology.

- The ADO architecture is comprised of nine major components. These components include the Connection object, the Command object, the Parameters collection and the Parameter object, the Recordset object, the Fields collection and Field object, the Record object, the Stream object, the Properties collection and the Property object, and finally, the Errors collection and the Error object.

The rest of this book walks you through the nitty gritty of application development using the ActiveX Data Objects technology. You will next learn how to access ADO through various different development languages, and then we will dive into the actual components of ADO.

3

Accessing ADO with Various Languages

Because ActiveX Data Objects expose their properties by means of COM interfaces, they can be accessed by any language that can utilize COM. In this book, we will look at accessing ADO from Visual Basic, Visual C++, and Visual J++, since these are the most commonly used tools for developing ADO applications on the Windows operating system.

In addition to these three languages, there are two scripting languages that are already well-established: VBScript and JScript. VBScript is a lightweight subset of Visual Basic that's designed specifically for adding script to HTML documents. JScript is Microsoft's implementation of JavaScript, designed for script development within HTML documents.

Although ADO is meant to offer the same development interface to each language from which it is accessed, some inconsistencies arise because of differences in their syntax and the development environments in which they are used. In this chapter, we will take a look at each of the five languages and learn how to get started developing ADO applications in each.

Accessing ADO with Visual Basic

Visual Basic is probably the most popular language in which to develop applications for ADO. It is also the language used in the examples and code throughout this book. Visual Basic is a very easy language to understand and excellent for both beginners and advanced developers.

Referencing ActiveX Data Objects

To write an application in Visual Basic using ActiveX Data Objects, you must first tell Visual Basic about them by adding ADO to the list of references that Visual Basic uses to run an application. You may do this by selecting the Project → References menu item so that the References dialog box appears, as shown in Figure 3-1. In the Available References list box, select the latest version of Microsoft ActiveX Data Objects Library that you have installed. Now you are ready to create and use ADO objects within your current Visual Basic application.

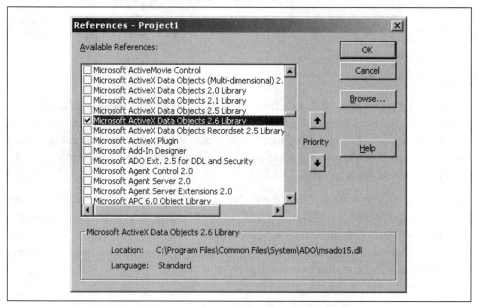

Figure 3-1. The References dialog box of Visual Basic

When redistributing ADO applications, you should use the MDAC redistributable package available for download from Microsoft's web site.

Creating ActiveX Data Objects

In Visual Basic, you can create new ADO objects by simply referencing the ADODB classes of the Microsoft ActiveX Data Objects Library. The following piece of code creates a Connection and a Recordset object in Visual Basic:

```
' create a reference to a Connection object
Dim con As ADODB.Connection

' create a reference to a Recordset object
Dim rst AS ADODB.Recordset
```

As with any other Visual Basic objects, you must instantiate them before they can be used, as in the following examples:

```
' create a new instance of the Connection object
Set con = New ADODB.Connection

' create a new instance of the Recordset object
Set rst = New ADODB.Recordset
```

In the previous examples, the ADODB prefix to the ADO objects is used in case your Visual Basic development environment references another object of the same class name in a different class library. The following code illustrates how a DAO Recordset and an ADO Recordset can be created within the same project:

```
' which object model is this from?
Dim rst As Recordset

' explicitly specifying the Data Access Object Model
Dim rstDAO As DAO.Recordset

' explicitly specifying the ActiveX Data Object Model
Dim rstADO As ADODB.Recordset
```

If you know for a fact that no other class library listed in the References dialog box of your current Visual Basic application has the same class names as ADO, you may remove the ADODB prefix when declaring and instantiating object variables. However, if you are using more than one object model with the same class definitions (as in the previous example), not specifying the library from which the class should be derived tells VB to instantiate the class from the library that comes first in the list of references to the project.

In Visual Basic, it is always a good idea to remove an object from memory once it is no longer being used. This is done by setting the object to Nothing, as follows:

```
' remove the objects
Set con = Nothing
Set rst = Nothing
```

Using ADO with Visual Basic: An Example

So that you can visualize how to work with ADO objects in Visual Basic, Example 3-1 uses ADO to open a connection to the Jet Biblio database and to return a recordset containing the names of its first ten authors. Each record is then written to a list box before both the Connection and Recordset objects are closed. Note that the example makes use of dynamic control creation supported by Visual Basic 6.0 or later; if you have an earlier version, simply delete the code that defines, instantiates, and sets the properties of the list box, and place a list box named *lstAuthors* on the form at design time.

To begin, create a new Application EXE project, and open the Project → References menu so that you see the References dialog box shown in Figure 3-1. Select the latest version of Microsoft ActiveX Data Objects that you have installed, and press the OK button.

Now, replace the existing source code for Form1 with the code shown in Example 3-1, and run the application. That's all there is to it. Make sure that you have a *Biblio.mdb* database located at *C:\Program Files\Microsoft Visual Studio\ VB98*, or if you have it in another location, simply change the path in the code that points to the Access database.

Example 3-1. A Simple Visual Basic Example

```
Option Explicit

Private WithEvents lstAuthors As ListBox

Private Sub Form_Load()

    ' create new instances of the Connection and Recordset objects

    Dim con As ADODB.Connection
    Dim rst As ADODB.Recordset

    ' instantiate the Connection and Recordset objects
    Set con = New ADODB.Connection
    Set rst = New ADODB.Recordset

    ' create two strings to define the connection and the recordset

    Dim sConString As String
    Dim sSQLString As String

    ' Create list box control

    Set lstAuthors = Me.Controls.Add("vb.listbox", _
                            "lstAuthors", _
                            Me)

    lstAuthors.Visible = True


    ' open the BiblioDSN data source with the Connection object

    sConString = "Provider=Microsoft.Jet.OLEDB.4.0; " _
            & "Data Source=C:\Program Files" _
                        & "\Microsoft Visual Studio" _
                        & "\VB98\Biblio.mdb"

    con.Open sConString

    Debug.Print "Connection opened."
```

Example 3-1. A Simple Visual Basic Example (continued)

```
    ' create a Recordset object from a SQL string

    sSQLString = "SELECT TOP 10 Author " & _
                 "FROM Authors"

    Set rst = con.Execute(sSQLString)

    Debug.Print "SQL statement processed."

    ' retrieve all the data within the Recordset object

    Debug.Print "Getting data now..."

    Do Until (rst.EOF)
        lstAuthors.AddItem rst("Author").Value
        rst.MoveNext
    Loop

    Debug.Print "End of data."

    ' close and remove the Recordset object from memory

    rst.Close
    Set rst = Nothing

    Debug.Print "Closed and removed " _
            & "Recordset object from memory."

    ' close and remove the Connection object from memory

    con.Close
    Set con = Nothing

    Debug.Print "Closed and removed " _
            & "Connection object from memory."

End Sub

Private Sub Form_Resize()

    ' this code is added for asthetics

    lstAuthors.Top = 0
    lstAuthors.Left = 0
    lstAuthors.Width = Me.Width
    lstAuthors.Height = Me.Height

End Sub
```

A lot of this information will not make much sense to you now, but it will start to as you begin to learn how to use ActiveX Data Objects from the rest of the chapters in this book. The important technique to notice from this example is how the ADO objects are created in the beginning of the code example, and how the ADO objects are removed at the end of the code example.

Accessing ADO with Visual C++

Visual C++ is a much more difficult language and environment with which to develop applications for ActiveX Data Objects. Because it is so difficult, Microsoft is constantly trying to provide developers with easier ways to access ADO components.

By far the easiest method (and the only method described here) is one that takes advantage of the #import keyword. This approach offers not only the most control to the developer, but it also allows the developer to code in a Visual Basic programming style.

Referencing ActiveX Data Objects

The #import keyword is used in Visual C++ applications to import information from a type library. To make ADO accessible to your C++ code, use the following #import directive:

```
#import <msado15.dll> no_namespace rename("EOF", "EOFile")
```

This statement assumes that the path to *msado15.dll* (usually *C:\Program Files\ Common Files\System\ADO*) is already set within the Visual C++ environment; if not, select the Directories tab of the Options dialog box (Tools → Options), and add it.

The #import statement does a couple of things. First, at compile time it creates a header file with a *.tlh* extension, which stands for Type Library Header. This header file is comprised of enumerated types and definitions for the objects contained in the type library for *msado15.dll.*

Secondly, it creates a file with a *.tli* (Type Library Implementation) extension that contains the wrappers for each function in the object model defined by the *msado15.dll* type library.

Finally, the rename attribute in the statement:

```
rename("EOF", "EOFile")
```

renames the EOF keyword from the type library and calls it EOFile so that it does not conflict with Visual C++'s definition of the EOF property.

Creating ActiveX Data Objects

In order to invoke an ActiveX Data Object, we must first start OLE so that we can use OLE DB. Remember that Chapter 2, *The ADO Architecture*, showed that ADO was simply a wrapper around the OLE DB technology. We do this with the following piece of code:

```
struct StartOLEProcess{
    StartOLEProcess() {
        ::CoInitialize(NULL);
    }
    ~StartOLEProcess() {
        ::CoUninitialize();
    }
} _start_StartOLEProcess;
```

Placing this structure definition anywhere in our application forces the application to call the **_start_StartOLEProcess** constructor once it has started. This constructor simply calls `CoInitialize` to initialize OLE. Once our application is complete, the destructor of **_start_StartOLEProcess** will be called. This in turn will call `CoUninitialize`, which will shut down OLE.

The next thing we must do to create an ActiveX Data Object is to declare a pointer to the object we wish to create, as follows:

```
// define a variable that will be used as a reference to the
// Connection object and set it to NULL
ADODB::_ConnectionPtr  con = NULL;

// define a variable that will be used as a reference to the
// Recordset object and set it to NULL
ADODB::_RecordsetPtr  rst = NULL;
```

We then can create an ActiveX Data Object by calling the **CreateInstance** function of our ADO pointer. This function returns a result of type **HRESULT** to inform us whether the creation of the object was successful. This is illustrated in the following code fragment:

```
' create a new instance of an ADO Connection object
hr = con.CreateInstance(__uuidof(ADODB::Connection));

' create a new instance of an ADO Recordset object
hr = rst.CreateInstance(__uuidof(ADODB::Recordset));
```

Finally, just as in Visual Basic, it is always a good idea to release objects once they are no longer needed. In Visual C++, we accomplish this with a couple of lines of code that look like the following:

```
' remove the objects
con = Null;
rst = Null;
```

Using ADO with Visual C++: An Example

Now let's take a look at a fully functional example of a Visual C++ application that utilizes ActiveX Data Objects. To try the following code, create a new Win32 Console Application from within Visual C++, choosing the Simple option from the wizard, and replace the contents of the main *.cpp* file with the code shown in Example 3-2.

Remember, just as with the Visual Basic example, make sure that a copy of *Biblio.mdb* is in the *C:\Program Files\Microsoft Visual Studio\VB98* directory, or that you change the directory in the following source code to reflect the proper path of the Access database. In addition, if you are having trouble with this code, make sure that you have the *MSADO15.DLL* file in the *C:\Program Files\Common Files\System\ado* directory or that you have the proper directory entered in the source code.

Example 3-2. A Simple Visual C++ Example

```
#include "stdafx.h"
#include <stdio.h>

#import "C:\Program Files\Common Files\System\ado\MSADO15.dll" _
    rename("EOF", "EOFile")

struct StartOLEProcess{
    StartOLEProcess() {
        ::CoInitialize(NULL);
    }
    ~StartOLEProcess() {
        ::CoUninitialize();
    }
} _start_StartOLEProcess;

void main(void)
{

    // define our variables which will be used as references to the
    // Connection and Recordset objects

    ADODB::_ConnectionPtr  con = NULL;
    ADODB::_RecordsetPtr   rec = NULL;

    // define variables to read the Author field from the recordset

    ADODB::FieldPtr        pAuthor;
    _variant_t             vAuthor;
    char                   sAuthor[40];

    // create two strings for use with the creation of a Connection
    // and a Recordset object
```

Example 3-2. A Simple Visual C++ Example (continued)

```
bstr_t              sConString;
bstr_t              sSQLString;

// create a variable to hold the result to function calls

HRESULT             hr              = S_OK;

// long variable needed for Execute method of Connection object

VARIANT             *vRecordsAffected = NULL;

// create a new instance of an ADO Connection object

hr = con.CreateInstance(__uuidof(ADODB::Connection));

printf("Connection object created.\n");

// open the BiblioDSN data source with the Connection object

sConString = L"Provider=Microsoft.Jet.OLEDB.4.0; "
             L"Data Source=C:\\Program Files\\"
                            L"Microsoft Visual Studio\\"
                            L"VB98\\Biblio.mdb";

con->Open(sConString, L"", L"", -1);

printf("Connection opened.\n");

// create a Recordset object from a SQL string

sSQLString = L"SELECT TOP 10 Author FROM Authors;";

rec = con->Execute(sSQLString,
                   vRecordsAffected,
                   1);

printf("SQL statement processed.\n");

// point to the Author field in the recordset

pAuthor = rec->Fields->GetItem("Author");

// retrieve all the data within the Recordset object

printf("Getting data now...\n\n");

while(!rec->EOFile) {

    // get the Author field's value and change it
    // to a multibyte type
    vAuthor.Clear();
```

Example 3-2. A Simple Visual C++ Example (continued)

```
    vAuthor = pAuthor->Value;

    WideCharToMultiByte(CP_ACP,
                        0,
                        vAuthor.bstrVal,
                        -1,
                        sAuthor,
                        sizeof(sAuthor),
                        NULL,
                        NULL);

    printf("%s\n", sAuthor);

    rec->MoveNext();

}

printf("\nEnd of data.\n");

// close and remove the Recordset object from memory

rec->Close();
rec = NULL;

printf("Closed an removed the "
       "Recordset object from memory.\n");

// close and remove the Connection object from memory

con->Close();
con = NULL;

printf("Closed and removed the "
       "Connection object from memory.\n");

}
```

Although much of the previous example will be very foreign to you until you have a thorough understanding of how to develop applications with ActiveX Data Objects, it is particularly important to notice how Visual C++ applications must convert datatypes returned by a field's value. In Example 3-2, a function called WideCharToMultiByte is used to convert a Variant datatype to a normal char string datatype (ASCII) so that it can in turn be passed to the printf function.

Accessing ADO with Visual J++

Like Visual C++, Visual J++ offers a number of ways to access ActiveX Data Objects. By far the easiest and most powerful is to use the Windows Foundation Classes, which expose the ADO objects and their members.

Referencing ActiveX Data Objects

To use the ActiveX Data Objects within your Visual J++ application through the WFC, you must import the type library with the following statement:

```
import com.ms.wfc.data.*;
```

Creating ActiveX Data Objects

In order to create an ActiveX Data Object in Visual J++, you must first create a variable to reference that object, as follows:

```
// define a variable which will be used as a reference to the
// Connection object
Connection  con;

// define a variable which will be used as a reference to the
// Recordset object
Recordset    rst;
```

Next, you can create a new instance of an ActiveX Data Object by using the **new** keyword and assigning it to the variable reference you just defined:

```
' create a new instance of an ADO Connection object
con = new Connection();

' create a new instance of an ADO Recordset object
rst = new Recordset();
```

These last two steps could be combined into one step with the following code (this is one of the beauties of Java):

```
// define a variable which will be used as a reference to the
// Connection object and create a new instance for that variable
Connection  con = new Connection();

// define a variable which will be used as a reference to the
// Recordset object and create a new instance for that variable
Recordset    rst = new Recordset();
```

As in any language, it is always a good idea to remove instances of objects that are no longer being used. You can do this in Java with the following lines of code:

```
' remove the objects
con = null;
rst = null;
```

Using ADO with Visual J++: An Example

Example 3-3 illustrates how an ActiveX Data Objects application may be written for the Visual J++ development environment. To create this project, open a Visual J++

Console Application project, and simply replace the code within the *Class1.java* file with the code from Example 3-3.

If you are having difficulty running this example, remember to have the *Biblio.mdb* file in the *C:\Program Files\Microsoft Visual Studio\VB98* directory, or have the correct directory for the Access database entered in the source code that you run.

Example 3-3. A Simple Visual J++ Example

```
import com.ms.wfc.data.*;

public class Class1
{

    public static void main(String args[]) {

        // define our variables which will be used as references to the
        // Connection and Recordset objects

        Connection  con = new Connection();
        Recordset   rst = new Recordset();


        // create two strings for use with the creation of a connection
        // and a recordset

        String      sConString;
        String      sSQLString;

        // create temporary variables for Execute method call

        long        lRecordsAffected;
        int         nCmdType;

        // create a new instance of an ADO Connection object

        System.out.println("Connection object created.\n");

        // open the BiblioDSN data source with the Connection object

        sConString = "Provider=Microsoft.Jet.OLEDB.4.0; " +
                    "Data Source=C:\\Program Files\\" +
                            "Microsoft Visual Studio\\" +
                            "VB98\\Biblio.mdb";

        con.open(sConString);

        System.out.println("Connection opened.\n");

        // create a Recordset object from a SQL string

        sSQLString = "SELECT TOP 10 Author FROM Authors";
```

Example 3-3. A Simple Visual J++ Example (continued)

```
rst = con.execute(sSQLString);

System.out.println("SQL statement processed.\n");

// retrieve all the data within the Recordset object

System.out.println("Getting data now...\n\n");

while (!rst.getEOF()) {
    System.out.println(rst.getField("Author").getValue());
    rst.moveNext();
}

System.out.println("\nEnd of data.\n");

// close and remove the Recordset object from memory

rst.close();
rst = null;

System.out.println("Closed and removed " +
                "Recordset object from memory.\n");

// close and remove the Connection object from memory

con.close();
con = null;

System.out.println("Closed and removed " +
                "Connection object from memory.\n");

    }

}
```

Notice that with the WFC, the implementation of ADO is just as easy as the implementation of ADO within Visual Basic.

Accessing ADO with VBScript

ActiveX Data Objects can be accessed from within server-side scripts via Active Server Pages, better known as ASP (which in this case does *not* stand for Application Service Provider). Although this book does not go into ASP in detail,* a brief

---

* For more detailed information, see *ASP in a Nutshell, Second Edition* by A. Keyton Weissinger (O'Reilly & Associates, 2000), which goes into depth about how to incorporate ADO into your ASP pages. In addition, *Developing ASP Components* by Shelley Powers (O'Reilly & Associates, 1999) covers accessing ADO from Visual Basic and Visual J++, discussing how to create an OLE DB simple data provider.

explanation of the technology is needed to understand how to develop VBScript code that uses ActiveX Data Objects.

When a client requests an ASP (Active Server Page) from a server, the ASP is "executed" before it is sent to the calling client. If there are any scripts embedded within the Active Server Page, they are executed. The result of this execution of different scripts is a static HTML page that can be viewed by virtually any web browser.

Active X Data Objects therefore can be embedded within a server-side script in order to gather and display information for the client in a low-resource-intensive manner. Because the ADO code is run on a server, the HTML page contains only the result, not the code. Once the page has been dynamically created by the server, it is passed back to the client for static reading. Because the web server does not pass actual recordsets, or rows of data, the potential savings in bandwidth can be considerable.

Referencing ActiveX Data Objects

In order to use ActiveX Data Objects from within your server-side scripts, your server must be running IIS (Internet Information Server) Version 3.0 or better. Along with IIS, you must of course have installed ADO, which is part of the MDAC installation. MDAC and IIS are included as part of the Windows 2000 operating system.

Also, in order to use ADO constants, you should copy the file *adovbs.inc* to the directory in which your HTML pages that use ADO reside. You can reference the *adovbs.inc* file by adding the following line of code to your HTML source:

```
<!--#include file="adovbs.inc"-->
```

Creating ActiveX Data Objects

In VBScript, the Variant is the only datatype. This type can represent just about any type of information that you could possibly want it to. Although in Visual Basic developers usually try to avoid using the Variant datatype at all costs, it is a necessary component of almost any VBScript code.

The first step in creating our ActiveX Data Objects in VBScript, as in Visual Basic, is to define the variables that will be used as references to our ActiveX Data Objects:

```
' define our variables which will be used as references to the
' Connection and Recordset objects
Dim con
Dim rst
```

You should notice that I did not use the **As** *datatype* notation in the variable-declaration statements. This is because VBScript does not allow us to define variables as a particular type. Because of this, we cannot directly create our variables as ADO objects. Instead, we must use late binding through the CreateObject method of the Server object to assign ActiveX Data objects to our Variant variables:

```
' create a new instance of an ADO Connection object
Set con = Server.CreateObject("ADODB.Connection")

' create a new instance of an ADO Recordset object
Set rst = Server.CreateObject("ADODB.Recordset")
```

Just as in Visual Basic, it is always good practice to remove your objects from memory before your code ends:

```
' remove the objects
Set con = Nothing
Set rst = Nothing
```

Using ADO with VBScript: An Example

Example 3-4 uses VBScript along with ActiveX Data Objects to create a static HTML sheet that can be passed from the Microsoft Internet Information Server to a client's web browser. It must be assigned a filename ending with an *.asp* extension and it must be stored in an IIS virtual directory so that IIS recognizes it as an Active Server Page.

As with the other projects, ensure that the *Biblio.mdb* file is located in the *C:\Program Files\Microsoft Visual Studio\VB98* directory or that the correct location is entered in the ASP page that you create.

Example 3-4. A Simple ASP Example Using VBScript

```
<% @LANGUAGE="VBScript" %>
<% Option Explicit %>
<!--#include file="adovbs.inc"-->

<html>

<head>
<title>Example of ADO using VBScript</title>
</head>

<body>
<%

    ' define our variables which will be used as references to our
    ' ActiveX Data Objects

    Dim con
    Dim rst
```

Example 3-4. A Simple ASP Example Using VBScript (continued)

```
' create two strings for use with the creation of a connection
' and a recordset

Dim sConString
Dim sSQLString


' create a new instance of an ADO Connection object

Set con = Server.CreateObject("ADODB.Connection")

Response.Write "Connection object created.<BR>"

' open the BiblioDSN data source with the Connection object

sConString = "Provider=Microsoft.Jet.OLEDB.4.0; " _
         & "Data Source=C:\\Program Files\\" _
         &                "Microsoft Visual Studio\\" _
         &                "VB98\\Biblio.mdb"

con.Open sConString

Response.Write "Connection opened.<BR>"

' create a Recordset object from a SQL string

sSQLString = "SELECT TOP 10 Author FROM Authors"

Set rst = con.Execute(sSQLString)

Response.Write "SQL statement processed.<BR>"

' retrieve all the data within the Recordset object

Response.Write "Getting data now...<BR><BR>"

Do Until (rst.EOF)
    Response.Write rst("Author") & "<BR>"
    rst.MoveNext
Loop

Response.Write "<BR>End of data.<BR>"

' close and remove the Recordset object from memory

rst.Close
Set rst = Nothing

Response.Write "Closed and removed " _
         & "Recordset object from memory.<BR>"
```

Example 3-4. A Simple ASP Example Using VBScript (continued)

```
' close and remove the Connection object from memory
con.Close
Set con = Nothing
Response.Write "Closed and removed " _
            & "Connection object from memory.<BR>"

%>

</body>
</html>
```

As with the other examples shown so far, the previous code may not mean too much to you yet. Right now, remember that when implementing ADO with VBScript, there are two important things that you should always remember. The first is that all variables are created as Variant datatypes. The second is that you must use late binding through the use of the Server.CreateObject method in order to assign a new instance of an ActiveX Data Object to a Variant datatype.

Accessing ADO with JScript

The JScript implementation of ActiveX Data Objects is almost identical to that of VBScript. The only difference is in the syntax. JScript server-side scripts are used within Active Server Pages and (with the help of Internet Information Server) are issued to a client web browser.

Referencing ActiveX Data Objects

Once difference between the VBScript and JScript implementations of ADO is the name of the include file for ActiveX Data Objects. In JScript, the filename is *adojavas.inc*. To add it to an Active Server Page, type the following line:

```
<!--#include file="adojavas.inc"-->
```

Creating ActiveX Data Objects

The first thing you need to do is create the variables that will hold your objects:

```
// define a variable which will be used as a reference to the
// Connection object
var con;

// define a variable which will be used as a reference to the
// Recordset object
var rec;
```

Once you have the variable references, you can create ActiveX Data Objects with the CreateObject function of the Server object just as in VBScript:

```
' create a new instance of an ADO Connection object
con = Server.CreateObject("ADODB.Connection");

' create a new instance of an ADO Recordset object
rst = Server.CreateObject("ADODB.Recordset");
```

Again, always remove your unused objects by setting them to null:

```
' remove the objects
con = null;
rst = null;
```

Using ADO with JScript: An Example

The last example in this chapter is very similar to the VBScript example. The JScript program in Example 3-5 illustrates how an Active Server Page can use the JScript scripting language to create and instantiate ActiveX Data Objects on an Internet Information Server in order to create standard static HTML pages to be sent back to a requesting client. The ASP page should be stored in a file with an *.asp* extension that is located in an IIS virtual directory.

Once again, ensure that the *Biblio.mdb* file resides in the *C:\Program Files\ Microsoft Visual Studio\VB98* directory or that the directory entered in the ASP source matches the location of the Access database file.

Example 3-5. A Simple ASP Page Using JScript

```
<% @LANGUAGE="JScript" %>
<!--#include file="adojavas.inc"-->
<html>

<head>
    <title>Example of ADO using JScript</title>
</head>

<body>
<script LANGUAGE="JScript" RUNAT="server">

    // define our variables which will be used as references to our
    // ActiveX Data Objects and instantiate a new Connection object

    var con = Server.CreateObject("ADODB.Connection");
    var rst;

    Response.write("Connection object created.<BR>");

    // create two strings for use with the creation of a connection
    // and a recordset
```

Example 3-5. A Simple ASP Page Using JScript (continued)

```jscript
var sConString;
var sSQLString;


// create temporary variable for Execute method call

var lRecordsAffected;

// open the BiblioDSN data source with the Connection object

sConString = "Provider=Microsoft.Jet.OLEDB.4.0; " +
             "Data Source=C:\\Program Files\\" +
                          "Microsoft Visual Studio\\" +
                          "VB98\\Biblio.mdb";

con.Open(sConString, "", "", -1);

Response.write("Connection opened.<BR>");

// create a Recordset object from a SQL string

sSQLString = "SELECT TOP 10 Author FROM Authors";

rst = con.Execute(sSQLString,
                  lRecordsAffected,
                  adCmdText);

Response.write("SQL statement processed.<BR>");

// retrieve all the data within the Recordset object

Response.write("Getting data now...<BR><BR>");

while (!rst.EOF) {
    Response.write(rst("Author") + "<BR>");
    rst.MoveNext();
}

Response.write("<BR>End of data.<BR>");

// close and remove the Recordset object from memory

rst.Close();
rst = null;

Response.write("Closed and removed " +
               "Recordset object from memory.<BR>");

// close and remove the Connection object from memory

con.Close();
con = null;
```

Example 3-5. A Simple ASP Page Using JScript (continued)

```
Response.write("Closed and removed " +
               "Connection object from memory.<BR>");

</script>

</body>
</html>
```

Summary

This chapter has explained how to access and use ActiveX Data Objects with the five most commonly used Microsoft development languages: Visual Basic, Visual C++, Visual J++, VBScript, and JScript. The following is a list of key points:

- Visual Basic is an easy language with which to develop ActiveX Data Object applications due to its minimal setup.

- Visual C++ offers a keyword, #import, to help create type library information for ADO enumerations (groups of constants) and interfaces. In addition, OLE must be instantiated before any ActiveX Data Objects are created at all.

- Visual J++ uses the Java Type Library Wizard to create type library information for ADO enumerations and interfaces.

- VBScript and JScript can be used through Active Server Pages to provide requesting clients with static HTML pages based upon an OLE DB data source.

- The interface for ActiveX Data Objects is extremely similar throughout all of the languages we have looked at, making it easy to move your skills from one language to another.

The next chapter in this book, Chapter 4, *The Connection Object*, deals with the most fundamental object within ADO, the Connection object. This object is used to create a session with a data source and to create different views with the data source's data.

4

The Connection Object

Within ADO, all activity is centered on the Connection object. A Connection object represents a unique physical connection to a data source. The characteristics of a connection are defined by the values that you pass to the Connection object.*

Opening and Closing a Connection: Implicit Versus Explicit

The Connection object is used to establish a unique physical connection to a given data source. This connection defines how you can obtain, interact with, and manipulate data from the specified source. While a Connection object is always required, you can choose whether to instantiate a connection explicitly or to allow ADO to create one implicitly on your behalf.

Opening a Connection

Example 4-1 illustrates how to open a `Recordset` object on a table in a data source without explicitly creating a Connection object.

Example 4-1. Implicit Creation of a Connection Object

```
' declare and instantiate a Recordset
Dim rst As ADODB.Recordset
Set rst = New ADODB.Recordset

' open the Recordset object and implicitly create a Connection
rst.Open "Titles", _
        "DSN=BiblioDSN", _
```

---

* For a complete list of the Connection object's methods, see Chapter 13, *ADO API Reference.*

Example 4-1. Implicit Creation of a Connection Object (continued)

```
        adOpenForwardOnly, _
        adLockReadOnly, _
        adCmdTable
'
' do something

' close the Recordset and clean up
rst.Close
Set rst = Nothing
```

Don't worry about not understanding the entire example now—I will explain everything soon. Do notice, however, how easy it is to open a table within a data source. Example 4-1 relies on no other code to first establish a connection; the simple connection string DSN=BiblioDSN tells ADO that the table, Titles, is in the BiblioDSN data source.

Some objects in ADO—in particular, the Recordset and the Command objects—do not require a pre-existing Connection object to operate. Both objects can read and write data to a data source, and both need a physical connection to a data source to do so. But the Recordset and the Command objects can create their own Connection objects in the background with information that you supply. The choice of declare and establish a connection with the Connection object or to let the Recordset or Command object handle the work for you.

By using your own Connection object, you gain greater control over your data access and manipulation. For instance, with a Connection object, you can execute queries through stored procedures that reside in a data source or through SQL statements that you explicitly declare to your application at runtime. The Connection object also offers transaction management so that at critical points in your data-manipulation code, the integrity of your data source can be preserved if an error were to occur.

Take a look at Example 4-2, which first explicitly creates and opens a Connection object to establish a connection before opening the table from the database.

Example 4-2. Explicit Creation of a Connection Object

```
' declare and instantiate a Connection and a Recordset
Dim con As ADODB.Connection
Dim rst As ADODB.Recordset

Set con = New ADODB.Connection
Set rst = New ADODB.Recordset

' first establish a connection to the data source
con.Open "DSN=BiblioDSN"
```

Example 4-2. Explicit Creation of a Connection Object (continued)

```
' now open the recordset using the established Connection
rst.Open "Titles", _
        con, _
        adOpenForwardOnly, _
        adLockReadOnly, _
        adCmdTable

' do something

' close the Recordset and clean up
rst.Close
Set rst = Nothing

' close the Connection and clean up
con.Close
Set con = Nothing
```

Notice the amount of extra work that is needed to open the Connection object before opening the Recordset object. Instead of passing a connection string to the Open method of the Recordset object, we are passing the already opened Connection object. This longer piece of code is accomplishing exactly what the previous example did in fewer lines. If a connection string is passed to a Recordset, the Recordset object creates its own Connection object from that string. If you pass a Connection object to a Recordset object, a new Connection object is not created. When opening a lot of Recordset objects, it would be advantageous to pass a Connection object, not a connection string, so that only one connection to the database is created. Figure 4-1 shows us the difference between creating Connection objects implicitly versus explicitly.

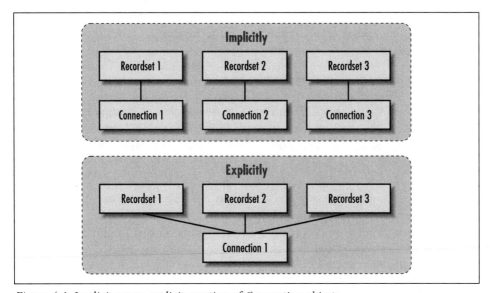

Figure 4-1. Implicit versus explicit creation of Connection objects

Creating a Connection object should be done implicitly when you need only one or a small number of connections to a data source. If you plan on having multiple recordsets, or views, of the same data source, you should create your own Connection object, which requires fewer system resources and offers better control, as you will learn in the following sections.

Closing a Connection

Although I have not specifically defined how to close a Connection object, you have seen it in all of the code presented thus far. You can use the Close method to close or disconnect the Connection object from the data source. When you use this method, the physical connection is lost, but the Connection object itself remains. It can be reopened with the same properties, or those properties can be altered before the Connection object is opened again. To fully remove the Connection object from memory, to free resources, and to remain respectable in the development community, set the object to the value **Nothing**, as shown here:

```
Set con = Nothing
```

Now that you know how to both establish and break a connection to a data source, we should take a look at the various options that we can use when connecting. These options dictate the ways in which our data is presented to us in the rest of our applications.

 When you are using a client-side Connection object with Remote Data Service (RDS), the connection with the server is not actually established by the Open method. Instead, RDS waits until a Recordset object is opened on the Connection object.

Configuring Connections

Let's now take a look at the different ways in which we can configure the connection to a data source through the use of a Connection object. In this section, I will explain how to work with connection strings and Data Source Names (DSNs). Connection strings are detailed explanations of how to open a data source, while Data Source Names are just a name of a definition that is stored on the current machine, by the operating system rather than the application. In addition, I will also talk about how to obtain the version number for the ADO library that you are using and how to set connection options such as the cursor location (whether to run the cursor on the server or the client), the default database setting, and the permission settings.

Working with Connection Strings

All connections revolve around connection strings, which contain all the pertinent information to ADO concerning the establishment of a connection to our data source. The connection string comprises a number of arguments. There are five standard ADO arguments that can be used in a connection string:

Provider

> Identifies the name of the data provider that you wish to use to establish a connection to a data source. The data provider indicates the type of data source. The Provider argument can be set to such things as Microsoft's OLE DB provider for SQL Server (SQLOLEDB.1) or Microsoft's OLE DB provider for Jet (Microsoft.Jet.OLEDB.4.0). (I will talk about the various types of data providers later in this chapter.)

File Name

> Specifies an exact filename (including a path) with which the connection should be established. Because this argument forces ADO to load the data provider that is associated with the data-source type of the file, the Provider argument cannot be used with the File Name argument; when the File Name argument is used, the data provider is implicit rather than explicit.

Remote Provider

> Used only when implementing RDS from a client-side Connection object to specify the name of a data provider. As a matter of fact, when using a client-side Connection object, you can use only the Remote Provider and Remote Server arguments.

Remote Server

> Used only when implementing RDS from a client-side Connection object to specify the path to a remote server. As a matter of fact, when using a client-side Connection object, you can use only the Remote Provider and Remote Server arguments.

URL

> Used to specify a resource, such as a file or a directory, as the data source. When using this argument, it must be in the form of an absolute URL (for example, *http://JROFF-NTLT/Documents/ADO.DOC.01*).

The ConnectionString is a public property of the Connection object that is set before the connection is opened. Here is an example of a ConnectionString that could be used to connect to an Oracle database, using the username of BigBear and the password, 1810:

```
"Provider=MSDAORA.1; Data Source=WidgetOracle; User ID=BigBear; Password=1810;"
```

The default data provider is the Microsoft OLE DB provider for ODBC drivers (or MSDASQL.1). Because it is the default provider, you don't necessarily have to name it in the ConnectionString. The following two connection strings are identical:

```
"Provider=MSDASQL.1; Data Source=WidgetsDSN; User ID=BigBear; Password=1810;"
```

and:

```
"Data Source=WidgetsDSN; User ID=BigBear; Password=1810;"
```

Example 4-3 shows the ways in which we can use the ConnectionString when we open the Connection object.

Example 4-3. The Two Different Ways of Opening a Connection Object

```
' declare and instantiate a Connection
Dim con As ADODB.Connection
Set con = New ADODB.Connection

' set the Connection String property
con.ConnectionString = "Provider=MSDASQL.1; " _
                    & "Data Source=BiblioDSN"

' open the Connection object using the connection string that was just set
con.Open

' display the version of ADO
MsgBox "Connection opened with ADO Version " & con.Version

' close the Connection
con.Close

' set the Connection String property with the Open method
con.Open "Provider=MSDASQL.1; " _
        & "Data Source=BiblioDSN"

' print the version of ADO and close the Connection object
MsgBox "Connection opened with ADO Version " & con.Version

' close the Connection and clean up
con.Close
Set con = Nothing
```

In the first part of the code, you can see that we set the ConnectionString as a property of the Connection object, and in the second part of the code, we passed the ConnectionString as an argument to the Open method of the Connection object. Either way works, and there is no real benefit to using one method over another.

The ConnectionString property of the Connection object has another useful function, however. Because it has read ability as well as write ability, we can use the

ConnectionString property to view the ConnectionString used by a Connection object that was implicitly created with another object, such as a Recordset object, as shown in Example 4-4.

Example 4-4. Reading the ConnectionString Property of the Connection Object

```
' declare and instantiate a Connection and a Recordset
Dim con As ADODB.Connection
Dim rst As ADODB.Recordset

Set con = New ADODB.Connection
Set rst = New ADODB.Recordset

' open the recordset, creating a Connection object implicitly
rst.Open "Titles", _
         "Provider=MSDASQL.1; Data Source=BiblioDSN", _
         adOpenForwardOnly, , _
         adCmdTable

' set con to the Connection object that was just created by
' the Recordset object in the above Method call
Set con = rst.ActiveConnection

' print the ConnectionString of the implicitly created Connection object
Debug.Print con.ConnectionString

' close and clean up the Recordset object
rst.Close
Set rst = Nothing

' close and clean up the Connection object
con.Close
Set con = Nothing
```

After running the previous code, the ConnectionString property of the implicitly created Connection object is printed to the Immediate window of the VB IDE. You should get an output message similar to the following:

```
Provider=MSDASQL.1;Data Source=BiblioDSN;
Extended Properties="DSN=BiblioDSN;DBQ=C:\Inetpub\wwwroot\BIBLIO.MDB;
DriverId=25;FIL=MS Access;MaxBufferSize=2048;PageTimeout=5;"
```

By reading the ConnectionString property, you can determine what settings are being used when connecting to a data source. For instance, in the previous example, you could parse the String for MaxBufferSize and see that it was set to 2048.

Working with Data Source Names

Another way in which to use the Open method of the Connection object is for the ConnectionString to be set to a valid Data Source Name (DSN). Valid DSNs are maintained in the ODBC applet in the Windows Control Panel. This is where all of the information regarding connections is stored. Using a DSN allows you to not worry about the actual definition of the connection string in your application. The details (such as the data-source type and location) are maintained by the ODBC applet on the system you are running your application. When using a DSN, ADO looks up the connection information through the ODBC applet.

Installing the DSNs

Throughout the rest of this book, I will be using two DSNs. The first of these two DSNs is BiblioDSN, which uses an ODBC driver for Microsoft Access to connect to the *Biblio.mdb* database usually located in the *C:\Program Files\Microsoft Visual Studio\VB98* directory when you install Visual Basic. The second is SQLNorthwindDSN, which uses an ODBC driver for SQL Server to connect to the Northwind database, installed with SQL Server.

To set up the BiblioDSN:

1. Open the Data Sources ODBC setup utility within the Control Panel (for Windows 9x and NT) or under Administrative Tools within the Control Panel for Windows 2000.

2. From this dialog box, select the System DSN tab, and click on the Add button so that you get the Wizard shown in Figure 4-2.

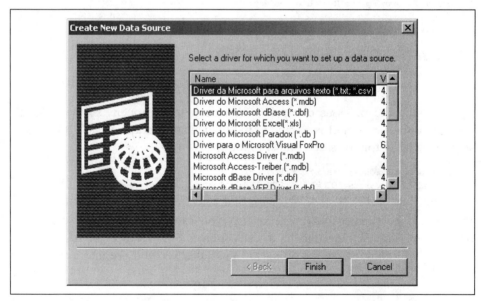

Figure 4-2. The Create New Data Source Wizard

3. From here, select the Microsoft Access driver, and click Finish. This should bring up the ODBC Microsoft Access Setup dialog box shown in Figure 4-3.

Fill out the Data Source Name (BiblioDSN) and the database (by clicking the Select button and navigating to the *Biblio.mdb* file).

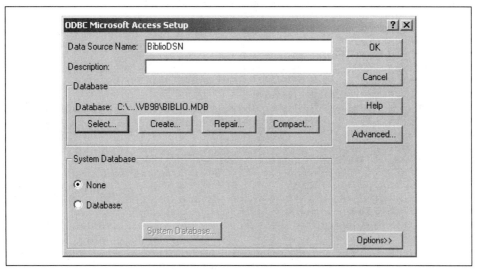

Figure 4-3. The ODBC Microsoft Access Setup dialog box

4. Once you have entered this information, hit the OK button to finish.

To set up the SQLNorthwindDSN:

1. Open the Data Sources ODBC setup utility within the Control Panel (for Windows 9x and NT) or under Administrative Tools within the Control Panel for Windows 2000.

2. From this dialog box, select the System DSN tab, and click the Add button so that you get the Wizard shown in Figure 4-1. Next, select the SQL Server driver and click the Finish button. You should see the "Create a New Data Source to SQL Server" dialog box, as shown in Figure 4-4. Fill in the Data Source Name (SQLNorthwindDSN), and choose your SQL Server of choice (I use my local machine).

3. Click the Next button, which brings up the panel in Figure 4-5. Here you must fill in a username and password to log on to the server. If you can click the Next button again, you don't have a problem with these settings.

4. The next screen, shown in Figure 4-6, allows you to choose your default database. Choose the Northwind database now, and click the Next button and then the Finish button so that you can see the summary screen shown in Figure 4-7. Here you can test your data source.

As soon as you choose the OK button, your new DSN is created for you to use.

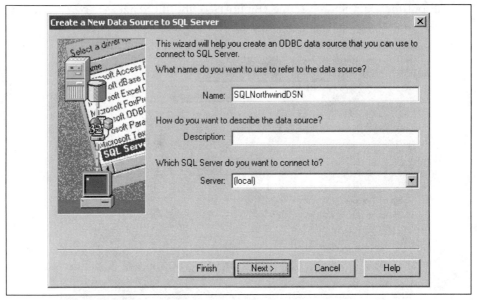

Figure 4-4. The Create New Data Source to SQL Server dialog box

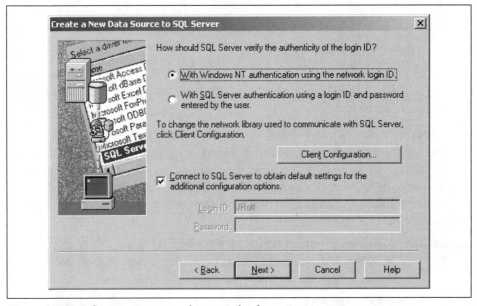

Figure 4-5. Specifying username and password information

Opening a connection with a DSN

Once a DSN has been created, all we have to supply ADO is the name of this DSN and logon information, as shown in Example 4-5.

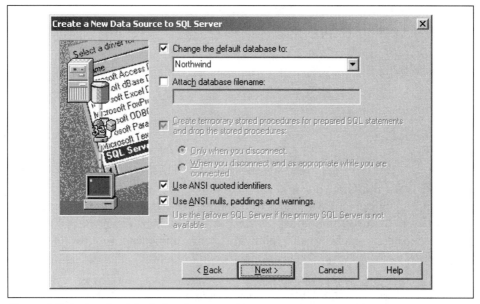

Figure 4-6. Setting the default database

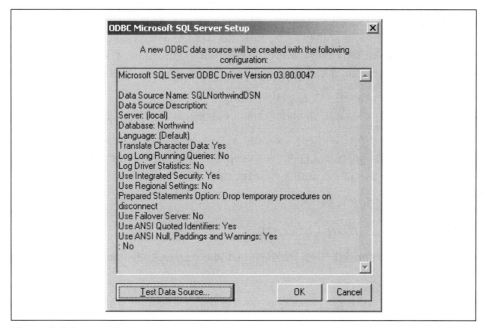

Figure 4-7. Summary screen

Example 4-5. Connecting to a Data Source Using a DSN

```
' instantiate a new instance of the Connection
Set con = ADODB.Connection
Set con = New ADODB.Connection
```

Example 4-5. Connecting to a Data Source Using a DSN (continued)

```
' establish a connection using only a DSN name and logon information
con.Open "BiblioDSN", _
         "Tammi", _
         "Rocks"

' print the ConnectionString used to establish this connection
Debug.Print con.ConnectionString

' close and clean up
con.Close
Set con = Nothing
```

This code calls the Open method of the Connection object with a Connection-String containing only a DSN name. In addition, the arguments Tammi and Rocks were used as the username and password. After running the previous code, you should see output similar to the following in the Immediate window of the VB IDE:

```
Provider=MSDASQL.1;Password=Rocks;User ID=Tammi;Data Source=BiblioDSN;
Extended Properties="DSN=BiblioDSN;DBQ=C:\Inetpub\wwwroot\BIBLIO.MDB;
DriverId=25;FIL=MS Access;MaxBufferSize=2048;PageTimeout=5;PWD=Rocks;
UID=admin;"
```

Obviously we did not send all of this information to ADO through the Connection-String, but regardless, it is there. The Provider argument was obtained through the ODBC applet in the Windows Control Panel along with some of the other information. These are the default values of the Connection object.

ADO determines that the ConnectionString argument being passed through the Open method is a DSN if it does not contain an equal sign (=).

It should be noted that you can use any valid connection string when opening a Connection object, not just a DSN. For simplicity in our examples for this chapter, I have chosen to use DSNs until you learn more about the details of a connection string.

Setting Connection Options

There are four connection properties that we can specify via the Connection object:

Default database

The DefaultDatabase property allows you to specify which database, on a multiple-database connection, is to be the default.

Data access permissions

By using the Mode property, you can either grant or read the permissions for accessing data for the given connection. In other words, you can determine whether the current user has read, write, or both read and write access to data over the given connection. In addition, you can deny others any of these rights.

Timeout setting

The ConnectionTimeout property provides a way of setting the number of seconds for which ADO will wait until it can establish a connection with the data source we specify.

Cursor location

The CursorLocation property specifies where the data will be processed when referenced by your application. We can specify that the cursor will reside either on the server (server-side) or on the client (client-side).

These properties are described in the following sections.

Default database

When the particular data provider that you are using allows the use of multiple databases per connection, I recommend that you set the DefaultDatabase property (shown in Example 4-6), because if you are using a DSN, it is possible that it will be pointing to a database that you do not care to use. This property indicates the database that is used for default access, via SQL statements, throughout any use of the Connection object. You should also set the DefaultDatabase for Recordset and Command objects that have been created with their ActiveConnection property set to such a Connection object.

If your data provider allows the use of multiple databases per connection, you must specify the name of alternate databases in SQL statements when you access them. All other statements (those that do not specify a database name) will revert to the default database specified by the DefaultDatabase property.

Example 4-6. Displaying the Default Database

```
' instantiate a new instance of the Connection
Set con = ADODB.Connection
Set con = New ADODB.Connection

' open a connection on a given DSN (Data Source Name)
con.Open "SQLNorthwindDSN"

' display the name of the current default database
MsgBox "The default database is: " & con.DefaultDatabase

' set the new default database of the currently open Connection object
con.DefaultDatabase = "Master"
```

Example 4-6. Displaying the Default Database (continued)

```
' display the name of the current default database
MsgBox "The default database is: " & con.DefaultDatabase

' close and clean up
con.Close
Set con = Nothing
```

In Example 4-6, the output of the DefaultDatabase property is **Master**, exactly as it is shown being set. The location (full qualified path) and filename (minus the database file extension) is reported.

If your data provider does not allow the use of multiple databases per connection, the DefaultDatabase property is read-only to your application. If your data provider does not support the DefaultDatabase property, either an empty string will be returned, or you will get an **adErrFeatureNotAvailable** error.

The DefaultDatabase property is not available to a client-side Connection object when using RDS.

Data-access permissions

With the Mode property, you can specify the types of permissions that are allowed on a connection. The Mode property can be set only while the Connection object is closed and is read-only once it is opened.

The Mode property can be set to one of the values specified by the **ConnectModeEnum** enumeration, which establishes the permissions for reading and writing data to the connection. The values of **ConnectModeEnum** are shown in Table 4-1.

Table 4-1. The ConnectModeEnum Values

Constant	Value	Description
AdModeUnkown	0	Default. Either the permissions of the current connection have not been set yet, or they are undeterminable.
AdModeRead	1	The user has read-only permission to the current connection.
AdModeWrite	2	The user has write-only permission to the current connection.
adModeReadWrite	3	The user has both read and write permissions to the current connection.

Table 4-1. The ConnectModeEnum Values (continued)

Constant	Value	Description
adModeShareDenyRead	4	Others are prevented from opening the current connection with read permissions.
adModeShareDenyWrite	8	Others are prevented from opening the current connection with write permissions.
adModeShareExclusive	12	Others are prevented from opening the current connection with either read or write permissions.
adModeShareDenyNone	16	Others are prevented from opening the current connection with any permissions at all.
adModeRecursive	&H400000	Used with the ShareDeny constants so that the permissions are recursively set to all children resources, such as in a file structure.

Example 4-7 demonstrates the setting of the Mode property on a Connection object. In addition, this example displays a message based on the current setting of the Mode property.

Example 4-7. Setting Data-Access Permissions

```
Dim con As ADODB.Connection
Dim sPermissions As String

Set con = New ADODB.Connection

' do not allow other users to write to the data source
con.Mode = adModeShareDenyWrite

' open the Connection object with a connection string
con.Open "DSN=SQLNorthwindDSN"

' print the current Mode property setting once the connection object
' is opened to verify the permissions
Select Case (con.Mode)

    Case adModeUnknown:
        sPermissions = "Unkown or unset permissions."

    Case adModeRead:
        sPermissions = "User cannot read data."

    Case adModeWrite:
        sPermissions = "User cannot write data."

    Case adModeReadWrite:
        sPermissions = "User cannot read nor write data."

    Case adModeShareDenyRead:
        sPermissions = "Other users cannot read data."
```

Example 4-7. Setting Data-Access Permissions (continued)

```
    Case adModeShareDenyWrite:
        sPermissions = "Other users cannot write data."

    Case adModeShareExclusive:
        sPermissions = "Other users cannot read or write data."

    Case adModeShareDenyNone:
        sPermissions = "Other users cannot do anything with data."

End Select

' close the connection to the data source
con.Close

' display permissions
MsgBox sPermissions

' clean up
Set con = Nothing
```

The Mode property is very useful when you need to restrict other users from accessing your data source. This usually occurs when yours needs to be the only application that allows changes to a particular database or when it is important that other applications do not change information that your application has changed.

The constant value of **adModeUnknown** is the only valid value for the Mode property when you are using a client-side Connection object with RDS.

Timeout setting

The Connection object uses the value of the ConnectionTimeout property to define the maximum number of seconds that ADO has to attempt to open a connection to a data source. The default value for this property is 15, or 15 seconds.

If the value of the ConnectionTimeout property is set to zero, then ADO will wait forever for a connection to complete. By setting the value of this property, you can abandon a connection when the network is too busy for this type of operation to take place. If the connection does not complete within the specified time interval, then an error is generated and ADO cancels the attempt.

The code in Example 4-8 illustrates how you can use the ConnectionTimeout property to abandon the opening of a connection to a data source. Notice how this subroutine handles errors. ADO can produce multiple errors; therefore, we must loop through a collection of errors and handle each one.

Example 4-8. Handling a Connection Timeout

```
Public Sub OpenDataSource()
On Error GoTo ERR_OpenDataSource:

    Dim con As ADODB.Connection
    Set con = New ADODB.Connection

    ' set the timeout period to 2 seconds
    con.ConnectionTimeout = 2

    ' attempt to open the Connection object with a connection string
    con.Open "DSN=SQLNorthwindDSN"

    '
    ' do something here
    '

    ' close the connection
    con.Close

' clean up
GoTo CleanUp:

' an error has occurred
ERR_OpenDataSource:

    Dim oErr As ADODB.Error

    ' there can be multiple errors in ADO;
    ' therefore, we must look at all of them
    For Each oErr In con.Errors

        Select Case (Err.Number)

            Case adErrStillConnecting:
                ' timeout error
                MsgBox "The connection timed out on attempting to open."

            Case Else:
                ' other type of error
                MsgBox "Other Error: " & oErr.Description

        End Select

    Next oErr

' this code will be run whether or not there was an error
CleanUp:

    ' clean up
    Set con = Nothing

End Sub
```

The ConnectionTimeout property is read-only once the Connection object is opened, and it can be used only if the specified data provider supports it. Writing to the ConnectionTimeout property while the Connection object is open will generate an error.

Cursor location

When opening a Connection object on a given data source, you can indicate whether you would like either a client-side or a server-side cursor for that object. Client-side cursors indicate that local cursor libraries will process the data from your connection locally. Server-side cursors indicate that the data provider will process the data from your connection on the server.

Your decision to use either client-side or server-side cursors should be based on the relative abilities of your local cursor libraries and those of the data provider. Usually, you would change the location of your cursor to take advantage of special features not available in another location.

Changing the location of your cursor is done with the CursorLocation property. By setting the CursorLocation property to **adUseClient** (or **adUseClientBatch** for earlier versions of ADO), you indicate to ADO that you want your data to be client-side, supplied by a local cursor library. By setting this property to **adUseServer**, which is the default, you indicate that you wish ADO to use the data provider or driver-supplied cursors for the given data source, residing wherever the data source resides.

CursorLocation is a read-write property. However, if you change its value, you will not see its effects until the Connection object's Open method is called. In other words, if the Connection object is already open when you change the value of the CursorLocation property, the location of the cursor will not change until that Connection object is closed and then reopened with the Open method, as Example 4-9 illustrates.

Example 4-9. Changing the Cursor Location

```
Dim con As ADODB.Connection
Set con = New ADODB.Connection

' set the ConnectionString property to use our DSN
con.ConnectionString = "SQLNorthwindDSN"

' set the cursor location to client-side
con.CursorLocation = adUseClient

' open the Connection object
con.Open
```

Example 4-9. Changing the Cursor Location (continued)

```
' we are using a client-side client

' do something here

' change the cursor location
con.CursorLocation = adUseServer

' this has no effect yet until we reopen the Connection object

con.Close

con.Open

' now we are using a server-side client
'
' do something here

' close the current connection
con.Close

' clean up
Set con = Nothing
```

When you are using a client-side Connection object with RDS, the CursorLocation property can be set only to adUseClient.

Determining ADO Version Number and Connection State

You can determine the version of ADO that you are using with the Version property of the Connection object. The value returned by the Version property is a read-only string. The following code fragment prints the version of ADO:

```
Dim con as ADODB.Connection
Set con = New ADODB.Connection

' print the current version of ActiveX Data Objects
Debug.Print con.Version
```

You can also determine whether the current connection is open or closed by reading the value of the State property of the Connection object. This property returns a long value that can be used to check the state of the Connection object. The connection can either be opened or closed, as represented by the constants adStateOpen and adStateClosed, respectively.

The following piece of code displays the state of the current Connection object:

```
If (con.State & adStateClosed) Then
    Debug.Print "The con object is currently closed."
End If

If (con.State & adStateConnecting) Then
    Debug.Print "The con object is currently connecting."
End If

If (con.State & adStateExecuting) Then
    Debug.Print "The con object is currently executing."
End If

If (con.State & adStateFetching) Then
    Debug.Print "The con object is currently fetching."
End If

If (con.State & adStateOpen) Then
    Debug.Print "The con object is currently open."
End If
```

Choosing a Data Provider

As of this writing, Microsoft supplies ten OLE DB providers with ADO. These providers are listed in Table 4-2. Other companies supply their own OLE DB providers. In this book, I will focus on the OLE DB provider for ODBC drivers and the OLE DB providers for SQL Server and Microsoft Access.

Table 4-2. Available Microsoft OLE DB Providers

Provider	Value
Microsoft OLE DB provider for ODBC	MSDASQL.1
Microsoft OLE DB provider for Microsoft Indexing Service	MSIDXS
Microsoft OLE DB provider for Microsoft Active Directory Service	ADSDSOObject
Microsoft OLE DB provider for Microsoft Jet	Microsoft.Jet.OLEDB.4.0
Microsoft OLE DB provider for SQL Server	SQLOLEDB
Microsoft OLE DB provider for Oracle	MSDAORA
Microsoft OLE DB provider for Internet Publishing	MSDAIPP.DSO
Microsoft Data Shaping Service for OLE DB (ADO Service Provider)	MSDataShape
Microsoft OLE DB Persistence Provider (ADO Service Provider)	MSPersist
Microsoft OLE DB Remoting Provider (ADO Service Provider)	MS Remote

The OLE DB provider for ODBC, supplied by Microsoft, is probably the most popular type of data source used today and is the default data provider of ADO. In other words, if you do not specify a data provider before opening a connection, ADO will assume you wish to use the ODBC OLE DB data provider. The ODBC OLE DB provider allows ADO to access any data source that has an ODBC-compliant driver, including, among others, flat files, Microsoft SQL Server, Microsoft Access, Microsoft FoxPro, Paradox, dBase, Oracle databases, and Microsoft Excel worksheets.

To explicitly choose the OLE DB provider for ODBC, set the value of the Provider argument in the ConnectionString of the Connection object to `MSDASQL.1`, as shown in Example 4-10. Additionally, this example illustrates the use of the ConnectionString to include arguments for usernames (UID) and passwords (PWD) with Connection objects `con1` and `con2`.

Example 4-10. Specifying the Microsoft OLE DB Provider for ODBC Drivers

```
Dim con1 As ADODB.Connection
Dim con2 As ADODB.Connection
Dim con3 As ADODB.Connection
Dim con4 As ADODB.Connection

Set con1 = New ADODB.Connection
Set con2 = New ADODB.Connection
Set con3 = New ADODB.Connection
Set con4 = New ADODB.Connection

' connect without using a DSN (Data Source Name)
con1.Open "Provider=MSDASQL.1; " _
        & "DRIVER={SQL Server}; " _
        & "Database=Northwind; " _
        & "Server=JROFF-NTLT; " _
        & "UID=sa; " _
        & "PWD="

' connect using a DSN and use the default provider
con2.Open "DSN=BiblioDSN; " _
        & "UID=BigBear; " _
        & "PWD=1810"

' connect using a DSN and specify the provider
con3.Open "Provider=MSDASQL.1; " _
        & "DSN=BiblioDSN; " _
        & "UID=Jason; " _
        & "PWD=1810; " _

' connect using a File DSN and specify the provider
con4.Open "Provider=MSDASQL.1; " _
        & "FileDSN=C:\Program Files\Common Files\ODBC\" _
                & "Data Sources\BiblioDSN.dsn"
```

Example 4-10. Specifying the Microsoft OLE DB Provider for ODBC Drivers (continued)

```
' close all connections
con1.Close
con2.Close
con3.Close
con4.Close

' clean up all connections
Set con1 = Nothing
Set con2 = Nothing
Set con3 = Nothing
Set con4 = Nothing
```

Data providers offer their own options for the syntax of the ConnectionString argument and property of the Connection object. The OLE DB provider for ODBC drivers is no exception. There are two ways to access a data source with this data provider through the connection string—the first with a DSN, the second without.

The following can be used to correctly specify a DSN:

```
    "Provider=MSDASQL.1; DSN=dsn_name; [DATABASE=database_name]; " _
 & "UID=user_name; PWD=password"

    "Provider=MSDASQL.1; FileDSN=dsn_file; [DATABASE=database_name]; " _
 & "UID=user_name; PWD=password"
```

As you can see, either a DSN name or a DSN filename can be given. The Provider argument is shown in both of these examples, but it is optional, since the OLE DB provider for ODBC drivers is the default data provider for ADO.

The DATABASE argument is optional. It refers to the name of the database to be used with the DSN, although one is already provided within the DSN itself. The DSN must be specified in the ODBC applet in the Windows Control Panel. Using the DATABASE argument in a DSN connection string actually alters the DSN definition, so it is important to use it whenever you can to ensure that you are getting the database that you need, in case someone else has altered the DSN definition.

An alternative syntax for an ODBC drivers data-provider connection string, a DSN-less connection, is as follows:

```
    "Provider=MSDASQL.1; DRIVER=driver; SERVER=server; " _
 & "DATABASE=database; UID=user_name; PWD=password;"
```

Connections of the preceding types do not need to include the Provider argument, because the OLE DB data provider for ODBC drivers is assumed to be the default. The DRIVER argument refers to the actual data-source driver for the connection. The SERVER argument refers to the name of the server chosen as the data source, and the DATABASE argument refers to the database name within the chosen server. See also the portion of code that opens the con1 Connection object in Example 4-10.

Executing Commands

ADO can work with data, or execute commands, in several ways:

1. Data can be queried or gathered based on a specific list of qualifications (selection commands).

2. Data can be manipulated with an action query that usually changes data in some common way throughout your data source (update commands).

3. Data can be restructured with statements that alter the way the data resides in a particular data source (restructuring commands).

These three types of data gathering and manipulation can be done through either SQL statements or stored procedures. The Connection object allows the execution of both SQL statements and stored procedures directly, through the use of an Execute method. The Execute method can also be used to open an entire table from your data source.

The following sections describe in detail execution of commands.

The Execute Method

There are two different syntaxes for the Connection object's Execute method. The first is for commands that return information in the form of a Recordset object (see Chapter 5, *The Recordset Object*), and the second is for commands that do not return anything.

The correct syntax for a call to the Execute method that returns a Recordset object is:

```
Set recordset = connection.Execute (CommandText, RecordsAffected, Options)
```

The correct syntax for a method call that does not return any records is:

```
connection.Execute CommandText, RecordsAffected, Options
```

Table 4-3 describes each of the components found in these syntaxes.

Table 4-3. The Components of the Execute Method

Component	Description
connection	A currently open Connection object.
CommandText	A string value containing a SQL statement, a table name, or a stored procedure command.
RecordsAffected	Optional. A long value that returns the number of records that were affected by the call to the Execute method.
Options	Optional. A long value that indicates the precise content of the CommandText argument. See Table 4-4.

Table 4-4 describes the different values for the Options argument of the Execute method, which are values of the CommandTypeEnum.

Table 4-4. The CommandTypeEnum Values

Constant	Value	Description
adCmdText	1	Indicates that the *CommandText* string is a data provider–specific command and will pass it onto that data provider for evaluation and execution. This value would be used when passing a SQL statement to a SQL data provider.
adCmdTable	2	Indicates that the *CommandText* string is evaluated as a name of a table in the current database. This type of *CommandText* string, when used with the Execute method of the Connection object, will result in a recordset that includes the entire table specified.
adCmdStoredProc	4	Indicates that the *CommandText* string is evaluated as a name of a stored procedure located within the current database.
adCmdUnknown	8	Default. Indicates that you have no clue what kind of information you are passing to the data provider and that the data provider will have to figure it out itself. This usually indicates that the Options flag was not set.
adCmdFile	256	Indicates that the *CommandText* string is evaluated as a name of a file that contains a previously persisted Recordset object. This option can be used only with the Open and Requery methods.
adCmdTableDirect	512	Indicates that the *CommandText* string is evaluated as a name of a table that you are requesting all of the columns to be returned. This option can be used only with the Open and Requery methods.

If you do not specify a value for the *Options* argument, then ADO has to communicate with your data provider to determine whether the *CommandText* string is a SQL statement, a stored procedure name, or a table name. This could take a considerable amount of time; therefore, it is recommended that you always specify the kind of information that you are sending to the data provider through the *CommandText* argument.

Example 4-11 illustrates how the Execute method can be used to execute each type of command matching those indicated in Table 4-4.

Example 4-11. Executing Different Command Types with the Connection Object

```
Dim con As ADODB.Connection
Dim rst As ADODB.Recordset

Set con = New ADODB.Connection
Set rst = New ADODB.Recordset
```

Example 4-11. Executing Different Command Types with the Connection Object (continued)

```
' use this variable to record the number of records affected by the
' Execute method
Dim lRecordsAffected As Long

' open the DSN (Data Source Name)
con.Open "SQLNorthwindDSN"

' execute a SQL statement on the database
Set rst = con.Execute("SELECT * FROM Orders;", _
                       lRecordsAffected, _
                       adCmdText)

' execute an open table command
Set rst = con.Execute("Orders", _
                       lRecordsAffected, _
                       adCmdTable)

rst.Close
Set rst = Nothing

' execute a stored proceudre
' notice that we did not specify the options argument, therefore,
' the data provider must determine what type of command this is
con.Execute "Invoices"

con.Close
Set con = Nothing
```

The OLE DB provider for ODBC can utilize the CommandText argument of the Execute method to access stored procedures with a special syntax. An example of this syntax appears in Example 4-12 where it is used to execute a Microsoft Access select query. (I will discuss the CommandText property of the Command object in Chapter 7, *The Command Object*.)

The Parameters collection belongs only to a Command object, not to a Connection object. For this reason, we cannot pass parameters to stored procedures via a Connection object. We can execute queries that do not require parameters, using this special syntax or by naming the stored procedure as in Example 4-12.

Example 4-12. Executing Stored Procedures

```
Dim con As ADODB.Connection
Dim rst As ADODB.Recordset

Set con = New ADODB.Connection
Set rst = New ADODB.Recordset

Dim lRecordsAffected As Long

con.Open "SQLNorthwindDSN"
```

Example 4-12. Executing Stored Procedures (continued)

```
' use just the name of the stored procedure
Set rst = con.Execute("[Ten Most Expensive Products]", _
                       lRecordsAffected, _
                       adCmdStoredProc)

' use OLE DB Provider for ODBC Drivers special stored procedure
' call syntax
Set rst = con.Execute("{call SalesByCategory(1)}", _
                       lRecordsAffected, _
                       adCmdText)

rst.Close
Set rst = Nothing

con.Close
Set con = Nothing
```

The code that is emphasized in Example 4-12 illustrates the syntax used for calling stored procedures with the OLE DB provider for ODBC drivers.

The CommandTimeout Property

The behavior of the Connection object's CommandTimeout property is very similar to the ConnectionTimeout property, although the setting for one does not affect the other. As described earlier, the ConnectionTimeout property indicates the maximum number of seconds allowed when completing a connection on a specified data source. The CommandTimeout property represents the maximum number of seconds allowed for ADO to complete a given command with the Execute method.

The default value for the CommandTimeout property is 30, representing 30 seconds. If the execution of a command exceeds the number of seconds specified in the CommandTimeout property, then the command is abandoned and an error is raised. This permits your command to timeout if network traffic is too busy to carry out such an operation.

Example 4-13 shows the use of the CommandTimeout property.

Example 4-13. The CommandTimeout Property

```
Public Sub CommandTimeout()
On Error GoTo ERR_CommandTimeout:

    Dim con As ADODB.Connection
    Set con = New ADODB.Connection

    ' set the timeout period to 2 seconds
    con.CommandTimeout = 2
```

Example 4-13. The CommandTimeout Property (continued)

```
    ' attempt to open the Connection object with a connection string
    con.Open "BiblioDSN"

    con.Execute "[All Titles]"

    ' close the connection
    con.Close

GoTo CleanUp:

' an error has occurred
ERR_CommandTimeout:

    Dim oErr As ADODB.Error

    ' there can be multiple errors in ADO; we must look at all of them
    For Each oErr In con.Errors

        Select Case (Err.Number)

            Case adErrStillConnecting:
                ' timeout error
                MsgBox "The command timed out on attempting to execute."

            Case Else:
                ' other type of error
                MsgBox "Other Error: " & oErr.Description

        End Select

    Next oErr

' this code will be ran whether there was an error or not
CleanUp:

    ' clean up
    Set con = Nothing

End Sub
```

The CommandTimeout property is read-only once the Connection object is opened, but while it is closed, you can either read or set its value.

Managing Multiple Transactions

Transaction management is used to maintain the integrity of a data source when operations on one or more data sources need to be treated as a single operation.

The most common example of transaction management comes from banking. Take, for instance, the steps involved in transferring money from a savings account to a checking account. First, you must remove the desired amount of money from the savings account, and then that amount must be added to your checking account. Suppose that somebody walked by and pulled the plug of the ATM machine just when it had completed removing your money from your savings account, but before it added it to your checking account.

By using three methods (BeginTrans, CommitTrans, and RollbackTrans), you can create single transactions from multiple operations.

The BeginTrans, CommitTrans, and RollbackTrans methods are not available when you are using a client-side Connection object with RDS.

Starting a Transaction: The BeginTrans and CommitTrans Methods

A transaction begins with a call to a Connection object's BeginTrans method and ends with a call to the CommitTrans method. The CommitTrans method indicates that the transaction is completed and that the data should be saved, or committed, to the data source.

The following code illustrates the use of the BeginTrans and CommitTrans methods:

```
' begin a new transaction
con.BeginTrans


'
' do some manipulation of the data here
'


' commit the manipulations of the data to the data source now
con.CommitTrans
```

Not all data providers support transactions, and you should check before using them. You can tell whether the current data provider supports transactions by checking for the Transaction DDL dynamic property by using the Properties collection of the Connection object. If it appears in the Connection object's Properties collection, then your data provider supports transaction management through the BeginTrans, CommitTrans, and RollbackTrans methods.

Example 4-14 shows how you can test for the support of transactions by your data provider, and how you can work with or without it depending on the result of your test.

Example 4-14. Testing for Transaction Support

```
Public Sub TestForTransactionSupport()

    Dim con As ADODB.Connection
    Set con = New ADODB.Connection

    ' open the connection on a given data source
    con.Open "BiblioDSN"

    ' if the data provider supports transactions, begin one
    If (SupportsTransactions(con)) Then con.BeginTrans

    ' manipulate data here
    '
    ' if the data provider supports transactions, commit changes
    If (SupportsTransactions(con)) Then con.CommitTrans

    ' close the Connection and clean up
    con.Close
    Set con = Nothing

End Sub

Private Function SupportsTransactions( _
                    conConnectionToTest As ADODB.Connection) As Boolean
On Error GoTo ERR_SupportsTransactions:

    Dim lValue As Long

    ' simply try to access the property to verify whether the data provider
    ' supports transactions
    lValue = conConnectionToTest.Properties("Transaction DDL").Value

    ' if we got this far, the property exists and the data provider
    ' supports transactions
    SupportsTransactions = True

Exit Function

ERR_SupportsTransactions:

    Select Case (Err.Number)

        ' property does not exist, therefore the data provider does not
        ' support transactions
        Case adErrItemNotFound:
            SupportsTransactions = False

        Case Else:
            ' another error

    End Select

End Function
```

Canceling a Transaction: The RollbackTrans Method

It doesn't make sense to keep track of transactions if you cannot cancel them, so the Connection object implements the RollbackTrans method. The RollbackTrans method cancels the current transaction, which is defined as the entire set of operations performed on the data source since the last call to the BeginTrans method. Once the RollbackTrans method is called, your data source will never see the changes that were made during the last transaction.

A common time to use the RollbackTrans method is immediately following an error that has occurred during the processing of data. Example 4-15 demonstrates the RollbackTrans method.

Example 4-15. The RollbackTrans Method

```
Public Sub Rollback()
On Error GoTo ERR_Rollback:

    Dim con As ADODB.Connection
    Set con = New ADODB.Connection

    ' open the connection on a given data source
    con.Open "BiblioDSN"

    ' begin a transaction
    con.BeginTrans

    '
    ' manipulate data here
    '

    ' commit changes
    con.CommitTrans

    ' skip rollback and close the connection
    GoTo CloseConnection

ERR_Rollback:

    ' an error has occurred, abort changes
    con.RollbackTrans

CloseConnection:

    ' close the Connection and clean up
    con.Close
    Set con = Nothing

End Sub
```

Nesting Transactions

If your data provider supports transactions, there is a good chance that it also supports nested transactions. For instance, Microsoft Access can support nested transactions up to five levels deep.

The BeginTrans method returns a Long value that represents the level of nesting for the newly created transaction. The first level is considered level one (1), not zero (0). When you nest transactions, you must resolve the more recently created transaction with either the CommitTrans or RollbackTrans method before you can resolve previously created transactions.

Example 4-16 illustrates the use of nested transactions.

Example 4-16. Nested Transactions

```
Dim con As ADODB.Connection

Dim lLevel As Long

Set con = New ADODB.Connection

' the connection must be open to utilize transactions
con.Open "Provider=Microsoft.Jet.OLEDB.4.0; " _
     & "Data Source=C:\Program Files" _
               & "\Microsoft Visual Studio" _
               & "\VB98\Biblio.mdb"

' record the level of the newly created transaction and print it
lLevel = con.BeginTrans()
Debug.Print lLevel

' inside level 1 transaction

     ' record the level of the newly created transaction and print it
     lLevel = con.BeginTrans()
     Debug.Print lLevel

     ' inside level 2 transaction

          ' record the level of the newly created transaction and print it
          lLevel = con.BeginTrans()
          Debug.Print lLevel

          ' inside level 3 transaction

          ' commit changes to the level 3 transaction
          con.CommitTrans

     ' commit changes to the level 2 transaction
     con.CommitTrans
```

Example 4-16. Nested Transactions (continued)

```
' commit changes to the level 1 transaction
con.CommitTrans

' close the Connection and clean up
con.Close
Set con = Nothing
```

Setting Transaction Options

There are two types of options that we can specify when using transactions through ADO:

Attributes
> The Attributes property specifies the automatic creation of new transactions. By using the Attributes property of the Connection object, we can define whether new transactions are created when the current one has ended.

IsolationLevel
> By setting the value of the IsolationLevel property, you can determine whether the current transaction can read the changes that are as of yet not committed by another transaction.

Automatic creation of new transactions

When you call either the CommitTrans or the RollbackTrans methods, you are ending the current transaction. By default, you must call BeginTrans once again to start another transaction, but you can change this behavior by setting the value of the Attributes property. Table 4-5 lists these values.

Table 4-5. The XactAttributeEnum Values of the Attributes Property

Constant	Value	Description
none	0	Default. Indicates that neither of the following constants have been chosen.
adXactCommitRetaining	131072	Indicates that a new transaction will be created after the CommitTrans method is called.
adXactAbortRetaining	262144	Indicates that a new transaction will be created after the RollBackTrans method is called.

You can use both the `adXactCommitRetaining` and the `adXactAbortRetaining` constants at the same time, as shown in Example 4-17.

Example 4-17. Using the Attributes Property with Multiple Constants

```
Dim con As ADODB.Connection
Set con = New ADODB.Connection
```

Example 4-17. Using the Attributes Property with Multiple Constants (continued)

```
' the connection must be open to utilize transactions
con.Open "BiblioDSN"

' set the attributes to automatically create a new transaction
' when both the CommitTrans and the RollbackTrans methods are
' called
con.Attributes = adXactCommitRetaining _
                + adXactAbortRetaining

' start transaction #1
con.BeginTrans

' do something here

' commit transaction #1, start transaction #2
con.CommitTrans

' do something here

' rollback transaction #2, start transaction #3
con.RollbackTrans

' do something here

' set the attributes so that neither CommitTrans nor RollbackTrans
' will create a new transaction
con.Attributes = 0

' commit transaction #3
con.CommitTrans

' close the Connection and clean up
con.Close
Set con = Nothing
```

 The Attributes property is not available to a client-side Connection object when using RDS. In addition, not all data providers support the transactions, and, therefore, they won't support the Attributes property. Be sure to check for the Transaction DDL property in the Properties collection of your Connection object to see whether your data provider supports transactions before you attempt to use the Attributes property.

Isolation level

The IsolationLevel property is used to indicate how transactions relate to each other. By setting its value, you can determine whether the current transaction can read the changes that are as of yet not committed by another transaction.

IsolationLevel is a read/write property that can take any one of the following IsolationLevelEnum constants shown in Table 4-6.

Table 4-6. The IsolationLevelEnum Values

Constant	Value	Description
adXactUnspecified	-1	Indicates that the data provider is using an isolation level that cannot be determined.
AdXactChaos	16	Indicates that you cannot write over changes that have been made by higher level transactions.
AdXactBrowse	256	Indicates that you can view changes that have not yet been committed by other transactions.
adXactReadUncommitted	256	Same as **adXactBrowse**. Kept for compatibility with earlier versions of ADO.
adXactCursorStability	4096	Default. Indicates that you can only view changes from other transactions once they have been committed.
adXactReadCommitted	4096	Same as **adXactCursorStability**. Kept for compatibility with earlier versions of ADO.
adXactRepeatableRead	65536	Indicates that from one transaction, you cannot see changes that have been made in other transactions until they are committed, but you can requery the data source to see newly created records.
AdXactIsolated	1048576	Indicates all transactions are completely isolated from each other.
adXactSerializable	1048576	Same as **adXactIsolated**. Kept for compatibility with earlier versions of ADO.

 The constant **adXactUnspecified** is the only valid value for the IsolationLevel property when you are using a client-side Connection object when using RDS.

Example 4-18 shows how you can use the IsolationLevel property to determine the level of isolation for the current transactions.

Example 4-18. Using the IsolationLevel Property

```
Dim con As ADODB.Connection
Set con = New ADODB.Connection

Dim sLevel As String

' open the connection
con.Open "BiblioDSN"
```

Example 4-18. Using the IsolationLevel Property (continued)

```
' select message based on the current isolation level
Select Case (con.IsolationLevel)

    Case adXactUnspecified:
        sLevel = "Isolation level cannot be determined."

    Case adXactChaos:
        sLevel = "You cannot write over changes that have been " _
                & "made by higher level transactions."

    Case adXactBrowse Or adXactReadUncommitted:
        sLevel = "You can view changes not yet committed by other " _
                & "transactions."

    Case adXactCursorStability Or adXactReadCommitted:
        sLevel = "You can only view changes from other " _
                & "transactions that have been committed."

    Case adXactRepeatableRead:
        sLevel = "You can only view changes from other " _
                & "transactions that have been committed and you " _
                & "can requery data to see new records."

    Case adXactIsolated Or adXactSerializable:
        sLevel = "All transactions are isolated from each other."

End Select

' display isolation level message
MsgBox sLevel

con.Close
Set con = Nothing
```

The IsolationLevel property is both read- and write-enabled, but it does not take effect until you call the BeginTrans method of the Connection object. It is possible that the data provider will automatically change the level of isolation when it cannot establish the level requested. In such a case, the level will be changed to the next higher level of isolation.

Determining the Layout of Your Data Source

Your data source has many characteristics that can be exposed to your applications via ADO. For instance, some data sources have table names, field names, and indexes. You can use the OpenSchema method of the Connection object to enumerate the characteristics that make up the structure of your data source. The OpenSchema method has the following syntax:

```
Set recordset_name = connection_name.OpenSchema(QueryType, Criteria, SchemaID)
```

Table 4-7 describes each of the components found in the previous syntax declaration.

Table 4-7. The Components of the OpenSchema Method

Component	Description
recordset_name	A valid Recordset object.
connection_name	A currently open Connection object.
QueryType	Indicates what type of schema query to perform on the associated connection object. This value must be a valid constant that belongs to the SchemaEnum enumeration. Not all QueryType values are supported by every data source. See the OpenSchema method in Appendix C, *ADO Errors*, for more information.
Criteria	Optional. Indicates a specific constraint used to perform the query as defined by the QueryType argument. Criteria values are specific to each QueryType value, and, because not all QueryTypes are supported by every data source, neither are all Criteria values.
SchemaID	Optional. A GUID for a provider-specific schema that is used only with the QueryType constant, adSchemaProviderSpecific.

In most cases, your data provider will not support all of the *Criteria* constraints. As a matter of fact, the data provider must supply you with only the **adSchemaTables**, **adSchemaColumns**, and **adSchemaProviderTypes** constants, according to the OLE DB specification. For a list of all the constraints available, refer to the SchemaEnum enumeration in Appendix E, *Enumeration Tables*.

Example 4-19 utilizes the OpenSchema method to create a viewer for all possible QueryType and Criteria combinations for a given data source.

To create this example, first open up a new Application EXE project within Visual Basic, and add the latest version of Microsoft ActiveX Data Objects through the Project → References tool item. Next, add the controls listed in Table 4-8, and name them accordingly.

Table 4-8. The Components of the OpenSchema Method

Control	Name
ListBox Control	lstQueryType
ListBox Control	lstCriteria
ListBox Control	lstValue
Command Button	cmdClose

Now, replacing the code that is already in the Form1 form dialog box, enter the code for the modular-level object variables, as shown in Example 4-19. This example will use the OLE DB provider for ODBC connections and the SQL Server DSN, SQLNorthwindDSN. If you do not have SQL Server, you can replace this DSN with the BiblioDSN DSN (see "Installing the DSNs" earlier in this chapter).

Example 4-19. The Schema Viewer Example

```
Option Explicit

Private con As ADODB.Connection
Private rst As ADODB.Recordset

Private Sub Form_Load()

    Set con = New ADODB.Connection
    Set rst = New ADODB.Recordset

    ' connect to our data source
    con.Open "SQLNorthwindDSN"

    ' populate the query types list box with valid query type values for
    ' this particular data source
    Call PopulateQueryTypes

End Sub

Private Sub PopulateQueryTypes()

    lstQueryType.Clear

    ' call the CheckQueryType function for each possible query type value
    CheckQueryType "adSchemaCatalogs: " & adSchemaCatalogs

    CheckQueryType "adSchemaCharacterSets: " & adSchemaCharacterSets
    CheckQueryType "adSchemaCheckConstraints: " & adSchemaCheckConstraints
    CheckQueryType "adSchemaCollations: " & adSchemaCollations
    CheckQueryType "adSchemaColumnPrivileges: " & adSchemaColumnPrivileges
    CheckQueryType "adSchemaColumns: " & adSchemaColumns
    CheckQueryType "adSchemaColumnsDomainUsage: " _
                & adSchemaColumnsDomainUsage
    CheckQueryType "adSchemaConstraintColumnUsage: " _
                & adSchemaConstraintColumnUsage
    CheckQueryType "adSchemaConstraintTableUsage: " _
                & adSchemaConstraintTableUsage
    CheckQueryType "adSchemaCubes: " & adSchemaCubes
    CheckQueryType "adSchemaDBInfoKeywords: " & adSchemaDBInfoKeywords
    CheckQueryType "adSchemaDBInfoLiterals: " & adSchemaDBInfoLiterals
    CheckQueryType "adSchemaDimensions: " & adSchemaDimensions
    CheckQueryType "adSchemaForeignKeys: " & adSchemaForeignKeys
    CheckQueryType "adSchemaHierarchies: " & adSchemaHierarchies
    CheckQueryType "adSchemaIndexes: " & adSchemaIndexes
    CheckQueryType "adSchemaKeyColumnUsage: " & adSchemaKeyColumnUsage
```

Example 4-19. The Schema Viewer Example (continued)

```
CheckQueryType "adschemaLevels: " & adSchemaLevels
CheckQueryType "adSchemaMeasures: " & adSchemaMeasures
CheckQueryType "adSchemaMembers: " & adSchemaMembers
CheckQueryType "adSchemaPrimaryKeys: " & adSchemaPrimaryKeys
CheckQueryType "adSchemaProcedureColumns: " & adSchemaProcedureColumns
CheckQueryType "adSchemaProcedureParameters: " _
              & adSchemaProcedureParameters
CheckQueryType "adSchemaProcedures: " & adSchemaProcedures
CheckQueryType "adSchemaProperties: " & adSchemaProperties
CheckQueryType "adSchemaProviderTypes: " & adSchemaProviderTypes
CheckQueryType "adSchemaReferentialContraints: " _
              & adSchemaReferentialContraints
CheckQueryType "adSchemaSchemata: " & adSchemaSchemata

CheckQueryType "adSchemaSQLLanguages: " & adSchemaSQLLanguages
CheckQueryType "adSchemaStatistics: " & adSchemaStatistics
CheckQueryType "adSchemaTableConstraints: " & adSchemaTableConstraints
CheckQueryType "adSchemaTablePrivileges: " & adSchemaTablePrivileges
CheckQueryType "adSchemaTables: " & adSchemaTables
CheckQueryType "adSchemaTranslations: " & adSchemaTranslations
CheckQueryType "adSchemaUsagePrivileges: " & adSchemaUsagePrivileges
CheckQueryType "adSchemaViewColumnUsage: " & adSchemaViewColumnUsage
CheckQueryType "adSchemaViews: " & adSchemaViews
CheckQueryType "adSchemaViewTableUsage: " & adSchemaViewTableUsage

End Sub
```

The CheckQueryType method determines if a schema is available by attempting to open it with the OpenSchema method:

```
Private Sub CheckQueryType(sQueryType As String)
On Error GoTo ERR_CheckQueryType:

    ' if we can open the schema without getting an error, the data source
    ' will support it, otherwise, do not add it to the list box
    Set rst = con.OpenSchema(GetQueryTypeValue(sQueryType))

ERR_CheckQueryType:
    Select Case Err.Number
        Case 0:
            lstQueryType.AddItem (sQueryType)
        Case adErrFeatureNotAvailable:
            ' not supported
    End Select

End Sub
```

When a user clicks on a query-type list box, the corresponding schema is opened and used to populate the criteria list box:

```
Private Sub lstQueryType_Click()

    Dim lTemp As Long
    Dim fld As ADODB.Field
```

```
        lstCriteria.Clear
        lstValue.Clear

        ' get the value of the query type from parsing the string
        ' that is selected
        lTemp = GetQueryTypeValue(lstQueryType.List(lstQueryType.ListIndex))

        ' open the schema for the query type chosen
        Set rst = con.OpenSchema(lTemp)

        ' add criterias that are available for the query type to the list box

        For Each fld In rst.Fields
            lstCriteria.AddItem fld.Name
        Next fld

    End Sub
```

In turn, as the criteria list box is selected, the individual values for the criteria are added to the values list box:

```
    Private Sub lstCriteria_Click()

        lstValue.Clear

        ' populate the values list box with the values for the selected
        ' query type and criteria
        If (Not (rst.EOF And rst.BOF)) Then rst.MoveFirst
        Do Until (rst.EOF)
            lstValue.AddItem _
                    ConvertToString(rst.Fields(lstCriteria.ListIndex).Value)
            rst.MoveNext
        Loop

    End Sub
```

Now enter the remaining utility and termination methods, and you are done:

```
    Private Function ConvertToString(vInput As Variant) As String

        ' return the 'Null' string if the value is null, otherwise return the
        ' actual string
        If IsNull(vInput) Then
            ConvertToString = "Null"
        Else
            ConvertToString = vInput
        End If

    End Function

    Private Function GetQueryTypeValue(sQueryType As String) As Long

        Dim sTemp As String
```

```
    ' take the number (value of the query type) off of the string
    sTemp = Right$(sQueryType, Len(sQueryType) - InStr(1, sQueryType, ":"))

    GetQueryTypeValue = Val(sTemp)

End Function

Private Sub cmdClose_Click()

    ' clean up recordset object
    rst.Close
    Set rst = Nothing

    ' clean up connection object
    con.Close
    Set con = Nothing

    ' end the application
    Unload Me

End Sub
```

When this application is compiled and run, it should produce a result similar to Figure 4-8, assuming your data source is similar to mine.

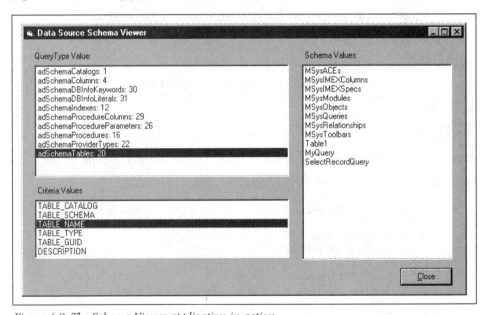

Figure 4-8. The Schema Viewer application in action

The OpenSchema method is very useful for finding such information about the data source as table names, stored procedure and query names, index information, table names, as well as a number of other valuable pieces of information. I suggest that you use the Schema Viewer application from Example 4-19 on your data source to see what is available and what you would find useful within your own application.

The OpenSchema method is not available to a client-side Connection object when using RDS.

Summary

This chapter has introduced the Connection object—the first of the nine major components of ActiveX Data Objects. You have learned how to establish connections with any type of OLE DB data provider. The following list summarizes key points:

- You can create a Connection object either explicitly within your own code, or implicitly, through instantiation of a Recordset or Command object.

- Each Connection object represents a single unique connection to a particular OLE DB data source through a data provider, both of which you have specified in a connection string.

- With the Connection object, you can execute commands against the associated data source. There are three types of commands that can be executed: a SQL statement, a stored procedure, or a parameterized query. In addition, you can open a simple table or pass a data provider–specific string to the particular data provider, which will provide its own analysis and resultset.

- The Connection object controls the utilization of transaction management through three methods: BeginTrans, CommitTrans, and RollbackTrans. Transactions are used to manage the integrity of one or multiple data sources when data is manipulated. Like `If...Then` statements, transactions can be nested.

- You can use the Connection object to obtain information about the structure of a given data source with the use of the OpenSchema method. This information can be helpful when querying for table, procedure, or index names.

The next chapter of this book, Chapter 5, explains how to manipulate and read data that is stored in record form, each of which is a collection of fields.

5

The Recordset Object

This chapter explains the Recordset object (familiar to users of DAO), which is used to access and manipulate data on the record level. As you learned earlier, all data can be broken down into logical rows, each containing one or more fields. Each field, in turn, describes one specific piece of data that falls into a specific category that is common throughout all the other rows in that rowset. For instance, the Authors table of the *Biblio.mdb* Access database supplied with Visual Basic contains one row per Author in the table. It also has a field called Name, which is an attribute of every Author.

With the Recordset object, you can navigate through the multiple rows that make up a rowset. You can search for particular rows, move to a row that you previously marked, or move to the beginning or the end of your logical rowset, all with the Recordset object.

The Recordset object is also used to add, edit, or delete records. We can specify how the data provider executes batch commands, and we can also run queries on our data source to provide a customized, filtered view of records.

ActiveX Data Objects allows us to view our records, selected from our data source, in a number of different ways. The way in which our data is presented to us is described by a cursor.

Cursors: Viewing a Recordset

Cursors present a logical view of a particular recordset. Once the records have been selected for us from our data source by opening our Recordset object, we must decide on how we would like them presented. This is done through a cursor. In ADO, there are four types of cursors:

- Dynamic cursor

- Keyset cursor

- Static cursor

- Forward-only cursor

In the following sections, the different cursor types are explained and an example at the end displays the various functions of each. To prepare your Recordset object to open with a particular cursor, use the CursorType property. The CursorType property is both read- and write-enabled while the Recordset object is closed, but once it is opened, the CursorType property becomes read-only.

Not all providers support all cursor types. When the data provider cannot provide you with the cursor that you have specified because prerequisites could not be met, the data provider may automatically assign a different cursor type. When this occurs, you can read the CursorType property to see the kind of cursor that was actually used when opening the recordset.

Dynamic Cursor

The first type of cursor is a *dynamic cursor*. A dynamic cursor allows you to move freely throughout your recordset, without restrictions, except when your provider does not support bookmarks—in this case, you cannot use bookmarks with the Dynamic cursor (see "Bookmarks" later in this chapter for more information).

"Moving freely through the recordset" means that you may move the record pointer forward or backwards and to the beginning and end of the recordset. This may seem like an obvious functionality, but as you will soon see, not all cursors allow you to move the record pointer this freely.

One of the biggest benefits of using the dynamic cursor is that it allows you to see, in real time, all additions, changes, and deletions made by other users in your recordset. For instance, if another user adds a row to a data source, and that row would have been part of your recordset if you recreated it, that row immediately becomes part of your recordset.

The dynamic cursor is by far the most versatile cursor available to the ADO developer. The major drawback of the dynamic cursor is that it is extremely resource- and time-intensive because of its ability to show, in real time, changes made by other users. I strongly recommend that you use the dynamic cursor only on the rare occasions when speed is not a concern and you need the added functionality that this cursor alone offers.

To prepare your Recordset object to open a dynamic cursor, set the CursorType property to adOpenDynamic:

```
rst.CursorType = adOpenDynamic
```

Keyset Cursor

The *keyset cursor* is very similar to the dynamic cursor in functionality, with the exception of the real-time viewing of new records created, deleted, and modified by other users. This cursor is the most resource-intensive cursor available in ADO.

The keyset cursor thus allows changes made by other users to be visible to your currently opened recordset and blocks access to records that have been deleted by other users, just as with a dynamic cursor. However, when a record is added by another user to your data source, when you have an open keyset cursor, you will not see the new record until you recreate the recordset.

Unlike with the dynamic cursor, the ability of the data provider to offer the use of bookmarks is mandatory. This is so that the keyset cursor can offer something called *batch updates*, which will be covered in more detail later in this chapter.

Use the keyset cursor instead of the dynamic cursor whenever possible to conserve resources.

To prepare your Recordset object to open a keyset cursor, set the CursorType property to adOpenKeyset:

```
rst.CursorType = adOpenKeyset
```

Figure 5-1 shows us the functionality supported by the keyset cursor. (The code for creating this informational dialog box is in the section "Cursor Type Example.")

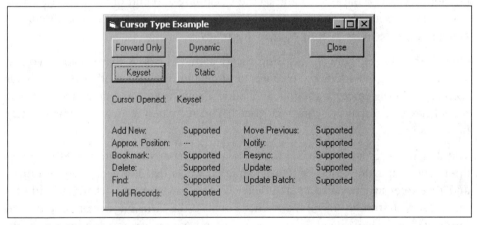

Figure 5-1. Keyset cursor functionality

Static Cursor

The *static cursor* is vastly different than the previous two. It still allows your application to move freely through the recordset. The difference is that you are unable to dynamically view changes made to the records by other users within your static recordset.

The static cursor is like a snapshot of the data within your data source at a specific point in time. You could open a static recordset on your data source and immediately afterward have the entire data source deleted, but your static cursor would never see the changes. To prepare your Recordset object to open a static cursor, set the CursorType property to adOpenStatic:

```
rst.CursorType = adOpenStatic
```

As with keyset cursors, Static cursors require that bookmarks are supported by the data provider. Figure 5-2 shows the functionality supported by the static cursor.

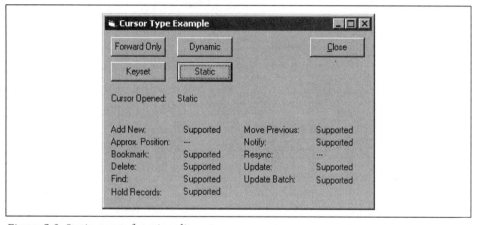

Figure 5-2. Static cursor functionality

The static cursor is excellent when you need to generate reports on data, which cannot dynamically change. It is also very good when you are using a data source that you know for sure no other users will access while you are.

The static cursor is significantly faster than both the dynamic and the keyset cursors because it does not constantly check the data source to ensure that changes have not been made.

 When you are using a client-side Recordset object with Remote Data Service (RDS), your only choice of cursor type is the static cursor.

Forward-Only Cursor

The *forward-only cursor* is the fastest available. It is similar to the static cursor in that it presents a snapshot of the data at a particular point in time, but it lacks the ability to move the record pointer backwards. The forward-only cursor is the only type of cursor that does not allow the record pointer to be moved in this way.

Because the forward-only cursor is so limited in its abilities, there are no prerequisites to opening one. To prepare your Recordset object to open a forward-only cursor, set the CursorType property to adOpenForwardOnly:

```
rst.CursorType = adOpenForwardOnly
```

Figure 5-3 indicates the functionality supported by the forward-only cursor.

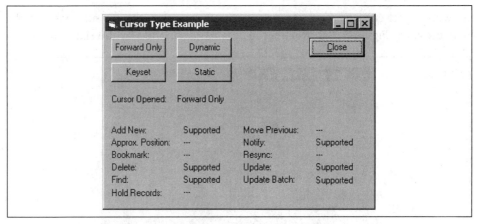

Figure 5-3. Forward-only cursor functionality

The forward-only cursor is very useful when you need to make only a single pass through your recordset, such as in some reporting scenarios. I strongly recommend using the forward-only cursor whenever your application can deal with its lack of abilities, because it is so fast.

CursorType Example

The example in this section will demonstrate the different available functions for each of the four cursor types.

First, create a new project with one form. Add the controls listed in Table 5-1, setting their values as specified in the second and third columns. Figure 5-4 shows the result.

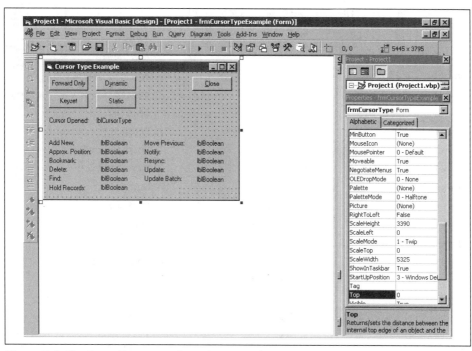

Figure 5-4. The CursorType example in design mode

Table 5-1. The CursorType Example Control Settings

Control	Property	Value
Command Button	Name	cmdCursorType
	Index	0
	Caption	ForwardOnly
Command Button	Name	cmdCursorType
	Index	1
	Caption	Keyset
Command Button	Name	cmdCursorType
	Index	2
	Caption	Dynamic
Command Button	Name	cmdCursorType
	Index	2
	Caption	Static
Command Button	Name	cmdClose
	Caption	&Close
Label	Caption	Cursor Opened:
Label	Name	lblCursorType

Table 5-1. The CursorType Example Control Settings (continued)

Control	Property	Value
Label	Caption	Add New:
Label	Caption	Approx. Position:
Label	Caption	Bookmark:
Label	Caption	Delete:
Label	Caption	Find:
Label	Caption	Hold Records:
Label	Caption	Move Previous:
Label	Caption	Notify:
Label	Caption	Resync:
Label	Caption	Update:
Label	Caption	Update Batch:
Label	Name	lblBoolean
	Index	0
	Tag	16778240
Label	Name	lblBoolean
	Index	1
	Tag	16384
Label	Name	lblBoolean
	Index	2
	Tag	8192
Label	Name	lblBoolean
	Index	3
	Tag	16779264
Label	Name	lblBoolean
	Index	4
	Tag	524288
Label	Name	lblBoolean
	Index	5
	Tag	256
Label	Name	lblBoolean
	Index	6
	Tag	512
Label	Name	lblBoolean
	Index	7
	Tag	262144

Table 5-1. The CursorType Example Control Settings (continued)

Control	Property	Value
Label	Name	lblBoolean
	Index	8
	Tag	131072
Label	Name	lblBoolean
	Index	9
	Tag	16809984
Label	Name	lblBoolean
	Index	10
	Tag	65536

Once you have all of the controls in place and you have set the necessary properties, you can begin to enter the code. Begin by entering the cmdClose_Click event to end the application:

```
Private Sub cmdClose_Click()
    Unload Me
End Sub
```

Next, enter the bulk of the code in the cmdCursorType_Click event:

```
Private Sub cmdCursorType_Click(Index As Integer)

    Dim rst As ADODB.Recordset
    Dim nCount As Integer

    Const FORWARD_ONLY = 0
    Const KEYSET = 1
    Const DYNAMIC = 2
    Const STATIC = 3

    Set rst = New ADODB.Recordset

    Select Case (Index)
        Case FORWARD_ONLY:
            rst.CursorType = adOpenForwardOnly
            lblCursorType.Caption = "Forward Only"
        Case KEYSET:
            rst.CursorType = adOpenKeyset
            lblCursorType.Caption = "Keyset"
        Case DYNAMIC:
            rst.CursorType = adOpenDynamic
            lblCursorType.Caption = "Dynamic"
        Case STATIC:
            rst.CursorType = adOpenStatic
            lblCursorType.Caption = "Static"
    End Select
```

```
        If (rst.State & adStateOpen) Then rst.Close
        rst.Open "Authors", _
                "DSN=BiblioDSN", _

                , _
                adLockPessimistic

        For nCount = 0 To 10
            If (rst.Supports(lblBoolean(nCount).Tag)) Then
                lblBoolean(nCount).Caption = "Supported"
            Else
                lblBoolean(nCount).Caption = "---"
            End If
        Next nCount

        rst.Close
        Set rst = Nothing

    End Sub
```

This code determines which button has been pressed by the Index variable passed to the function. With this information, the application opened the Authors table of the DSN with the correct cursor type. Once the recordset is opened, the application loops through all of the lblBoolean labels on the form. Each label represents a function that the current cursor may or may not support. By the value stored in that label's Tag property, the Recordset can determine whether the functionality is supported. Each of the values in the Tag properties directly corresponds to the functions enumeration value from the CursorOptionEnum enumeration shown in Table 5-2.

Table 5-2. The CursorOptionEnum Enumeration

Value	Description
adAddNew	Indicates that the recordset can use the AddNew method to add new records.
adApproxPosition	Indicates that the recordset supports the AbsolutePosition and AbsolutePage properties.
adBookmark	Indicates that the recordset supports the Bookmark property.
adDelete	Indicates that the recordset can use the Delete method to delete records.
adHoldRecords	Indicates that the recordset allows more records to be modified before committing current changes.
adMovePrevious	Indicates that the recordset can use the MovePrevious method to step backwards in a recordset.
adResync	Indicates that the recordset can use the Resync method to update the records in the recordset from the underlying data source.
adUpdate	Indicates that the recordset can use the Update method to update information that has been modified within the recordset.
adUpdateBatch	Indicates that the recordset can use the UpdateBatch and CancelBatch methods to support batch processing of edits.

Finally, enter the code for the Form_Load event, which kicks off the application by invoking the Forward Only command button:

```
Private Sub Form_Load()
    cmdCursorType_Click (0)
End Sub
```

Once this project is built, press the Dynamic button to see the application illustrated in Figure 5-5.

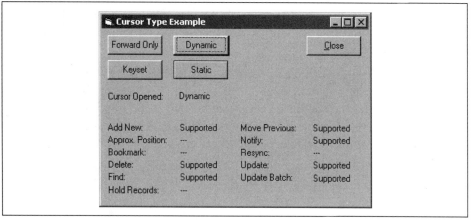

Figure 5-5. Dynamic cursor functionality

If you are having trouble starting the application, you may need to set up a System DSN (Data Source Name)—see "Installing the DSNs" in Chapter 4, *The Connection Object.*

The examples in this chapter use the *Biblio.mdb* Access database extensively. In order for these examples to work correctly (and to maintain their simplicity), it is necessary to remove all relationships from within the tables of the *Biblio.mdb* database. It is suggested that you make a copy of the *Biblio.mdb* database (in a working directory), open it up with Access, and remove all of the relationships. Once this is done, you can use the ODBC Data Source Administrator to set the System DSN, BiblioDSN, to your copy of the *Biblio.mdb* database as described in Chapter 4.

Working with Recordsets

The first thing you want to do with a recordset is open it, of course. In order to open a recordset, you must specify, with the Recordset object, what information you want, where your information is located, and how to open your information.

The Open Method

The following syntax describes the Open method of the Recordset object:

```
Recordset.Open [Source], [ActiveConnection], [CursorType], _
        [LockType], [Options]
```

Notice that all of the parameters of the Open method are optional. The parameters all relate directly to the respective properties of the Recordset object. You can set their values through the corresponding parameter or property. However, specifying the parameter will override previously set properties. In addition, these properties are read/write while the Recordset object is closed but read-only once the object has been opened.

Setting the Source property of the Recordset object indicates the information you wish to open in your recordset. The ActiveConnection property tells the Recordset object where it can find the information that you want to open. Both the Cursor-Type and LockType properties tell the Recordset how to open and use the information in the recordset. The following code opens a Recordset object and sets its properties:

```
rst.Source = "Authors"
rst.ActiveConnection = "DSN=BiblioDSN"
rst.CursorType = adOpenKeyset
rst.LockType = adLockOptimistic

rst.Open
' do something here
rst.Close
```

As you can see, there is not much involved with opening recordsets.

All of the examples in this chapter are assuming that you have already instantiated the Recordset object with the New keyword.

Alternatively, you can specify all of these values as parameters to the Open method of the Recordset object as shown:

```
rst.Open "Authors", _
        "DSN=BiblioDSN", _
        adOpenKeyset, _
        adLockOptimistic, _
        adCmdTable

' do something here
rst.Close
```

Notice that this example has an extra parameter (adCmdTable), called the Options parameter. This parameter is used to indicate the type of the Source property or parameter's value. In the previous example, the `adCmdTable` value indicates that the "`Authors`" Source is a table name. The complete list of valid Options is shown in Table 5-3.

Table 5-3. The CommandTypeEnum Enumeration

Value	Description
AdCmdFile	Indicates that the Source value will be evaluated as a filename.
adCmdStoredProc	Indicates that the Source value will be evaluated as a stored procedure.
adCmdTable	Indicates that ADO will create a SQL statement to return all rows of the table specified by Source.
adCmdTableDirect	Indicates that the Source value will be evaluated as a table name.
AdCmdText	Indicates that the Source value will be evaluated as a SQL statement or another string value that should be understood by the data source.
adCmdUnknown	Indicates that the type of the Source value is unknown.

The following piece of code shows us how we can pass a SQL statement through the Source parameter of the Open method. Notice that the fifth parameter, Options, is set to `adCmdText` to indicate that the Source parameter contains a string that should be evaluated as a SQL statement by the data source:

```
rst.Open "SELECT * FROM Authors;", _
        "DSN=BiblioDSN", _
        , _
        , _
        adCmdText

Debug.Print "Number of records: " & _
        CStr(rst.RecordCount)

rst.Close
```

There is no member property for the Options parameter of the Open method as there is for Source, ActiveConnection, CursorType, and LockType. Although it is optional, I recommend that you always specify the Options parameter. If you do not specify its value, ADO has to make several calls to the data source to determine how to open the Source, which can cause significant delays in performance.

 The Option parameter has been omitted from most of the remaining code examples for simplicity and ease of reading. Although this chapter's examples rarely use the Option parameter, it is a good idea to indicate it in your applications.

The ActiveConnection property can be set to a Variant value that evaluates to an open Connection object or a String value that evaluates to a valid connection string (see "Working with Connection Strings" in Chapter 4).

The following piece of code demonstrates how the ActiveConnection property can be set to an already opened connection object:

```
con.Open "DSN=BiblioDSN"

rst.Source = "Authors"
rst.ActiveConnection = con
rst.Open

rst.Close
con.Close
```

If the ActiveConnection property is not set to an already open Connection object, you can pass the Recordset object a connection string. The Recordset object will then use the connection string to create its own Connection object:

```
rst.Open "Authors", _
         "DSN=BiblioDSN"

Set con = rst.ActiveConnection

If (con.State & adStateOpen) Then
    Debug.Print "Connection object open."
End If

Debug.Print "Number of records: " & _
            CStr(rst.RecordCount)

rst.Close
con.Close
```

Notice that the previous example also indicates how the Connection object can be referenced directly through the ActiveConnection property of the Recordset object.

In the previous two examples, you should notice that the ActiveConnection property accepts either a String or a Connection object. When a String is passed (a valid connection string), the code is telling ADO to create a new Connection object with the connection string for the Recordset object. When you pass the Connection object, the code is telling ADO to use the reference to the existing Connection object for the Recordset object.

The Save Method

A very interesting method of the Recordset object is the Save method, which saves the recordset to a file. This method takes two optional parameters: the first is a filename to which to save the recordset. The second is a parameter, PersistFormat, indicating the format of the saved recordset. The two options for this parameter are adPersistADTG (default) and adPersistXML. The following code illustrates how to use the Save method:

```
rst.CursorLocation = adUseClient
rst.Open "Authors", _
        "DSN=BiblioDSN"

rst.Save "AuthorsRecordset", adPersistXML

' alter recordset

rst.Save

rst.Close
```

It is not necessary to specify a filename in subsequent calls to the Save method. This example's second call to Save will save the recordset to the same location as the first.

It is always a wise idea to set the CursorLocation property to **adUseClient** (to use a cursor engine recordset). When you do this, you get better behavior, as some providers have limitations when saving metadata. In addition, you are bringing all the records locally anyways, so you'll get a little better performance when letting the cursor engine handle the entire rowset.

To open the saved recordset from a file, specify the filename in either the Source property of the Recordset object (while the object is closed) or the Source parameter of the Open method of the Recordset object. It is not necessary to indicate the Options parameter as adCmdFile, because this is the default value of the parameter if the ActiveConnection property is not set.

```
rst.Open "AuthorsRecordset"

Debug.Print "Number of records: " & _
            CStr(rst.RecordCount)

rst.Close
```

Determining the State of the Recordset Object: The State Property

You can determine the state of a Recordset object with the State property. The State property returns a value from the ObjectStateEnum enumeration as shown in Table 5-4.

Table 5-4. The ObjectStateEnum Enumeration

Value	Description
adStateClosed	Indicates that the object is closed. This is the default value.
adStateConnecting	Indicates that the object is still connecting.
adStateExecuting	Indicates that the object is still executing a command.
adStateFetching	Indicates that the object is still fetching rows from the source.
adStateOpen	Indicates that the object is opened.

Example 5-1 shows how the State property of the Recordset object can be used to print the object's state.

Example 5-1. The PrintRecordState Subroutine

```
Private Sub PrintRecordsetState(rst As Recordset)

If (rst.State & adStateClosed) Then
    Debug.Print "The rst object is currently closed."
End If

If (rst.State & adStateConnecting) Then
    Debug.Print "The rst object is currently connecting."
End If

If (rst.State & adStateExecuting) Then
    Debug.Print "The rst object is currently executing."
End If

If (rst.State & adStateFetching) Then
    Debug.Print "The rst object is currently fetching."
End If

If (rst.State & adStateOpen) Then
    Debug.Print "The rst object is currently open."
End If
End Sub
```

The following code uses the PrintRecordState subroutine shown in Example 5-1 to let us see the state of a Recordset during the process of opening and closing a data source:

```
    PrintRecordsetState rst          ' State & adStateClosed

    rst.Open "Authors", _
          "DSN=BiblioDSN"            ' Open the recordset

    PrintRecordsetState rst          ' State & adStateOpen

    rst.Close                        ' Close the recordset

    PrintRecordsetState rst          ' State & adStateClosed
```

The output from running this piece of code first shows that the recordset is closed prior to the Open method call. Once the call has been made, the recordset is opened (the State property is equal to adStateOpen) and then closed once the Close method is called.

Fine-Tuning Performance of the Recordset Object

The Recordset object has numerous properties used to fine-tune performance with the connection to the data source. One of these properties is the CacheSize property.

The CacheSize property

The CacheSize property can be set at any time, while the Recordset object is opened or closed.

The CacheSize property indicates how many records are cached by ADO. The default setting for this property is 1, and its value cannot be set to 0. If the value of the CacheSize property is changed while the Recordset is open, it will not affect the caching of records until the Recordset object needs to cache more records when the record pointer moves to a location outside the cached group of records. In other words, if the CacheSize property has been set to 5 and then to 10, the Recordset will not cache 10 records until it reaches the sixth record.

The following code illustrates how to use the CacheSize property:

```
rst.Open "Authors", _
        "DSN=BiblioDSN"

rst.CacheSize = 10
Do Until (rst.EOF)
    Debug.Print "Author: " & rst.Fields("Author").Value
    rst.MoveNext
Until

rst.Close
```

The MaxRecords property

The number of records returned by a Recordset object can be limited by using the MaxRecords property. The MaxRecords property accepts a Long value, which indicates the maximum number of records to be returned to the recordset.

The following code counts the number of records returned after setting the MaxRecords property to 100:

```
Dim lRecords As Long

rst.MaxRecords = 100
```

```
rst.Open "SELECT Au_ID FROM Authors;", _
        "DSN=BiblioDSN"

lRecords = 0

Do Until (rst.EOF)
    lRecords = lRecords + 1
    rst.MoveNext
Loop

Debug.Print "There were " & CStr(lRecords) & " retrieved."

rst.Close
```

The default value of the MaxRecords property is 0, which indicates that there is no limit to the number of records returned to the Recordset object.

The CursorLocation property

Another useful property of the Recordset object is the CursorLocation property, which tells ADO where to create the recordset, either on the server (**adUseServer**—the default) or the client (**adUseClient**).

The following example prints the time it takes to establish a connection to the Author table using a server-side cursor:

```
rst.CursorLocation = adUseServer

dTime = Now

rst.Open "Authors", _
        "DSN=BiblioDSN", _
        , _
        , _
        adCmdTableDirect

' do something
rst.Close

Debug.Print "Time taken: " & _
        Format$(Now - dTime, "hh:mm:ss")
```

The next code fragment indicates the time taken to establish a connection to the Author table using a client-side cursor:

```
rst.CursorLocation = adUseClient

dTime = Now

rst.Open "Authors", _
        "DSN=BiblioDSN", _
        , _
        , _
        adCmdTableDirect
```

```
' do something
rst.Close

Debug.Print "Time taken: " & _
            Format$(Now - dTime, "hh:mm:ss")
```

The CursorLocation property is both read- and write-enabled while the Recordset object is closed, but is read-only once the object has been opened.

The Connection object also has a CursorLocation property (see "Cursor location" under "Setting Connection Options" in Chapter 4). If you decide to open your Recordset object with an already opened Connection object and the ActiveConnection property, the Recordset object will automatically inherit the value of the CursorLocation property from the Connection object.

 When you are using a client-side Recordset object with RDS, your only choice of cursor location is the client.

Sorting, Filtering, and Finding Rows in a Recordset

The Recordset objects also include properties that allow recordset manipulation, such as sorting and filtering records in already created recordsets.

The Filter property

The Filter property of the Recordset object allows you to filter a recordset even after it has been created. This very useful property allows us to filter our recordset down into a smaller subset of records.

The Filter property can be set to a number of values. The first of these values is the criteria search string. This is a value that closely resembles the WHERE clause of a SQL statement. The following code illustrates how the Filter property is used with a criteria search string:

```
rst.Open "Authors", _
         "DSN=BiblioDSN", _
         adOpenKeyset

Debug.Print "Number of records: " & _
            CStr(rst.RecordCount)

rst.Filter = "[Year Born]=1970"

Debug.Print "Number of records: " & _
            CStr(rst.RecordCount)

rst.Close
```

When this piece of code is executed, the number of records in the Recordset object is originally very large (assuming there are a large number of records still in the *Biblio.mdb* database). Once the filter is applied with the [Year Born]=1970 clause, the number of records drops significantly because the Recordset is now filtering out all other values.

Other acceptable values for the Filter property include the values of the Filter-GroupEnum enumeration shown in Table 5-5.

Table 5-5. The FilterGroupEnum Enumeration

Value	Description
adFilterNone	Indicates that there is no filter on the recordset. This value is equivalent to an empty string ("") and can be used to remove a filter and restore the recordset to its original contents.
adFilterPendingRecords	Indicates that the filter on the recordset is for records that have changed and have not yet been sent to the server. This value is for batch update mode only (see "Batch Optimistic" later in this chapter for more information).
adFilterAffectedRecords	Indicates that the filter on the recordset is for records that have been affected by the last call to Delete, Resync, UpdateBatch, or CancelBatch methods.
adFilterFetchedRecords	Indicates that the filter on the recordset is only for those records in the current cache.
adFilterConflictingRecords	Indicates that the filter on the recordset is for those records that have failed the last attempt at batch update.

The next piece of code illustrates the use of the adFilterPendingRecords constant as the value for the Filter property in order to see only those records that have not yet been posted to the data source:

```
rst.Open "Authors", _
        "DSN=BiblioDSN", _
        adOpenKeyset, _
        adLockBatchOptimistic

rst.AddNew "Author", "Steven"
rst.AddNew "Author", "Patrice"
rst.AddNew "Author", "Tammi"

rst.Filter = adFilterPendingRecords
Debug.Print "Number of records: " & _
        CStr(rst.RecordCount)

rst.Filter = ""
Debug.Print "Number of records: " & _
        CStr(rst.RecordCount)
```

```
rst.UpdateBatch
Debug.Print "Number of records: " & _
         CStr(rst.RecordCount)

rst.Close
```

In this example, after the filter is applied, only the three newly added records are visible through the Recordset object because the `adFilterPendingRecords` constant value was used.

The Sort property

You can also sort an opened recordset by the Recordset object by using the Sort property. The Sort property accepts a list of comma-delimited fields that correspond to fields in the recordset. In addition, a space followed by either `DESC` or `ASC` can be added to each field in the list to specify the order in which the records will be sorted. The Sort property works only with client-side cursors.

The following code uses a client-side cursor to create a temporary index on the local machine based upon the sorting criteria `[Year Born] DESC, Author`:

```
rst.CursorLocation = adUseClient

rst.Open "Authors", _
         "DSN=BiblioDSN"

rst.Sort = "[Year Born] DESC, Author"

Do Until (rst.EOF)
    Debug.Print rst.Fields("Author").Value, _
             "" & rst.Fields("Year Born").Value
    rst.MoveNext
Loop

rst.Close
```

The Resync method

Another useful method of the Recordset object is the Resync method. The Resync method repopulates the Recordset object with data from the data source. The Resync method accepts two parameters, AffectRecords and ResyncValues.

The values for the AffectRecords parameter can be one of the AffectEnum enumeration values listed in Table 5-6.

Table 5-6. The AffectEnum Enumeration

Value	Description
adAffectCurrent	Indicates that only the current record will be refreshed.
adAffectsGroup	Indicates that the records within the group specified by the Filter property will be refreshed.

Table 5-6. The AffectEnum Enumeration (continued)

Value	Description
adAffectAll	Indicates that all of the records within the Recordset object (even those outside of the applied Filter) will be updated. This is the default value.

The value for the second parameter, ResyncValues, can be set to one of the ResyncEnum enumeration values shown in Table 5-7.

Table 5-7. The ResyncEnum Enumeration

Value	Description
adResyncAllValues	Indicates that the recordset is populated with the data from the data source, overwriting any pending changes. This is the default value.
adResyncUnderlyingValues	Indicates that pending changes are saved to the database and then the recordset is repopulated.

In the following code example, the Resync method is called with the adAffect-Group value for the AffectRecords parameter so that only the modified record is repopulated. In addition, the adResyncAllValues value is used for the Resync-Values parameter. This value causes the record that has been modified to be repopulated with the original data from the data source, thus canceling the update batch:

```
Dim lNumRecords As Long

rst.Open "Authors", _
        "DSN=BiblioDSN", _
        adOpenKeyset, _
        adLockBatchOptimistic

rst.Find "Author='Jason'"
rst.Update "Author", "Joey"
rst.Filter = adFilterPendingRecords
Debug.Print "Number of records: " & _
        CStr(rst.RecordCount)

rst.Resync adAffectGroup, _
            adResyncAllValues
Debug.Print "Number of records: " & _
        CStr(rst.RecordCount)

Debug.Print rst.Fields("Author").Value

rst.Close
```

In order to repopulate the recordset with the one record that was modified and to post the update to the data source, the Resync method should be called with the `adResyncUnderlyingValues` value for the ResyncValues parameter. This is shown in the following code:

```
rst.Open "Authors", _
         "DSN=BiblioDSN", _
         adOpenKeyset, _
         adLockBatchOptimistic

rst.Find "Author='Jason'"
rst.Update "Author", "Joey"
rst.Filter = adFilterPendingRecords
Debug.Print "Number of records: " & _
         CStr(rst.RecordCount)

rst.Resync adAffectGroup, _
            adResyncUnderlyingValues
Debug.Print "Number of records: " & _
         CStr(rst.RecordCount)

Debug.Print rst.Fields("Author").Value

rst.Close
```

The Find method

The Find method of the Recordset object can be used to locate the first occurrence of a condition within a Recordset object. The Find method has four arguments:

Criteria (String)

Indicates a column name from the Recordset, a comparison operator (<, >, =, >=, <=, <>, or like).

SkipRows (Long)

Optional. Indicates how many records to skip before beginning the search. The default value for this argument is 0.

SearchDirection

Optional. A SearchDirectionEnum (`adSearchBackward` or `adSearchForward`).

Start (Variant)

Optional. A bookmark that specifies where the search should begin.

The following example illustrates how the Find method can be used to find the first author in the Authors table, named **Jason**:

```
rst.Open "Authors", _
         "DSN=BiblioDSN", _
         adOpenKeyset, _
         adLockBatchOptimistic
```

```
rst.Find "Author='Jason'"

    .
    .
    .

rst.Close
```

Working with Multiple Recordset Objects

You can clone a Recordset object with the Clone method of the Recordset object.

By cloning Recordset objects, as shown in the next code fragment, you can easily look at multiple records within the same recordset. If you add records to the original or to the clone, the new records are instantaneously available to the other:

```
Dim rstClone As ADODB.Recordset
Set rstClone = ADODB.Recordset

rst.Open "Authors", _
        "DSN=BiblioDSN", _
        adOpenKeyset, _
        adLockOptimistic

Set rstClone = rst.Clone

Debug.Print "Number of records before AddNew (original): " & _
        CStr(rst.RecordCount)

Debug.Print "Number of records before AddNew (clone): " & _
        CStr(rstClone.RecordCount)

rst.AddNew "Author", "Jason"

Debug.Print "Number of records after AddNew (original): " & _
        CStr(rst.RecordCount)

Debug.Print "Number of records after AddNew (clone): " & _
        CStr(rstClone.RecordCount)

rst.Close
rstClone.Close
```

Recordsets can be cloned as many times as you wish. You can close the clones or the originals without affecting the other. When a clone is created, the record pointer is moved to the first record of the cloned recordset.

The Clone method accepts an optional parameter, the LockType parameter. The default value for this parameter is adLockUnspecified, which tells ADO to use the same locking scheme on the clone as was used on the original. The only other value specified for this property is adLockReadOnly, which, as it sounds, sets the locking scheme of the clone to read-only.

Another method that is of some interest within the Recordset object is the Next-Recordset method. This method allows you to query multiple SQL statements from within a single compound recordset. The following code illustrates how to use the NextRecordset method:

```
rst.Open "SELECT * FROM Authors; " & _
         "SELECT * FROM Publishers;", _
         "DSN=BiblioDSN", _
         adOpenForwardOnly, _
         adLockReadOnly, _
         adCmdText

While (Not rst)
    Do Until (rst.EOF)
        Debug.Print rst.Fields(1).Value
        rst.MoveNext
    Until

    Set rst = rst.NextRecordset
Wend

rst.Close
```

Notice that the two SQL statements in this code example are separated by a semi-colon (;). The first time through, the **rst** Recordset object is set to a recordset created by the first SQL statement. With the first call to the NextRecordset method (which returns a Recordset object), the **rst** Recordset object is set to a recordset created by the second SQL statement. Upon the second call to the NextRecordset method, the **rst** Recordset object is set to Nothing.

Navigating a Recordset

Moving around in a recordset is one of the most basic actions. There are many ways you can move within a recordset, but the basic concept for each technique is the same.

Regardless of where or how you want to move around in a recordset, there is always a place pointed to by a record pointer.

The Record Pointer

The *record pointer* indicates the current record. Imagine a record pointer as the needle on a record player. It points to the current song so that you can access that song's information. In a recordset, a record pointer points to a record (most of the time) so that you can access that records information.

Two important properties of a Recordset object, which have appeared in previous examples without full explanation, are the BOF (Beginning Of File) and EOF (End

Of File) properties. These are Boolean properties that indicate that you have stepped out of the bounds of the recordset. Figure 5-6 shows you that the BOF property is True when the record pointer is before the first record in the recordset and that the BOF property is True when the record pointer is past the last record in the recordset.

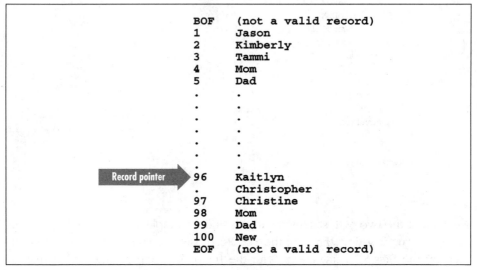

Figure 5-6. A typical recordset with BOF and EOF Properties

If, when you open a recordset, there are no records in that recordset, both the BOF and EOF properties are set to True. We can check for this situation with the following code:

```
If (Not (rst.BOF And rst.EOF)) Then ...
```

The BOF and EOF properties are very important when moving around within a recordset. We will take a closer look at them in the next section as we begin to explore how they interact with functions that allow us to change the position of the record pointer.

The MoveFirst, MovePrevious, MoveNext, and MoveLast Methods

The four most common methods for moving the record pointer in a recordset are the MoveFirst, MovePrevious, MoveNext and MoveLast methods. The functionalities of these methods are described in Table 5-8.

Table 5-8. The MoveFirst, MovePrevious, MoveNext, and MoveLast Methods

Method	Description
MoveFirst	The MoveFirst method moves the record pointer to the first record in a recordset.
MovePrevious	The MovePrevious method moves the record pointer to the ordinal position located directly before the current one. If there is no record at this location (meaning that the current record is the first record in the recordset), the BOF property is set to **True** and the record pointer no longer points to a valid record.
MoveNext	The MoveNext method moves the record pointer to the ordinal position located directly after the current one. If there is no record at this location (meaning that the current record is the last record in the recordset), the EOF property is set to **True** and the record pointer no longer points to a valid record.
MoveLast	The MoveLast method moves the record pointer to the last record in the recordset.

The following code is a typical example of how the MoveFirst and MoveNext methods can be used (with the BOF and EOF properties) to step from the beginning to the end of a recordset:

```
rst.Open "Authors", _
         "DSN=BiblioDSN"

Do Until (rst.EOF)
    Debug.Print "Author: " & rst.Fields("Author").Value
    rst.MoveNext
Loop

rst.Close
```

Notice what is happening in this code. First, we check the recordset to see whether it is empty. If it's not, the record pointer is set to the first record in the recordset. Next, a **Do Until** statement, while the record pointer points to a valid record, prints the Author name and moves to the next record (by means of the MoveNext method). If the recordset is empty, the **Do Until** statement never executes, because the EOF property is true.

Use the same concept to move from the end of a recordset to the beginning:

```
rst.Open "Authors", _
         "DSN=BiblioDSN", _
         adOpenKeyset

Do Until (rst.BOF)
    Debug.Print "Author: " & rst.Fields("Author").Value
    rst.MovePrevious
Loop

rst.Close
```

In this example, if the recordset is not empty, a call to the MoveLast method moves the record pointer to the end of the recordset. Also, the `Do Until` statement checks whether the record pointer is pointing to the beginning of the file, thus making the BOF property `True`.

During each call to the MovePrevious method, the record pointer is moved to the record directly before the record to which it was pointing. When the record pointer points to the first record in the recordset and the MovePrevious method is called, the record pointer moves to the position located directly before the first record. When the record pointer is in this position, the BOF property is set to True as shown in Figure 5-6. The `Do Until` loop does not execute again because there are no more records available in the recordset.

Notice that in the last example, we opened the recordset with a keyset cursor. Remember from the previous section on cursors ("Cursors: Viewing a Recordset") that the keyset cursor is one of the three cursors that allow you to move the record pointer backward within a recordset.

Sometimes it is necessary to check for the ability to move backward within a recordset. We can do this with the Supports method:

```
rst.Open "Authors", _
        "DSN=BiblioDSN", _
        adOpenForwardOnly

If (rst.Supports(adMovePrevious)) Then
    rst.MoveLast

    Do Until (rst.BOF)
        Debug.Print "Author: " & rst.Fields("Author").Value
        rst.MovePrevious
    Loop
Else
    Debug.Print "Cursor does not support bookmarks."
End If

rst.Close
```

This code never prints an Author name, because a forward-only cursor does not support the MovePrevious method.

The Move Example

This example uses a model that is very typical to many database applications. Figure 5-7 shows the Move Example in action.

Each of the four buttons that allow the user to move to a different record in the recordset are called navigation buttons. Each of these buttons corresponds to a Move method introduced in the last section.

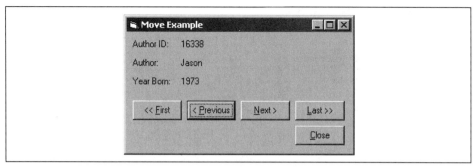

Figure 5-7. The Move Example

Begin by adding the controls and setting their property values as shown in Table 5-9. Remember to make the four navigation buttons part of a control array.

Table 5-9. The Move Example Control Settings

Control	Property	Value
Label	Caption	`Author ID:`
Label	Name	`lblAuthorID`
Label	Caption	`Author:`
Label	Name	`lblAuthorName`
Label	Caption	`Year Born:`
Label	Name	`lblYearBorn`
Command Button	Name	`cmdMove`
	Index	`0`
	Caption	`<< &First`
Command Button	Name	`cmdMove`
	Index	`1`
	Caption	`< &Previous`
Command Button	Name	`cmdMove`
	Index	`2`
	Caption	`&Next >`
Command Button	Name	`cmdMove`
	Index	`3`
	Caption	`&Last >>`
Command Button	Name	`cmdClose`
	Caption	`&Close`

Now enter the code shown in Example 5-2.

Example 5-2. The Move Next Example

```
Option Explicit

Private m_rst As ADODB.Recordset

Const FIRST = 0
Const PREVIOUS = 1
Const NEXT = 2
Const LAST = 3

Private Sub cmdClose_Click()
    m_rst.Close
    Set m_rst = Nothing

    Unload Me
    End
End Sub

Private Sub cmdMove_Click(Index As Integer)

    Select Case (Index)
        Case FIRST:
            m_rst.MoveFirst
        Case PREVIOUS:
            m_rst.MovePrevious
        Case NEXT:
            m_rst.MoveNext
        Case LAST:
            m_rst.MoveLast
    End Select

    PopulateAuthorInformation

    AdjustNavigationButtons

End Sub

Private Sub PopulateAuthorInformation()

    lblAuthorID.Caption = m_rst.Fields("Au_ID").Value
    lblAuthorName.Caption = "" & m_rst.Fields("Author").Value
    lblYearBorn.Caption = "" & m_rst.Fields("Year Born").Value

End Sub

Private Sub AdjustNavigationButtons()

    m_rst.MovePrevious
    If (m_rst.BOF) Then
        cmdMove(FIRST).Enabled = False
        cmdMove(PREVIOUS).Enabled = False
    Else
        cmdMove(FIRST).Enabled = True
        cmdMove(PREVIOUS).Enabled = True
```

Example 5-2. The Move Next Example (continued)

```
    End If
    m_rst.MoveNext

    m_rst.MoveNext
    If (m_rst.EOF) Then
        cmdMove(LAST).Enabled = False
        cmdMove(NEXT).Enabled = False
    Else
        cmdMove(LAST).Enabled = True
        cmdMove(NEXT).Enabled = True
    End If
    m_rst.MovePrevious

End Sub

Private Sub Form_Load()

    Set m_rst = New ADODB.Recordset

    m_rst.Open "Authors", _
            "DSN=BiblioDSN", _
            adOpenKeyset, _
            adLockReadOnly

    If (m_rst.BOF And m_rst.EOF) Then
        MsgBox "There are no records in this recordset.", _
            vbOKOnly, _
            "Error"
        cmdClose_Click
    End If

    cmdMove_Click FIRST

End Sub
```

In this example, the navigation buttons move the record pointer within the recordset. The AdjustNavigationButtons method changes the Enabled property for the buttons based on whether they can be used. If the record pointer is before the first record in the recordset, then the First and Previous button's Enabled property is set to `False`. If the record pointer is past the last record in the recordset, then the Last and Next button's Enabled property is set to `False`.

Take a close look at the code in the AdjustNavigationButtons method. Notice that when testing to determine if BOF is True, the record pointer is first moved back one ordinal position and then is moved back to its original position once the test is completed:

```
    m_rst.MovePrevious
    If (m_rst.BOF) Then
    .
    .
    .
```

```
End If
m_rst.MoveNext
```

The reason for this, as you may recall, is that the BOF property is **True** when the record pointer is at the position immediately before the first record in the recordset. What this code does is disable the First and Previous buttons before the user moves the record pointer to the position after the last record in the recordset, which would be an invalid record.

The same goes for the EOF property. In this example, the record pointer is moved forward one position to check to see whether it is at position directly after the last record in the recordset. Once this check is complete, the record pointer moves back to the original record position. If the EOF property becomes **True** during this check, it means that the original position pointed to was the last record in the recordset.

Notice that in the Form_Load event, after the recordset is opened, there is a check whether there are any records in the recordset at all. The reason for this is simple. If the recordset was empty when it was opened, the code just described would not work properly. You cannot use MoveFirst, MovePrevious, MoveNext, or MoveLast in an empty recordset. In an empty recordset, the BOF and EOF properties are set to **True**.

Ordinal Position

The ordinal position of the record pointer can be set with the AbsolutePosition property as shown:

```
rst.Open "Authors", _
        "DSN=BiblioDSN", _
        adOpenKeyset

rst.AbsolutePosition = 1234

Debug.Print "Author at record 1234: " & _
        rst.Fields("Author").Value

rst.Close
```

The AbsolutePosition property returns a value ranging from 1 to the number of records in the recordset. To obtain the number of records in a recordset, use the RecordCount property:

```
rst.Open "Authors", _
        "DSN=BiblioDSN", _
        adOpenKeyset

Debug.Print "Number of records: " & _
        CStr(rst.RecordCount)

rst.Close
```

The AbsolutePosition property can also return one of the constants from the PositionEnum enumeration shown in Table 5-10.

Table 5-10. The PositionEnum Enumeration

Value	Description
adPosBOF	Indicates that the record pointer is at the position directly before the first record in the recordset, and that the BOF property is True. This value is not returned if the recordset is empty.
adPosEOF	Indicates that the record pointer is at the position directly after the last record in the recordset and that the EOF property is True. This value is not returned if the recordset is empty.
AdPosUnknown	Indicates one of three things: • The recordset is empty. • The current position of the record pointer is unknown. • The data provider does not support the AbsolutePosition property.

Once the AbsolutePosition property has changed, ADO recaches the number of records indicated by the CacheSize property, the first record in the cache being that pointed to by the AbsolutePosition property.

The value of the AbsolutePosition property should never be used as a marker or a record number, because you cannot rely on the value of this property being the same even if you read it twice for the same record. Once a record is added or deleted from the recordset, this value changes. Instead, use the Bookmark property to perform such actions.

Bookmarks

When a recordset is created, each record is given a unique identifier, called a *bookmark*, which can be accessed with the Bookmark property. The Bookmark property returns a Variant datatype, which does not always evaluate to a readable String. The Bookmark property is not meant to be read directly: its implementation is dependent upon the data provider. The data provider is required only to allow you to read and set the values properly—not to allow you to read and make sense of the value.

Not all data providers or cursors support bookmarks. Use the Supports method of the Recordset object to check for the availability of bookmarks within a recordset. However, when you are using a client-side Recordset object with RDS, the Bookmark property is always supported.

The following code illustrates how the Bookmark property is used:

```
Dim vBookmark As Variant

rst.Open "Authors", _
         "DSN=BiblioDSN", adOpenKeyset

rst.Find "Author='Jason'"

If (rst.Supports(adBookmark)) Then

    vBookmark = rst.Bookmark
    rst.MoveFirst
    rst.Bookmark = vBookmark

    Debug.Print rst.Fields("Author").Value

End If

rst.Close
```

The value of a recordset's bookmark is unique to the currently opened recordset. You cannot use a bookmark within two different recordsets or even two instances of the same recordset and expect predictable results. (The only exception to this rule is when you create one recordset from another with the Clone method.)

The same record can be pointed to by two different bookmarks; therefore, you should never directly compare two bookmark's values. Instead, use the Compare-Bookmark property:

```
Dim vFirstBookmark As Variant
Dim vSecondBookmark As Variant
Dim lCompareResult As Long

rst.Open "Authors", _
         "DSN=BiblioDSN", _
         adOpenKeyset

rst.MoveFirst
rst.Find "Author='Jason'"
vFirstBookmark = rst.Bookmark

rst.MoveFirst
rst.Find "Author='Tammi'"
vSecondBookmark = rst.Bookmark

lCompareResult = rst.CompareBookmarks(vFirstBookmark, _
                                      vSecondBookmark)

If (lCompareResult = adCompareLessThan) Then
    Debug.Print "Jason comes before Tammi"
```

```
Else
    Debug.Print "Tammi comes before Jason"
End If

rst.Close
```

In this example, the result of the CompareBookmarks method was compared to the `adCompareLessThan` constant to see the position of one bookmark in relation to the other. In addition to this constant, the CompareBookmark method can also return any value from the CompareEnum enumeration shown in Table 5-11.

Table 5-11. The CompareEnum Enumeration

Value	Description
adCompareLessThan	Indicates that the first bookmark comes before the second in order.
adCompareGreaterThan	Indicates that the second bookmark comes before the first in order.
adCompareEqual	Indicates that the first bookmark is in the same position as the second.
adCompareNotEqual	Indicates that the first bookmark is not in the same position as the second and furthermore that the records are not ordered.
adCompareNotComparable	Indicates that the first bookmark cannot be compared to the second bookmark.

The Move method

Another method for navigating a recordset is the Move method. This method takes two parameters. The first parameter is a Long value that indicates the number of records to move. The second parameter can be either a valid bookmark Variant value or a valid value from the BookmarkEnum enumeration shown in Table 5-12.

Table 5-12. The BookmarkEnum Enumeration

Value	Description
adBookmarkCurrent	Indicates that the Move method should begin counting records from the current record pointed to by the record pointer. This is the default value.
adBookmarkFirst	Indicates that the Move method should begin counting records from the first record in the recordset.
adBookmarkLast	Indicates that the Move method should begin counting records from the last record in the recordset.

For you to pass a bookmark for the second parameter of the Move method, the recordset must support bookmarks. The following example illustrates how the Move method is used:

```
Dim lNumRecords As Long

rst.Open "Authors", _
         "DSN=BiblioDSN", _
         adOpenKeyset

lNumRecords = 230

rst.Move lNumRecords, adBookmarkFirst

Do Until (rst.EOF)
    Debug.Print "Author: " & _
                rst.Fields("Author").Value
    rst.Move lNumRecords, adBookmarkCurrent
Loop

rst.Close
```

This code starts at the first record in the recordset (indicated by the
adBookmarkFirst constant value) and moves ahead 230 record positions. Within
the **Do Until** loop, the Move method is continually called with the
adBookmarkCurrent value that tells ADO to start from the current position within
the recordset. This continues until the EOF property is **True**.

If the number of records in the recordset is not evenly divisible by 230, attempting
to move past the last record in the recordset sets the EOF property to **True**.
Another attempt to move forward in a recordset by the Move method would result
in an error, as would a call to the MoveNext method.

You can also pass a negative number to the Move method as its first parameter:

```
rst.Open "Authors", _
         "DSN=BiblioDSN", _
         adOpenKeyset

lNumRecords = -230

rst.Move lNumRecords, adBookmarkLast

Do Until (rst.BOF)
    Debug.Print "Author: " & _
                rst.Fields("Author").Value
    rst.Move lNumRecords, adBookmarkCurrent
Until

rst.Close
```

Notice the second parameter to the Move method, the **adBookmarkLast** constant.
This constant indicates that the Move method will begin counting records from the
last record in the recordset. This example is almost identical to the previous one,

except the negative number passed to the Move method indicates that the record pointer is moving backwards in the recordset. The Move method then uses the `adBookmarkCurrent` constant, as in the last example, from within the `Do Until` loop to move from the position to which the record pointer is currently pointing. When the Move method attempts to move the record pointer before the first record in the recordset, the BOF property is set to `True`.

Paging

Pages logically divide the recordset into groups. The size of a page is determined by the value passed to the PageSize property. The number of logical pages within a recordset is indicated by the PageCount property. These properties are not available in a forward-only cursor.

Both of these properties are illustrated in the following code:

```
rst.Open "Authors", _
        "DSN=BiblioDSN", _
        adOpenKeyset, _
        adLockOptimistic

rst.PageSize = 25

Debug.Print "Pages: " & CStr(rst.PageCount)
Debug.Print "Page Size: " & CStr(rst.PageSize)

rst.Close
```

You can jump to the beginning of any page by using the AbsolutePage property to set the current page:

```
Dim lPageNumber As Long

rst.Open "Authors", _
        "DSN=BiblioDSN", _
        adOpenKeyset, _
        adLockOptimistic

rst.PageSize = 25

For lPageNumber = 1 To rst.PageCount
    rst.AbsolutePage = lPageNumber
    Debug.Print "The first author on page " & _
            CStr(lPageNumber) & " is " & _
            rst.Fields("Author").Value
Next lPageNumber

rst.Close
```

Working with Records

When working with data sources, the majority of your work revolves around adding, editing, or deleting records. In addition, you may find the need to retrieve many records at once. Let us begin learning how to work with records by learning how to add them to our recordset.

Adding New Records

To add a new record to a recordset, use the AddNew method. The AddNew method creates a new record at the end of your recordset and points the record pointer to it. The following code illustrates the most basic way in which the AddNew method can be used:

```
rst.Open "Authors", _
         "DSN=BiblioDSN", _
         adOpenKeyset, _
         adLockOptimistic

rst.AddNew
rst.Fields("Author") = "Jason"
rst.Fields("Year Born") = 1973
rst.Update

rst.Close
```

Notice that before the recordset is closed and after the information has been loaded into the fields of the recordset, the Update method is called. The Update method tells ADO that the record currently being edited is ready to be updated in the database.

The AddNew method can also be used with a set of parameters as shown in this example:

```
rst.Open "Authors", _
         "DSN=BiblioDSN", _
         adOpenKeyset, _
         adLockOptimistic

rst.AddNew "Author", "Kimberly"

rst.Close
```

This example passes two parameters to the AddNew method. The first parameter is the name of a field and the second parameter is the value for that field. There is no need to call the Update method when using this syntax because ADO knows that you are creating a new record with only one field value specified.

Finally, the third and final syntax for adding new records with the AddNew method also accepts two parameters, but it allows you to set multiple fields' values in a single method call. This is accomplished with the use of arrays as follows:

```
Dim sFields(1) As Variant
Dim sValues(1) As Variant

rst.Open "Authors", _
         "DSN=BiblioDSN", _
         adOpenKeyset, _
         adLockOptimistic

sFields(0) = "Author"
sFields(1) = "Year Born"

sValues(0) = "Tamara"
sValues(1) = "1975"

rst.AddNew sFields, sValues

rst.Close
```

Notice that the **sFields** array has the same dimension as the **sValues** array and that each ordinal position in the **sFields** array (beginning with 0) corresponds to an ordinal position in the **sValues** array.

As in the previous example, there is no need to call the Update method, because ADO assumes that it has all the information it needs and automatically updates this information in the data source.

It may seem obvious, but it is important to realize that a read-only data source does not allow you to update the recordset. This includes adding new records. The ability of a recordset to add new records can be checked with the Supports method by passing the adAddNew constant:

```
rst.Open "Authors", _
         "DSN=BiblioDSN", _
         adOpenKeyset, _
         adLockReadOnly     ' read only... cannot add a record

If (rst.Supports(adAddNew)) Then
    rst.AddNew "Author", "New Author"
Else
    Debug.Print "Cannot add a new record."
End If

rst.Close
```

As stated earlier, once a new record has been added to the recordset, the record pointer points to this new record so that the application can immediately read information from the newly added record. The following code displays the name

of the newly added record, illustrating that the record pointer is automatically
moved to point to the new record:

```
rst.Open "Authors", _
        "DSN=BiblioDSN", _
        adOpenKeyset

If (rst.Supports(adAddNew)) Then
    rst.AddNew
    rst.Fields("Author") = "John"
    rst.Update

    Debug.Print rst.Fields("Author")
Else
    Debug.Print "Cannot add a new record."
End If

rst.Close
```

Updating and Editing Records

Earlier in this chapter, the Update method was described as the method that indicates to ADO that the application is ready for it to save the information for the
edited record. There is also a method that tells ADO to cancel the pending modifications and to discard any new information to the data source. This method is the
CancelUpdate method, which is illustrated in the following code:

```
rst.Open "Authors", _
        "DSN=BiblioDSN", _
        adOpenKeyset, _
        adLockOptimistic

Dim lResponse As Long

If (rst.Supports(adAddNew)) Then

    rst.AddNew
    rst.Fields("Author") = "Kaitlyn"
    rst.Fields("Year Born") = "1997"

    lResponse = MsgBox("Are you sure you want to add this record?", _
                    vbYesNo, _
                    "Add Record")

    If (lResponse = vbYes) Then
        rst.Update
    Else
        rst.CancelUpdate
    End If

End If

rst.Close
```

This example creates a new record in the recordset and then asks the user to confirm that they want to create a new record. If the answer is yes, the Update method is called. If the answer is no, the CancelUpdate method is called.

Besides working in conjunction with the AddNew method, the Update method can also be used to edit an existing record in the recordset. By passing two parameters (just like the AddNew method), the Update method can alter the contents of a single field.

The following example queries a data source to create a recordset that contains all records where Author is equal to **Tamara**. The **Do Until** loop then changes each of the records in the recordset so that the Author field is **Tammi**, instead of **Tamara**.

```
rst.Open "SELECT Author " & _
        "FROM Authors " & _
        "WHERE Author='Tamara';", _
        "DSN=BiblioDSN", _
        adOpenKeyset, _
        adLockOptimistic

Do Until (rst.EOF)
    rst.Update "Author", "Tammi"
    rst.MoveNext
Loop

rst.Close
```

Just as the AddNew method had various syntaxes for its parameters, so does the Update method. Two Variant arrays can be passed to the Update method so that multiple fields can be updated immediately within a single record. The following piece of code illustrates how this can be done:

```
Dim sFields(1) As Variant
Dim sValues(1) As Variant

rst.Open "SELECT Author, [Year Born] " & _
        "FROM Authors " & _
        "WHERE Author='Kimberly';", _
        "DSN=BiblioDSN", _
        adOpenKeyset, _
        adLockOptimistic

sFields(0) = "Author"
sFields(1) = "Year Born"

sValues(0) = "Kim"
sValues(1) = "1975"

Do Until (rst.EOF)
    rst.Update sFields, sValues
```

```
    rst.MoveNext
Until

rst.Close
```

This example changes the value of the Author field to Kim and the Year Born field to 1975 for all records where the Author field was originally Kimberly.

The EditMode property returns a value representing the current state of the recordset; this value is a valid EditModeEnum enumeration value as shown in Table 5-13.

Table 5-13. The EditModeEnum Enumeration

Value	Description
AdEditAdd	Indicates that the AddNew method has been called to add a new record to the current recordset, but either the Update or the CancelUpdate methods have not yet been called to save the new record to the underlying data source.
AdEditDelete	Indicates that the record that is pointed to by the record pointer has been deleted.
AdEditInProgress	Indicates that the data within the record that is currently being pointed to has been edited but not yet saved.
AdEditNone	Indicates that there is no editing taking place on the current record.

The EditMode property can be used to print a text message indicating the mode of editing for a given recordset, at any time, by using a procedure like this one:

```
Private Sub PrintEditMode(rst As Recordset)

    Select Case (rst.EditMode)
        Case adEditNone:
            Debug.Print "Edit None"
        Case adEditInProgress:
            Debug.Print "Edit In Progress"
        Case adEditAdd:
            Debug.Print "Edit Add"
        Case adEditDelete:
            Debug.Print "Edit Delete"
    End Select

End Sub
```

Now, take a look at a piece of code that has utilizes the PrintEditMode function to indicate the mode of a recordset at particular key places in our editing routines:

```
rst.Open "Authors", _
        "DSN=BiblioDSN"

If (rst.Supports(adAddNew)) Then
```

```
        PrintEditMode rst                ' EditMode = adEditNone

        rst.AddNew                       ' Add a new record
        PrintEditMode rst                ' EditMode = adEditAdd

        rst.Fields("Author") = "Justin"
        rst.Update                       ' Update the new record
        PrintEditMode rst                ' EditMode = adEditNone

        rst.AddNew "Author", "Tyler"     ' Add a new record (and update it)
        PrintEditMode rst                ' EditMode = adEditNone

        rst.AddNew                       ' Add a new record
        rst.Fields("Author") = "Lisa"
        PrintEditMode rst                ' EditMode = adEditAdd

        rst.AddNew                       ' Add a new record (update the other)
        PrintEditMode rst                ' EditMode = adEditAdd

        rst.Fields("Author") = "Jessie"
        rst.Update                       ' Update the last new record
        PrintEditMode rst                ' EditMode = adEditNone

    End If

    rst.Close
```

Deleting Records

In ADO, the Delete method is used to remove records from the underlying data source. The Delete method can accept one of the AffectEnum enumeration values shown in Table 5-6.

The following code shows how the Delete method can be used to delete a number of records. In this case, the Delete method is used to delete all records from the data source whose Year Born field is equal to 1975:

```
rst.Open "SELECT Author, [Year Born] " & _
         "FROM Authors " & _
         "WHERE [Year Born]=1975;", _
         "DSN=BiblioDSN"

Do Until (rst.EOF)
    rst.Delete adAffectCurrent
    rst.Requery
Loop

rst.Close
```

Retrieving Records

Multiple records of a recordset can be retrieved with a single call to ADO in one of two ways. The first is by using the GetRows method. This method accepts three parameters. The first parameter is the number of rows that you would like to retrieve. The second parameter indicates the position in the recordset from which ADO should begin to retrieve rows. The third parameter indicates which fields to return from the recordset.

The following example shows how the GetRows method is used:

```
Dim vAuthor As Variant
Dim lCount As Long

rst.Open "Authors", _
        "DSN=BiblioDSN", _
        adOpenKeyset, adLockOptimistic

vAuthor = rst.GetRows(20, _
                        adBookmarkFirst, _
                        "Author")

For lCount = 0 To UBound(vAuthor, 2)
    Debug.Print vAuthor(0, lCount)
Next lCount

rst.Close
```

The first parameter in the previous example indicates that 20 records should be returned. The second parameter, **adBookmarkFirst**, indicates to the GetRows method that ADO should start retrieving records starting from the first record. In addition to the example shown, the second parameter of the GetRows method can be a valid bookmark or any one of the BookmarkEnum enumeration values indicated in Table 5-14.

Table 5-14. The BookmarkEnum Enumeration

Value	Description
adBookmarkCurrent	Indicates that the GetRows method will begin retrieving records starting with the current record in the recordset.
adBookmarkFirst	Indicates that the GetRows method will begin retrieving records starting with the first record in the recordset.
adBookmarkLast	Indicates that the GetRows method will begin retrieving records starting with the last record in the recordset.

The third and last parameter of the GetRows method can set to a valid field name—as in the last example, an ordinal position of a field name, an array of field names, or an array of ordinal positions of field names.

Along with the GetRows method, there is a method that returns the entire recordset in a string format. This method is called the GetString method:

```
Dim vRecordset As Variant

rst.Open "SELECT * FROM Authors " & _
         "WHERE ([Year Born]<1970) " & _
         "AND   ([Year Born]<>0); ", _
         "DSN=BiblioDSN", _
         adOpenKeyset, _
         adLockOptimistic

vRecordset = rst.GetString

Debug.Print vRecordset

rst.Close
```

Although not shown in this example, the GetString method can accept as many as five parameters:

- The first parameter, the StringFormat parameter, can be set to a valid String-FormatEnum enumeration value. Currently, the only value defined within ADO for this enumeration is adClipString.

- The second parameter, the NumRows parameter, indicates the number of rows in the recordset that should be returned by the GetString method. If the Num-Rows value is not specified (or if it is greater than the number of records in the recordset), then the entire recordset will be returned in a string format.

- The third parameter, the ColumnDelimiter parameter, is used to indicate the character in which the columns are divided. If this parameter is omitted, the TAB character is used.

- The fourth parameter, the RowDelimiter parameter, is used to indicate the character in which the rows are divided. If this parameter is omitted, the CARRIAGE RETURN character is used.

- The fifth parameter, the NullExpr parameter, is used to indicate the character in which to display a NULL value. An empty string is used if this parameter is omitted.

Lock Types: Managing Access to a Recordset

There are four record-locking schemes in ADO. Each has its own advantages and disadvantages, as described in the following sections. The record lock type is indicated by either the LockType property of the Recordset object or the LockType parameter of the Open method of the Recordset object. The LockType parameter of the Open method is the fourth parameter in the parameter list.

Either one of these (the parameter or the property) can be set to one of the four valid constants from the LockTypeEnum enumeration shown in Table 5-15.

Table 5-15. The LockTypeEnum Enumeration

Value	Description
adReadOnly	Indicates that the recordset will use a read-only record-locking scheme.
adLockOptimistic	Indicates that the recordset will use an optimistic record-locking scheme.
adLockPessimistic	Indicates that the recordset will use a pessimistic record-locking scheme.
adLockBatchOptimistic	Indicates that the recordset will use a batch optimistic record-locking scheme.

Read-Only Locks

A read-only record-locking scheme is the simplest locking scheme of the four available. Basically, a read-only recordset does not allow adding or editing of records; therefore, the records themselves do not need to be locked for editing at all.

The following example illustrates how to open a recordset with the read-only record-locking scheme:

```
rst.Open "Authors", _
        "DSN=BiblioDSN", _
        adOpenKeyset, _
        adLockReadOnly

' cannot alter data

rst.Close
```

You should use read-only locking whenever you do not plan on updating the data with the recordset. This can save system resources and speed up the data access because ADO does not have to handle multiple users editing the data.

Pessimistic Locks

A pessimistic record-locking scheme is one in which the data provider usually locks the data source, record by record, as soon as a record begins to be edited:

```
rst.Open "Authors", _
        "DSN=BiblioDSN", _
```

```
              adOpenKeyset, _
              adLockPessimistic

rst.AddNew                             ' record locked
rst.Fields("Author").Value = "Lindsay"
rst.Update
                                       ' record unlocked
rst.Close
```

The previous example illustrates how the data provider locks a newly created record immediately while the call to AddNew is made. The record is unlocked once the Update method (or the CancelUpdate method) is called.

You might choose to use pessimistic locking when your updates are going to be quick, as with an automated import process. Since pessimistic locking locks the record immediately, you don't have to wait until you have processed all the data and attempt to update the record to find out that it is locked by another user. However, pessimistic locking can cause delays in multi-update applications, creating lock contention.

Optimistic Locks

An optimistic record-locking scheme is one in which the data provider usually locks the data source, record by record, only during the Update method call:

```
rst.Open "Authors", _
        "DSN=BiblioDSN", _
        adOpenKeyset, _
        adLockOptimistic

rst.AddNew
rst.Fields("Author").Value = "Lindsay"
rst.Update                             ' record locked
                                       ' record unlocked
rst.Close
```

Notice how this example differs from that of the pessimistic locking example. The newly created record is locked only during the Update method call rather than during the entire time between the AddNew and Update method calls.

You might use optimistic locking when the user has interaction with the editing process. Because optimistic locking does not lock the record until the update is being performed, you can tie your code that modifies field values directly to the user interface that the user is modifying. By using optimistic locking, you don't need to lock a record if the user decides to take an hour to modify data—instead, when the user attempts to save the data, the record would be locked momentarily.

Batch Optimistic Locks

Batch optimistic locking is very similar to optimistic locking in that the data provider locks the underlying data source only when updates are made, rather than
when editing begins. The difference, however, is that updates are done in batches.

Batch optimistic locking is advantageous when the user is making a lot of changes
and wants to commit them all at once:

```
rst.Open "Authors", _
        "DSN=BiblioDSN", _
        adOpenKeyset, _
        adLockBatchOptimistic

rst.AddNew "Author", "Christopher"
rst.AddNew "Author", "Charlie"
rst.AddNew "Author", "Frankie"
rst.UpdateBatch

rst.Close
```

Notice how the previous example adds three new records. Because the LockType
parameter of the Open method call of the Recordset object was set to
`adLockBatchOptimistic`, the records aren't actually written to the data source
until the UpdateBatch method of the Recordset object is called. In addition, the
data source is not locked until this method is called.

Just as the Update method has a CancelUpdate method, the UpdateBatch method
has the CancelBatch method, which accomplishes basically the same job:

```
rst.Open "Authors", _
        "DSN=BiblioDSN", _
        adOpenKeyset, _
        adLockBatchOptimistic

rst.AddNew "Author", "David"
rst.AddNew "Author", "Danny"
rst.CancelBatch

rst.Close
```

In the preceding example, neither of the two records created by the AddNew
method was added to the recordset because the CancelBatch method was called.

The UpdateBatch and CancelBatch methods can also accept a valid AffectEnum
enumeration value as shown in Table 5-6. The following example illustrates the
use of a parameter with the CancelBatch and UpdateBatch methods:

```
rst.Open "Authors", _
        "DSN=BiblioDSN", _
        adOpenKeyset, _
        adLockBatchOptimistic
```

```
rst.AddNew "Author", "David"
rst.AddNew "Author", "Danny"
rst.CancelBatch adAffectCurrent        ' cancels Danny

rst.AddNew "Author", "Marie"
rst.UpdateBatch adAffectAllChapters ' updates David and Marie

rst.Close
```

Notice that the call to the CancelBatch method only cancels the last editing function, the AddNew method that was used to add a record with an Author field set to **Danny**. The UpdateBatch method uses the **adAffectAllChapters** value to update the two remaining, newly created records.

The Status property displays the status of the current record's editing by returning a sum of one or more valid RecordStatusEnum enumeration values as shown in Table 5-16.

Table 5-16. The RecordStatusEnum Enumeration

Value	Description
adRecCanceled	Indicates that the record was not saved because the last batch operation was canceled.
adRecCantRelease	Indicates that the new record was not saved because of conflicts with record locks.
adRecConcurrencyViolation	Indicates that the record was not saved because optimistic concurrency was used.
adRecDBDeleted	Indicates that the record has already been removed from the data source.
adRecDeleted	Indicates that the record has been deleted.
adRecIntegrityViolation	Indicates that the record was not saved because the application violated integrity constraints.
adRecInvalid	Indicates that the record was not saved because its bookmark was invalid.
adRecMaxChangesExceeded	Indicates that the record was not saved because there were more pending records than the data provider supported.
adRecModified	Indicates that the record was not modified.
adRecMutlipleChanges	Indicates that the record was not saved because it would have affected multiple records.
adRecNew	Indicates that the record is new.
adRecObjectOpen	Indicates that the record was not saved because it conflicted with an open storage object.
adRecOK	Indicates that the record was successfully updated.
adRecOutOfMemory	Indicates that the record was not saved because the computer has run out of memory.
adRecPendingChanges	Indicates that the record was not saved because it references a pending insert.

Table 5-16. The RecordStatusEnum Enumeration (continued)

Value	Description
adRecPermissionDenied	Indicates that the record was not saved because the application did not have sufficient permissions.
adRecSchemaViolation	Indicates that the record was not saved because it conflicted with the underlying structure of the database.
adRecUnmodified	Indicates that the record was not modified.

The Status property can be used to print a textual description of the status of the Recordset object, at any time, by using a subroutine similar to the one listed here:

```
Private Sub PrintRecordStatus(rst As Recordset)

    Select Case (rst.Status)
        Case adRecUnmodified:
            Debug.Print "Record is unmodified"
        Case adRecNew:
            Debug.Print "New record"
        Case adRecDBDeleted:
            Debug.Print "Record has been deleted"
        Case Else:
            Debug.Print "Other"
    End Select
```

The PrintRecordStatus method can be used in our code to see the status of our records as we constantly add and edit them, as shown in this example:

```
rst.Open "Authors", _
        "DSN=BiblioDSN", _
        adOpenKeyset, _
        adLockBatchOptimistic

PrintRecordStatus rst' Status = adRecUnmodified

rst.AddNew "Author", "David"' Add a new record
PrintRecordStatus rst' Status = adRecNew

rst.AddNew "Author", "Danny"' Add a new record
PrintRecordStatus rst' Status = adRecNew

rst.CancelBatch adAffectCurrent' Remove the previous record
PrintRecordStatus rst' Status = adRecDBDeleted

rst.AddNew "Author", "Marie"' Add a new record
PrintRecordStatus rst' Status = adRecNew

rst.UpdateBatch adAffectAllChapters' Update all pending records
PrintRecordStatus rst' Status = adRecUnmodified

rst.Close
```

When working with client-side cursors, an Update method of some kind can send a lot of unnecessary information back to the server. In particular, by default, the Update methods return all of the records to the server, even if they were not modified. To alter this behavior, the MarshallOptions property can be set to `adMarshallModifiedOnly` value, which allows the client-side cursor to return only the modified records to the server—this setting can potentially save a lot of time and resources:

```
rst.Open "Authors", _
         "DSN=BiblioDSN", _
         adOpenStatic, _
         adLockBatchOptimistic

rst.MarshalOptions = adMarshalModifiedOnly
rst.AddNew "Author", "Patrice"

rst.Close
```

The MarshalOptions property is used only when you are using a client-side Recordset object with RDS.

Summary

This chapter showed you the second of the seven major components of ActiveX Data Objects, the Recordset object and its functions. After reading this chapter, you should be able to fully understand the Recordset object and the following key points:

- There are four different types of views, or cursors, into a data source's information. These are the dynamic, keyset, static, and forward-only cursors.

- Recordsets are opened with the Open method. Before a recordset is opened, the way in which it can be opened can be fine-tuned with multiple properties, and once a recordset is opened, it can be filtered and sorted.

- The standard ways in which you can move around within a recordset are the MoveFirst, MovePrevious, MoveNext, and MoveLast methods. In addition, the record pointer can be set to a particular ordinal position within a recordset or a valid bookmark.

- Records can be added, modified, and deleted. The status of a particular record can be identified—and multiple records can be returned—by the single method calls GetRows and GetString.

- There are four different types of record-locking schemes: read-only, pessimistic, optimistic, and batch optimistic record locking.

The next chapter of this book, Chapter 6, *Fields*, explains how to work with individual fields of a recordset. In addition, this chapter will show how these fields can be manipulated from within an application.

6

Fields

The Fields Collection Object

Every Recordset object contains a collection of fields represented by the Fields collection object. Within the Fields collection object, there is a collection of Field objects, each representing a column in the recordset. Through the Fields collection object, each individual Field object can be accessed.

Every value within one column of a recordset shares a common group of characteristics, which define that field. These characteristics for each column are stored in a corresponding Field object within the recordset's Fields collection object.

The Field Object

In its simplest form, a Field object has a name and a value. A field's name uniquely identifies a column within the recordset. The name of a given field can be accessed through Field object's Name property, for example:

```
Dim fld As Field

rst.Open "Authors", _
        "DSN=BiblioDSN"

Set fld = rst.Fields(1)

Debug.Print fld.Name

rst.Close
Set fld = Nothing
```

The value of a Field object changes depending on which record the record pointer is pointing to. The value of a field can be obtained by the Value property of the Field object:

```
Debug.Print rst.Fields!Author.Value
Debug.Print rst.Fields!Author
```

Both of these statements would print the same value, because the two lines are identical in meaning: because the Value property is the default property for the Field object.

When you add new records to a recordset, you can use the Value property to set the value for a particular field in the new record:

```
rst.AddNew
rst.Fields("Author").Value = "Jason"
rst.Update
```

And, as mentioned earlier, since the Value property is the default property for the Field object, it can be omitted, as in the following example:

```
rst.AddNew
rst.Fields("Author") = "Kimberly"
rst.Update
```

Working with the Fields Collection

The Fields collection object of a Recordset object contains a collection of Field objects for the given recordset, once the Recordset object is opened. The number of Field objects with the Fields collection object can be obtained with the Count property:

```
rst.Open "Authors", _
         "BiblioDSN", _
         adOpenKeyset, _
         adLockOptimistic

Debug.Print rst.Fields.Count

rst.Close
```

Individual Field objects can be accessed with the Item method of the Fields collection object:

```
Debug.Print rst.Fields.Item(1).Name
Debug.Print rst.Fields.Item("Author").Name
```

Alternatively, the Item method can be omitted, because it is the default property of the Fields collection object:

```
Debug.Print rst.Fields(1).Name
Debug.Print rst.Fields("Author").Name
```

In addition, the following syntax can be used to access a particular Field object in the Fields collection object:

```
Debug.Print rst.Fields!Author.Name
```

To add a new Field object to the Fields collection object, use the Append method:

```
rst.Fields.Append "Dirty", _
                adChar, _
                10, _
                adFldMayBeNull + adFldUpdatable
```

Notice the use of the parameters in this example. The first parameter gives the newly created Field object a name. The second parameter indicates the new Field object's datatype. The optional third parameter indicates the defined size of the new Field object. The fourth and last parameter is a combination of `FldAttributesEnum` values. All of these parameters are described later in this chapter.

The Append method cannot be called on a recordset that is already open or has had the ActiveConnection property previously set.

To remove a Field object from the Fields collection object, use the Delete method of the Fields object with a single parameter indicating the name of the Field to delete from the collection:

```
rst.Fields.Delete "Dirty"
```

Field Specifics

The Field object, as stated earlier, contains all of the information that corresponds to a single column of data within the recordset. The most important type of field characteristic is the field's *datatype*.

Field Datatypes

The datatype of a field specifies the type of information stored in the field within the recordset. There are many different datatypes available from many different data sources. ADO contains a list of datatypes that encompasses the majority of the datatypes known to developers. This list is shown in Table 6-1. These values are constants that represent the different datatype values that the Type property of the Field object can be set to.

Table 6-1. The DataTypeEnum Enumeration

Value	Description
adArray	Indicates that the datatype of the Field object is a safe array of another type that is joined to the adArray value by a logical Or.
adBigInt	Indicates that the datatype of the Field object is an 8-byte signed integer value.
adBinary	Indicates that the datatype of the Field object is a binary value.
adBoolean	Indicates that the datatype of the Field object is a Boolean value.
adByRef	Indicates that the datatype of the Field object is a pointer to another type which is joined to the adByRef value by a logical Or.
adBSTR	Indicates that the datatype of the Field object is a null-terminated character-string value.
adChar	Indicates that the datatype of the Field object is a String value.
adCurrency	Indicates that the datatype of the Field object is a currency value, which is stored in an 8-byte, signed integer.
adDate	Indicates that the datatype of the Field object is a date value, which is stored in a Double.
adDBDate	Indicates that the datatype of the Field object is a date value represented in the format *yyyymmdd*.
adDBTime	Indicates that the datatype of the Field object is a date value represented in the format *hhmmss*.
adDBTimeStamp	Indicates that the datatype of the Field object is a date-time stamp represented in the format *yyyymmddhhmmss* and a fraction value that represents billionths of a second.
adDecimal	Indicates that the datatype of the Field object is an exact numeric value with a fixed precision and scale.
adDouble	Indicates that the datatype of the Field object is a double-precision floating-point value.
adEmpty	Indicates that the datatype of the Field object is unspecified.
adError	Indicates a 32-bit error code.
adGUID	Indicates that the datatype of the Field object is a globally unique identifier (GUID).
adIDispatch	Indicates that the datatype of the Field object is a pointer to an Idispatch interface on an OLE object.
adInteger	Indicates that the datatype of the Field object is a 4-byte signed integer value.
adIUnknown	Indicates that the datatype of the Field object is a pointer to an unknown interface on an OLE object.
adLongVarBinary	Indicates that the datatype of the Field object is a long binary value.
adLongVarChar	Indicates that the datatype of the Field object is long String value.

Table 6-1. The DataTypeEnum Enumeration (continued)

Value	Description
adLongVarWChar	Indicates that the datatype of the Field object is a long null-terminated string value.
adNumeric	Indicates that the datatype of the Field object is an exact numeric value with a fixed precision and scale.
adSingle	Indicates that the datatype of the Field object is a single precision floating-point value.
adSmallInt	Indicates that the datatype of the Field object is a 2-byte signed-integer value.
adTinyInt	Indicates that the datatype of the Field object is a 1-byte signed-integer value.
adUnsignedBigInt	Indicates that the datatype of the Field object is an 8-byte unsigned-integer value.
adUnsignedInt	Indicates that the datatype of the Field object is a 4-byte unsigned-integer value.
adUnsignedSmallInt	Indicates that the datatype of the Field object is a 2-byte unsigned-integer value.
adUnsignedTinyInt	Indicates that the datatype of the Field object is a 1-byte unsigned-integer value.
adUserDefined	Indicates that the datatype of the Field object is a user-defined variable.
adVarBinary	Indicates that the datatype of the Field object is a binary value.
adVarChar	Indicates that the datatype of the Field object is a String value.
adVariant	Indicates that the datatype of the Field object is an Automation Variant value.
adVector	Indicates that the datatype of the Field object is a structure that contains a count of elements and a pointer to a value of another other type, which is joined to the adVector value by a logical Or.
adVarWChar	Indicates that the datatype of the Field object is a null-terminated Unicode character-string value.
adWVhar	Indicates that the datatype of the Field object is a null-terminated Unicode character-string value.

You can use the Type property of the Field object to print the datatype for a given object with a function, as shown here:

```
Private Sub PrintFieldDataType(fld As Field)

    Dim sTemp As String

    Select Case (fld.Type)
        Case adBigInt:
            sTemp = "8-Byte Signed Integer"
        Case adBinary:
            sTemp = "Binary"
```

```
          Case adBoolean:
              sTemp = "Boolean"
          Case adBSTR:
              sTemp = "Null Terminated String"
          Case adChar:
              sTemp = "String"
          Case adCurrency:
              sTemp = "Currency"
          Case adDate:
              sTemp = "Date (Double)"
          Case adDBDate:
              sTemp = "Date (yyyymmdd)"
          Case adDBTime:
              sTemp = "Time (hhmmss)"
          Case adDBTimeStamp:
              sTemp = "Date/Time (yyyymmddhhmmss and a billionths " _
                  & "of a second fraction)"
          Case adDecimal:
              sTemp = "Decimal"
          Case adDouble:
              sTemp = "Double Precision Floating Point"
          Case adEmpty:
              sTemp = "Not Specified"
          Case adError:
              sTemp = "32-Bit Error code"
          Case adGUID:
              sTemp = "Globally Unique Identifier"
          Case adIDispatch:
              sTemp = "Pointer to an IDispatch Interface"
          Case adInteger:
              sTemp = "4-Byte Signed Integer"
          Case adIUnknown:
              sTemp = "Pointer to an IUnknown Interface"
          Case adLongVarBinary:
              sTemp = "Long Binary"
          Case adLongVarChar:
              sTemp = "Long String"
          Case adLongVarWChar:
              sTemp = "Long Null Terminated String"
          Case adNumeric:
              sTemp = "Numeric"
          Case adSingle:
              sTemp = "Single Precision Floating Point"
          Case adSmallInt:
              sTemp = "2-Byte Signed Integer"
          Case adTinyInt:
              sTemp = "1-Byte Signed Integer"
          Case adUnsignedBigInt:
              sTemp = "8-Byte Unsigned Integer"
          Case adUnsignedInt:
              sTemp = "4-Byte Unsigned Integer"
          Case adUnsignedSmallInt:
              sTemp = "2-Byte Unsigned Integer"
```

```
        Case adUnsignedTinyInt:
            sTemp = "1-Byte Unsigned Integer"
        Case adUserDefined:
            sTemp = "User Defined Variable"
        Case adVarBinary:
            sTemp = "Binary"
        Case adVarChar:
            sTemp = "String"
        Case adVariant:
            sTemp = "Variant"
        Case adWChar:
            sTemp = "Null Terminated Unicode String"
    End Select

    Debug.Print fld.Name & ":", _
            sTemp

End Sub
```

The PrintFieldDataType function can be used to display the datatype of each of the Field objects in a given Fields collection object:

```
For Each fld In rst.Fields
    PrintFieldDataType fld
Next fld
```

If we were to take a look at the output of running the previous code segment, we might see something like this:

```
Au_ID:      4-Byte Signed Integer
Author:     String
Year Born:  2-Byte Signed Integer
```

For fields with numeric datatypes, the Precision property allows you to see the number of bytes that can be used to represent the information within the field. The following code will print the precision for each of the three fields in the Fields collection object:

```
For Each fld In rst.Fields
    Debug.Print fld.Name & ":", _
            fld.Precision
Next fld
```

with output something like:

```
Au_ID:      10
Author:     255
Year Born:  5
```

The Au_ID field can hold the maximum value that can be shown in 10 digits (2,147,483,647). The Author field does not have precision—thus the 255 value. The Year Born field's largest value (32,767) can be shown in a maximum of 5 bytes.

The NumericScale property is used to determine how many bytes are used after the decimal point for fields with numeric datatypes. If the following code was run on the same table, values of 255 would appear for each since Long Integers, Strings, and Integers do not have a numeric scale:

```
For Each fld In rst.Fields
    Debug.Print fld.Name & ":", _
                fld.NumericScale
Next fld
```

Field Sizes

There are two sizes associated with each Field object: defined and actual.

The defined size of a field is the size, in bytes, that the field obtains within a data source to hold the field's information. The actual size of a field is the size, in bytes, that is used by the field to hold the field's information. In other words, the defined size indicates the allotted space for the field information while the actual size is the space that is actually used. The actual size can be equal to or less than the defined size.

The defined size of a field can be obtained by using the DefinedSize property. The actual size of a field is determined by the ActualSize property:

```
For Each fld In rst.Fields

    Debug.Print "Name:", _
                fld.Name

    Debug.Print "Value:", _
                fld.Value

    Debug.Print "Actual Size:", _
                fld.ActualSize

    Debug.Print "Defined Size:", _
                fld.DefinedSize

    Debug.Print "Room Left:", _
                (fld.DefinedSize - fld.ActualSize)

    Debug.Print

Next fld
```

If this code were run on our data source, the following output would be generated:

```
Name:          Au_ID
Value:         16587
Actual Size:   4
Defined Size:  4
Room Left:     0
```

```
Name:          Author
Value:         Kimberly
Actual Size:   8
Defined Size:  50
Room Left:     42

Name:          Year Born
Value:         0
Actual Size:   2
Defined Size:  2
Room Left:     0
```

Notice that the fields that are of numeric datatypes have no room left, even if they aren't holding any information (Year Born). Also notice how the actual size is different from the defined size for the field Author, which is a string datatype.

Large Datatypes

Sometimes a field's data is too large to obtain all at once. Sometimes we don't know the actual size of a field's data. A good example of this is the Microsoft Access datatype "Memo." This datatype is used to hold a large amount of string information, and the amount varies from record to record.

Conventional field access would tell us to use the Value property to obtain this data, but ADO gives us a couple more functions to deal with these datatypes. The AppendChunk and GetChunk methods are used to store and retrieve chunks of information in datatypes that contain large binary information. In order to use either the AppendChunk or GetChunk methods, the field must be able to support them. To check for this functionality, use the Attributes property as shown in the following example:

```
If (rst.Fields("BigField").Attributes And adFldLong) Then

    rst.MoveFirst

    rst.Fields("BigField").AppendChunk "This is the first part of the data"
    rst.Fields("BigField").AppendChunk "This is another"
    rst.Fields("BigField").AppendChunk "This is another"
    rst.Fields("BigField").AppendChunk "This is another"

    rst.Update

End If
```

This code segment moves to the first record within a recordset and appends data to a field, BigField, if the field has an attribute of **adFldLong**. The first AppendChunk method call replaces the information within the field, while each subsequent call adds information onto the last. Finally, the Update method of the recordset is called to save the information.

After running this code, the value of the BigField field would be, "This is the first part of the dataThis is anotherThis is anotherThis is another". In this example, this value makes little sense, but in real-world applications, the AppendChunk method can be used to append log information, note fields, or even binary image information.

The sister method of AppendChunk, GetChunk, is used to retrieve the information within a large binary field. Just as with AppendChunk, the attribute flag adFldLong must be set in order to use the method. The following example uses the GetChunk method to retrieve the information stored within the BigField field:

```
If (rst.Fields("BigField").Attributes And adFldLong) Then

    Dim sTemp As String

    rst.MoveFirst
    sTemp = rst.Fields("BigField").GetChunk(5) & ""
    While (sTemp <> "")
        Debug.Print sTemp;
        sTemp = rst.Fields("BigField").GetChunk(2) & ""
    Wend
    Debug.Print

End If
```

In this example, an initial call to the GetChunk method is made with the parameter 5, which indicates how many bytes of information to retrieve from the field. With this method call, GetChunk will return five bytes of information if it exists. If less than five bytes of information exists, then the remainder will be returned. If there is no more information to return, the value returned from the GetChunk method is Null.

This return value from the GetChunk method is concatenated with an empty string ("") so that we do not get an error if this information returned Null. We cannot assign a Null value to a String, but by concatenating a Null value and empty string, we are left with an empty string, which can be assigned to a String variable.

The previous code then performs a While loop, which checks for an empty string value to indicate completion. Within the loop, the GetChunk method retrieves two bytes at a time, until a Null value is returned and concatenated with our empty string, thus ending the While loop.

Batch Updates

When working with batch updates, sometimes it is desirable to know what was in the field before changes were made. ADO offers two different properties to check this value: UnderlyingValue and OriginalValue.

The OriginalValue property returns the value that was originally returned to the Recordset object. This value is used to restore the field value when a Cancel-Update or CancelBatch method is called. If the Update or UpdateBatch method is called, then the OriginalValue will return this new value.

The UnderlyingValue property returns the value that is stored in the data source. This value can change (perhaps by another user) and differs from the Original-Value, which returns the value last stored in the recordset.

To see the difference between the two properties, look at the following code fragment:

```
rst.Open "Authors", _
        "DSN=BiblioDSN", _
        adOpenKeyset, _
        adLockBatchOptimistic

rst.MoveFirst
PrintFieldValues rst.Fields("Author")

rst.Fields("Author") = "Jason"
PrintFieldValues rst.Fields("Author")

rst.Fields("Author") = "Kimberly"
PrintFieldValues rst.Fields("Author")

    ' modify the first record, assuming its Year Born field is 1973
    con.Open "DSN=BiblioDSN"
    con.Execute "UPDATE Authors SET Author = 'Tammi' WHERE [Year Born] = 1973;"
    con.Close

PrintFieldValues rst.Fields("Author")

rst.Fields("Author") = "Kaitlyn"
PrintFieldValues rst.Fields("Author")

rst.UpdateBatch
PrintFieldValues rst.Fields("Author")

rst.Close
```

Here the record pointer is positioned to the first record in the recordset. Its value is changed to Jason, then to Kimberly. At this time, a second transaction updates all records to Tammi, where the Year Born field value is 1973 (we are assuming the first record has this value for Year Born). Next, the Author name is changed to Kaitlyn and then updated.

Between the commotion, calls to the method PrintFieldValues are made. This method simply displays the name, value, underlying value, and original value of the field as follows:

```
Private Sub PrintFieldValues(fld As Field)

    Debug.Print "Name:             " & fld.Name
    Debug.Print "Value:            " & fld.Value
    Debug.Print "Underlying Value: " & fld.UnderlyingValue
    Debug.Print "Original Value:   " & fld.OriginalValue
    Debug.Print


End Sub
```

If we took a look at the output of the previous pieces of code, we would see something like this:

```
Name:             Author
Value:            Sydow, Dan Parks
Underlying Value: Sydow, Dan Parks
Original Value:   Sydow, Dan Parks
```

The first call to the PrintFieldValues prints what we would expect—the value, underlying value, and original value are all the same:

```
Name:             Author
Value:            Jason
Underlying Value: Sydow, Dan Parks
Original Value:   Sydow, Dan Parks
```

Now, the code has changed the value of the field to **Jason**. Notice that the recordset is in batch updating mode and the information will not be saved until the UpdateBatch method is called.

```
Name:             Author
Value:            Kimberly
Underlying Value: Sydow, Dan Parks
Original Value:   Sydow, Dan Parks
```

Again, the value of the field is changed, this time to **Kimberly**:

```
Name:             Author
Value:            Kimberly
Underlying Value: Tammi
Original Value:   Sydow, Dan Parks
```

Notice how the underlying value and the original value part ways. Now the underlying value in the data source has been changed by the Update method from a separate transaction. The original value is the value that was originally returned to the recordset.

```
Name:             Author
Value:            Kaitlyn
Underlying Value: Tammi
Original Value:   Sydow, Dan Parks
```

Once again, the value of the field is changed—this time to **Kaitlyn**:

```
Name:             Author
Value:            Kaitlyn
```

```
Underlying Value: Kaitlyn
Original Value:   Kaitlyn
```

Finally, the UpdateBatch method is called, resetting all three values to the value that is in the field, in the data source, and the value that has been returned to the recordset.

Determining Field Object Functionality

Earlier, the Attributes property of the Field object was introduced as a method to identify functionality available to a particular field. In the earlier example, the Attributes property was used to see whether a field contained long binary data prior to using the AppendChunk and GetChunk methods.

In addition to this attribute, the Attributes property can identify any combination of valid FieldAttributeEnum enumeration values as listed in Table 6-2.

Table 6-2. The FieldAttributeEnum Enumeration

Value	Description
adFldMayDefer	Indicates that the field value is returned only when the value is accessed rather than with the rest of the record.
adFldUpdatable	Indicates that the field value is updateable.
adFldUnknownUpdatable	Indicates that ADO cannot determine if the field value is updateable.
adFldFixed	Indicates that the field contained a fixed length of data.
adFldIsNullable	Indicates that the field value can be set to Null.
adFldKeyColumn	Indicates that the field value is a key in the data source.
adFldMayBeNull	Indicates that the Null values can be returned by this field value.
adFldLong	Indicates that the field value is a long binary value. This attribute must be set in order to use AppendChunk and GetChunk methods on a field.
adFldRowID	Indicates that the field value is a unique row identifier that cannot be set.
adFldRowVersion	Indicates that the field value is a type of time and/or date stamp used to track changes in the record.
adFldCacheDeferred	Indicates that the field value is cached.

In order to check for a particular FieldAttributeEnum value, use the logical **And** operator on the Attributes property as shown in the following code segment:

```
For Each fld In rst.Fields

    Debug.Print "Name:", _
                fld.Name
```

```
Debug.Print "Attributes:"

If (fld.Attributes And adFldMayDefer) Then
    Debug.Print , "Deferred"
End If

If (fld.Attributes And adFldUpdatable) Then
    Debug.Print , "Updateable"
End If

If (fld.Attributes And adFldUnknownUpdatable) Then
    Debug.Print , "Update capability unknown"
End If

If (fld.Attributes And adFldFixed) Then
    Debug.Print , "Fixed-length data"
End If

If (fld.Attributes And adFldIsNullable) Then
    Debug.Print , "Accepts Null values"
End If

If (fld.Attributes And adFldMayBeNull) Then
    Debug.Print , "Field may be null"
End If

If (fld.Attributes And adFldLong) Then
    Debug.Print , "Long binary data"
End If

If (fld.Attributes And adFldRowID) Then
    Debug.Print , "Row identifier"
End If

If (fld.Attributes And adFldKeyColumn) Then
    Debug.Print , "Key column"
End If

If (fld.Attributes And adFldRowVersion) Then
    Debug.Print , "Time or date stamp for versioning"
End If

If (fld.Attributes And adFldMayBeNull) Then
    Debug.Print , "Cached"
End If

Debug.Print

Next fld
```

In this code, separate If...Then clauses are needed to check for each FieldAttributeEnum value. Because the Attributes property can contain multiple FieldAttributeEnum values, I do not recommend checking for an attribute

with equality. For instance, if the following code were used to check for the
`adFldRowVersion` value, it would not work if the Attributes property contained
both the `adFldRowVersion` and `adFldKeyColumn` flags:

```
' will not detect adFldRowVersion + adFldKeyColumn
If (fld.Attributes = adFldRowVersion) Then
        Debug.Print , "Time or date stamp for versioning"
End If
```

Summary

After reading this chapter, you should understand the Fields collection object, as
well as the Field object, and the following key points about the two:

- The Fields collection object contains a collection of Field objects, which each
  represent a column in the data source.

- There are many different datatypes for fields, all of which can be identified
  with the Type property. For many types, alternate properties such as Precision and NumericScale can be used to better explain the definition of the field.

- The supported functionality of a given Field object can be obtained using the
  Attributes property.

The next chapter of this book, Chapter 7, *The Command Object*, explains how
commands can be sent to the data source in order to execute SQL statements,
stored procedures, and other data source–specific commands.

7

The Command Object

The Command object performs one of three tasks. First, it can query the data source and return a Recordset object. By giving the Command object the name of a parameterized query, a stored procedure, or even a table, the Command object can execute instructions and return to your application a Recordset object with the results of the operation. Although we have learned to pass SQL statements and open tables with other objects from ADO (e.g., Recordset objects), as we will soon learn, the Command object is the only object that can use Parameter objects.

Second, the Command object can execute bulk operations such as an **UPDATE** or **INSERT INTO SQL** statement. Again, the Recordset object can provide the same functionality, but the Command object will allow the persistence of its command text for re-execution, unlike the Recordset object.

Finally, the Command object can alter the state of the underlying data source using SQL statements. Appendix A, *Introduction to SQL*, introduces the Structured Query Language (SQL) and provides examples of commands that can alter the structure of a data source.

Specifying Commands

Commands are set, through Command objects, with two properties. The first of these properties, CommandText, holds either the String value representing the command's text or the name of a stored command text as the data provider references it. In other words, either the SQL statement **SELECT * FROM Authors;** can be assigned to the CommandText property, or this string can be stored in the data source and referenced, through the data provider, by a name such as "Get All From Authors". The CommandType property tells ADO what kind of value resides in the CommandText property. This property would indicate if the value within the CommandText property was a SQL statement or a name of a stored SQL statement. The value of the CommandType property can be set to any valid CommandTypeEnum values as shown in Table 7-1.

Table 7-1. The CommandTypeEnum Enumeration

Value	Description
adCmdText	Indicates that the value of the CommandText property is a definition of a command that the data provider will understand.
adCmdTable	Indicates that the value of the CommandText property is the name of a table within the data source. ADO will create a SQL statement from the table name specified to return all fields within the table.
adCmdTableDirect	Indicates that the value of the CommandText property is the name of a table within the data source. This value is very similar to that of adCmdFile except that the table name is used to return all of the fields within the table rather than a generated SQL statement.
adCmdStoredProc	Indicates that the value of the CommandText property is the name of a stored procedure accessible by the data provider.
adCmdUnknown	Indicates that the value of the CommandText property is of an unknown type. This is the default value for the CommandType property.
adCmdFile	Indicates that the value of the CommandText property is the name of a file that has been created by a persisted Recordset.

One of the most common uses of the CommandText and CommandType properties involves passing textual definitions of commands to the data source.

Textual Definitions as Commands

When working with textual definitions of a command, we usually think of SQL statements. Although it is a topic well beyond the scope of this book, many other types of textual definitions can be defined within the CommandText property, depending on your data provider. Particular command information should be available within your data provider's documentation. In this book, we are working with Access and SQL Server databases; therefore, we are going to stick with SQL statements as the sole example of textual definitions of commands.

The following piece of code illustrates how a SQL **SELECT** statement can be assigned to the CommandText property and how it can be executed to return a Recordset object to the application:

```
com.ActiveConnection = "driver={SQL Server}; " _
                     & "server=JROFF_LAPTOP; " _
                     & "uid=sa; " _
                     & "database=Northwind"

com.CommandText = "SELECT * " _
```

```
                & "FROM Customers " _
                & "WHERE (ContactTitle = 'Sales Representative') " _
                & "AND (Country = 'USA'); "
com.CommandType = adCmdText

Set rst = com.Execute

Do Until (rst.EOF)
    Debug.Print rst.Fields("ContactName")
    rst.MoveNext
Loop

rst.Close
```

In this example, the Execute method of the Command object instructed ADO to query the data source with the SQL statement defined within the CommandText property and to return a Recordset object. Notice that ADO also knew the CommandText property held a textual definition of a command because the CommandType property had been set to **adCmdText**.

It is also important to note that the ActiveConnection property, in the last piece of code, was used to indicate the SQL Server data source that we are using to execute our query. Although the ActiveConnection property is explained in greater detail later in this chapter, all Command objects have to have an associated connection to a data source to use the Execute method.

The next piece of code is somewhat similar to the last, except that the SQL statement being executed by the Command object is considered an Action query (see Appendix A for more information):

```
com.ActiveConnection = "driver={SQL Server}; " _
                & "server=JROFF_LAPTOP; " _
                & "uid=sa; " _
                & "database=Northwind"

com.CommandText = "UPDATE customers " _
                & "SET Country = 'UK' " _
                & "WHERE (CustomerID = 'HUNGC'); "

com.CommandType = adCmdText

Set rst = com.Execute

If (rst.State & adStateOpen) Then
    Debug.Print "Recordset is open... records returned."
    rst.Close
Else
    Debug.Print "Recordset not open... no records."
End If
```

Since an Action query does not return records, the Recordset object returned from the Execute method is closed. Furthermore, if we attempt to use the Close method on a closed Recordset object, we get an error. The previous example illustrates how you can use the Command object to modify a group of records with a single command.

Stored Procedures as Commands

Another type of value that can be passed to the CommandText property is a name of a stored definition of a command—a stored procedure. Stored procedures are used a lot in today's database applications and used quite heavily within ADO implementations of these applications.

To execute a stored procedure with a Command object in ADO, pass the name of the stored procedure to the CommandText property, and set the CommandType property to **adCmdStoredProc** as shown:

```
com.ActiveConnection = "driver={SQL Server}; " _
                     & "server=JROFF_LAPTOP; " _
                     & "uid=sa; " _
                     & "database=Northwind"

com.CommandText = "[Ten Most Expensive Products]"
com.CommandType = adCmdStoredProc

Set rst = com.Execute

Do Until (rst.EOF)
    Debug.Print rst.Fields("TenMostExpensiveProducts")
    rst.MoveNext
Loop
```

In this code, we are assuming that the stored procedure "Ten Most Expensive Products" returns records. In addition, because the name of this stored procedure has spaces within it, we have to put this name within brackets. This is a requirement of SQL Server, not ADO. ADO simply passes this information to SQL Server.

Table Names as Commands

Table names can be used as the command text of a Command object in two different ways. First, when the **adCmdTable** value is used within the CommandType property, ADO constructs a SQL statement based on the table name that is passed to it through the ComandText property, as in the following code:

```
com.ActiveConnection = "driver={SQL Server}; " _
                     & "server=JROFF_LAPTOP; " _
                     & "uid=sa; " _
                     & "database=Northwind"

com.CommandText = "Orders"
com.CommandType = adCmdTable
```

```
Set rst = com.Execute

Debug.Print "CommandText property value: " & com.CommandText

rst.Close
```

The output from this code is:

```
CommandText property value:
SELECT * FROM ORDERS
```

As you can see, ADO has generated a SQL statement and has placed it directly within the CommandText property.

The second way tables can be accessed with a Command object is with the **adCmdTableDirect** setting for the CommandType property. This setting is not available with all data providers, including SQL Server, but it does exist:

```
com.ActiveConnection = "DSN=SupportedDSN"

com.CommandText = "ATableName"
com.CommandType = adCmdTableDirect

Set rst = com.Execute

Debug.Print "CommandText property value: "
Debug.Print UCase$(com.CommandText)

rst.Close
```

When this code is executed on a data provider that supports the **adCmdTableDirect** flag of the CommandType property, its output is:

```
CommandText property value:
ATableName
```

Notice how ADO does not change the value of the CommandText property value when communicating with the data provider.

Unknown Command Types

Another valid setting for the CommandType property is **adCmdUnknown**. What this value indicates to ADO is that the application does not know what it is sending to the data provider. It could be a SQL statement, a stored procedure, or a table name. It doesn't know. Although ADO will accept this, it is not a wise value to use unless absolutely necessary.

When you do use the **adCmdUnknown** value, ADO has to try to figure out what it has and perform additional communications with SQL Server to determine the type of command it is, an unnecessary and time-consuming activity.

Nevertheless, if for some reason you don't know the type of command that you are asking ADO to execute, you can use the **adCmdUnknown** value as follows:

```
com.ActiveConnection = "driver={SQL Server}; " _
                       & "server=JROFF_LAPTOP; " _
                       & "uid=sa; " _
                       & "database=Northwind"

com.CommandText = "[Ten Most Expensive Products]"
com.CommandType = adCmdUnknown

Set rst = com.Execute

If (rst.State & adStateOpen) Then
    Debug.Print "Recordset is open... records returned."
    rst.Close
Else
    Debug.Print "Recordset not open... no records."
End If
```

As you can see, the only difference is the change of the CommandType property value to **adCmdUnknown**.

Executing Commands

You can execute a command with the Command object, the Connection object, or the Recordset object. Command objects allow you the greatest flexibility by allowing you to specify how the returned Recordset is defined. Connection objects and Recordset objects offer very little fine-tuning capabilities, but they are excellent for retrieving simple recordsets using the default settings.

Executing Commands with the Command Object

A command can be executed with a Command object by using its Execute method. The Execute method has three parameters. The first is a number indicating how many records were affected by the command once it had been executed. If the command being executed deleted records, this number would indicate how many were deleted. If it was a command to update records, this number would indicate how many were updated. The second is an array of variant data representing one or more parameter values (parameters are discussed in the next section of this chapter). The third is an integer value representing a CommandTypeEnum value listed in Table 7-1 and an optional ExcecuteOption-Enum value.

The ExecuteOptionEnum value used with the Execute method of the Command object allows you to specify how a provider should execute a command. The valid values for the ExecuteOptionEnum enumeration can be found in Table 7-2.

Table 7-2. The ExecuteOptionEnum Enumeration

Enumeration (ADO/WFC)	Value	Description
AdAsyncExecute (ASYNCEXECUTE)	16 (&H10)	Instructs ADO to execute the command asynchronously.
adAsyncFetch (ASYNCFETCH)	32 (&H20)	Instructs ADO to fetch the records returned from this command asynchronously after the initial number of rows (indicated by the CacheSize property) are returned.
adAsyncFetchNonBlocking (ASYNCFETCHNONBLOCKING)	64 (&H40)	Instructs ADO never to block the main thread while executing, and if the row that is requested has not been read, it is automatically moved to the end of the file.
adExecuteNoRecords (NORECORDS)	128 (&H80)	Instructs ADO that the CommandText property does not return rows, and if it does, to discard them. This value is always combined with adCmdText or adCmdStoredProc of the CommandTypeEnum enumeration.
adExecuteStream (no ADO/WFC equivalent)	1024 (&H400)	Indicates that the returned object of the Command object's Execute method will be a Stream object. This value is invalid for all other uses.

Although a Command object is independent of other objects, it must be connected to a data source before it can execute its command. The Command object uses the ActiveConnection property to establish this connection.

The ActiveConnection can be set to any valid, open Connection object, as shown in the following example:

```
con.ConnectionString = "DSN=BiblioDSN"
con.Open

Set com.ActiveConnection = con

com.CommandText = "Authors"

Set rst = com.Execute(, , adCmdTable)

Debug.Print "First author's name: " & rst.Fields("Author")

rst.Close
con.Close
```

In this example, once the Connection object is open, a reference of the object is given to the Command object to use as a connection to the data source (this is merely one way of establishing a connection). If the Close method of the Connection object were to be called prior to the Execute method of the Command object, an error would occur.

A Command object's ActiveConnection property can also accept a String value representing a connection string. With this value, the Command object can create its own Connection object, internally:

```
com.ActiveConnection = "DSN=BiblioDSN"

Set con = com.ActiveConnection

Debug.Print "Command Object's Connection String:"

sTemp = con.ConnectionString & ";"

While (sTemp <> "")
    nPosition = InStr(1, sTemp, ";", vbTextCompare)
    Debug.Print , Left$(sTemp, nPosition)
    sTemp = Right$(sTemp, Len(sTemp) - nPosition)
Wend

com.CommandText = "Authors"

Set rst = com.Execute(, , adCmdTable)

Debug.Print "First author's name: " & rst.Fields("Author")

rst.Close
con.Close
```

Notice that in this code segment, the internally created Connection object is actually retrieved from the Command object by reading the ActiveConnection property.

The following example is the output that describes the ConnectionString property of the newly created Connection object, all derived from the original **"DSN=BiblioDSN"** connection string passed to the ActiveConnection of the Command object:

```
Command Object's Connection String:
        Provider=MSDASQL.1;
        Connect Timeout=15;
        Extended Properties="DSN=BiblioDSN;
        DBQ=c:\My Documents\Book\Chapter 5\BIBLIO.MDB;
        DriverId=25;
        FIL=MS Access;
        MaxBufferSize=512;
        PageTimeout=5;
        ";
        Locale Identifier=1033;
```

If a Connection object is not specified for a Command object's ActiveConnection property, a new Connection object is created each time, even if the connection string used is the same. It is wiser to create a single Connection object and pass it to the Command object each time you need to execute a command to save resources and connection time.

Executing Commands with the Connection Object

The second way of executing a command is through the Connection object. Although it is not necessary to explicitly instantiate an instance of a Command object in order to execute a command through the Connection object, it does not mean that one is not being used.

The Execute method of the Connection object accepts three parameters. The first is the equivalent of the CommandText property of the Command object. The second is a variable used to store the number of records affected by the execution. The third and final parameter is equivalent to the CommandType property of the Command object, specifying the type of command that has been passed in the first parameter:

```
con.Open "DSN=BiblioDSN"

Set rst = con.Execute("Authors", _

                ' _
                adCmdTable)

Debug.Print "First author's name: " & rst.Fields("Author")

rst.Close
```

When the Execute method is called, it returns a Recordset object just as the Command's Execute method does. This is done with a Command object that is created internally by the Connection object. The Command object created by the Connection object cannot be retrieved like the Connection object from the Command object in the last section.

Executing Commands with the Recordset Object

The third and final way of executing a command within ADO is with the use of a Recordset object. In this way, a Command object is created by specifying at least the connection and the command itself. This Command object is then passed to the Open method of the Recordset object as the first parameter, representing the source of the recordset. The following piece of code represents this method:

```
com.ActiveConnection = "DSN=BiblioDSN"
com.CommandText = "Authors"

rst.Open com, _

        ' _
        adOpenDynamic, _
        adLockBatchOptimistic, _
        adCmdTable

Debug.Print "First author's name: " & rst.Fields("Author")

rst.Close
```

Note that if a Command object is being passed to the Open method of the Recordset object, a connection must already be established within the Command object. The connection cannot be present in the second parameter of the Open method. This situation would result in an error.

In addition, it is also very important to note that this final method of executing commands is the only method that allows the developer to specify how the recordset is returned to the application. It is the only way in which the cursor type and locking scheme can be specified for the resulting recordset.

Parameters

Parameterized queries are used frequently in today's databases. Parameters allow queries to be stored within the data source and to be altered based upon different values at runtime.

Passing Parameters

Like most things in ADO, there are a couple ways of passing parameter values to the data provider.

The first way, and probably the easiest, is to specify the value of a parameter in CommandText property of a Command object, like a function call:

```
com.ActiveConnection = "driver={SQL Server}; " _
                     & "server=JROFF_LAPTOP; " _
                     & "uid=sa; " _
                     & "database=Northwind"

com.CommandText = "CustOrderHist('ALFKI')"
com.CommandType = adCmdStoredProc

Set rst = com.Execute

Do Until (rst.EOF)
    Debug.Print rst.Fields("ProductName")
    rst.MoveNext
Loop

rst.Close
```

In this code, the value **'ALFKI'** is passed to the stored procedure **CustOrderHist**. This method can also be used when executing commands through a Connection object, as in the following example:

```
con.Open "driver={SQL Server}; " _
       & "server=JROFF_LAPTOP; " _
       & "uid=sa; " _
       & "database=Northwind"
```

```
Set rst = con.Execute("CustOrderHist('ALFKI')", _
                      , _
                      adCmdStoredProc)

Do Until (rst.EOF)
    Debug.Print rst.Fields("ProductName")
    rst.MoveNext
Loop

rst.Close
```

Although easy to understand, this method leaves much to be desired. Suppose that you wish to pass a parameter value from within a variable, rather than hard-coding it into the string as shown in the last two examples. In this case, of course it can be done. However, you will have to do string concatenation, and things can get sloppy in the code. Why bother?

Through the Command object only, ADO allows us to specify the values of parameters as an array (or a string if there is only one parameter), as in the following example:

```
com.ActiveConnection = "driver={SQL Server}; " _
                       & "server=JROFF_LAPTOP; " _
                       & "uid=sa; " _
                       & "database=Northwind"

com.CommandText = "CustOrdersDetail"

Set rst = com.Execute(, "10255", adCmdStoredProc)

Do Until (rst.EOF)
    Debug.Print rst.Fields("ProductName")
    rst.MoveNext
Loop

rst.Close
```

In this code, the value 10255 has been passed as the parameter to the Execute method of the Command object. Notice that the third and final parameter, CommandType, must be specified if the second parameter is being used. This method is a lot neater than the first.

The Parameters collection of the Command object allows us to view information about parameters in addition to setting them. The Parameters collection has a method called Refresh. The Refresh method must be called before you can read the properties of any given parameter. In fact, the Refresh method must be called in order to obtain the individual parameters.

In the previous examples, the Command object called the Refresh method on its own to obtain information about the parameters for the given stored procedure.

Once the Refresh method has been called, parameters can be accessed via their index in the collection, as shown in the following example:

```
com.ActiveConnection = "driver={SQL Server}; " _
                     & "server=JROFF_LAPTOP; " _
                     & "uid=sa; " _
                     & "database=Northwind"

com.CommandText = "CustOrdersDetail"
com.CommandType = adCmdStoredProc

com.Parameters.Refresh
com.Parameters(1).Value = "10255"

Set rst = com.Execute

Do Until (rst.EOF)
    Debug.Print rst.Fields("ProductName")
    rst.MoveNext
Loop

rst.Close
```

Here, the Refresh method is called after the stored procedure name is specified in order to obtain information regarding its parameters. The value of the first parameter is set to 10255, and then the command is executed.

In addition to the Value property of the Parameter object, if the particular parameter accepts long binary data, the AppendChunk method can be used to set the value of the parameter as explained in "Large Datatypes" in Chapter 6, *Fields*.

The Attributes property can determine whether the particular parameter accepts long binary data by using the logical **And** keyword and the value **adParamLong** as shown:

```
com.ActiveConnection = "driver={SQL Server}; " _
                     & "server=JROFF_LAPTOP; " _
                     & "uid=sa; " _
                     & "database=Northwind"

com.CommandText = "CustOrdersDetail"
com.CommandType = adCmdStoredProc

com.Parameters.Refresh

If (com.Parameters(1).Attributes And adParamLong) Then
    com.Parameters(1).AppendChunk "First piece of data"
    com.Parameters(1).AppendChunk "Second piece of data"
    com.Parameters(1).AppendChunk "Third piece of data"
    com.Parameters(1).AppendChunk "Fourth piece of data"
Else
    com.Parameters(1).Value = "10255"
```

```
   End If

   Set rst = com.Execute

   Do Until (rst.EOF)
       Debug.Print rst.Fields("ProductName")
       rst.MoveNext
   Loop

   rst.Close
```

If a parameter accepts long binary values, the AppendChunk method, called in succession, appends data to the value. The first time the AppendChunk method is called on a parameter, the value of that parameter is set to the value passed with the method. Every succeeding call to the AppendChunk method adds data to that value. In addition, by passing a **Null** value to the AppendChunk method, the value of the parameter is cleared.

Parameter Properties

Once the Parameters collection has all the information about the individual Parameter objects that are within it, you can use any of the Parameter properties shown in Table 7-3.

Table 7-3. The Parameter Object's Properties

Property	Description
Attributes	Indicates particular properties of a Parameter object, including whether it accepts signed values, nulls, or long binary data.
Direction	Indicates if the parameter is an input parameter, an output parameter, both an input and an output parameter, or a return value from a stored procedure.
Name	Indicates the name of the parameter.
NumericScale	Indicates the number of decimal places that are used if the type of the particular Parameter object is numeric.
Precision	Indicates the number of bytes that are used to present the largest numeric value that the Parameter object can hold.
Size	Indicates the maximum number of bytes that the Parameter object can hold.
Type	Indicates the type of the Parameter object's value by a DataTypeEnum value.
Value	Indicates the value of the Parameter object.

Although we can ask ADO to obtain information about the parameters belonging to a stored procedure, it is not always such a good idea. In most cases, obtaining information about parameters on its own causes ADO to spend a lot of time communicating with the data provider when it doesn't have to. The following section explains how to specify known parameters.

Specifying Parameters

In the cases in which you know the details about a specific parameter, it saves time tell ADO before attempting to execute a command.

The Parameters collection contains all the parameters for a command. Parameters can be added to this collection with the use of the CreateParameter method of the collection. The CreateParameter method accepts three parameters itself: the name, the datatype, and the direction of the parameter to be created.

The datatype parameter must be a valid DataTypeEnum value (see Table 6-1). The direction parameter must be a valid ParameterDirectionEnum value shown in Table 7-4.

Table 7-4. The ParameterDirectionEnum Enumeration

Value	Description
adParamUnknown	Indicates that the parameter direction is unknown.
adParamInput	Indicates that the parameter is an input parameter. This is the default value for the Direction property and parameter.
adParamOutput	Indicates that the parameter is an output parameter.
adParamInputOutput	Indicates that the parameter is both an input and an output parameter.
adParamReturnValue	Indicates that the parameter is a return value from the stored procedure.

The following example illustrates the use of the CreateParameter method:

```
com.ActiveConnection = "driver={SQL Server}; " _
                     & "server=JROFF_LAPTOP; " _
                     & "uid=sa; " _
                     & "database=Northwind"

com.CommandText = "CustOrdersDetail"
com.CommandType = adCmdStoredProc

Set par = com.CreateParameter("@OrderID", adInteger, adParamInput)
com.Parameters.Append par

par.Value = "10255"
Set rst = com.Execute

Do Until (rst.EOF)
    Debug.Print rst.Fields("ProductName")
    rst.MoveNext
```

```
Loop
rst.Close

par.Value = "10260"
Set rst = com.Execute

Do Until (rst.EOF)
    Debug.Print rst.Fields("ProductName")
    rst.MoveNext
Loop
rst.Close
```

As you can see, the CreateParameter method returns a Parameter object. A reference to the Parameter object is appended, using the Append method, to the Parameters collection. Once this is done, the Parameter object's value is changed before each execution of the stored procedure.

The previous code fragment potentially executes faster than code using the Refresh method of the Parameters collection to determine the parameter specifications of a stored procedure.

The Parameters Project

Now that you understand Parameter objects, this section will walk you though a project that allows you to view all available properties and attributes of any given stored procedure.

Begin by creating a form that looks like that of the one shown in Figure 7-1.

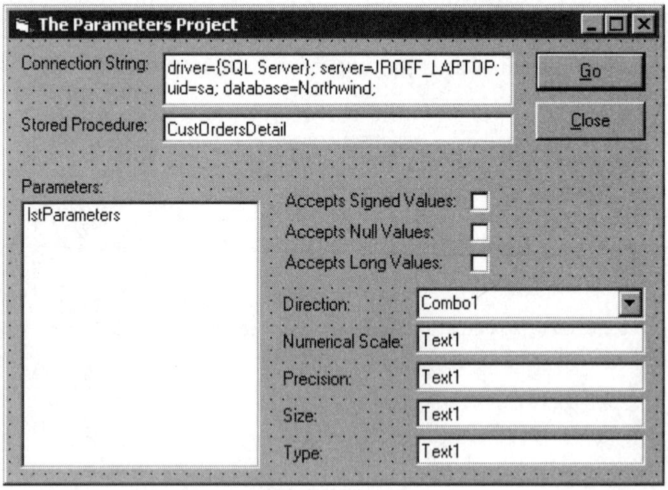

Figure 7-1. The Parameters Project in design mode

Now set the values of the controls as listed in Table 7-5.

Table 7-5. The Parameters Project Example Control Settings

Control	Property	Value
Command Button	Name	cmdGo
	Caption	"&Go"
	Default	-1 'True
Command Button	Name	CmdClose
	Caption	"&Close"
	Cancel	-1 'True
Text Box	Name	TxtConnectionString
	MultiLine	-1 'True
	Text	A valid connection string
Text Box	Name	TxtCommandString
	Text	A valid stored procedure name
Check Box	Name	chkSigned
	Alignment	1 'Right Justify
	Caption	"Accepts Signed Values:"
Check Box	Name	chkNull
	Alignment	1 'Right Justify
	Caption	"Accepts Null Values:"
Check Box	Name	chkLong
	Alignment	1 'Right Justify
	Caption	"Accepts Long Values:"
Combo Box	Name	CboDirection
	Enabled	0 'False
List Box	Name	lstParameters
Text Box	Name	TxtType
	Enabled	0 'False
Text Box	Name	TxtSize
	Enabled	0 'False
Text Box	Name	TxtPrecision
	Enabled	0 'False
Text Box	Name	TxtNumericScale
	Enabled	0 'False
Label	Caption	"Connection String:"
Label	Caption	"Stored Procedure:"

Table 7-5. The Parameters Project Example Control Settings (continued)

Control	Property	Value
Label	Caption	"Parameters:"
Label	Caption	"Direction:"
Label	Caption	"Numerical Scale:"
Label	Caption	"Precision:"
Label	Caption	"Size:"
Label	Caption	"Type:"

Now that the controls are in place and their values have been set, begin by entering the Declarations section of the Parameters project as follows:

```
Option Explicit

Private com As ADODB.Command
Private par As ADODB.Parameter
```

Enter the code for the Close button's Click event, which unloads the global Command object instance from memory:

```
Private Sub cmdClose_Click()
    Set com = Nothing
    Unload Me
End Sub
```

The form's Load event clears the controls by calling the SetFields method:

```
Private Sub Form_Load()
    Set com = New ADODB.Command

    Call SetFields
End Sub

Private Sub SetFields()

    chkSigned.Value = 0
    chkNull.Value = 0
    chkLong.Value = 0

    cboDirection.Clear
    cboDirection.AddItem "Unknown direction", adParamUnknown
    cboDirection.AddItem "Input Parameter", adParamInput
    cboDirection.AddItem "Output Parameter", adParamOutput
    cboDirection.AddItem "Input/Output Parameter", adParamInputOutput
    cboDirection.AddItem "Return Value", adParamReturnValue

    txtNumericScale.Text = ""
    txtPrecision.Text = ""
    txtSize.Text = ""
    txtType.Text = ""

End Sub
```

Now enter the following code for the Go button's Click event. This code clears the contents of the controls on the form and attempts to refresh the Parameters collection of a Command object based upon the connection string and stored procedure name entered in the form:

```
Private Sub cmdGo_Click()
On Error GoTo ERR_cmdGo_Click:

    Screen.MousePointer = vbHourglass

    lstParameters.Clear
    SetFields

    com.ActiveConnection = txtConnectionString.Text
    com.CommandText = txtCommandText.Text
    com.CommandType = adCmdStoredProc
    com.Parameters.Refresh

    lstParameters.Clear
    For Each par In com.Parameters
        lstParameters.AddItem par.Name
    Next

ERR_cmdGo_Click:

    Screen.MousePointer = vbDefault

    Select Case (Err.Number)
        Case 0: ' no error
        Case Else:
            MsgBox "Error #" & Err.Number _
                & " " & Err.Description
    End Select
End Sub
```

The only thing left to enter now is the Click event for the list control containing the parameters belonging to the stored procedure. This event basically fills in the controls on the form, based on the information gathered from the parameter that was chosen from the list:

```
Private Sub lstParameters_Click()

    Call SetFields

    Set par = com.Parameters( _
            lstParameters.List( _
                lstParameters.ListIndex))

    If (par.Attributes And adParamSigned) Then chkSigned.Value = 1
    If (par.Attributes And adParamNullable) Then chkNull.Value = 1
    If (par.Attributes And adParamLong) Then chkLong.Value = 1

    cboDirection.ListIndex = par.Direction
```

```
txtNumericScale.Text = par.Direction
txtPrecision.Text = par.Precision
txtSize.Text = par.Size

Select Case (par.Type)
    Case adBigInt:
        txtType.Text = "adBigInt"
    Case adBinary:
        txtType.Text = "adBinary"
    Case adBoolean:
        txtType.Text = "adBoolean"
    Case adBSTR:
        txtType.Text = "adBSTR"
    Case adChar:
        txtType.Text = "adChar"
    Case adCurrency:
        txtType.Text = "adCurrency"
    Case adDate:
        txtType.Text = "adDate"
    Case adDBDate:
        txtType.Text = "adDBDate"
    Case adDBTime:
        txtType.Text = "adDBTime"
    Case adDBTimeStamp:
        txtType.Text = "adDBTimeStamp"
    Case adDecimal:
        txtType.Text = "adDecimal"
    Case adDouble:
        txtType.Text = "adDouble"
    Case adEmpty:
        txtType.Text = "adEmpty"
    Case adError:
        txtType.Text = "adError"
    Case adGUID:
        txtType.Text = "adGUID"
    Case adIDispatch:
        txtType.Text = "adIDispatch"
    Case adInteger:
        txtType.Text = "adInteger"
    Case adIUnknown:
        txtType.Text = "adIUnknown"
    Case adLongVarBinary:
        txtType.Text = "adLongVarBinary"
    Case adLongVarChar:
        txtType.Text = "adLongVarChar"
    Case adLongVarWChar:
        txtType.Text = "adLongVarWChar"
    Case adNumeric:
        txtType.Text = "adNumeric"
    Case adSingle:
        txtType.Text = "adSingle"
    Case adSmallInt:
        txtType.Text = "adSmallInt"
    Case adTinyInt:
        txtType.Text = "adTinyInt"
```

```
        Case adUnsignedBigInt:
            txtType.Text = "adUnsignedBigInt"
        Case adUnsignedInt:
            txtType.Text = "adUnsignedInt"
        Case adUnsignedSmallInt:
            txtType.Text = "adUnsignedSmallInt"
        Case adUnsignedTinyInt:
            txtType.Text = "adUnsignedTinyInt"
        Case adUserDefined:
            txtType.Text = "adUserDefined"
        Case adVarBinary:
            txtType.Text = "adVarBinary"
        Case adVarChar:
            txtType.Text = "adVarChar"
        Case adVariant:
            txtType.Text = "adVariant"
        Case adVarWChar:
            txtType.Text = "adVarWChar"
        Case adWChar:
            txtType.Text = "adWChar"
    End Select

    Set par = Nothing

End Sub
```

Once you have entered all of the code, run the application. If the connection string and stored procedure values are not already entered, do so now. Click the Go button to refresh the Parameters collection of the newly created Command object, and then choose a parameter from the list to the left to view its specific attributes and property values. Figure 7-2 shows what this project might look like in action.

Asynchronous Execution

Asynchronous execution allows you to execute commands in the background of the client or server, while allowing the application to continue executing other commands. Asynchronous execution is vital when dealing with large data sources over a large network.

In most cases, users will not wait more than a few seconds—let alone two or three minutes—for a response from your application indicating that a command is finally done. For instance, suppose an administrator of a large company determines to increase the prices of all items by one dollar. Suppose that this company has 10,000 products. When the user presses a button confirming the price change, she shouldn't have to wait for all products to be updated before she can continue her work. Instead, once she confirms the price change, the application should issue an asynchronous command to the server to execute the update.

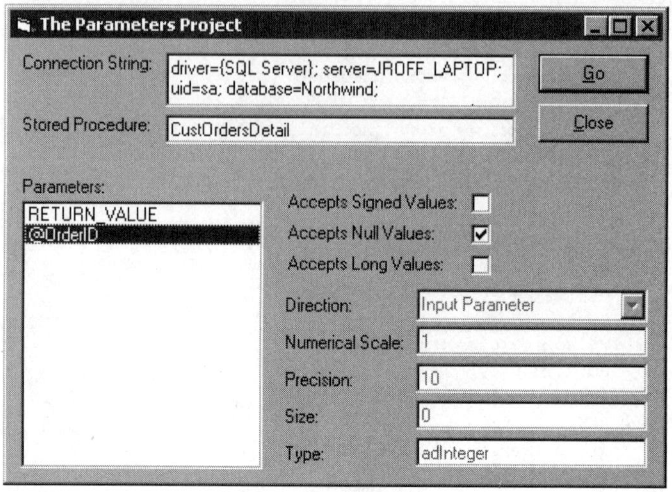

Figure 7-2. The Parameters project executing

Executing a Command Asynchronously

Before you learn how to execute commands asynchronously, first take a look at a piece of code that takes a significant amount of time to execute:

```
com.ActiveConnection = "driver={SQL Server}; " _
                  & "server=JROFF_LAPTOP; " _
                  & "uid=sa; " _
                  & "database=Northwind"

com.CommandText = "DELETE [Order Details (Backup)]; "

sSQL = "INSERT INTO [Order Details (Backup)] " _
    & "      (OrderID, ProductID, UnitPrice, Quantity, Discount) " _
    & "SELECT OrderID, ProductID, UnitPrice, Quantity, Discount " _
    & "FROM [Order Details]; "

com.CommandText = com.CommandText + sSQL

Debug.Print "Time execution began:     " & Now

Set rst = com.Execute(lNumberOfRecords, _
                  , _
                  adCmdText)

Debug.Print "  Number of records:      " & lNumberOfRecords

Debug.Print "Time execution completed: " & Now
```

This code actually executes two action queries on the data source with one command execution. First, all the records of the "Order Details (Backup)" table are deleted. Second, all of the records located in the "Order Details" record are copied to the blank table.

On my machine, this takes about 3 seconds and inserts 2,155 records into the backup table. Although 3 seconds is not a tremendous amount of time, imagine if it were to insert 21550 records. This could take 30 seconds on a single machine. It could take a minute over the network.

To execute a command asynchronously, add the **adAsyncExecute** constant value to the CommandType parameter of the Execute method:

```
com.ActiveConnection = "driver={SQL Server}; " _
                   & "server=JROFF_LAPTOP; " _
                   & "uid=sa; " _
                   & "database=Northwind"

com.CommandText = "DELETE [Order Details (Backup)]; "

sSQL = "INSERT INTO [Order Details (Backup)] " _
     & "     (OrderID, ProductID, UnitPrice, Quantity, Discount) " _
     & "SELECT OrderID, ProductID, UnitPrice, Quantity, Discount " _
     & "FROM [Order Details]; "

com.CommandTimeout = 0
com.CommandText = com.CommandText + sSQL

Set rst = com.Execute(lNumberOfRecords, _
                   , _
                   adCmdText + adAsyncExecute)

PrintObjectState "Command", com

While (com.State & adStateExecuting)
    ' empty loop
Wend

PrintObjectState "Command", com
```

You will also need the following code for the PrintObjectState method to display the current state of the Command object in the last example:

```
Private Sub PrintObjectState(sObjectType As String, _
                   oObject As Object)

    Debug.Print "The " & sObjectType & " object is ";
    Select Case (oObject.State)
        Case adStateClosed:
            Debug.Print "closed."
        Case adStateOpen:
            Debug.Print "open."
        Case adStateConnecting:
            Debug.Print "connecting."
        Case adStateExecuting:
```

```
            Debug.Print "executing."
      Case adStateFetching:
            Debug.Print "fetching."
    End Select

  End Sub
```

Notice that when this example is executed, the processing of the application still continues. Visual Basic does not wait for ADO to return from the Execute method and announce its completion; rather, Visual Basic continues to process while the data provider does its thing in the background.

Also, notice that the CommandTimeout property was used in the last example. As we will see next, the CommandTimeout property is used to indicate the length, in seconds, to wait for an execution to complete. In the previous example, the CommandTimeout property was set to zero, which indicates that there is no time limit.

Canceling a Command

If a command's execution is taking longer than expected, or too long for your needs, you can always cancel its execution with the Cancel method of the Command object. The following example illustrates the use of the Cancel method:

```
Private Sub ExecuteCancelQuery()

    Dim com As ADODB.Command
    Dim rst As ADDOB.Recordset
    Dim sSQL As String

    Set com = New ADODB.Command

    com.ActiveConnection = "driver={SQL Server}; " _
                    & "server=JROFF_LAPTOP; " _
                    & "uid=sa; " _
                    & "database=Northwind"

    com.CommandText = "DELETE [Order Details (Backup)]; "

    sSQL = "INSERT INTO [Order Details (Backup)] " _
        & "     (OrderID, ProductID, UnitPrice, Quantity, Discount) " _
        & "SELECT OrderID, ProductID, UnitPrice, Quantity, Discount " _
        & "FROM [Order Details]; "

    com.CommandText = com.CommandText + sSQL

    Set rst = com.Execute(, , adCmdText + adAsyncExecute)

    PrintObjectState "Command", com

    If (com.State = adStateExecuting) Then
```

```
        com.Cancel
        Debug.Print "  The execution took too long, "
        Debug.Print "  it has been canceled."
    End If

    PrintObjectState "Command", com

End Sub
```

In this example, ExecuteCancelQuery executes an asynchronous query and immediately cancels it to illustrate how to use the Cancel method. Notice, however, that
the state of the command's execution is checked prior to the Cancel method call.

We can also use the CommandTimeout property of a Command object to explicitly state the length in seconds to wait to complete a command's execution. In the
following example, the CommandTimeout property is set to one second, assuming
that the time to execute the following command will take longer than this:

```
Private Sub ExecuteTimeoutQuery()
On Error GoTo ERR_ExecuteTimeoutQuery:

    Dim com As ADODB.Command
    Dim rst As ADODB.Recordset
    Dim sSQL As String

    Set com = New ADODB.Command

    com.ActiveConnection = "driver={SQL Server}; " _
                         & "server=JROFF_LAPTOP; " _
                         & "uid=sa; " _
                         & "database=Northwind"

    com.CommandText = "DELETE [Order Details (Backup)]; "

    sSQL = "INSERT INTO [Order Details (Backup)] " _
        & "      (OrderID, ProductID, UnitPrice, Quantity, Discount) " _
        & "SELECT OrderID, ProductID, UnitPrice, Quantity, Discount " _
        & "FROM [Order Details]; "

    com.CommandText = com.CommandText + sSQL

    com.CommandTimeout = 1 ' one second to execute command

    Set rst = com.Execute(, _
                        , _
                        adCmdText + adAsyncExecute)

    PrintObjectState "Command", com

    While (com.State & adStateExecuting)
        ' empty loop
    Wend

    PrintObjectState "Command", com
```

```
ERR_ExecuteTimeoutQuery:
    Select Case Err.Number
        Case 0:                        ' No error
        Case -2147217871:              ' Timeout error
            MsgBox "Execution timeout."
        Case Else:                     ' Unknown error
            MsgBox "Error #: " & Err.Number _
                & " " & Err.Description
    End Select
End Sub
```

When executed in the previous example, ExecuteCancelQuery will timeout and raise error number –2147217871, which is trapped in the error-handling section of the function. If this were a complete application, you would inform the user that the execution did not complete.

Summary

This chapter explains the Command object and its use of Parameter objects to help you understand how to execute different types of commands and pass parameters to stored procedures. After reading this chapter, you should be able to fully understand how commands are executed using ADO and the following key points about their execution:

- Although Command objects can be created independently of other ADO objects, they still need to connect to a data source.

- Commands can be executed with the Command object, the Recordset object, or the Connection object.

- Specifying parameters ahead of time can significantly increase performance when executing commands.

- Asynchronous execution of commands allows applications to continue processing while ADO and the data provider continue to work in the background of the client machine or on a server.

The next chapter of this book, Chapter 8, *The ADO Event Model*, explains how to use the Errors collection of the Connection object, which contains all of the Error objects for specific failures of the data provider.

8

The ADO Event Model

With Version 2.0 of ActiveX Data Objects came the introduction of the ADO Event Model. Coupled with the power of ADO to handle asynchronous operations, this new event model gives developers greater control over their applications.

Introduction to Events

There are two different types of events:

Will event

Raised when an operation will occur. For instance, the WillConnect event is raised when a connection to a data source will occur. All Will events begin with the word Will.

Complete event

Raised once the operation is completed (successfully or not). An example of a Complete event is the ConnectComplete event that is raised once a connection to a data source has been attempted. Some, but not all, Complete events end with the word Complete.

All Will events have a matching Complete event, but the opposite is not true. Matching Will and Complete events (e.g., WillConnect and ConnectComplete) are usually referred to as "Will/Connect pairs." Those Complete events that do not have a corresponding Will event are usually referred to as "Standalone events."

Events belong to either the ConnectionEvent family or the RecordsetEvent family, each of which represents the events that are raised by operations on the respective object.

Within the ConnectionEvent family, there are nine events broken into four categories, as shown in Table 8-1.

Table 8-1. The ConnectionEvent Family of Events

Event Group	Event	Description
Connection Events	WillConnect	Indicates that a connection will occur.
	ConnectComplete	Indicates that a connection has occurred.
	Disconnect	Indicates that a connection has ended.
Execution Events	WillExecute	Indicates that an execution will occur.
	ExecuteComplete	Indicates that an execution has occurred.
Transaction Events	BeginTransComplete	Indicates that a transaction has begun.
	CommitTransComplete	Indicates that a transaction has been committed.
	RollbackTransComplete	Indicates that a transaction has been rolled back.
Informational Event	InfoMessage	Provides additional information about an operation.

The RecordsetEvent family has eleven events broken into five categories, as shown in Table 8-2.

Table 8-2. The RecordsetEvent Family of Events

Event Group	Event	Description
Retrieval Events	FetchProgress	Indicates the progress of an asynchronous fetch.
	FetchComplete	Indicates that an asynchronous fetch has completed.
Movement Events	WillMove	Indicates that the record pointer within the recordset will move to a new record.
	MoveComplete	Indicates that the record pointer within the recordset has moved to a new record.
	EndOfRecordset	Indicates that the record pointer within the recordset has moved past the last record.
Field Change Events	WillChangeField	Indicates that a field's value will change.
	FieldChangeComplete	Indicates that a field's value has changed.

Table 8-2. The RecordsetEvent Family of Events (continued)

Event Group	Event	Description
Record Change Events	WillChangeRecord	Indicates that the current record will change.
	RecordChangeComplete	Indicates that the current record has changed.
Recordset Change Events	WillChangeRecordset	Indicates that the current recordset will change.
	RecordsetChangeComplete	Indicates that the current recordset has changed.

The events and their categories are described in more detail in the following sections.

The ConnectionEvent Family

The ConnectionEvent family contains a group of events that belong to the Connection object. To instantiate a connection object that implements events, declare it as follows:

```
Private WithEvents con As ADODB.Connection
```

As stated earlier, the events within the ConnectionEvent family can be broken into four categories:

- Connection events
- Execution events
- Transaction events
- Informational events

Each category of events contains events pertaining to one specific task.

Connection Events

The Connection events category of the ConnectionEvent family comprises three events:

- The WillConnect event is raised when a connection to a data source is about to be attempted.
- The ConnectComplete event is raised after a connection to a data source has been attempted.
- The Disconnect event is raised after a connection to a data source has been terminated.

The WillConnect and ConnectComplete events are a Will/Complete event pair. Notice there is not a Will event for the Disconnect event, making it a standalone event.

To illustrate when each of these events is fired, enter a call to the PrintStatus function (which I will describe in a minute) to the three events:

```
Private Sub con_WillConnect(ConnectionString As String, _
                    UserID As String, _
                    Password As String, _
                    Options As Long, _
                    adStatus As ADODB.EventStatusEnum, _
                    ByVal pConnection As ADODB.Connection)

    PrintStatus "WillConnect", adStatus

End Sub

Private Sub con_ConnectComplete(ByVal pError As ADODB.Error, _
                    adStatus As ADODB.EventStatusEnum, _
                    ByVal pConnection As ADODB.Connection)

    PrintStatus "ConnectComplete", adStatus, pError

End Sub

Private Sub con_Disconnect(adStatus As ADODB.EventStatusEnum, _
                    ByVal pConnection As ADODB.Connection)

    PrintStatus "Disconnect", adStatus

End Sub
```

This code assumes that there is already a member variable, con, which is declared as a Connection object supporting events. To declare this member variable, enter the following code in the module's General Declaration section:

```
Option Explicit

Private WithEvents con As ADODB.Connection
```

Now enter the PrintStatus method that will indicate when an event has been fired. This method outputs to the Immediate Window the name and status of the event that was fired, as well as any error information that was passed to the method:

```
Private Sub PrintStatus(sEventName As String, _
                    ByRef adStatus As ADODB.EventStatusEnum, _
                    Optional ByVal pError As ADODB.Error)

    Debug.Print
    Debug.Print sEventName & " event raised."

    Debug.Print "  Status: ";
```

```
Select Case (adStatus)

    Case adStatusOK:
        Debug.Print "Okay."

    Case adStatusCantDeny:
        Debug.Print "Can't deny."

    Case adStatusErrorsOccurred:
        Debug.Print "Errors have occurred."
        Debug.Print "  Error:  " & pError.Description
        adStatus = adStatusCancel

    End Select

End Sub
```

The PrintStatus method accepts three arguments. The first of these arguments is a String value that represents the name of the event that has been fired. This value is shown in the three preceding event declarations.

The second parameter is a reference to a variable that contains the event's status at the time it was fired. This variable can return one of the valid EventStatusEnum enumeration values shown in Table 8-3.

Table 8-3. The EventStatusEnum Enumeration, Initial Values

Value	Description
adStatusOK	Indicates that the operation that caused the event to fire has succeeded.
adStatusErrorsOccurred	Indicates that the operation that caused the event to fire has resulted in one or more errors or that a corresponding Will event has canceled the operation.
adStatusCantDeny	Indicates that the Will event cannot request that the operation that caused the event to fire be canceled.

The third parameter is optional and works in conjunction with the status parameter. If the status parameter returned a value of **adStatusErrorOccurred**, the third parameter (a pointer to an Error object) displays the error's description.

If you look back at the PrintStatus method calls that were inserted into the Connection events, you will notice that only the ConnectComplete event returned an Error object. This is the only event that can pass this information to the PrintStatus method, because there are plenty of errors that can occur while attempting to connect to a data source. The ConnectComplete event can return either **adStatusOk** or **adStatusErrorsOccurred** for the status parameter. If the **adStatusErrors-Occurred** value is set for the status flag, the Error object is populated with the information regarding the error.

The WillConnect event does not return an Error object. There are no errors to report. The WillConnect event simply says that a connection to the data source will be attempted. Being a Will event, WillConnect can return a value of adStatusOk or adStatusCantDeny only for the status parameter.

The Disconnect event does not return an Error object. The Disconnect event just indicates when a connection to a data source has been terminated. The Disconnect event returns a value of adStatusOk only for the status parameter.

Let's take a look at a very simple example of how these three events are fired:

```
con.Open "DSN=BiblioDSN"

con.Close
```

This example establishes a connection to a data source by opening the BiblioDSN data source name. When this code is run, the following output is sent to the Immediate Window:

```
WillConnect event raised.
  Status: Okay.

ConnectComplete event raised.
  Status: Okay.

Disconnect event raised.
  Status: Okay.
```

Notice the order in which the events are fired. If you were to step through the execution of this example, you would be able to see how the con method calls fell into this order:

```
con.Open "DSN=BiblioDSN"
WillConnect
ConnectComplete
con.Close
Disconnect
```

The following code attempts to open a data-source name that does not exist. (If by some chance you do have a data-source name *MissingDSN*, you should select better DSNs!):

```
con.Open "DSN=MissingDSN"

con.Close
```

When this code is executed, the following output results:

```
WillConnect event raised.
  Status: Okay.
```

```
ConnectComplete event raised.
   Status: Errors have occurred.
   Error: [Microsoft][ODBC Driver Manager] Data source name not found and no
          default driver specified
```

Notice how the error occurred within the ConnectComplete event. This can be a little misleading—when the connection fails, the ConnectComplete event is fired with an error. Furthermore, the con.Close method call will return a runtime error because you cannot close a Connection object that is not open.

In addition to the values shown in Table 8-3, the EventStatusEnum enumeration contains the values shown in Table 8-4, which can be used to set the status of an event prior to its completion. These values cannot be combined.

Table 8-4. The EventStatusEnum Enumeration, Additional Values

Value	Description
adStatusUnwantedEvent	Indicates that the event is no longer fired.
adStatusCancel	Indicates that the code within the event has requested to cancel the operation.

You can set the status parameter of Will events to **adStatusOK** (tells the Will event to continue executing and raising), **adStatusCancel** (cancel the pending operation on the current object), or **adStatusUnwantedEvent** (suppress further firing of the current event for the current Connection instance). You can set the status parameter of Complete events to **adStatusOK** or **adStatusUnwantedEvent**.

Now look at a similar piece of code that establishes a connection to a SQL Server database by passing the user ID **sa**:

```
con.Open "driver={SQL Server}; " _
      & "server=JROFF_LAPTOP; " _
      & "database=Northwind" _
      , "sa"

con.Close
```

Assuming that there is no password for the user **sa** and that the ConnectionString information passed to the Open method of the Connection object is correct, executing this code will send the following output to the Immediate Window:

```
WillConnect event raised.
   Status: Okay.

ConnectComplete event raised.
   Status: Okay.

Disconnect event raised.
   Status: Okay.
```

Now change the code to pass an invalid user ID:

```
con.Open "driver={SQL Server}; " _
      & "server=JROFF_LAPTOP; " _
      & "database=Northwind" _
      , "WrongUserID"

con.Close
```

Again, if you have a valid user named `"WrongUserID"` (without a password) for the Northwind database of your SQL Server on JROFF_LAPTOP, something is fishy.

The following error will be reported to the Immediate Window upon execution of the previous code:

```
WillConnect event raised.
   Status: Okay.

ConnectComplete event raised.
   Status: Errors have occurred.
   Error:  [Microsoft][ODBC SQL Server Driver][SQL Server]Login failed for user
           'WrongUserID'.
```

A runtime error will be generated for the attempt to call the Close method of **con** while the Connection is not opened.

To illustrate a point, modify the code again to attempt to open the data source without specifying a user ID:

```
con.Open "driver={SQL Server}; " _
      & "server=JROFF_LAPTOP; " _
      & "database=Northwind"

con.Close
```

Now modify the WillConnect event:

```
Private Sub con_WillConnect(ConnectionString As String, _
                      UserID As String, _
                      Password As String, _
                      Options As Long, _
                      adStatus As ADODB.EventStatusEnum, _
                      ByVal pConnection As ADODB.Connection)

    PrintStatus "WillConnect", adStatus

    If (UserID = "") Then UserID = "sa"

End Sub
```

This code checks for a user ID before it allows Connection to complete. If the user ID is missing, it fills it in. As you would expect, this code allows the previous attempt to connect to the data source to succeed, as we see from the output in the Intermediate Window:

```
WillConnect event raised.
   Status: Okay.

ConnectComplete event raised.
   Status: Okay.

Disconnect event raised.
   Status: Okay.
```

FetchProgress events are dependent upon the provider, and Microsoft tells us that ADO almost never gets an accurate portrayal of the progress of an asynchronous fetch. The FetchProgress event is useful to know that your code hasn't hung—but it is not reliable enough for a progress bar.

Execution Events

Two events belong to the Execution events category of the ConnectionEvent family:

* The WillExecute event is raised when an execution of a command is going to be attempted.

* The ExecuteComplete event is raised after an execution of a command has been attempted.

The WillExecute and ExecuteComplete events are a Will/Complete event pair. So that we can track the firing of these two events, add the code shown to call the PrintStatus method with information from the events:

```
Private Sub con_WillExecute(Source As String, _
                         CursorType As ADODB.CursorTypeEnum, _
                         LockType As ADODB.LockTypeEnum, _
                         Options As Long, _
                         adStatus As ADODB.EventStatusEnum, _
                         ByVal pCommand As ADODB.Command, _
                         ByVal pRecordset As ADODB.Recordset, _
                         ByVal pConnection As ADODB.Connection)

    PrintStatus "WillExecute", adStatus

End Sub

Private Sub con_ExecuteComplete(ByVal RecordsAffected As Long, _
                         ByVal pError As ADODB.Error, _
                         adStatus As ADODB.EventStatusEnum, _
                         ByVal pCommand As ADODB.Command, _
                         ByVal pRecordset As ADODB.Recordset, _
                         ByVal pConnection As ADODB.Connection)

    PrintStatus "ExecuteComplete", adStatus, pError

End Sub
```

Now look at a piece of code that executes a command from the Connection object:

```
con.Open "DSN=BiblioDSN"

Set rst = con.Execute("SELECT * FROM Authors")

con.Close
```

When this code is executed, the following output is sent to the Immediate Window:

```
WillConnect event raised.
   Status: Okay.

ConnectComplete event raised.
   Status: Okay.

WillExecute event raised.
   Status: Okay.

ExecuteComplete event raised.
   Status: Okay.

Disconnect event raised.
   Status: Okay.
```

This output also shows the Connection events fired from the last piece of code. (For the remainder of this section, I will stop showing these events and will focus on the Execution events.)

To see how an error is reported while executing a command, alter the code to request a table that does not exist:

```
Set rst = con.Execute("SELECT * FROM AMissingTable")
```

When this code is executed, the error is reported to the Complete event of the pair, the ExecuteComplete event:

```
WillExecute event raised.
   Status: Okay.

ExecuteComplete event raised.
   Status: Errors have occurred.
   Error:  [Microsoft][ODBC Microsoft Access 97 Driver] The Microsoft Jet
           database engine cannot find the input table or query 'AMissingTable'.
           Make sure it exists and that its name is spelled correctly.
```

Now, for the sake of illustration, alter the code once again to a valid command text value:

```
Set rst = con.Execute("DELETE * FROM Authors " _
                 & "WHERE (Author = 'Jason')")
```

Alter the WillExecute event as shown:

```
Private Sub con_WillExecute(Source As String, _
                    CursorType As ADODB.CursorTypeEnum, _
                    LockType As ADODB.LockTypeEnum, _
                    Options As Long, _
                    adStatus As ADODB.EventStatusEnum, _
                    ByVal pCommand As ADODB.Command, _
                    ByVal pRecordset As ADODB.Recordset, _
                    ByVal pConnection As ADODB.Connection)


    PrintStatus "WillExecute", adStatus

    Debug.Print "  The Source of this execution is:"
    Debug.Print "     " & Source

    Debug.Print "  The ConnectionString used for this execution is:"
    Debug.Print "     " & pConnection.ConnectionString

    CursorType = adOpenKeyset
    LockType = adLockOptimistic
    Options = adCmdText

End Sub
```

This code sends the command text and the ConnectionString used to execute the command to the Immediate Window as output. In addition, the properties of the resulting recordset can be altered, as shown, by setting the CursorType, Lock-Type, and Options variables. An example of output from the previous code is:

```
WillExecute event raised.
  Status: Okay.
  The Source of this execution is:
    DELETE * FROM Authors WHERE (Author = 'Jason')
  The ConnectionString used for this execution is:
    Provider=MSDASQL.1;User ID=sa;Connect Timeout=15;Extended
    Properties="DSN=BiblioDSN;DBQ=c:\My Documents\BIBLIO.MDB;DriverId=25;
    FIL=MS Access;MaxBufferSize=512;PageTimeout=5;UID=admin;";
    Locale Identifier=1033

ExecuteComplete event raised.
  Status: Okay.
```

Notice how the ConnectionString information is a lot longer than you might have expected. This is because ADO sets many of the default characteristics of a connection for you.

Now, execute a non-row-returning command as shown next:

```
Set rst = con.Execute("DELETE * FROM Authors " _
                    & "WHERE (Author = 'Kaitlyn')")
```

Alter the ExecuteComplete event to output the number of records the command affected:

```
Private Sub con_ExecuteComplete(ByVal RecordsAffected As Long, _
                                ByVal pError As ADODB.Error, _
                                adStatus As ADODB.EventStatusEnum, _
                                ByVal pCommand As ADODB.Command, _
                                ByVal pRecordset As ADODB.Recordset, _
                                ByVal pConnection As ADODB.Connection)

    PrintStatus "ExecuteComplete", adStatus, pError

    If (RecordsAffected >= 0) Then
        Debug.Print "  Records Affected: " & RecordsAffected
    End If
End Sub
```

Notice that the records affected are only printed if the number is greater than or equal to zero. This is because the variable, RecordsAffected, is very often set to −1 (usually when ADO cannot determine the number of records that have been affected). The following output results from the previous code:

```
WillExecute event raised.
  Status: Okay.
  The Source of this execution is:
    DELETE * FROM Authors WHERE (Author = 'Kaitlyn')
  The ConnectionString used for this execution is:
    Provider=MSDASQL.1;User ID=sa;Connect Timeout=15;Extended
    Properties="DSN=BiblioDSN;DBQ=c:\My Documents\BIBLIO.MDB;DriverId=25;
    FIL=MS Access;MaxBufferSize=512;PageTimeout=5;UID=admin;";
    Locale Identifier=1033

ExecuteComplete event raised.
  Status: Okay.
  Records Affected: 4
```

You can also use the Execute events when working with a Command object, although the events belong to a Connection object.

As you may recall, each Command object has to have an associated Connection object. If this Connection object is external to the Command object rather than internally created by the Command object, the Execute events can be fired for a Command object's execution, as illustrated in the following code:

```
com.CommandText = "SELECT * FROM Authors"
com.CommandTimeout = 10
com.CommandType = adCmdText
com.ActiveConnection = con

Set rst = com.Execute
```

Notice that in this piece of code, the **con** variable is set to the ActiveConnection property of the Command object that will be executed. This **con** variable is where the actual firing of the Execute events takes place.

Now alter the WillExecute event so that we may verify that it is fired for the correct Command object:

```
Private Sub con_WillExecute(Source As String, _
                            CursorType As ADODB.CursorTypeEnum, _
                            LockType As ADODB.LockTypeEnum, _
                            Options As Long, _
                            adStatus As ADODB.EventStatusEnum, _
                            ByVal pCommand As ADODB.Command, _
                            ByVal pRecordset As ADODB.Recordset, _
                            ByVal pConnection As ADODB.Connection)

    PrintStatus "WillExecute", adStatus

    Debug.Print "  The CommandText used for this execution is:"
    Debug.Print "    " & pCommand.CommandText

End Sub
```

This code results in the following (partial) output:

```
WillExecute event raised.
  Status: Okay.
  The CommandText used for this execution is:
    SELECT * FROM Authors
```

We can verify that the WillExecute method was fired for the Command object because the CommandText is identical.

Transaction Events

Three events belong to the Transaction events category of the ConnectionEvent family:

- The BeginTransComplete event is raised when a new transaction has been created.

- The CommitTransComplete event is raised when a transaction has been committed to the data source.

- The RollbackTransComplete event is raised when a transaction has been rolled back to restore the information within the data source prior to the creation of a new transaction.

Just as you have for the other events introduced thus far, add the method call to PrintStatus for each of the Transaction events:

```
    Private Sub con_BeginTransComplete(ByVal TransactionLevel As Long, _
                           ByVal pError As ADODB.Error, _
                           adStatus As ADODB.EventStatusEnum, _
                           ByVal pConnection As ADODB.Connection)

        PrintStatus "BeginTransComplete", adStatus, pError

    End Sub

    Private Sub con_CommitTransComplete(ByVal pError As ADODB.Error, _
                           adStatus As ADODB.EventStatusEnum, _
                           ByVal pConnection As ADODB.Connection)

        PrintStatus "CommitTransComplete", adStatus, pError

    End Sub

    Private Sub con_RollbackTransComplete(ByVal pError As ADODB.Error, _
                           adStatus As ADODB.EventStatusEnum, _
                           ByVal pConnection As ADODB.Connection)

        PrintStatus "RollbackTransComplete", adStatusCancel, pError

    End Sub
```

To illustrate how the Transaction events are fired, enter the following code, which
establishes a connection, begins a transaction, commits the transaction, and closes
the connection to the data source:

```
    con.Open "DSN=BiblioDSN"

    con.BeginTrans
    '
    ' do something here...
    '
    con.CommitTrans

    con.Close
```

This code results in the following output in the Immediate Window:

```
    WillConnect event raised.
       Status: Okay.

    ConnectComplete event raised.
       Status: Okay.

    BeginTransComplete event raised.
       Status: Okay.

    CommitTransComplete event raised.
       Status: Okay.

    Disconnect event raised.
       Status: Okay.
```

Again, the WillConnect, ConnectComplete, and Disconnect events are shown here to illustrate where the Transaction events are fired in comparison. For the remainder of this section, the Connection events will not be shown.

Now look at something slightly different. The following piece of code attempts to commit a transaction that has already been rolled back:

```
con.BeginTrans
'
' do something here...
'
con.RollbackTrans
'
' do something here...
'
con.CommitTrans
```

Upon execution of the above piece of code, the following output is sent to the Immediate Window:

```
BeginTransComplete event raised.
   Status: Okay.

RollbackTransComplete event raised.
   Status: Okay.

CommitTransComplete event raised.
   Status: Errors have occurred.
   Error:  No transaction is active.
```

By changing the Attributes property of the Connection object, we can allow transactions to be created automatically after any call to RollbackTrans or CommitTrans. This change eliminates the previous error.

The following code adds the **adXactCommitRetaining** and **adXactAbortRetaining** flags to the Attributes property to allow for just this (refer to the "Managing Multiple Transactions" in Chapter 4, *The Connection Object*, for more information):

```
con.Attributes = adXactCommitRetaining _
            + adXactAbortRetaining

con.BeginTrans
'
' do something here...
'
con.RollbackTrans
'
' do something here...
'
con.CommitTrans
```

When this code is executed, a new transaction is created after the RollbackTrans method call, therefore allowing it to be committed with the CommitTrans method call. The following output results:

```
BeginTransComplete event raised.
   Status: Okay.

RollbackTransComplete event raised.
   Status: Okay.

CommitTransComplete event raised.
   Status: Okay.
```

As we can see, the transaction code no longer generates an error.

Informational Events

The final category in ConnectionEvents is the Informational events category. The only event currently in the Informational Events category is the InfoMessage event, which is fired whenever a warning has occurred during any other Connection-Events operation.

To track the firing of the InfoMessage event and to display the warning that has been raised, modify the InfoMessage event as shown:

```
Private Sub con_InfoMessage(ByVal pError As ADODB.Error, _
                       adStatus As ADODB.EventStatusEnum, _
                       ByVal pConnection As ADODB.Connection)

    PrintStatus "InfoMessage", adStatus, pError

    Debug.Print "  Error: " & pError.Description
    Debug.Print

End Sub
```

Now, enter code that you thought executed previously without any problems:

```
con.Open "DSN=BiblioDSN"

Set rst = con.Execute("SELECT * FROM Authors")

con.Close
```

When this code is executed, notice the following InfoMessage event:

```
WillConnect event raised.
   Status: Okay.

ConnectComplete event raised.
   Status: Okay.
```

```
InfoMessage event raised.
  Status: Okay.
  Error: [Microsoft][ODBC Driver Manager] Driver's SQLSetConnectAttr failed

WillExecute event raised.
  Status: Okay.
  The Source of this execution is:
    SELECT * FROM Authors
  The ConnectionString used for this execution is:
    Provider=MSDASQL.1;User ID=sa;Connect Timeout=15;Extended
    Properties="DSN=BiblioDSN;DBQ=c:\My Documents\BIBLIO.MDB;DriverId=25;
    FIL=MS Access;MaxBufferSize=512;PageTimeout=5;UID=admin;";
    Locale Identifier=1033

ExecuteComplete event raised.
  Status: Okay.

Disconnect event raised.
  Status: Okay.
```

The InfoMessage event has posted a warning, not an error. This warning was placed in the pError object just as an error is. When the InfoMessage event is raised, it is known that a warning has occurred, and therefore the pError object will be populated with its information; however, the adStatus flag is set to **adStatusOK**. Our code in the PrintStatus method prints the information from the pError object only if the adStatus flag is set to **adStatusErrorsOccurred**. This is why we printed the warning from within the InfoMessage event itself.

The RecordsetEvent Family

The RecordsetEvent family contains a group of events that belong to the Recordset object. To instantiate a Recordset object that implements events, declare it as follows:

```
Private WithEvents rst As ADODB.Recordset
```

As stated earlier, the events within the Recordset family can be broken into five categories:

- Retrieval events
- Movement events
- Field Change events
- Record Change events
- Recordset Change events

Each category of events contains events pertaining to one specific task. The first of these tasks is retrieving records from a data source.

Retrieval Events

Two events belong to the Retrieval events category of the RecordsetEvent family:

- The FetchProgress event is raised to indicate the progress of a lengthy asynchronous fetch operation.

- The FetchComplete event is raised when an asynchronous fetch operation is complete.

So that we can track how ADO raises these two events, add the PrintStatus method call to each, as shown in the following code. In addition, we will put an **End** keyword within the FetchComplete event so that the application will terminate once all of the records have been fetched:

```
Private Sub rst_FetchProgress(ByVal Progress As Long, _
                      ByVal MaxProgress As Long, _
                      adStatus As ADODB.EventStatusEnum, _
                      ByVal pRecordset As ADODB.Recordset)

     PrintStatus "FetchProgress", adStatus

End Sub

Private Sub rst_FetchComplete(ByVal pError As ADODB.Error, _
                      adStatus As ADODB.EventStatusEnum, _
                      ByVal pRecordset As ADODB.Recordset)

     PrintStatus "FetchComplete", adStatus

     ' End the application
     End

End Sub
```

Now enter the following code to create a recordset that returns all of the records from the Orders table. In this example, we are passing the **adAsyncFetch** option to the Open method of the Recordset object in order to retrieve the records asynchronously:

```
Dim con As ADODB.Connection

Set con = New ADODB.Connection
Set rst = New ADODB.Recordset

con.CursorLocation = adUseClient

con.Open "driver={SQL Server}; " _
      & "server=JROFF_LAPTOP; " _
      & "database=Northwind; " _
      & "uid=sa;"
```

```
rst.rst.Open "SELECT * FROM Orders", _
        con, _
        ' _
        ' _
        adAsyncFetch

While True
    DoEvents
Wend
```

The last piece of code had a forced **While...Wend** statement that assures us that our application is still running. Periodically, while the fetch is taking place, the FetchProgress event should be raised; once the operation is complete, the Fetch-Complete event should be raised.

Once the last piece of code is executed, the following output is sent to the Immediate Window:

```
FetchProgress event raised.
    Status: Okay.


.
. (about 20 more times)
.

FetchProgress event raised.
    Status: Okay.

FetchProgress event raised.
    Status: Okay.

FetchComplete event raised.
    Status: Okay.
```

For clarity, I have removed about twenty statements declaring that the Fetch-Progress event has been raised. The last piece of code executed exactly as we had planned.

Movement Events

Three events belong to the Movement events category of the RecordsetEvent family:

- The WillMove event is raised when an operation is going to execute that will move the record pointer to a different location within the recordset.

- The MoveComplete event is raised when an operation that moves the record pointer to a different location within the recordset has completed.

- The EndOfRecordset event is raised when an operation has completed that moved the record pointer to the EOF marker within the recordset.

We will first look at the WillMove and MoveComplete events of the Recordset object. For both of these events, an adReason parameter is returned, containing a constant value that represents the reason why the event was raised. This parameter can contain any valid EventReasonEnum enumeration value listed in Table 8-5.

Table 8-5. The EventReasonEnum Enumeration Values for the adReason Parameter

Value	Description
adRsnMoveFirst	The event was raised because of a MoveFirst method call.
adRsnMoveLast	The event was raised because of a MoveLast method call.
adRsnMoveNext	The event was raised because of a MoveNext method call.
adRsnMovePrevious	The event was raised because of a MovePrevious method call.
adRsnMove	The event was raised because of a Move method call.
adRsnRequery	The event was raised because of a Requery method call.

Enter the following code for both the WillMove and the WillComplete events so that we can track the raising of these events. In addition, place a call to the Print-Reason function (which I will define next) within the WillMove event:

```
Private Sub rst_WillMove(ByVal adReason As ADODB.EventReasonEnum, _
                         adStatus As ADODB.EventStatusEnum, _
                         ByVal pRecordset As ADODB.Recordset)

    PrintStatus "WillMove", adStatus
    PrintReason adReason

End Sub

Private Sub rst_MoveComplete(ByVal adReason As ADODB.EventReasonEnum, _
                             ByVal pError As ADODB.Error, _
                             adStatus As ADODB.EventStatusEnum, _
                             ByVal pRecordset As ADODB.Recordset)

    PrintStatus "MoveComplete", adStatus, pError

End Sub
```

The EventReasonEnum contains many more constants than those shown in Table 8-3, but they do not apply to the WillMove and MoveComplete events. The following code for the PrintReason method includes all of the possible Event-ReasonEnum values, because it will be used for other RecordsetEvent events later in this chapter:

```
Private Sub PrintReason(adReason As ADODB.EventReasonEnum)

    Debug.Print "  Reason for event: ";
    Select Case (adReason)
```

```
        Case adRsnAddNew:
            Debug.Print "AddNew"
        Case adRsnClose:
            Debug.Print "Close"
        Case adDelete:
            Debug.Print "Delete"
        Case adRsnFirstChange:
            Debug.Print "First Change"
        Case adRsnMove:
            Debug.Print "Move"
        Case adRsnMoveFirst:
            Debug.Print "MoveFirst"
        Case adRsnMoveLast:
            Debug.Print "MoveLast"
        Case adRsnMoveNext:
            Debug.Print "MoveNext"
        Case adRsnMovePrevious:
            Debug.Print "MovePrevious"
        Case adRsnOpen:
            Debug.Print "Open"
        Case adRsnRequery:
            Debug.Print "Requery"
        Case adRsnResynch:
            Debug.Print "Resynch"
        Case adRsnUndoAddNew:
            Debug.Print "Undo AddNew"
        Case adRsnUndoDelete:
            Debug.Print "Undo Delete"
        Case adRsnUndoUpdate:
            Debug.Print "Undo Update"
        Case adRsnUpdate:
            Debug.Print "Update"
    End Select

End Sub
```

The following code and its output illustrate the events that are called when a recordset is simply opened and then closed:

```
Debug.Print "---------- Before the recordset is opened."
rst.rst.Open "Authors", _
        "DSN=BiblioDSN", _
        adOpenKeyset, _
        adLockOptimistic, _
        adCmdTable

Debug.Print
Debug.Print "---------- Before the recordset is closed."
rst.rst.Close
```

When this example is run, the following output is sent to the Immediate Window:

```
---------- Before the recordset is opened.

WillMove event raised.
```

```
Status: Can't deny.
  Reason for event: Move

MoveComplete event raised.
  Status: Okay.

---------- Before the recordset is closed.

WillMove event raised.
  Status: Okay.
  Reason for event: Move

MoveComplete event raised.
  Status: Okay.
```

In analyzing the output from the previous piece of code, when the Recordset is opened, the WillMove event is raised for the first time. This event is raised with a status of `Can't deny`. The reason displayed for the event being raised is a Move method. We did not code a Move method in our code example; however, when the Recordset is first opened, the record pointer is moved for the first record, and you can't do anything about it. This is why its status is `'Can't deny'`. The Move-Complete event is then raised once the move has been completed.

When the Recordset is closed, the Move event is raised again, followed by the MoveComplete event.

Now look at a piece of code that does a little more. After the Recordset is opened, the MoveNext method is called and followed by the Close method. Enter the following code to see how the WillMove and MoveComplete events are called in this situation:

```
Debug.Print "---------- Before the recordset is opened."
rst.Open "Authors", _
            "DSN=BiblioDSN", _
            adOpenKeyset, _
            adLockOptimistic, _
            adCmdTable
Debug.Print
Debug.Print "---------- MoveNext Call"
rst.MoveNext

Debug.Print
Debug.Print "---------- Before the recordset is closed."
rst.Close
```

Once this code has been entered and run, the following output is sent to the Immediate Window:

```
---------- Before the recordset is opened.

---------- MoveNext Call
```

```
WillMove event raised.
   Status: Okay.
   Reason for event: MoveNext

MoveComplete event raised.
   Status: Okay.

---------- Before the recordset is closed.
```

The output for the Open and Close method calls have been omitted in the most recent example output because it is the same as the output in the previous example. The only output that is shown earlier is that for the MoveNext method to illustrate the events that are fired for the previous example's MoveNext statement.

The third event belonging to the Movement events category of the Recordset-Events family is the EndOfRecordset event. This event, as stated earlier in this section, is raised once the record pointer has moved one position past the last record in the recordset to the EOF marker. Add the PrintStatus method to the EndOf-Recordset event, as shown in the following example, so that we can track when this event is being raised:

```
Private Sub rst_EndOfRecordset(fMoreData As Boolean, _
                               adStatus As ADODB.EventStatusEnum, _
                               ByVal pRecordset As ADODB.Recordset)

      PrintStatus "EndOfRecordset", adStatus

End Sub
```

Assuming that a recordset is already open, enter the following methods to move the record pointer around within the recordset:

```
Debug.Print
Debug.Print "---------- MoveLast Call"
rst.MoveLast

Debug.Print
Debug.Print "---------- First MoveNext Call"
rst.MoveNext

Debug.Print
Debug.Print "---------- Second MoveNext Call"
rst.MoveNext
```

Run this code to see which Movement events are being raised for each Recordset method call in the previous piece of code. The following is sent as output to the Immediate Window from the last piece of code:

```
---------- MoveLast Call

WillMove event raised.
   Status: Okay.
   Reason for event: MoveLast
```

```
MoveComplete event raised.
   Status: Okay.

---------- First MoveNext Call

WillMove event raised.
   Status: Okay.
   Reason for event: MoveNext

EndOfRecordset event raised.
   Status: Okay.

MoveComplete event raised.
   Status: Okay.

---------- Second MoveNext Call

WillMove event raised.
   Status: Okay.
   Reason for event: MoveNext

EndOfRecordset event raised.
   Status: Okay.

MoveComplete event raised.
   Status: Errors have occurred.
   Error:  Either BOF or EOF is True, or the current record has been deleted;
           the operation requested by the application requires a current record.
```

The MoveLast method call continues successfully, as does the first call to Move-Next. This call to MoveNext effectively places the record pointer at the end of file marker, located directly past the last record in the recordset.

The second call to the MoveNext method generates an error after it raises the End-OfRecordset event. The error is reported through the MoveComplete event, which indicates that neither BOF nor EOF is **True**.

Now, modify the EndOfRecordset event as shown:

```
Private Sub rst_EndOfRecordset(fMoreData As Boolean, _
                        adStatus As ADODB.EventStatusEnum, _
                        ByVal pRecordset As ADODB.Recordset)

    PrintStatus "EndOfRecordset", adStatus

    pRecordset.AddNew
    pRecordset.Update

    fMoreData = True

End Sub
```

The fMoreData flag of the EndOfRecordset event allows you to indicate that more data has been added to the recordset and that the record pointer no longer points to an invalid record. If you want to do this, you must add the new records (with the AddNew method) and then set the fMoreData flag to **True**. When the application exits the EndOfRecordset event, the MoveComplete event does not report an error, but completes successfully.

By changing the EndOfRecordset event as shown before and re-executing the code, the following event output is sent to the Immediate Window:

```
---------- MoveLast Call

WillMove event raised.
  Status: Okay.
  Reason for event: MoveLast

MoveComplete event raised.
  Status: Okay.

---------- First MoveNext Call

WillMove event raised.
  Status: Okay.
  Reason for event: MoveNext

EndOfRecordset event raised.
  Status: Okay.

MoveComplete event raised.
  Status: Okay.

---------- Second MoveNext Call

WillMove event raised.
  Status: Okay.
  Reason for event: MoveNext

EndOfRecordset event raised.
  Status: Okay.

MoveComplete event raised.
  Status: Okay.
```

Notice how the last MoveNext method call executed without an error.

Field Change Events

Two events make up the Field Change events category of the RecordsetEvent family:

- The WillChangeField event is raised when one or more fields are about to change due to an operation.

- The ChangeFieldComplete event is raised when one or more fields were changed due to an operation.

The WillChangeField event, shown next, passes two important parameters. The first of these parameters is a Long value indicating the number of fields that will be changed. The second parameter, Fields, is a Variant value that contains an array of Field objects that are about to be changed.

The code in the following WillChangeField event not only calls the PrintStatus method to indicate that the event has been raised, but it also prints the old value of each field that is about to be modified:

```
Private Sub rst_WillChangeField(ByVal cFields As Long, _
                                ByVal Fields As Variant, _
                                adStatus As ADODB.EventStatusEnum, _
                                ByVal pRecordset As ADODB.Recordset)

    Dim lCount As Long

    PrintStatus "WillChangeField", adStatus

    For lCount = 1 To cFields
        Debug.Print "  Field " & lCount & ": " & Fields(lCount - 1)
    Next lCount

End Sub
```

The FieldChangeComplete event is called after the operation has changed the field (or has failed trying):

```
Private Sub rst_FieldChangeComplete(ByVal cFields As Long, _
                                    ByVal Fields As Variant, _
                                    ByVal pError As ADODB.Error, _
                                    adStatus As ADODB.EventStatusEnum, _
                                    ByVal pRecordset As ADODB.Recordset)

    PrintStatus "FieldChangeComplete", adStatus, pError

End Sub
```

Now enter the following code to see how the Field Change events are raised when a single Field is modified:

```
rst.MoveFirst

rst.Update "Author", "Kimberly"
```

When this code is executed, the following output is sent to the Immediate Window:

```
WillChangeField event raised.
  Status: Okay.
  Field 1: Jason

FieldChangeComplete event raised.
  Status: Okay.
```

Notice that the value of Field 1 output during the WillChangeField event is `Jason`, although the code has changed it to the value of `Kimberly`. This is because during the WillChangeField event, the value of the Field has not changed yet; therefore, the original value of the field is outputted.

Record Change Events

Two events make up the Record Change events category of the RecordsetEvent family:

- The WillChangeRecord event is raised when the current record is about to change due to an operation.

- The ChangeRecordComplete event is raised when the current record has changed due to an operation.

Both of the Record Change events pass the `adReason` flag that we saw earlier in the Movement events. The WillChangeRecord and RecordChangeComplete events can be raised because of any of the values of the EventReasonEnum values in Table 8-6.

Table 8-6. The EventReasonEnum Enumeration for Record Change Events

Value	Description
adRsnAddNew	The event was raised because of an AddNew method call.
adRsnDelete	The event was raised because of a Delete method call.
adRsnUpdate	The event was raised because of an Update method call.
adRsnUndoUpdate	The event was raised because of a CancelUpdate method call.
adRsnUndoAddNew	The event was raised because of a CancelBatch method call (concerning a previous AddNew method call).
adRsnUndoDelete	The event was raised because of a CancelBatch method call (concerning a previous Delete method call).
adRsnFirstChange	The event was raised because it was the first time that this recordset has been set.

Enter the following code for both the WillChangeRecord and the RecordChange-Complete events. It will be used to track when and why the events are raised.

```
Private Sub rst_WillChangeRecord(ByVal adReason As ADODB.EventReasonEnum, _
                                 ByVal cRecords As Long, _
                                 adStatus As ADODB.EventStatusEnum, _
                                 ByVal pRecordset As ADODB.Recordset)

    PrintStatus "WillChangeRecord", adStatus
    PrintReason adReason
    Debug.Print "  Records: " & cRecords

End Sub
```

```
Private Sub rst_RecordChangeComplete(ByVal adReason As ADODB.EventReasonEnum, _
                            ByVal cRecords As Long, _
                            ByVal pError As ADODB.Error, _
                            adStatus As ADODB.EventStatusEnum, _
                            ByVal pRecordset As ADODB.Recordset)

    PrintStatus "RecordChangeComplete", adStatus, pError
    PrintReason adReason
    Debug.Print "  Records: " & cRecords

End Sub
```

Now enter some code that would fire the two previous events. The following piece of code uses a single Update method call to modify two fields within the current record:

```
Dim vFields(1) As Variant
Dim vValues(1) As Variant

vFields(0) = "Author"
vFields(1) = "Year Born"

vValues(0) = "Tamara"
vValues(1) = "1975"

rst.Update vFields, vValues
```

When the previous code is run, the following is sent as output to the Immediate Window:

```
WillChangeRecord event raised.
   Status: Okay.
   Reason for event: First Change
   Records: 1

WillChangeField event raised.
   Status: Okay.
   Field 1: Jason
   Field 2: 1973

FieldChangeComplete event raised.
   Status: Okay.

RecordChangeComplete event raised.
   Status: Okay.
   Reason for event: First Change
   Records: 1

WillChangeRecord event raised.
   Status: Okay.
   Reason for event: Update
   Records: 1
```

```
RecordChangeComplete event raised.
   Status: Okay.
   Reason for event: Update
   Records: 1
```

When we break down this output, we see that the WillChangeRecord event is raised before any other. Then the WillChangeField and FieldChangeComplete events are fired, indicating that the two Fields shown (with values of **Jason** and **1973**) are changed. Then the RecordChangeComplete event is raised. This grouping of events has indicated that the values have changed, but not necessarily been updated to the data source.

When the last WillChangeRecord and RecordChangeComplete events are raised, the update is made (indicated by the Update output for the reason for the event).

Recordset Change Events

Two events make up the final set of events—the Record Change events category of the RecordsetEvent family:

- The WillChangeRecordset event is raised when the current recordset is about to change due to an operation.

- The ChangeRecordsetComplete event is raised when the current recordset has changed due to an operation.

Both of these events include a parameter, adReason, which can be set to any of the EventReasonEnum values indicated in Table 8-7.

Table 8-7. The EventReasonEnum Enumeration for Recordset Change Events

Value	Description
adRsnReQuery	The event was raised because of a Requery method call.
adRsnReSynch	The event was raised because of a Resynch method call.
adRsnOpen	The event was raised because of an Open method call.
adRsnClose	The event was raised because of a Close method call.

Now enter the code that is necessary in order to track the raising of the WillChangeRecordset and the RecordsetChangeComplete events:

```
Private Sub rst_WillChangeRecordset(ByVal adReason As ADODB.EventReasonEnum, _
                         adStatus As ADODB.EventStatusEnum, _
                         ByVal pRecordset As ADODB.Recordset)

   PrintStatus "WillChangeRecordset", adStatus
   PrintReason adReason

End Sub
```

```
Private Sub rst_RecordsetChangeComplete(ByVal adReason As ADODB.EventReasonEnum, _
                                ByVal pError As ADODB.Error, _
                                adStatus As ADODB.EventStatusEnum, _
                                ByVal pRecordset As ADODB.Recordset)

    PrintStatus "RecordsetChangeComplete", adStatus, pError
    PrintReason adReason

End Sub
```

Now enter code that will illustrate how these two events are raised. The following piece of code opens and closes a recordset:

```
rst.Open "Authors", _
        "DSN=BiblioDSN", _
        adOpenDynamic, _
        adLockOptimistic, _
        adCmdTable

rst.Close
```

When this code is run, the following is sent as output to the Immediate Window:

```
WillChangeRecordset event raised.
  Status: Okay.
  Reason for event: Move

RecordsetChangeComplete event raised.
  Status: Okay.
  Reason for event: Move

WillMove event raised.
  Status: Okay.
  Reason for event: Move

MoveComplete event raised.
  Status: Okay.

RecordsetChangeComplete event raised.
  Status: Okay.
  Reason for event: Close
```

Looking at this output, we see that the record pointer moving from one record to another has caused the WillChangeComplete and RecordsetChangeComplete events to be raised. Once the recordset is closed, the RecordsetChangeComplete event is raised again.

Canceling Operations

Your application can deny the execution of any operation that triggers a Will event. By changing the status parameter passed to any Will event to adStatusCancel, the operation will not execute. However, if the adStatus property is set to adStatusCantDeny, you cannot cancel the operation.

For instance, assume that you want to restrict the connection to a data source. By entering the following code for the WillConnect event, the connection will never occur:

```
Private Sub con_WillConnect(ConnectionString As String, _
                    UserID As String, _
                    Password As String, _
                    Options As Long, _
                    adStatus As ADODB.EventStatusEnum, _
                    ByVal pConnection As ADODB.Connection)

    ' cancel the connection
    adStatus = adStatusCancel

End Sub
```

Now enter the following code in a method to test the connection:

```
On Error GoTo ERR_Connection:

    Set con = New Connection

    con.Open "DSN=BiblioDSN"

    con.Close

ERR_Connection:
    If (Err.Number = 3712) Then
        Debug.Print "Connection canceled."
    End If

    Set con = Nothing
```

Output from this code produces the message `Connection canceled`. Of course, you would not logically deny every connection attempt made by an application, but you might deny Connections if you know that you already have many connections made to the same data source.

Turning Events Off

In addition to canceling operations by altering the status parameter of an event, you can also turn the events off completely for an open instance of an object. By setting any event's status parameter to `adStatusUnwantedEvent`, you are informing ADO that you no longer want to be notified of a particular event.

To illustrate this ability, alter the WillMove event as shown:

```
Private Sub rst_WillMove(ByVal adReason As ADODB.EventReasonEnum, _
                    adStatus As ADODB.EventStatusEnum, _
                    ByVal pRecordset As ADODB.Recordset)
```

```
Debug.Print
Debug.Print "  WillMove Event Raised"
adStatus = adStatusUnwantedEvent
Debug.Print "  Turned WillMove Event Off"

End Sub
```

Now enter and execute a piece of code that raises the WillMove event at least once:

```
Debug.Print "--------- Before Opening Recordset"
rst.Open "Authors", _
        "DSN=BiblioDSN"

Debug.Print
Debug.Print "--------- Before MoveFirst"
rst.MoveFirst

Debug.Print
Debug.Print "--------- Before MoveNext"
rst.MoveNext

Debug.Print
Debug.Print "--------- Before Closing Recordset"
rst.Close
```

When this code is executed, the following output is sent to the Immediate Window:

```
--------- Before Opening Recordset

  WillMove Event Raised
  Turned WillMove Event Off

--------- Before MoveFirst

--------- Before MoveNext

--------- Before Closing Recordset
```

Note that once a Recordset object (or a Connection object for that matter) is closed and then reopened, the event will be raised again.

In the case of events that can be raised for more than one reason, you must indicate that the event is not wanted for each possible reason as each type occurs. At the very least, each event can occur one time for each possible reason.

Summary

This chapter was written to help you understand how to trap and potentially alter executions prior to their completion, as well as develop applications that are notified once an operation is complete. After reading this chapter, you should be able to fully understand how the ADO Event Model works and the following key points about it:

- There are two different types of events, Will/Complete events and Standalone events.

- The Connection object supports events that deal with connecting to a data source, executing commands, transaction management, and informational events that belong to the ConnectionEvent family.

- The Recordset object supports events that deal with the asynchronous fetching of records, movement through a recordset, and Field, Record, and Recordset Change events that belong to the RecordsetEvent family.

- Within a given event, an operation can be canceled or an event can be turned off so that the application will no longer receive them.

The next chapter of this book, Chapter 9, *Data Shaping*, explains how to use one or more data providers to construct a hierarchical view (shaped view) of your data.

9

Data Shaping

Introduced with ADO 2.0, *data shaping* allows creation of hierarchical or nested sets of recordsets with a single ADO object. The data shaping specifies the relation between columns and recordsets (i.e., parent-child relationships).

An Introduction to Data Shaping

Each of the columns within a shaped recordset can be defined as one of the following:

- Data from a data provider

- A reference to another recordset

- A solution to an operation on a single row of this recordset

- A solution to an operation on an entire column of a recordset

- A completely new defined column

A recordset whose column contains another recordset is called a *hierarchical recordset*. Hierarchical recordsets can be nested to any depth. The recordset that contains another recordset is called the *parent*, while the contained recordset is called the *child*. When a parent recordset's field (column), which represents another recordset, is read, ADO actually returns an instance of another Recordset object as the value of the field.

The field in the parent recordset that refers to a child recordset is called a *chapter*. This Field object is appended to the parent recordset and given a datatype of adChapter.

To create shaped recordsets, ADO 2.0 introduced the Shape command syntax, which is explained later in this chapter ("Shaping Commands"). Shape commands are used in conjunction with the OLE DB provider's native command set, usually SQL. A Shape command is passed to the Source property of a Recordset object just like any other SQL statement.

In Version 2.1, ADO introduced the concept of *reshaping*. Reshaping allows a newly created recordset to have existing shaped recordsets as its children. There are four restrictions to reshaping:

- You cannot add columns to an existing recordset.

- You cannot reshape a parameterized query.

- You cannot reshape any of the Recordset objects within an intervening Compute clause.

- You cannot perform aggregate options on the children or the recordset that is being reshaped.

Each recordset in a hierarchical recordset can have an alias. Any field within any of these recordsets can be referenced through a fully qualified name. For instance, if a hierarchical recordset has three recordsets—Customers, Orders, and Products—a product's cost may be referenced with the name Customers.Orders. Products.Cost. This name can also be used as an argument to one of the aggregate functions mentioned later in this chapter. This concept is referred to as *grandchild aggregates.*

The Microsoft Data Shaping Service

The Microsoft Data Shaping Service is one of two providers necessary to create a shaped recordset with a connection to a data source. The other is a data provider such as SQL Server. In this case, SQL Server would supply the data to the MS Data Shaping service, which would supply it to the application, through ADO.

To specify the MS Data Shaping Service, in the ConnectionString property, set the Provider keyword to `MSDataShape`. When the Provider property is set to `MSDataShape`, the connection string gains a dynamic property called Data Provider, used to specify the source of the data provided to the MS Data Shaping Service.

The following example shows how the MS Data Shaping Service property is used in conjunction with the MS Jet Engine:

```
Dim con As ADODB.Connection

Set con = New ADODB.Connection

con.ConnectionString = "Provider=MSDataShape; " _
                & "Data Provider=Microsoft.Jet.OLEDB.4.0; " _
                & "Data Source=C:\My Documents\Biblio.mdb; "
```

```
con.Open

'
' do something here
'
con.Close
Set con = Nothing
```

Shaping Commands

Shaping commands allow you to create hierarchical recordsets in two ways. The first way is done through the APPEND command. The APPEND command can be used to attach a child recordset to a parent based upon a common field value or values. One field value in the parent recordset is equivalent to all of the field values in its child recordset. The APPEND command can add not only chapter columns (pointing to child recordsets), it can also add calculated, aggregated, and fabricated columns.

The second method of creating hierarchical recordsets in ADO is to use the COMPUTE command. This method generates a parent recordset from a child recordset. Parent columns are created by aggregation operations over a column of the child, an expression on an entire row of the recordset, a grouping column (using the keyword BY), or by creating a new blank column. In addition, one of the parent recordset's columns must be a chapter column pointing to the child recordset. The parent can also be a calculated, aggregated, or fabricated column.

APPEND Command

The APPEND command is used to append a child recordset to a column within a parent recordset. The syntax of the APPEND command is as follows:

```
SHAPE {parent-command} [[AS] parent-alias]
APPEND ({child-command} [AS] child-alias
RELATE parent-column TO child-column) [[AS] chapter-alias]...
```

In this syntax, the parent-command and child-commands can be one of four things:

- A command that is translated by the underlying data provider (usually a SQL Statement)

- A table name preceded by the keyword TABLE

- Another Shape command in (...)

- The name of a recordset that has already been shaped

The first type of command can be translated by the underlying data provider. In the following example, two tables from the *Nwind.mdb* database supplied with

Visual Basic 6.0 will be shaped. To better visualize the hierarchical recordset that is a result of this Shape command, we will create a form with only one control: the Microsoft Hierarchical FlexGrid control.

Create a new project, and rename the main form to *frmShapeExample*. Add the component Microsoft Hierarchical FlexGrid Control 6.0 (OLE DB) and the reference to ADO, Microsoft ActiveX Data Objects 2.6 Library.

Next, add an instance of the MSHFlexGrid control to the form, and rename it *mshFlexGrid*. Now enter the following code to resize the control along with the form:

```
Private Sub Form_Resize()

    mshFlexGrid.Top = 0
    mshFlexGrid.Left = 0
    mshFlexGrid.Width = Me.ScaleWidth
    mshFlexGrid.Height = Me.ScaleHeight

End Sub
```

Now save this project as *prjShapeExample*. This project will be used throughout this chapter to view the hierarchical recordsets that we will create.

The simplest hierarchical recordset that we can create is one that appends one SQL statement to another:

```
SHAPE    {SELECT * FROM Orders;}
APPEND ({SELECT * FROM [Order Details];}
RELATE   OrderID TO OrderID)
```

This statement uses the Orders and Order Details tables from the *Nwind.mdb* MS Access database file distributed with MS Visual Basic 6.0.

To view this recordset in action, enter the following code for the FirstExample method:

```
Private Sub FirstExample()

    Dim con As  ADODB.Connection
    Dim rst As ADODB.Recordset

    Dim sSource As String

    Set con = New ADODB.Connection
    Set rst = New ADODB.Recordset

    con.ConnectionString = "Provider=MSDataShape; " _
                    & "Data Provider=Microsoft.Jet.OLEDB.4.0; " _
                    & "Data Source=D:\My Documents\Nwind.mdb; "

    con.Open
```

```
        sSource = "SHAPE    {SELECT * FROM Orders;} " _
              & "APPEND ({SELECT * FROM [Order Details];} " _
              & "RELATE   OrderID TO OrderID) "

        rst.Open sSource, _
               con, _
               adOpenForwardOnly, _
               adLockReadOnly

        Set mshFlexGrid.Recordset = rec

        rst.Close
        Set rst = Nothing

        con.Close
        Set con = Nothing

    End Sub
```

Now, enter a call to the FirstExample method within the Form_Load event, and run this example. If this example doesn't work immediately, ensure that the path set in the `con.ConnectionString` property points to your copy of the *Nwind. mdb* database file.

If this example does work properly for you, you should see a form similar to that shown in Figure 9-1.

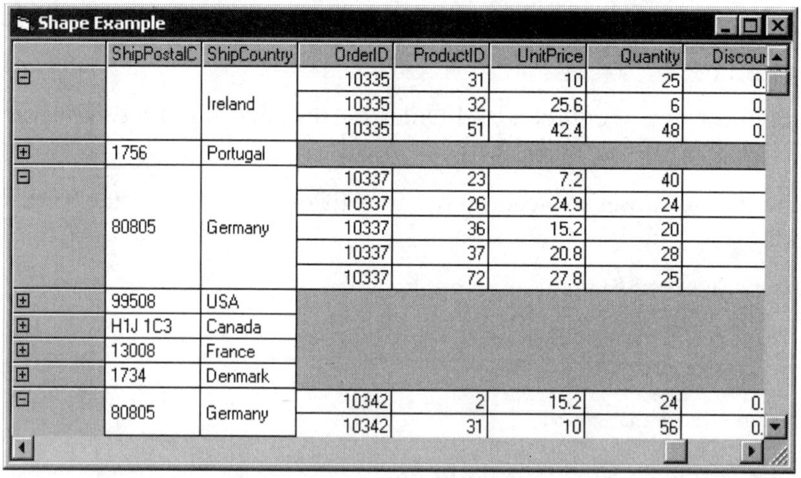

	ShipPostalC	ShipCountry	OrderID	ProductID	UnitPrice	Quantity	Discour
⊟			10335	31	10	25	0.
		Ireland	10335	32	25.6	6	0.
			10335	51	42.4	48	0.
⊞	1756	Portugal					
⊟			10337	23	7.2	40	
			10337	26	24.9	24	
	80805	Germany	10337	36	15.2	20	
			10337	37	20.8	28	
			10337	72	27.8	25	
⊞	99508	USA					
⊞	H1J 1C3	Canada					
⊞	13008	France					
⊞	1734	Denmark					
⊟			10342	2	15.2	24	0.
	80805	Germany	10342	31	10	56	0.

Figure 9-1. The first Shape example in action

Another valid value for either the parent-command or the child-command would be a table name preceded with the **TABLE** keyword. By replacing the following lines of code in the FirstExample method shown earlier, the application is performing the same function:

```
sSource = "SHAPE    TABLE Orders; " _
        & "APPEND (TABLE [Order Details] " _
        & "RELATE   OrderID TO OrderID) "
```

In addition, either the parent-command or the child-command can be another valid Shape command as in the following example:

```
sSource = "SHAPE TABLE Customers " _
        & "APPEND (( " _
        & "   SHAPE TABLE Orders " _
        & "   APPEND (TABLE [Order Details]; " _
        & "   RELATE OrderID TO OrderID)) " _
        & "RELATE CustomerID TO CustomerID) "
```

This example creates a three-level hierarchical recordset starting with the Customers table, then the Orders table, and finally the Order Details table.

You can enter the previous code lines into the project that you have set up and run it. You will notice that you have a lot of column headers now—three tables worth. To ease the readability for the example, you can selectively choose the columns that you would like to see, as with the following lines of code:

```
sSource = "SHAPE {SELECT CustomerID, ContactName " _
        & "        FROM Customers;} " _
        & "APPEND (( " _
        & "   SHAPE {SELECT OrderID,CustomerID " _
        & "          FROM Orders;} " _
        & "   APPEND (TABLE [Order Details] " _
        & "   RELATE OrderID TO OrderID)) " _
        & "RELATE CustomerID TO CustomerID) "
```

If you were to run this code within the project that you have created, you would see a window similar to that shown in Figure 9-2.

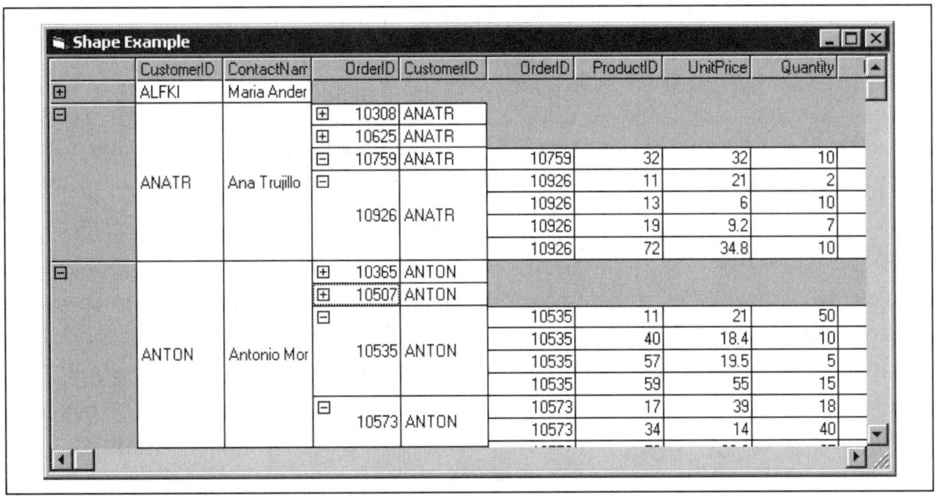

Figure 9-2. A three-level hierarchical recordset example

When a Recordset object is opened on an ordinary Shape command, both the parent and the child recordsets are opened immediately. You might expect to achieve better performance by using a Shaped recordset.

The main advantage to a shaped recordset is the amount of information that is returned to the application. Every Shaped recordset could be replaced with a JOINed SQL statement. With a Shaped recordset, parent records are not duplicated; with a JOINed SQL statement, a parent recordset could contain much more data than necessary. For instance, take a look at Figure 9-2, at CustomerID ANATR. With a Shaped recordset, only one record is returned from the parent recordset for this customer. If this recordset was created with JOINed SQL statements, there would be four records (one for each of the orders) that are duplicated for the parent. In addition, if a third recordset was appended, as in the example shown in Figure 9-2, there would be a duplicated record for each of the order detail records.

The shape commands can also use the **PARAMETER** keywords. Don't mistake the Shape **PARAMETER** keyword with the Parameters collection object or the **PARAMETER** object of ADO; it has nothing to do with them. The Shape **PARAMETER** keyword is interpreted by the Microsoft Data Shaping Engine. Try placing the following lines of code into the example project that you have created:

```
sSource = "SHAPE    TABLE Orders " _
        & "APPEND ({SELECT * " _
        & "          FROM [Order Details] " _
        & "          WHERE (OrderID = ?);} " _
        & "RELATE   OrderID TO PARAMETER 0) "
```

The question mark (?) in the SQL statement **SELECT * FROM [Order Details] WHERE (OrderID = ?)**; acts like an ordinary parameter. The **PARAMETER** keyword, with the index zero, is supplied by the Data Shaping Engine to the child recordset before ADO returns it. The result is that the child recordset is not read until it is needed. This is different than the shaped recordsets that we have seen so far, in that the entire child recordset is read immediately.

By using the **PARAMETER** keyword, ADO isn't expecting an actual value for the parameter from the application. In the preceding example, the data shaping engine knows to relate the OrderID value of the Orders Detail table with the OrderID of the current Orders table.

The are two advantages to using the **PARAMETER** keyword. First, it offers faster initial execution since the child rowset is not populated at execute time. Second, only the child data you actually need is fetched from the server. If your application needs to use all of the children from a Shaped recordset, you will most likely be better off without using the **PARAMETER** keyword because it will require many small trips to the server versus fewer larger trips.

COMPUTE Command

The **COMPUTE** command is used to create a parent recordset based upon a given child recordset. The syntax of the **COMPUTE** command is as follows:

```
SHAPE {child-command} [AS] child-alias
COMPUTE child-alias [, additional-fields-list]
[BY group-field-list]
```

In this syntax, the child-command can be one of four things:

- A command that is translated by the underlying data provider (usually a SQL statement)

- A table name preceded by the keyword TABLE

- Another Shape command

- The name of a recordset that has already been shaped

If a **COMPUTE** Shape command does not use the optional BY keyword, then only one record will be returned in the recordset. The columns for this record would include chapter column pointing to the entire child recordset.

By using the project skeleton that was introduced earlier in this chapter, replace the **sSource** variable assignment with the following code:

```
sSource = "SHAPE {SELECT * FROM Orders;} " _
        & "        AS Orders " _
        & "COMPUTE Orders, " _
        & "        SUM(Orders.Freight) AS TotalFreight"
```

In this code, the following Shape command is being assigned to the sSource variable:

```
SHAPE {SELECT * FROM Orders;} AS Orders
COMPUTE Orders, SUM(Orders.Frieght) AS TotalFreight
```

The child-command in this example is a SQL statement that returns all of the columns of the Orders table to the MS Data Shaping Service. The MS Data Shaping Service is going to create a parent recordset for this child-command because the **COMPUTE** command is being used. Within this parent recordset, there are two fields. The first is a chapter field pointing to the child-recordset, Orders. The second field is a summation of all the Freight field values within the child recordset. This command will return only one record with the total freight cost as the TotalFreight field value.

In order to return more than one record within the created parent-recordset, you must use the **BY** keyword. The **BY** keyword groups by a column value within the child recordset producing one record in the parent recordset for each unique value within the child recordset.

As an example, replace the **sSource** variable assignment in our sample application with the following code:

```
sSource = "SHAPE {SELECT OrderID, ShipCountry " _
       & "         FROM Orders;} " _
       & "           AS Orders " _
       & "COMPUTE Orders, " _
       & "         COUNT(Orders.OrderID) AS [Number Of Orders], " _
       & "BY ShipCountry"
```

This code produces the following Shape statement:

```
SHAPE {SELECT OrderID, ShipCountry FROM Orders;"
       AS Orders
COMPUTE Orders, COUNT(Orders.OrderID) AS [Number Of Orders]
BY ShipCountry
```

This example uses a child-command that only returns two columns, the OrderID and the ShipCountry. The **COMPUTE** command causes a parent recordset to be created with three fields. The first field is a chapter field pointing to the child-recordset that was created by the SQL statement. The second field displays a count of the number of orders within the chapter of that record. Finally, the third field comes from the **BY** clause of the Shape command, the ShipCountry field. This **BY** clause causes the parent recordset to have a distinct record for each unique ShipCountry within the child-command specified. For each of these parent recordset records, the chapter field returns a subset of the overall child command. Each child recordset contains only recordsets whose ShipCountry field values match that of the current parent recordset's ShipCountry field value. Figure 9-3 illustrates how this parent-child hierarchical recordset looks once it is created.

Let us go one step further and create another nested level within our hierarchical recordset. In the next example, the parent recordset is grouped by countries, and its child recordset contains all of the regions within each country. Furthermore, each recordset broken down by regions acts as a parent recordset whose child recordset contains all of the individual orders within each region.

To create such a nested Shape command, replace the **sSource** assignment in our example framework with the following two assignments:

```
sSource = "SHAPE {SELECT OrderID, ShipCountry, ShipRegion " _
       & "         FROM Orders;} " _
       & "           AS Orders " _
       & "COMPUTE Orders, " _
       & "         COUNT(Orders.OrderID) AS [Number Of Orders], " _
       & "         ANY(Orders.ShipCountry) as Country " _
       & "BY ShipRegion "

sSource = "SHAPE (" & sSource & ") " _
       & "         AS OrderRegion " _
       & "COMPUTE OrderRegion, " _
```

```
   & "          SUM(OrderRegion.[Number Of Orders]) " _
   & "              AS [Number Of Country Orders] " _
   & "BY Country"
```

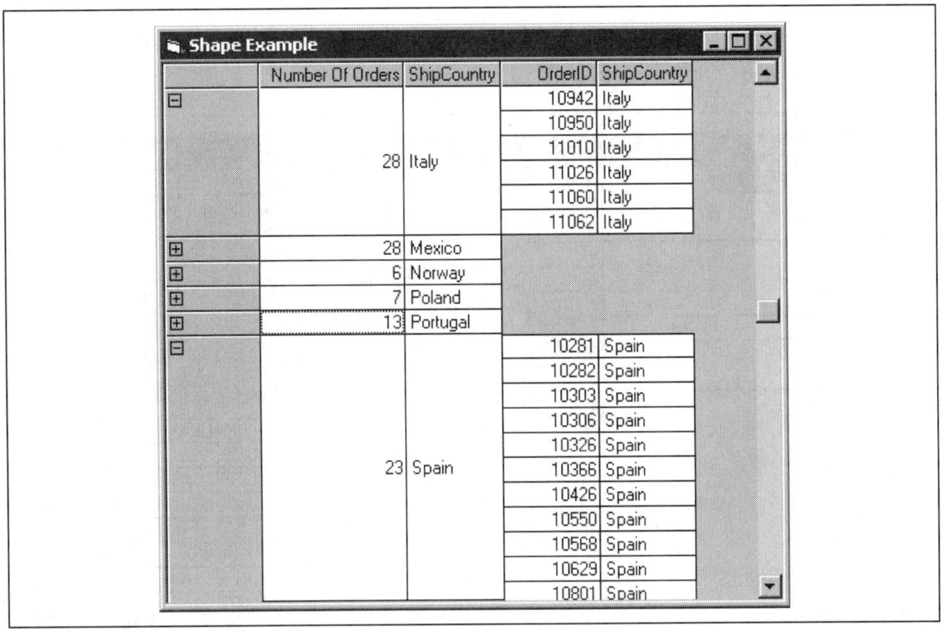

Figure 9-3. A simple COMPUTE Shape command

As you can see, the **sSource** variable is first set to a Shape command that will group the orders by region. The second **sSource** variable is assigned to another Shape command that takes the first shape command and groups it by country.

The following output is generated by the code:

```
SHAPE (
    SHAPE {SELECT OrderID, ShipCountry, ShipRegion
           FROM Orders;}
             AS Orders
    COMPUTE Orders,
            COUNT(Orders.OrderID) AS [Number Of Orders],
            ANY(Orders.ShipCountry) AS Country
    BY ShipRegion
)
  AS OrderRegion
COMPUTE OrderRegion,
        SUM(OrderRegion.[Number Of Orders])
          AS [Number Of Country Orders]
BY Country
```

Notice that within the nested Shape statement the inner nest, or the first Shape statement, returns four fields: the Orders chapter, the Count field, the ShipCountry value for the given row, and the ShipRegion for its child recordset. It is important to have this Shape statement include the ShipCountry value to the outer Shape command so that it can group by it.

When the application is run with this statement, you should see a dialog box very similar to that shown in Figure 9-4.

	Country Orders	Country	ier Of Orders	Country	ShipRegion	OrderID	ShipCountry	ShipRegion
⊟	83	Brazil	⊞ 34	Brazil	RJ			
			⊞ 49	Brazil	SP			
⊟	30	Canada	⊞ 17	Canada	BC			
			⊞ 13	Canada	Québec			
⊞	507	France						
⊞	19	Ireland						
⊟	23	UK	⊞ 13	UK	Essex			
			⊞ 10	UK	Isle of Wight			
⊟			⊞ 10	USA	AK			
			⊟ 4	USA	CA	10579	USA	CA
						10719	USA	CA
						10735	USA	CA
						10884	USA	CA
			⊞ 31	USA	ID			
	122	USA	⊟ 3	USA	MT	10624	USA	MT
						10775	USA	MT
						11003	USA	MT
			⊞ 18	USA	NM			
			⊞ 28	USA	OR			
			⊞ 19	USA	WA			
			⊞ 9	USA	WY			
⊞	46	Venezuela						

Figure 9-4. A nested COMPUTE Shape command

Notice that we have introduced another aggregate function, ANY. The purpose of the ANY aggregate function is to return a value for a column that is the same for all of the child recordset's rows. For instance, notice that in Figure 9-4, the Ship-Country value is the same for all records of a chapter by looking at the last three columns shown in the dialog box. In this example, USA is the value for all of the child records.

Shape Functions

In total, the Shape command syntax supports seven aggregate functions as shown in Table 9-1.

Table 9-1. The Shape Aggregate Functions

Function Syntax	Description
ANY (chapter-alias. field-name)	Returns the value of the column that matches all the values of the child's column of the same name. The ANY function has a well-defined result only when all of the rows in the child recordset have the identical value for the specified column. If the rows in the child recordset don't all have the same value for the specified column, one of the values will be picked as the value of the ANY aggregate. Which value is picked is not defined, so ANY in this case has unpredictable results.
AVG (chapter-alias. field-name)	Returns an average value within the child recordset.
COUNT (chapter-alias.field-name)	Returns a count of all child's records. The field name is optional for the COUNT function. If it is omitted, the value of COUNT is the number of rows in the child recordset. If a field name is provided, then the value of COUNT is the number of rows in the child recordset for which the specified column is non-Null.
MAX (chapter-alias. field-name)	Returns the maximum value within the child recordset.
MIN (chapter-alias. field-name)	Returns the minimum value within the child recordset.
STDEV (chapter-alias.field-name)	Returns the standard deviation based upon the values within the child recordset.
SUM (chapter-alias. field-name)	Returns the sum of all the values within the child recordset.

In addition, the Shape command syntax also supports all VBA function or expressions through the use of the **CALC** function. The **CALC** function can be used only upon the row of the recordset that contains the **CALC** function itself, as in the following example:

```
sSource = "SHAPE    {SELECT OrderID, OrderDate FROM Orders;} " _
        & "APPEND ({SELECT OrderID, ProductID FROM [Order Details];} " _
        & "RELATE   OrderID TO OrderID), " _
        & "         CALC(Format(OrderDate, 'mmm-dd-yyyy'))"
```

In this example, the VBA function **Format$** was used to return the OrderDate field with the format **mmm-dd-yyyy**.

Example: Accessing Shaped Recordsets

The example in this chapter allows you to navigate manually through a three-level hierarchical recordset with the use of non-bound controls. Although the MS Hierarchical Flex Grid is very useful in some situations, as we see throughout this chapter, this control frequently offers us no help at all in our real-world applications.

Figure 9-5 shows what the Access example looks like during runtime.

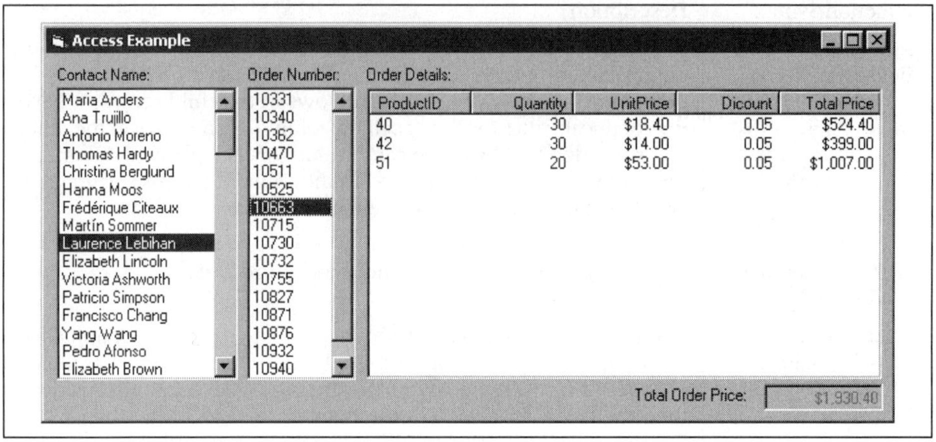

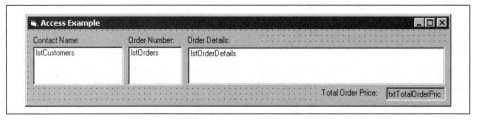

Figure 9-5. The Access Shape recordset example in action

This example allows the user to select a contact name, or customer, from a list box on the left. Programmatically, this action accesses a chapter field within the recordset that passes a child recordset to the individual orders shown in the second list box. When you select an order from this list box, another chapter field is read to return the second child recordset, the Order Details table. The Total Order Price shown in the bottom-right corner of the form is calculated using an aggregation method on the Order Details child recordset.

To begin this example, create a new project and call it *prjAccessExample*. Use the Project → References . . . menu item to add a reference to Microsoft ActiveX Data Objects 2.1 Library, or the most recent version that you have. In addition, you should use the Project → Components . . . menu item to add the Microsoft Windows Common Controls 6.0 to your project for the use of the List View control.

Once you are done with these steps, add four labels, two list boxes, a List View, and a text box as shown in Figure 9-6. The lstOrderDetails control shown is the List View control.

Figure 9-6. The Access Shape recordset example at design time

After adding the controls to the form, go to the Property Pages of the List View control by right-clicking on the control and selecting Properties from the pop-up menu. Change the View property on the first tab to 3-lvwReport, and then add five columns to the Column Headers tab. Name the columns ProductID, Quantity, Unit-Price, Discount, and Total Price. Set all but the ProductID column headers alignment to 1-lvwColumnRight because they will be displaying numeric values.

Once you are done with all of this, you can continue to set the properties of the controls as specified by Table 9-2.

Table 9-2. The Access Shape Recordset Example Form Control Settings

Control	Property	Value
Form	Name	`frmAccessExample`
	Caption	`Access Example`
Label	Caption	`Contact Name:`
List Box	Name	`lstCustomers`
Label	Caption	`Order Number:`
List Box	Name	`lstOrders`
Label	Caption	`Order Details:`
List View	Name	`lstOrderDetails`
Label	Caption	`Total Order Price:`
Text Box	Name	`txtTotalOrderPrice`
	Enabled	`False`
	BackColor	`Button Face`

Now begin entering the code. Enter the following Private declarations for the connection and the three recordsets:

```
Private con As ADODB.Connection

Private rstCustomers As ADODB.Recordset
Private rstOrders As ADODB.Recordset
Private rstOrderDetails As ADODB.Recordset
```

Now add the code to kick off the Form_Load event:

```
Public Sub Form_Load()

    Set con = New ADODB.Connection
    Set rstCustomers = New ADODB.Recordset
    Set rstOrders = New ADODB.Recordset
    Set rstOrderDetails = New ADODB.Recordset

    SpaceOrderDetailColumns
    CreateRecordset
    PopulateCustomersList

End Sub
```

The code for the Form_Unload event simply closes any open recordsets, as well as the connection. It also sets all of these objects to **Nothing**. Notice that for only two Recordset objects, **rstOrderDetails** and **rstOrders**, the state of the object is checked to make sure it is open before it is closed. This is done because these recordsets are opened as you click on the list boxes; if you do not click on them and close the application, they will never be opened. In such a case, attempting to close them would result in an error; therefore, the State property of each is compared to the constant enumeration value, adStateOpen, to attempt to close them only if they are already open. The rstCustomers Recordset and the con Connection aren't checked because we are assuming that they both are open at the application startup:

```
Private Sub Form_Unload(Cancel As Integer)

    If (rstOrderDetails.State = adStateOpen) Then rstOrderDetails.Close
    Set rstOrderDetails = Nothing

    If (rstOrders.State = adStateOpen) Then rstOrders.Close
    Set rstOrders = Nothing

    rstCustomers.Close
    Set rst = Nothing

    con.Close
    Set con = Nothing

End Sub
```

Now enter the following code for SpaceOrderDetailColumns method. This automatically resizes the column headers of the List View control so that all are shown on the screen at once. This is done only for aesthetics:

```
Private Sub SpaceOrderDetailColumns()

    Dim lColumnCount As Long
    Dim lColumnWidth As Long

    With lstOrderDetails

        lColumnWidth = (.Width - 100) / .ColumnHeaders.Count

        For lColumnCount = 1 To .ColumnHeaders.Count
            .ColumnHeaders(lColumnCount).Width = lColumnWidth
        Next lColumnCount

    End With

End Sub
```

The following method, ClearContents, has been added to clear the contents of everything but the lstCustomers List Box control. This example will use this method in a couple of places.

```
Private Sub ClearContents()

    lstOrders.Clear
    lstOrderDetails.ListItems.Clear
    txtTotalOrderPrice.Text = ""

End Sub
```

The second method to be called from the Form_Load event is the CreateRecordset method shown next. This method establishes a connection to the data source—in this case, the *Nwind.mdb* database supplied with MS Visual Basic 6.0. After the connection is established, a shaped recordset is created. You may need to change the path of the *Nwind.mdb* database file in order to get this example to work correctly on your machine.

```
Private Sub CreateRecordset()

    Dim sSource As String

    con.ConnectionString = "Provider=MSDataShape; " _
                    & "Data Provider=Microsoft.Jet.OLEDB.4.0; " _
                    & "Data Source=D:\My Documents\Nwind.mdb; "

    con.Open

    sSource = "SHAPE TABLE Customers " _
            & "APPEND (( " _
            & "    SHAPE TABLE Orders " _
            & "    APPEND ({SELECT OrderID, ProductID, Quantity, " _
            & "                    UnitPrice, Discount, " _
            & "                    ((UnitPrice * Quantity * (1 - Discount) " _
            & "                                        / 100) * 100) " _
            & "                    AS TotalUnitPrice " _
            & "            FROM [Order Details];} " _
            & "    RELATE OrderID TO OrderID) AS cptOrderDetails, " _
            & "        SUM(cptOrderDetails.TotalUnitPrice) " _
            & "            AS TotalOrderPrice) " _
            & "RELATE CustomerID TO CustomerID) AS cptOrders"

    rstCustomers.Open sSource, _
                    con, _
                    adOpenForwardOnly, _
                    adLockReadOnly

End Sub
```

I tried very hard to get the shaped recordset that is set to the **sSource** String variable to be as readable as I could, but just in case you still cannot read it, here it is without the mess:

```
SHAPE TABLE Customers
APPEND ((
   SHAPE TABLE Orders
   APPEND (({SELECT OrderID, ProductID, Quantity, UnitPrice, Discount,
         ((UnitPrice * Quantity * (1 - Discount) / 100) * 100)
                                               AS TotalUnitPrice
      FROM [Order Details];}
   RELATE OrderID TO OrderID) AS cptOrderDetails,
        SUM(cptOrderDetails.TotalUnitPrice) AS TotalOrderPrice)
RELATE CustomerID TO CustomerID) AS cptOrders
```

Let's take a look at this Shape command. There are three recordsets being shaped in all. The parent recordset is made up of all the columns of the Customers table (**TABLE Customers;**), and its child recordset is the Orders table (**TABLE Orders;**). The two of these tables are related by the CustomerID field shown on the last line of the Shape command, and the chapter field that refers to the child recordset is referred to as **cptOrders**.

The third recordset, created from the Order Details table with a complex SELECT statement, is a child recordset of the Orders table, which is now a parent recordset. The two tables are related by the OrderID field and the child recordset is accessed through the chapter field, TotalOrderPrice.

In addition, the SELECT statement, which is done on the Order Details table to create the third-level recordset, has an additional field, the TotalUnitPrice field. This field is calculated for each row of the Order Details table based upon the Quantity, UnitPrice, and Discount field values. This TotalUnitPrice field is used within an aggregate function, **SUM**, which in turn is used to append another field to each order record in the Orders table.

In short, this Shape command relates customers to their orders and the orders to the order details. For each order detail, a total unit price is calculated, and for each order, all the total unit prices are summed in order to generate a total order price.

Now we can continue to the third and last method that is called by the Form_Load event, the PopulatCustomersList method:

```
Private Sub PopulateCustomersList()

   With rstCustomers

      If (Not (.BOF And .EOF)) Then .MoveFirst

      Do Until (.EOF)
         lstCustomers.AddItem .Fields("ContactName").Value
         .MoveNext
      Loop
```

```
        End With

        ClearContents

    End Sub
```

This method simply fills the lstCustomers list box with the ContactName property values of the rstCustomers Recordset object. It then calls ClearContents to remove anything else that is shown on the form.

When a user clicks on the lstCustomers list box, the lstCustomers_Click event, shown next, is fired to populate the lstOrders list box for the customer selected:

```
    Private Sub lstCustomers_Click()

        Dim sCustomer As String

        ClearContents

        sCustomer = lstCustomers.List(lstCustomers.ListIndex)

        With rstCustomers

            If (Not (.BOF And .EOF)) Then .MoveFirst
            .Find "ContactName='" & sCustomer & "'"

            Set rstOrders = .Fields("cptOrders").Value

        End With

        PopulateOrdersList

    End Sub
```

First, the customer name is extracted from the list box and then used to find the correct record within the lstCustomers recordset. Once it is found, the rstOrders Recordset object is opened with the cptOrders chapter field of that record. This chapter field returns a child recordset of the rstCustomers recordset for the current customer. Once the recordset has been extracted, the PopulateOrdersList method is called, as follows:

```
    Private Sub PopulateOrdersList()

        With rstOrders

            If (Not (.BOF And .EOF)) Then .MoveFirst

            Do Until (.EOF)
                lstOrders.AddItem .Fields("OrderID").Value
                .MoveNext
            Loop

        End With

    End Sub
```

When the lstOrders list box is clicked, the lstOrders_Click event is fired. Fill in the code for this event as it appears here:

```
Private Sub lstOrders_Click()

    Dim sOrderID As String

    sOrderID = lstOrders.List(lstOrders.ListIndex)

    With rstOrders

        If (Not (.BOF And .EOF)) Then .MoveFirst
        .Find "OrderID='" & sOrderID & "'"

        Set rstOrderDetails = .Fields("cptOrderDetails").Value

        txtTotalOrderPrice.Text = FormatCurrency(.Fields("TotalOrderPrice"))

    End With

    PopulateOrderDetailInformation

End Sub
```

The code for the lstOrders_Click event is very similar to that of the lstCustomers_ Click event. It finds the order that has been selected from the list, and it locates it in the rstOrders child recordset. Once the record has been located, the rstOrder-Details Recordset object is set to the chapter field cptOrderDetails. This chapter field returns another child recordset, this time for the parent rstOrders. The returned child recordset contains the detail records for the current order selected from the rstOrders recordset.

In addition, the aggregate field, TotalOrderPrice, is used to populate the txtTotal-OrderPrice text box on the form indicating the total price of the order.

Finally, the PopulateOrderDetailInformation method is called to show the detail records contained within this new child recordset. The following code is used for this method:

```
Private Sub PopulateOrderDetailInformation()

    Dim lListItem As Long
    Dim lFieldCount As Long

    lstOrderDetails.ListItems.Clear

    rstOrderDetailsDo Until (rstOrderDetails.EOF)

        With lstOrderDetails

            .ListItems.Add , , rstOrderDetails.Fields("ProductID").Value

            lListItem = .ListItems.Count
```

```
      With .ListItems(lListItem).ListSubItems

          .Add , , rstOrderDetails.Fields("Quantity").Value
          .Add , , FormatCurrency( _
                   rstOrderDetails.Fields("UnitPrice").Value)
          .Add , , rstOrderDetails.Fields("Discount").Value
          .Add , , FormatCurrency( _
                   rstOrderDetails.Fields("TotalUnitPrice").Value)

      End With

    End With

    rstOrderDetails.MoveNext

  Loop

End Sub
```

For each record within the rstOrderDetails recordset, another list item is added to the List View control.

Summary

This chapter introduced and explained the concepts of Data Shaping and Hierarchical Recordset with the use of the Microsoft Data Shaping Service provided with ADO 2.0 and 2.1, how to create Shaped statements, and how to use them in your applications. After reading this chapter, you should be able to connect to the MS Data Shaping Service and fully understand the Shape command syntax and the following key points about it:

- There are two types of Shape commands: APPEND and COMPUTE.
- The APPEND Shape command allows you to append a child recordset to a parent recordset.
- The COMPUTE Shape command allows you to create a parent recordset to a child recordset based upon computations specified in the Shape statement.
- Shape commands can be nested to any level that you need.

10

Records and Streams

The Record object represents either a single record of a Recordset object or of a resource on a web server (such as a file or a directory). The Stream object represents a buffer of either binary or text data.

Together the Record and Stream objects can be used to navigate hierarchical data sources, such as a directory structure. Each file and directory within this hierarchical data source is considered a resource and therefore can be opened as a Record object. The Record object allows you to copy, move, and delete files and directories of a data source. Within such a resource, there is a stream (or buffer) of information that can be read, thus the Stream object. The Stream object allows you to manipulate the contents of a stream by editing the text or binary data directly. One of the most interesting features about these two new objects is the ability to connect to their data source with the use of URLs as a connection string. Both the Record and Stream objects were introduced with ActiveX Data Objects 2.5.

The Record Object

The Record object is used to navigate hierarchical data sources, such as a file directory. Think of a file directory as a tree with nodes. The Record object can represent any node within that tree—either a leaf node (a file), or a nonleaf node (a directory).

As a leaf node, the Record object contains information about a file or document. The properties of the file or document are accessed through the Record object's Fields collection. The contents of the file or document is accessed through the default stream for the Record Object (covered later in this chapter under "Opening a Stream with an Open Record Object").

As a nonleaf node, the Record object contains information about a directory, which may contain other files and directories. As such, the Record object will provide information about the directory through its Fields collection. The files and directories belonging to the directory represented by this Record object can be returned within a Recordset object, containing individual Record objects for each resource. I will discuss this later in this chapter (see "Navigating Hierarchies").

Opening a Record Object

To begin working with a Record object, you first have to open it, of course. Following is the prototype for the Record.Open method:

```
record.Open [Source], _
            [ActiveConnection], _
            [Mode], _
            [CreateOptions], _
            [Options], _
            [UserName], _
            [Password]_
```

The Record object can be opened by passing one of five different items to the Source argument:

- A Command object
- A SQL statement
- A table name
- An open Recordset object
- A URL representing the resource to open served by a web site

This chapter focuses on opening a Record object with a URL, but I will first briefly discuss the other four ways of opening a Record object, all of which return a single row when used with the Record object.

Opening a Record object with a Command object

To open a Record object with a Command object, you must create a common Connection object that uses a data provider that supports executing commands through the Record object. The OLE DB provider for SQL Server does just that.

After the Connection object is opened, it must be passed to both the Command object and the Record object. Assign your CommandText property of the Command object with the correct SQL statement, and then pass the Command object to the Record object's open method. Finally, the fifth parameter to the Open method, the Options parameter, must be set to the ADODB.RecordOpenOptionsEnum value adOpenExecuteCommand:

```
con.Open "Provider=SQLOLEDB; " _
      & "Data Source=JROFF-NTLT; " _
      & "Initial Catalog=Northwind; " _
      & "UID=sa"

com.ActiveConnection = con
com.CommandText = "SELECT * " _
              & "FROM Shippers " _
              & "WHERE CompanyName='United Package'"

rec.Open com, _
      con, , , _
      adOpenExecuteCommand
```

Make sure that you have done the following:

- Declared the con, com, and rec object variables as ADODB Connection, Command, and Record objects, respectively.

- Set each of the three object variables to a new instance of its respective ADODB object type.

- Have a SQL Server running on JROFF-NTLT (or change it to your own).

- Have an OLE DB provider for SQL Server driver installed.

- Have a database named *Northwind* (one comes with SQL Server).

- Have the username and password of the SQL Server set to "**sa**" and "", respectively.

Before running the previous code, add the following code so that you can see whether the Record object was opened by looking at the Record.State property:

```
If (rec.State & adStateOpen) Then
    MsgBox "Record successfully opened."
Else
    MsgBox "Record was not opened."
End If
```

Finally, add the following function to your project so that you can see the output of the Fields collection of the Record object:

```
Private Function DisplayFields(Flds As ADODB.Fields)

    Dim fld As ADODB.Field

    For Each fld In Flds
        Debug.Print Left$(fld.Name & Space(25), 25) & ": " & fld.Value
    Next fld

End Function
```

Now add a call to the DisplayFields function that you have just entered, and add the code to close all of the objects that you were using:

```
DisplayFields rec.Fields

rec.Close
com.Close
con.Close
```

After running all of the previous code, you should see the following output in your Immediate window within Visual Basic:

```
ShipperID           : 2
CompanyName         : United Package
Phone               : (503) 555-3199
```

If you got this far, you have successfully opened your first Record object—and used a Command object while you were at it. If you are experiencing errors with this first example, go back and make sure that your prerequisites listed in the beginning are correct (do you have the right server name? did you declare and instantiate your variables correctly? and so on).

Opening a Record object with a SQL statement

Now that you are getting the hang of opening Record objects, the next one should be a snap. To open a Record object with a SQL statement, do the exact same thing you did when opening a Record object with a Command object, except that you leave out the Command object. Instead of setting the SQL statement to the Command.CommandText property, you can pass it directly to the Record.Open method's Source argument as shown here:

```
con.Open "Provider=SQLOLEDB; " _
       & "Data Source=JROFF-NTLT; " _
       & "Initial Catalog=Northwind; " _
       & "UID=sa"

rec.Open "SELECT * " _
       & "FROM Customers " _
       & "WHERE CustomerID='CHOPS'", _
         con, , , _
         adOpenExecuteCommand

DisplayFields rec.Fields

rec.Close
con.Close
```

Running this code fragment gives you the fields you would expect from the Customer's table:

```
CustomerID          : CHOPS
CompanyName         : Chop-suey Chinese
ContactName         : Yang Wang
ContactTitle        : Owner
Address             : Hauptstr. 29
```

```
City                   : Bern
Region                 :
PostalCode             : 3012
Country                : Switzerland
Phone                  : 0452-076545
Fax                    :
```

Opening a Record object with a table name

Opening a Record object with a table name is just as easy—simply pass the table name instead of the SQL statement, and you are done:

```
con.Open "Provider=SQLOLEDB; " _
       & "Data Source=JROFF-NTLT; " _
       & "Initial Catalog=Northwind; " _
       & "UID=sa"

rec.Open "Orders", _
         con, , , _
         adOpenExecuteCommand

DisplayFields rec.Fields

rec.Close
con.Close
```

The output of this code fragment yields the following:

```
OrderID                : 10248
CustomerID             : VINET
EmployeeID             : 5
OrderDate              : 7/4/1996
RequiredDate           : 8/1/1996
ShippedDate            : 7/16/1996
ShipVia                : 3
Freight                : 32.38
ShipName               : Vins et alcools Chevalier
ShipAddress            : 59 rue de l'Abbaye
ShipCity               : Reims
ShipRegion             :
ShipPostalCode         : 51100
ShipCountry            : France
```

Opening a Record object with an open Recordset object

Now let's try to open a Record object with an already open Recordset object. Remember that a Record object can represent a single row within a Recordset object.

To use the Recordset object as a Source to the Record.Open method, the Recordset must be opened on a file using the OLE DB Internet Publishing Provider. To do so, you must specify a valid URL address of the file you want to open.

I have IIS 5.1 running on my machine, and my server's root directory is *C:\Inetpub\ WWWroot*; however, to access this directory, it is specified in IIS as the *JROFF-NTLT* server. With this information, the correct URL pointing to this directory is *http:// JROFF-NTLT/*. Precede this with the URL keyword as in the following code fragment, and you should be on your way:

```
rst.Open "index.htm", _
        "URL=http://JROFF-NTLT/", , , _
        adCmdTableDirect

rec.Open rst

DisplayFields rec.Fields

rec.Close
rst.Close
```

Notice that the Recordset object takes the URL statement within the ActiveConnection argument to the Open method, while it accepts the name of the individual file *index.htm* as the source. Also notice that the option `adCmdTableDirect` is used.

Once the Recordset object is opened, it can be passed to the Record object's Open method. Calling the DisplayFields function displays the following output to the Immediate window:

```
RESOURCE_PARSENAME          : index.htm
RESOURCE_PARENTNAME         : http://jroff-ntlt
RESOURCE_ABSOLUTEPARSENAM: http://jroff-ntlt/index.htm
RESOURCE_ISHIDDEN           : False
RESOURCE_ISREADONLY         :
RESOURCE_CONTENTTYPE        :
RESOURCE_CONTENTCLASS       : text/html
RESOURCE_CONTENTLANGUAGE :
RESOURCE_CREATIONTIME       : 3/19/2000 5:08:35 PM
RESOURCE_LASTACCESSTIME  :
RESOURCE_LASTWRITETIME      : 3/19/2000 5:08:36 PM
RESOURCE_STREAMSIZE         : 13715
RESOURCE_ISCOLLECTION       : False
RESOURCE_ISSTRUCTUREDDOCU:
DEFAULT_DOCUMENT            :
RESOURCE_DISPLAYNAME        : index.htm
RESOURCE_ISROOT             :
RESOURCE_ISMARKEDFOROFFLI: False
DAV:getcontentlength        : 13715
DAV:creationdate            : 3/19/2000 5:08:35 PM
DAV:displayname             : index.htm
DAV:getetag                 : "0240c3c591bf1:aec6"
DAV:getlastmodified         : 3/19/2000 5:08:36 PM
DAV:ishidden                : False
DAV:iscollection            : False
DAV:getcontenttype          : text/html
```

All of the previous fields are specific to the OLE DB provider for Internet Publishing. Each will be explained in "Internet Publishing Provider Fields" later in this chapter, but you should be able to guess what a lot of these fields indicate already.

Opening a Record object with a URL

Now let's apply the same information regarding a URL ActiveConnection to the Record object. The following code fragment opens up the root directory of the *JROFF-NTLT* server:

```
rec.Open , "URL=http://JROFF-NTLT/"

DisplayFields rec.Fields

rec.Close
```

The output from calling the DisplayFields function should look familiar to you now:

```
RESOURCE_PARSENAME         :
RESOURCE_PARENTNAME        : http://jroff-ntlt
RESOURCE_ABSOLUTEPARSENAM: http://jroff-ntlt
RESOURCE_ISHIDDEN          : False
RESOURCE_ISREADONLY        :
RESOURCE_CONTENTTYPE       :
RESOURCE_CONTENTCLASS      : application/octet-stream
RESOURCE_CONTENTLANGUAGE :
RESOURCE_CREATIONTIME      : 1/15/2000 12:46:22 AM
RESOURCE_LASTACCESSTIME    :
RESOURCE_LASTWRITETIME     : 1/15/2000 12:46:24 AM
RESOURCE_STREAMSIZE        : 0
RESOURCE_ISCOLLECTION      : True
RESOURCE_ISSTRUCTUREDDOCU:
DEFAULT_DOCUMENT           :
RESOURCE_DISPLAYNAME       : /
RESOURCE_ISROOT            :
RESOURCE_ISMARKEDFOROFFLI: False
DAV:getcontentlength       : 0
DAV:creationdate           : 1/15/2000 12:46:22 AM
DAV:displayname            : /
DAV:getetag                : "0709af2f15ebf1:aec6"
DAV:getlastmodified        : 1/15/2000 12:46:24 AM
DAV:ishidden               : False
DAV:iscollection           : True
DAV:getcontenttype         : application/octet-stream
```

The last example opened up what ADO refers to as a *collection*, or a directory. This is indicated by the **RESOURCE_ISCOLLECTION** field's value of **True**.

Open up a file, which is considered a noncollection resource. You can do this by specifying the resource in the Source argument of the Record.Open method.

Additionally, I have added a path to locate the resource. (I don't expect you to have a *Documents* directory containing a file named *ADO.01.DOC*—unless you are writing a competing ADO book and don't need my help!) In any case, change the Source argument in the remaining examples to directories and files that you have on your server. The important point about the next example is that it is pointing to a file—it doesn't necessarily have to be a Word document:

```
rec.Open "Documents/ADO.01.DOC", _
        "URL=http://JROFF-NTLT/"


DisplayFields rec.Fields


rec.Close
```

Running this code will cause the following output in your Immediate Window:

```
RESOURCE_PARSENAME          : ADO.01.DOC
RESOURCE_PARENTNAME         : http://jroff-ntlt/Documents
RESOURCE_ABSOLUTEPARSENAM: http://jroff-ntlt/Documents/ADO.01.DOC
RESOURCE_ISHIDDEN           : False
RESOURCE_ISREADONLY         :
RESOURCE_CONTENTTYPE        :
RESOURCE_CONTENTCLASS       : application/msword
RESOURCE_CONTENTLANGUAGE :
RESOURCE_CREATIONTIME       : 4/15/2000 9:10:55 PM
RESOURCE_LASTACCESSTIME     :
RESOURCE_LASTWRITETIME      : 4/5/1999 3:02:56 PM
RESOURCE_STREAMSIZE         : 123392
RESOURCE_ISCOLLECTION       : False
RESOURCE_ISSTRUCTUREDDOCU:
DEFAULT_DOCUMENT            :
RESOURCE_DISPLAYNAME        : ADO.01.DOC
RESOURCE_ISROOT             :
RESOURCE_ISMARKEDFOROFFLI: False
DAV:getcontentlength        : 123392
DAV:creationdate            : 4/15/2000 9:10:55 PM
DAV:displayname             : ADO.01.DOC
DAV:getetag                 : "090e462757fbe1:aec6"
DAV:getlastmodified         : 4/5/1999 3:02:56 PM
DAV:ishidden                : False
DAV:iscollection            : False
DAV:getcontenttype          : application/msword
```

Notice a couple of newly populated properties. First, **RESOURCE_STREAMSIZE** is now populated with the file size of your resource. This indicates that we can open a Stream object to access the data within the file specified. We will do this later in this chapter, in "Opening a Stream with an open Record object."

We can create files and directories with the Record.Open method by passing the right values to the CreateOptions argument. The following example creates a new file, the appropriately named *New File* within the *Documents* directory of the

JROFF-NTLT server. As a matter of fact, if the file already exists on the server, in the same location, this code will overwrite it:

```
rec.Open "Documents/NewFile", _
        "URL=http://JROFF-NTLT", , _
        adCreateOverwrite
  '
  '
  '
rec.Close
```

Similarly, we can create a collection (a directory), by adding the **adCreate-Collection** enumeration value to the CreateOptions argument:

```
rec.Open "Documents/NewDirectory", _
        "URL=http://JROFF-NTLT/", , _
        adCreateOverwrite + adCreateCollection
  '
  '
  '
rec.Close
```

You can also specify the ActiveConnection and the Source property values separately, by using the corresponding Record object property values, as in the following example:

```
rec.ActiveConnection = "URL=http://JROFF-NTLT/"
rec.Source = "Documents/ADO.01.DOC"
rec.Open

Debug.Print "ParentUrl: " & rec.ParentURL

rec.Close
```

In addition, the Record object has a nifty property called ParentURL, which, when read (unsurprisingly), outputs the parent URL for the opened resource. Running the previous results in the following output:

```
ParentURL: http://jroff-ntlt/Documents
```

Another important property of the Record object is the Mode property. The Mode property indicates the read/write permissions the Record object should use to open the resource. The following two examples produce the same effect. One uses the Record properties, and the other uses the Record.Open method arguments:

```
rec.Mode = adModeReadWrite
rec.ActiveConnection = "URL=http://JROFF-NTLT/Documents/"
rec.Source = "ADO.01.DOC"
rec.Open
  '
  '
  '
rec.Close
```

```
rec.Open "ADO.01.DOC", _
         "URL=http://JROFF-NTLT/Documents/", _
         adModeReadWrite
   '
   '
   '
rec.Close
```

The RecordType property of the Record object returns a RecordTypeEnum enumeration value indicating the record type of the opened resource. The following source code indicates that the *ADO.01.DOC* file is a Simple Record—or a text file:

```
sSource = "http://JROFF-NTLT/Documents/ADO.01.DOC"

rec.Open sSource

Select Case (rec.RecordType)
    Case ADODB.RecordTypeEnum.adCollectionRecord
        sRecordType = "Collection"
    Case ADODB.RecordTypeEnum.adSimpleRecord
        sRecordType = "Simple Record"
    Case ADODB.RecordTypeEnum.adStructDoc
        sRecordType = "Structured Document"
End Select

MsgBox "The source: " & sSource & " has a record type of " & sRecordType

rec.Close
```

Navigating Hierarchies

Now that we've seen the basic steps for opening a Record object, let's do something with it. When a Record object is opened on a collection resource (such as a directory), the GetChildren method of the Record object can be used to return a Recordset containing the subdirectories and files belonging to that directory.

The following two functions use the GetChildren method to build a display of the directory structure for the *JROFF-NTLT* server:

```
Public Sub NavigatingHierarchies()

    Set rec = New ADODB.Record

    rec.Open "http://JROFF-NTLT"

    DisplaySubLevels rec, 0

    rec.Close

    Set rec = Nothing

End Sub
```

```
Private Sub DisplaySubLevels(RecordIn As ADODB.Record, _
                             Level As Long)

    Dim rst As ADODB.Recordset
    Dim rec As ADODB.Record

    If (Level = 0) Then Debug.Print RecordIn.ParentURL

    If (RecordIn.RecordType = adCollectionRecord) Then

        '
        ' Display resource name
        '
        Debug.Print Space(Level * 2);
        Debug.Print RecordIn.Fields("RESOURCE_PARSENAME").Value

        '
        ' loop through collection
        '
        Set rst = RecordIn.GetChildren

        If (Not (rst.BOF And rst.EOF)) Then rst.MoveFirst

        Set rec = New ADODB.Record

        While (Not rst.EOF)
            rec.Open rst
            DisplaySubLevels rec, Level + 1
            rec.Close
            rst.MoveNext
        Wend

        Set rec = Nothing
        rst.Close

    End If

End Sub
```

This example outputs only the directories; however, it can be modified to also output the files within each directory. Running the previous code on my server resulted in the following output:

```
http://jroff-ntlt

  scripts
  webpub
  msadc
    Samples11
      AddressBook
    Samples
      Tutorial
      Selector
        Middle_Tier
```

```
              VBBusObj
           Client
            VB
               VBtoADF
                  Setup
               VBtoVB
                  Setup
             IE
          AddressBook
       doc11
    iishelp
      iis
        misc
        winhelp
        htm
          tutorial
            template
          core
'
'
'
' continued...
```

File and Directory Manipulation with the Record Object

The Record object has three methods designed to manipulate files and directories on a server: the CopyRecord, DeleteRecord, and MoveRecord methods.

Copying

The CopyRecord method accepts a source, a destination, and an ADODB.Copy-RecordOptionsEnum enumeration value, which indicates how the copy should proceed. The following code copies the *index.htm* file to the *Copy of index.htm* file, overwriting the destination file if it already exists:

```
rec.Open "http://JROFF-NTLT/"

rec.CopyRecord "http://JROFF-NTLT/index.htm", _
               "Copy of index.htm", , , _
               adCopyOverWrite

rec.Close
```

The following code does the same thing; this time, a relative URL path is passed for the Source argument, instead of an absolute URL path:

```
rec.Open "http://JROFF-NTLT/"

rec.CopyRecord "index.htm", _
               "Copy of index.htm", , , _
               adCopyOverWrite

rec.Close
```

The CopyRecord method can also be used to copy directories, as in the following example:

```
rec.Open "http://JROFF-NTLT/"

rec.CopyRecord "Documents", _
               "Copy of Documents", , , _
               adCopyOverWrite

rec.Close
```

The previous code fragment will copy the Documents folder and any other recursive folders and files beneath it. To avoid this, and to simply copy the directory name to another location, add the adCopyOverwrite enumeration value to the CopyOptions argument of the Record.CopyRecord method.

```
rec.CopyRecord "Backup of Documents", _
               "Documents Folder", , , _
               adCopyNonRecursive + adCopyOverWrite

rec.Close
```

Another option when copying files with the Record.CopyRecord method is to allow for emulation, which means that while the files and directories are being copied, other applications will see the files as if they were already there, through simulation:

```
rec.CopyRecord "Backup of Documents", _
               "Documents Folder", , , _
               adCopyOverWrite + adCopyAllowEmulation

rec.Close
```

Deleting

To delete a file on a server, call the Record.Delete method with the name of that file:

```
rec.Open "http://JROFF-NTLT/"

rec.DeleteRecord "Copy of Index.htm"

rec.Close
```

Moving

To move a file from one place to another (but still within the scope of the server), use the Record.MoveRecord method:

```
rec.Open "http://JROFF-NTLT/"

rec.MoveRecord "index.htm", _
```

```
              "index.htm Renamed", , , _
              adMoveOverWrite

     rec.Close
```

This example overwrites the destination file if it already exists because the Move-Record method was called with the **adMoveOverWrite** value.

When you move files from one location to another on a web server, think about hyperlinks between these files. By default, the MoveRecord method updates links, if your provider can handle it. If for some reason you don't want to update the hyperlinks based on the new location of the resource, you can add the **adMoveDontUpdateLinks** enumeration value to the MoveOptions parameter:

```
     rec.Open "http://JROFF-NTLT/"

     rec.MoveRecord "Documents", _
               "Documents Renamed", , , _
               adMoveOverWrite + adMoveDontUpdateLinks

     rec.Close
```

Finally, the MoveRecord method also allows for emulation, just as the Copy-Record method does, as shown in the next code fragment:

```
     rec.Open "http://JROFF-NTLT/"

     rec.MoveRecord "Backup of Documents", _
               "Documents Folder", , , _
               adMoveAllowEmulation + adMoveOverWrite

     rec.Close
```

Record Object Properties

Although the Record object has a Properties collection, it doesn't seem to contain anything. As a matter of fact, Microsoft's documentation doesn't even show that properties exist for the Record object.

Record Object Fields

Each Record object has a Fields collection. The Fields collection of the Record object is just like the Fields collection of the Recordset object, which is covered in detail in Chapter 6, *Fields*.

What is unique about the Record object's Fields collection is the type of Fields that are present when using the OLE DB provider for Internet Publishing, as described in the following sections.

Internet Publishing provider fields

As in previous examples throughout this chapter, the OLE DB provider for Internet Publishing has a set of standard field values that provide information about the resource that is open. Table 10-1 describes each of these fields.

Table 10-1. Standard Record Object Fields

Field	Description
RESOURCE_PARSENAME	If the Record object represents a simple record (noncollection-type resource), represents the name of this resource.
RESOURCE_PARENTNAME	Indicates the parent URL of the given non-collection resource or the entire URL if the Record object represents a collection resource.
RESOURCE_ABSOLUTEPARSENAME	Combination of RESOURCE_PARSENAME and RESOURCE_PARENTNAME: returns an absolute URL to the resource represented by the Record object.
RESOURCE_ISHIDDEN	Indicates if the resource is hidden.
RESOURCE_ISREADONLY	Indicates if the resource is read-only.
RESOURCE_CONTENTTYPE	Indicates the type of the resource, such as text/html.
RESOURCE_CONTENTCLASS	Indicates the type of resource, such as text/html, application/octet-stream, application/msword.
RESOURCE_CONTENTLANGUAGE	Indicates the language of the resource.
RESOURCE_CREATIONTIME	Indicates the time the resource was created.
RESOURCE_LASTACCESSTIME	Indicates the time the resource was last accessed.
RESOURCE_LASTWRITETIME	Indicates the time the resource was last written to.
RESOURCE_STREAMSIZE	Indicates the size of the default stream of the Record object, if the Record object represents a noncollection-type resource.
RESOURCE_ISCOLLECTION	Indicates if the Record object represents a collection-type resource.
RESOURCE_ISSTRUCTUREDDOCUMENT	Indicates if the Record object represents a structured document-type resource.
DEFAULT_DOCUMENT	Indicates that the resource contains a URL to a simple document (folder or structured document) that is the default. This is used when the default stream is requested and blank for a simple file.
RESOURCE_DISPLAYNAME	Indicates the name that is displayed for the current resource.

Table 10-1. Standard Record Object Fields (continued)

Field	Description
RESOURCE_ISROOT	Indicates if the current resource is a root.
RESOURCE_ISMARKEDFOROFFLINE	Indicates if the current resource is marked for offline browsing.
DAV:getcontentlength	Same as RESOURCE_STREAMSIZE.
DAV:creationdate	Same as RESOURCE_CREATIONTIME.
DAV:displayname	Same as RESOURCE_DISPLAYNAME.
DAV:getetag	The entity tag associated with a cached entity.
DAV:getlastmodified	Same as RESOURCE_LASTWRITETIME.
DAV:ishidden	Same as RESOURCE_ISHIDDEN.
DAV:iscollection	Same as RESOURCE_ISCOLLECTION.
DAV:getcontenttype	Same as RESOURCE_CONTENTCLASS.

Standard Record object fields

There are two special Field objects accessed via the FieldEnum enumeration. The first of these special Field objects is the RecordURL field, accessed via the adRecordURL enumeration value, as shown in the following code fragment:

```
rec.Open "http://JROFF-NTLT/index.htm"

MsgBox "Record opened on " & _
        rec.Fields.Item(ADODB.FieldEnum.adRecordURL).Value

rec.Close
```

This code returns the Source parameter that was passed to the Record.Open method call.

The second of the two special Field objects is the default stream that belongs to Record objects representing noncollection-type resources. This field is accessed via the adDefaultStream enumeration value and returns a Stream object:

```
rec.Open "Documents/ADO.01.DOC", "URL=http://JROFF-NTLT/"

Set stm = rec.Fields.Item(ADODB.FieldEnum.adDefaultStream).Value

If (stm.State & adStateOpen) Then
    MsgBox "Stream successfully opened."
Else
    MsgBox "Stream was not opened."
End If

rec.Close
stm.Close
```

The Stream object returned from the default stream field of the Record object represents the data within the resource opened. Let us now take a closer look at the Stream object.

The Stream Object

The Stream object is used to view and manipulate text or binary data. A stream object can exist as a type of resource (such as a noncollection file) or as a buffer in memory.

Opening a Stream Object

The prototype for the Stream object is:

```
stream.Open [Source], _
            [Mode], _
            [OpenOptions], _
            [UserName], _
            [Password]
```

The Stream object can be retrieved in four ways:

*   By setting it to the default Stream property of the Record object, as seen in the last section of this chapter.

*   By passing an open Record object to the Source argument of the Stream.Open method.

*   By passing an absolute URL to the Source argument of the Stream.Open method.

*   By opening the Stream in memory; that is, by calling the Stream.Open method without a Source argument.

This chapter focuses on opening a Record object with a URL, but I will first describe the other four ways of opening a Record object.

Obtaining a Stream with the Default Stream from a Record object

The following example recaps what we saw earlier regarding the Record object returning the default string for a noncollection-type resource through the use of the Default Stream field:

```
rec.Open "Documents/ADO.01.DOC", "URL=http://JROFF-NTLT/"

Set stm = rec.Fields.Item(ADODB.FieldEnum.adDefaultStream).Value

MsgBox "Stream is " & stm.Size & " bytes."

rec.Close
stm.Close
```

In this example, we see that we can get the size of the Stream in bytes through the Stream.Size property.

Opening a Stream with an open Record object

Similarly, we can pass the opened Record object to the Source argument of the Stream.Open method to accomplish the same task as the previous example:

```
rec.Open "Documents/ADO.01.DOC", "URL=http://JROFF-NTLT/"

stm.Open rec, , _
        adOpenStreamFromRecord

If (stm.State & adStateOpen) Then MsgBox "Stream open."

stm.Close
rec.Close
```

Here, the Stream is checked to see whether it is open, by means of the State property.

Opening a Stream with an absolute URL

A Stream object can accept an absolute URL to a noncollection-type resource within the Source argument of the Stream.Open method as shown:

```
Set stm = New ADODB.Stream

stm.Open "URL=http://JROFF-NTLT/Documents/ADO.01.DOC"

Select Case (stm.Type)
    Case (ADODB.StreamTypeEnum.adTypeBinary):
        sMessage = "binary"
    Case (ADODB.StreamTypeEnum.adTypeText):
        sMessage = "text"
End Select

MsgBox "The stream is " & sMessage

stm.Close
```

This example determines whether the newly opened Stream is a binary or a text resource by checking the Stream.Type property.

Opening a Stream in memory

One of the most interesting ways in which we can use the Stream object is without connecting to a web server at all. In this case, the Stream can be used to contain either text or binary data locally. As we will see in the upcoming "Stream persistence" section, we can use these types of Stream objects to persist the data to a file locally and later retrieve this information in the same state. In this way, the Stream object doubles as a nifty buffer utility:

```
stm.Type = adTypeBinary
stm.Open

If (stm.State & adStateOpen) Then MsgBox "Stream open."

'

'

'

stm.Close
```

Reading and Writing with Streams

Once we have opened a Stream, we can either read from it or write to it. We can do so with either text or binary information, depending upon how the Stream was created.

Textual data

Let's first take a look at writing to a newly created text file. In the following example, we create a new text file using the Record object. Next, we open a Stream object, but not before we set the Stream.Type property to text and the Stream.CharSet property to ASCII. Once the Stream is opened, we can use the WriteText method to send data to the stream:

```
rec.Open "TextFile.txt", _
        "URL=http://JROFF-NTLT/", _
        adModeReadWrite, _
        adCreateNonCollection + adCreateOverwrite

stm.Type = adTypeText
stm.Charset = "ASCII"

stm.Open rec, _
        adModeReadWrite, _
        adOpenStreamFromRecord

stm.WriteText "This is the first line of text.", adWriteLine
stm.WriteText "This is the second line of text.", adWriteLine
stm.WriteText "This is the third line of text.", adWriteLine
stm.WriteText "ABC", adWriteChar
stm.WriteText "DEF", adWriteChar
stm.WriteText "GHI", adWriteLine
stm.WriteText "This is the fifth line of text.", adWriteLine
stm.WriteText "This is the sixth and last line of text.", adWriteLine

stm.Flush

stm.Close
rec.Close
```

As you can see, this example used two different parameters in the WriteText method calls. The first parameter used, adWriteLine, indicates that a line separator should be appended to the end of the data being written. The second parameter, adWriteChar, indicates that the next call to WriteText should append to the location that this call last left off. This technique is similar to adding a semicolon at the end of a Debug.Print statement.

To verify the contents of the newly created text file, enter the following code to print its contents:

```
stm.Open "URL=http://JROFF-NTLT/TextFile.txt", _
        adModeReadWrite

Debug.Print stm.ReadText(ADODB.StreamReadEnum.adReadAll)

stm.Close
```

You should see the following output in the Immediate window:

```
This is the first line of text.
This is the second line of text.
This is the third line of text.
ABCDEFGHI
This is the fifth line of text.
This is the sixth and last line of text.
```

Notice that in the first example, the Stream.Flush method is called prior to the Stream.Close method. This isn't completely necessary. The Flush method forces data entered with the WriteText method (and the Write method—described in the next section) to the data source. By calling the Close method, the Flush method is implicitly called. This example was redundant in order to show you the Stream. Flush method.

The previous example read the entire file by passing the adReadAll parameter to the Stream.ReadText method. We can also read a file line-by-line with the adReadLine method:

```
stm.Open "URL=http://JROFF-NTLT/TextFile.txt", _
        adModeReadWrite

While (Not stm.EOS)
    Debug.Print stm.ReadText(ADODB.StreamReadEnum.adReadLine)
Wend

stm.Close
```

In this code fragment, the Stream.EOS property is used to indicate whether the end of the Stream has been reached. The first time the ReadText method is called, the Stream is read from the beginning of the file until a line separator or the end of the Stream is reached. If the end of the Stream is not reached and the second call to Stream.ReadText is made, the Stream's pointer picks up where is last left off, at the beginning of the next line.

Finally, we can read a section of characters with the ReadText method by specifying a number of characters to retrieve. In the following example, one character is obtained at a time:

```
Dim sChar As String

stm.Open "URL=http://JROFF-NTLT/TextFile.txt", _
        adModeReadWrite

While (Not stm.EOS)
    sChar = stm.ReadText(1)
    If (Asc(sChar) <> 10) Then Debug.Print sChar;
Wend

stm.Close
```

This example contains a little bit more code than the others. The reason for this is simple: by reading one character at a time, we get two characters at the end of a line (carriage return and linefeed). Both of these characters, outputed with Debug. Print, cause a carriage return, resulting in blank lines in between each line. To avoid this, the code suppresses characters with an ASCII code of 10 (line feeds), but keeps the carriage returns.

Another interesting method of the Stream object that has to do with reading text data is the SkipLine method. It does exactly what it seems to do—skips lines:

```
stm.Open "URL=http://JROFF-NTLT/TextFile.txt", _
        adModeReadWrite

Debug.Print stm.ReadText(ADODB.StreamReadEnum.adReadLine)

stm.SkipLine

Debug.Print stm.ReadText(ADODB.StreamReadEnum.adReadLine)

stm.SkipLine
stm.SkipLine

Debug.Print stm.ReadText(ADODB.StreamReadEnum.adReadLine)

stm.Close
```

Running this code on the same text file returns the following output to the Immediate window:

```
This is the first line of text.
This is the third line of text.
This is the sixth and last line of text.
```

The Stream.Position property can be read to indicate where the stream pointer is located within a Stream, or it can be set to force the stream pointer to a particular location. Using the Position property in conjunction with the SetEOS method (which truncates files, giving them a new EOS marker), we can change the size of a file as in the next example:

```
stm.Open "URL=http://JROFF-NTLT/TextFile.txt"

stm.Position = Abs(stm.Size / 2)
stm.SetEOS
stm.Position = 0

Debug.Print stm.ReadText(ADODB.StreamReadEnum.adReadAll)

stm.Close
```

This example cuts the file in half by obtaining the size of the stream, and dividing it by two—and thereby moving the stream pointer to the halfway mark and calling the SetEOS method. After this, the stream pointer is moved back to the beginning of the Stream so that the Stream can be sent as output to the Immediate window as shown:

```
This is the first line of text.
This is the second line of text.
This is the third line of
```

Binary data

Reading and writing binary data is almost identical to reading and writing text data, except that instead of a String value, the Write and Read methods accept and return an array of Byte values. Since there is no sense of line separators with binary data, the Write method doesn't have the second parameter that the Write-Text method has to indicate if a line separator should be added:

```
Dim byBuffer(5) As Byte

rec.Open "BinaryData.dat", _
        "URL=http://JROFF-NTLT/", _
        adModeReadWrite, _
        adCreateNonCollection + adCreateOverwrite

stm.Type = adTypeBinary

stm.Open rec, _
        adModeReadWrite, _
        adOpenStreamFromRecord

byBuffer(0) = 100
byBuffer(1) = 110
byBuffer(2) = 120
```

```
byBuffer(3) = 130
byBuffer(4) = 140

stm.Write byBuffer

stm.Flush

stm.Close
rec.Close
```

To read and output the data, use the following code fragment:

```
Dim byBufferIn() As Byte
Dim lCount As Long

stm.Open "URL=http://JROFF-NTLT/BinaryData.dat"

byBufferIn = stm.Read(ADODB.StreamReadEnum.adReadAll)

For lCount = 0 To UBound(byBuffer)
    Debug.Print "Byte #" & lCount + 1 & ": " & byBuffer(lCount)
Next lCount

stm.Close
```

This code results in the following output:

```
Byte #1: 100
Byte #2: 110
Byte #3: 120
Byte #4: 130
Byte #5: 140
Byte #6: 0
```

Notice the last Byte value, 0. This is the end-of-file marker.

Stream persistence

When we create a Stream in memory without specifying a Source argument, we can persist the information within the Stream object by using the SaveToFile, LoadToFile, and CopyTo methods.

The first of these methods, SaveToFile, persists the Stream to a file of your choice (which does not have to be within a web server's scope because we are not using the OLE DB provider for Internet Publishing):

```
stm.Type = adTypeText
stm.Open

stm.WriteText "This is the first line of text.", adWriteLine
stm.WriteText "ABC", adWriteChar
stm.WriteText "DEF", adWriteChar
stm.WriteText "GHI", adWriteLine
stm.WriteText "This is the third line of text.", adWriteLine
```

```
stm.SaveToFile "Stream Output.txt", _
    adSaveCreateOverWrite

stm.Close
```

To reread the data into a Stream object, we can use the LoadFromFile method—but not until the Stream is already opened as shown:

```
stm.Open

stm.LoadFromFile "Stream Output.txt"

Debug.Print stm.ReadText(ADODB.StreamReadEnum.adReadAll)

stm.Close
```

This code fragment sends the following output to the Immediate window:

```
This is the first line of text.
ABCDEFGHI
This is the third line of text.
```

The CopyTo method copies the contents or a portion of one Stream to another. In the following example, the CopyTo method is used to copy the first 10 bytes to another open Stream object:

```
Dim stmCopy As ADODB.Stream

Set stmCopy = New ADODB.Stream

stm.Open
stm.LoadFromFile "Stream Output.txt"

stmCopy.Open

stm.CopyTo stmCopy, 10
stm.Close

stmCopy.Position = 0

Debug.Print stmCopy.ReadText(ADODB.StreamReadEnum.adReadAll)
```

Summary

This chapter introduced the Record and Stream objects, explaining how they can be used to access hierarchical data sources such as directory and file structures. The Record and Stream objects are primarily designed to work in conjunction with the OLE DB provider for Internet Publishing; however, each has their own methods and properties, which add functionality way beyond the scope of Internet Publishing. After reading this chapter, you should be able to open both Record and Stream objects and understand the following key points about each:

- There are five ways in which a Record object can be opened.

- The Record object can be used to navigate hierarchical data sources.

- The Record object can be used to manipulate directories and files within a web server.

- The OLE DB provider for Internet Publishing provides a standard set of Fields for the Record object, which contain additional information about the Record object's represented resource.

- The Stream object can be obtained four different ways.

- The Stream object can be used to read and write text and binary data.

- The Stream object can be used to persist and retrieve information to local files.

11

Remote Data Services

With ADO, you typically create two-tier applications in which your application is the first tier and the data source is the second. In this scenario, your application can access data directly.

In some cases, you may wish to create a three-tier application in which a separate middle-tier is added to handle communication with the data source on behalf of the application. In web applications, this functionality of the optional middle tier requires IIS (Internet Information Server) or some other web server to mediate communication between the browser-based client and the data source. Remote Data Service (RDS) allows you to provide this functionality in a middle tier.

This chapter provides a brief overview of RDS.

RDS Object Model

Remote Data Service is a set of three objects used to provide client-side access to functionality running on the middle tier, especially over the Internet or an intranet.

By using a third middle tier, your application written in VBScript need not access the data source directly. Instead, by using RDS, the client application can instruct IIS to connect to the database itself, optimally processing the data on the server instead of tying up client resources.

The following three objects are provided with RDS:

DataSpace object
> Allows the client access to business objects, such as the DataFactory object, located on the middle tier of an application through the generation of proxies.

DataFactory object

> Provides a client-side application with access to the data. This object can be replaced with a custom object that implements its methods differently than the default.

DataControl object

> Binds one or more HTML controls to a Recordset object so that they are automatically populated with the data retrieved from the Recordset object.

When the client application requests a query from the data source indirectly through RDS, IIS establishes a proxy connection to the data source through either the DataSpace object or the DataControl object, depending upon which one you use in your code.

With the DataControl object, this proxy is used internally and allows the DataControl object access to the data source without the use of the DataSpace or the DataFactory objects. On the client side, the DataFactory object can be bound to one or more visual controls on the HTML page, just as VB controls can be bound to an instance of the ADO Data Control.

If your application is not using the DataControl object, the proxy that is returned to the client application can be used with the DataFactory object that allows your application to remotely control the manipulation of a Recordset that was created on the middle tier. This Recordset can be sent to the client for manipulation, and just the changes can be sent back to the middle tier to be persisted by passing back this same instance of the Recordset object.

The DataSpace Object

The DataSpace object establishes a proxy with a business object located in the middle tier of an application. A proxy allows the client application to communicate with objects created in the middle tier. Remote Data Service supports HTTP, HTTPS, and DCOM protocols through the use of proxies. In addition, if the middle tier is accessible to the client without the use of the Internet or a network (usually on the same machine), then a proxy is not necessary; instead, the DataSpace simply returns an instance of the business object requested. The use of proxies is illustrated in Figure 11-1.

When a new request is made from the DataSpace object, a new instance of the specified business object is instantiated on the middle tier, a proxy is created (for HTTP, HTTPS, and DCOM protocols) and returned to the client. This proxy is used by the client to access the functionality of the business object just as it was instantiated locally.

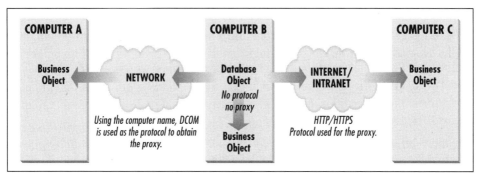

Figure 11-1. The use of proxies with the DataSpace object

Once a request is completed with the business object, and since the Internet is stateless, RDS automatically removes the instance of the business object. If another request is made from the same DataSpace object, a new business object is automatically created on the middle tier. Although this activity is transparent to the client, it is the reason the client cannot use properties of the business object to carry over application data from request to request.

DataSpace object members

The following method and property are the only members of the DataSpace object:

CreateObject method (String)

Instantiates an instance of a business object for use in the front-end code by accepting a String value as the programmatic ID of the business object to create and a String value as the computer name or URL to the web server where the instance of the business object is created. In doing this, a proxy is created if the protocol specified is HTTP (standard Internet protocol), HTTPS (secure Internet protocol), or DCOM (for a network without HTTP). The proxy handles the packaging of data from the server and unpacks it on the client. In addition, the CreateObject method can use an in-process protocol that is used when the business object is on the same machine and a network is unnecessary. In this case, a proxy is bypassed, and a pointer to the instantiated business object is returned.

InternetTimeout property

Specifies, in milliseconds, the time to wait before a connection to the server will timeout. The InternetTimeout property applies only to HTTP and HTTPS protocols.

Instantiating an object with the DataSpace object

To instantiate a business object from the client using the HTTP protocol, you might use code similar to the following:

```
Dim dsp As RDS.DataSpace
Dim dfy As Object

Set dsp = New RDS.DataSpace

dsp.InternetTimeout = 10
Set dfy = dsp.CreateObject("RDSServer.DataFactory", _
                           "http://production/")


'
' place your code here
'

Set dfy = Nothing
Set dsp = Nothing
```

In this code, the CreateObject method of the DataSpace object indicates that the business object to create is the DataFactory object and that it should be created on the production server using an HTTP protocol to obtain the proxy.

Before you use the DataSpace object in Visual Basic, you need to add a reference (from the Project → References . . . menu) to the Microsoft Remote Data Services 2.6 library.

The DataFactory Object

The DataFactory object provides access to the underlying data source from the client. It is created as an Automation object on the server side that processes requests from the client.

The DataFactory and the DataControl objects share some members. If you call these members from within your client-side application, the DataControl object's members are called by default.

The DataFactory object can be replaced with a custom business object that will implement some or all of the methods provided by the default DataFactory object and that is customized for the data source. From this custom business object, the default DataFactory's methods can be called if the custom business object doesn't implement them itself.

DataFactory object members

The following four methods are the only members of the DataFactory object:

ConvertToString method

Accepts a Recordset object and converts it into a MIME string that can be sent via HTTP to the client. Microsoft suggests that you use this process only for recordsets with 400 or fewer records with each record containing no more than 1024 bytes.

CreateRecordset method

Creates an empty Recordset object that can be used by a server-side business object. This method accepts an array of columns to be used in the creation of the Recordset object. Each column is an array of attributes containing the name, type, size, and nullability of the column. On the server side, this Recordset object can be populated with data from a file, data from a data source, or hard-coded data from the application.

Query method

Accepts a connection string and a valid SQL statement (for the specified data source) and returns a Recordset object.

SubmitChanges method

Sends changes to a Recordset object back to the server so that they can be persisted. This method accepts a connection string and a Recordset object.

Creating an empty recordset on the client side

The following example illustrates how an empty Recordset object can be created from the client-side application:

```
Dim dfy As RDSServer.DataFactory
Dim rst As ADODB.Recordset

Dim vFieldInfo1(3) As Variant
Dim vFieldInfo2(3) As Variant
Dim vFieldInfo3(3) As Variant
Dim vFields(2) As Variant
Dim vValues(2) As Variant
Dim vFieldNames(2) As Variant

Set dfy = New RDSServer.DataFactory

'
' define the recordset
'
vFieldInfo1(0) = "Name"
vFieldInfo1(1) = CInt(ADODB.DataTypeEnum.adVarChar)
vFieldInfo1(2) = CInt(30)
vFieldInfo1(3) = False
```

```
vFields(0) = vFieldInfo1

vFieldInfo2(0) = "Age"
vFieldInfo2(1) = CInt(ADODB.DataTypeEnum.adInteger)
vFieldInfo2(2) = CInt(-1)
vFieldInfo2(3) = True

vFields(1) = vFieldInfo2

vFieldInfo3(0) = "Married"
vFieldInfo3(1) = CInt(ADODB.DataTypeEnum.adBoolean)
vFieldInfo3(2) = CInt(-1)
vFieldInfo3(3) = True

vFields(2) = vFieldInfo3

Set rst = dfy.CreateRecordSet(vFields)

'
' populate the recordset
'
vFieldNames(0) = vFieldInfo1(0)
vFieldNames(1) = vFieldInfo2(0)
vFieldNames(2) = vFieldInfo3(0)

vValues(0) = "Jason"
vValues(1) = CInt(27)
vValues(2) = True
rst.AddNew vFieldNames, vValues

vValues(0) = "Kimberly "
vValues(1) = 25
vValues(2) = True
rst.AddNew vFieldNames, vValues

vValues(0) = "Zachary "
vValues(1) = 0
vValues(2) = False
rst.AddNew vFieldNames, vValues

'
' do something with the Recordset
'

Set rst = Nothing
Set dfy = Nothing
```

Roundtrip querying and updating

The DataFactory object allows a query to the server and an update from the client in a single roundtrip communication, as shown in the following example:

```
Dim dsp As RDS.DataSpace
Dim dfy As Object
```

```
Dim rst As ADODB.Recordset

Dim sCon As String

Set dsp = New RDS.DataSpace

dsp.InternetTimeout = 10

'
' create the data factory from the data space
'
Set dfy = dsp.CreateObject("RDSServer.DataFactory", "")

'
' retrieve the data from the server
'
sCon = "driver={SQL Server};" _
     & "server=jroff-laptop;" _
     & "database=NORTHWIND"

Set rst = dfy.Query(sCon, _
                    "SELECT * FROM Orders")

'
' update the data
'
rst.Find "OrderID=10268", _
         0, _
         adSearchForward, _
         0

rst!Freight = rst!Freight + 1.27

'
' send the data back to the server
'
dfy.SubmitChanges sCon, rst

Set dfy = Nothing
Set dsp = Nothing
```

The DataControl Object

The RDS DataControl object allows your project easy access to data without your explicitly creating and working with the DataSpace object and a DataFactory object. In addition, the DataControl object links one or more controls on an HTML page to a query.

The DataControl object is for web applications only and has no purpose in a Visual Basic desktop application. If you have multiple queries, you need multiple DataControl objects. There is no restriction on the number of DataControl objects that you can use in a single HTML page.

All of the properties of the DataControl object are optional, since custom business objects can be developed to replace any of the functionality. With the DataControl object, you can query a data source with a SQL statement; move around within the created recordset; and update, sort, and filter records.

DataControl object members

The following list of methods, properties, and events constitute the members of the DataControl object:

Cancel method

    Cancels the execution of an asynchronous method call that is still running. After calling this method, the Recordset object is empty.

CancelUpdate method

    Cancels any pending changes to the current record or the new record. After calling this method, the bound control is refreshed from the original data.

Connect property

    Connects to a data source against which queries and updates will be executed. The Connect property can be set during design time (by using HTML tags) or runtime.

CreateRecordset method

    Creates an empty Recordset object that can be used by a server-side business object. On the server side, this Recordset object can be populated with data from a file, data from a data source, or hard-coded data from the application.

ExcecuteOptions property

    Indicates whether the next refresh of the Recordset will be asynchronous (adcExecAsync, the default value) or synchronous (adcExecSync).

FetchOptions property

    Indicates the type of asynchronous fetching that should occur. The default value for this property is adcFetchAsync, which returns control immediately to the application while the records are being fetched. This is the setting recommended by Microsoft for web applications. For a compiled client application, the Microsoft-recommended setting is adcFetchBackground, which returns control to the application as soon as the first batch of records has been fetched. The remaining setting, adcFetchUpFront, fetches all of the records before control is returned. You should choose this last setting if you need the entire recordset to continue your code.

FilterColumn property

    Used with the FilterValue and FilterCriterion properties, indicates the column on which to evaluate the filter criteria for the Recordset. The Reset method must be called to update the data in the Recordset.

FilterCriterion property

Is set to a String value of <, <=, >, >=, =, or <> to indicate the filter-criteria operator used in the filter specified by the FilterValue and FilterColumn properties. The Reset method must be called to update the data in the Recordset.

FilterValue property

Is set to a String value that indicates the data value to filter on. The Filter-Value property is used in conjunction with the FilterColumn and the FilterCriterion properties. The Reset method must be called to update the data in the Recordset.

Handler property

Indicates the name of a server-side custom program (or handler) that is used to extend the functionality of the DataFactory object. Included in this string can be parameters for the handler, separated by commas (for example, "handler_name, parameter1, parameter2").

InternetTimeout property

Specifies, in milliseconds, the time to wait before a request to the server will timeout. The InternetTimeout property applies only to HTTP and HTTPS protocols.

MoveFirst method

Moves to the first record in the Recordset.

MoveLast method

Moves to the last record in the Recordset.

MoveNext method

Moves to the next record in the Recordset.

MovePrevious method

Moves to the previous record in the Recordset.

onError event

Called whenever an error occurs with an operation.

onReadyStateChange event

Fired when a change occurs in the DataControl's ReadyState property value.

ReadyState property

Indicates the current state of the DataControl object as it receives data. If no records have been fetched yet and the query is still executing, the ReadyState property is set to adcReadyStateLoaded. If the initial set of records is loaded in the DataControl object and the remaining records are still loading, the Recordset object can be used, and the ReadyState property is set to adReadyStateInteractive. If all the records have been returned to the DataControl object or an error has occurred in the execution of the last command, the ReadyState property will be set to adcReadyStateComplete. To determine whether an error has occurred, in addition to checking the Ready-State property, check the State property for the adStateClosed enumeration value.

Recordset property

Read-only. Returns the Recordset object that was returned from a custom business object. To set the Recordset object, use the SourceRecordset object.

Refresh method

Refreshes the data in the Recordset object by querying the data source again. Any controls on the page that are tied to the DataControl object are refreshed automatically.

Reset method

Re-executes the sort and filter query for a Recordset object for a client-side cursor. This method accepts a Boolean value to indicate if the re-execution of the query should include the current filter (**True**) or if it should re-execute on the original data (**False**) and clear out the current filter.

SourceRecordset property

Write-only. Sets the Recordset object that was returned from a custom business object. To read the Recordset object, use the Recordset object.

Server property

Indicates on which server the DataControl's request is processed. This property can be set at design time or runtime.

SortColumn property

Indicates which column is to be used when sorting the Recordset.

SortDirection property

Indicates the direction of the sort for the Recordset. A value of **True** indicates that the sort order is ascending; **False** indicates descending.

SQL property

Indicates the SQL statement that is used to populate the Recordset object.

SubmitChanges method

Sends only the changed records from a Recordset object to the server to be updated. Either all or none of the records are updated.

URL property

Indicates a String that contains either a relative or an absolute URL. This URL usually points to an ASP page that returns a Recordset object. If the URL property is indicated, the SubmitChanges method will return records to the URL.

Binding a control to the DataControl object

The DataControl object binds a query easily to one or more visual controls on an HTML page, as demonstrated in the next example. To run this example, you must first create an ASP page. Within this page, create a table with the following HTML code:

```
<TABLE DATASRC=#OrderTable>
<TBODY>
  <TR>
    <TD><SPAN DATAFLD="OrderID"></SPAN></TD>
    <TD><SPAN DATAFLD="ShipName"></SPAN></TD>
    <TD><SPAN DATAFLD="Freight"></SPAN></TD>
  </TR>
</TBODY>
</TABLE>
```

In this code, three columns are names based upon three columns in the recordset that we will be creating.

The next thing you need to do is to create a DataControl object. To do this, you must create an object with the class ID of **BD96C556-65A3-11D0-983A-00C04FC29E33**, as in the following code:

```
<OBJECT classid="clsid:BD96C556-65A3-11D0-983A-00C04FC29E33"
    ID=OrderTable HEIGHT=1 WIDTH=1>
</OBJECT>
```

Within the VBScript section of your ASP page, enter the following code to set the server, SQL statement, and connection string:

```
OrderTable.Server = "http://JROFF-LAPTOP/"

OrderTable.SQL = "SELECT * FROM Orders;"

OrderTable.Connect = "DRIVER={SQL SERVER}; " _
                   & "SERVER=JROFF-LAPTOP; " _
                   & "DATABASE=Northwind; "


OrderTable.Refresh
```

When this page is viewed, the table is populated with all the records from the Orders table.

Filtering and sorting the recordset

With the DataControl object, you can filter and sort the recordset, as shown:

```
'
' set the filter
'
OrderTable.FilterColumn = "Freight"
```

```
OrderTable.FilterCriterion = ">="
OrderTable.FilterValue = "20.00"

'
' set the sort order
'
OrderTable.SortColumn = "Freight"
OrderTable.SortDirection = False

'
' populate
'
OrderTable.Refresh
```

An Example in RDS

Example 11-1 displays the entire Orders table of the *Northwind* database in a table within an ASP page. To run this example, create an ASP page and replace the entire contents of the page with the following code. Make sure that this ASP page is within a virtual directory of your web server, such as *RDSExample*. To execute this page, go to Internet Explorer and type in the full URL to the ASP—for example, *http://servername/RDSExample/example.asp*.

Example 11-1. Displaying a Table with RDS

```
<%@ Language=VBScript %>
<html>
<head>
    <title>RDS Code Example</title>
</head>

<body>

<h1>RDS Code Example</h1>

<H2>Orders Table</H2>
<P>

<INPUT TYPE=button NAME="View" VALUE="View">

<SCRIPT Language="VBScript">
<!--

Sub View_OnClick

    '
    ' connect to the server and query
    '
    OrderTable.Server = "http://JROFF-LAPTOP/"

    OrderTable.SQL = "SELECT * FROM Orders;"
```

Example 11-1. Displaying a Table with RDS (continued)

```
    OrderTable.Connect = "DRIVER={SQL SERVER}; " _
                       & "SERVER=JROFF-LAPTOP; " _
                       & "DATABASE=Northwind; "


    '
    ' set the filter
    '
    OrderTable.FilterColumn = "Freight"
    OrderTable.FilterCriterion = ">="
    OrderTable.FilterValue = "20.00"


    '
    ' set the sort order
    '
    OrderTable.SortColumn = "Freight"
    OrderTable.SortDirection = False


    '
    ' populate
    '
    OrderTable.Refresh

End Sub

-->
</SCRIPT>
 </P>

<TABLE DATASRC=#OrderTable
       align=left
       border=1
       style="LEFT: 11px; TOP: 115px">
<TBODY>
  <TR>
    <TD><SPAN DATAFLD="OrderID"></SPAN></TD>
    <TD><SPAN DATAFLD="ShipName"></SPAN></TD>
    <TD><SPAN DATAFLD="Freight"></SPAN></TD>
  </TR>
</TBODY>
</TABLE>

<P>
<OBJECT classid=clsid:BD96C556-65A3-11D0-983A-00C04FC29E33
       height=1
       id=OrderTable
       width=1>

    <PARAM NAME="ExecuteOptions" VALUE="2">
    <PARAM NAME="FetchOptions" VALUE="3">
    <PARAM NAME="InternetTimeout" VALUE="100">
```

Example 11-1. Displaying a Table with RDS (continued)

```
</OBJECT></P>

<P> </P>
<P> </P>
<P> </P>

</body>
</html>
```

More Information About RDS

This chapter by no means covers RDS in full. RDS has more capabilities that are not mentioned here. For instance, RDS allows you to create custom business objects to use in place or in addition to the standard objects supplied by RDS. RDS also has many features that allow customization of security rights. For more information see *Professional ADO 2.5 RDS Programming with ASP 3.0* by John Papa (Wrox Press, Inc., 2000).

Summary

This chapter introduced to you the component of ADO called Remote Data Services or RDS. You have learned that RDS allows client-side applications to access and manipulate data sources through a third middle tier such as IIS. After reading this chapter, you should be able to fully understand RDS and the following key points:

- There are three objects that make up RDS: the DataSpace object, the Data-Factory object, and the DataControl object.

- The DataSpace object manages the connection through the middle tier to the data source by providing a proxy to the client application.

- The DataFactory object allows the manipulation and the access to the underlying data source by using the proxy returned from the DataSpace object.

- The DataControl object is used as a simple way to access a data source through a middle tier without using the DataSpace and the DataFactory objects. This object also allows your client HTML page to be bound to the results of the query that has been executed by the DataControl.

12

The Microsoft
.NET Framework
and ADO.NET

At the Professional Developer's Conference 2000, Microsoft announced a new development platform called the .NET Framework. One of the components of the new .NET Framework is ADO.NET, Microsoft's successor to ADO. In this chapter, I will provide a brief introduction to the .NET Framework and ADO.NET's place within it. For more information on .NET, see *http://msdn.microsoft.com*, as well as *C# Essentials* (O'Reilly, 2001) and the upcoming *.NET Framework Essentials* (O'Reilly, 2001).

The Microsoft .NET Framework

The Microsoft .NET Framework consists of three new components of interest to the ADO developer:

- The Common Language Runtime (CLR) and its base class library (BCL)
- C#, a new unified programming language
- ASP.NET, a new framework for web application development

Each of these three components plays a key role in the .NET Framework.

The Common Language Runtime

The Common Language Runtime has two roles, one for the execution environment and one for the development environment.

For the execution environment, the CLR is the provider of .NET's functionality. This functionality includes, but is not limited to: compilation of Intermediate

Language (IL) to native code, handling of security, memory allocation, and thread and process management.

For the development environment, the CLR supports any language compiler that generates the IL code that it understands and the metadata it uses to make runtime decisions. In its first release, .NET will support VB.NET (the new C# language), managed C++, and JScript.NET. The CLR also allows the developer to write less code because so much is handled by the runtime, such as garbage collection and serialization of objects to and from XML.

C#: Unified Programming Language

In the current Microsoft development framework, C++, Visual Basic, and Java all have different APIs that achieve the same functionality. With the .NET Framework, Microsoft is attempting to combine the APIs into one class framework.

This gives developers more power than they have ever had by allowing them to mix and match languages very easily. In fact, it will allow cross-language inheritance, debugging, and error handling.

This common class framework (or set of APIs) that every language can use as its own will make the language used for developing an application virtually meaningless, allowing you to create applications in JScript that are just as powerful as applications written in C++.

ASP.NET

ASP.NET is the Microsoft .NET Framework for developing web applications. ASP. NET, like its predecessor, allows developers to combine HTML and programming languages to create web pages on the server that function as middle-tier business objects. ASP.NET also simplifies the task of interacting with browser clients a range of devices including PDAs and cell phones, as well as PCs.

ASP.NET controls are objects that run on the server but broadcast simple HTML controls to the client, such as a text box or a button. These ASP.NET controls have object models so that they can be programmed using normal development techniques on the server and any of the .NET-compliant languages.

In addition, ASP.NET provides application context through its own object model to the web developer, such as session state.

From COM to .NET: The Creation of ADO.NET

One of the main purposes of the Microsoft .NET Framework is to make development of COM objects and applications easier. This is done through an abstraction level that automates the creation, management, interaction, and registration of COM objects so that the developer can do other things.

Because of this abstraction, Microsoft was able to create ADO.NET, a simpler successor to ADO that is geared towards web applications. Because web applications are stateless, ADO.NET focuses on disconnected data, while traditional ADO focuses on connected data.

ADO will continue to play an important role in traditional desktop and client-server applications where the data-services code is tightly coupled with the data source itself. Microsoft provides access to ADO and other COM/ActiveX object libraries through the use of the .NET/COM interoperability services, which allow direct access to a COM object from within the .NET Framework, without using the abstraction layer that is normally applied to COM objects. By using these services, your application can access traditional ADO as it always has.

ADO.NET

ADO.NET is comprised of two main components, DataSets and managed providers. *DataSets* can store an entire database in memory, while *managed providers* provide the ability to establish a connection between the data source and a DataSet. In addition, managed providers provide a means of populating, manipulating, and accessing the data within the DataSet.

DataSets

A DataSet is a memory-resident version of a database containing tables, rows, relationships, constraints, and keys. In ADO.NET, all work is done with a DataSet. The DataSet has three main collection classes and numerous child classes belonging to each:

TablesCollection object

A collection of one or more DataTable objects that represent individual tables from the data source. In these DataTable objects, both columns and rows are stored as separate objects. Each DataTable object represents one table within memory. The DataSet is able to persist the contents of the TablesCollection and reload it using XML. The TablesCollection automatically keeps track of any changes made to the data stored in the individual DataTables.

RelationsCollection object

A collection of one or more relations between rows from different tables. Relations can be navigated from one table to another.

Extended Properties object
> A collection of user-customized properties such as a password or the time data was last updated.

Managed Providers

A managed provider establishes a connection between a data source, such as SQL Server and DataSet. There are three main components to managed providers:

DataSetCommand object
> Connections, commands, and parameters that access and populate the DataSet with the data.

DataReader object
> Provides fast, simple, forward-only access to data.

Low-level objects
> Connect to the database to issue data-specific commands.

There are two managed providers provided with .NET: the SQL managed provider, which creates a connection between the DataSet and SQL Server, and the ADO managed provider, which bridges the DataSet object to any data source that has an OLE DB driver.

ADO.NET Features

As the name implies, ADO.NET is an extension built upon the existing, traditional ADO object model. While ADO.NET will be very familiar to an ADO developer, several new features have been added to facilitate use with disconnected data sources:

- ADO.NET focuses on disconnected data.
- ADO.NET allows strongly typed language.
- ADO.NET works with hierarchical and relational data through XML.

Each of these differences have their own benefits, as explained in the following sections.

Disconnected Data

ADO.NET allows you to create disconnected *n*-tier applications. This feature is probably the biggest draw of ADO.NET. Traditional ADO was designed to work with tightly coupled application tiers, where state is maintained. In the web development paradigm, state is nonexistent.

With ADO.NET, the DataSet object is populated with the entire data that is needed in your application, and then the connection is closed, even if you are going to work with this data for a long time. When the data needs to be persisted to the data source, another connection is created, and then the data is persisted.

In ADO, you must state explicitly that you want to work with a disconnected Recordset, which can be done only with RDS objects: with ADO.NET, this choice is the default.

Strongly Typed Language

ADO.NET provides for a strongly typed language, which allows you to access collection classes and data that are normally parameterized with the actual name. For instance, to display the first name of the current author in a table, you could type:

```
Msgbox Authors.Firstname
```

With ADO, you must specify the parametered value, such as:

```
Msgbox rst("FirstName").Value
```

In addition, ADO.NET syntax allows you to use the actual datatype of the member, rather than just a Variant—this is the definition of a strongly typed language. This feature allows the development IDE to use IntelliSense and display the actual table and column names as you are developing, thus enabling faster and smoother development.

XML Integration

Both .NET and ADO.NET allow you to work easily with hierarchical data (compared to the relational data that ADO works so well with). The ability to work with hierarchical data is important, as the computing population is moving closer and closer to XML, a hierarchical data-storage method.

ADO.NET provides the ability to access relational data through the use of a DataSet. The DataSet also allows data to be saved and restored in its native format, including XML, making the DataSet an ideal candidate for tier communication in a client/server application.

.NET provides the ability to access hierarchical data, with XML, through the use of the XmlDocument. A third component, XmlDataDocument, allows the developer to bridge the two types of data access. This object allows the developer to load either relational or hierarchical data and manipulate it using DOM (Document Object Model). The XmlDataDocument handles the synchronization between the DataSet and the DOM.

Summary

This chapter briefly introduced the Microsoft .NET Framework and its ADO.NET component. I also listed the key components and features of the ADO.NET component:

- The Microsoft .NET Framework is a development and runtime environment that promises ease of development and stronger Internet applications, based upon its ability to abstract COM details.

- ADO.NET is the .NET Framework's replacement for ADO. ADO.NET maintains in memory a copy of data in use, allowing disconnected access to a data source—ideal for today's web applications.

- Some of the features of ADO.NET include the ability to work disconnected data, promotion of a strongly typed language, and XML integration.

II

Reference Section

13

ADO API Reference

This reference chapter lists all of the methods, properties, and events that belong to ActiveX Data Objects.

Finding the Reference Page

This reference section is arranged in alphabetical order, and all properties, methods, and events are alphabetized by their fully qualified name, which includes the name of the object which they are part of. For instance, if you want to read about the Open method of the Recordset object, look up "Recordset. Open", not "Open."

Table 13-1 contains a directory that will help if you do not know the object to which your method, property, or event belongs, or if the reference page is not where you expected. The table of contents lists, in the left column, the properties, methods, and events within ADO. The right column gives you the full name of the object and the member—here's where you'll find the correct reference page. Note that some members are used by more than one object. For example, the State property belongs to the Command, Connection, Record, Recordset, and Stream objects.

Table 13-1. Reference Contents

For	See
AbsolutePage	Recordset.AbsolutePage
AbsolutePosition	Recordset.AbsolutePosition
ActiveCommand	Recordset.ActiveCommand
ActiveConnection	Command.ActiveConnection, Record.ActiveConnection, Recordset.ActiveConnection

Table 13-1. Reference Contents (continued)

For	See
ActualSize	Field.ActualSize
AddNew	Recordset.AddNew
Append	Fields.Append, Parameters.Append
AppendChunk	Field.AppendChunk, Parameter.AppendChunk
Attributes	Connection.Attributes, Field.Attributes, Parameter.Attributes, Property.Attributes
BeginTrans	Connection.BeginTrans
BeginTransComplete	Connection.BeginTransComplete
BOF	Recordset.BOF
Bookmark	Recordset.Bookmark
CacheSize	Recordset.CacheSize
Cancel	Command.Cancel, Connection.Cancel, Record.Cancel, Recordset.Cancel, Stream.Cancel
CancelBatch	Recordset.CancelBatch
CancelUpdate	Fields.CancelUpdate, Recordset.CancelUpdate
CharSet	Stream.CharSet
Clear	Errors.Clear
Clone	Recordset.Clone
Close	Connection.Close, Record.Close, Recordset.Close, Stream.Close
CommandStream	Command.CommandStream
CommandText	Command.CommandText
CommandTimeout	Command.CommandTimeout, Connection.CommandTimeout
CommandType	Command.CommandType
CommitTrans	Connection.CommitTrans
CommitTransComplete	Connection.CommitTransComplete
CompareBookmarks	Recordset.CompareBookmarks
ConnectionString	Connection.ConnectionString
ConnectionTimeout	Connection.ConnectionTimeout
CopyRecord	Record.CopyRecord
CopyTo	Stream.CopyTo
Count	Fields.Count, Parameters.Count, Properties.Count
CreateParameter	Command.CreateParameter
CursorLocation	Connection.CursorLocation, Recordset.CursorLocation
CursorType	Recordset.CursorType
DataFormat	Field.DataFormat

Table 13-1. Reference Contents (continued)

For	See
DataMember	Recordset.DataMember
DataSource	Recordset.DataSource
DefaultDatabase	Connection.DefaultDatabase
DefinedSize	Field.DefinedSize
Delete	Fields.Delete, Parameters.Delete, Recordset.Delete
DeleteRecord	Record.DeleteRecord
Description	Error.Description
Dialet	Command.Dialet
Direction	Parameter.Direction
Disconnect	Connection.Disconnect
EditMode	Recordset.EditMode
EndOfRecordset	Recordset.EndOfRecordset
EOF	Recordset.EOF, Stream.EOS
Errors	Connection.Errors
Execute	Command.Execute, Connection.Execute
ExecuteComplete	Connection.ExecuteComplete
FetchComplete	Recordset.FetchComplete
FetchProgress	Recordset.FetchProgress
FieldChangeComplete	Recordset.FieldChangeComplete
Fields	Fields, Record.Fields, Recordset.Fields
Find	Recordset.Find
Flush	Stream.Flush
GetChildren	Record.GetChildren
GetChunk	Field.GetChunk
GetRows	Recordset.GetRows
GetString	Recordset.GetString
HelpContext	Error.HelpContext
HelpFile	Error.HelpFile
Index	Recordset.Index
InfoMessage	Connection.InfoMessage
IsolationLevel	Connection.IsolationLevel
Item	Errors.Item. Fields.Item, Parameters.Item, Properties. Item
LineSeparator	Stream.LineSeparator
LoadFromFile	Stream.LoadFromFile
LockType	Recordset.LockType

Table 13-1. Reference Contents (continued)

For	See
MarshallOptions	Recordset.MarshallOptions
MaxRecords	Recordset.MaxRecords
Mode	Connection.Mode, Record.Mode, Stream.Mode, Recordset.Move
MoveComplete	Recordset.MoveComplete
MoveFirst	Recordset.MoveFirst
MoveLast	Recordset.MoveLast
MoveNext	Recordset.MoveNext
MovePrevious	Recordset.MovePrevious
MoveRecord	Record.MoveRecord
Name	Command.Name, Field.Name, Parameter.Name, Property.Name
NamedParameters	Command.NamedParameters
NativeError	Error.NativeError
NextRecordset	Recordset.NextRecordset
Number	Error.Number
NumericScale	Field.NumericScale, Parameter.NumericScale
Open	Connection.Open, Record.Open, Recordset.Open, Stream.Open
OpenSchema	Connection.OpenSchema
OriginalValue	Field.OriginalValue
PageCount	Recordset.PageCount
PageSize	Recordset.PageSize
Parameters	Command.Parameters, Parameters Collection
ParentURL	Record.ParentURL
Position	Stream.Position
Precision	Field.Precision, Parameter.Precision
Prepared	Command.Prepared
Properties	Connection.Properties, Field.Properties, Parameter. Properties, Properties, Record.Properties, Recordset. Properties
Provider	Connection.Provider
Read	Stream.Read
ReadText	Stream.ReadText
RecordChangeComplete	Recordset.RecordChangeComplete
RecordCount	Recordset.RecordCount
RecordsetChangeComplete	Recordset.RecordsetChangeComplete

Table 13-1. Reference Contents (continued)

For	See
RecordType	Record.RecordType
Refresh	Errors.Refresh, Fields.Refresh, Parameters.Refresh, Properties.Refresh
Requery	Recordset.Requery
Resync	Fields.Resync, Recordset.Resync
RollbackTrans	Connection.RollbackTrans
Save	Recordset.Save
SaveToFile	Stream.SaveToFile
Seek	Recordset.Seek
SetEOS	Stream.SetEOS
Size	Parameter.Size, Stream.Size
SkipLine	Stream.SkipLine
Sort	Recordset.Sort
Source	Error.Source, Record.Source, Recordset.Source
SQLState	Error.SQLState
State	Command.State, Connection.State, Record.State, Recordset.State, Stream.State
Status	Field.Status, Recordset.Status
StayInSync	Recordset.StayInSync
Supports	Recordset.Supports
Type	Field.Type, Parameter.Type, Property.Type, Stream.Type
UnderlyingValue	Field.UnderlyingValue
Update	Fields.Update, Recordset.Update
UpdateBatch	Recordset.UpdateBatch
Value	Field.Value, Parameter.Value, Property.Value
Version	Connection.Version
WillChangeField	Recordset.WillChangeField
WillChangeRecord	Recordset.WillChangeRecord
WillChangeRecordset	Recordset.WillChangeRecordset
WillConnect	Connection.WillConnect
WillExecute	Connection.WillExecute
WillMove	Recordset.WillMove
Write	Stream.Write
WriteText	Stream.WriteText

Using the Reference Pages

Each object and collection within ADO has its own section. The first reference page is titled "Sample Object"; it explains the structure of each reference page representing an ADO object or collection.

Each member (method, property, or event) of an ADO object and collection has its own section. The second reference page is titled "Sample Object.Property"; it explains the structure of each reference page representing an ADO property.

The third reference page is titled "Sample Object.Method"; it explains the structure of each reference page representing an ADO method or event.

Sample Object   (Versions)

Title, Versions, and Description

Each entry begins with a title, the versions of ADO in which the object or collection is found, and a description. Entries are listed in alphabetical order with a quick summary of the item; this feature helps ensure that you've found the correct entry.

Collections

Some ADO objects contain references to ADO collections. For instance, the Recordset object has a reference to the Fields collection. In this section, the referenced Collections for the currently referenced ADO object are listed in alphabetical order with a brief description.

Methods

Lists the methods, if any, for the currently referenced ADO object or collection in alphabetical order with a brief description.

Properties

Lists the properties, if any, for the currently referenced ADO object or collection in alphabetical order with a brief description.

Events

Lists the events, if any, for the currently referenced ADO object in alphabetical order with a brief description.

Description

Provides the pertinent information for the given ADO object or collection with an overview of what the object or collection can do and an idea of the capabilities of each member method, property, and event.

Examples

One or more examples on using the ADO object or collection.

Sample Object.Property   (Versions)

Title, Versions, and Description

Each property reference entry includes a title, the versions of ADO the property can be found in, and a description. Entries in the reference are listed in alphabetical order and contain the fully qualified name of the property. For instance, the State property of the Recordset object is titled "Recordset.State Property."

Datatype

Lists the datatype for the given property.

Description

Provides a detailed description of the property.

See Also

Lists the objects, collections, methods, properties, and events that are related to the current property.

Sample Object.Method   (Versions)

Title, Versions, and Description

Each method and event reference entry includes a title, the versions of ADO the property can be found in, and a description. Entries in the reference are listed in alphabetical order and contain the fully qualified name of the method. For instance, the Open method of the Recordset object is titled "Recordset.Open Method."

Arguments

Lists the arguments, if any, for the current method or event, with a datatype and a description.

Returns

Lists the possible datatypes that can be returned for the method. Events do not have Returns sections.

Description

Provides a detailed description of the method.

See Also

Lists the objects, collections, methods, properties, and events that are related to the current method or event.

Command Object   (Versions 2.0, 2.1, 2.5, 2.6)

```
Dim object As ADODB.Command
```

The Command object executes a SQL statement, query, or stored procedure against a specified data source. A Command object can alter the structure of the data source, execute large batch operations, or select records to be returned within a Recordset object.

Collections

Parameters

The Parameters collection returns a collection of parameters for the given Command object.

Properties

The Properties property returns a Properties Collection class that contains characteristics specific to the Command object for the currently used provider.

Methods

Cancel

The Cancel method cancels the pending asynchronous command that is executing.

CreateParameter

The CreateParameter creates and returns a new parameter with the information that is supplied.

Execute

The Execute method executes a SQL statement, query, or stored procedure specified in the Command.CommandText property value.

Properties

ActiveConnection

The ActiveConnection property specifies the Connection object for the current Command object.

CommandStream

The CommandStream property sets or returns the data provider–specific stream that is used as the Command's input just as the CommandText property identifies the command to use as the input.

CommandText

The CommandText property sets or returns a valid SQL statement, table name, stored procedure name, relative URL, or any other command text that the data provider may recognize.

CommandTimeout

The CommandTimeout property indicates how long ADO waits, in seconds, before it generates an error when executing an asynchronous command.

CommandType

The CommandType property indicates the current type of Command object.

Dialect

The Dialect property is used with the CommandText and the CommandStream properties to indicate the data provider–specific syntax of the Command's source.

Name

The Name property specifies the name for the current Command object.

NamedParameters

The NamedParameters property indicates whether the data provider should use parameter names to match the Command object's parameters or if it should match them in the order that they appear.

Prepared

The Prepared property indicates whether a prepared statement should be created by the current Command object before it is executed.

State

The Status property determines the status of the current record when using batch updates or bulk operations.

Description

A Command object must have a value for its ActiveConnection property that either associates it with an existing, open ActiveConnection object or uses a connection string to create a new, independent Connection object within the Command object.

Once a Command object is associated to an open Connection object, the Command object can be executed from the Connection object, by name. A Connection object can also execute a command, without a Command object at all, by using the Execute method. In this case, ADO is actually creating and using a Command object internally within the Connection object, but it does not expose it to your application.

When you execute a command without a Command object, you cannot persist (save the data to the datasource) and re-execute the command text or use parameters with your command.

If two or more Command objects are associated to the same Connection object and one of them is a stored procedure with output parameters, an error will occur. To avoid this, use separate Connection objects for each Command object, or make sure that all other Command objects are disconnected from their Connection objects before executing others.

Examples

In this section, we will be looking at three examples that will show us how to:

- Execute SQL statements.
- Execute a Command object from an associated Connection object.
- Use parameters in queries.

To use the Command examples for this section, you must define the following connection string Const value for the examples to work properly:

```
Private Const DATASOURCE_BIBLIO = "Provider=Microsoft.Jet.OLEDB.4.0; " _
                    & "Data Source=C:\Program Files\" _
                    & "Microsoft Visual Studio\VB98\Biblio.mdb;"
```

Example 13-1 illustrates how a Command object can be used to execute a simple SQL statement. Notice how the connection string Const value is assigned to the ActiveConnection property. This value will be used by ADO to create the Command object and its own Connection object.

Example 13-1. Executing a SQL Statement with a Command Object

```
Dim com As ADODB.Command
Dim rst As ADODB.Recordset


'
' instantiate a new instance of the Command Object
'
Set com = New ADODB.Command


'
' pass the previously defined connection string to the object
'
' this will create a new internal Connection object
'
com.ActiveConnection = DATASOURCE_BIBLIO


'
' specify the command text and tell the object to evaluate it
' as a SQL statement
'
com.CommandText = "SELECT * FROM Authors;"
com.CommandType = adCmdText


'
' instruct ADO to prepare the statement and timeout after 30 seconds
'
com.Prepared = True
com.CommandTimeout = 30


'
' execute the command and return the results to the Recordset object
'
Set rst = com.Execute


'
' the Recordset object now contains the results from the Command's query
'
MsgBox "The first author in the recordset is: " & rst.Fields.Item("Author").Value


'
' like always, clean up
'
rst.Close

Set rst = Nothing
Set com = Nothing
```

A Command object can also be associated with a Connection object and be invoked directly as you will see in Example 13-2. Note that by using this method, the method created by the associated Command object—in this example, MyCommand—is not available in the Intellisense feature offered by VB. This is because the Command object is being bounded late to the Connection object.

Example 13-2. Executing a Command Object from a Connection Object

```
Dim con As ADODB.Connection
Dim com As ADODB.Command
Dim rst As ADODB.Recordset

'
' open an external Connection object
'
Set con = New ADODB.Connection
con.Open DATASOURCE_BIBLIO

'
' instantiate a new instance of the Command Object and give it a name
'
Set com = New ADODB.Command
com.Name = "MyCommand"

'
' associate the Command object with the already opened Connection object
'
Set com.ActiveConnection = con

'
' specify the command text and tell the object to evaluate it
' as a SQL statement
'
com.CommandText = "SELECT * FROM Authors WHERE Author=AuthorName;"
com.CommandType = adCmdText

'
' execute the command and return the results to the Recordset object
'
Set rst = New ADODB.Recordset
con.MyCommand "Ingham, Kenneth", rst

'
' the Recordset object now contains the results from the Command's query
'
MsgBox "The first author in the recordset is: " & rst.Fields("Author")

Debug.Print rst.Fields.Item("Author").Value

'
' like always, clean up
'
rst.Close
con.Close

Set rst = Nothing
Set com = Nothing
Set con = Nothing
```

Example 13-3 illustrates how parameters are used with the object. Each Command object has its own collection class, Parameters. By using the CreateParameter method, we can create an instance of a Parameter class and append it to the Command's Parameters collection.

Example 13-3. Using Parameters with the Command Object

```
Dim con As ADODB.Connection
Dim com As ADODB.Command
Dim par As ADODB.Parameter
Dim rst As ADODB.Recordset

'
' open an external Connection object
'
Set con = New ADODB.Connection
con.Open DATASOURCE_BIBLIO

'
' instantiate a new instance of the Command Object and give it a name
'
Set com = New ADODB.Command
com.Name = "MyCommand"

'
' associate the Command object with the already opened Connection object
'
Set com.ActiveConnection = con

'
' specify the command text and tell the object to evaluate it
' as a SQL statement
'
com.CommandText = "SELECT * FROM Authors WHERE Author=AuthorName;"
com.CommandType = adCmdText

'
' create the parameter and add it to the Parameters collection
'
Set par = com.CreateParameter("AuthorName", _
                              adChar, _
                              adParamInput, _
                              20, _
                              "Ingham, Kenneth")

com.Parameters.Append par

'
' execute the command and return the results to the Recordset object
'
Set rst = New ADODB.Recordset
con.MyCommand , rst

'
```

Example 13-3. Using Parameters with the Command Object (continued)

```
' the Recordset object now contains the results from the Command's query
'
MsgBox "The first author in the recordset is: " & rst.Fields("Author")

Debug.Print rst.Fields.Item("Author").Value

'
' like always, clean up
'
rst.Close
con.Close

Set rst = Nothing
Set com = Nothing
Set par = Nothing
Set con = Nothing
```

Command.ActiveConnection Property   (Versions 2.0, 2.1, 2.5, 2.6)

```
Command.ActiveConnection = ConnectionString
Set Command.ActiveConnection = ConnectionObject
```

The ActiveConnection property specifies the Connection object for the current Command object.

Datatype

String or Variant (containing the current Connection object)

Description

The ActiveConnection property can be set to either a String, representing a connection string, or a Variant, representing an open Connection object.

The ActiveConnection property can be set to either a String or a reference to a Connection object. If a String value is used, then it should be a valid connection string that could be passed to the ConnectionString property of a Connection object. You must set the Active-Connection property before you attempt to execute a Command object. Before it is set, the value of the ActiveConnection property is a Null object reference, by default.

If you set the ActiveConnection property to a closed Connection object, ADO will generate an error. If you set it to Nothing, ADO will disassociate the Command object from the Connection object and release any resources that are associated with the data source. If the ActiveConnection property is set to either Nothing or a different Connection object, those Parameter objects that were supplied by the data provider, residing in the Command's Parameters collection class, will be lost. However, those Parameter objects that were manually added to the Parameters collection class will not.

If you close the Connection object associated with a Command object, the Command object's ActiveConnection will automatically be set to Nothing.

See Also

Connection.ConnectionString Property

Command.Cancel Method   (Versions 2.0, 2.1, 2.5, 2.6)

`Command.Cancel`

The Cancel method cancels the pending asynchronous command that is executing.

Description

The Cancel method cancels an asynchronous executing command that was initiated with the Execute method using the **adAsyncExecute** option.

If the Cancel method is called on a command that was not executed with the **adAsyncExecute** option set, an error will occur.

See Also

Command.Execute Method

Command.CommandStream Property   (Version 2.6)

`Command.CommandStream = Stream`

The CommandStream property sets or returns the data provider–specific stream that is used as the Command's input just as the CommandText property identifies the command to use as the input.

Datatype

Variant

Description

The CommandStream property is used to specify the stream used as a Command's input. If this property is set, then the CommandText property is set to an empty String (""). Similarly, if the CommandText property is set, the CommandStream property is set to **Nothing**.

If a Command object whose source is a stream is used to create a Recordset object, reading the Recordset object's Source property would return an empty String (""), because it returns the value of the Command object's CommandText property.

You must use either the **adCmdText** or **adCmdUnknown** enumeration values for the CommandType property if the CommandStream property is set.

The format of the stream being set to the CommandStream property is data provider–specific, as is the behavior of both the Command.Parameters.Refresh and Command.Prepare methods.

See Also

Command.CommandText Property, Comand.CommandDialect Property, Command-TypeEnum Enumeration, Recordset.Source

Command.CommandText Property   (Versions 2.0, 2.1, 2.5, 2.6)

`Command.CommandText = CommandText`

The CommandText property sets or returns a valid SQL statement, table name, stored procedure name, relative URL, or any other command text that the data provider may recognize.

Datatype

String

Description

The CommandText property contains a String value that by default contains a zero-length string (""). This string can be set to a SQL statement, table name, stored procedure call, relative URL, or any other command text that the data provider may recognize.

The CommandType property is used to indicate to ADO what type of information resides within the CommandText property. If the CommandType property is set to adCmdText, it indicates to the provider that the CommandText property value contains a text command that the provider will understand. This will usually be a SQL statement, but not necessarily.

If you set the CommandText property, ADO prepares the specified query on the Execute or Open methods whenever the Prepared property of the Command object is set to True, and it is bound to an open connection.

The value of CommandText may be changed by ADO, depending on the value of the CommandType property. Retrieve the value of the CommandText property at any time if you question its value.

If the CommandStream property is set to a value, then the CommandText property is automatically set to an empty string ("").

See Also

Command.CommandStream, Command.CommandType Property, Command.Dialect Property, Command.Prepared Property

Command.CommandTimeout Property   (Versions 2.0, 2.1, 2.5, 2.6)

`Command.CommlandTimeout = Seconds`

The CommandTimeout property indicates how long ADO waits, in seconds, before it generates an error when executing an asynchronous command.

Datatype

Long

Description

The CommandTimeout property is read- and write-enabled. With the CommandTimeout property, you can specify how long ADO will wait for a command to execute. The setting for the CommandTimeout property is represented in seconds, and the default value is 30. By setting this property to zero, you are allowing ADO to wait indefinitely for a specified command to execute. If a command does timeout, an error is generated.

The CommandTimeout property of the Command object is unrelated to the Command-Timeout property of the Connection object.

Note

Not all providers support the CommandTimeout property. Check your data provider's documentation to see if it supports this property. When developing an application with ADO, it might be a good idea to go as far as checking the capabilities of your planned data provider to see whether it matches your needs before you write most of your code—and it becomes too late.

See Also

Command.Execute Method, Connection.CommandTimeout Property

Command.CommandType Property (Versions 2.0, 2.1, 2.5, 2.6)

Command.CommandType = CommandTypeEnum

The CommandType property indicates the current type of Command object.

Datatype

CommandTypeEnum

Description

The CommandType property indicates the type of Command object you are using. The value of this property can be set to one of the CommandTypeEnum enumeration values. If the source of the Command object is a stream (set via the Command.CommandStream property), the CommandType property must be set to either adCmdText or adCmdUnknown.

In addition, the ExecuteOptionEnum value of adExecuteNoRecords can be combined with the adCmdText or adCmdStoredProc constants to improve performance. This value cannot be used with the Open method of the Recordset object.

If you know the type of Command object that you are using, set this property manually to prevent unwanted delays in performance when ADO tries to figure it out for itself. If the property is set incorrectly, an error is generated upon a call to the Execute method.

See Also

Command.CommandStream, Command.CommandText Property, CommandTypeEnum Enumeration

Command.CreateParameter Method (Versions 2.0, 2.1, 2.5, 2.6)

Set parameter = command.CreateParameter(Name, Type, Direction, Size, Value)

The CreateParameter method creates and returns a new parameter with the information supplied.

Arguments

Name (String)
> Optional. Contains the desired name of the new parameter. This argument is mapped to the Parameter.Name property.

Type (DataTypeEnum)

Optional. Indicates the desired datatype of the new parameter. This argument is mapped to the Parameter.Type property. The default value is adEmpty.

Direction (ParameterDirectionEnum)

Optional. Indicates the desired direction of the new parameter. This argument is mapped to the Parameter.Direction property. The default value is adParamImput.

Size (Long)

Optional. Specifies the maximum length of the newly created parameter in either characters or bytes if the Type parameter is set to a variable-length datatype. This argument is mapped to the Parameter.Size property.

Value (Variant)

Optional. Is used to initialize the value of the newly created Parameter object. This argument is mapped to the Parameter.Value property.

Returns

Parameter object

Description

With the CreateParameter method of the Command object, you can create a new Parameter object with the information that you specify, including name, type, direction, size, and value. When you create a new Parameter object with this method, the parameter is not automatically added to the Parameters collection of the chosen Command object. The Append method of the Command.Parameters property must be used to do this.

When assigning variable-length datatypes, you must set the Size property at either creation or some other time before appending it to the Parameters collection to avoid an error.

If the Type property is set to either adNumeric or adDecimal, the Parameter.NumericScale and Parameter.Precision properties must be set to fully specify the parameter's datatype. For instance, a NumericScale of 3 would indicate that there are three digits after the decimal point and a Precision of 5 would mean that there are five digits, total, representing the number.

See Also

DataTypeEnum Enumeration, ParameterDirectionEnum Enumeration, Parameter.Direction Property, Parameter.Name Property, Parameter.NumericScale Property, Parameter.Precision Property, Parameter.Size Property, Parameter.Type Property, Parameter.Value Property

---

Command.Dialect Property   (Version 2.6)

Command.*Dialect* = *GUID*

The Dialect property is used with the CommandText and the CommandStream properties to indicate the data provider–specific syntax of the Command's source.

Datatype

String

Description

The default value for the Dialect property is {C8B521FB-5CF3-11CE-ADE5-00AA0044773D}, which indicates to ADO that the provider will attempt to figure out how to interpret the Command's source specified in either the CommandStream or the CommandText property.

Note

You must check your data provider's documentation to see what the valid values of the Dialect property must be specified as, depending upon the value in the CommandStream or CommandText properties.

See Also

Command.CommandStream Property, Command.CommandText Property

Command.Execute Method   (Versions 2.0, 2.1, 2.5, 2.6)

```
Set recordset = command.Execute(RecordsAffected, Parameters, Options)
Set stream = command.Execute(RecordsAffected, Parameters, Options)
command.Execute RecordsAffected, Parameters, Options
```

The Execute method executes a SQL statement, query, or stored procedure specified in the Command.CommandText property value.

Arguments

RecordsAffected (Long)
> Optional. Populated, by the data provider, with the number of records that were affected by the action SQL statement, query, or stored procedure (result-returning commands do not populate this parameter).

Parameters (Variant Array)
> Optional. Contains the values to be passed to the SQL statement, query, or stored procedure for the parameters in which it holds.

Options (Long)
> Optional. A combination of one or more CommandTypeEnum and ExecuteOption-Enum values indicating how the data provider should treat the command. The default value is −1 (no options set). The CommandTypeEnum values can also be set with the Command.CommandType property.

Returns

> Recordset object
> Stream object
> Nothing

Description

The Execute method executes a stored procedure, SQL statement, or query against a data source. The command that is executed is dependent upon the value of the Command.CommandText property. The way in which ADO evaluates this CommandText is dependent upon the Options parameter to the Execute method.

If the CommandText value causes the Execute method to return records from the data source, these records are returned in the form of a Recordset object from the Execute method. A returned Recordset object from the Command.Execute method is always a read-only, forward-only cursor.

When the Execute method's Options parameter includes the `adAsyncExecute`, `adAsyncFetch`, or `adAsyncFetchNonBlocking` values, operations continue in the background of the application flow. While these operations are continuing, the Command. Cancel method can be called to cancel all pending asynchronous operations.

See Also

Command.Cancel Method, Command.CommadText Property, Command.CommandType Property, CommandTypeEnum Enumeration, ExecuteOptionEnum Enumeration, ExecuteOptionEnum Enumeration

---

Command.Name Property   (Versions 2.0, 2.1, 2.5, 2.6)

`command.Name = Name`

The Name property specifies the name for the current Command object.

Datatype

String

Description

The Name property is both read- and write-enabled for the Command object. The Name property is used to assign a name to the associated Command object or retrieve a Command object from the Commands collection.

Names do not have to be unique within collections.

Command.NamedParameters Property   (Version 2.6)

`command.NamedParameters = Boolean`

The NamedParameters property indicates whether the data provider should use parameter names to match the Command object's parameters or if it should match them in the order that they appear.

Datatype

Boolean

Description

If the NamedParameters property is set to `True`, the name properties of each Parameter object in the current Command objects, Parameters collection, will be passed to the data provider so that they can be used to map the parameters to the values in either the CommandText or the CommandStream Property.

If this property is set to `False`, then the parameters are not matched by name, but rather by the order in which they appear.

See Also

Command.CommandText Property, Command.CommandStream Property, Parameters Collection

---

Command.Parameters Collection
(Versions 2.0, 2.1, 2.5, 2.6)

```
Set parameters = command.Parameters
```

The Parameters collection returns a collection of parameters for the given Command object.

Datatype

Parameters (Collection object)

Applies To

Command object

Description

The Parameters property of the Command object is read-only. It returns a reference to the Parameters collection object, which can contain zero or many Parameter objects that represent parameters for the given command.

Command.Prepared Property
(Versions 2.0, 2.1, 2.5, 2.6)

```
command.Prepared = Boolean
```

The Prepared property indicates whether a prepared statement should be created by the current Command object before it is executed.

Datatype

Boolean

Description

If the value of the Prepared property is set to **True**, then before the first execution of a query defined by the CommandText property of the Command object, the query is compiled and saved. From then on the Execute statement will refer to the compiled version of the query to perform. This may slow the initial call to Execute, but all calls that follow will benefit from this.

If the value of the Prepared property is set to **False**, then the query is never compiled; instead the query is done directly from the Command object.

Note

Not all providers support the Prepared property. Some providers raise an error as soon as the Prepared property is set to **True**, while others do not raise an error and simply replace the Prepared property's value with **False**.

Command.Properties Collection

Set *properties* = *command*.Properties

The Properties property returns a Properties Collection class that contains characteristics specific to the Command object for the currently used provider.

Datatype

Properties (Collection object)

Applies To

Command object

Description

The Properties collection class contains a Property class instance for each property specific to the Command object for the data provider.

The Properties collection of the Command object is not populated until the ActiveConnection property of the Command object has been set to an open Connection object or a valid connection string value.

See Also

Command.ActiveConnection Property

Command.State Property

state = *command*.State

The Status property is used to determine the status of the current record when using batch updates or bulk operations.

Datatype

RecordStatusEnum

Description

The Type property is used to check the changes that are pending for records that have changed during a batch update. In addition, you can check the status of records that have failed during bulk operations such as what might happen with a call to the Delete, Resync, UpdateBatch, or CancelBatch methods or when a Filter property is set to an array of bookmarks.

The Type property returns a sum of one or more of the RecordStatusEnum enumerations, listed in Appendix E, *Enumeration Tables*.

See Also

Recordset.CancelBatch, Recordset.Delete Method, Recordset.Filter Property, Recordset. Resync Method, Recordset.UpdateBatch, RecordStatusEnum Enumeration, ObjectStateEnum Enumeration

Connection Object   (Versions 2.0, 2.1, 2.5, 2.6)

Dim *connection* As ADODB.Connection

A Connection object represents a unique connection to a data source. Connection objects are independent of all other ADO objects.

Collections

Errors

> The Errors collection is a collection of individual errors and warnings that have occurred for the last operation on the current Connection object.

Properties

> The Properties collection contains characteristics specific to the Connection object for the currently used provider.

Methods

BeginTrans

> Manages transaction processing for the current Connection object by starting a transaction.

Cancel

> Cancels the pending asynchronous connection or execution.

Close

> Closes either a Connection or Recordset object, including any dependent objects that they may have.

CommitTrans

> Manages transaction processing for the current Connection object by committing a transaction.

Execute

> Executes a specified SQL statement, query, stored procedure, URL, or provider-specific command against the data source.

Open

> For the Connection object, opens a connection to a particular data source. For the Recordset object, opens a cursor.

OpenSchema

> Returns a Recordset object containing information about the data source's schema.

RollbackTrans

> Manages transaction processing for the current Connection object by rolling back a transaction.

Properties

Attributes

> Sets or returns specific characteristics about the Connection object.

CommandTimeout

> Indicates how long ADO waits before it generates an error when executing a particular command.

ConnectionString

Defines the connection used to access a data source.

ConnectionTimeout

Indicates how long in seconds ADO will wait while attempting a connection to a data source.

CursorLocation

Indicates the location of the cursor service.

DefaultDatabase

Indicates the database that is chosen as the default for the current connection.

IsolationLevel

Sets the level of isolation used when utilizing transaction management.

Mode

Identifies the available permissions for modifying data within the specified connection.

Provider

Indicates the name of the data provider for the current Connection object.

State

Indicates the current status of a Command, Connection, Record, Recordset, or Stream object.

Version

Indicates the current version of ActiveX Data Objects that is being used.

Events

BeginTransComplete

Raised after the BeginTrans method has completed its operation.

CommitTransComplete

Raised after the CommitTrans method completes its operation.

ConnectComplete

Raised once a connection has been made.

Disconnect

Raised once a connection has ended.

ExecuteComplete

Called when the execution of a command has completed.

InfoMessage

Called when a warning is produced during a ConnectionEvent operation.

RollbackTransComplete

Raised after the RollbackTrans method has completed its operation.

WillConnect

Raised before a connection is made.

WillExecute

Raised before an execution of a command has begun.

Description

A Connection object can execute commands on its own or with the use of an associated Command object. In addition, Connection objects are used to manage transaction locking, view ADO errors, and inspect the schema of a data source.

The Connection is one of the two ADO objects that support events at this time. By responding to the Connection events, your application can be notified when transactions are being used, when connections are made and lost, and when commands are executed.

Examples

In this section, we will be looking at four examples that will show us how to:

- Establish an asynchronous connection to a data source.

- Manage transactions with the Connection object.

- Issue SQL statements without the use of a Command object.

- Inspect the schema of a data source.

Before we take a look at these examples that use the Connection object, let's first add some code to show us when our Connection events are fired. With this code, we can see how events are reported as we look at the upcoming examples in this section.

For all examples, add a new Class to your current project and declare the Connection object WithEvents as shown:

```
Private WithEvents con As ADODB.Connection
```

Now, you should be able to see the con variable in the first combo box in the code pane. Selecting this object, you will be given a choice of nine events that can be fired for your Connection object. For each event, we are going to add code to output the parameters passed to that event to the Immediate Window.

Add the following code for the nine events to the new Class:

```
Private Sub con_BeginTransComplete(ByVal TransactionLevel As Long, _
                        ByVal pError As ADODB.Error, _
                        adStatus As ADODB.EventStatusEnum, _
                        ByVal pConnection As ADODB.Connection)


    Debug.Print "Event: BeginTransComplete"
    Debug.Print "  TransLevel: " & TransactionLevel
    Debug.Print "  Status:     " & GetStatusString(adStatus)
    Debug.Print "  Connection: " & pConnection.ConnectionString
    Debug.Print

End Sub

Private Sub con_CommitTransComplete(ByVal pError As ADODB.Error, _
                        adStatus As ADODB.EventStatusEnum, _
                        ByVal pConnection As ADODB.Connection)


    Debug.Print "Event: CommitTransComplete"
    Debug.Print "  Status:     " & GetStatusString(adStatus)
    Debug.Print "  Connection: " & pConnection.ConnectionString
    Debug.Print
```

```
    End Sub

    Private Sub con_ConnectComplete(ByVal pError As ADODB.Error, _
                        adStatus As ADODB.EventStatusEnum, _
                        ByVal pConnection As ADODB.Connection)

        Debug.Print "Event: ConnectComplete"
        Debug.Print "  Status:     " & GetStatusString(adStatus)
        Debug.Print "  Connection: " & pConnection.ConnectionString
        Debug.Print

    End Sub

    Private Sub con_Disconnect(adStatus As ADODB.EventStatusEnum, _
                        ByVal pConnection As ADODB.Connection)

        Debug.Print "Event: Disconnect"
        Debug.Print "  Status:     " & GetStatusString(adStatus)
        Debug.Print "  Connection: " & pConnection.ConnectionString
        Debug.Print

    End Sub

    Private Sub con_ExecuteComplete(ByVal RecordsAffected As Long, _
                        ByVal pError As ADODB.Error, _
                        adStatus As ADODB.EventStatusEnum, _
                        ByVal pCommand As ADODB.Command, _
                        ByVal pRecordset As ADODB.Recordset, _
                        ByVal pConnection As ADODB.Connection)

        Debug.Print "Event: ExecuteComplete"
        Debug.Print "  RecordsAff: " & RecordsAffected
        Debug.Print "  Status:     " & GetStatusString(adStatus)
        Debug.Print "  Command:    " & pCommand.CommandText
        Debug.Print "  Recordset:  " & pRecordset.Source
        Debug.Print "  Connection: " & pConnection.ConnectionString
        Debug.Print

    End Sub

    Private Sub con_InfoMessage(ByVal pError As ADODB.Error, _
                        adStatus As ADODB.EventStatusEnum, _
                        ByVal pConnection As ADODB.Connection)

        Debug.Print "Event: InfoMessage"
        Debug.Print "  Error:      " & pError.Description
        Debug.Print "  Status:     " & GetStatusString(adStatus)
        Debug.Print "  Connection: " & pConnection.ConnectionString
        Debug.Print

    End Sub

    Private Sub con_RollbackTransComplete(ByVal pError As ADODB.Error, _
                        adStatus As ADODB.EventStatusEnum, _
                        ByVal pConnection As ADODB.Connection)
```

```
        Debug.Print "Event: RollbackTransComplete"
        Debug.Print "  Status:      " & GetStatusString(adStatus)
        Debug.Print "  Connection: " & pConnection.ConnectionString
        Debug.Print

    End Sub

    Private Sub con_WillConnect(ConnectionString As String, _
                                UserID As String, _
                                Password As String, _
                                Options As Long, _
                                adStatus As ADODB.EventStatusEnum, _
                                ByVal pConnection As ADODB.Connection)

        Debug.Print "Event: WillConnect"
        Debug.Print "  UserID:      " & UserID
        Debug.Print "  Password:    " & Password
        Debug.Print "  Options:     " & Options
        Debug.Print "  Status:      " & GetStatusString(adStatus)
        Debug.Print "  Connection: " & pConnection.ConnectionString
        Debug.Print

    End Sub

    Private Sub con_WillExecute(Source As String, _
                                CursorType As ADODB.CursorTypeEnum, _
                                LockType As ADODB.LockTypeEnum, _
                                Options As Long, _
                                adStatus As ADODB.EventStatusEnum, _
                                ByVal pCommand As ADODB.Command, _
                                ByVal pRecordset As ADODB.Recordset, _
                                ByVal pConnection As ADODB.Connection)

        Debug.Print "Event: WillExecute"
        Debug.Print "  CursorType: " & CursorType
        Debug.Print "  LockType:   " & LockType
        Debug.Print "  Options:    " & Options
        Debug.Print "  Status:      " & GetStatusString(adStatus)
        If (Not (pCommand Is Nothing)) Then
            Debug.Print "  Command:    " & pCommand.CommandText
        End If
        If (Not (pRecordset Is Nothing)) Then
            Debug.Print "  Recordset: " & pRecordset.Source
        End If
        Debug.Print "  Connection: " & pConnection.ConnectionString
        Debug.Print

    End Sub
```

The only other code that you will need for the following examples is the code for the GetStatusString function, which accepts an EventStatusEnum value and returns a String describing the enumeration value:

```
        Private Function GetStatusString(adStatus As ADODB.EventStatusEnum) _
                                                    As String

            Select Case (adStatus)

                Case ADODB.EventStatusEnum.adStatusCancel:
                    GetStatusString = "Cancel"

                Case ADODB.EventStatusEnum.adStatusCantDeny:
                    GetStatusString = "Can't Deny"

                Case ADODB.EventStatusEnum.adStatusErrorsOccurred
                    GetStatusString = "Errors Occurred"

                Case ADODB.EventStatusEnum.adStatusOK:
                    GetStatusString = "Status Okay"

                Case ADODB.EventStatusEnum.adStatusUnwantedEvent:
                    GetStatusString = "Unwanted Event"

            End Select

        End Function
```

Example 13-4 illustrates how we can establish a connection to a data source, asynchronously, by adding the **adAsyncExecute** enumeration value to the Open method of the Connection object.

Example 13-4. Establishing an Asynchronous Connection

```
' instantiate a new Connection object
'
Set con = New ADODB.Connection

'
' open the Biblio database with Jet as read/write enabled
'

con.Mode = adModeReadWrite

con.Provider = "Microsoft.Jet.OLEDB.4.0"

con.Open "C:\Program Files\Microsoft Visual Studio\VB98\Biblio.mdb", _
        ' _
        ' _
        ADODB.ExecuteOptionEnum.adAsyncExecute

While (con.State <> ADODB.ObjectStateEnum.adStateOpen)
    '
    ' do something while the connection is being opened
    '
Wend

'
```

Example 13-4. Establishing an Asynchronous Connection (continued)

```
' do something with the connection object _

'


'
' close and clean up
'
con.Close


Set con = Nothing
```

Notice that all the examples for the Connection object do not declare their own **con** variable—rather, they simply instantiate the module-level variable that has already been declared so that we can trap the events for that object. Example 13-4 sends the following output to the Immediate Window:

```
Event: WillConnect
  UserID:
  Password:
  Options:    16
  Status:     Status Okay
  Connection: C:\Program Files\Microsoft Visual Studio\VB98\Biblio.mdb


Event: ConnectComplete
  Status:     Status Okay
  Connection: Provider=Microsoft.Jet...... ir=False;Jet OLEDB:SFP=False


Event: Disconnect
  Status:     Status Okay
  Connection: C:\Program Files\Microsoft Visual Studio\VB98\Biblio.mdb
```

I'm sure that you will notice that the connection string for the **ConnectComplete** event has been shorted to save trees.

Example 13-5 shows how transactions are used and managed with the Connection object.

Example 13-5. Managing Transactions with the Connection Object

```
Dim sCon As String

'
' instantiate and open a new Connection object
'
Set con = New ADODB.Connection


sCon = "Provider=Microsoft.Jet.OLEDB.4.0; " _
    & "Data Source=C:\Program Files\Microsoft " _
    & "Visual Studio\VB98\Biblio.mdb; "


con.Open sCon

'
' begin the first level of the transaction
'
```

Example 13-5. Managing Transactions with the Connection Object (continued)

```
con.BeginTrans

    '
    ' begin the second level of the transaction
    '
    con.BeginTrans

        '
        ' begin the third level of the transaction
        '
        con.BeginTrans

        '
        ' commit the third level of the transaction
        '
        con.CommitTrans

    '
    ' rollback the second level of the transaction
    '
    con.RollbackTrans

'
' commit the third level of the transaction
'
con.CommitTrans

'
' close and clean up
'
con.Close

Set con = Nothing
```

This example uses three levels of transactions, as we can see from the Immediate Window's tell-tale account:

```
Event: WillConnect
  UserID:
  Password:
  Options:    -1
  Status:     Status Okay
  Connection: Provider=Microsoft.Jet.OLEDB.4.0; Data Source=C:\Program Files\
Microsoft Visual Studio\VB98\Biblio.mdb;

Event: ConnectComplete
  Status:     Status Okay
  Connection: Provider=Microsoft.Jet...... ir=False;Jet OLEDB:SFP=False

Event: BeginTransComplete
  TransLevel: 1
  Status:     Status Okay
  Connection: Provider=Microsoft.Jet...... ir=False;Jet OLEDB:SFP=False
```

```
Event: BeginTransComplete
  TransLevel: 2
  Status:      Status Okay
  Connection: Provider=Microsoft.Jet...... ir=False;Jet OLEDB:SFP=False

Event: BeginTransComplete
  TransLevel: 3
  Status:      Status Okay
  Connection: Provider=Microsoft.Jet...... ir=False;Jet OLEDB:SFP=False

Event: CommitTransComplete
  Status:      Status Okay
  Connection: Provider=Microsoft.Jet...... ir=False;Jet OLEDB:SFP=False

Event: RollbackTransComplete
  Status:      Status Okay
  Connection: Provider=Microsoft.Jet...... ir=False;Jet OLEDB:SFP=False

Event: CommitTransComplete
  Status:      Status Okay
  Connection: Provider=Microsoft.Jet...... ir=False;Jet OLEDB:SFP=False

Event: Disconnect
  Status:      Status Okay
  Connection: Provider=Microsoft.Jet.OLEDB.4.0; Data Source=C:\Program Files\
Microsoft Visual Studio\VB98\Biblio.mdb;
```

Although the connection strings for the transaction events have been shortened, you might notice that the connection events WillConnect and Disconnect used the original connection string that was used with the Connection object. The other events used a modified String that contained much more detail about the connection once it was made.

Example 13-6 shows how the Connection object can be used to issue SQL statements without the use of a Command object.

Example 13-6. Issuing SQL Statements Without the Use of a Command Object

```
Dim sCon As String

Dim com As ADODB.Command
Dim rst As ADODB.Recordset

'
' instantiate and open a new Connection object
'
Set con = New ADODB.Connection

sCon = "Provider=Microsoft.Jet.OLEDB.4.0; " _
    & "Data Source=C:\Program Files\Microsoft " _
    & "Visual Studio\VB98\Biblio.mdb; "

con.Open sCon

'
```

Example 13-6. Issuing SQL Statements Without the Use of a Command Object (continued)

```
' execute a SQL statement without a Command object
'
con.CommandTimeout = 3
Set rst = con.Execute("SELECT * FROM Authors;")


' the Recordset object now contains the results from the Command
'
MsgBox "The first author in the recordset is: " & rst("Author")


' close and clean up
'
rst.Close
con.Close

Set rst = Nothing
Set con = Nothing
```

Events fired by our Connection object cause the following message to be printed:

```
    Event: WillConnect
      UserID:
      Password:
      Options:    -1
      Status:     Status Okay
      Connection: Provider=Microsoft.Jet.OLEDB.4.0; Data Source=C:\Program Files\
    Microsoft Visual Studio\VB98\Biblio.mdb;

    Event: ConnectComplete
      Status:     Status Okay
      Connection: Provider=Microsoft.Jet...... ir=False;Jet OLEDB:SFP=False

    Event: WillExecute
      CursorType: -1
      LockType:   -1
      Options:    -1
      Status:     Status Okay
      Connection: Provider=Microsoft.Jet...... ir=False;Jet OLEDB:SFP=False

    Event: ExecuteComplete
      RecordsAff: 0
      Status:     Status Okay
      Command:    SELECT * FROM Authors;
      Recordset:  SELECT * FROM Authors;
      Connection: Provider=Microsoft.Jet...... ir=False;Jet OLEDB:SFP=False

    Event: Disconnect
      Status:     Status Okay
      Connection: Provider=Microsoft.Jet.OLEDB.4.0; Data Source=C:\Program Files\
    Microsoft Visual Studio\VB98\Biblio.mdb;
```

Example 13-7, our final example for the Connection object, illustrates how we can inspect the schema of a data source with the Connection object and display its tables. Notice that the Connection object is being used to check the version of ADO in use.

Example 13-7. Inspecting a Data Source's Schema

```
Dim sCon As String
Dim sTables As String

Dim com As ADODB.Command
Dim rst As ADODB.Recordset
Dim fld As ADODB.Field

'
' instantiate and open a new Connection object
'
Set con = New ADODB.Connection

sCon = "Provider=Microsoft.Jet.OLEDB.4.0; " _
    & "Data Source=C:\Program Files\Microsoft " _
    & "Visual Studio\VB98\Biblio.mdb; "

con.Open sCon

'
' display the ADO version
'
MsgBox "ADO Version " & CStr(con.Version)

'
' open the schema for the database tables which is returned as a
'   Recordset
'
Set rst = con.OpenSchema(adSchemaTables)

'
' record the field names and values
'
If (Not (rst.BOF And rst.EOF)) Then rst.MoveFirst

For Each fld In rst.Fields
    sTables = sTables & Left$(fld.Name & Space(20), 20) & vbTab
Next fld

sTables = sTables & vbCr

While (Not rst.EOF)

    For Each fld In rst.Fields
        sTables = sTables & Left$((fld.Value & "") & Space(20), 20)
        sTables = sTables & vbTab
    Next fld

    sTables = sTables & vbCr
```

Example 13-7. Inspecting a Data Source's Schema (continued)

```
    rst.MoveNext

Wend

'
' display the table information
'
Debug.Print sTables

'
' close and clean up
'
rst.Close
con.Close

Set rst = Nothing
Set con = Nothing
```

Now, we have output from both the events and the schema data. Because the amount of schema data returned in this example is tremendous, we kept only a couple of columns for readability:

```
Event: WillConnect
  UserID:
  Password:
  Options:     -1
  Status:      Status Okay
  Connection: Provider=Microsoft.Jet.OLEDB.4.0; Data Source=C:\Program Files\
Microsoft Visual Studio\VB98\Biblio.mdb;

Event: ConnectComplete
  Status:      Status Okay
  Connection: Provider=Microsoft.Jet...... ir=False;Jet OLEDB:SFP=False
```

TABLE_NAME	TABLE_TYPE
All Titles	VIEW
Authors	TABLE
MSysACEs	SYSTEM TABLE
MSysIMEXColumns	ACCESS TABLE
MSysIMEXSpecs	ACCESS TABLE
MSysModules	ACCESS TABLE
MSysModules2	ACCESS TABLE
MSysObjects	SYSTEM TABLE
MSysQueries	SYSTEM TABLE
MSysRelationships	SYSTEM TABLE
Publishers	TABLE
Title Author	TABLE
Titles	TABLE

```
Event: Disconnect
  Status:      Status Okay
  Connection: Provider=Microsoft.Jet.OLEDB.4.0; Data Source=C:\Program Files\
Microsoft Visual Studio\VB98\Biblio.mdb;
```

Connection.Attributes Property   (Versions 2.0, 2.1, 2.5, 2.6)

Connection.Attributes = XactArgumentsEnum [+ XactArgumentsEnum...]

The Attributes property is used to set or return specific characteristics about the Connection object.

Datatype

XactArgumentsEnum (Long)

Description

The Attributes property is read- and write-enabled. The value of the Attributes property can be set to any sum of the XactArgumentsEnum enumeration values, listed in Appendix E.

The default value of the Attributes property is zero.

Note

Not all providers support the functionality of the Attributes property.

See Also

Connection.BeginTrans Method, Connection.CommitTrans Method, Connection.RollBack-Trans Method, XactAttributeEnum Enumeration

---

Connection.BeginTrans Method   (Versions 2.0, 2.1, 2.5, 2.6)

Connection.CommitTrans Method   (Versions 2.0, 2.1, 2.5, 2.6)

Connection.RollbackTrans Method   (Versions 2.0, 2.1, 2.5, 2.6)

connection.BeginTrans
level = connection.BeginTrans()
connection.CommitTrans
connection.RollbackTrans

The BeginTrans, CommitTrans, and RollbackTrans methods are used to manage transaction processing for the current Connection object.

The BeginTrans method begins a transaction, as you might expect.

The CommitTrans method ends the current transaction, while first saving any changes and then possibly starting another transaction altogether.

The RollbackTrans method ends the current transaction, but rolls back any changes made during the current transaction. In addition, the RollbackTrans method can start another transaction, just as the CommitTrans method can.

Description

The BeginTrans, CommitTrans, and RollbackTrans methods of the Connection object perform transaction management within a particular connection. The most common example of a need for transaction management is a banking system. When you transfer money from one account to another, it is important that the two steps involved (a withdraw followed by a deposit) occur as a single transaction. By using these three transaction-management methods, we can ensure that both or none (but not either alone) of the bank steps are performed. If there is a problem with the deposit after the withdraw has completed, we can in effect roll back time with the RollbackTrans method.

. The BeginTrans method begins a new transaction within the current Connection object. By using the BeginTrans method, you can create nested transactions much like you can create nested If . . . Then statements in your code. A return value can be received from the Begin-Trans method in the form of a Long, if the data provider supports nested transactions. This return value indicates the level of the nested transaction that was created, one being the first.

The CommitTrans method commits any changes since the beginning of the last transaction. While the RollbackTrans method performs the opposite, it cancels any changes made to the last transaction. In both cases, the last transaction is ended. In addition, the last transaction created must end before either the CommitTrans or RollbackTrans methods can end an earlier transaction.

If the Arguments property of the Connection object is set to `adXactCommitRetaining`, a new transaction is automatically created after a CommitTrans method call. If this property is set to `adXactAbortRetaining`, a new transaction is created automatically after a Rollback-Trans method call.

See Also

Connection.Arguments Property

Connection.BeginTransComplete Event   (Versions 2.0, 2.1, 2.5, 2.6)

```
Private Sub BeginTransComplete(ByVal TransactionLevel As Long, _
                    ByVal pError As ADODB.Error, _
                    adStatus As ADODB.EventStatusEnum, _
                    ByVal pConnection As ADODB.Connection)
```

The BeginTransComplete event is raised after the BeginTrans method has completed its operation.

Arguments

TransactionLevel
> A Long value indicating the nesting level of the new transaction.

pError
> An Error object containing details about an error that occurred if the *adStatus* parameter is set to `adStatusErrorsOccurred`.

adStatus
> An EventStatusEnum value indicating the status of the current operation. If the *adStatus* parameter is set to `adStatusOK`, the operation was successful. If the *adStatus* parameter is set to `adStatusErrorsOccurred`, the operation failed, and the *pError* object contains the details regarding the error. By setting the *adStatus* parameter to `adStatusUnwantedEvent`, this event will not be called again.

pConnection
> The Connection object that fired this event.

See Also

Connection.BeginTrans Method, Connection.CommitTransComplete Event, Connection.Roll-backTransComplete Event, EventStatusEnum Enumeration

Connection.Cancel Method   (Versions 2.0, 2.1, 2.5, 2.6)

connection.Cancel

The Cancel method cancels the pending asynchronous connection or execution.

Description

If the Execute or Open methods of a Connection object where called with the adAsyncConnect, adAsyncExecute, or adAsyncFetch options, the Cancel method will cancel the pending asynchronous operation.

If the Cancel method is called for an operation that was not executed with the adAsyncExecute option set, an error will occur.

See Also

Connection.Execute Method, Connection.Open Method

Connection.Close Method   (Versions 2.0, 2.1, 2.5, 2.6)

connection.Close

The Close method is used to close either a Connection or Recordset object, including any dependent objects that they may have.

Description

The Close method terminates a connection with a data source. After a Connection object is closed, properties can be adjusted, and the object can be opened again. Calling methods that require a connection while the Connection object is closed generates an error.

Closing a Connection object that one or more Recordset objects were created from causes those Recordset objects to close as well. All pending changes are lost. If there is a pending transaction, an error occurs.

Closing a Connection object does not remove it from memory, it only frees the resources that it is using. To remove the Connection object from memory in Visual Basic, set it to Nothing.

Connection.CommandTimeout Property   (Versions 2.0, 2.1, 2.5, 2.6)

connection.CommandTimeout = *timeout*

The CommandTimeout property indicates how long ADO waits before it generates an error when executing a particular command.

Datatype

Long

Description

The CommandTimeout property is read- and write-enabled. By using the Command-Timeout property, you can specify how long ADO will wait for a command to execute. The setting for the CommandTimeout property is represented in seconds, and the default value is 30. By setting this property to zero, you are allowing ADO to wait indefinitely for a specified command to execute. If a command does time out, an error will be generated.

The CommandTimeout property of the Command object is unrelated to the Command-Timeout property of the Connection object.

The Connection object's CommandTimeout is read- and write-enabled even when the Connection object is open.

Note

Not all providers support the CommandTimeout property.

Connection.CommitTrans Method   (Versions 2.0, 2.1, 2.5, 2.6)

See the Connection.BeginTrans Method.

Connection.CommitTransComplete Event   (Versions 2.0, 2.1, 2.5, 2.6)

```
Private Sub CommitTransComplete(ByVal pError As ADODB.Error, _
                                adStatus As ADODB.EventStatusEnum, _
                                ByVal pConnection As ADODB.Connection)
```

The CommitTransComplete event is raised after the CommitTrans method completes its operation.

Arguments

pError
> An Error object containing details about an error that occurred if the *adStatus* parameter is set to adStatusErrorsOccurred.

adStatus
> An EventStatusEnum value indicating the status of the current operation. If the *adStatus* parameter is set to adStatusOK, the operation was successful. If the *adStatus* parameter is set to adStatusErrorsOccurred, the operation failed, and the *pError* object contains the details regarding the error. By setting the *adStatus* parameter to adStatusUnwantedEvent, this event will not be called again.

pConnection
> The Connection object that fired this event.

See Also

Connection.BeginTransComplete Event, Connection.CommitTrans Method, Connection.RollbackTransComplete Event, EventStatusEnum Enumeration

Connection.ConnectComplete Event   (Versions 2.0, 2.1, 2.5, 2.6)

```
Private Sub ConnectComplete(ByVal pError As ADODB.Error, _
                            adStatus As ADODB.EventStatusEnum, _
                            ByVal pConnection As ADODB.Connection)
```

The ConnectComplete event is raised once a connection has been made.

Arguments

pError
> An Error object containing details about an error that occurred if the *adStatus* parameter is set to adStatusErrorsOccurred.

adStatus
> An EventStatusEnum value indicating the status of the current operation. If the *adStatus* parameter is set to adStatusOK, the operation was successful. If the *adStatus* parameter is set to adStatusErrorsOccurred, the operation failed, and the *pError* object contains the details regarding the error. If the *adStatus* parameter is set to adStatusUnwantedEvent, this event will not be called again.

pConnection
> The Connection object that fired this event.

See Also

Connection.Disconnect Event, Connection.WillConnect Event, ConnectOptionEnum Enumeration, EventStatusEnum Enumeration

Connection.ConnectionString Property   (Versions 2.0, 2.1, 2.5, 2.6)

```
connection.ConnectionString = connectionstring
```

The ConnectionString property defines the connection used to access a data source.

Datatype

String

Description

The ConnectionString property indicates the data source to be used by your connection. You may pass either a DSN (data source name) or a detailed connection string, which is a list of arguments. The arguments must be in the form of *argument=value*, with multiple arguments separated by a semicolon. If ADO finds an equal sign in the ConnectionString property, it assumes that you are passing a detailed connection string.

Arguments

The three supported arguments are listed next. If you pass additional arguments, they are passed directly to the data provider and are not checked by ADO:

Provider
> Specifies the name of the data provider to use for the particular connection.

`Filename`

Specifies the name of a data provider–specific file containing connection information. This argument cannot be used with the `Provider` argument.

URL

Identifies the absolute URL of a file or directory.

The contents of the ConnectionString property can be altered by ADO at any time after opening the Connection object, so read the property if you are unsure of its contents.

If the ConnectionString argument was used in the Open method of the Connection object, the value is placed within the ConnectionString property of the Connection object.

While the Connection object is open, the ConnectionString is read-only, but when it is closed, it is both read- and write-enabled.

See Also

Connection.Open Method

Connection.ConnectionTimeout Property   (Versions 2.0, 2.1, 2.5, 2.6)

`connection.ConnectionTimeout = timeout`

The ConnectionTimeout property indicates how long in seconds ADO will wait while attempting a connection to a data source.

Datatype

Long

Description

By using the ConnectionTimeout property, you can specify how long ADO will wait for a connection to a data source. The setting for the ConnectionTimeout property is represented in seconds. By setting this property to zero, you are allowing ADO to wait indefinitely for a specified connection. If the connection does time out, an error is generated.

The ConnectionTimeout property is read- and write-enabled while the Connection object is closed, but read-only once it is opened.

Note

Not all providers support the ConnectionTimeout property.

See Also

Connection.Open Method

Connection.CursorLocation Property   (Versions 2.0, 2.1, 2.5, 2.6)

`connection.CursorLocation = CursorLocationEnum`

The CursorLocation property indicates the location of the cursor service.

Datatype

CursorLocationEnum (Long)

Description

The value of the CursorLocation property can be set to one of the valid Cursor-LocationEnum values, listed in Appendix E.

The value of the CursorLocation property is both read- and write-enabled. However, changing the value of this property affects only Connections that are opened after the value has changed.

See Also

Connection.Open Method

Connection.DefaultDatabase Property   (Versions 2.0, 2.1, 2.5, 2.6)

connection.DefaultDatabase = *database*

The DefaultDatabase property indicates the database that is chosen as the default for the current connection.

Datatype

String

Description

The DefaultDatabase property allows the application to specify which database is the default for a Connection object.

Unqualified syntax automatically refers to the database specified by the DefaultDatabase property. Qualifying the object names with the desired database name must be done to access all other databases.

Note

Not all providers support the DefaultDatabase property. If they do not, they may raise an error or return an empty String value.

Connection.Disconnect Event   (Versions 2.0, 2.1, 2.5, 2.6)

```
Private Sub Disconnect(adStatus As ADODB.EventStatusEnum, _
                   ByVal pConnection As ADODB.Connection)
```

The Disconnect event is raised once a connection has ended.

Arguments

adStatus

> An EventStatusEnum value indicating the status of the current operation. The *adStatus* parameter is always set to adStatusOK when the event is fired. Setting the *adStatus* parameter to adStatusUnwantedEvent before leaving the event code means that this event will not be called again.

`pConnection`
> The Connection object that fired this event.

See Also

Connection.ConnectComplete Event, EventStatusEnum Enumeration

---

Connection.Errors Collection   (Versions 2.0, 2.1, 2.5, 2.6)

`Set errors = connection.Errors`

The Errors collection is a collection of individual errors and warnings that have occurred for the last operation on the current Connection object.

Datatype

Errors (Collection Object)

Description

The Errors property of the Connection object is read-only. It returns a reference to the Errors collection object that can contain zero or many Error objects that indicate ADO or provider-specific errors.

Connection.Execute Method   (Versions 2.0, 2.1, 2.5, 2.6)

`connection.Execute CommandText, RecordsAffected, Options`
`Set recordset = connection.Execute(CommandText, RecordsAffected, Options)`

The Execute method is used to execute a specified SQL statement, query, stored procedure, URL, or provider-specific command against the data source.

Arguments

`CommandText (String)`
> Optional. Contains the SQL statement, query, stored procedure, URL, or provider-specific command to be executed. The parameter is similar to the Command.CommandText property.

`RecordsAffected (Long)`
> Optional. Contains the number of records that the executed command affected.

`Options (Long)`
> Optional. Represents a combination of one or more CommandTypeEnum and ExecuteOptionEnum values indicating how the data provider should treat the command. The default value is −1 (no options set).

> The CommandTypeEnum and ExecuteOptionEnum enumeration values are listed in Appendix E.

Returns

RecordsetObject

Description

The Execute method executes the command specified by the CommandText parameter, which in turn is evaluated based upon the Options parameter. When the execution of the command is complete, the Connection.ExecuteComplete event is raised.

If the execution of the command returns records, a new Recordset object is returned from the Execute method. If the execution of the command does not return records, an empty Recordset object is returned from the Execute method. Regardless, the Recordset returned is always read-only with a forward-only cursor.

When the Execute method's Options parameter includes one of the **adAsyncExecute**, **adAsyncFetch**, or **adAsyncFetchNonBlocking** values, operations continue in the background of the application flow. While these operations are continuing, the Connection. Cancel method can be called to cancel all pending asynchronous operations.

Note

Although the documentation for ADO 2.6 (beta 2) has specified that the CommandText arguments and property can be set to a relative URL, I have found that whatever you set this value to, it is irrelevant. If you wish to obtain the contents of a directory, you must specify the directory in the ConnectionString property. No matter what you specify as the CommandText arguments of the Execute method or the CommandText property of the Connection object, it is ignored. However, if you use an empty String ("") as a value, you will receive the error "Errors Occurred."

The following example illustrates how the CommandText property value is irrelevant when calling the Execute method:

```
Dim con As ADODB.Connection
Dim rec As ADODB.Recordset

Set con = New ADODB.Connection

con.Open "URL=http://jroff_laptop/"

Set rec = con.Execute("nothing really matters")

'
' rec contains contents of jroff_laptop
'

rec.Close
con.Close

Set rec = Nothing
Set con = Nothing
```

See Also

Connection.Cancel Method, Command.CommandText Property, Connection.ExecuteComplete Event, CommandTypeEnum Enumeration, ExecuteOptionEnum Enumeration

Connection.ExecuteComplete Event   (Versions 2.0, 2.1, 2.5, 2.6)

```
Private Sub con_ExecuteComplete(ByVal RecordsAffected As Long, _
                                ByVal pError As ADODB.Error, _
                                adStatus As ADODB.EventStatusEnum, _
                                ByVal pCommand As ADODB.Command, _
                                ByVal pRecordset As ADODB.Recordset, _
                                ByVal pConnection As ADODB.Connection)
```

The ExecuteComplete event is called when the execution of a command has completed.

Arguments

RecordsAffected (Long)
> Indicates how many records are affected by the executed command.

pError (Error)
> Contains details about an error that occurred if the *adStatus* parameter is set to
> adStatusErrorsOccurred.

adStatus (EventStatusEnum)
> Indicates the status of the current operation. If the *adStatus* parameter is set to
> adStatusOK, the operation was successful. If the *adStatus* parameter is set to
> adStatusErrorsOccurred, the operation failed, and the *pError* object contains the
> details regarding the error. If the *adStatus* parameter is set to
> adStatusUnwantedEvent, this event will not be called again.

pCommand
> Represents the Command object that was executed (if there was one).

pRecordset
> Represents the Recordset object that results from the commands execution. This
> Recordset object can be empty.

pConnection
> Represents the Connection object that fired this event.

See Also

Connection.Execute Method, Command.Execute Method, Recordset.NextRecordset Method,
Recordset.Open Method, EventStatusEnum Enumeration

Connection.InfoMessage Event   (Versions 2.0, 2.1, 2.5, 2.6)

```
Private Sub InfoMessage(ByVal pError As ADODB.Error, _
                        adStatus As ADODB.EventStatusEnum, _
                        ByVal pConnection As ADODB.Connection)
```

The InfoMessage event is called when a warning is produced during a ConnectionEvent
operation.

Arguments

pError
> An Error object containing details about an error that occurred if the *adStatus* param-
> eter is set to adStatusErrorsOccurred.

adStatus

> An EventStatusEnum value indicating the status of the current operation. If the *adStatus* parameter is set to *adStatusOK*, the operation was successful. If the *adStatus* parameter is set to *adStatusErrorsOccurred*, the operation failed, and the *pError* object contains the details regarding the error. If the *adStatus* parameter is set to *adStatusUnwantedEvent*, this event will not be called again.

pRecordset

> The Recordset object that fired this event.

See Also

EventStatusEnum Enumeration

Connection.IsolationLevel Property   (Versions 2.0, 2.1, 2.5, 2.6)

connection.IsolationLevel = IsolationLevelEnum

The IsolationLevel property is used to set the level of isolation used when utilizing transaction management.

Datatype

IsolationLevelEnum (Long)

Description

The IsolationLevel property is both read- and write-enabled. If the value of this property is changed, the effects will not take place until you call the BeginTrans method. If the level of isolation requested couldn't be granted by the data provider, then the next level may be set automatically.

The IsolationLevel property can be set to one of the IsolationLevelEnum enumerations listed in Appendix E.

See Also

Connection.BeginTrans Method, IsolationLevelEnum Enumeration

Connection.Mode Property   (Versions 2.0, 2.1, 2.5, 2.6)

connection.Mode = ConnectModeEnum

The Mode property identifies the available permissions for modifying data within the specified connection.

Datatype

ConnectModeEnum (Long)

Description

The Mode property is read- and write-enabled while the Connection object is closed, but read-only once it is opened.

The Mode property can be set to one of the ConnectModeEnum enumerations listed in Appendix E.

Connection.Open Method (Versions 2.0, 2.1, 2.5, 2.6)

`connection.Open ConnectionString, UserID, Password, Options`

The Open method for the Connection object opens a connection to a particular data source. The Open method for the Recordset object opens a cursor.

Arguments

ConnectionString (String)
> Optional. Contains the information needed for ADO to connect to the data provider. This property is mapped to the Connection.ConnectionString property.

UserID (String)
> Optional. Contains a username that is used to establish the desired connection.

Password (String)
> Optional. Contains a password that is used to establish the desired connection.

Options (Long)
> Optional. Represents a ConnectOptionEnum enumeration value. Currently, the only defined value for the ConnectOptionEnum enumeration is **adAsyncConnect** (16) which instructs ADO to connect to the data source asynchronously. The default value is –1 (no options set).

Description

The Open method establishes a connection with a data provider. Once a connection is established, you can issue commands against the data provider and obtain information from the data source.

The connection to a data provider can be established asynchronously by passing the **adConnectAsync** value to the Options parameter of the Open method. Once the operation has started, the application can call the Connection.Cancel method to cancel the pending asynchronous connection if the application has determined that the connection is taking too long.

The connection to the data provider is defined by the value of the ConnectionString parameter. In addition, the *UserName* and *Password* parameters authenticates the user within the data provider. It is possible to set the *UserName* and *Password* values in both the ConnectionString and as parameters to the Open method. In such a case, the parameters will override those specified in the ConnectionString property.

The ConnectionString parameter overwrites any value previously set to the Connection.ConnectionString property. In most cases, the ConnectionString property contains more detailed information about the connection then you would pass through the ConnectionString parameter of the Open method. You can read the ConnectionString property to see this added detail.

The ConnectionString parameter, like the ConnectionString property, is constructed of a services of *argument=value* statements separated by semicolons. The arguments that are used within the ConnectionString parameter (and property) are completely dependent upon the data provider to which you are connecting.

The Connection.Close method is used to close an opened Connection object once the application is done with it. A Connection object that is closed can be altered and reopened again. To remove the Connection object from memory in Visual Basic, set it to **Nothing**.

See Also

Connection.Cancel Method, Connection.Close Method, Connection.ConnectionString Property, ConnectModeEnum Enumeration, ConnectOptionEnum Enumeration

---

Connection.OpenSchema   (Versions 2.0, 2.1, 2.5, 2.6)

`Set recordset = ` *`connection`*`.OpenSchema(`*`Schema, Criteria, SchemaID`*`)`

The OpenSchema method returns a Recordset object containing information about the data source's schema.

Arguments

Schema (SchemaEnum)
>   Indicates the type of schema the OpenSchema method will provide in the returned Recordset object.
>
>   SchemaEnum contains the enumeration values listed in Table F-1.

Criteria (Variant Array)
>   Optional. Indicates which constraint columns to use for the Schema requested. A list of each available constraint column for each schema type is listed in Table G-1.

SchemaID (Long)
>   Optional. Represents a GUID of a provider-specific schema query. If the Schema parameter is set to **adSchemaProviderSpecific** (–1), then this parameter is mandatory; otherwise, it is not used.

Description

The OpenSchema method is used to obtain information about a data source's structure—its schema.

By setting the *Schema* parameter to a SchemaEnum value, ADO can determine which information the application is requesting. In addition, the *Criteria* parameter can be set to narrow the search. For instance, by passing the **adSchemaTables** enumeration value, the OpenSchema method will only return the table names.

Some providers may support their own schema query types. To use this feature, set the *Schema* parameter to **adSchemaProviderSpecific**, and set the *SchemaID* parameter to the GUID of the provider-specific schema query. If the *Schema* parameter is set to the **adSchemaProviderSpecific** value and the *SchemaID* parameter is not specified, an error will occur.

Not all providers will support all of the schema queries defined in Table G-1. As a matter of fact, only the adSchemaTables, adSchemaColumns, and adSchemaProviderTypes schema queries are supported by all providers. But this still does not guarantee that any of the constraint columns are supported.

See Also

SchemaEnum Enumeration

Connection.Properties Collection (Versions 2.0, 2.1, 2.5, 2.6)

`Set properties = connection.Properties`

The Properties collection contains characteristics specific to the Connection object for the currently used provider.

Datatype

Properties (Collection Object)

Description

The Properties collection class contains a Property class instance for each property specific to the Connection object for the data provider.

The Properties collection of the Connection object contains only the following properties until the Connection is opened:

- Password
- Persist Security Info
- User ID
- Data Source
- Window Handle
- Location
- Mode
- Prompt
- Connect Timeout
- Extended Properties
- Locale Identifier
- Initial Catalog
- OLE DB Services
- General Timeout

Connection.Provider Property (Versions 2.0, 2.1, 2.5, 2.6)

`connection.Provider = provider`

The Provider property indicates the name of the data provider for the current Connection object.

Datatype

String

Description

The Provider property sets the provider for the current Connection object. It can also be specified in the ConnectionString property of the Connection object or the ConnectionString argument to the Open method of the Connection object. It is recommended that the provider be specified in only one of these places, however, because the results can be unpredictable.

The Provider property of the Connection object is read- and write-enabled when the associated Connection object is closed, but read-only once it is open.

The Provider property is not used until the Connection object is opened or the Properties collection of the Connection object is used.

If no provider is specified, ADO will default to MSDASQL, the Microsoft ODBC Provider for OLE DB.

See Also

Connection.ConnectionString Property, Connection.Open Method

Connection.RollbackTrans Method   (Versions 2.0, 2.1, 2.5, 2.6)

See the Connection.BeginTrans Method.

Connection.RollbackTransComplete Event   (Versions 2.0, 2.1, 2.5, 2.6)

```
Private Sub con_RollbackTransComplete(ByVal pError As ADODB.Error, _
                        adStatus As ADODB.EventStatusEnum, _
                        ByVal pConnection As ADODB.Connection)
```

The RollbackTransComplete event is raised after the RollbackTrans method has completed its operation.

Arguments

pError
An Error object containing details about an error that occurred if the *adStatus* parameter is set to adStatusErrorsOccurred.

adStatus
An EventStatusEnum value indicating the status of the current operation. If the *adStatus* parameter is set to adStatusOK, the operation was successful. If the *adStatus* parameter is set to adStatusErrorsOccurred, the operation failed, and the *pError* object contains the details regarding the error. If the *adStatus* parameter is set to adStatusUnwantedEvent, this event will not be called again.

pConnection
The Connection object that fired this event.

See Also

Connection.BeginTransComplete Event, Connection.CommitTransComplete Event, Connection.RollbackTrans Method, EventStatusEnum Enumeration

---

Connection.State Property   (Versions 2.0, 2.1, 2.5, 2.6)

state = connection.State

The State property indicates the current status of a Command, Connection, Record, Recordset, or Stream object.

Datatype

ObjectStateEnum (Long)

Description

The State property returns a combination of the ObjectStateEnum values, listed in Appendix E, which indicate the current state of an object.

See Also

ObjectStateEnum Enumeration

Connection.Version Property   (Versions 2.0, 2.1, 2.5, 2.6)

`version = connection.Version`

The Version property indicates the current version of ADO in use.

Datatype

String

Description

The Version property returns the version information for the version of ADO that you are using in your application, in the form of a String.

Connection.WillConnect Event   (Versions 2.0, 2.1, 2.5, 2.6)

```
Private Sub WillConnect(ConnectionString As String, _
                        UserID As String, _
                        Password As String, _
                        Options As Long, _
                        adStatus As ADODB.EventStatusEnum, _
                        ByVal pConnection As ADODB.Connection)
```

The WillConnect event is raised before a connection is made.

Arguments

ConnectionString (String)
    Contains the connection information for the awaiting connection operation.

UserID (String)
    Contains the username for the awaiting connection operation.

Password (String)
    Contains the password for the awaiting connection operation.

Options (Long)
    Indicates how the ConnectionString parameter should be evaluated. For this parameter, the only valid value is **adAsyncOpen**.

adStatus (EventStatusEnum)
    Indicates the status of the current operation. The *adStatus* parameter is set to adStatusOK if the operation causing this event was successful. If the *adStatus*

parameter is set to `adStatusCantDeny`, the event cannot request that the operation be canceled. If the *adStatus* parameter is set to `adStatusUnwantedEvent`, this event will not be called again. If the *adStatus* parameter is set to `adStatusCancel`, a cancelation request will be made for this operation.

pConnection

Represents the Connection object that fired this event.

Note

The *ConnectionString*, *UserID*, and *Password* parameters can be changed by the application within this event before the operation finishes execution.

See Also

Connection.ConnectComplete Event, EventStatusEnum Enumeration

---

Connection.WillExecute Event   (Versions 2.0, 2.1, 2.5, 2.6)

```
Private Sub WillExecute(Source As String, _
                        CursorType As ADODB.CursorTypeEnum, _
                        LockType As ADODB.LockTypeEnum, _
                        Options As Long, _
                        adStatus As ADODB.EventStatusEnum, _
                        ByVal pCommand As ADODB.Command, _
                        ByVal pRecordset As ADODB.Recordset, _
                        ByVal pConnection As ADODB.Connection)
```

The WillExecute event is raised before an execution of a command has begun.

Arguments

Source (String)

Contains the source of the command that is to be executed. This value is usually a SQL statement or a stored procedure name.

CursorType (CursorTypeEnum)

Indicates the type of Recordset object that will be opened. This value can be changed within the event to change the type of cursor that gets used when the Recordset.Open method is called. This parameter is ignored for any other method that causes this event.

LockType (LockTypeEnum)

Indicates the locking scheme that will be used when the Recordset object is opened. This value can be changed within the event to change the locking scheme that gets used when the Recordset.Open method is called. This parameter is ignored for any other method that causes this event.

Options (Long)

Indicates any other options used to execute the command or open the recordset.

adStatus (EventStatusEnum)

Indicates the status of the current operation. The *adStatus* parameter is set to `adStatusOK` if the operation causing this event was successful. If the *adStatus* parameter is set to `adStatusCantDeny`, the event cannot request that the operation be canceled. If the *adStatus* parameter is set to adStatusUnwantedEvent, this event will not be called again. By setting the *adStatus* parameter to adStatusCancel, a cancelation request will be made for this operation.

pCommand
Represents the Command object to which this event applies. Set to Nothing if this event was raised because of a Connection.Execute method or a Recordset.Open method.

pRecordset
Represents the Recordset object to which this event applies. Set to Nothing if this event was raised because of a Connection.Execute method or a Command.Execute method.

pConnection
Represents the Connection object that fired this event.

See Also

Connection.Execute Method, Command.Execute Method, Recordset.Open Method, EventStatusEnum Enumeration, LockTypeEnum Enumeration

---

Error Object

Dim *error* As ADODB.Error

The Error object contains information regarding a particular error or warning that was raised by a data provider during an ADO operation.

Applies To

Errors
Contains one or more Error objects that hold information about errors or warnings raised by ADO during an operation.

Properties

Description
Describes the error or warning either ADO or the data provider has generated.

HelpContext
Indicates the topic within a help file for a particular error within an Error object.

HelpFile
Indicates the name of a help file that contains a topic for a particular error within an Error object.

NativeError
Returns the error code supplied by the data provider for the current Error object.

Number
Uniquely identifies the error specified by the current Error object.

Source
Returns the name of an object or application that generated an error within ADO.

SQLState
Returns the SQL state of the current Error object.

Description

It is important to remember that these errors are not ADO errors, but rather data-provider errors. ADO errors are reported by the development languages default error-handling mechanism (in Visual Basic, this is the On Error statement and the Err object).

When a data provider reports an error for a single ADO operation, ADO clears the contents of the Errors collection and populates the collection with an Error object for each error or warning. Data providers can generate warnings, but they do not halt the execution of an operation.

Because the Errors collection is cleared by ADO only when a new error or warning is generated, it is a good idea to call the Errors.Clear method (to remove all Error objects from the collection) before calling an ADO member that can cause an error or warning, such as Recordset.CancelBatch, Recordset.Filter, Recordset.Resync, Recordset.UpdateBatch, or Connection.Open.

Examples

Example 13-8 generates an ADO error (reported by VB) and a data-provider error (reported through the Errors collection).

Example 13-8. Error Reporting

```
Public Sub ErrorExample()
On Error GoTo ErrorHandler

    Dim con As ADODB.Connection
    Dim ero As ADODB.Error

    Dim sMes As String

    Set con = New ADODB.Connection
    con.Open "DSN=MissingDSN"

    '
    ' process flow will never get here
    '

Exit Sub

ErrorHandler:

    sMes = "Error Number:" & vbTab & Err.Number & vbCr _
        & "Source:" & vbTab & vbTab & Err.Source & vbCr _
        & "Last DLL Error:" & vbTab & Err.LastDllError & vbCr _
        & "Description:" & vbCr & vbCr & Err.Description

    MsgBox sMes, _
            vbCritical + vbMsgBoxHelpButton, _
            "VB/ADO Error", _
            Err.HelpFile, _
            Err.HelpContext

    For Each ero In con.Errors
```

Example 13-8. Error Reporting (continued)

```
        sMes = "Error Number:" & vbTab & ero.Number & vbCr _
             & "Source:" & vbTab & vbTab & ero.Source & vbCr _
             & "SQL State:" & vbTab & ero.SQLState & vbCr _
             & "Native Error:" & vbTab & ero.NativeError & vbCr _
             & "Description:" & vbCr & vbCr & ero.Description & vbCr

        MsgBox sMes, _
                vbCritical + vbMsgBoxHelpButton, _
                "Data Provider Error", _
                ero.HelpFile, _
                ero.HelpContext

    Next ero

    Set con = Nothing

End Sub
```

Error.Description Property   (Versions 2.0, 2.1, 2.5, 2.6)

description = *error.*Description

The Description property describes the error or warning either ADO or the data provider has generated.

Datatype

String

Description

The Description property of the Error object is read-only. It offers error or warning information in a String form so that you can notify the user of your application that an error or warning has occurred.

The value of the Description property can come from either ADO or the provider.

Error.HelpContext Property   (Versions 2.0, 2.1, 2.5, 2.6)

Error.HelpFile Property   (Versions 2.0, 2.1, 2.5, 2.6)

helpcontext = *error.*HelpContext
helpfile = *error.*HelpFile

The HelpContext and HelpFile properties indicate the topic and the name, respectively, of a particular error within an Error object.

Datatype

Long (HelpContext Property)
String (HelpFile Property)

Description

The HelpFile property contains a fully qualified path to a Windows Help file.

The HelpContext property automatically displays a Help topic from the Windows Help file that is indicated through the HelpFile property.

If no Help topic is relevant to the generated error, the HelpContext property returns zero, and the HelpFile property returns an empty string ("").

Error.NativeError Property   (Versions 2.0, 2.1, 2.5, 2.6)

`nativeerror = error.NativeError`

The NativeError property returns the error code supplied by the data provider for the current Error Object.

Datatype

Long

Description

Use this property to retrieve error codes that pass from the data source to the data provider and then to ADO.

Error.Number Property   (Versions 2.0, 2.1, 2.5, 2.6)

`number = error.Number`

The Number property is used to uniquely identify the error specified by the current Error object.

Datatype

Long or ErrorValueEnum (Long)

Description

The value of the Number property is a unique number that describes an error that has occurred. The value can be one of the ErrorValueEnum enumeration values shown in Table E-18.

See Also

ErrorValueEnum Enumeration

Error.Source Property   (Versions 2.0, 2.1, 2.5, 2.6)

`source = error.Source`

The Source property returns the name of an object or application that generated an error within ADO.

Datatype

The Error object returns a String.

Description

For the Errors object, the Source property indicates the name of the object or application that originally generated an error within ADO.

ADO errors will have a source value beginning with the value **ADODB.** followed by the name of the object that generated the error.

Error.SQLState Property

(Versions 2.0, 2.1, 2.5, 2.6)

sqlstate = error.SQLState

The SQLState property returns the SQL state of the current Error object.

Datatype

String (five characters)

Description

Use this property to retrieve the five-character error code that the data provider returns to ADO when an error occurs processing a SQL statement. These error codes should be ANSI SQL standard, but they may not be, depending on the particular data provider.

Errors Collection

(Versions 2.0, 2.1, 2.5, 2.6)

`Set errors = connection.Errors`

See the Error Object for more information and examples pertaining to the Errors collection.

Objects

Error
  Contains information regarding a particular error or warning that was raised by ADO during an operation.

Methods

Clear
  The Clear method erases all errors stored in the Errors collection.

Refresh
  The Refresh method of the Errors collection is an undocumented method of ADO that has been around since Version 2.0.

Properties

Count
  Indicates how many Error objects belong to the associated Errors collection.

Item
  Accesses a particular Error object belonging to the Errors collection.

Errors.Clear Method

(Versions 2.0, 2.1, 2.5, 2.6)

`errors.Clear`

The Clear method erases all errors stored in the Errors collection.

Description

The Clear method clears the current collection of ADO errors. When a new runtime error is generated, the Errors collection is automatically cleared and then populated with the error information.

Use the Clear method when you are going to make calls to a Recordset object that might return multiple warnings. These calls include Delete, Resync, UpdateBatch, and Cancel-Batch. Once you have made any of these calls, after clearing the Errors collection, you can determine whether any warnings were generated by the call in question.

See Also

Recordset.CancelBatch Method, Recordset.Delete Method, Recordset.Resync Method, Recordset.UpdateBatch Method

---

Errors.Count Property

(Versions 2.0, 2.1, 2.5, 2.6)

`count = errors.Count`

The Count property indicates how many Error objects belong to the associated Errors collection.

Datatype

Long

Description

If the value of the Count property is zero, there are no Error objects within the associated Errors collection. However, Error objects that do belong to the associated Errors collection are indexed from 0 to one less than the value of the Count property.

Errors.Item Property

(Versions 2.0, 2.1, 2.5, 2.6)

`Set error = errors.Item(Index)`
`Set error = errors (Index)`

The Item property accesses a particular Error object belonging to the Errors collection.

Datatype

Error object

Description

The *Index* placeholder represents a Variant datatype that represents the ordinal position of an Error object within the Errors collection. If the Errors collection does not contain the item requested, an error is generated.

Note

Some languages do not support the Item property in its first syntax. For these languages, use the second syntax, without the Item method name.

Errors.Refresh Method (Versions 2.0, 2.1, 2.5, 2.6)

`errors.Refresh`

The Refresh method of the Errors collection is an undocumented method of ADO that has been around since Version 2.0.

Description

The Errors.Refresh method appears to requery for errors within ADO.

Field Object (Versions 2.0, 2.1, 2.5, 2.6)

`Dim field As ADODB.Field`

The Field object represents an individual column within a Recordset or a Record object's Fields collection. A Field contains metadata properties that define its datatype, size, and precision.

Applies To

Fields
Contains a group of Field objects that represent the fields of the current record in an open Recordset object.

Collections

Properties
Contains characteristics specific to the Field object for the currently used provider.

Methods

AppendChunk
Appends data to a large data or binary field.

GetChunk
Returns the specified number of bytes or characters from the specified field.

Properties

ActualSize
Returns the actual length of a field's value.

Attributes
Sets or returns specific characteristics about the Field object.

DataFormat
The DataFormat property for the Field object is not documented at all in the ADO help files—however, the DataFormat property is used in other Microsoft objects outside of ADO.

DefinedSize
> Represents the size, in bytes, of the capacity of a Field object's datatype.

Name
> Specifies the name for the current Field object.

NumericScale
> Indicates the scale of numeric values in the current Field object.

OriginalValue
> Returns the value that belonged to a field before any changes were made to it.

Precision
> Represents the degree of precision of a numeric value within the current Field object.

Status
> Indicates the status of the current Field object.

Type
> Indicates the datatype of the Field's Value property.

UnderlyingValue
> Returns the current value of the Field object's Value property.

Value
> Indicates the value assigned to the current Field object.

Description

A Field object can be used to inspect the value of data within the current row in a Recordset or the row represented by the Record object.

For a Record object, the Fields collection contains two special fields. The first is the URL of the resource that is represented by the Record object, and the second is the default stream for the Record object.

The Fields collection can be used to add or remove fields with the Append and Delete method and can be finalized with the Update method. Attempting to access fields that do not exist causes ADO to append the field to the collection to await a call to Update.

Examples

In this section, we will be looking at three examples that will show us how to:

*   Examine a Field object's attributes.
*   Use long datatypes, such as Memo, with the Field object.
*   Add Field objects to a Recordset object without a data source.

Before we begin looking at the Field examples for this section, we define the following connection string Const value so that the examples will work properly:

```
Private Const DATASOURCE_BIBLIO = "Provider=Microsoft.Jet.OLEDB.4.0; " _
                        & "Data Source=C:\Program Files\" _
                        & "Microsoft Visual Studio\VB98\Biblio.mdb;"
```

Now that we have this constant defined, we can begin to look at some examples. Example 13-9 displays the information for each of the Field objects in a Fields collection of a Recordset object.

Example 13-9. Examining a Field Object's Attributes

```
Dim con As ADODB.Connection
Dim rst As ADODB.Recordset
Dim fld As ADODB.Field

Dim sMes As String

'
' open an external Connection object
'
Set con = New ADODB.Connection
con.Open DATASOURCE_BIBLIO

'
' obtain a recordset with data
'
Set rst = con.Execute("SELECT * FROM Authors;")

'
' display the names of the fields within the Recordset object
'
sMes = ""
For Each fld In rst.Fields
    sMes = sMes & fld.Name & vbCr
Next fld

MsgBox "Field names:" & vbCr & vbCr & sMes

'
' display the values of the fields for the first record
'
sMes = ""
For Each fld In rst.Fields
    sMes = sMes & fld.Name & ": " & vbTab & fld.Value & vbCr
Next fld

MsgBox "The values for the first record's fields are: " _
      & vbCr & vbCr & sMes

'
' clean up
'
rst.Close
con.Close

Set rst = Nothing
Set con = Nothing
```

Example 13-10 illustrates how you can use the Field object's AppendChunk and GetChunk methods to read and write to columns that have a long datatype, such as Memo.

Example 13-10. Using Long Datatypes with the Field Object

```
Dim con As ADODB.Connection
Dim rst As ADODB.Recordset
Dim fld As ADODB.Field

Dim sMes As String
Dim sChunk As String

'
' open an external Connection object
'
Set con = New ADODB.Connection
con.Open DATASOURCE_BIBLIO

'    *
' obtain a recordset with data
'
Set rst = New ADODB.Recordset
rst.Open "Publishers", con, adOpenDynamic, adLockPessimistic

'
' use the AppendChunk method to add to a Long type field
'
rst.MoveFirst
rst.Fields.Item("Comments").AppendChunk "This is the first piece."
rst.Fields.Item("Comments").AppendChunk "This is the second piece."
rst.Fields.Item("Comments").AppendChunk "This is the third piece."
rst.Fields.Item("Comments").AppendChunk "This is the fourth piece."
rst.Fields.Item("Comments").AppendChunk "This is the fifth piece."
rst.Update

rst.MoveFirst

'
' now read the Long type field, one chunk at a time
'
sMes = rst.Fields.Item("Comments").GetChunk(10)
MsgBox "The first chunk is: '" & sMes & "'"

sMes = rst.Fields.Item("Comments").GetChunk(10)
MsgBox "The second chunk is: '" & sMes & "'"

sMes = rst.Fields.Item("Comments").GetChunk(10)
MsgBox "The third chunk is: '" & sMes & "'"

sChunk = rst.Fields.Item("Comments").GetChunk(10)
While (sChunk <> "")
    sMes = sMes & sChunk
    sChunk = rst.Fields.Item("Comments").GetChunk(10) & ""
Wend
sMes = sMes & sChunk
```

Example 13-10. Using Long Datatypes with the Field Object (continued)

```
MsgBox "The remaining data is: '" & sMes & "'"

'
' clean up
'
rst.Close
con.Close

Set rst = Nothing
Set con = Nothing
```

Example 13-11 shows how Field objects can be added to a Recordset object that has been instantiated without a connection to a physical data source. After the Fields are appended, the Recordset object is populated with three rows and then saved to an XML file.

Example 13-11. Adding Field Objects to a Recordset Object

```
Dim rst As ADODB.Recordset
Dim fld As ADODB.Field

'
' create a new Recordset object
'
Set rst = New ADODB.Recordset

MsgBox "There are " & CStr(rst.Fields.Count) & " fields."

'
' add four fields to it dynamically
'
rst.Fields.Append "FirstField", adChar, 20
rst.Fields.Append "SecondField", adBoolean
rst.Fields.Append "ThirdField", adInteger
rst.Fields.Append "FourthField", adBinary, 10
MsgBox "There are " & CStr(rst.Fields.Count) & " fields."

'
' remove one of the fields
'
rst.Fields.Delete 3
MsgBox "There are " & CStr(rst.Fields.Count) & " fields."

rst.Open

'
' add three records
'
rst.AddNew
rst.Fields("FirstField").Value = "Jason T. Roff"
rst!SecondField = True
rst.Fields(2) = 27
rst.Update
```

Example 13-11. Adding Field Objects to a Recordset Object (continued)

```
rst.AddNew
rst.Fields("FirstField").Value = "Kimberly A. Roff"
rst!SecondField = True
rst.Fields(2) = 25
rst.Update

rst.AddNew
rst.Fields("FirstField").Value = "??? Roff"
rst!SecondField = True
rst.Fields(2) = 0
rst.Update

'
' save the data to an XML file
'
rst.Save "Data.xml", adPersistXML


'
' clean up
'
rst.Close

Set rst = Nothing
```

In the previous example, numerous ways of accessing a Field object from the Recordset object are shown. Example 13-11 produces the following XML file:

```
<xml xmlns:s='uuid:BDC6E3F0-6DA3-11d1-A2A3-00AA00C14882'
    xmlns:dt='uuid:C2F41010-65B3-11d1-A29F-00AA00C14882'
    xmlns:rs='urn:schemas-microsoft-com:rowset'
    xmlns:z='#RowsetSchema'>
<s:Schema id='RowsetSchema'>
    <s:ElementType name='row' content='eltOnly' rs:updatable='true'>
        <s:AttributeType name='FirstField' rs:number='1' rs:write='true'>
            <s:datatype dt:type='string' rs:dbtype='str' dt:maxLength='20' rs:
precision='0' rs:fixedlength='true' rs:maybenull='false'/>
        </s:AttributeType>
        <s:AttributeType name='SecondField' rs:number='2' rs:write='true'>
            <s:datatype dt:type='boolean' dt:maxLength='2' rs:precision='0' rs:
fixedlength='true' rs:maybenull='false'/>
        </s:AttributeType>
        <s:AttributeType name='ThirdField' rs:number='3' rs:write='true'>
            <s:datatype dt:type='int' dt:maxLength='4' rs:precision='0' rs:
fixedlength='true' rs:maybenull='false'/>
        </s:AttributeType>
        <s:extends type='rs:rowbase'/>
    </s:ElementType>
</s:Schema>
<rs:data>
```

```
    <rs:insert>
        <z:row FirstField='Jason T. Roff       ' SecondField='True'
ThirdField='27'/>
        <z:row FirstField='Kimberly A. Roff    ' SecondField='True'
ThirdField='25'/>
        <z:row FirstField='??? Roff            ' SecondField='True'
ThirdField='0'/>
    </rs:insert>
</rs:data>
</xml>
```

Field.ActualSize Property   (Versions 2.0, 2.1, 2.5, 2.6)

actualsize = field.ActualSize

The ActualSize property returns the actual length of a field's value.

Datatype

Long

Description

The ActualSize property returns a number indicating how many bytes are stored in the specified field, as opposed to the maximum number of bytes allowed (indicated through the DefinedSize property). If the length of the Field object's value cannot be determined by ADO, adUnknown is returned.

See Also

Field.DefinedSize Property

Field.AppendChunk   (Versions 2.0, 2.1, 2.5, 2.6)

field.AppendChunk Data

The AppendChunk method is used to append data to a large data or binary field.

Arguments

Data (Variant)
    Contains the large amount of data that you wish to append to the current Field object.

Description

The AppendChunk method appends large amounts of either text or binary data to an existing Field object. This can come in very useful when the current system contains limited system memory with regard to the amount needed for the operation to be performed. With the AppendChunk method, you can add the data to your Field object in increments as you see fit.

You can use the AppendChunk method with a Field object only if the adFldLong bit of the Arguments property of that Field object is set to True.

By calling the AppendChunk method for the first time, you overwrite any data that may already be in that field. With each additional call to the AppendChunk method, the data is appended to the end of the pre-existing data. ADO assumes that you are finished appending to a particular field in a recordset if you then read or write data in another field in the same recordset. What this means is that if you call the AppendChunk method again on the original field, the data is once again cleared, as if it were the first call to the method. Reading or writing data in another Recordset object will not cause this action to occur, unless it is a clone of the original Recordset object.

See Also

Field.Attributes Property, FieldAttributeEnum Enumeration

Field.Attributes Property   (Versions 2.0, 2.1, 2.5, 2.6)

`field.Attributes = attributes`

The Attributes property sets or returns specific characteristics about the Field object.

Datatype

Long

Description

The Attributes property is read-only; it can be a sum of the values from the FieldAttributes-Enum enumeration listed in Appendix E indicating the characteristics of the Field object, such as whether it is updatable or represents a row identifier.

See Also

FieldAttributesEnum Enumeration

Field.DataFormat Property   (Versions 2.0, 2.1, 2.5, 2.6)

The DataFormat property links the current Field object to a data-bound control.

Datatype

StdDataFormat

Description

The DataFormat property is both read- and write-enabled. It accepts and returns a StdDataFormat object that is used to attach a bound object.

The DataFormat property for the Field object is not documented at all in the ADO help files—however, the DataFormat property is used in other Microsoft objects outside of ADO.

Field.DefinedSize Property   (Versions 2.0, 2.1, 2.5, 2.6)

`definedsize = field.DefinedSize`

The DefinedSize property represents the size, in bytes, of the capacity of a Field object's datatype.

Datatype

Long

Description

The DefinedSize property is used to determine the data capacity of a Field object's Value property, in bytes. This property differs from the ActualSize property, which indicates how many bytes of the defined datatype size are actually being used.

See Also

Field.ActualSize Property

Field.GetChunk Method   (Versions 2.0, 2.1, 2.5, 2.6)

`Set value = field.GetChunk(NumBytes)`

The GetChunk method returns the specified number of bytes or characters from the specified field.

Arguments

NumBytes

The *NumBytes* parameter is a Long value representing the number of bytes or characters that you want to receive.

Returns

Variant

Description

The GetChunk method gets pieces of information from a Field object that belongs to a Fields collection of an open Recordset object. If the Arguments property of the Field object is set to **adFldLong**, you can use the GetChunk method on that field.

The first call to GetChunk retrieves the number of bytes specified in the method call, from the beginning of the field. All subsequent calls to GetChunk will return data starting from where the last call to GetChunk left off. If the amount of bytes or characters in the Field object is fewer than the amount that you requested, only the remainder is returned without padding for the difference.

When you read or write to another field within the same Recordset object (one that is not a clone of that recordset), ADO assumes that you are done retrieving chunks from that particular Field object. The next call to GetChunk will perform as if it were the first, retrieving the first number of bytes or characters that you request.

See Also

Field.Arguments Property

Field.Name Property   (Versions 2.0, 2.1, 2.5, 2.6)

```
Set value = field.GetChunk(NumBytes)
```

The Name property specifies the name for the current Field object.

Datatype

String

Description

The Name property retrieves a Field object from the Fields collection. Names do not have to be unique within collections.

Field.NumericScale Property   (Versions 2.0, 2.1, 2.5, 2.6)

```
field.NumericScale = numericscale
```

The NumericScale property indicates the scale of numeric values in the current Field object.

Datatype

Byte

Description

The read-only NumericScale property identifies how many bytes are used to the right of the decimal point for a Field object containing a numeric value.

Field.OriginalValue Property   (Versions 2.0, 2.1, 2.5, 2.6)

```
originalvalue = field.OriginalValue
```

The OriginalValue property returns the value that belonged to a field before any changes were made to it.

Datatype

Variant

Description

In Immediate mode, the OriginalValue property returns the value of a field in the current record before any changes were made to it. In other words, the OriginalValue property is the value of the field when the last Update method was called. This is the value that is replaced in the Field object when the CancelUpdate method is called.

In Batch Update mode, the OriginalValue property returns the value of a field in the current record before any changes were made to it. In other words, the OriginalValue property is the value of the field when the last UpdateBatch method was called. This is the value that is replaced in the Field object when the CancelBatch method is called.

See Also

Recordset.CancelBatch Method, Recordset.CancelUpdate Method, Recordset.Update Method, Recordset.UpdateBatch Method

Field.Precision Property   (Versions 2.0, 2.1, 2.5, 2.6)

`precision = field.Precision`

The Precision property represents the degree of precision of a numeric value within the current Field object.

Datatype

Byte

Description

The Precision property is read-only for the Field object. This property returns a Byte value that indicates the total number of digits used to represent a value for a numeric Field object.

Field.Properties Collection   (Versions 2.0, 2.1, 2.5, 2.6)

`Set properties = field.Properties`

The Properties collection contains characteristics specific to the Field object for the currently used provider.

Datatype

Properties (Collection object)

Description

The Properties collection class contains a Property class instance for each property specific to the Field object for the data provider.

Field.Status Property   (Versions 2.5, 2.6)

`status = field.Type`

The Status property indicates the status of the current Field object.

Datatype

FieldStatusEnum

Description

The default value for the Status property is **adFieldOK**.

After a call to the Record or Recordset's Update method if an error has occurred the Status property of each Field object is set to a value from the FieldStatusEnum enumeration, describing the problem.

If you are adding and deleting Field objects to and from the Fields collection, the Status property can tell you whether they have been successfully added or deleted.

The Status property can hold more than one FieldStatusEnum enumeration value at a time.

See Also

FieldStatusEnum Enumeration, Record.Update Method, Recordset.Update Method

Field.Type Property   (Versions 2.0, 2.1, 2.5, 2.6)

`datatype = field.Type`

The Type property indicates the datatype of the Field's Value property.

Datatype

DataTypeEnum

Description

The Type property is read-only unless it is for a new Field object that has been appended to the Fields collection of a Record object, of which it is only read/write after the Value property of the Field object has already been specified and the data provider has added the Field object to the data source (by using the Update method of the Fields collection).

See Also

DataTypeEnum Enumeration, Field.Value Property, Fields.Update Method

Field.UnderlyingValue Property   (Versions 2.0, 2.1, 2.5, 2.6)

`underlyingvalue = field.UnderlyingValue`

The UnderlyingValue property returns the current value of the Field object's Value property.

Datatype

Variant

Description

The UnderlyingValue property returns the value—from the current record—of the associated Field object. This value may differ from the OriginalValue property as it shows the value of a field for the current transaction.

This is the same value that the Resync method uses to replace the value of the Value property.

See Also

Field.OriginalValue, Field.Value Property, Recordset.Resync Method

Field.Value Property   (Versions 2.0, 2.1, 2.5, 2.6)

`field.Value = value`

The Value property indicates the value assigned to the current Field object.

Datatype

Variant

Description

The Value property is used to read and set the value of the associated Field object. The Value property supports long binary data through ADO.

Fields Collection   (Versions 2.0, 2.1, 2.5, 2.6)

```
Set fields = record.Fields
Set fields = recordset.Fields
```

See the Field object for more information and examples pertaining to the Fields collection.

Applies To

Recordset
> Offers a particular view of a group of records from the associated connection.

Objects

Field
> Contains information about a single field in the current record of an open Recordset object.

Methods

Append
> Adds a new Field object to the collection.

CancelUpdate
> Cancels any pending changes to the individual Field objects of the Record object's Fields collection.

Delete
> Removes a Field object from the current Fields collection.

Refresh
> Does not perform any visible function according to the Microsoft documentation.

Resync
> Updates the current collection based upon the underlying database.

Update
> Persists any changes made to the current Fields collection of a Record object.

Properties

Count
> Indicates how many Field objects belong to the associated Fields collection.

Item
> Accesses a particular Field object belonging to the Fields collection.

Fields.Append Method   (Versions 2.0, 2.1, 2.5, 2.6)

```
fields.Append Name, Type, DefinedSize, Attrib, FieldValue
```

The Append method adds a new Field object to the collection.

Arguments

Name (String)
> Represents the name of the field to append to the Fields collection. This name must not already exist within the collection.

Type (DataTypeEnum)

Specifies the datatype of the Field's Value property. The default value for this parameter is adEmpty.

DefinedSize (String)

Optional. Dictates the length of the value stored within the Field object. The value of this parameter is derived from the Type property.

Attrib (FieldAttributeEnum)

Optional. Specifies additional information regarding the new Field object. The default value for this parameter is adFldDefault.

FieldValue (Variant)

Optional. Gives the new Field object a value. The default for this parameter is Null. This parameter is valid only when adding a Field object to a Record object's Fields collection, not a Recordset object's.

Description

The following datatypes are not supported by ADO and cannot be used when adding new Field objects to the collection class: adIDispatch, adIUnknown, and adVariant.

The following datatypes cannot be added to the Field's collection and will generate an error: adArray, adChapter, adEmpty, adPropVariant, and adUserDefined.

When using the Append method with a Fields collection of a Recordset object, you cannot use the FieldValue parameter. Instead, you must add the Field objects while the Recordset object is closed and then assign them values after it is opened.

When appending Field objects to the Fields collection of a Record object, you must first set the Field.Value property and call the Update method before accessing any other Field properties such as Type.

See Also

DataTypeEnum Enumeration, FieldAttributeEnum Enumeration

Fields.CancelUpdate Method   (Versions 2.5, 2.6)

`record.Fields.CancelUpdate`

The CancelUpdate method cancels any pending changes to the individual Field objects of the Record object's Fields collection.

Description

After calling the CancelUpdate method, all of the Field Objects will have a status of adFieldOK.

See Also

Record Object

Fields.Count Property (Versions 2.0, 2.1, 2.5, 2.6)

`count = fields.Count`

The Count property indicates how many Field objects belong to the associated Fields collection.

Datatype

Long

Description

If the value of the Count property is zero, there are no Field objects within the associated Fields collection. However, Field objects that do belong to the associated Fields collection are indexed from 0 to one less than the value of the Count property.

Fields.Delete Method (Versions 2.0, 2.1, 2.5, 2.6)

`Fields.Delete Field`

The Delete method removes a Field object from the current Fields collection.

Arguments

`Field`

Either the name of a valid Field object within the current Field's collection or the ordinal position of a Field object within the collection to be removed.

Description

You can call the Field.Delete method only on a closed Recordset object.

Fields.Item Property (Versions 2.0, 2.1, 2.5, 2.6)

`Set field = fields.Item(Index)`
`Set field = fields(Index)`

The Item property accesses a particular Field object belonging to the Fields collection.

Datatype

Object

Description

The Index placeholder represents a Variant datatype that represents the ordinal position of a Field object within the Fields collection. If the Fields collection does not contain the item requested, an error is generated.

Note

Some languages do not support the Item property in its first syntax. For these languages, use the second syntax, without the Item method name.

Fields.Refresh Method

(Versions 2.0, 2.1, 2.5, 2.6)

Fields.Refresh

The Refresh method does not perform any visible function according to the Microsoft documentation.

Description

In order to update the Fields collection with changes from the underlying database, use the Resync method or the MoveFirst method if the Recordset object doesn't support bookmarks.

See Also

Recordset.MoveFirst Method, Recordset.Resync Method

Fields.Resync Method

(Versions 2.5, 2.6)

record.Fields.Resync *ResyncValues*

The Resync method updates the current collection based upon the underlying database.

Arguments

ResyncValues (ResyncEnum)
> Optional. Specifies whether the underlying values within the Fields collection are over-written. The default value for this parameter is **adResyncAllValues**.

Description

The Resync method resynchronizes the Field objects of a Record object's Fields collection with those within the underlying database.

The default value for the only parameter to this method, **adResyncAllValues** synchronizes all of the values within the UnderlyingValue, Value, and OriginalValue properties.

If a Field object within the collection has a Status property equal to either **adFieldPendingUnknown** or **adFieldPendingInsert**, then the Resync method is ignored for those Field objects.

See Also

Field.OriginalValue Property, Field.Status Property, Field.UnderlyingValue Property, Field. Value Property, ResyncEnum Enumeration

---

Fields.Update Method

(Versions 2.5, 2.6)

record.Fields.Update

Description

The Update method persists any pending changes to the current Fields collection of a Record object.

```
Dim parameter As ADODB.Parameter
```

Parameter Object   (Versions 2.0, 2.1, 2.5, 2.6)

The Parameter object contains information for one variable within a SQL statement or stored procedures. Combined, Parameter objects belong to the Parameters collection of Command objects.

Applies To

Parameters
> This collection contains a group of Parameter objects that describe parameters belonging to the associated Command object.

Collections

Properties
> Returns a Properties collection class that contains characteristics specific to the Parameter object for the currently used provider.

Methods

AppendChunk
> Append data to a large data or binary field within the current Parameter object.

Properties

Attributes
> Sets or returns specific characteristics about the Parameter object.

Direction
> Specifies whether the current parameter is an input parameter, an output parameter, both an input and an output parameter, or a return value from a stored procedure.

Name
> Specifies the name for the current Parameter object.

NumericScale
> Indicates the scale of numeric values in the current Parameter object.

Precision
> Represents the degree of precision of a numeric value within the current Parameter object.

Size
> Returns the maximum size of a Parameter object's value.

Type
> Identifies the current object's datatype.

Value
> Indicates the value assigned to the current Parameter object.

Description

Parameters allow SQL statements or stored procedures to be created that can be "altered" at runtime by plugging in values for specific variables. A Parameter object contains metadata about the variable (datatype, attributes, direction, numeric scale, and size). Parameters can be input, output, or both input and output variables.

When using a Command object with a parameterized query, you can either call the Refresh method of the Parameters collection before specifying values for each parameter, or you can call the CreateParameter method of the Command object for each parameter that belongs to the query.

By calling the CreateParameter method for each parameter, you can potentially save tremendous amounts of time that would otherwise be used by ADO when the Refresh method is called, communicating with the data source to find the parameters and their metadata information for a parameterized query.

Examples

In this section, we will be looking at two examples that will show how to:

- Execute a parameterized query without first identifying the parameters.

- Execute a parameterized query with explicitly specified parameters.

Before we begin looking at the Parameter examples for this section, please make sure that you have the following connection string **Const** value defined so that the examples will work properly:

```
Private Const DATASOURCE_NWIND = "Provider=Microsoft.Jet.OLEDB.4.0; " _
                        & "Data Source=C:\Program Files\" _
                        & "Microsoft Visual Studio\VB98\NWind.mdb;"
```

Now that we have this constant defined, we can begin to look at some examples. Example 13-12 will show you how to execute a parameterized query without specifying the parameters beforehand.

Example 13-12. Executing a Parameterized Query Without First Identifying the Parameters

```
Dim con As ADODB.Connection
Dim com As ADODB.Command
Dim rst As ADODB.Recordset

Dim vParameters() As Variant

'
' open the connection
'
Set con = New ADODB.Connection
con.Open DATASOURCE_NWIND


'
' create a new Command object and assign the stored procedure
'
Set com = New ADODB.Command
Set com.ActiveConnection = con

com.CommandText = "[Employee Sales by Country]"
com.CommandType = adCmdStoredProc


'
' there are two parameters for this stored procedure, start and end date
'
```

Example 13-12. Executing a Parameterized Query Without First Identifying the Parameters (continued)

```
ReDim vParameters(1)

vParameters(0) = "1/1/1995"
vParameters(1) = "12/31/1996"

'
' execute the command with the parameters
'
Set rst = com.Execute(, vParameters)

'
' the Recordset object now contains the results from the Command's query
'
MsgBox "The first order to ship in the time frame specified was: " _
        & CStr(rst.Fields("OrderID").Value)

'
' clean up
'
rst.Close
con.Close

Set com = Nothing
Set rst = Nothing
Set con = Nothing
```

Example 13-13 executes the same parameterized query as Example 13-12, but it does so by first explicitly specifying the parameters with the CreateParameter example.

Example 13-13. Executing a Query with Explicitly Specified Parameters

```
Dim con As ADODB.Connection
Dim com As ADODB.Command
Dim par As ADODB.Parameter
Dim rst As ADODB.Recordset

Dim vParameters() As Variant

'
' open the connection
'
Set con = New ADODB.Connection
con.Open DATASOURCE_NWIND

'
' create a new Command object and assign the stored procedure
'
Set com = New ADODB.Command
Set com.ActiveConnection = con

com.CommandText = "[Employee Sales by Country]"
com.CommandType = adCmdStoredProc
```

Example 13-13. Executing a Query with Explicitly Specified Parameters (continued)

```
'
' now manually create the two parameters and append them to the
'   collection
'

Set par = com.CreateParameter("Start Date", _
                                adDate, _
                                adParamInput, _
                                , _
                                "1/1/1995")
com.Parameters.Append par

Set par = com.CreateParameter("End Date", _
                                adDate, _
                                adParamInput, _
                                , _
                                "12/31/1995")
com.Parameters.Append par

'
' execute the command
'
Set rst = com.Execute

'
' the Recordset object now contains the results from the Command's query
'
MsgBox "The first order to ship in the time frame specified was: " _
        & CStr(rst.Fields("OrderID").Value)

'
' clean up
'
rst.Close
con.Close

Set com = Nothing
Set par = Nothing
Set rst = Nothing
Set con = Nothing
```

Parameter.AppendChunk Method   (Versions 2.0, 2.1, 2.5, 2.6)

parameter.AppendChunk *Data*

The AppendChunk method appends data to a large data or binary field within the current Parameter object.

Arguments

Data

The only parameter, *Data*, is a Variant datatype that contains the large amount of data that you wish to append to the current Parameter object.

Description

The AppendChunk method appends large amounts of either text or binary data to an existing Parameter object. This can be very useful when the current system contains limited system memory in respect to the amount needed for the operation to be performed. With the AppendChunk method, you can add the data to your Field object in increments as you see fit.

The adFldLong bit of the Arguments property belonging to the Parameter object must be set in order for the AppendChunk method of the Parameter object to be called.

By calling the AppendChunk method multiple times on a Parameter object, you append the data to the pre-existing data in the object. The only way to clear the data in a Parameter object is set it to a zero-length string. By passing a Null value to the AppendChunk method of a Parameter object, you generate an error.

See Also

Parameter.Arguments Property

Parameter.Attributes Property   (Versions 2.0, 2.1, 2.5, 2.6)

parameter.Attributes = *ParameterAttributesEnum*

The Attributes property is used to set or return specific characteristics about the Parameter object.

Datatype

ParameterAttributesEnum (Long)

Description

The Arguments property is read- and write-enabled. The value of the Arguments property can be set to any sum of the values from the ParameterArgumentsEnum enumeration listed in Appendix E. The default value for the Arguments property is adParamSigned.

See Also

ParameterAttributesEnum Enumeration

Parameter.Direction Property   (Versions 2.0, 2.1, 2.5, 2.6)

parameter.Direction = *ParameterDirectionEnum*

The Direction property specifies whether the current parameter is an input parameter, an output parameter, both an input and an output parameter, or a return value from a stored procedure.

Datatype

ParameterDirectionEnum (Long)

Description

The Direction property is both read- and write-enabled. It is to your advantage to add parameters manually to a Parameters collection so that ADO does not have to make additional calls to the data provider to locate this information itself. In some cases, you must specify the Direction property manually because the particular data provider may not be able to determine this information itself.

The Direction property may be set to one of the ParameterDirectionEnum enumerations listed in Appendix E.

Note

Not all providers can determine the value of the Direction property; therefore, for such providers the application must manually set the value of the Direction property for parameters before they are used.

See Also

ParameterDirectionEnum Enumeration

Parameter.Name Property (Versions 2.0, 2.1, 2.5, 2.6)

`parameter.Name = Name`

The Name property specifies the name for the current Parameter object.

Datatype

String

Description

The Name property is both read- and write-enabled for the Parameter object. You can set the Name property only if the Parameter object is not already appended to a Parameters collection.

The Name property assigns a name to the associated Parameter object or retrieves a Parameter object from the Parameters collection.

Names do not have to be unique within the Parameters collection object.

Parameter.NumericScale Property (Versions 2.0, 2.1, 2.5, 2.6)

`numberscale = parameter.NumericScale`

The NumericScale property indicates the scale of numeric values in the current Parameter object.

Datatype

Byte

Description

The NumericScale property is both read- and write-enabled for the Parameter object. It is used to identify how many bytes are used to the right of the decimal point for a numeric Parameter object.

Parameter.Precision Property   (Versions 2.0, 2.1, 2.5, 2.6)

```
precision = parameter.Precision
```

The Precision property represents the degree of precision of a numeric value within the current Parameter object.

Datatype

Byte

Description

The Precision property is both read- and write-enabled for the Parameter object. This property returns a Byte value that indicates the total number of digits used to represent a value for a numeric Parameter object.

Parameter.Properties Collection   (Versions 2.0, 2.1, 2.5, 2.6)

```
Set properties = parameter.Properties
```

The Properties collection returns a Properties collection class that contains characteristics specific to the Parameter object for the currently used provider.

Datatype

Properties (Collection object)

Description

The Properties collection class contains a Property class instance for each property specific to the Parameter object for the data provider.

Parameter.Size Property   (Versions 2.0, 2.1, 2.5, 2.6)

```
parameter.Size = size
```

The Size property returns the maximum size of a Parameter object's value.

Datatype

Long

Description

The Size property returns the maximum size of a parameter's value, in bytes. This property is both read- and write-enabled.

If a Parameter object is of variable length datatype, the Size property must be set before it is appended to the Parameters collection, or an error will be generated.

If you attempt to change the datatype of a Parameter object to a variable-length datatype, be sure to set the Size property first so that an error will not be generated.

You should also set the Size property of the Parameter object before calling the Execute method of the Command object, since if you don't and a variable-length datatype exists, ADO may try to allocate memory based on the maximum amount needed, causing an error.

Parameter.Type Property

(Versions 2.0, 2.1, 2.5, 2.6)

parameter.Type = DataTypeEnum

The Type property identifies the current object's datatype.

Datatype

DataTypeEnum (Long)

Description

The Type property is both read- and write-enabled for the Parameter object. This property returns a Byte value that indicates the total number of digits used to represent a value for a numeric Parameter object.

See Also

DataTypeEnum Enumeration

Parameter.Value Property

(Versions 2.0, 2.1, 2.5, 2.6)

parameter.Value = value

The Value property indicates the value assigned to the current Parameter object.

Datatype

Variant

Description

The Value property reads and sets the value of the associated Parameter object. The Value property supports long binary data through ADO.

ADO reads Parameter objects' Value property only once. If you execute a command containing a parameter with an empty Value property—and it creates a recordset—be sure to close the recordset before you read the Value property.

Parameters Collection

```
Set parameters = command.Parameters
Set fields = recordset.Fields
```

See the Parameter Object for more information and examples pertaining to the Parameters collection.

Objects

Parameter

Contains information about a particular parameter belonging to a SQL statement, query, or stored procedure.

Methods

Append

Appends a new Parameter object to the current Parameters collection class.

Delete

Removes a Parameter object from the Parameters collection class.

Refresh

Updates the collection with the parameters of the current stored procedure or parameterized query associated with the Command object to which the Parameters collection belongs.

Properties

Count

Indicates how many Parameter objects belong to the associated Parameters collection.

Item

Accesses a particular Parameter object belonging to the Parameters collection.

Parameters.Append Method   (Versions 2.0, 2.1, 2.5, 2.6)

`parameters.Append Object`

The Append method appends a new Parameter object to the current Parameters collection class.

Arguments

Object

The only parameter of the Append method is a Parameter object. The Type property of the Parameter object must be set before the Append method is actually called. In addition, if the datatype of your Parameter is of variable length, you must also set the Size property of the Parameter object to a value greater than zero.

Description

The Append method of the Parameters collection informs ADO of the type of parameters that are included in stored procedures or parameterized queries. You would do this for a couple of reasons: one is that it decreases the time that a stored procedure or parameterized query takes to perform its duty by minimizing the calls to the data provider for this information. Another reason for declaring the parameters in advance—by adding them to the Parameters collection—is that not all data providers actually make this information known to ADO. For this reason, unless you populate the Parameters collection yourself, you stand a strong chance of not being able to use these stored procedures or queries at all.

It is my advice (as well as Microsoft's) to always declare the parameters of a stored procedure or parameterized query in advance whenever possible, because you may not always be able to rely on the information being available to ADO (and it can't hurt having the extra speed advantage).

See Also

Command.CreateParameter Method, Parameter.Size Property, Parameter.Type Property

Parameters.Count Property   (Versions 2.0, 2.1, 2.5, 2.6)

`count = parameters.Count`

The Count property indicates how many Parameter objects belong to the associated Parameters collection.

Datatype

Long

Description

If the value of the Count property is zero, there are no Parameter objects within the associated Parameters collection. However, Parameter objects that do belong to the associated Parameters collection are indexed from 0 to one less than the value of the Count property.

Parameters.Delete Method   (Versions 2.0, 2.1, 2.5, 2.6)

`parameters.Delete Index`

The Delete method removes a Parameter object from the Parameters collection class.

Arguments

Index
> The *Index* parameter can be either the name of the Parameter object to be removed or its ordinal position.

Description

The Delete method of the Parameters collection class removes a Parameter object from the collection. By passing either the name of a valid Parameter object within the collection or its ordinal position, the Delete method removes the specified Parameter object from the associated Parameters collection class.

See Also

Parameter.Name Property

Parameters.Item Property   (Versions 2.0, 2.1, 2.5, 2.6)

`Set error = errors.Item(Index)`
`Set error = errors (Index)`

The Item property accesses a particular Parameter object belonging to the Parameters collection.

Datatype

Object

Description

The *Index* placeholder is a Variant datatype that represents the ordinal position of a Parameter object within the Parameters collection. If the Parameters collection does not contain the item requested, an error is generated.

Note

Some languages do not support the Item property in its first syntax. For these languages, use the second syntax, without the Item method name.

Parameters.Refresh Method   (Versions 2.0, 2.1, 2.5, 2.6)

```
parameters.Refresh
```

The Refresh method of the Parameters collection class updates the collection with the parameters of the current stored procedure or parameterized query associated with the Command object to which the Parameters collection belongs.

Description

The Refresh method updates the Parameters collection class with the parameters of the associated Command object's stored procedure or parameterized query.

If you attempt to access the Parameters collection class before calling the Refresh method, it is automatically called by ADO.

Properties Collection   (Versions 2.0, 2.1, 2.5, 2.6)

```
Set properties = connection.Properties
Set properties = command.Properties
Set properties = recordset.Properties
Set properties = field.Properties
```

See the Property Object for more information and examples pertaining to the Properties collection.

Objects

Property
 Contains information about a particular feature supported by the associated data provider.

Methods

Refresh
 Updates the Properties collection with properties that are specific to the data provider.

Properties

Count
 Indicates how many Property objects belong to the associated Properties collection.

Item
 Accesses a particular Property object belonging to the Properties collection.

Properties.Count Property   (Versions 2.0, 2.1, 2.5, 2.6)

*count = properties.*Count

The Count property indicates how many Property objects belong to the associated Properties collection.

Datatype

Long

Description

If the value of the Count property is zero, there are no Property objects within the associated Properties collection. However, Property objects that do belong to the associated Properties collection are indexed from 0 to one less than the value of the Count property.

Properties.Item Property   (Versions 2.0, 2.1, 2.5, 2.6)

Set *property = properties.*Item(*Index*)
Set *property = properties*(*Index*)

The Item property accesses a particular Property object belonging to the Properties collection.

Datatype

Property object

Description

The *Index* placeholder is a Variant datatype that represents the ordinal position of a Property object within the Properties collection. If the Properties collection does not contain the item requested, an error is generated.

Note

Some languages do not support the Item property in its first syntax. For these languages, use the second syntax, without the Item method name.

Properties.Refresh Method   (Versions 2.1, 2.5, 2.6)

*properties.*Refresh

The Refresh method updates the Properties collection with properties that are specific to the data provider.

Property Object   (Versions 2.0, 2.1, 2.5, 2.6)

Dim *property* As ADODB.Property

The Property object contains information about dynamic properties implemented by the associated data provider.

Applies To

Properties

This collection contains a group of Property objects that hold information about the functionality of a data provider.

Properties

Attributes

Sets or returns specific characteristics about the Property object.

Name

Specifies the name for the current Property object.

Type

Indicates the datatype of the Property object's value.

Value

Indicates the value of the current Property object.

Description

Individual Property objects are part of Properties collections for the Connection, Command, Recordset, and Field objects.

An instance of a Property object represents a single Dynamic property for the given data provider. The values of these properties, when changed, can alter the behavior of a data provider to a lower level than with the built-in properties of the given ADO object.

Examples

In this section, we will be looking at two examples that show how to do the following:

- Display the dynamic properties of the Connection object.
- Modify the value of a dynamic property.

Before we begin looking at the Property examples for this section, define the following connection string Const value so that the examples will work properly:

```
Private Const DATASOURCE_NWIND = "Provider=Microsoft.Jet.OLEDB.4.0; " _
                    & "Data Source=C:\Program Files\" _
                    & "Microsoft Visual Studio\VB98\NWind.mdb;"
```

Now that we have this constant defined, we can begin to look at some examples. Example 13-14 displays all of the dynamic properties for the Connection object when it connects to the Northwind database with Jet 4.0.

Example 13-14. Displaying the Dynamic Properties of the Connection Object

```
Dim con As ADODB.Connection
Dim prp As ADODB.Property


' open the NWind database with Jet

Set con = New ADODB.Connection
con.Open DATASOURCE_NWIND
```

Example 13-14. Displaying the Dynamic Properties of the Connection Object (continued)

```
'
' display each dynamic property of the Connection object
'
For Each prp In con.Properties
    Debug.Print Left$(prp.Name & ":" & Space(45), 45) & " " & prp.Value
Next prp


'
' clean up
'
con.Close

Set con = Nothing
```

As we can see from the output of this example, there are plenty of properties to play with:

```
Current Catalog:
Active Sessions:                             128
Asynchable Commit:                           False
Catalog Location:                            1
Catalog Term:                                Database
Column Definition:                           1
NULL Concatenation Behavior:                 2
Data Source Name:                            C:\Program......\NWind.mdb
Read-Only Data Source:                       False
DBMS Name:                                   MS Jet
DBMS Version:                                04.00.0000
GROUP BY Support:                            4
Heterogeneous Table Support:                 2
Identifier Case Sensitivity:                 8
Maximum Index Size:                          255
Maximum Row Size:                            4049
Maximum Row Size Includes BLOB:              False
Maximum Tables in SELECT:                    0
Multiple Storage Objects:                    False
Multi-Table Update:                          True
NULL Collation Order:                        4
OLE Object Support:                          1
ORDER BY Columns in Select List:             False
Prepare Abort Behavior:                      1
Prepare Commit Behavior:                     2
Procedure Term:                              STORED QUERY
Provider Name:                               MSJETOLEDB40.DLL
OLE DB Version:                              02.10
Provider Version:                            04.00.2927
Schema Term:                                 Schema
Schema Usage:                                0
SQL Support:                                 512
Structured Storage:                          9
Subquery Support:                            63
Isolation Levels:                            4096
Isolation Retention:                         9
Table Term:                                  Table
User Name:                                   Admin
```

```
Pass By Ref Accessors:                          False
Transaction DDL:                                16
Asynchable Abort:                               False
Data Source Object Threading Model:             1
Output Parameter Availability:                  1
Persistent ID Type:                             4
Multiple Parameter Sets:                        True
Rowset Conversions on Command:                  True
Multiple Results:                               0
Provider Friendly Name:                         Microsoft......der for Jet
Alter Column Support:                           36
Open Rowset Support:                            2
Cache Authentication:                           True
Encrypt Password:                               False
Mask Password:                                  False
Password:
User ID:                                        Admin
Data Source:                                    C:\Program......\NWind.mdb
Window Handle:                                  0
Mode:                                           16
Prompt:                                         4
Extended Properties:
Locale Identifier:                              1033
Jet OLEDB:System database:
Jet OLEDB:Registry Path:
Jet OLEDB:Database Password:
Jet OLEDB:Engine Type:                          4
Jet OLEDB:Database Locking Mode:                0
Jet OLEDB:Global Partial Bulk Ops:              2
Jet OLEDB:Global Bulk Transactions:             1
Jet OLEDB:New Database Password:
Jet OLEDB:Create System Database:               False
Jet OLEDB:Encrypt Database:                      False
Jet OLEDB:Don't Copy Locale on Compact:         False
Jet OLEDB:Compact Without Replica Repair:        False
Jet OLEDB:SFP:                                   False
Jet OLEDB:Compact Reclaimed Space Amount:        0
Autocommit Isolation Levels:                     4096
Jet OLEDB:ODBC Command Time Out:                 0
Jet OLEDB:Max Locks Per File:                    0
Jet OLEDB:Implicit Commit Sync:                  False
Jet OLEDB:Flush Transaction Timeout:             0
Jet OLEDB:Lock Delay:                            0
Jet OLEDB:Max Buffer Size:                       0
Jet OLEDB:User Commit Sync:                      True
Jet OLEDB:Lock Retry:                            0
Jet OLEDB:Exclusive Async Delay:                 0
Jet OLEDB:Shared Async Delay:                    0
Jet OLEDB:Page Timeout:                          0
Jet OLEDB:Recycle Long-Valued Pages:             False
Jet OLEDB:Reset ISAM Stats:                      True
Jet OLEDB:Connection Control:                    2
Jet OLEDB:ODBC Parsing:                          False
Jet OLEDB:Page Locks to Table Lock:              0
```

```
Jet OLEDB:Sandbox Mode:                    False
Jet OLEDB:Transaction Commit Mode:         0
```

Example 13-15 shows how one of the previous properties can be modified to change the behavior of the data provider, particularly the **Prompt** dynamic property which allows you to instruct ADO to prompt the user for connection information.

Example 13-15. Modifying a Dynamic Property Object

```
Dim con As ADODB.Connection

'
' create a new instance of the Connection object
'
Set con = New ADODB.Connection

'
' ask to always show the prompt
'
con.Properties.Item("Prompt") = ADODB.ConnectPromptEnum.adPromptAlways

'
' attempt to open the Connection without any information
'
con.Open

'
' do something here
'

'
' clean up
'
con.Close

Set con = Nothing
```

Property.Attributes Property   (Versions 2.0, 2.1, 2.5, 2.6)

property.Attributes = PropertyArgumentsEnum

The Attributes property sets or returns specific characteristics about the Property object.

Datatype

PropertyArgumentsEnum (Long)

Description

The Attributes property is read-only. The value of the Arguments property can be set to any sum of the values from the PropertyArgumentsEnum enumerations listed in Appendix E.

See Also

PropertyAttributesEnum Enumeration

Property.Name Property (Versions 2.0, 2.1, 2.5, 2.6)

```
property.Name = name
```

The Name property specifies the name for the current Property object.

Datatype

String

Description

The Name property is read-only for the Property object. The Name property retrieves a Property object from the Properties collection. Names do not have to be unique within a Properties collection class.

Property.Type Property (Versions 2.0, 2.1, 2.5, 2.6)

```
type = property.Type
```

The Type property indicates the datatype of the Property object's value.

Datatype

DataTypeEnum

Description

The Type property is read-only for Property objects.

See Also

DataTypeEnum Enumeration

Property.Value Property (Versions 2.0, 2.1, 2.5, 2.6)

```
value = property.Value
```

The Value property indicates the value of the current Property object.

Datatype

Variant

Description

Sets or returns the value of the current Property object.

Record Object (Versions 2.5, 2.6)

```
Dim record As ADODB.Record
```

The Record object represents either a single row within a Recordset object or a resource in a semistructured data source, such as a file directory.

Collections

Fields

Contains individual field objects for the current Record object.

Properties

Contains characteristics specific to the Record object for the currently used provider.

Methods

Cancel

Cancels an asynchronous operation for the Record object.

Close

Closes an opened Record object.

CopyRecord

Represents a member method of the Recordset object that cancels the currently pending batch update.

DeleteRecord

Deletes the resource represented by the current Record object, or another if specified.

GetChildren

Returns the children of a collection Record object in the form of a Recordset object.

MoveRecord

Moves a resource to another location.

Open

Opens an individual record in a recordset or a resource within a data source.

Properties

ActiveConnection

Indicates to which Connection object the current Record object belongs.

Mode

Indicates the permissions for modifying data within a Record object.

ParentURL

Indicates the parent record of the current Record object by means of an absolute URL.

RecordType

Indicates the type of the current record.

Source

Indicates from which object the Record object is created.

State

Indicates the current state of the Record object.

Description

A Record object contains a collection of Fields, just as a Recordset object does. When a Record object is opened with a Recordset object, the Record object contains all of the fields of the Recordset object plus two extra (one for the default stream and one for the URL representing the resource identified by the Record object).

If a Record object is created from a Recordset object, the Source property can be used to return to the original Recordset object.

When a Record object is representing a structured data source such as a filesystem, the Record object can be used to represent a leaf node (file) or nonleaf node (directory). In each case, the fields within the Fields collection may mean different things. As a nonleaf node (directory), the Field objects usually represent attributes of the resource. As a leaf node (file), the Field objects contain not only attributes of the resource, but also a default Stream object that contains the binary data for the resource. Although this is usually the case, a nonleaf node may also contain binary data.

A Record object can be opened by a URL that uniquely represents a resource. In such a case, a Connection object is implicitly created within the Record object, unless one is explicitly stated with the ActiveConnection property. In the latter case, the Connection object would dictate the context of the files and directories accessible from the Record object.

The Record object can be used to copy, move, and delete resources within the context of its associated Connection object. These resources can be, but don't necessarily have to be, the resource that is being represented by the current Record object.

 MSDAIPP is needed to browse filesystem data sources; it is the Microsoft OLE DB Provider for Internet Publishing.

Examples

In this section, we will be looking at three examples that show how to do the following:

- Open a Record object from a Recordset object.
- Work with files using the Record object.
- Return the children of a resource with the Record object.

Example 13-16 shows how a Record object can be opened from an already opened Recordset object. This example opens a Recordset object using a URL from the root directory of your localhost. Please note that for this example to work, you must be running a Internet Information Server or an equivalent Web Server.

Example 13-16. Opening a Record Object from a Recordset Object

```
Dim rst As ADODB.Recordset
Dim rec As ADODB.Record
Dim fld As ADODB.Field

'
' open a Recordset object for the root of the local host
'
Set rst = New ADODB.Recordset
rst.Open "URL=http://localhost"

'
' open the Record object with the current record of the Recordset
'
Set rec = New ADODB.Record
```

Example 13-16. Opening a Record Object from a Recordset Object (continued)

```
rec.Open rst

'
' display the fields for the single record of the Recordset object
'
For Each fld In rec.Fields
    Debug.Print Left$(fld.Name & ":" & Space(35), 35) & " " & fld.Value
Next fld

'
' clean up
'
rec.Close
rst.Close

Set rec = Nothing
Set rst = Nothing
```

After running this example, notice that the following information is outputed to the Immediate Window. The Record object had been opened for the first resource in the root directory of the localhost, the Gallery directory (collection):

```
RESOURCE_PARSENAME:                    Gallery
RESOURCE_PARENTNAME:                   http://localhost
RESOURCE_ABSOLUTEPARSENAME:            http://localhost/Gallery
RESOURCE_ISHIDDEN:
RESOURCE_ISREADONLY:
RESOURCE_CONTENTTYPE:
RESOURCE_CONTENTCLASS:
RESOURCE_CONTENTLANGUAGE:
RESOURCE_CREATIONTIME:
RESOURCE_LASTACCESSTIME:
RESOURCE_LASTWRITETIME:
RESOURCE_STREAMSIZE:
RESOURCE_ISCOLLECTION:                 True
RESOURCE_ISSTRUCTUREDDOCUMENT:
DEFAULT_DOCUMENT:
RESOURCE_DISPLAYNAME:                  Gallery
RESOURCE_ISROOT:                       True
RESOURCE_ISMARKEDFOROFFLINE:           False
```

Example 13-17 shows how files can be created, copied, moved, and deleted within the context of the connection—in this case, the root directory of the localhost machine.

Example 13-17. Working with Files Using the Record Object

```
Dim rec As ADODB.Record

'
' create a new resource on the local host
'
Set rec = New ADODB.Record

rec.Open "newfile", _
```

Example 13-17. Working with Files Using the Record Object (continued)

```
            "URL=http://localhost/", _
            adModeReadWrite, _
            adCreateOverwrite

'
' copy the new resource to another file
'
rec.CopyRecord , _
                "http://localhost/anotherfile", _
                , _
                , _
                adCopyOverWrite

'
' move the file to a new file name
'
rec.MoveRecord "http://localhost/anotherfile", _
                "http://localhost/movedfile", _
                , _
                , _
                adMoveOverWrite

'
' delete the moved file
'
rec.DeleteRecord "http://localhost/movedfile"

'
' clean up
'
rec.Close

Set rec = Nothing
```

Example 13-18 shows how the Record object can return children for a given resource. In this example, the Record object is opened for the root directory (a collection resource) of the localhost machine. Calling the GetChildren method returns a Recordset object containing multiple records, each representing a single resource that is considered a child of the root directory resource.

Example 13-18. Returning the Children of a Resource Using the Record Object

```
Dim rec As ADODB.Record
Dim rst As ADODB.Recordset
Dim fld As ADODB.Field

Set rec = New ADODB.Record

rec.Open "Gallery", "URL=http://localhost"

Set rst = rec.GetChildren

If (Not (rst.BOF And rst.EOF)) Then rst.MoveFirst
```

Example 13-18. Returning the Children of a Resource Using the Record Object (continued)

```
While (Not rst.EOF)
    Debug.Print rst.Fields.Item("RESOURCE_ABSOLUTEPARSENAME").Value
    rst.MoveNext
Wend

'

' clean up
'

rst.Close
rec.Close

Set rst = Nothing
Set rec = Nothing
```

Running the previous example outputs the following data to the Immediate Window:

```
http://localhost/Gallery/survey
http://localhost/Gallery/guestbk
http://localhost/Gallery/usernote
http://localhost/Gallery/timeline
http://localhost/Gallery/themes
http://localhost/Gallery/shopcart
http://localhost/Gallery/randomad
http://localhost/Gallery/quote
http://localhost/Gallery/query
http://localhost/Gallery/prefer
http://localhost/Gallery/mmedia
http://localhost/Gallery/ie4
http://localhost/Gallery/grid
http://localhost/Gallery/dentry
http://localhost/Gallery/counter
http://localhost/Gallery/controls
http://localhost/Gallery/applet
http://localhost/Gallery/images
http://localhost/Gallery/_private
http://localhost/Gallery/VIEWSRC.ASP
http://localhost/Gallery/USERNTB.HTM
http://localhost/Gallery/USERNTA.HTM
http://localhost/Gallery/TIMELNB.HTM
http://localhost/Gallery/TIMELNA.HTM
http://localhost/Gallery/THEMEB.HTM
http://localhost/Gallery/THEMEA.HTM
http://localhost/Gallery/SURVEYB.HTM
http://localhost/Gallery/SURVEYA.HTM
http://localhost/Gallery/SHOPCRTB.HTM
http://localhost/Gallery/SHOPCRTA.HTM
http://localhost/Gallery/SAMPTOC.HTM
http://localhost/Gallery/SAMPLE.ASP
http://localhost/Gallery/SAMPINTR.HTM
http://localhost/Gallery/SAMPHDR.ASP
http://localhost/Gallery/RANDADB.HTM
http://localhost/Gallery/RANDADA.HTM
http://localhost/Gallery/QUOTEB.HTM
```

```
http://localhost/Gallery/QUOTEA.HTM
http://localhost/Gallery/QUERYB.HTM
http://localhost/Gallery/QUERYA.HTM
http://localhost/Gallery/PREFB.HTM
http://localhost/Gallery/PREFA.HTM
http://localhost/Gallery/MMEDIAB.HTM
http://localhost/Gallery/MMEDIAA.HTM
http://localhost/Gallery/LEGEND.ASP
http://localhost/Gallery/IE4B.HTM
http://localhost/Gallery/IE4A.HTM
http://localhost/Gallery/GUESTBKB.HTM
http://localhost/Gallery/GUESTBKA.HTM
http://localhost/Gallery/GRIDB.HTM
http://localhost/Gallery/GRIDA.HTM
http://localhost/Gallery/Global.asa
http://localhost/Gallery/DENTRYB.HTM
http://localhost/Gallery/DENTRYA.HTM
http://localhost/Gallery/DEFAULT.HTM
http://localhost/Gallery/COUNTERB.HTM
http://localhost/Gallery/COUNTERA.HTM
http://localhost/Gallery/CONTROLB.HTM
http://localhost/Gallery/CONTROLA.HTM
http://localhost/Gallery/CODE.ASP
http://localhost/Gallery/APPLETB.HTM
http://localhost/Gallery/APPLETA.HTM
```

Record.ActiveConnection Property   (Versions 2.5, 2.6)

```
Record.ActiveConnection = ConnectionString
Set Record.ActiveConnection = ConnectionObject
```

The ActiveConnection property indicates to which Connection object the current Record object belongs.

Datatype

String or Variant (containing the current Connection object)

Description

The ActiveConnection property of the Record object is both read- and write-enabled while the Record object is closed and read-only once it is opened. This property can be set to either a connection string or a Connection object and returns a Connection object when it is read.

If the Record object was opened from an existing Record object or a Recordset object, then the Record object gains its Connection object from this object. If the Record object is opened by using a URL, a Connection object is automatically created for the Record object and is accessible from the ActiveConnection property.

See Also

Record.Open Method

Record.Cancel Method   (Versions 2.5, 2.6)

`record.Cancel`

The Cancel method cancels an asynchronous operation for the Record object.

Description

The Cancel method can be called to cancel an asynchronous operation of the Record object invoked by the CopyRecord, DeleteRecord, MoveRecord, and Open methods.

See Also

Record.CopyRecord Method, Record.DeleteRecord Method, Record.MoveRecord Method, Record.Open Method

---

Record.Close Method   (Versions 2.5, 2.6)

`record.Close`

The Close method closes an opened Record object.

Description

The Close method can be called only on an open Record object. After calling the Close method, the Open method can be called again to reopen the Record object. Calling the Close method releases any resources allocated to the Record object.

Record.CopyRecord Method   (Versions 2.5, 2.6)

```
record.CopyRecord (Source, _
                   Destination, _
                   UserName, _
                   Password, _
                   Options, _
                   Async) As String
```

The CancelBatch is a member method of the Recordset object that cancels the currently pending batch update.

Arguments

Source (String)
> Optional. Indicates the URL of a resource to be copied. If this argument is omitted, then the resource represented by the current Record object is copied.

Destination (String)
> Optional. Represents a URL value that indicates where the resource will be copied to.

UserName (String)
> Optional. Indicates, if necessary, the username that will be used to access the resource indicated by the *Destination* argument.

Password (String)
> Optional. Indicates, if necessary, the password to verify the *UserName* argument.

Options (CopyRecordOptionsEnum)
> Optional. Indicates the behavior of the copy operation. The default value for this argument is `adCopyUnspecified`.

Async (Boolean)
> Optional. Indicates whether this operation should be executed asynchronously.

Returns

String

Description

By default, the CopyRecord method will not overwrite a resource that already exists. To force the replacement of the destination resource, use the `adCopyOverWrite` option.

By default, the CopyRecord method will copy all subdirectories and files beneath the source resource unless the `adCopyNonRecursive` option is specified.

If the source and the destination resources are identical, an error will occur. If the destination resource is a child of the source resource, the operation will never complete.

The return value, although provider-specific, is usually the name of the destination resource.

See Also

CopyRecordOptionsEnum Enumeration

Record.DeleteRecord Method (Versions 2.5, 2.6)

`record.DeleteRecord Source, Async`

The DeleteRecord method deletes the resource represented by the current Record object, or another if specified.

Arguments

Source (String)
> Optional. Specifies which resource to delete. If this argument is omitted, the resource represented by the current Record object will be deleted.

Async (Boolean)
> Optional. Indicates whether this operation should be executed asynchronously.

Description

The DeleteRecord method deletes all children resources of the current resource as well.

The Record object should be closed immediately after calling the DeleteRecord method because its behavior would be unpredictable. At the very least, an error will occur when trying to work with a Record object that represents a deleted resource.

If the Record object was created from a Recordset object, you should either close and reopen the Recordset object or call Resync or Requery for the resource to be removed from it.

See Also

Recordset.Open Method, Recordset.Requery Method, Recordset.Resync Method

Record.Fields Collection   (Versions 2.5, 2.6)

`record.Fields`

The Fields collection contains individual Field objects for the current Record object.

Datatype

Fields (Collection object)

Description

The Fields collection contains multiple Field objects for the current Record object. There are two special Field objects, `adDefaultStream` and `adRecordURL`,that can be accessed by specifying the FieldEnum enumeration. One returns the default string for the current Record object, and the other returns the URL.

Field objects can be added to the collection either by calling the Field.Append method or by referencing a Field by name that is not already part of the collection. Calling the Field. Update method will add the field to the collection, if possible, within the data source. Until this moment, the Field.Status property will return `adFieldPendingInsert`.

See Also

Field.Append Method, Field.Update Method, FieldEnum Enumeration

Record.GetChildren Method   (Versions 2.5, 2.6)

`Set recordset = record.GetChildrean`

The GetChildren method returns the children of a collection Record object in the form of a Recordset object.

Returns

Recordset object

Description

The GetChildren method returns a Recordset object containing children of the current Record object. Each record within the returned Recordset object represents a single resource that is a child of the resource represented by the associated Record object.

Record.Mode Property   (Versions 2.5, 2.6)

`record.Mode = ConnectModeEnum`

The Mode property indicates the permissions for modifying data within a Record object.

Datatype

ConnectModeEnum

Description

The default value for the Mode property of a Record object is adModeRead. The Mode property is read- and write-enabled while the Record object is closed, but read-only once it is opened.

See Also

ConnectModeEnum Enumeration

Record.MoveRecord Method

(Versions 2.5, 2.6)

```
record.MoveRecord   (Source, _
                     Destination, _
                     UserName, _
                     Password, _
                     Options, _
                     Async) As String
```

The MoveRecord method moves a resource to another location.

Arguments

Source (String)
> Optional. Indicates the URL of a resource to be moved. If this argument is omitted, then the resource represented by the current Record object is moved.

Destination (String)
> Optional. Represents a URL value that indicates where the resource will be moved.

UserName (String)
> Optional. Indicates, if necessary, the username that will be used to access the resource indicated by the *Destination* argument.

Password (String)
> Optional. Indicates, if necessary, the password to verify the *UserName* argument.

Options (CopyRecordOptionsEnum)
> Optional. Indicates the behavior of the move operation. The default value for this argument is adMoveUnspecified.

Async (Boolean)
> Optional. Indicates whether this operation should be executed asynchronously.

Returns

String

Description

By default, the MoveRecord method does not overwrite a resource that already exists. To force the replacement of the destination resource, use the adCopyOverWrite option. All hypertext links in the file are automatically updated unless otherwise specified in the *Options* argument.

If the source and the destination resources are identical, an error will occur.

If the Record object was created from a Recordset object, you should close and reopen the Recordset object or call Resync or Requery for the resource to be removed from the recordset.

Not all properties of the Record object will be automatically repopulated—to do this, close and reopen the Record object.

The return value, although provider-specific, is usually the name of the destination resource.

See Also

MoveRecordOptionsEnum Enumeration, Record.Close Method, Record.Open Method, Recordset.Open Method, Recordset.Requery Method, Recordset.Resync Method

---

Record.Open Method   (Versions 2.5, 2.6)

```
record.Open  (Source, _
              ActiveConnection, _
              Mode, _
              CreateOptions, _
              Options, _
              UserName, _
              Password)
```

The Open method opens an individual record in a recordset or a resource within a data source.

Arguments

Source (Variant)
> Optional. Indicates the source of the resource to open. This can be a URL, a Command object returning a single row, an open Recordset object, or a String containing a SQL statement or a table name.

ActiveConnection (Variant)
> Optional. Indicates the connection to the data source by either a connection string or an open Connection object.

Mode (ConnectModeEnum)
> Optional. Indicates the access permissions to open the Record object with. The default value is adModeUnknown.

CreateOptions (CreateModeEnum)
> Optional. This argument is used only when the Source argument represents a URL. This argument can be used to indicate whether to open an existing resource or to create a new one. The default value for this argument is adFailIfNotExist.

Options (RecordOpenOptionsEnum)
> Optional. Can contain multiple RecordOpenOptionsEnum enumeration values that indicate special options for opening the Record object. The default value for this method is adOpenRecordUnspecified.

UserName (String)
> Optional. Indicates, if necessary, the username that will be used to access the resource indicated by the source argument.

Password (String)

Optional. Indicates, if necessary, the password to verify the *UserName* argument.

Description

If the Record object represents a resource that cannot be represented by a URL, then the ParentURL property and the adRecordURL default field both return Null.

See Also

ConnectModeEnum Enumeration, RecordCreateOptionsEnum Enumeration, Record-OpenOptionsEnum Enumeration

---

Record.ParentURL Property (Versions 2.5, 2.6)

`record.ParentURL = ParentURL`

The ParentURL is used to indicate the parent record of the current Record object by means of an absolute URL.

Datatype

String

Description

The ParentURL property indicates the parent resource of the current resource represented by the Record object. This property is read-only.

The ParentURL can be Null if there is no parent for the current resource represented by the Record object or if the resource cannot be expressed in terms of a URL.

Record.Properties Collection (Versions 2.5, 2.6)

`record.Properties`

The Properties collection contains characteristics specific to the Record object for the currently used provider.

Datatype

Properties (Collection object)

Description

The Properties collection class contains a Property class instance for each property specific to the Record object for the data provider.

Record.RecordType Property (Versions 2.5, 2.6)

`record.RecordType = RecordTypeEnum`

The RecordType property indicates the type of the current record.

Datatype

RecordTypeEnum

Description

The RecordType property is read-only; it indicates the type of the current Record object.

See Also

RecordTypeEnum Enumeration

Record.Source Property   (Versions 2.5, 2.6)

```
Set record.Source = object
```

The Source property indicates from which object the Record object is created.

Datatype

Variant

Description

The Source property is read-only when the Record object is open, but read- and write-enabled while it is closed.

The Source property can be set to a Recordset or Command object. If the Source property is set to a Recordset object, the Record object will be opened based upon the current record of the Recordset object. If the Source property is set to a Command object, the Command object must return a single row.

If the ActiveConnection property is also set, then the Source property must be set to an object that is within the connection's scope.

The Source property returns the Source argument of the Record.Open method.

See Also

Record.ActiveConnection Property, Record.Open Method

Record.State Property   (Versions 2.5, 2.6)

```
state = record.State
```

The State property indicates the current state of the Record object.

Datatype

Long (ObjectStateEnum)

Description

The read-only State property returns a Long value that can be evaluated as an ObjectStateEnum enumeration value. The default value for the Record object is closed (adStateClosed).

For the Record object, the State property can return multiple values when the object is executing an operation asynchronously (i.e., `adStateOpen` and `adStateExecuting`).

See Also

ObjectStateEnum Enumeration

Recordset Object   (Versions 2.0, 2.1, 2.5, 2.6)

`Dim recordset As ADODB.Recordset`

The Recordset object represents a complete group of rows within a table or a group of records that have been returned from an executed command.

Collections

Fields

Contains multiple Field objects for the current Recordset object, one for each column in the Recordset object.

Properties

Contains characteristics specific to the Recordset object for the currently used provider.

Methods

AddNew

Creates a new record within the current Recordset object and sets it to the specified value.

Cancel

Cancels an asynchronous operation for the Recordset object.

CancelBatch

Cancels the currently pending batch update for the current Recordset object.

CancelUpdate

Cancels any changes to the current batch update made since the last AddNew or Update method calls.

Clone

Returns a clone of the current recordset.

Close

Closes a recordset and releases any resources used by it.

CompareBookmarks

Determines the position of two bookmarks in a recordset in relationship to one another.

Delete

Deletes specified records within the recordset.

Find

Moves the record pointer to a row within the current recordset that matches the single-column search criteria specified.

GetRows

Returns multiple records from an open Recordset object in the form of an array.

GetString
Returns the entire Recordset object as a String value.

Move
Moves the position of the record pointer within the desired Recordset object.

MoveFirst
Moves the record pointer to the first record in a recordset.

MoveLast
Moves the record pointer to the last record in a recordset.

MoveNext
Moves the record pointer to the next record in a recordset.

MovePrevious
Moves the record pointer to the previous record in a recordset.

NextRecordset
Returns the next recordset by advancing through a series of commands.

Open
Opens a cursor within a Recordset object.

Requery
Re-executes the command that created the recordset in the first place, in order to cause a refresh of the recordset.

Resync
Refreshes the data in the recordset from the underlying data source.

Save
Saves the current Recordset object to a file or to a Stream object.

Seek
Quickly changes the record pointer to the record in the Recordset object that matches the index provided.

Supports
Determines whether the current data provider supports specified functionality.

Update
Saves the changes made to fields within the current record when one or more fields have been changed or a call to AddNew was made.

UpdateBatch
Writes all pending batch updates to disk when called.

Properties

AbsolutePage
Returns or sets a value that indicates the current page in the recordset.

AbsolutePosition
Returns or sets a value that indicates the current record position within the recordset.

ActiveCommand
Returns the Command object that was used to populate a Recordset object.

ActiveConnection
Specifies the Connection object for the current Recordset object.

BOF

Indicates that the record pointer is located before the first record in the recordset.

Bookmark

Returns a unique identifier for the current record within a recordset. By setting the Bookmark property to a previously read value, the record pointer can be repositioned to the original record.

CacheSize

Indicates the number or records that are cached by ADO locally in system memory.

CursorLocation

Indicates the location of the cursor service.

CursorType

Indicates the type of cursor being used for the current recordset.

DataMember

Indicates the object, within the data source specified by the DataSource property, with which the Recordset object should be created.

DataSource

Indicates the source with which the Recordset object should be created.

EditMode

Indicates the current editing status for a given record.

EOF

Indicates that the record pointer is located directly after the last record in the recordset.

Filter

Filters a selection of records within the current Recordset object.

Index

Sets the current index for a given recordset.

LockType

Indicates the type of locks that are set on records when they are being edited.

MarshalOptions

Indicates which records are to be marshaled back to the server.

MaxRecords

Indicates the maximum number of records to be returned to a recordset from a query.

PageCount

Returns the number of logical pages that are in the current Recordset object.

PageSize

Indicates how many records belong to a logical page.

RecordCount

Returns the number of records in the current Recordset object.

Sort

Sorts a recordset on one or more field names.

Source

Returns the source for the data in a Recordset object.

State

Indicates the current state of the Recordset object.

Status

Indicates the status of the current record in relation to bulk operations.

StayInSync

Indicates whether the references to chapter recordsets change when the record pointer moves to a different parent row for hierarchical recordsets.

Events

EndOfRecordset

Called when an attempt to move the record pointer past the end of the recordset has occurred.

FetchComplete

Called when a long asynchronous operation (fetch) has completed and all of the records have been returned.

FetchProgress

Called during a long asynchronous operation (fetch) to report the progress of the fetch.

FieldChangeComplete

Called after an operation changes one or more Field object values.

MoveComplete

Called after an operation changes the position of the record pointer within the Recordset object.

RecordChangeComplete

Called after an operation changes one or more records in the Recordset object.

RecordsetChangeComplete

Called after an operation changes the Recordset object.

WillChangeField

Called before an operation changes one or more Field object values.

WillChangeRecord

Called before an operation changes one or more records in the Recordset object.

WillChangeRecordset

Called before an operation changes the Recordset object.

WillMove

Called before an operation changes the position of the record pointer within the Recordset object.

Description

The Recordset object needs a connection to a data source through the ActiveConnection property or the ActiveConnection argument of the Open method. Either can be set to an open Connection object or a valid connection string. If used with a connection string, the Recordset object implicitly creates its own Connection object behind the scenes. When using multiple Recordset objects for the same data source, create a Connection object, and use it with the ActiveConnection property or argument. By passing a connection string to each Recordset object, multiple connections to the data source are maintained, even if the connection string is identical.

Before opening a Recordset object, you can set the type of cursor that is used to view the data. There are four types of cursors available: Dynamic, Keyset, Static, and Forward Only.

(See Chapter 5, *The Recordset Object*, for more information on these cursor types.) The Forward Only cursor is the default.

The Dynamic cursor allows the application to see all changes including additions, deletions, and modifications to records. You can move in any direction within a Dynamic cursor, even if the data provider being used doesn't support bookmarks.

The Keyset cursor is very similar to the Dynamic cursor, except that it doesn't allow you to see newly added rows or to access rows that have been deleted by other users. Changes to existing rows can still be seen by the application. Because the Keyset cursor supports bookmarks, you can move in any direction.

The Static cursor takes a snapshot of the data within a data source and therefore doesn't allow the application to see additions, changes, or deletions by other users. The Static cursor also supports bookmarks and allows full movement within it. The Static cursor is the only cursor that can be chosen when using a client-side Recordset object (the CursorLocation property is equal to adUseClient).

The Forward Only cursor is the default cursor and does not allow backwards movement through a Recordset object. It also does not support viewing changes by other users. This cursor is very popular because of its speed when a single pass through the Recordset object is needed.

You can navigate through a Recordset object with the MoveFirst, MoveNext, MovePrevious, MoveLast, and Move methods in conjunction with the BOF and EOF properties, which indicate the beginning and the end of the recordset, respectively. If the current Recordset object is empty, then both the BOF and EOF properties will be set to True.

The Filter property can be set to specify which records are visible within the Recordset object. You can search for a particular record by using the Find and Seek methods.

A Recordset object can be used to modify data by means of updating. There are two types of updating supported by the Recordset object, Immediate and Batch.

Immediate updating is done by calling the Update method. Batch updating is done with the UpdateBatch method. Batch updating can be used to persist multiple record changes at one time to the data source.

Examples

In this section, we will be looking at three examples that show how to do the following:

- Open and navigate a Recordset object.
- Add new records to a Recordset object.
- Find and filter data in a Recordset object.

Before we take a look at any examples of the Recordset object, let's first add some code to our application to show us when our Recordset events are fired. With this code, we can see how events are reported as we look at the upcoming examples in this section.

Add a new Class to your current project, declare the Recordset object With Events as shown, and add the necessary ConnectionString Const for the examples:

```
Private WithEvents rst As ADODB.Recordset

Private Const DATASOURCE_NWIND = "Provider=Microsoft.Jet.OLEDB.4.0; " _
```

```
                                    & "Data Source=C:\Program Files\" _
                                    & "Microsoft Visual Studio\VB98\NWind.mdb;"
```

Now you should be able to see the `rst` variable in the first combo list box over your code. After selecting this object, you will be given a choice of eleven events that can be fired for your Recordset object. For each event, we are going to add code to output the parameters passed to that event to the Immediate Window.

Add the code from Example 13-19 for the 11 events[*] to the new Class.

Example 13-19. The 11 Events to the New Class

```
Private Sub rst_EndOfRecordset(fMoreData As Boolean, _
                               adStatus As ADODB.EventStatusEnum, _
                               ByVal pRecordset As ADODB.Recordset)

    Debug.Print "Event: EndOfRecordset"
    Debug.Print "  More Data: " & fMoreData
    Debug.Print "  Status:    " & GetStatusString(adStatus)
    Debug.Print "  Recordset: " & pRecordset.Source
    Debug.Print

End Sub


Private Sub rst_FetchComplete(ByVal pError As ADODB.Error, _
                              adStatus As ADODB.EventStatusEnum, _
                              ByVal pRecordset As ADODB.Recordset)

    Debug.Print "Event: FetchComplete"
    Debug.Print "  Error:     " & pError.Description
    Debug.Print "  Status:    " & GetStatusString(adStatus)
    Debug.Print "  Recordset: " & pRecordset.Source
    Debug.Print

End Sub


Private Sub rst_FetchProgress(ByVal Progress As Long, _
                              ByVal MaxProgress As Long, _
                              adStatus As ADODB.EventStatusEnum, _
                              ByVal pRecordset As ADODB.Recordset)

    Debug.Print "Event: FetchProgress"
    Debug.Print "  Progress:  " & Progress
    Debug.Print "  Maximum:   " & MaxProgress
    Debug.Print "  Status:    " & GetStatusString(adStatus)
    Debug.Print "  Recordset: " & pRecordset.Source
    Debug.Print

End Sub


Private Sub rst_FieldChangeComplete(ByVal cFields As Long, _
                                    ByVal Fields As Variant, _
```

---

* Available for download from the book's web site, *http://www.oreilly.com/catalog/ado*.

Example 13-19. The 11 Events to the New Class (continued)

```
                                    ByVal pError As ADODB.Error, _
                                    adStatus As ADODB.EventStatusEnum, _
                                    ByVal pRecordset As ADODB.Recordset)

    Debug.Print "Event: FieldChangeComplete"
    Debug.Print "  Changed:   " & cFields
    If (Not (pError Is Nothing)) Then
        Debug.Print "  Error:     " & pError.Description
    End If
    Debug.Print "  Status:    " & GetStatusString(adStatus)
    Debug.Print "  Recordset: " & pRecordset.Source
    Debug.Print

End Sub

Private Sub rst_MoveComplete(ByVal adReason As ADODB.EventReasonEnum, _
                        ByVal pError As ADODB.Error, _
                        adStatus As ADODB.EventStatusEnum, _
                        ByVal pRecordset As ADODB.Recordset)

    Debug.Print "Event: MoveComplete"
    Debug.Print "  Reason:    " & GetReasonString(adReason)
    If (Not (pError Is Nothing)) Then
        Debug.Print "  Error:     " & pError.Description
    End If
    Debug.Print "  Status:    " & GetStatusString(adStatus)
    Debug.Print "  Recordset: " & pRecordset.Source
    Debug.Print

End Sub

Private Sub rst_RecordChangeComplete( _
                        ByVal adReason As ADODB.EventReasonEnum, _
                        ByVal cRecords As Long, _
                        ByVal pError As ADODB.Error, _
                        adStatus As ADODB.EventStatusEnum, _
                        ByVal pRecordset As ADODB.Recordset)

    Debug.Print "Event: RecordChangeComplete"
    Debug.Print "  Reason:    " & GetReasonString(adReason)
    Debug.Print "  Changed:   " & cRecords
    If (Not (pError Is Nothing)) Then
        Debug.Print "  Error:     " & pError.Description
    End If
    Debug.Print "  Status:    " & GetStatusString(adStatus)
    Debug.Print "  Recordset: " & pRecordset.Source
    Debug.Print

End Sub

Private Sub rst_RecordsetChangeComplete( _
                        ByVal adReason As ADODB.EventReasonEnum, _
```

Example 13-19. The 11 Events to the New Class (continued)

```
                                ByVal pError As ADODB.Error, _
                                adStatus As ADODB.EventStatusEnum, _
                                ByVal pRecordset As ADODB.Recordset)

    Debug.Print "Event: RecordsetChangeComplete"
    Debug.Print "  Reason:    " & GetReasonString(adReason)
    If (Not (pError Is Nothing)) Then
        Debug.Print "  Error:     " & pError.Description
    End If
    Debug.Print "  Status:    " & GetStatusString(adStatus)
    Debug.Print "  Recordset: " & pRecordset.Source
    Debug.Print

End Sub

Private Sub rst_WillChangeField(ByVal cFields As Long, _
                                ByVal Fields As Variant, _
                                adStatus As ADODB.EventStatusEnum, _
                                ByVal pRecordset As ADODB.Recordset)

    Debug.Print "Event: WillChangeField"
    Debug.Print "  Changed:   " & cFields
    Debug.Print "  Status:    " & GetStatusString(adStatus)
    Debug.Print "  Recordset: " & pRecordset.Source
    Debug.Print

End Sub

Private Sub rst_WillChangeRecord( _
                        ByVal adReason As ADODB.EventReasonEnum, _
                        ByVal cRecords As Long, _
                        adStatus As ADODB.EventStatusEnum, _
                        ByVal pRecordset As ADODB.Recordset)

    Debug.Print "Event: WillChangeRecord"
    Debug.Print "  Reason:    " & GetReasonString(adReason)
    Debug.Print "  Changed:   " & cRecords
    Debug.Print "  Status:    " & GetStatusString(adStatus)
    Debug.Print "  Recordset: " & pRecordset.Source
    Debug.Print

End Sub

Private Sub rst_WillChangeRecordset( _
                        ByVal adReason As ADODB.EventReasonEnum, _
                        adStatus As ADODB.EventStatusEnum, _
                        ByVal pRecordset As ADODB.Recordset)

    Debug.Print "Event: WillChangeRecordset"
    Debug.Print "  Reason:    " & GetReasonString(adReason)
```

Example 13-19. The 11 Events to the New Class (continued)

```
    Debug.Print "  Status:    " & GetStatusString(adStatus)
    Debug.Print "  Recordset: " & pRecordset.Source
    Debug.Print

End Sub

Private Sub rst_WillMove(ByVal adReason As ADODB.EventReasonEnum, _
                    adStatus As ADODB.EventStatusEnum, _
                    ByVal pRecordset As ADODB.Recordset)

    Debug.Print "Event: WillMove"
    Debug.Print "  Reason:    " & GetReasonString(adReason)
    Debug.Print "  Status:    " & GetStatusString(adStatus)
    Debug.Print "  Recordset: " & pRecordset.Source
    Debug.Print

End Sub
```

The only other code that you need for the following examples is the code for the GetStatusString and GetReasonString functions, which accept an enumeration value and returns a String describing the value:

```
    Private Function GetStatusString(adStatus As ADODB.EventStatusEnum) As String

        Select Case (adStatus)

            Case ADODB.EventStatusEnum.adStatusCancel:
                GetStatusString = "Cancel"

            Case ADODB.EventStatusEnum.adStatusCantDeny:
                GetStatusString = "Can't Deny"

            Case ADODB.EventStatusEnum.adStatusErrorsOccurred
                GetStatusString = "Errors Occurred"

            Case ADODB.EventStatusEnum.adStatusOK:
                GetStatusString = "Status Okay"

            Case ADODB.EventStatusEnum.adStatusUnwantedEvent:
                GetStatusString = "Unwanted Event"

        End Select

    End Function

    Private Function GetReasonString(adReason As ADODB.EventReasonEnum) As String

        Select Case (adReason)

            Case ADODB.EventReasonEnum.adRsnAddNew
                GetReasonString = "Add New"
```

```
        Case ADODB.EventReasonEnum.adRsnClose
            GetReasonString = "Close"

        Case ADODB.EventReasonEnum.adRsnDelete
            GetReasonString = "Delete"

        Case ADODB.EventReasonEnum.adRsnFirstChange
            GetReasonString = "First Change"

        Case ADODB.EventReasonEnum.adRsnMove
            GetReasonString = "Move"

        Case ADODB.EventReasonEnum.adRsnMoveFirst
            GetReasonString = "Move First"

        Case ADODB.EventReasonEnum.adRsnMoveLast
            GetReasonString = "Move Last"

        Case ADODB.EventReasonEnum.adRsnMoveNext
            GetReasonString = "Move Next"

        Case ADODB.EventReasonEnum.adRsnMovePrevious
            GetReasonString = "Move Previous"

        Case ADODB.EventReasonEnum.adRsnRequery
            GetReasonString = "Requery"

        Case ADODB.EventReasonEnum.adRsnResynch
            GetReasonString = "Resynch"

        Case ADODB.EventReasonEnum.adRsnUndoAddNew
            GetReasonString = "Undo Add New"

        Case ADODB.EventReasonEnum.adRsnUndoDelete
            GetReasonString = "Undo Delete"

        Case ADODB.EventReasonEnum.adRsnUndoUpdate
            GetReasonString = "Undo Update"

        Case ADODB.EventReasonEnum.adRsnUpdate
            GetReasonString = "Update"

    End Select

    End Function
```

Example 13-20 illustrates how to open a Recordset object with an existing Connection object and how to navigate the newly opened object with the Move methods and bookmarks.

Example 13-20. Opening and Navigating a Recordset Object

```
Dim con As ADODB.Connection

Dim vBookmark1 As Variant
```

Example 13-20. Opening and Navigating a Recordset Object (continued)

```
Dim vBookmark2 As Variant

'
' instantiate and open a new Connection object
'
Set con = New ADODB.Connection
con.Open DATASOURCE_NWIND

'
' instantiate and open a new Recordset object with:
'
'    currently opened connection
'    Suppliers table
'    Server side cursor
'    Dynamic cursor
'    Read-only locking
'

Set rst = New ADODB.Recordset

rst.ActiveConnection = con
rst.Source = "Suppliers"
rst.CursorLocation = adUseServer
rst.CursorType = adOpenKeyset
rst.LockType = adLockReadOnly
rst.Open , , , , adCmdTable

'
' move to the first record in the recordset
'
If (Not (rst.BOF And rst.EOF)) Then rst.MoveFirst

'
' begin to move around
'
rst.MoveLast
rst.MovePrevious

'
' save the first bookmark
'
vBookmark1 = rst.Bookmark
MsgBox "Bookmark 1 is at position " & CStr(rst.AbsolutePosition)

'
' move around a little
'
rst.MoveFirst
rst.MoveNext

'
' save the second bookmark
'
```

Example 13-20. Opening and Navigating a Recordset Object (continued)

```
vBookmark2 = rst.Bookmark
MsgBox "Bookmark 2 is at position " & CStr(rst.AbsolutePosition)


'
' compare the two bookmarks
'
If (rst.CompareBookmarks(vBookmark1, _
                         vBookmark2) = adCompareLessThan) Then
    MsgBox "Bookmark 1 comes before Bookmark 2."
Else
    MsgBox "Bookmark 2 comes before Bookmark 1."
End If


'
' set the record pointer to a prevously saved bookmark
'
rst.Bookmark = vBookmark1
MsgBox "Now located at position " & CStr(rst.AbsolutePosition)
MsgBox "Now located at page " & CStr(rst.AbsolutePage)


'
' clean up
'
rst.Close
con.Close

Set rst = Nothing
Set con = Nothing
```

Remember not to declare the `rst` variable in a member function. It is already declared at a module level, allowing the events that are triggered for it to be displayed in the Immediate Window, as shown for the output from the previous example:

```
Event: WillMove
   Reason:    Move
   Status:    Can't Deny
   Recordset: select * from Suppliers

Event: MoveComplete
   Reason:    Move
   Status:    Status Okay
   Recordset: select * from Suppliers

Event: WillMove
   Reason:    Move
   Status:    Status Okay
   Recordset: select * from Suppliers

Event: MoveComplete
   Reason:    Move
   Status:    Status Okay
   Recordset: select * from Suppliers
```

```
Event: WillMove
  Reason:     Move First
  Status:     Status Okay
  Recordset: select * from Suppliers

Event: MoveComplete
  Reason:     Move First
  Status:     Status Okay
  Recordset: select * from Suppliers

Event: WillMove
  Reason:     Move Last
  Status:     Status Okay
  Recordset: select * from Suppliers

Event: MoveComplete
  Reason:     Move Last
  Status:     Status Okay
  Recordset: select * from Suppliers

Event: WillMove
  Reason:     Move Previous
  Status:     Status Okay
  Recordset: select * from Suppliers

Event: MoveComplete
  Reason:     Move Previous
  Status:     Status Okay
  Recordset: select * from Suppliers

Event: WillMove
  Reason:     Move First
  Status:     Status Okay
  Recordset: select * from Suppliers

Event: MoveComplete
  Reason:     Move First
  Status:     Status Okay
  Recordset: select * from Suppliers

Event: WillMove
  Reason:     Move Next
  Status:     Status Okay
  Recordset: select * from Suppliers

Event: MoveComplete
  Reason:     Move Next
  Status:     Status Okay
  Recordset: select * from Suppliers

Event: WillMove
  Reason:     Move
  Status:     Status Okay
  Recordset: select * from Suppliers
```

```
Event: MoveComplete
   Reason:    Move
   Status:    Status Okay
   Recordset: select * from Suppliers

Event: RecordsetChangeComplete
   Reason:    Close
   Status:    Status Okay
   Recordset: select * from Suppliers
```

Example 13-21 shows how records can be added to a Recordset object in immediate update mode, the default.

Example 13-21. Adding Records to a Recordset Object

```
'
' instantiate and open a Recordset on the Suppliers table
'
Set rst = New ADODB.Recordset

rst.Open "Suppliers", _
         DATASOURCE_NWIND, _
         adOpenKeyset, _
         adLockOptimistic, _
         adCmdTable


'
' add a new record to the Suppliers table
'
rst.AddNew
rst.Fields("CompanyName").Value = "Roff's Supplies"
rst.Fields("ContactName").Value = "Roff, Jason T."
rst.Update


'
' add another record to the Suppliers table
'
rst.AddNew
rst.Fields("CompanyName").Value = "Kimberly's Supplies"
rst.Fields("ContactName").Value = "Roff, Kimberly A."
rst.Update


'
' clean up
'
rst.Close

Set rst = Nothing
```

When running Example 13-21, the following output is displayed in the Immediate Window:

```
Event: WillMove
   Reason:    Move
   Status:    Can't Deny
   Recordset: select * from Suppliers
```

```
Event: MoveComplete
  Reason:    Move
  Status:    Status Okay
  Recordset: select * from Suppliers

Event: WillMove
  Reason:    Move
  Status:    Status Okay
  Recordset: select * from Suppliers

Event: MoveComplete
  Reason:    Move
  Status:    Status Okay
  Recordset: select * from Suppliers

Event: WillMove
  Reason:    Move
  Status:    Status Okay
  Recordset: select * from Suppliers

Event: WillChangeRecord
  Reason:    Add New
  Changed:   1
  Status:    Status Okay
  Recordset: select * from Suppliers

Event: RecordChangeComplete
  Reason:    Add New
  Changed:   1
  Status:    Status Okay
  Recordset: select * from Suppliers

Event: MoveComplete
  Reason:    Move
  Status:    Status Okay
  Recordset: select * from Suppliers

Event: WillChangeField
  Changed:   1
  Status:    Status Okay
  Recordset: select * from Suppliers

Event: FieldChangeComplete
  Changed:   1
  Status:    Status Okay
  Recordset: select * from Suppliers

Event: WillChangeField
  Changed:   1
  Status:    Status Okay
  Recordset: select * from Suppliers

Event: FieldChangeComplete
  Changed:   1
```

```
      Status:    Status Okay
      Recordset: select * from Suppliers

Event: WillChangeRecord
   Reason:    Update
   Changed:   1
   Status:    Status Okay
   Recordset: select * from Suppliers

Event: RecordChangeComplete
   Reason:    Update
   Changed:   1
   Status:    Status Okay
   Recordset: select * from Suppliers

Event: WillMove
   Reason:    Move
   Status:    Status Okay
   Recordset: select * from Suppliers

Event: WillChangeRecord
   Reason:    Add New
   Changed:   1
   Status:    Status Okay
   Recordset: select * from Suppliers

Event: RecordChangeComplete
   Reason:    Add New
   Changed:   1
   Status:    Status Okay
   Recordset: select * from Suppliers

Event: MoveComplete
   Reason:    Move
   Status:    Status Okay
   Recordset: select * from Suppliers

Event: WillChangeField
   Changed:   1
   Status:    Status Okay
   Recordset: select * from Suppliers

Event: FieldChangeComplete
   Changed:   1
   Status:    Status Okay
   Recordset: select * from Suppliers

Event: WillChangeField
   Changed:   1
   Status:    Status Okay
   Recordset: select * from Suppliers

Event: FieldChangeComplete
   Changed:   1
```

```
      Status:    Status Okay
      Recordset: select * from Suppliers

   Event: WillChangeRecord
      Reason:    Update
      Changed:   1
      Status:    Status Okay
      Recordset: select * from Suppliers

   Event: RecordChangeComplete
      Reason:    Update
      Changed:   1
      Status:    Status Okay
      Recordset: select * from Suppliers

   Event: RecordsetChangeComplete
      Reason:    Close
      Status:    Status Okay
      Recordset: select * from Suppliers
```

Example 13-22, our final example for the Recordset object, illustrates how data can be found and filtered very easily.

Example 13-22. Filtering and Finding Data

```
Dim sInfo As String

'
' instantiate and open a Recordset on the Suppliers table
'   using Batch locking
'
Set rst = New ADODB.Recordset

rst.Open "Suppliers", _
         DATASOURCE_NWIND, _
         adOpenKeyset

If (Not (rst.BOF And rst.EOF)) Then rst.MoveFirst

'
' find the first record with the contact, Jason T. Roff
'
rst.Find "ContactName = 'Roff, Jason T.'", _
         0, _
         adSearchForward

MsgBox "Jason's company: " & rst.Fields("CompanyName")

'
' display some information about the current Recordset objet
'
sInfo = sInfo & "Page size:   " & vbTab & rst.PageSize & vbCr
sInfo = sInfo & "Page count:  " & vbTab & rst.PageCount & vbCr
sInfo = sInfo & "Cache size:  " & vbTab & rst.CacheSize & vbCr
sInfo = sInfo & "Recordcount: " & vbTab & rst.RecordCount
```

Example 13-22. Filtering and Finding Data (continued)

```
MsgBox sInfo

'
' filter records for just the Managers
'
rst.Filter = "ContactTitle Like '*Manager*'"
MsgBox "There are " & CStr(rst.RecordCount) & " managers as contacts."

'
' clean up
'
rst.Close

Set rst = Nothing
```

The Immediate Window is populated with the following event-debug information:

```
    Event: WillMove
      Reason:    Move
      Status:    Can't Deny
      Recordset: Suppliers

    Event: MoveComplete
      Reason:    Move
      Status:    Status Okay
      Recordset: Suppliers

    Event: WillMove
      Reason:    Move
      Status:    Status Okay
      Recordset: Suppliers

    Event: MoveComplete
      Reason:    Move
      Status:    Status Okay
      Recordset: Suppliers

    Event: WillMove
      Reason:    Move First
      Status:    Status Okay
      Recordset: Suppliers

    Event: MoveComplete
      Reason:    Move First
      Status:    Status Okay
      Recordset: Suppliers

    Event: WillMove
      Reason:    Move Last
      Status:    Status Okay
      Recordset: Suppliers
```

```
Event: MoveComplete
   Reason:     Move Last
   Status:     Status Okay
   Recordset: Suppliers

Event: WillMove
   Reason:     Requery
   Status:     Status Okay
   Recordset: Suppliers

Event: MoveComplete
   Reason:     Requery
   Status:     Status Okay
   Recordset: Suppliers

Event: RecordsetChangeComplete
   Reason:     Close
   Status:     Status Okay
   Recordset: Suppliers
```

Recordset.AbsolutePage Property
(Versions 2.0, 2.1, 2.5, 2.6)

absolutepage = *recordset*.AbsolutePage

The AbsolutePage property returns or sets a value that indicates the current page in the recordset.

Datatype

Long

Description

By setting the AbsolutePage property, you are instructing ADO to move the record pointer to the first record within the page that you specified. The AbsolutePage property can be set from 1 to the number returned by the PageCount property, which is the total number of logical pages. The size of each page is determined by the PageSize property.

By reading the AbsolutePage property, you can determine in which logical page the record pointer is located. The AbsolutePage property can return a Long value indicating the current page or a PositionEnum value.

If when reading the AbsolutePage property, the record pointer is pointing to the BOF marker, then the value adPosBOF (–2) is returned. If the record pointer is at the EOF marker, then the adPosEOF (–3) value is returned. If the recordset is empty, if the record pointer's position is unknown or if the data provider does not support the AbsolutePage property, then the value adPosUnknown (–1) is returned.

The AbsolutePage property is 1-based, meaning that a value of 1 indicates the first page in the recordset.

Note

Not all providers support the AbsolutePage property.

See Also

CursorOptionEnum Enumeration, PositionEnum Enumeration, Recordset.Count Property, Recordset.Filter Property, Recordset.PageSize Property, Recordset.Supports Method

---

Recordset.AbsolutePosition Property   (Versions 2.0, 2.1, 2.5, 2.6)

absoluteposition = recordset.AbsolutePosition

The AbsolutePosition property returns or sets a value that indicates the current record position within the recordset.

Datatype

Long

Description

By setting the AbsolutePosition property, you are instructing ADO to move to the record with the ordinal position that you specified. The AbsolutePosition property can be set from 1 to the number returned by the RecordCount property, which is the total number of records in the recordset.

When you set the AbsolutePosition property, ADO reloads the cache with a new set of records, the first one of which is the record that you specify. The number of records that are loaded in the cache is determined by the CacheSize property.

By reading the AbsolutePosition property, you can determine at which ordinal position the record pointer is located by the Long or the PositionEnum value.

If, when reading the AbsolutePosition property, the record pointer is pointing to the BOF marker, then the value **adPosBOF** (–2) is returned. If the record pointer is at the EOF marker, then the **adPosEOF** (–3) value is returned. If the recordset is empty, if the record pointer's position is unknown, or if the data provider does not support the AbsolutePosition property, then the value **adPosUnknown** (–1) is returned.

It is important to note that the AbsolutePosition can change in the event that a previous record is deleted or even if the recordset is required. I recommend using bookmarks to keep track of records by position.

The AbsolutePosition property is 1-based, meaning that the value 1 indicates the first record in the recordset.

Note

Not all providers support the AbsolutePosition property.

See Also

CursorOptionEnum Enumeration, PositionEnum Enumeration, Recordset.CacheSize Property, Recordset.RecordCount Property, Recordset.Supports Method

Recordset.ActiveCommand Property (Versions 2.0, 2.1, 2.5, 2.6)

`activecommand = recordset.ActiveCommand`

The ActiveCommand property returns the Command object that was used to populate a Recordset object.

Datatype

Variant (containing a Command object)

Description

The read-only ActiveCommand property is used to return the Command object that was used to populate a Recordset object.

If a Command object was not used to populate a Recordset object, a reference to a Null object is returned.

Recordset.ActiveConnection Property (Versions 2.0, 2.1, 2.5, 2.6)

`Set recordset.ActiveConnection = connection`
`recordset.ActiveConnection = connenctionstring`

The ActiveConnection property specifies the Connection object for the current Recordset object.

Datatype

String or a Variant (containing the current Connection object)

Description

The ActiveConnection property can be read to return either a String or a reference to a Connection object. The ActiveConnection property cannot be read if the Recordset object is open or if the Recordset object was created with a Command object (its Source property set to a Command object). At any other time, the ActiveConnection property can be set to either a String or a reference to a Connection object. If a String value is used, then it should be a valid connection string that could be passed to the ConnectionString property of a Connection object. You must set the ActiveConnection property before you attempt to open a Recordset object. Before it is set, the default value for the ActiveConnection property is a Null object reference.

If you specify the ActiveConnection as a parameter to the Open method of the Recordset object, the ActiveConnection property will access the same value. If you opened a Recordset object with a Command object as the Source property value, the Recordset object's ActiveConnection property will access the Command object's ActiveConnection property value.

See Also

Conection.ConnectionString Property, Recordset.Open Method, Recordset.Source Property

Recordset.AddNew Method   (Versions 2.0, 2.1, 2.5, 2.6)

recordset.AddNew Fields, Values

The AddNew method creates a new record within the current Recordset object that is set to the value that you specify.

Arguments

Fields

As the optional first parameter to the AddNew method, supply either a Variant or a Variant array. This object represents the name of the field or an array of fields, respectively, for which you wish to initialize values. If this parameter is a Variant array, then the next parameter, *Values*, must also be a Variant array of the same dimension.

Values

The optional second parameter works in correspondence with the first parameter, *Fields*. This parameter is also either a Variant or a Variant array that specifies the values of the fields that you included in your first parameter. It is important to remember that if this parameter contains a Variant array, then the Fields parameter must also be an array of the same dimension. In addition, each ordinal position of both arrays must match the proper fields to the correct values.

Description

The AddNew method is a member method of the Recordset object. Its purpose is to add a new record to the recordset specified by the Recordset object. With the AddNew method, you may choose to include either a single field name and initialization value or a list of fields, in the form of a Variant array, along with a corresponding Variant array of values, which match these fields.

After calling the AddNew method, you can call either the Update method or the AddNew method again to add the current record to the Recordset object. If you call the AddNew method before calling the Update method, then ADO automatically calls the Update method and proceeds with the AddNew method call. Simply adding the record to the Recordset object does not guarantee that your new record is in your data source. This case depends on the updating mode of your Recordset object.

If the Recordset object is set for immediate update mode and you do not include parameters with the AddNew call, then your changes are made immediately after the following Update or AddNew method call. If you call AddNew with parameters, the values are cached locally until the next Update is called. During the period between the AddNew and Update method calls, the EditMode property is set to `adEditAdd` and is not reset to `adEditNone` until the update is completed, either by calling the Update method or AddNew once again.

If the Recordset object is set for batch update mode, your changes are made only when the UpdateBatch method of the Recordset object is called. In this mode, the changes are cached locally if the AddNew method does not include parameters. This also sets the EditMode property to `adEditAdd`. The changes are sent to the provider—but still not posted to the data source—when the Update method is called, in turn setting the EditMode property to `adEditNone`. On the other hand, if you call the AddNew method with parameters, the changes are immediately sent to the provider to be posted with the next UpdateBatch method call.

If your Recordset object supports bookmarks, your new record will be added to the end of your recordset and can be accessed at any time. If your Recordset object does not support bookmarks, there is a good chance that you may not be able to access the record once you move away from it, so never rely on it being there. Instead, use the Requery method of the Recordset object to enable your application to find the field.

See Also

EditModeEnum Enumeration, Recordset.EditMode Property, Recordset.Requery Method, Recordset.Update Method, Recordset.UpdateBatch Method

---

Recordset.BOF Property   (Versions 2.0, 2.1, 2.5, 2.6)

Recordset.EOF Property   (Versions 2.0, 2.1, 2.5, 2.6)

```
Boolean = recordset.BOF
Boolean = recordset.EOF
```

The BOF property indicates that the record pointer is located before the first record in the recordset. The EOF property indicates that the record pointer is located directly after the last record in the recordset.

Datatype

Boolean

Description

The BOF and EOF properties are both read-only.

If both the BOF and EOF properties are **True**, then the current recordset is empty. Using any Move method (Move, MovePrevious, MoveFirst, MoveNext, or MovePrevious) generates an error.

If both the BOF and EOF properties are **False**, then the record pointer can be pointing to any record within the recordset. If this is the case, you can use any of the Move methods without generating an error.

If the BOF property is **True** and the EOF property is **False**, then the record pointer is pointing to the position directly before the first record within the recordset. When this happens, you cannot use the MovePrevious method or the Move method with a negative number without generating an error.

If the EOF property is **True** and the BOF property is **False**, then the record pointer is pointing to the position directly after the last record within the recordset. When this happens, you cannot use the MoveFirst method or the Move method with a positive number without generating an error.

If you delete the last record in the recordset, the BOF and EOF properties will remain set to **False** until you move the record pointer.

If either a call to MoveFirst or a call to MoveLast results in not being able to find a record, both the EOF and BOF properties will be set to **True**.

If MovePrevious or Move—with a value of less than zero—cannot find a record, the BOF property is set to **True**.

If MoveNext or Move—with a value of greater than zero—cannot find a record, the EOF property is set to True.

See Also

Recordset.Move Method, Recordset.MoveFirst Method, Recordset.MoveLast Method, Recordset.MoveNext Method, Recordset.MovePrevious Method, Recordset.Open Method

Recordset.Bookmark Property   (Versions 2.0, 2.1, 2.5, 2.6)

bookmark = recordset.Bookmark

The Bookmark property returns a unique identifier for the current record within a recordset. By setting the Bookmark property to a previously read value, the record pointer can be repositioned to the original record.

Datatype

Variant

Description

The Bookmark property is available only through recordsets that support bookmarks. Bookmarks are used to record the position of the current record and later to set the current record back to the specified bookmark.

Bookmarks can be used interchangeably within Recordset objects that are clones of each other, but not with other Recordset objects, even if they were created from the same source.

The return value of the Bookmark property is not readable and shouldn't be used in comparisons because two bookmarks of the same record may not be the same.

Note

Not all recordsets support the Bookmark property.

See Also

CursorOptionEnum Enumeration, Recordset.Supports Method

Recordset.CacheSize Property   (Versions 2.0, 2.1, 2.5, 2.6)

recordset.CacheSize = cachesize

The CacheSize property indicates the number or records that are cached by ADO locally in system memory.

Datatype

Long

Description

The CacheSize property sets or reads the number of records that are kept in local memory at one time by ADO. The value of CacheSize must be at least 1, otherwise an error will occur. The default value of the CacheSize property is 1.

When a recordset is first opened, the number of records specified by the CacheSize property is gathered. After the record pointer moves beyond this number, another set of records is returned, the first being the next record in the recordset. If fewer records are available, the CacheSize requests only those records that are gathered.

The CacheSize property can be changed throughout the life of a recordset; however, the number of records retrieved into the cache does not change until the record pointer is moved outside the current cache.

The values within the cache do not reflect changes made by other users. To accomplish this, use the Resync method.

See Also

Recordset.Resync Method

Recordset.Cancel Method

(Versions 2.0, 2.1, 2.5, 2.6)

```
recordset.Cancel
```

The Cancel method cancels an asynchronous operation for the Recordset object.

Description

The Cancel method can be called to cancel an asynchronous operation of the Recordset object invoked by the Open method.

See Also

Recordset.Open Method

Recordset.CancelBatch Method

(Versions 2.0, 2.1, 2.5, 2.6)

```
recordset.CancelBatch AffectRecords
```

The CancelBatch method cancels the currently pending batch update for the current Recordset object.

Arguments

AffectRecords (AffectEnum)

Optional. Enumerator with the value of `adAffectCurrent`, `adAffectGroup`, or `adAffectAll`.

If the value of *AffectRecords* is `adAffectCurrent`, the CancelBatch method call affects only the pending updates for the current record of the recordset.

If the value of *AffectRecords* is `adAffectGroup`, the CancelBatch method call affects only the pending records that are dictated through the Filter property of the current Recordset object. This property must be already set for the CancelBatch method to be called with the *adAffectGroup* parameter.

If the value of *AffectRecords* is `adAffectAll`, all records pending updates within the current Recordset object (including those hidden by the Filter property) are affected by the CancelBatch method.

Description

With the CancelBatch method, you can cancel any or all pending updates in the current Recordset object from batch update mode; however, in immediate update mode, calling this method will generate an error.

The CancelUpdate method is called when the CancelBatch method is called, thus removing any updates or new records that were added within the batch. For this reason, the current record position may be invalid, and it is suggested that you move to a reliable record position, either by a valid bookmark or by using a method such as MoveFirst.

If a runtime error occurs during the call to the CancelBatch method, then there are conflicts with all of the records that were requested from the current recordset. In addition, if only one or a few records are in conflict, then the Errors collection is populated, but a runtime error does not occur.

Note

Not all providers support the CancelBatch property.

See Also

CursorOptionEnum Enumeration, Recordset.CancelUpdate Method, Recordset.Filter Property, AffectEnum Enumeration, Recordset.Supports Method

---

Recordset.CancelUpdate Method   (Versions 2.0, 2.1, 2.5, 2.6)

recordset.CancelUpdate

The CancelUpdate method cancels any changes to the current batch update made since the last AddNew or Update method calls.

Description

The CancelUpdate method of the Recordset object cancels any changes that were made to a record since a call to the Update method of that Recordset. In addition, the CancelUpdate method cancels the creation of a new record by the AddNew method.

The CancelUpdate method must be called before the Update method for the current record. The only other way to cancel the changes to a record is by using transaction management through the BeginTrans and RollbackTrans methods of the Recordset object.

See Also

Recordset.AddNew Method, Recordset.Update Method

Recordset.Clone Method   (Versions 2.0, 2.1, 2.5, 2.6)

Set *cloned_recordset* = *original_recordset*.Clone

The Clone method of the Recordset object returns a clone of the current Recordset.

Returns

Recordset object

Description

The Clone method of the Recordset object creates an exact multiple copy of the original Recordset object. Use this method when you want to access more than one record at a time within the same recordset. This is more efficient than creating another new Recordset object for the same recordset.

When a clone is created, the clone's record position will be set to the first record in the recordset.

Only recordsets that support bookmarks can be cloned. Bookmarks from one recordset are valid for clones of that recordset, and vice versa. Closing a clone does not close the original recordset, and vice versa.

See Also

LockTypeEnum Enumeration

Recordset.Close Method   (Versions 2.0, 2.1, 2.5, 2.6)

recordset.Close

The Close method closes a Recordset object.

Description

The Close method closes either a Connection or a Recordset object. When you invoke this method on either object, all dependant objects of your connection or recordset are also closed. You would use the Close method to free system resources although the resource still remains in memory. After closing a Connection or Recordset object, you can still open it again. To completely remove the object from memory, set it to Nothing.

When calling the Close method of the Connection object, all associated Recordset objects will be closed, but the associated Command object will persist, thus setting the Active-Connection property to Nothing and clearning the Parameters collection of the Command object. You can still use the Open method to connect to a data source.

If you close a Connection object that has any associated open Recordset objects, any pending changes of the Recordset objects will be rolled back. By calling the Close method of the Connection object while a transaction is in progress, you generate an error. If a Connection object falls out of scope while a transaction is in progress, the transaction is automatically rolled back.

When you use the Close method on the Recordset object, that object releases any exclusive access you may have to the data and releases any associated data. You can still use the Open method of that Recordset object later, after the Close method.

If your data source is in immediate update mode and the Close method is called while editing, an error occurs. To avoid this error, call either the Update method or the Cancel-Update method. If you are in batch update mode, the data since the last UpdateBatch will be lost.

If you have cloned a Recordset object whose Close method you called, the cloned Recordset object will not be closed, and vice versa.

See Also

Recordset.ActiveConnection Property, Recordset.CancelUpdate Method, Recordset.Open Method, Recordset.Update Method

---

Recordset.CompareBookmarks Method   (Versions 2.0, 2.1, 2.5, 2.6)

```
result = recordset.CopmareBookmarks (Bookmark1, Bookmark2)
```

The CompareBookmarks method determines the position of two bookmarks in a recordset relative to one another.

Arguments

Bookmark1 (Variant)
> A bookmark of the first row to be compared.

Bookmark2 (Variant)
> A bookmark of the second row to be compared.

Returns

CompareEnum

Description

The CompareBookmark method returns a value that indicates which of the two passed bookmarks come first in ordinal position. Bookmarks are unique to rows within the same Recordset and clones of a Recordset object. Comparing bookmarks from two different Recordsets (not created by cloning another) will not return reliable results.

Obtain the current row's bookmark by reading the Bookmark property.

See Also

CompareEnum Enumeration, Recordset.Bookmark Property, Recordset.Clone Method

---

Recordset.CursorLocation Property   (Versions 2.0, 2.1, 2.5, 2.6)

```
recordset.CursorLocation = cursorlocation
```

The CursorLocation property indicates the location of the cursor service.

Datatype

CursorLocationEnum (Long)

Description

The value of the CursorLocation property can be set to one of the valid Cursor-LocationEnum values listed in Appendix E.

The value of the CursorLocation property is read- and write-enabled for closed Recordset objects and read-only for open Recordset objects.

A recordset returned from an Execute method inherits the value for the CursorLocation from the original object. Recordset objects automatically inherit this value from the Connection object that established it.

See Also

Command.Object Method, Connection.Execute Method, CursorLocationEnum Enumeration, Recordset.Open Method

Recordset.CursorType Property   (Versions 2.0, 2.1, 2.5, 2.6)

`recordset.CursorLocation = cursorlocation`

The CursorType property indicates the type of cursor to be used for the current recordset.

Datatype

CursorTypeEnum (Long)

Description

The CursorType property indicates the type of cursor that should be used when the Recordset object is opened. The value of this property is read- and write-enabled when the Recordset object is closed and read-only when it is opened. The value of the CursorType property can be one of the CursorType enumerations listed in Appendix E.

If the current data provider does not support the selected cursor type, the value of the CursorType property changes when the Recordset object is opened. This value can be read by the application if need be. In this case, once the Recordset object is closed, the original selected value will be returned to the CursorType property.

You can use the Supports method of the Recordset object to see what functionality is supported by the chosen cursor type. (See Chapter 5 for more information on cursor types.)

The Dynamic cursor supports the adMovePrevious functionality as described by the Supports method. The Forward Only cursor does not support any of the functionality that the Supports method indicates. The Keyset cursor and the Static cursor support adBookmark, adHoldRecords, adMovePrevious, and adResync functionality as described by the Supports method.

The Forward Only cursor type does not support bookmarks, because you do not have the functionality to move back to a bookmarked record. The Keyset and Static cursor records support bookmarks through ADO, and the Dynamic cursor supports bookmarks through the data provider (if it supports them).

Note

If the CursorLocation property has been set to **adUseClient**, only the **adOpenStatic** CursorType value can be used.

See Also

Connection.CursorLocation Property, CursorTypeEnum Enumeration, Recordset.CursorLocation Property, Recordset.Open Method, Recordset.Supports Method

Recordset.DataMember Property (Versions 2.0, 2.1, 2.5, 2.6)

Recordset.DataSource Property (Versions 2.0, 2.1, 2.5, 2.6)

```
recordset.DataMember = datamember
recordset.DataSource = datasource
```

The DataMember property indicates the object, within the data source specified by the Data Source property, that the Recordset object should be created with.

Datatype

> String (DataMember property)
> DataSource (DataSource property)

Description

The DataMember and DataSource properties are always used together.

The DataSource property indicates the data source in which the object specified by Data-Member resides.

The DataMember property indicates which object within the data source should be used to create the Recordset object.

The Recordset must be closed when the DataMember property is being set. In addition, an error will be raised if the DataSource property is set before the DataMember property.

Recordset.Delete Method (Versions 2.0, 2.1, 2.5, 2.6)

```
recordset.Delete AffectRecords
```

The Delete method deletes specified records within the recordset.

Arguments

AffectRecords (Affect Enum)
> Optional. Indicates either the value of **adAffectCurrent** or **adAffectGroup**.
>
> If the value of *AffectRecords* is **adAffectCurrent**, the CancelBatch method call affects only the pending updates for the current record of the recordset.
>
> If the value of AffectRecords is **adAffectGroup**, the CancelBatch method call affects only the pending records that are dictated through the Filter property of the current Recordset object. This property must be already set for the CancelBatch method to be called with the *adAffectGroup* parameter.

Description

The Delete method removes a record or a group of records when used with the Recordset object. The Delete method removes a specified Parameter object from the Parameters collection when used with it.

When using the Delete method with the Recordset object, records that are to be deleted are actually marked for deletion. If the particular recordset does not allow deletion, an error occurs. In immediate update mode, the deletion occurs immediately. However, in batch update mode, the records are marked deleted and are cached until the UpdateBatch method is called. You can view the deleted records by using the Filter property.

After you delete a record, the current record position is still on that record. Once you move from that record position, the records are no longer accessible, and attempting to read a deleted record results in an error. If you are using transaction management with Begin-Trans, you can cancel the deletion of records with the RollbackTrans method. In addition, in batch update mode, you can cancel deletion by using the CancelBatch method.

If you attempt to delete a record that has already been deleted by another user, a runtime error does not occur; instead, the Errors collection is populated with warnings. A runtime error occurs only if all of the requested records to be deleted have a conflict for some reason. You can use the Filter property with the `adFilterAffectedRecords` value and the Status property to locate any records with conflicts.

The Delete method is valid only for the Parameters collection of the Command object. Specify the name of the parameter to be deleted from the collection in the form of a String.

Note

Not all providers support the Delete method.

See Also

AffectEnum Enumeration, Connection.RollbackTrans Method, CursorOptionEnum Enumeration, Recordset.CancelBatch Method, Recordset.Filter Property, Recordset.Status Property, Recordset.Supports Method

---

Recordset.EditMode Property   (Versions 2.0, 2.1, 2.5, 2.6)

`recordset.EditMode = editmode`

The EditMode property indicates the current editing status for a given record.

Datatype

EditModeEnum (Long)

Description

Use the EditMode property to determine whether the current record is being edited when an editing process has been interrupted. With this information, you can determine whether you need to call the Update method or the CancelUpdate method.

The value of the EditMode property can be one of the EditModeEnum enumerations listed in Appendix E.

See Also

EditModeEnum Enumeration, Recordset.AddNew Method, Recordset.CancelUpdate Method, Recordset.Update Method

Recordset.EndOfRecordset Event   (Versions 2.0, 2.1, 2.5, 2.6)

```
EndOfRecordset(fMoreData As Boolean, _
               adStatus As ADODB.EventStatusEnum, _
               ByVal pRecordset As ADODB.Recordset)
```

The EndOfRecordset event is called when an attempt to move the record pointer past the end of the recordset has occurred.

Arguments

fMoreData

> A VARIANT_BOOL value that can be set to **True** if more data was added by the application to invalidate the current event. In other words, when this event is fired, it is an indication that the record pointer has gone outside the recordset. At this time, you can append more records to the recordset and set this *fMoreData* parameter to **True**, so that the operation can be attempted again.

adStatus

> An EventStatusEnum value indicating the status of the current operation. The *adStatus* parameter is set to **adStatusOK** if the operation causing this event was successful. If the *adStatus* parameter is set to **adStatusCantDeny**, the event cannot request that the operation be canceled. If the *adStatus* parameter is set to **adStatusUnwantedEvent**, this event will not be called again.

pRecordset

> The Recordset object that fired this event.

See Also

EventStatusEnum Enumeration, Recordset.MoveNext Method

Recordset.EOF Property   (Versions 2.0, 2.1, 2.5, 2.6)

See Recordset.BOF Property.

Recordset.FetchComplete Event   (Versions 2.0, 2.1, 2.5, 2.6)

```
FetchComplete(ByVal pError As ADODB.Error, _
              adStatus As ADODB.EventStatusEnum, _
              ByVal pRecordset As ADODB.Recordset)
```

The FetchComplete event is called when a long asynchronous operation (fetch) has completed and all of the records have been returned.

Arguments

pError

> An Error object containing details about an error that occurred if the *adStatus* parameter is set to **adStatusErrorsOccurred**.

adStatus

> An EventStatusEnum value indicating the status of the current operation. If the *adStatus* parameter is set to **adStatusOK** the operation was successful. If the

adStatus parameter is set to `adStatusErrorsOccurred`, the operation failed and the *pError* object contains the details regarding the error. By setting the *adStatus* parameter to `adStatusUnwantedEvent`, this event will not be called again.

pRecordset
   The Recordset object that fired this event.

See Also

EventStatusEnum Enumeration

Recordset.FetchProgress Event   (Versions 2.0, 2.1, 2.5, 2.6)

```
FetchProgress(ByVal Progress As Long, _
             ByVal MaxProgress As Long, _
             adStatus As ADODB.EventStatusEnum, _
             ByVal pRecordset As ADODB.Recordset)
```

The FetchProgress event is called during a long asynchronous operation (fetch) to report the progress of the fetch.

Arguments

Progress
   A Long value that indicates the number of records that have been retrieved so far by the operation.

MaxProgress
   A Long value that indicates the maximum number of records that are expected to be retrieved.

adStatus
   An EventStatusEnum value indicating the status of the current operation. The *adStatus* parameter is set to `adStatusOK` if the operation causing this event was successful. If the *adStatus* parameter is set to `adStatusCantDeny`, the event cannot request that the operation be canceled. If the *adStatus* parameter is set to `adStatusUnwantedEvent`, this event will not be called again.

pRecordset
   The Recordset object that fired this event.

See Also

EventStatusEnum Enumeration, Recordset.FetchProgress Event

Recordset.FieldChangeComplete Event   (Versions 2.5, 2.6)

```
FieldChangeComplete(ByVal cFields As Long, _
                   ByVal Fields As Variant, _
                   ByVal pError As ADODB.Error, _
                   adStatus As ADODB.EventStatusEnum, _
                   ByVal pRecordset As ADODB.Recordset)
```

The FetchChangeComplete event is called after an operation changes one or more Field object values.

Arguments

cFields (Long)
Indicates the number of Field objects within the Fields parameter.

Fields (Variant array)
Contains the Field objects that are waiting to be changed.

pError (Error)
Contains details about an error that occurred if the *adStatus* parameter is set to adStatusErrorsOccurred.

adStatus (EventStatusEnum)
Indicates the status of the current operation. If the *adStatus* parameter is set to adStatusOK, the operation was successful. If the *adStatus* parameter is set to adStatusErrorsOccurred, the operation failed, and the *pError* object contains the details regarding the error. If the *adStatus* parameter is set to adStatusCancel, then the operation has been canceled before completion by the application. If the *adStatus* parameter is set to **adStatusUnwantedEvent**, this event will not be called again.

pRecordset
Represents the Recordset object that fired this event.

See Also

EventStatusEnum Enumeration, Recordset.WillChangeField Event, Recordset.Value, Recordset.Update

---

Recordset.Fields Collection   (Versions 2.0, 2.1, 2.5, 2.6)

record.Fields

The Field collection contains multiple Field objects for the current Recordset object, one for each column in the Recordset object.

Datatype

Fields (Collection object)

Description

The Fields collection of a Recordset object can be populated before opening a Recordset object by calling the Refresh method of the Fields collection.

Field objects can be added to the collection either by calling the Field.Append method or by referencing by name a Field object that is not already part of the collection. Calling the Field.Update method will add the field to the collection, if possible, within the data source. Until this moment, the Field.Status property will return **adFieldPendingInsert**.

See Also

Field.Append Method, Field.Refresh Method, Field.Update Method

Recordset.Filter Property

(Versions 2.0, 2.1, 2.5, 2.6)

```
recordset.CancelBatch AffectRecords
```

The Filter property filters a selection of records within the current Recordset object.

Datatype

Variant

Description

When you set the Filter property, the cursor type is changed to the current filtered recordset. In this case, the AbsolutePosition, AbsolutePage, RecordCount, and PageCount properties are affected, since the current record is changed to the first record that meets the requirements dictated by the Filter property.

The Filter property can have one of three types of values:

- A set of clauses that are connected with the AND or OR keywords.
- An array of bookmark values.
- A FilterGroupEnum enumeration value.

Clauses are similar to WHERE clauses in SQL statements. They consist of a field name, an operator, and a value. Multiple clauses can be grouped and joined together with the AND and OR keywords. The field name in a clause has to be a valid field name within the current recordset and if it contains spaces, it has to be placed in brackets ([First Name]). The operator within a clause can be any of the following: <, >, <=, >=, <>, =, or LIKE. The value within a clause is similar to the data within the field specified. Numbers can use decimal points, dollar signs, and scientific notation. Dates are surrounded by pound signs (#) (#06/20/1973#) and strings are surrounded by single quotes ('Jason T. Roff').

If you are using the LIKE keyword as an operator, only the asterisk (*) and percent sign (%) can be used as wildcards, as long as one of the two is at the end of the value (Jason* or *as*).

When setting the Filter property to an array of bookmarks, the bookmarks must be unique—pointing to different records—within the associated recordset.

When setting the Filter to a FilterGroupEnum enumeration value, choose from one of the constants listed in Table E-25.

The Filter property can fail because of a record that has been deleted by another user. In this case, a runtime error does not occur. Instead, the Errors collection is populated with warnings. A runtime error occurs only if all of the requested records to be filtered have a conflict for some reason. You can use the Status property to locate any records with conflicts.

See Also

AffectEnum Enumeration, FilterGroupEnum Enumeration, Recordset.AbsolutePage Property, Recordset.AbsolutePosition Property, Recordset.CancelBatch Method, Recordset.Delete Property, Recordset.PageCount Property, Recordset.RecordCount Property, Recordset.Resync Method, Recordset.UpdateBatch Method

Recordset.Find Method   (Versions 2.0, 2.1, 2.5, 2.6)

`recordset.Find (Criteria, SkipRows, SearchDirections, Start)`

The Find method moves the record pointer to a row within the current recordset that matches the single-column search criteria specified.

Arguments

Criteria (String)

Specifies a single-column search criteria in the form of `'Column Operator Value'`. The Column portion is a name of a column in the Recordset object. The Operator can be >, <, =, >=, <=, <>, or `LIKE`. The value can be written as a string, floating point number, or date. Strings are deliminated with single strings or number signs (#) and dates are deliminated with number signs (#). When using the `LIKE` operator, asterisks (*) can be used at the end or both the beginning and the end of the value (`'*jr*'`, `'jr*'`). If the asterisks is used at the beginning only, an error will occur.

SkipRows (Long)

Optional. Indicates how many rows to skip before searching the recordset for a match to the *Criteria* argument. The default is 0, meaning the search will begin on the current row.

SearchDirection (SearchDirectionEnum)

Optional. Indicates whether to search forward or backward through the recordset. If a match is not found and a forward search is being done, the record pointer will point to the EOF marker. If a backward search is done and a match is not found, the record pointer will point to the BOF marker. By default, a forward search is done.

Start (Variant)

Optional. Specifies a starting position for the search in the form of a bookmark. The default value for this argument is the current row.

Description

If a current record is not set prior to calling the Find method, an error will occur. It is good practice to call the MoveFirst method prior to the Find method.

The Find method works only with single-column search critierias.

Not all providers support Bookmarks and, therefore, cannot search backwards. Use the Supports method to determine whether your current data provider can support the Find operation that you want to use.

See Also

CursorOptionEnum Enumeration, Recordset.MoveFirst Method, Recordset.Supports Method, SearchDirectionEnum Enumeration

Recordset.GetRows Method   (Versions 2.0, 2.1, 2.5, 2.6)

`Set record_array = recordset.GetRows(Rows, Start, Fields)`

The GetRows method of the Recordset object returns multiple records from an open Recordset object in the form of an array.

Arguments

Rows (Long)

> Optional. Indicates the number of records to retrieve. The default value for this argument is `adGetRowsRest` (value of –1).

Start (String or Variant)

> Optional. Evaluates to a bookmark where the GetRows method should begin.

Fields (Variant)

> Optional. Specifies which fields should be returned for each record by the GetRows method. Represents a single field name, a single field-ordinal number, an array of field names, or an array of field-ordinal numbers.

Returns

> Variant (two-dimensional array)

Description

The GetRows method of the Recordset object returns multiple records from the same Recordset object into a two-dimensional array. The records are returned in the form of a Variant array that is automatically dimensioned by ADO. The first subscript is the field; the second is the record number. The data returned is read-only.

You can specify the number of records to be returned through the first argument. If this value is larger than the number of records, only the remaining records are returned.

If the selected Recordset object supports bookmarks, you can specify the starting location by passing the value of the record's Bookmark property.

After the call to GetRows, the record pointer is set to the next unread record, unless there is no more records, in which case the EOF property is set to **True**.

The last argument, *Fields*, can represent a single field or a group of fields to be returned by the GetRows method. This is done with a field name, a field-ordinal position, an array of field names, or an array of field-ordinal positions.

Note

Not all providers support the Find method.

See Also

BookmarkEnum Enumeration, CursorOptionEnum Enumeration, GetRowsOptionEnum Enumeration, Recordset.Bookmark Property, Recordset.EOF Property, Recordset.Supports Method

---

Recordset.GetString Method   (Versions 2.0, 2.1, 2.5, 2.6)

```
Set Variant = recordset.GetString(StringFormat, NumRows, ColumnDelimiter, _
                                  RowDelimiter, NullExpr)
```

The GetString method returns the entire Recordset object as a String value.

Arguments

`StringFormat (StringFormatEnum)`
  Indicates the format of the returned Recordset in String form.

`NumRows`
  Optional. Indicates the number of rows to be converted to a String. If the value of this parameter is either missing or greater than the total number of records in the Recordset object, then all of the records are converted.

`ColumnDelimeter`
  Optional. Used only when the `StringFormat` parameter is set to `adClipString`. Indicates the delimeter used between columns. The tab character is the default character.

`RowDelimeter`
  Optional. Used only when the `StringFormat` parameter is set to `adClipString`. Indicates the delimeter used between rows. The carriage return character is the default character.

`NullExpr`
  Optional. Used only when the `StringFormat` parameter is set to `adClipString`. Indicates the String used to replace `Null` characters. The default for this parameter is the empty String.

Returns

Variant

Description

The GetString method converts the contents of the Recordset object to a String value.

See Also

StringFormatEnum Enumeration

Recordset.Index Property   (Versions 2.1, 2.5, 2.6)

`recordset.Index = index`

The Index property sets the current index for a given recordset.

Datatype

String

Description

The Index property is both read- and write-enabled. However, it cannot be set within a WillRecordsetChange or RecordsetChangeComplete event or during an asynchronous execution.

The Index property is used in conjunction with the Seek method to take advantage of the underlying table's indexed structure (as compared to the Find method, which operates sequentially).

The position of the record pointer may change when the Index is set (changing the Absolute Position property value). In addition, the following events occur: WillRecordsetChange, RecordsetChangeComplete, WillMove, and MoveComplete.

If the LockType property is set to `adLockPessimistic` or `adLockOptimistic`, then the UpdateBatch method is called releasing any filter that may be applied. In addition, the record pointer is moved to the first record in the indexed recordset.

Note

Not all providers support indexes; therefore, they do not all support the Index property.

See Also

CursorOptionEnum Enumeration, Recordset.MoveComplete Event, Recordset.RecordsetChangeComplete Event, Recordset.Seek Method, Recordset.UpdateBatch Method, Recordset.WillMove Event, Recordset.WillRecordsetChange Event, Recordset.Supports Method

---

Recordset.LockType Property (Versions 2.0, 2.1, 2.5, 2.6)

```
locktype = recordset.LockType
```

The LockType property indicates the type of locks that are set on records when they are being edited.

Datatype

LockTypeEnum (Long)

Description

The LockType property is read- and write-enabled when the Recordset object is closed, but read-only once it is opened. The LockType property may be any one of the values in Table E-29.

Note

Not all data providers support every type of record locking. In this case, the data provider may automatically select a different type of lock type. Check the available functionality of a data provider with the Supports property.

See Also

LockTypeEnum Enumeration, Recordset.Open Method, Recordset.Supports Method, Recordset.Update Method

---

Recordset.MarshalOptions Property (Versions 2.0, 2.1, 2.5, 2.6)

```
recordset.MarshalOptions = marshaloptions
```

The MarshalOptions property indicates which records are to be marshaled back to the server.

Datatype

MarshalOptionsEnum (Long)

Description

The MarshalOptions property can be one of the MarshalOptionsEnum enumeration values listed in Appendix E.

See Also

MarshalOptionsEnum Enumeration

Recordset.MaxRecords Property   (Versions 2.0, 2.1, 2.5, 2.6)

`recordset.MaxRecords = maxrecords`

The MaxRecords property indicates the maximum number of records to be returned to a recordset from a query.

Datatype

Long

Description

The MaxRecords property is read- and write-enabled when the Recordset object is open, but read-only when it is closed. A value of 0 (default) indicates that all of the valid records will be returned from a query.

Recordset.Move Method   (Versions 2.0, 2.1, 2.5, 2.6)

`recordset.Move NumRecords, Start`

The Move method of the Recordset object moves the position of the record pointer within the specified Recordset object.

Arguments

NumRecords (Long)
    Specifies the number of records you want the record pointer to move.

Start (String or Variant)
    Optional. Represents the bookmark from which you want the record pointer to move.

Description

The Move method of the Recordset object moves the record pointer a specified number of records. If the *NumRecords* argument is less than zero, the pointer is moved forward the desired number. If the *NumRecords* argument is greater than zero, the record pointer is moved forward the desired number of records.

If the current Recordset object supports bookmarks, then you can indicate a beginning position to start moving from with the Start argument. The Start argument should be set to a valid bookmark within the current Recordset object, and the record pointer will be moved the desired number of records from that point. If no bookmark is used, the record pointer will move from the current record.

Attempting to move to a point before the first record will result in moving to the record before the first record, which is a BOF. Attempting to move past the last record will result in the record pointer moving to the record after the last record, which is the EOF. In either case, if the Move method is used to attempt to move past the BOF or EOF, an error is generated.

If the CacheSize property is set to cache records locally from the data provider and you pass a NumRecords that ventures outside of the cache, ADO is forced to retrieve a new group of records from the data provider. The number of records received is dependent upon the CacheSize property. This also happens if you are using a local cache and use the Start argument. The first record to be received, in this case, would be the desired destination record.

Even if the Recordset object is forward-only, you can still pass a NumRecords value that is less than zero, as long as the destination record is within the current cache. If it is before the current cache, an error is generated.

Note

Not all providers support the Move method.

See Also

BookmarkEnum Enumeration, Recordset.Bookmark Property, Recordset.CacheSize Property

---

Recordset.MoveComplete Event (Versions 2.0, 2.1, 2.5, 2.6)

```
MoveComplete(ByVal adReason As ADODB.EventReasonEnum, _
             ByVal pError As ADODB.Error, _
             adStatus As ADODB.EventStatusEnum, _
             ByVal pRecordset As ADODB.Recordset)
```

The MoveComplete event is called after an operation changes the position of the record pointer within the Recordset object.

Arguments

adReason (EventReasonEnum)

Indicates the reason for this event. Proper values for the *adReason* parameter are: adRsnMoveFirst, adRsnMoveLast, adRsnMoveNext, adRsnMovePrevious, adRsn-Move, and adRsnRequery.

pError (Error)

Contains details about an error that occurred if the *adStatus* parameter is set to adStatusErrorsOccurred.

adStatus (EventStatusEnum)

Indicates the status of the current operation. If the *adStatus* parameter is set to adStatusOK, the operation was successful. If the *adStatus* parameter is set to adStatusErrorsOccurred, the operation failed, and the *pError* object contains the details regarding the error. If the *adStatus* parameter is set to adStatusCancel, the operation has been canceled before completion by the application. If the *adStatus* parameter is set to adStatusUnwantedEvent, this event will not be called again.

pRecordset
Represents the Recordset object that fired this event.

See Also

EventReasonEnum Enumeration, EventStatusEnum Enumeration, Recordset.AbsolutePage Property, Recordset.AbsolutePosition Property, Recordset.AddNew Method, Recordset.Bookmark Method, Recordset.Filter Property, Recordset.Index Property, Recordset.Open Method, Recordset.Move Method, Recordset.MoveFirst Method, Recordset.MoveLast Method, Recordset.MoveNext Method, Recordset.MovePrevious Method, Recordset.Requery Method, Recordset.WillMove Event

---

Recordset.MoveFirst Method   (Versions 2.0, 2.1, 2.5, 2.6)

Recordset.MoveLast Method   (Versions 2.0, 2.1, 2.5, 2.6)

Recordset.MoveNext Method   (Versions 2.0, 2.1, 2.5, 2.6)

Recordset.MovePrevious Method   (Versions 2.0, 2.1, 2.5, 2.6)

```
recordset.MoveFirst
recordset.MoveLast
recordset.MoveNext
recordset.MovePrevious
```

The MoveFirst, MoveLast, MoveNext, and MovePrevious methods of the Recordset object move the record pointer to the first, last, next, and previous records, respectively, and make that record the current record.

Description

The MoveFirst, MoveLast, MoveNext, and MovePrevious methods of the Recordset object allow you to move freely throughout the specified open Recordset object.

The MoveFirst method moves to the first record in the recordset, making it the current record.

The MoveLast method moves to the last record in the recordset, making it the current record. This method requires the Recordset object to support bookmarks. If it does not, an error is generated when attempting to use the MoveLast method.

The MoveNext method moves to the next record in the recordset, making it the current record. If the current record is the last record in the recordset before the call to MoveNext, then the record pointer is moved to the record after the last in the recordset and sets the EOF property to True. Attempting to move past the EOF results in an error.

The MovePrevious method moves to the record directly before the current record in the recordset. This record is then set to the current record. This method requires that the recordset support either bookmarks or backward cursor movement; otherwise, an error is generated. If the current record—before calling the MovePrevious method—is the first record in the recordset, the record pointer is set to the record directly before the first record, and the BOF property is set to True. Attempting to move before the beginning of the recordset results in an error.

Note

Not all providers support the MoveFirst and MovePrevious methods.

See Also

CursorOptionEnum Enumeration, Recordset.BOF Property, Recordset.EOF Property, Recordset.Supports Method

---

Recordset.NextRecordset Method   (Versions 2.0, 2.1, 2.5, 2.6)

```
Set resulting_recordset = recordset.NextRecordset(RecordsAffected)
```

The NextRecordset method of the Recordset object returns the next recordset by advancing through a series of commands:

```
recordset.MoveFirst
```

Arguments

RecordsAffected (Long)
> Set to the number of records that the current operation affected. The data provider does this.

Description

Use the NextRecordset method of the Recordset object to obtain the next recordset in a compound command statement or a stored procedure that returns multiple results. An example of a compound command statement is:

```
SELECT * FROM upstairs; SELECT * FROM downstairs
```

The recordset that is originally created with either the Execute or Open methods returns a Recordset object based only on the first SQL statement in this compound statement. You must call NextRecordset to obtain each additional recordset. If the Recordset object is closed and there are remaining statements, those statements will never be executed.

The NextRecordset method continues to return recordsets as long as there are more in the list. If a row-returning statement successfully executes, and the result is zero records, then the Recordset object's EOF and BOF properties are both be set to True. If a non-row-returning statement successfully executes, then the Recordset object should not be set to Nothing, but the EOF property should be True.

If there are no more statements in the compound command statement, the returned Recordset object is set to Nothing.

You must call the Update or the CancelUpdate methods before requesting the next recordset if you are in immediate update mode and editing. Otherwise, an error will be generated.

Parameters for compound command statements are passed like those of regular statements; all parameters must be filled in the Parameters collection in the proper order across statements. In addition, you must read all the results of a recordset before reading output parameter values.

See Also

Recordset.Update Method, Recordset.CancelUpdate Method, Recordset.BOF Property, Recordset.EOF Property

---

Recordset.Open Method   (Versions 2.0, 2.1, 2.5, 2.6)

`recordset.Open Source, ActiveConnection, CursorType, LockType, Options`

The Open method opens a cursor within a Recordset object.

Arguments

Source (Variant)
> Optional. Indicates the actual data that is used to open the Recordset object. This can be a Command object, a SQL statement, a table name, a stored procedure, a URL, a filename, or a Stream object that contains a previously persisted Recordset object.

ActiveConnection (Variant)
> Optional. Specifies either an open Connection object or a connection string to be used when the Recordset object creates its own Connection object.

CursorType (CursorTypeEnum)
> Optional. Indicates the type of cursor that is to be used when opening the Recordset object. By default this value is `adLockReadOnly`.

LockType (LockTypeEnum)
> Optional. Specifies the locking to be used on the opened Recordset object. The `adLockReadOnly` enumeration value is the default value for this argument.

Options (Long—CommandTypeEnum and ExecuteOptionEnum)
> Optional. Specifies the type of data that is to be specified by the Source argument; additionally, can indicate that the Recordset object is to be opened asynchronously. The default value for the Options argument if a Command object is not the source of the Recordset object is `adCmdFile`.

Description

The Source, ActiveConnection, CursorType, and LockType arguments have matching properties within the Recordset object. If the arguments are omitted in the Open method call, the individual values are obtained from the corresponding properties. If a value is specified for a given argument, however, it will overwrite the previous value stored in the property value.

The source of a Recordset object can be one of the following:

- Command object
- SQL statement
- Stored procedure
- Table name
- URL
- Filename
- Stream object (with the contents of a previously persisted Recordset object)

If anything other than a Command object is used to open a Recordset, specify the data source by using the Options argument. If you do not, ADO must call the data provider repeatedly to determine the type of data that it is opening.

When specifying a file as a Recordset object's source, you can do so with a full pathname, a relative pathname, or even a URL value (*http://www.domain.com*).

The ActiveConnection argument is used only if you do not specify a Command object. In fact, it is read-only if a valid Command object is set to the Source property.

The ActiveConnection argument can be either an already opened Connection object or a connection string, which will be used to open a new Connection object for the Recordset object.

It is possible to change the value of the ActiveConnection property after a Recordset object is opened, in order to send the updates to the recordset to another data source. However, the remaining arguments and their corresponding properties become read-only once the Recordset object is opened.

You can also open a Recordset asynchronously by adding the **adAsyncFetch** enumeration value (from the ExecuteOptionEnum enumeration).

Once the Recordset is opened if it is empty, both the BOF and the EOF properties will be set **True**. Close the Recordset object by calling the Close method. This doesn't remove the Recordset object from memory because you can reopen a Recordset object. To remove the Recordset from memory, set the object to **Nothing**.

When opening a Recordset object with a Stream object, the Recordset will automatically be opened synchronously regardless of the ExecuteOptionEnum values specified. In addition, you should not specify any other arguments to the Open method when opening a Recordset object from a Stream object.

See Also

CommandTypeEnum Enumeration, CursorTypeEnum Enumeration, ExecuteOptionEnum, LockTypeEnum Enumeration, Recordset.ActiveConnection Property, Recordset.BOF Property, Recordset.Close Method, Recordset.CursorType Property, Recordset.EOF Property, Recordset.LockType Property, Recordset.Source Property

---

Recordset.PageCount Property   (Versions 2.0, 2.1, 2.5, 2.6)

pagecount = recordset.PageCount

The PageCount property returns the number of logical pages that are in the current Recordset object.

Datatype

Long

Description

The PageCount property returns a value indicating how many logical pages of data are contained within the recordset. A page is determined by the number of records in the recordset divided by the number of records per page (determined by the PageSize property).

If the last page does not contain the number of records in the PageSize property, that page is still counted as a page in the PageCount property.

Returns

If the Recordset object does not support the PageCount property, the return value is –1. This indicates that the number of pages could not be determined.

See Also

Recordset.AbsolutePage Property, Recordset.PageSize Property

Recordset.PageSize Property   (Versions 2.0, 2.1, 2.5, 2.6)

pagesize = recordset.PageSize

The PageSize property indicates the number of records in a logical page.

Datatype

Long

Description

The PageSize property determines how many records belong to a logical page within your recordset. The default value is 10. This property can be set at any time and is used with the AbsolutePage property to move to the first record within a specified page.

See Also

Recordset.AbsolutePage Property, Recordset.PageCount Property

---

Recordset.Properties Collection   (Versions 2.0, 2.1, 2.5, 2.6)

Set *properties = recordset*.Properties

The Properties collection contains characteristics specific to the Recordset object for the currently used provider.

Datatype

Properties (Collection object)

Description

The Properties collection class contains a Property class instance for each property specific to the Recordset object for the data provider.

The Properties collection of the Command object is not populated until the ActiveConnection property of the Command object has been set to an open Connection object or a valid connection string value.

See Also

Command.ActiveConnection Property

Recordset.RecordChangeComplete Event (Versions 2.0, 2.1, 2.5, 2.6)

```
RecordChangeComplete(ByVal adReason As ADODB.EventReasonEnum, _
                     ByVal cRecords As Long, _
                     ByVal pError As ADODB.Error, _
                     adStatus As ADODB.EventStatusEnum, _
                     ByVal pRecordset As ADODB.Recordset)
```

The RecordChangeComplete event is called after an operation changes one or more records in the Recordset object.

Arguments

adReason (EventReasonEnum)
Indicates the reason for this event. Proper values for the *adReason* parameter are: adRsnAddNew, adRsnDelete, adRsnUpdate, adRsnUndoUpdate, adRsnUndoAddNew, adRsnUndoDelete, and adRsnFirstChange.

cRecords (Long)
Indicates how many records are affected by the operation causing this event.

pError (Error)
Contains details about an error that occurred if the *adStatus* parameter is set to adStatusErrorsOccurred.

adStatus(EventStatusEnum)
Indicates the status of the current operation. If the *adStatus* parameter is set to adStatusOK, the operation was successful. If the *adStatus* parameter is set to adStatusErrorsOccurred, the operation failed, and the *pError* object contains the details regarding the error. If the *adStatus* parameter is set to adStatusCancel, the operation has been canceled before completion by the application. If the *adStatus* parameter is set to adStatusUnwantedEvent, this event will not be called again.

pRecordset
Represents the Recordset object that fired this event.

See Also

EventReasonEnum Enumeration, EventStatusEnum Enumeration, Recordset.AddNew Method, Recordset.CancelBatch Method, Recordset.CancelUpdate Method, Recordset.Delete Method, Recordset.WillChangeRecord Event, Recordset.Update Method, Recordset.Update-Batch Method

Recordset.RecordsetChangeComplete Event (Versions 2.0, 2.1, 2.5, 2.6)

```
RecordsetChangeComplete(ByVal adReason As ADODB.EventReasonEnum, _
                        ByVal pError As ADODB.Error, _
                        adStatus As ADODB.EventStatusEnum, _
                        ByVal pRecordset As ADODB.Recordset)
```

The RecordsetChangeComplete event is called after an operation changes the Recordset object.

Arguments

adReason (EventReasonEnum)
> Indicates the reason for this event. Proper values for the *adReason* parameter are: adRsnReQuery, adRsnReSynch, adRsnClose, and adRsnOpen.

pError (Error)
> Contains details about an error that occurred if the *adStatus* parameter is set to adStatusErrorsOccurred.

adStatus (EventReasonEnum)
> Indicates the status of the current operation. If the *adStatus* parameter is set to adStatusOK, the operation was successful. If the *adStatus* parameter is set to adStatusErrorsOccurred, the operation failed, and the *pError* object contains the details regarding the error. If the *adStatus* parameter is set to adStatusCancel, the operation has been canceled before completion by the application. If the *adStatus* parameter is set to adStatusUnwantedEvent, this event will not be called again.

pRecordset
> Represents the Recordset object that fired this event.

See Also

EventReasonEnum Enumeration, EventStatusEnum Enumeration, Recordset.Open Method, Recordset.Requery Method, Recordset.WillChangeRecordset Event

---

Recordset.RecordCount Property   (Versions 2.0, 2.1, 2.5, 2.6)

recordcount = recordset.RecordCount

The RecordCount property returns the number of records in the current Recordset object.

Datatype

Long

Description

If the provider or the cursor does not support the RecordCount property, or if the number of records cannot be determined by ADO, –1 is returned.

The actual number of records is always returned by the RecordCount property for Keyset or Static cursors, but –1 is always returned for a Forward Only cursor. Dynamic cursors can return either –1 or the actual number of records, depending upon the data source.

The RecordCount efficiently reports the number of records in a recordset only if the current Recordset object supports approximate positioning (Supports—adApproxPosition) or bookmarks (Supports—adBookmark); otherwise, this property uses a lot of resources because ADO must load all of the records to count them.

Recordset.Requery Method   (Versions 2.0, 2.1, 2.5, 2.6)

`recordset.Requery`

Description

The Requery method of the Recordset object re-executes the command that created the recordset in the first place in order to cause a refresh of the recordset. This method has the same effect as calling the Close method followed by the Open method.

If you are adding a new record or editing an existing one, when you call the Requery method, an error is generated.

If you wish to change properties that are read-only while a Recordset object is open (CursorType, LockType, etc.), you must manually close and reopen the Recordset object by calling the Close method, editing the properties, and calling the Open method.

See Also

ExecuteOptionEnum

Recordset.Resync Method   (Versions 2.0, 2.1, 2.5, 2.6)

`recordset.Resync AffectRecords`

The Resync method of the Recordset object refreshes the data in the recordset from the underlying data source.

Arguments

AffectRecords (AffectEnum)

Optional. An enumerator of type AffectEnum having the value of `adAffectCurrent` (1), `adAffectGroup` (2), or `adAffectAll` (3, the default).

If the value of *AffectRecords* is `adAffectCurrent`, the Resync method call affects only the pending updates for the current record of the recordset.

If the value of *AffectRecords* is `adAffectGroup`, the Resync method call affects only the pending records that are dictated through the Filter property of the current Record-set object. This property must be already set for the Resync method to be called with the `adAffectGroup` parameter.

If the value of *AffectRecords* is `adAffectAll`, all records pending updates within the current Recordset object (including those hidden by the Filter property) are affected by the Resync method.

Description

The Resync method of the Recordset object is used to resynchronize the records in the current recordset with those found in the underlying data source. This is very useful when you have either a Static or a Forward Only cursor and you want to check whether anyone else has altered the records in the data source.

The Resync method does not show you records that have been added to the data source; rather, it simply updates the ones that you already have. Therefore, the Resync method does not re-execute the underlying command that created the recordset in the first place.

If the Resync method attempts to read a record that has been deleted by another user, a runtime error does not occur. Instead, the Errors collection is populated with warnings. A runtime error occurs only if all of the requested records to be updated have a conflict for some reason. You can use the Filter property with the `adFilterAffectedRecords` value and the Status property to locate any records with conflicts.

Note

Not all providers support the Resync method.

See Also

ADCPROP_UPDATERESYNC_ENUM Enumeration, AffectEnum Enumeration, Cursor-OptionEnum Enumeration, Recordset.Supports Method, ResyncEnum Enumeration

---

Recordset.Save Method   (Versions 2.0, 2.1, 2.5, 2.6)

`recordset.Save Destination, PersistFormat`

The Save method saves the current Recordset object to a file or to a Stream object.

Arguments

Destination (Variant)
> Optional. Can be either a name of a file to create or a Stream object that is to accept the saved Recordset object.

PersistFormat (PersistFormatEnum)
> Optional. Indicates the format of the Recordset object when it is saved. The default is ADTG, but XML can also be used.

Description

The Save method must be invoked on an Open Recordset object. The first time Save is called, you can specify the Destination argument, but subsequent calls should be made omitting this argument. If the same destination name is used on the same Recordset object, an error will occur, but if two different names are used, both files will remain open until the Close method is called. Omitting the Destination name on the initial call to Save causes a file to be created with the name of the Source to the Recordset object.

When saving a Recordset object with a Filter, only visible records are saved. When saving a hierarchical recordset, the current child Recordset, its children, and the parent Recordset are all saved. When saving a child Recordset, only the child and its children are saved.

If the Save method is called while an asynchronous operation is in effect for the Recordset object, the Save method waits until that operation is complete before attempting to persist the Recordset object. After the Recordset object is persisted, the record pointer points to the first record in the Recordset.

You should obtain better results by setting the CursorLocation property to the client. If the data provider does not support the functionality necessary to save the Recordset object, then the cursor service will. When using the server as the cursor location, you can typically only insert, delete, or update a single table. In addition, the Resync method is not available.

Microsoft warns that when persisting hierarchical recordsets in XML format, you cannot save the Recordset if it contains pending updates or is a parameterized hierarchical Recordset object.

See Also

PersistFormatEnum Enumeration, Recordset.Close Method, Recordset.CursorLocation Property, Recordset.Filter Property, Recordset.Source Property

Recordset.Seek Method

(Versions 2.1, 2.5, 2.6)

`recordset.Seek KeyValues, SeekOptions`

The Seek method quickly changes the record pointer to the record in the Recordset object that matches the index provided.

Arguments

KeyValues (Variant)
   Indicates the values that are used in conjunction with the Recordset.Index value to locate a record.

SeekOptions (SeekEnum)
   Indicates the type of comparison used when seeking a record.

Description

The Seek method is used with the Index property of the Recordset object. If the current Recordset supports indexes, you can use the Seek method. Check the value of the Recordset.Supports (adSeek) method call to determine whether the current Recordset object will support this method.

The Index property indicates which Index is used with the Seek method. The Seek method's first parameter, an array of Variant values, should contain one value for each column within the currently used Index.

If the record cannot be found, the record pointer is placed at the EOF marker.

Notes

The Seek method can be used only on server-side clients, which are opened with the CommandTypeEnum enumeration value, *adCmdTableDirect*.

Not all providers support the Seek method.

See Also

CommandTypeEnum Enumeration, CursorOptionEnum Enumeration, Recordset.EOF Property, Recordset.Index Property, SeekEnum Enumeration, Recordset.Supports Method

Recordset.Sort Property　　　　　　　(Versions 2.0, 2.1, 2.5, 2.6)

recordset.Sort = *sortstring*

The Sort property sorts a recordset on one or more field names.

Datatype

String

Description

The Sort property can be set to sort a recordset based upon one or more fields in either ascending or descending order. The Sort property accepts a String value identical to a sort clause of a SQL statement. Fields are separated by commas with either the ASC or DESC keywords following each field name. If the ASC or DESC keyword is absent, ASC is inferred.

Setting the Sort property to an empty String value ("") removes the sort from the recordset and returns the order to the default.

For instance, the following value for the Sort property, "Company ASC, Contact DESC," would sort the recordset by the company in ascending order and then by the contact in descending order.

The Sort property does not rearrange data within the recordset; instead, it creates a temporary index for each field that does not already have an index if the CursorLocation property is set to adUseClient.

Note

Not all providers support the Sort property.

See Also

Recordset.CursorLocation Property

Recordset.Source Property　　　　　　(Versions 2.0, 2.1, 2.5, 2.6)

recordset.Source = *source*

The Source property returns the source for the data in a Recordset object.

Datatype

String (Let, Get)
Command (Set)

Description

For a Recordset object, the Source property specifies from where a recordset's data comes. The Source property for the Recordset object is read- and write-enabled while the Recordset object is closed, but read-only once it is opened.

The value of the Source property for the Recordset object can contain one of the following:

- Command object variable
- SQL statement

- Stored procedure name
- Table name
- File or URL

If the Source property is set to a Command object, the ActiveConnection property of the Recordset object gets its value from the ActiveConnection property of the Command object, but reading the Source property does not return a Command object. Instead, it returns the CommandText property of the associated Command object from which you set the Source property.

If the Source property is set to a SQL statement, a stored procedure name, or a table name, you would be better off specifying it in the Options argument of the Open method, in order for the Recordset object to optimize performance.

See Also

Recordset.Open Method

Recordset.State Property   (Versions 2.0, 2.1, 2.5, 2.6)

*state = recordset.*State

The State property indicates the current state of the Recordset object.

Datatype

ObjectStateEnum

Description

The read-only State property indicates whether the current Recordset object is opened or closed.

See Also

ObjectStateEnum Enumeration

Recordset.Status Property   (Versions 2.0, 2.1, 2.5, 2.6)

*status = recordset.*Status

The Status property indicates the status of the current record in relation to bulk operations.

Datatype

RecordStatusEnum

Description

The Status property can be set to one or more of the RecordStatusEnum enumeration values listed in Appendix E.

The Status property indicates changes still pending for records that have been updated during a batch operation.

In addition, the Status property indicates why the following functions have failed: Resync, UpdateBatch, CancelBatch, and Filter (setting equal to an array of bookmarks).

See Also

Recordset.CancelBatch Method, Recordset.Filter Property, Recordset.Resync Method, Recordset.UpdateBatch Method, RecordStatusEnum Enumeration

---

Recordset.StayInSync Property   (Versions 2.0, 2.1, 2.5, 2.6)

`recordset.Resync AffectRecords`

The StayInSync property indicates when the references to chapter recordsets change if the record pointer moves to a different parent row for hierarchical recordsets.

Datatype

Boolean

Description

The StayInSync property is both read- and write-enabled. The default value for this property is **True**.

If the value of the StayInSync property is set to **True**, the references of chapter recordsets change when the parent recordset is changed.

If the value of the StayInSync property is set to **False**, the references of chapter recordsets point to the previous parent recordset when moving the record pointer within a hierarchical recordset changes the parent recordset.

Recordset.Supports Method   (Versions 2.0, 2.1, 2.5, 2.6)

`Set boolean = recordset.Supports(CursorOptions)`

The Supports method determines whether the current data provider supports specified functionality.

Arguments

`CursorOptions (Long)`
Represents the type functionality that you are testing for. This value can be one or more of the CursorOptionEnum values listed in Appendix E.

Returns

Boolean

Description

The Supports method of the Recordset object tests whether the Recordset object supports individual types of functionality.

If the values of the CursorOptionEnum values are added and passed as the sole argument to the Supports function, a return value indicates whether all of the questioned functionality is supported.

See Also

CursorOptionEnum Enumeration

Recordset.Update Method

(Versions 2.0, 2.1, 2.5, 2.6)

`recordset.Update Fields, Values`

The Update method of the Recordset object saves the changes made to fields within the current record since a call to AddNew changes the contents of a field or array of fields.

Arguments

Fields (Variant or Variant array)
> This argument can hold the field, ordinal position, array of fields, or an array of ordinal positions that you wish to update in the current record. The *Fields* argument must be of the same type and dimension as that of the *Values* argument.

Values (Variant or Variant array)
> Optional. This argument can hold the value or values of the fields specified in the *Fields* argument. The *Values* argument must be of the same type and dimension as that of the *Fields* argument.

Description

The current record remains the current record after the call to the Update method.

If you specify an array of field names for the *Fields* argument to the Update method, the *Values* argument must have the same dimensional array passed to it, containing the corresponding values for each field listed in the Fields array. Otherwise, an error will be generated.

If you move to another record while editing a record, that record will be saved—by an automatic call to the Update method—before the record position is changed. In addition, if you are editing the current record and you call the UpdateBatch method, the Update method will again—automatically be called.

Conversely, the CancelUpdate method cancels any changes made to the current record.

Note

Not all providers support the Update method.

See Also

CursorOptionEnum Enumeration, Recordset.Supports Method

Recordset.UpdateBatch Method

(Versions 2.0, 2.1, 2.5, 2.6)

`recordset.UpdateBatch AffectRecords`

The UpdateBatch method of the Recordset object writes all pending batch updates to disk when called.

Arguments

AffectRecords (AffectEnum)
> The optional parameter to the UpdateBatch method is an enumerator of type AffectEnum having the value of `adAffectCurrent` (1), `adAffectGroup` (2), or `adAffectAll` (3, the default).

If the value of *AffectRecords* is adAffectCurrent, the UpdateBatch method call affects only the pending updates for the current record of the recordset.

If the value of *AffectRecords* is adAffectGroup, the UpdateBatch method call affects only the pending records that are dictated through the Filter property of the current Recordset object. This property must be already set for the UpdateBatch method to be called with the adAffectGroup parameter.

If the value of *AffectRecords* is adAffectAll, all records pending updates within the current Recordset object (including those hidden by the Filter property) are affected by the UpdateBatch method.

Description

The UpdateBatch method transmits all pending batch updates to the data source. This method is for use only when in batch update mode, which should be used only with a Keyset or Static cursor.

It is possible to update cached field values multiple times before committing the changes of the pending batch updates. The Update method is automatically called if the UpdateBatch method is called while in edit mode.

If you attempt to update a record that has already been deleted by another user, a runtime error does not occur; instead, the Errors collection is populated with warnings. A runtime error occurs only if all of the requested records to be updated have a conflict for some reason. You can use the Filter property with the adFilterAffectedRecords value and the Status property to locate any records with conflicts.

Conversely, the CancelBatch method cancels all pending batch updates,

Note

Not all providers support the UpdateBatch method.

See Also

AffectEnum Enumeration, Recordset.Supports Method, CursorOptionEnum Enumeration

---

Recordset.WillChangeField Event   (Versions 2.0, 2.1, 2.5, 2.6)

```
WillChangeField(ByVal cFields As Long, _
                ByVal Fields As Variant, _
                adStatus As ADODB.EventStatusEnum, _
                ByVal pRecordset As ADODB.Recordset)
```

The WillChangeField event is called before an operation changes one or more Field object values.

Arguments

cFields (Recordset object)
    Represents the actual recordset that you wish to refresh.

Fields (Variant array)
    Contains the Field objects that are waiting to be changed.

adStatus (EventStatusEnum)

Indicates the status of the current operation. The *adStatus* parameter is set to adStatusOK if the operation causing this event was successful. If the *adStatus* parameter is set to adStatusCantDeny, the event cannot request that the operation be canceled. If the *adStatus* parameter is set to adStatusUnwantedEvent, this event will not be called again. If the *adStatus* parameter is set to adStatusCancel, a cancellation request will be made for this operation.

pRecordset

Represents the Recordset object that fired this event.

See Also

EventStatusEnum Enumeration, Recordset.FieldChangeComplete Event, Recordset.Update Method, Recordset.Value Property

---

Recordset.WillChangeRecord Event   (Versions 2.0, 2.1, 2.5, 2.6)

```
WillChangeRecord(ByVal adReason As ADODB.EventReasonEnum, _
                 ByVal cRecords As Long, _
                 adStatus As ADODB.EventStatusEnum, _
                 ByVal pRecordset As ADODB.Recordset)
```

The WillChangeRecord event is called before an operation changes one or more records in the Recordset object.

Arguments

adReason (EventStatusEnum)

Indicates the reason for this event. Proper values for the *adReason* parameter are: adRsnAddNew, adRsnDelete, adRsnUpdate, adRsnUndoUpdate, adRsnUndoAddNew, adRsnUndoDelete, and adRsnFirstChange.

cRecords (Long)

Indicates how many records are affected by the operation causing this event.

adStatus (EventStatusEnum)

Indicates the status of the current operation. The *adStatus* parameter is set to adStatusOK if the operation causing this event was successful. If the *adStatus* parameter is set to adStatusCantDeny, the event cannot request that the operation be canceled. If the *adStatus* parameter to adStatusUnwantedEvent, this event will not be called again. If the *adStatus* parameter is set to adStatusCancel, a cancellation request will be made for this operation.

pRecordset

Represents the Recordset object that fired this event.

See Also

EventReasonEnum Enumeration, EventStatusEnum Enumeration, Recordset.AddNew Method, Recordset.CancelBatch Method, Recordset.CancelUpdate Method, Recordset.Delete Method, Recordset.RecordChangeComplete Event, Recordset.Update Method, Recordset.UpdateBatch Method

Recordset.WillChangeRecordset Event   (Versions 2.0, 2.1, 2.5, 2.6)

```
WillChangeRecordset(ByVal adReason As ADODB.EventReasonEnum, _
                    adStatus As ADODB.EventStatusEnum, _
                    ByVal pRecordset As ADODB.Recordset)
```

The WillChangeRecordset event is called before an operation changes the Recordset object.

Arguments

adReason (EventReasonEnum)
> Indicates the reason for this event. Values for the *adReason* parameter are: adRsnReQuery, adRsnReSynch, adRsnClose, and adRsnOpen.

adStatus (EventReasonEnum)
> Indicates the status of the current operation. The *adStatus* parameter is set to adStatusOK if the operation causing this event was successful. If the *adStatus* parameter is set to adStatusCantDeny, the event cannot request that the operation be canceled. If the *adStatus* parameter is set to adStatusUnwantedEvent, this event will not be called again. If the *adStatus* parameter is set to adStatusCancel, a cancellation request will be made for this operation.

pRecordset
> Represents the Recordset object that fired this event.

See Also

EventReasonEnum Enumeration, EventStatusEnum Enumeration, RecordsetChangeComplete Event, Recordset.Requery, Recordset.Open

---

Recordset.WillMove Event   (Versions 2.0, 2.1, 2.5, 2.6)

```
WillMove(ByVal adReason As ADODB.EventReasonEnum, _
         adStatus As ADODB.EventStatusEnum, _
         ByVal pRecordset As ADODB.Recordset)
```

The WillMove event is called before an operation changes the position of the record pointer within the Recordset object.

Arguments

adReason (EventReasonEnum)
> Indicates the reason for this event. Values for the *adReason* parameter are: adRsnMoveFirst, adRsnMoveLast, adRsnMoveNext, adRsnMovePrevious, adRsnMove, adRsnRequery.

adStatus
> Holds an EventStatusEnum value indicating the status of the current operation. The *adStatus* parameter is set to adStatusOK if the operation causing this event was successful. If the *adStatus* parameter is set to adStatusCantDeny, the event cannot request that the operation be canceled. If the *adStatus* parameter is set to adStatusUnwantedEvent, this event will not be called again. If the *adStatus* parameter is set to adStatusCancel, a cancellation request will be made for this operation.

pRecordset

Represents the Recordset object that fired this event.

See Also

EventReasonEnum Enumeration, EventStatusEnum Enumeration, Recordset.AbsolutePage Property, Recordset.AbsolutePosition Property, Recordset.AddNew Method, Recordset.Bookmark Method, Recordset.Filter Property, Recordset.Index Property, Recordset.Move Method, Recordset.MoveFirst Method, Recordset.MoveLast Method, Recordset.MoveNext Method, Recordset.MovePrevious Method, Recordset.Open Method, Recordset.Requery Method, Recordset.WillMove Event

---

Stream Object

(Versions 2.5, 2.6)

```
Dim stream As ADODB.Stream
```

A Stream object represents a stream of data that is obtained from a URL, a Record object, or nothing at all.

Methods

Cancel

Cancels an asynchronous operation for the Stream object.

Close

Closes an opened Stream object.

CopyTo

Copies data from one stream to another.

Flush

Ensures that all changes made to a Stream object have been persisted to the resource that the Stream object represents.

LoadFromFile

Loads a file's contents into an already open Stream object.

Open

Opens a Stream object from a URL, an opened Record object, or without a source at all, in memory.

Read

Reads a number of bytes from a binary stream.

ReadText

Reads a number of characters from a binary stream.

SaveToFile

Persists the data of a binary stream to a local file.

SetEOS

Changes the EOS within a given Stream object and to truncate any data that lies past the new EOS pointer.

SkipLine

Skips entire lines when reading text streams.

Write

Writes a number of bytes to a binary stream.

WriteText

Writes a number of bytes to a binary stream.

Properties

CharSet

Indicates the character set to which the contents of a text Stream should be translated.

EOS

Indicates that the stream pointer is currently at the end of the stream.

LineSeparator

Indicates the character (or characters) that are used to indicate the end of a line in text streams.

Mode

Indicates the permissions for modifying data within a Stream object.

Position

Indicates the position of the stream pointer within the Stream object.

Size

Represents the number of bytes in a Stream object.

State

Indicates the current state of the Stream object.

Type

Indicates how a Stream object's data should be analyzed.

Description

A Stream object created with no source can be instantiated in memory without a data provider.

A Stream object can contain binary or textual data. It can be persisted to a file, retrieved from a file, or copied to a file or another Stream object in memory.

 MSDAIPP is needed to browse filesystem data sources; it is the Microsoft OLE DB Provider for Internet Publishing.

Examples

In this section, we will be looking at three examples that show how to do the following:

- Open a Stream object with a URL.
- Open a Stream object with a Record object.
- Open a Stream object without a physical data source.

The examples for the Stream object require you to create a test text file placed at the root directory of your web server. For these examples, our text file is named *text.txt* and contains the following information:

```
This is the first line of the file.
This is the second line of the file.
```

```
abcdefghijklmnopqrstuvwxyz
1234567890
This is the sixth line of the file.
This is the last line of the file.
```

Example 13-23 opens the *test.txt* file with a URL, which means that you must have Internet Information Server running (or equivalent). Once the file is opened, it is sent to the Immediate Window with the ReadText method. After this is done, we write to and read from the file a little bit more, displaying its size as we go along.

Example 13-23. Opening a Stream Object with a URL

```
Dim sText As String

Dim str As ADODB.Stream

'
' instantiate and open the Stream object for a resource
'
Set str = New ADODB.Stream

str.Open "URL=http://localhost/test.txt", _
        adModeReadWrite

'
' set the characterset and data type of the stream
'
str.Charset = "iso-8859-1"
str.Type = adTypeText

'
' output the entire resource
'
Debug.Print str.ReadText

'
' add a line of data
'
str.Position = 0
str.WriteText "<some added data>", adWriteLine

'
' output the entire resource and display the size
'
str.Position = 0
Debug.Print
Debug.Print str.ReadText

MsgBox "The size of the stream is: " & CStr(str.Size)

'
' write a piece of text to the resource and set a new EOS
'
str.Position = 10
str.WriteText "New text"
```

Example 13-23. Opening a Stream Object with a URL (continued)

```
str.SetEOS

'
' output the entire resource and display the size
'
str.Position = 0
Debug.Print
Debug.Print str.ReadText

MsgBox "The size of the stream is: " & CStr(str.Size)

'
' clean up
'
str.Close

Set str = Nothing
```

The following is sent as output to the Immediate Window once the example has executed:

```
This is the first line of the file.
This is the second line of the file.
abcdefghijklmnopqrstuvwxyz
1234567890
This is the sixth line of the file.
This is the last line of the file.

<some added data>
ine of the file.
This is the second line of the file.
abcdefghijklmnopqrstuvwxyz
1234567890
This is the sixth line of the file.
This is the last line of the file.

<some addeNew text
```

Example 13-24 illustrates how a Stream object can be opened from a Record object in two different ways. The first method passes the Record object to the Open method of the Stream object, while the second method requests the default Stream object from the Record object's Fields collection.

Example 13-24. Opening a Stream Object from a Record Object

```
Dim rec As ADODB.Record
Dim str As ADODB.Stream

'
' open a stream from a Record object
'
Set rec = New ADODB.Record
rec.Open "test.txt", _
        "URL=http://localhost/"
```

Example 13-24. Opening a Stream Object from a Record Object (continued)

```
Set str = New ADODB.Stream
str.Open rec, _
        , _
        adOpenStreamFromRecord

'
' do something
'

str.Close
Set str = Nothing

'
' open a stream from the default stream for a Record object
'
Set str = rec.Fields.Item(ADODB.FieldEnum.adDefaultStream).Value

'
' do something
'

str.Close
Set str = Nothing

Set str = New ADODB.Stream
str.Open
str.LoadFromFile "C:\autoexec.bat"

'
' clean up
'
str.Close
rec.Close

Set str = Nothing
Set rec = Nothing
```

Example 13-25 illustrates how a stream can be created without a physical data source (resource) associated with it; instead, the stream is created from memory. After opening the Stream object without a resource, data is written to it and saved to a local file on the local machine.

Example 13-25. Creating a Stream Object Without a Physical Data Source

```
Dim str As ADODB.Stream

'
' instantiate and open a Stream object in memory
'
Set str = New ADODB.Stream
str.Open
```

Example 13-25. Creating a Stream Object Without a Physical Data Source (continued)

```
'
' add some data to the Stream object
'
str.WriteText "This is a test.", adWriteLine
str.WriteText "Just want to see something...", adWriteChar
str.WriteText "hopefully this will work...", adWriteLine
str.WriteText "(I bet it does)", adWriteLine


'
' save the Stream object to a file
'
str.SaveToFile "C:\newfile.txt", _
            adSaveCreateOverWrite


'
' clean up
'
str.Close

Set str = Nothing
```

The following text represents the contents of the file created after running Example 13-25:

```
This is a test.
Just want to see something...hopefully this will work...
(I bet it does)
```

Stream.Cancel Method   (Versions 2.5, 2.6)

```
record.Cancel
```

The Cancel method cancels an asynchronous operation for the Stream object.

Description

The Cancel method cancels an asynchronous operation of the Record object invoked by the Open method.

See Also

Stream.Open Method

Stream.CharSet Property   (Versions 2.5, 2.6)

```
stream.CharSet = characterset
```

The CharSet property indicates the character set to whioch the contents of a text Stream should be translated.

Datatype

String

Description

The CharSet property can be set to a valid character set only if the Position property of the Stream object is set to 0. Valid character sets for a system are defined in the `HKEY_CLASSES_ROOT\MIME\Database\CharSet` subkeys.

The default value for the CharSet property is "unicode". If the character set is changed on the fly, the data is translated as it is read from the stream and passed to the application. When writing data, the information is translated before being saved to the data source.

This property is only valid for text streams, which are Stream objects having a value of `adTypeText` for their Type property value.

See Also

Stream.Type Property

Stream.Close Method   (Versions 2.5, 2.6)

`record.Close`

The Close method closes an opened Stream object.

Description

The Close method can be called only on an open Stream object. After calling the Close method, the Open method can be called again to reopen the Stream object. Calling the Close method releases any resources allocated to the Stream object.

Stream.CopyTo Method   (Versions 2.5, 2.6)

`stream.CopyTo DestStream, NumChars`

The CopyTo method copies data from one stream to another.

Arguments

DestStream (Stream Object)
    Must be set to a valid open Stream object, otherwise a runtime error occurs.

NumChars (Integer)
    Optional. Specifies the number of characters to copy from the source to the destination Stream object. The default value is –1, which indicates that all remaining data should be copied.

Description

The CopyTo method copies data from the source Stream object starting at the current stream pointer position (indicated by the Stream.Position property). The number of characters copied is either the number indicated by the *NumChars* argument or the rest of the source stream if the *NumChars* argument is greater than the number of remaining characters in the source stream or the *NumChars* argument value is –1.

The stream pointer position of the destination Stream object is automatically set to the next byte available in the Stream object. The CopyTo method will not remove excess data from the destination Stream object past the copy. To do this, call the SetEOS method.

You can copy data from a textual Stream to a binary Stream object, but not from a binary Stream to a textual Stream object.

See Also

Stream.Position Property, Stream.SetEOS Method

Stream.EOS Property   (Versions 2.5, 2.6)

`Boolean = stream.EOS`

The EOS property indicates that the stream pointer is currently at the end of the stream.

Datatype

Boolean

Description

The EOS property is True when the stream pointer is located directly after the last piece of information within the stream and is now pointing to the End-Of-Stream pointer.

Stream.Flush Method   (Versions 2.5, 2.6)

`stream.Flush`

The Flush method ensures that all changes made to a Stream object have been persisted to the resource that the Stream object represents.

Description

The Flush method persists any outstanding changes of the Stream object to the resource that is represented by the Stream object. Microsoft claims that this is very rarely necessary, as ADO calls this method internally in the background whenever possible. In addition, when closing a Stream object, the stream is first flushed to the data source.

Stream.LineSeparator Property   (Versions 2.5, 2.6)

`stream.LineSeparator = lineseparator`

The LineSeparator indicates the character (or characters) that are used to indicate the end of a line in text streams.

Datatype

LineSeparatorEnum

Description

The default value for the LineSeparator property is adCRLF, which indicates both a carriage return and a line feed.

This property is valid only for text streams, which are Stream objects having a value of adTypeText for their Type property value.

See Also

LineSeparatorEnum Enumeration, Stream.SkipLine Method

Stream.LoadFromFile Method (Versions 2.5, 2.6)

stream.LoadFromFile *FileName*

The LoadFromFile method loads a file contents into an already open Stream object.

Arguments

FileName (String)
> Must contain a name of a valid file to be loaded into the currently opened Stream object. If the file specified by this argument cannot be found, a runtime error occurs.

Description

The LoadFromFile method works only with an already opened Stream object, replacing the contents of the object with the contents of the file specified within the LoadFromFile argument, *FileName*. All pre-existing data is overwritten, and any extra data is truncated. However, the Stream object does not lose its relationship to the resource with which it was originally opened.

The LoadFromFile method can be used to upload a file to a server from a client.

Stream.Mode Property (Versions 2.5, 2.6)

stream.Mode = ConnectModeEnum

The Mode property indicates the permissions for modifying data within a Stream object.

Datatype

ConnectModeEnum

Description

The default value for the Mode property of a Stream object that is associated with an underlying source is adModeRead. Stream objects that are instantiated in memory have a default value of adModeUnknown for the Mode property.

The Mode property is read- and write-enabled while the Stream object is closed, but read-only once it is opened.

If the Mode property is not specified for a Stream object, it is inherited from the source used to open the object, such as a Record object.

See Also

ConnectModeEnum Enumeration, Stream.Open Method

Stream.Open Method   (Versions 2.5, 2.6)

`stream.Open` *Source, Mode, OpenOptions, UserName, Password*

The Open method opens a Stream object from a URL, an opened Record object, or without a source at all, in memory.

Arguments

Source (Variant)

Optional. Indicates the source of the resource to open. This can be a URL or an open Record object. Omitting this argument instructs ADO to open the Stream object in memory only.

Mode (ConnectModeEnum)

Optional. Indicates the access permissions with which to open the Stream object. The default value is **adModeUnknown**; if the Stream object is opened with a Record object, the Mode value is taken from that object, ignoring this argument.

OpenOptions (StreamOpenOptions)

Optional. Can be one or more StreamOpenOptions enumeration values, which indicate whether the Stream object should be opened asynchronously or if it is being opened from a Record object, but the default value is **adOpenStreamUnspecified**.

UserName (String)

Optional. Indicates, if necessary, the username that will be used to access the resource indicated by the source argument. If the Stream object is being opened with a Record object, this value is ignored because access is already available for the resource.

Password (String)

Optional. Indicates, if necessary, the password to verify the *UserName* argument. If the Stream object is being opened with a Record object, this value is ignored because access is already available for the resource.

Description

The Open method of the Stream object can be invoked with a URL source, an already opened Record object, or without a source at all, indicating that the Stream object is opened in memory. If this last method is used, you can read and write to the Stream object just as you can any other way, but you can persist and retrieve data only by using the SaveToFile or LoadFromFile methods.

When opening a Stream object from an already opened Record object, the Mode value is taken from the Record object, and the *UserName* and *Password* properties, if specified, are ignored because access has to be already granted to the Record object if it is open. If opening a Stream from a Record object, specify the **adOpenStreamFromRecord** enumeration value as the OpenOptions argument, and ADO will use the Record's default stream to populate the Stream object.

If you are opening the Stream object with a URL, you must use the URL keyword (URL=scheme://server/folder).

See Also

ConnectModeEnum Enumeration, Stream.LoadFromFile Method, Stream.Mode Property, Stream.SaveToFile Method, StreamOpenOptionsEnum Enumeration

Stream.Position Property   (Versions 2.5, 2.6)

`stream.Position = number`

The Position property indicates the position of the stream pointer within the Stream object.

Datatype

Long

Description

The Position property can be set to any positive number or 0. It can also be set to a value greater than the size of the current Stream object. In doing so, for streams with write permissions you may increase the size of a Stream object by automatically adding Null values. You can, although you are not advised to, do the same for read-only streams, but the size is not altered.

The Position property indicates the number of bytes the stream pointer is located away from the first byte in the stream. If your character set contains multiple bytes for each character, you must multiply this number by the position desired to get the actual character position. For example, when using Unicode, 0 represents the first character, and 2 represents the second.

Stream.Read Method   (Versions 2.5, 2.6)

`bytes = stream.Read (NumBytes)`

The Read method reads a number of bytes from a binary stream.

Arguments

NumBytes (Long or StreamReadEnum)
  Optional. Specifies the number of bytes to read from the binary stream. The default value is adReadAll, which returns all the remaining bytes in the stream.

Returns

Variant (array)

Description

The Read method is used to read binary streams (Stream.Type property is equal to adTypeBinary), while the ReadText method is used to read textual streams (Stream.Type property is equal to adTypeText).

The return value is a Variant array of bytes, which will equal the number of bytes requested or the number of remaining bytes in the stream if the number of remaining bytes is less than the requested number of bytes. If there is no data to return, a Null Variant value is returned.

See Also

Stream.ReadText Method, Stream.Type Property, StreamReadEnum Enumeration

Stream.ReadText Method   (Versions 2.5, 2.6)

`string = stream.ReadText (NumChars)`

The ReadText method reads a number of characters from a binary stream.

Arguments

NumChars (Long or StreamReadEnum)
> Optional. Specifies the number of characters to read from the text stream. The default value is `adReadAll`, which returns all the remaining characters in the stream. You can also specify to return the next line of data with the `adReadLine` enumeration value.

Returns

String

Description

The ReadText method reads textual streams (Stream.Type property is equal to `adTypeText`), while the Read method is used to read binary streams (Stream.Type property is equal to `adTypeBinary`).

The return value is a String of values, which equals the number of characters requested or the number of remaining characters in the stream if the number of remaining characters is less than the requested number of characters. If there is no data to return, a Null Variant value is returned.

See Also

Stream.Read Method, Stream.Type Property, StreamReadEnum Enumeration

---

Stream.SaveToFile Method   (Versions 2.5, 2.6)

`stream.SaveToFile (FileName, SaveOptions)`

The SaveToFile method persists the data of a binary stream to a local file.

Arguments

FileName (String)
> Indicates where the contents of the current Stream object are to be persisted.

SaveOptions (SaveOptionsEnum)
> Specifies whether a file is to be created if one doesn't exist, if an existing file should be overwritten, or, if a file already exists, whether an error should occur.

Description

The SaveToFile method completely overwrites an existing file if the `adSaveCreate-Overwrite` enumeration value is used in the SaveOptions argument.

Using this method does not change the contents of the Stream object nor its association to the original resource with which the Stream object was opened. The only difference from the Stream object is that the Position property is set to the beginning of the stream (0).

See Also

SaveOptionsEnum Enumeration, Stream.Position Property

Stream.SetEOS Method   (Versions 2.5, 2.6)

`stream.SetEOS`

The SetEOS method changes the EOS within a given Stream object and truncates any data that lies past the new EOS pointer.

Description

The SetEOS method can shorten a Stream object's length when using the Write, WriteText, and CopyTo methods, which cannot truncate the stream themselves.

See Also

Stream.CopyTo Method, Stream.Write Method, Stream.WriteText Method

Stream.Size Property   (Versions 2.5, 2.6)

`size = stream.Size`

The Size property represents the number of bytes in a Stream object.

Datatype

Long

Description

Because the Stream object's size is only restricted by resources, a Long value may not correctly contain the size of a Stream if it exceeds the largest possible number a Long value can contain.

If the size of a stream is unknown, −1 is returned.

Stream.SkipLine Method   (Versions 2.5, 2.6)

`stream.SkipLine`

The SkipLine method skips entire lines when reading text streams.

Description

The SkipLine method skips an entire line in a textual stream (Stream.Type is equal to **adTypeText**). This is done by searching for the next occurrence of a line separator (indicated by the LineSeparator property which is, by default, set to **adCRLF**) or the EOS pointer.

See Also

LineSeparatorEnum Enumeration, Stream.LineSeparator Property, Stream.Type Property

Stream.State Property   (Versions 2.5, 2.6)

state = record.State

The State property indicates the current state of the Stream object.

Datatype

Long (ObjectStateEnum)

Description

The State property is read-only; returning a Long value that can be evaluated as an Object-StateEnum enumeration value. The default value for the Stream object is closed.

For the Stream object, the State property can return multiple values when the object is executing an operation asynchronously (i.e., **adStateOpen** and **adStateExecuting**).

See Also

ObjectStateEnum Enumeration

Stream.Type Property   (Versions 2.5, 2.6)

streamtype = *stream*.Type

The Type property indicates how a Stream object's data should be analyzed.

Datatype

StreamTypeEnum Enumeration

Description

The default value for a Stream object is **adTypeText**, but if binary data is written to a new Stream object, the Type property will automatically be changed to **adTypeBinary**.

The Type property is read- and write-enabled while the stream pointer is at zero (Position property equals 0) and read-only at any other position.

If the Type property is set to **adTypeText**, you should use the ReadText and WriteText methods for data manipulation and retrieval. If the Type property is set to **adTypeBinary**, you should use the Read and Write methods for data manipulation and retrieval.

See Also

Stream.Read Method, Stream.ReadText Method, Stream.Write Method, Stream.WriteText method, StreamTypeEnum Enumeration

Stream.Write Method   (Versions 2.5, 2.6)

stream.Write *Buffer*

The Write method writes a number of bytes to a binary stream.

Arguments

Buffer (Variant)
   Contains an array of Byte values to be written to the current binary stream.

Description

After writing the specified bytes to the Stream object, the Position property is set to the next byte following the last byte written. If there is existing data past the end of what has been written, it is not truncated. If you want to truncate this data, call the SetEOS method.

If the written data exceeds the length of the Stream object, the new data is appended to the Stream object, the length of the stream is increased, and the EOS pointer is moved to the new end of the stream.

The Write method is used to write to binary streams (Stream.Type property is equal to **adTypeBinary**), while the WriteText method is used to write textual streams (Stream.Type property is equal to **adTypeText**).

See Also

Stream.EOS Property, Stream.SetEOS Method, Stream.Type Property, Stream.WriteText Method, StreamWriteEnum Enumeration

---

Stream.WriteText Method   (Versions 2.5, 2.6)

```
stream.WriteText Data, Options
```

The WriteText method writes a number of bytes to a binary stream.

Arguments

Data (String)
    Represents the String data to be written to the Stream object.

Options (StreamWriteEnum)
    Optional. Indicates whether just the data is written to the Stream object or if the data and a line separator (indicated by the LineSeparator property) are added to the Stream object. The default is not to add the line separator.

Description

After writing the specified string to the Stream object, the Position property is set to the next character following the last character written. If there is existing data past the end of what has been written, it is not truncated. If you want to truncate this data, call the SetEOS method.

If the written data exceeds the length of the Stream object, the new data is appended to the Stream object, the length of the stream is increased, and the EOS pointer is moved to the new end of the stream.

The WriteText method is used to write to text streams (Stream.Type property is equal to **adTypeText**), while the Write method is used to write binary streams (Stream.Type property is equal to **adTypeBinary**).

See Also

Stream.EOS Property, Stream.SetEOS Method, Stream.Type Property, Stream.WriteText Method, StreamWriteEnum Enumeration

III

Appendixes

Introduction to SQL

The SQL, or Structured Query Language, specification has many varieties. All are used for either data selection, data manipulation, or database modification. Through this language we can gracefully create queries, store procedures, filter recordsets, create tables—you name it. Just about everything that you can do with a database, you can do with SQL.

In this appendix, you will learn the Microsoft Jet Engine SQL language. This form of SQL is very similar to the ANSI SQL specification. Differences exist between these two specifications in a number of places, the most important difference being *datatypes*. ANSI SQL and Microsoft use different names for datatypes. The SQL language described in this appendix uses the Microsoft datatypes, for obvious reasons.

Other differences arise when ANSI SQL conflicts with Microsoft standards. In addition, some functions have been removed from the ANSI standard by Microsoft because there are already ways to accomplish these functions through ADO. Also, some statements (listed next) are unique to Microsoft, including TRANSFORM, PARAMETERS, STDEV, and STDEVP. We will be taking a look at these statements and functions shortly.

Record Selection

The most basic SQL statements are constructed through *selection statements*. Selection statements return a group of records whose values can be filtered, grouped, ordered, or altered. To jump into the basics of SQL, you must first learn how to create a simple selection query.

Selection Statements

Statements that select records all begin with the keyword **SELECT**. The syntax for a simple select statement is as follows:

```
SELECT [predicate] {* |
                    field_name1 [AS alias_name1]
                    [field_name2 [AS alias_name2]] [, ...]]}
FROM table_expression
 [IN external_database]
```

This syntax declaration might be slightly intimidating if you have never seen SQL before, but rest assured, you will know this like the back of your hand before long.

Let's begin by taking a look at the simplest of all select statements, one without any predicate (or secondary keyword), the **SELECT** statement.

SELECT

The **SELECT** statement is used to return selected fields from all records, in one or more tables, located in the current database or an external database. Let's image that we have a table named *Employees* in our current database. The *Employees* table has the following field names: FirstName, LastName, and EmployeeID. The *Employees* table is populated as in Table A-1.

Table A-1. The Employees Table

FirstName	LastName	EmployeeID
Jason	Roff	100
Tammi	Roff	101
Kimberly	Roff	102
John	DelWhatta	200
John	Katsosing	201

By using a simple **SELECT** statement, we can list all of the employees and their IDs:

```
SELECT *
FROM Employees;
```

The asterisk (*) in the preceding SQL statement indicates that you want all of the fields that belong to the chosen record to be returned. The **FROM** portion of this statement indicates that you want to select the fields from the *Employees* table. Results of this statement look like this:

```
FirstName  LastName   EmployeeID
Jason      Roff       100
Tammi      Roff       101
```

```
Kimberly   Roff        102
John       DelWhatta   200
John       Katsosing   201
```

The first line of the preceding output should be the field names as the SQL statement returned them. Now let's suppose that we want to return partial data on the given table. Let's face it: we are not always going to need every field in a particular table, and by requesting them all, we waste resources. Take a look at this statement:

```
SELECT LastName AS Name,
       EmployeeID AS Number
FROM Employees;
```

This time, we have added a new keyword, **AS**, to the statement. The **AS** keyword alters the field name in the resulting recordset to the new name. The results of this query are:

Name	Number
Roff	100
Roff	101
Roff	102
DelWhatta	200
Katsosing	201

Notice how the field names on the first line of the result set have changed to the names indicated in the SQL statement.

SELECT ALL

In the Microsoft Jet Engine SQL Language, **SELECT ALL** has the same effects as the **SELECT** statement. You can use them interchangeably; the predicate **ALL** is the default for the **SELECT** statement. In other words, if you leave out the predicate altogether, the Jet Engine inserts the **ALL** keyword.

SELECT DISTINCT

The **SELECT DISTINCT** phrase is very commonly used in SQL. The purpose of the **DISTINCT** keyword is to filter the selected records down to those that have unique values. Take a look at the following statement and its results:

```
SELECT DISTINCT LastName
FROM Employees;
```

LastName
Roff
Ann
DelWhatta
Katsosing

Notice how one two of the Roffs were left out because we used the `DISTINCT` predicate within the SQL statement. Now take a look at this SQL statement and result combination:

```
SELECT DISTINCT FirstName, LastName
FROM Employees;
```

FirstName	LastName
Jason	Roff
Tammi	Roff
Kimberly	Roff
John	DelWhatta
John	Katsosing

The Roff records are still in the result set. This is because the `DISTINCT` predicate returns distinct rows based on the sum of its fields. In this example, Jason Roff and Tammi Roff are two unique records and should both be included.

SELECT DISTINCTROW

The `DISTINCTROW` predicate is used with joins within your SQL statement. This concept is explained later under "Joining Tables."

SELECT TOP

The `TOP` predicate is used to return only the first number of fields specified, based on records or on a percentage of the records in the table. The `TOP` predicate works with the `ORDER BY` clause and is discussed under "Grouping and Ordering" later in this appendix.

Aggregate Functions

Aggregate functions are a very powerful feature of any SQL language. They report numeric statistics on a field for the entire record set that is a product of a SQL statement.

AVG

The `AVG` function returns a value that is the average of all of the records selected, for a particular field. Let's suppose that we have the table *Sales* as shown in Table A-2.

Table A-2. The Sales Table

EmployeeID	CrossStitch	Hammocks	Automobiles	TotalRevenue
100	1,012	1,234	456	21,100
101	450	345	45	62,758
102	21,018	3,234	765	1,154,001

Table A-2. The Sales Table (continued)

EmployeeID	CrossStitch	Hammocks	Automobiles	TotalRevenue
200	17	32	143	991
201	3	1	0	17

By using the AVG function, we can obtain important statistics from our *Sales* table:

```
SELECT AVG(CrossStitch) AS Average
FROM Sales;
```

Average
4500

Notice that the SQL statement returns a single record. You can also create AVG functions for other fields in the SQL statement.

COUNT

The COUNT function displays a count of the number of records selected from a recordset. The COUNT function takes as an argument a string expression that evaluates to one or more field names. It accepts the asterisk (*), which specifies all fields to be included. If a string is used, only records that have no NULL values in the fields indicated are counted. If the asterisk is used, all records are counted as long as at least one field in each record has a non-NULL value. This is the fastest method of using the COUNT function. Following is an example of using COUNT:

```
SELECT COUNT(*) AS CountOfPeople
FROM Employees;
```

CountOfPeople
5

MIN and MAX

The MIN and MAX functions return the minimum and the maximum value, respectively, within a chosen recordset. Take a look at an example of both the MIN and MAX functions:

```
SELECT MIN(CrossStitch) AS Minimum,
       MAX(Hammocks) AS Maximum
FROM Sales;
```

Minimum Maximum
3   3234

STDEV and STDEVP

The STDEV and STDEVP functions are not part of the ANSI SQL specification. These functions are used to report the standard deviation of a sample (STDEV) and the standard deviation of a population (STDEVP). The following is an example of both these functions:

```
SELECT STDEV(CrossStitch) AS Sample,
       STDEVP(Hammocks) AS Population
FROM Sales;

Sample           Population
9243.01447039871 1216.94854451616
```

SUM

The SUM function returns a sum of a field in a selection statement:

```
SELECT SUM(CrossStitch) AS CrossStitchSum,
       SUM(CrossStictch + Hammocks) AS Both
FROM Sales;

CrossStitchSum  Both
22500           27346
```

In this example, a sum was taken from a single field and from the sum of two fields.

VAR and VARP

The VAR and VARP functions return the variance of a sample and the variance of a population, respectively:

```
SELECT VAR(CrossStitch) AS Sample,
       VARP(Hammocks) AS Population
FROM Sales;

Sample      Population
85433316.5 88855543.76
```

If you can find a reason to use this . . . go for it.

Setting Conditions

Conditions can be set in a number of places to specify which records the SQL statement returns. The most common place for these conditions is in the WHERE clause.

WHERE

The WHERE clause can contain expressions that limit the amount of records returned. In the following example, I filter the records with ordinary comparison operators:

```
SELECT EmployeeID,
       CrossStitch,
```

```
        Hammocks
FROM    Sales
WHERE ((CrossStitch >= 450)
       AND (Hammocks < 2000));
```

EmployeeID	CrossStitch	Hammocks
100	1012	1234
101	450	345

In the next example, I limit the records returned with the **IN** keyword:

```
SELECT FirstName
FROM Employees
WHERE LastName NOT IN (Roff, Katsosing);
```

FirstName
John

In this example, I limit the records returned with the **LIKE** keyword:

```
SELECT FirstName
FROM Employees
WHERE ((FirstName LIKE "[A-M]*")
       AND (LastName LIKE "RO*"));
```

FirstName
Jason
Kimberly

WHERE

Another useful clause is the **BETWEEN...AND...** clause. The following two statements are equivalent:

```
SELECT...
WHERE ((Field >= 100)
       AND (Field <= 200))

SELECT...
WHERE Field BETWEEN 100 AND 200
```

Take a look at the **BETWEEN...AND...** clause in action with the optional **NOT** keyword:

```
SELECT EmployeeID,
       TotalRevenue
WHERE TotalRevenue NOT Between 10000 AND 100000;
```

EmployeeID TotalRevenue
1154001
991
17

Grouping and Ordering

With other SQL clauses, you can group records in your recordset or order them according to a particular field or group of fields. You can also perform conditional statements on the groups that you have formed or limit the amount of records that are returned to your recordset with the TOP predicate of the SELECT statement. Table A-3 contains the *Automobile* table, which will serve as our recordset for the following sections.

Table A-3. The Automobile Table

EmployeeID	Year	Make	Model	Color	Cost
102	1998	BMW	323I	Black	40,000
100	1989	Mercury	Sable	Blue	0
100	1987	Ford	Mustang	Red	4,500
100	1979	Chevy	Nova	Red	800
100	1975	Chevy	Camaro	Blue	800
100	1981	Mercury	Capri	Brown	0

GROUP BY

The GROUP BY clause of a selection statement combines records based on the fields that you specify. The following combination of SQL statement and result uses the GROUP BY clause:

```
SELECT Make,
       COUNT(Make) AS NumOfMake
FROM Automobile
GROUP BY Make;
```

```
Make      NumOfMake
BMW       1
Mercury   2
Ford      1
Chevy     2
```

Notice how the Make field was unique, while the NumOfMake field contained the number of records for each Make in the recordset.

HAVING

The HAVING clause works with the GROUP BY clause to set one or more conditions on the groups created by the SQL statement. In this example, the HAVING clause restricts the outputed records to those that represent more than one car for the same Make value:

```
SELECT Make
FROM Automobile
```

```
GROUP BY Make
HAVING (COUNT(Make) < 1);
```

Make   NumOfMake
Mercury 2
Chevy   2

ORDER BY

The ORDER BY clause sets the order of the resulting records of a SQL statement. The syntax for an ORDER BY clause of a SQL statement is as follows:

```
SELECT field_name1 [, field_name2 ...]
FROM table_expression
ORDER BY field_name1 [ASC | DESC] [, field_name2 [ASC | DESC]...]
```

The ASC and DESC keywords tell the SQL statement to order the records, by the specified field, in either ascending or descending order. Both of these are optional; however, if you do not specify one, ascending order is the default. Here are some examples:

```
SELECT DISTINCT Make
FROM Automobile
ORDER BY Make;
```

Make
BMW
Chevy
Ford
Mercury

```
SELECT Make, Model, Color
FROM Automobile
ORDER BY Color DESC, Make ASC;
```

Make	**Model**	**Color**
Chevy	Nova	Red
Ford	Mustang	Red
Mercury	Capri	Brown
Chevy	Camaro	Blue
Mercury	Sable	Blue
BMW	323I	Black

In this last example, the ORDER BY clause sorts first by the Color field in descending order and then sorts multiple Color records by the Make field in ascending order.

SELECT TOP

The TOP predicate returns a subset of fields—it returns the first x fields from the recordset, or the first y percentage of fields from the recordset. The TOP predicate works in conjunction with the ORDER BY clause. The syntax for the TOP predicate of the SELECT statement is as follows:

```
SELECT TOP number [PERCENT] field_name1 [, field_name2 ...]
FROM table_expression
ORDER BY field_name1 [ASC | DESC] [, field_name2 [ASC | DESC]...]
```

The first form of the SELECT TOP clause is illustrated here:

```
SELECT TOP 2 Model,
             Cost
FROM Automobile
ORDER BY Cost DESC;
```

Model	Cost
323I	40,000
Mustang	4,500

As you can see, the number 2 is placed after the TOP predicate to indicate that you want only the top two records based on the ORDER BY clause, which specifies that the records should be sorted in descending order based on the Cost field.

In the next example, we see the second form of the SELECT TOP clause, with the use of the PERCENT keyword:

```
SELECT TOP 50 PERCENT Model,
                      Cost
FROM Automobile
ORDER BY Cost ASC;
```

Model	Cost
Sable	0
Capri	0
Nova	800

Here, the SQL statement returns the top 50 percent of the records, based on the ORDER BY clause. This example highlights a very useful piece of information about the TOP predicate: even if there are more than the specified number or percentage of records available, only the amount requested is returned. In this last example, you could argue that the Camaro also had a Cost value of 800, as did the Nova. The thing to remember is that no matter what, the TOP predicate will return the number or percentage of records *from the top of the recordset*. In this case 50 percent meant 3 records.

Joining Tables

Joins are used to include multiple tables in the same result set from a SQL statement. Technically, there is no limit to the number of tables that you can join together in a single query, but practically speaking, it is greatly limited by the abilities of your data provider. There are two major types of joins.

INNER JOIN

The first type of join is the *inner join*, which joins two tables that have one or more matching fields. One record is chosen from each table when all of the conditions are met in the ON clause.

The following example uses the INNER JOIN clause:

```
SELECT Employees.FirstName,
       Employees.LastName,
       Sales.TotalRevenue
FROM Employees
INNER JOIN Sales
ON (Employees.EmployeeID = Sales.EmployeeID);
```

FirstName	LastName	TotalRevenue
Jason	Roff	21,100
Tammi	Roff	62,758
Kimberly	Roff	1,154,001
John	DelWhatta	991
John	Katsosing	17

As you can see, by using the INNER JOIN clause, you can greatly expand the number of tricks in your bag.

LEFT JOIN and RIGHT JOIN

The second type of join is the *outer join*. An outer join can be categorized as either a *left outer join* or a *right outer join*. A left outer join includes all the records from the first table, even if there is not a matching record, based on the ON clauses in the second table. A right outer join includes all the records in the second table, regardless of whether they are present in the first.

The following query represents the use of the LEFT JOIN clause:

```
SELECT Employees.FirstName,
       Employees.LastName,
       Automobile.Make
FROM Employees
LEFT JOIN Automobile
ON (Employees.EmployeeID = Automobile.EmployeeID);
```

FirstName	LastName	Make
Jason	Roff	Mercury
Jason	Roff	Ford
Jason	Roff	Chevy
Jason	Roff	Chevy
Jason	Roff	Mercury
Tammi	Roff	
Kimberly	Roff	BMW
John	DelWhatta	
John	Katsosing	

Notice how in this query, Jason Roff comes up five times, and other people don't have a car associated to them. The outer join gathers all data from one table, regardless of whether there is a matching record in the second table.

SELECT DISTINCTROW

The `DISTINCTROW` predicate is used with joins in your SQL statement to weed out distinct rows within a recordset of two or more tables. Look back at the previous example. If the `LEFT JOIN` had been an `INNER JOIN`, people without a car would not have been included. Now, if we include the `DISTINCTROW` predicate of the `SELECT` statement, we also weed out duplicate rows:

```
SELECT Employees.FirstName,
       Employees.LastName,
       Automobile.Make
FROM Employees
LEFT JOIN Automobile
ON (Employees.EmployeeID = Automobile.EmployeeID);
```

FirstName	LastName	Make
Jason	Roff	Mercury
Jason	Roff	Ford
Jason	Roff	Chevy
Kimberly	Roff	BMW

The `DISTINCTROW` predicate operates just as the `DISTINCT` predicate does, but it spans across tables when they are joined. Remember, a record's uniqueness is determined by the sum of all of its displayed fields.

Subqueries

Subqueries are very useful statements. They are actually one or more nested SQL statements. Subqueries are frequently very resource-intensive, especially in large databases, because the data provider must gather a lot of information in memory to determine which fields the SQL statement returns.

The following is an example of a subquery:

```
SELECT FirstName,
       LastName
FROM Employees
WHERE EmployeeID IN
  (SELECT EmployeeID
   FROM Sales
   WHERE (TotalRevenues > 10,000));
```

FirstName	LastName
Jason	Roff
Tammi	Roff
Kimberly	Roff

Unions

Unions are used to produce the combination of one or more queries into one resultset of a SQL statement.

UNION

Use the UNION keyword with the following syntax:

```
[TABLE] query_expression1 UNION [ALL]
[TABLE] query_expression2
[UNION [ALL] [TABLE] query_expression3 [...]]
```

Does this look a little overwhelming? Well, let's take a look at a typical UNION query:

```
(SELECT EmployeeID,
        TotalRevenue
 FROM Employees
 WHERE (TotalRevenue < 1000))
 UNION
(SELECT EmployeeID,
        TotalRevenue
 FROM Employees
 WHERE (TotalRevenue > 100000));
```

EmployeeID	TotalRevenue
1154001	
991	
17	

Notice that the two queries report the same field names. This output looks like one query. You can also use the UNION keyword with the TABLE and ALL keywords, as in this senseless query:

```
TABLE Employees
UNION ALL
(SELECT *
 FROM Employees
 WHERE (TotalRevenue < 20));
```

EmployeeID	CrossStitch	Hammocks	Automobiles	TotalRevenue
100	1012	1234	456	21100
101	450	345	45	62758
102	21018	3234	765	1154001
200	17	32	143	991
201	3	1	0	17

I called this query "senseless" because no matter what records the second query returns, the resulting recordset contains all of the records of the *Employees* table. In real-world applications, use two different tables with the same structure when using the TABLE...UNION ALL clause.

When using the UNION clause, only distinct records (unique based on the sum of all the fields) are returned.

Other Options

There are additional capabilities for selection statements that I have not yet covered. These include parameter capabilities, the creation of stored procedures, and an option that allows the user of a query to have the same access privileges as its owner.

PARAMETERS

The PARAMETERS clause is used to insert variables into your SQL statement so that it can be used under different conditions. Here is an example of the PARAMETERS clause in action:

```
PARAMETERS
[First Name Parameter] AS STRING,
[Last Name Parameter] AS STRING;
SELECT FirstName,
       LastName
FROM Employees
WHERE ((FirstName LIKE [First Name Parameter])
       AND (LastName LIKE [Last Name Parameter]));

[First Name Parameter] = "*"
[Last Name Parameter] = "Roff"
```

FirstName	LastName
Jason	Roff
Tammi	Roff
Kimberly	Roff

As you can see, the PARAMETERS clause can be very helpful when creating complex queries within a large database application.

PROCEDURE

The PROCEDURE clause creates and names stored procedures from a SQL statement. The PROCEDURE clause can also accept parameters, much like the PARAMETERS clause:

```
PROCEDURE ReturnEmployeeID
[First Name Parameter] AS STRING,
[Last Name Parameter] AS STRING;
SELECT FirstName,
       LastName,
       EmployeeID
FROM Employees
WHERE ((FirstName LIKE [First Name Parameter])
       AND (LastName LIKE [Last Name Parameter]));
```

```
[First Name Parameter] = "Jason"
[Last Name Parameter] = "Roff"
```

FirstName	LastName	EmployeeID
Jason	Roff	100

WITH OWNERACCESS OPTION

The WITH OWNERACCESS OPTION is used at the end of any SQL statement to allow the user of the query to access information for which she otherwise would not have the proper permissions. Of course, this is all dependent on the owner of the query having the proper permissions to access the information.

The WITH OWNERACCESS OPTION appears in a SQL statement as shown here:

```
PROCEDURE GetFinancialInformation
[First Name Parameter] AS STRING,
[Last Name Parameter] AS STRING;
SELECT Employees.FirstName,
       Employees.LastName,
       Sales.TotalRevenue
FROM Employees
INNER JOIN Sales
ON (Employees.EmployeeID = Sales.EmployeeID)
WHERE ((Employees.FirstName = [First Name Parameter])
       AND (Employees.LastName = [Last Name Parameter]))
WITH OWNERACCESS OPTION;

[First Name Property] = "Kimberly"
[Last Name Property] = "Roff"
```

FirstName	LastName	TotalRevenue
Kimberly	Roff	1154001

Data Manipulation

SQL is much more than just a data-retrieving language. It is also manipulates data within a given data source. The three types of data manipulation are the addition of data, the modification of data, and the removal of data.

Adding Records

Adding records in SQL is very easy. It is done through an *append query*. This type of query can add one or more records to an existing table through the INSERT... INTO clause.

INSERT ... INTO

The INSERT...INTO clause syntax for appending a single record is as follows:

```
INSERT INTO target_table
[IN external_database]
            [(field_name1 [, field_name2 [, ...]])]
SELECT [source_table].field_name1 [, field_name2 [, ...]
FROM source_table
```

The following example inserts multiple records into the *Automobile* table, based on cost, from an additional table, *NewAutomobiles*:

```
INSERT INTO Automobile
SELECT *
FROM NewAutomobiles
WHERE (Cost >= 100000);
```

The **INSERT...INTO** clause syntax for appending multiple records is as follows:

```
INSERT INTO target_table
            [(field_name1 [, field_name2 [, ...]])]
VALUES (value1 [, value2 [, ...]])
```

The following SQL statement adds a new record to the *Automobile* table:

```
INSERT INTO Automobile
            (EmployeeID,
            Year,
            Make,
            Model,
            Color,
            Cost)
VALUES      (100,
            1997,
            Chevy
            Cavalier,
            Teal,
            14000);
```

Modifying Records

To modify values of a field in an existing table, use an *update query*.

UPDATE

The **UPDATE** clause syntax is:

```
UPDATE table_name
SET new_value_of_field
WHERE criteria_for_update
```

The following example increments the value of the TotalRevenue field of the *Sales* table based on the amount of hammocks sold:

```
UPDATE Sales
SET (TotalRevenue = TotalRevenue + (Hammocks * 1.25))
WHERE (Hammocks >= 1000);
```

This example makes changes to the indicated records:

Hammocks	TotalRevenue (Before)	TotalRevenue (After)
21100	22642.5	
3234	1154001	11548043.5

The UPDATE clause can also update multiple fields within the qualifying records (based upon the WHERE clause) with the same SQL statement, as demonstrated in the following example:

```
UPDATE Sales
SET (TotalRevenue = TotalRevenue + (Hammocks * 1.25)),
    (UnitsSold = UnitsSold + 1)
WHERE (Hammocks >= 1000);
```

Deleting Records

The DELETE method deletes one or more records of a specified table with optional conditions.

DELETE

The DELETE clause syntax is:

```
DELETE [table_name.*]
FROM table_name
WHERE criteria_for_delete
```

The following examples delete all records from the *Automobile* table:

```
DELETE
FROM Automobile;

DELETE *
FROM Automobile;

DELETE Automobile.*
FROM Automobile;
```

The following example deletes blue cars from the *Automobile* table:

```
DELETE Automobile.*
FROM Automobile
WHERE (Automobile.Color = "Blue");
```

Database Modification

The last part of the functionality of SQL is *database modification*. With SQL, you can dynamically change the structure of a database by adding, modifying, and deleting tables. When you perform database modification on tables, either by adding or modifying them, you can add or modify indexes and constraints.

CREATE TABLE

The **CREATE TABLE** statement creates a new table in the current data source. This statement has the following syntax:

```
CREATE TABLE table_expression
          (field_name1 data_type [(size)] [NOT NULL]
          [, field_name2 data_type [(size)] [NOT NULL] [, ...]])
```

The following **CREATE TABLE** statement creates the *Automobile* table:

```
CREATE TABLE Automobile
          (Year LONG NOT NULL,
          Make TEXT (12) NOT NULL,
          Model TEXT (15) NOT NULL,
          Color TEXT (10) NOT NULL,
          Cost LONG);
```

The **NOT NULL** keywords in the preceding example tell the data provider to create the particular field so that it does not accept NULLs as legal values for that field.

ALTER TABLE

The **ALTER TABLE** clause alters an existing table in your current data source. The syntax for the **ALTER TABLE** clause is:

```
ALTER TABLE table_expression
   [ADD COLUMN field_name1 data_type [(size)] [NOT NULL]
              [CONSTRAINT index_name1 | CONSTRAINT multifield_index_name]] |
   [DROP {COLUMN field_name1 | CONSTRAINT index_name1}]
```

The **ALTER TABLE** statement is very powerful. You can add or delete a particular field in a table or add or delete a **CONSTRAINT** within a table. The following example illustrates adding a field to the *Automobile* table:

```
ALTER TABLE Automobile
    ADD COLUMN MotorSize TEXT(5);
```

The following example shows you how to remove that field from the *Automobile* table:

```
ALTER TABLE Automobile
    DROP COLUMN MotorSize;
```

The following example illustrates how to add a **CONSTRAINT** to the *Automobile* table:

```
ALTER TABLE Employees
    ADD CONSTRAINT EmployeeIDConst REFERENCES Automobile (EmployeeID);
```

The following example shows you how to remove this last **CONSTRAINT** from the *Automobile* table:

```
ALTER TABLE Automobile
    DROP CONSTRAINT Automobile;
```

CONSTRAINT

The CONSTRAINT clause can be used with either the CREATE TABLE statement or the ALTER TABLE statement. The CONSTRANT clause can be used to create both single-field constraints and multiple-field constraints. The syntax for the single-field CONSTRAINT clause is as follows:

```
CONSTRAINT constraint_name
   {PRIMARY KEY |
    UNIQUE |
    NOT NULL |
    REFERENCES foreign_table [(foreign_field1, foreignfield2)]}
```

An example of a CONSTRAINT is shown in this SQL statement, which adds the EmployeeID field to the *Sales* table:

```
ALTER TABLE Sales
   ADD COLUMN EmployeeID LONG NOT NULL
       CONSTRAINT EmployeeIDConst
       REFERENCES Employees (EmployeeID);
```

The syntax for a multiple-field constraint is as follows:

```
CONSTRAINT constraint_name
   {PRIMARY KEY (primary1 [, primary2 [, ...]]) |
    UNIQUE (unique1 [, unique2, [, ...]]) |
    NOT NULL (not_null1, [, not_null2 [, ...]]) |
    FOREIGN KEY (ref1 [, ref2 [, ...]]) |
    REFERENCES foreign_table [(foreign_field1, foreignfield2)]}
```

CREATE INDEX

The CREATE INDEX statement creates an index within the current data source with the information that you provide. The syntax for the CREATE INDEX statement is as follows:

```
CREATE [UNIQUE] INDEX index_name
   ON table_name (field_name1 [ASC | DESC] [,field_name2 [ASC | DESC] [, ...]])
   [WITH {PRIMARY |
          DISALLOW NULL |
          IGNORE NULL}]
```

The following two examples show you how to use the CREATE INDEX statement within your SQL statements:

```
CREATE UNIQUE INDEX EmployeeIDIndex
ON Employees (EmployeeID ASC)
WITH PRIMARY;

CREATE INDEX CarType
ON Automobile (Make ASC, Model ASC)'
```

DROP

The DROP statement removes either a table from the associated data source or an index from the indicated table. The following statement removes the *Automobile* table from our data source:

```
DROP TABLE Automobile;
```

This example removes the CarTypeIndex from the *Automobile* table:

```
DROP TABLE CarTypeIndex
ON Automobile;
```

B

The Properties Collection

The Properties collection exists within the Connection, Command, Recordset, and Field objects. This collection provides dynamic property information about its corresponding ADO object directly from the underlying data provider.

The Properties collection is not very complicated. Because the capabilities with the Properties collection is limited, so are the number of properties and methods. In fact, there is only one property, Count, which returns the number of Property objects within the Properties collection. Only two methods belong to the Properties collection: Item and Refresh. Item, as its name implies, accesses an individual Property object within the Properties collection. The Refresh method repopulates the corresponding ADO object with the dynamic Property objects that describe the characteristics of the underlying data provider.

Each Property object within the Properties collection represents a single attribute of the underlying data provider that pertains to the associated ADO object, whether it is the Connection, Command, Recordset, or Field object.

An individual Property object does not have any methods, but it does have four properties of its own:

Name
    Returns a string value representing the name of the property.

Type
    Returns a valid DataTypeEnum value indicating the datatype of the property's value.

Value
    Sets or returns a variant value representing the value of the datatype.

Attributes

> Returns a valid PropertyAttributesEnum value that indicates the attributes associated with the given Property object. The Attributes property can contain a sum of any of the valid PropertyAttributesEnum values shown in Table B-1.

Table B-1. The PropertyAttributesEnum Enumeration

Value	Description
adPropNotSupported	Indicates that the characteristic defined by the current Property object is not supported by the data provider.
adPropRequired	Indicates that the characteristic defined by the current Property object must be set by the application before connecting to the data source. Most of the time, a required field has a default value so that actually populating the Property object with a value is unnecessary.
adPropOptional	Indicates that the characteristic defined by the current Property object is optional and does not have to be set in order to establish a connection to the data source.
adPropRead	Indicates that the value of the characteristic defined by the current Property object can be read.
adPropWrite	Indicates that the value of the characteristic defined by the current Property object can be written by the application.

Now that we understand Property objects and the Properties collection, let's take a look at a neat example that allows you to view the contents of different ADO objects' Properties collections.

The Property Example

The Property Example is a simple application that utilizes the Properties collection and the Property object to report in a user-friendly manner the dynamic characteristics that are exposed by a data provider for any of the given ADO objects that support the Properties collection. Figure B-1 shows the Property Example main dialog box when the program is executing.

To begin, create a new Visual Basic project, select the Standard EXE project type, name the default form frmPropertyExample, and change its Caption property to "Property Example". Next, add two labels, a List View control, and five command buttons. For each of these controls, set the values of the properties shown in Table B-2.

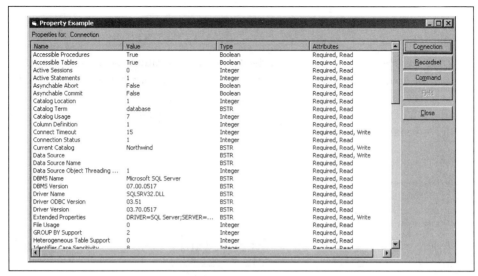

Figure B-1. The Property Example

Table B-2. The Property Example Control Settings

Control	Property	Value
Label	Caption	Properties for:
Label	Name	lblObject
List View	Name	lvwProperties
	View	3 - lvwReport
Command Button	Name	cmdConnection
	Caption	Co&nnection
Command Button	Name	cmdRecordset
	Caption	&Recordset
Command Button	Name	cmdCommand
	Caption	Co&mmand
Command Button	Name	cmdField
	Caption	&Field
Command Button	Name	cmdClose
	Caption	&Close

Next, you need to add the four column headers through the Custom property in the property dialog box in the Visual Basic IDE for the List View. The four columns that you need to create are:

- Name
- Value

- Type
- Attributes

Now we are ready for the code.* In the General Declarations section of the form, declare the four variables shown in the following code, one for each of the ADO objects that contains the Properties collection. Remember to include the ADO runtime DLL within the References dialog box of your Visual Basic project, or you will have some trouble when it comes time to compile:

```
Option Explicit

Private m_oCon As Connection
Private m_oCom As Command
Private m_oRst As Recordset
Private m_oFld As Field
```

Make sure that all of the objects are set to **Nothing** when the application exits by adding the following code to the **cmdClose_Click** event:

```
Private Sub cmdClose_Click()
    Set m_oCon = Nothing
    Set m_oRst = Nothing
    Set m_oCom = Nothing
    Unload Me
End Sub
```

Now enter the following code for the **cmdConnection_Click** event, which is used to establish a connection with a data source. The form **frmConnnection** is used to gather the ConnectionString and CursorLocation information for the Connection object. We will enter the **frmConnection** code later. After the connection is established, the DisplayProperties method is called with the Connection object as a parameter. We will soon see that the DisplayProperties method is used to populate the List View control with the Properties collection of the ADO object that is passed to it:

```
Private Sub cmdConnection_Click()

    frmConnection.Show vbModal
    If (frmConnection.Canceled) Then Exit Sub

    Set m_oCon = New Connection
    m_oCon.ConnectionString = frmConnection.ConnectionString
    m_oCon.CursorLocation = frmConnection.CursorLocation
    Unload frmConnection

    m_oCon.Open
```

* This and all other code examples from this book are available for download from the book's web site, *http://www.oreilly.com/catalog/ado/.*

```
cmdRecordset.Enabled = True
cmdCommand.Enabled = True
cmdField.Enabled = False
Set m_oRst = Nothing

DisplayProperties m_oCon, "Connection"
```

End Sub

The code for the **cmdRecordset_Click** event is very similar to that for the **cmdConnection_Click** event. To open a Recordset object, the application uses the form **frmRecordset** to gather the CursorType, LockType, and Source property values. Once the Recordset object is opened, the DisplayProperties method is called to populate the List View control:

```
Private Sub cmdRecordset_Click()

    frmRecordset.Show vbModal
    If (frmRecordset.Canceled) Then Exit Sub

    Set m_oRst = New ADODB.Recordset

    m_oRst.ActiveConnection = m_oCon
    m_oRst.CursorType = frmRecordset.CursorType
    m_oRst.LockType = frmRecordset.LockType
    m_oRst.Source = frmRecordset.Source
    Unload frmRecordset

    m_oRst.Open

    cmdField.Enabled = True

    DisplayProperties m_oRst, "Recordset"

End Sub
```

The **cmdCommand_Click** event uses the **frmCommand** form to gather the CommandText to open a Command object:

```
Private Sub cmdCommand_Click()

    frmCommand.Show vbModal
    If (frmCommand.Canceled) Then Exit Sub

    Set m_oCom = New ADODB.Command
    Set m_oRst = New ADODB.Recordset

    m_oCom.ActiveConnection = m_oCon
    m_oCom.CommandText = frmCommand.CommandText
    Unload frmCommand

    Set m_oRst = m_oCom.Execute
```

```
cmdField.Enabled = True

DisplayProperties m_oCom, "Command"
```

End Sub

Finally, enter the code for the **cmdField_Click** event, which displays the **frmField** form so that the user can select a field from the currently opened Recordset or Command object to display its Properties collection:

```
Private Sub cmdField_Click()

    Set frmField.Recordset = m_oRst
    frmField.Show vbModal
    If (frmField.Canceled) Then Exit Sub

    Set m_oFld = m_oRst.Fields(frmField.Field)
    Unload frmField

    DisplayProperties m_oFld, "Field"
```

End Sub

Now enter the following code for the **DisplayProperties** method. The following code sets the width of the columns within the List View control then loops through each of the Property objects in the Properties collection of the ADO object that has been passed to the method. For each property, a **ListItem** is added to the List View control. The ListItem contains all of the Property object's properties: Name, Value, Type, and Attributes. Because the values returned from the Type and Attributes properties are numeric, the GetPropertyType and GetAttributes methods are used to return a string value that is easy for the user to understand:

```
Private Sub DisplayProperties(oObject As Object, _
                              sUsing As String)

    Dim lColumnCount As Long
    Dim lColumnWidth As Long

    Dim oProperty As Property
    Dim oListItem As ListItem

    lblObject.Caption = sUsing

    lColumnWidth = lvwProperties.Width / 4
    For lColumnCount = 1 To 4
        lvwProperties.ColumnHeaders.Add
        lvwProperties.ColumnHeaders(lColumnCount).Width = lColumnWidth
    Next lColumnCount

    lvwProperties.ListItems.Clear

    For Each oProperty In oObject.Properties
```

```
                Set oListItem = lvwProperties.ListItems.Add()
                oListItem.Text = oProperty.Name
                oListItem.SubItems(1) = oProperty.Value & ""
                oListItem.SubItems(2) = GetPropertyType(oProperty.Type)
                oListItem.SubItems(3) = GetAttributes(oProperty.Attributes)
            Next oProperty

        End Sub
```

The code for the GetAttributes method is as follows:

```
    Private Function GetAttributes(lAttributes As Long) As String

        If (lAttributes And adPropNotSupported) Then _
            GetAttributes = "Not Supported, "

        If (lAttributes And adPropRequired) Then _
            GetAttributes = GetAttributes & "Required, "

        If (lAttributes And adPropOptional) Then _
            GetAttributes = GetAttributes & "Optional, "

        If (lAttributes And adPropRead) Then _
            GetAttributes = GetAttributes & "Read, "

        If (lAttributes And adPropWrite) Then _
            GetAttributes = GetAttributes & "Write, "

        If (Right$(GetAttributes, 2) = ", ") Then _
            GetAttributes = Left$(GetAttributes, Len(GetAttributes) - 2)

    End Function
```

Because the value within the Attributes property of a Property object can be the sum of any of the PropertyAttributesEnum values, the Attributes value is logically Anded with each enumeration constant to see whether that particular flag is set. For each flag that is set, a string value is appended to the description of the attributes.

The code for the GetPropertyType method is as follows. This code also returns a string value to describe the enumeration value that is passed to it:

```
    Private Function GetPropertyType(lType As Long) As String
        Select Case (lType)
            Case adBigInt:              GetPropertyType = "BigInt"
            Case adBinary:              GetPropertyType = "Binary"
            Case adBoolean:             GetPropertyType = "Boolean"
            Case adBSTR:                GetPropertyType = "BSTR"
            Case adChar:                GetPropertyType = "Char"
            Case adCurrency:            GetPropertyType = "Currency"
            Case adDate:                GetPropertyType = "Date"
            Case adDBDate:              GetPropertyType = "DBDate"
            Case adDBTime:              GetPropertyType = "DBTime"
            Case adDBTimeStamp:         GetPropertyType = "DBTimeStamp"
```

```
            Case adDecimal:            GetPropertyType = "Decimal"
            Case adDouble:             GetPropertyType = "Double"
            Case adEmpty:              GetPropertyType = "Empty"
            Case adError:              GetPropertyType = "Error"
            Case adGUID:               GetPropertyType = "GUID"
            Case adIDispatch:          GetPropertyType = "IDispatch"
            Case adInteger:            GetPropertyType = "Integer"
            Case adIUnknown:           GetPropertyType = "IUnknown"
            Case adLongVarBinary:      GetPropertyType = "LongVarBinary"
            Case adLongVarChar:        GetPropertyType = "LongVarChar"
            Case adLongVarWChar:       GetPropertyType = "LongVarWChar"
            Case adNumeric:            GetPropertyType = "Numeric"
            Case adSingle:             GetPropertyType = "Single"
            Case adSmallInt:           GetPropertyType = "SmallInt"
            Case adTinyInt:            GetPropertyType = "TinyInt"
            Case adUnsignedBigInt:     GetPropertyType = "UnsignedBigInt"
            Case adUnsignedInt:        GetPropertyType = "UnsignedInt"
            Case adUnsignedSmallInt:   GetPropertyType = "UnsignedSmallInt"
            Case adUnsignedTinyInt:    GetPropertyType = "UnsignedTinyInt"
            Case adUserDefined:        GetPropertyType = "UserDefined"
            Case adVarBinary:          GetPropertyType = "VarBinary"
            Case adVarChar:            GetPropertyType = "VarChar"
            Case adVariant:            GetPropertyType = "Variant"
            Case adVarWChar:           GetPropertyType = "VarWChar"
            Case adWChar:              GetPropertyType = "WChar"
            Case Else:                 GetPropertyType = "Unknown"
        End Select
    End Function
```

Finally, enter the code for the Form_Load event, which sets the Enabled property of the command buttons:

```
Private Sub Form_Load()
    cmdConnection.Enabled = True
    cmdRecordset.Enabled = False
    cmdCommand.Enabled = False
    cmdField.Enabled = False
End Sub
```

Now that the main form, frmPropertiesExample, is complete, add another form to your project, name it frmConnection, and change its Caption property to "Connection Information". This form gathers the ConnectionString and CursorLocation property values from the user so that the frmPropertiesExample form can open a Connection object. Figure B-2 shows the frmConnection form at runtime.

Add two frames to your new form. Within the first frame, add a control array of four option buttons. Within this frame, create a text box next to the last option button in the control array. Within the second frame, add a control array of two option buttons. Add two command buttons in the area outside of the frames, and then set the properties of all the controls as shown in Table B-3.

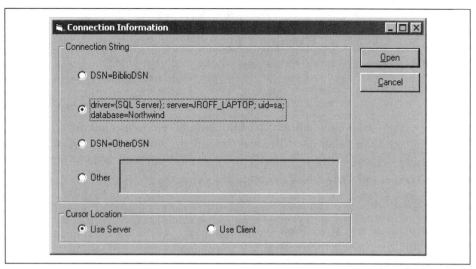

Figure B-2. The Connection Information dialog box

Table B-3. The Connection Information Dialog Box Control Settings

Control	Property	Value
Frame	Caption	Connection String
Option Button	Name	optConnectionString
	Index	0
Option Button	Name	optConnectionString
	Index	1
Option Button	Name	optConnectionString
	Index	2
Option Button	Name	optConnectionString
	Index	3
	Caption	Other
Text Box	Name	txtConnectionString
	MultiLine	True
Option Button	Name	optCursorLocation
	Index	0
	Caption	Use Server
Option Button	Name	optCursorLocation
	Index	1
	Caption	Use Client
Command Button	Name	cmdOpen
	Caption	&Open
	Default	True

Table B-3. The Connection Information Dialog Box Control Settings (continued)

Control	Property	Value
Command Button	Name	CmdCancel
	Caption	&Cancel
	Cancel	True

Once all of the properties are set for the controls, enter the following code to handle the command button's Click events and the Cancel property. When the user clicks the Cancel command button, the Canceled property will be set to `True`, but it will be set to `False` when the user clicks Open:

```
Option Explicit

Private m_bCanceled As Boolean

Private Sub cmdCancel_Click()
    m_bCanceled = True
    Me.Hide
End Sub

Private Sub cmdOpen_Click()
    m_bCanceled = False
    Me.Hide
End Sub

Public Property Get Canceled() As Boolean
    Canceled = m_bCanceled
End Property
```

The code for the Form_Load event, shown next, populates the ConnectionString option button array with different connection strings. In addition, the User Server CursorLocation value is chosen as the default for startup:

```
Private Sub Form_Load()

    optConnectionString(0).Caption = "DSN=BiblioDSN"

    optConnectionString(1).Caption = "driver={SQL Server}; " _
                                   & "server=JROFF_LAPTOP; " _
                                   & "uid=sa; " _
                                   & "database=Northwind"

    optConnectionString(2).Caption = "DSN=OtherDSN"

    optConnectionString(0).Value = True
    optCursorLocation(0).Value = True

End Sub
```

When the fourth option button is pressed (indicated by an *Index* value of 3), the Connection String text box has to be enabled. The Connection String text box allows users to enter their own connection string rather than picking one of the "hard-coded" choices. The following code takes care of this:

```
Private Sub optConnectionString_Click(Index As Integer)
    If (Index = 3) Then
        txtConnectionString.Enabled = True
        txtConnectionString.BackColor = vbWhite
    Else
        txtConnectionString.Enabled = False
        txtConnectionString.BackColor = &H8000000F  ' light grey
    End If
End Sub
```

Next, enter the code for the CursorLocation property, which returns a valid Cursor-LocationEnum enumeration value based upon which option button the user has selected:

```
Public Property Get CursorLocation() As ADODB.CursorLocationEnum
    If (optCursorLocation(0).Value = True) Then
        CursorLocation = adUseServer
    Else
        CursorLocation = adUseClient
    End If
End Property
```

The code for the ConnectionString property returns a connection string based upon the option button selected by the user or the connection string entered into the Connection text box next to the last option button:

```
Public Property Get ConnectionString() As String

    If (optConnectionString(0).Value = True) Then _
        ConnectionString = optConnectionString(0).Caption

    If (optConnectionString(1).Value = True) Then _
        ConnectionString = optConnectionString(1).Caption

    If (optConnectionString(2).Value = True) Then _
        ConnectionString = optConnectionString(2).Caption

    If (optConnectionString(3).Value = True) Then _
        ConnectionString = txtConnectionString.Text

End Property
```

That's it for the frmConnection form.

Now move onto the frmRecordset form, which allows the user to select the Source, CursorType, and LockType property values prior to opening a new Recordset object. The frmRecordset form is shown in Figure B-3.

To begin, add a new form to your project, name it frmRecordset, and change its Caption property to "Recordset Information". Now add the three frames and the

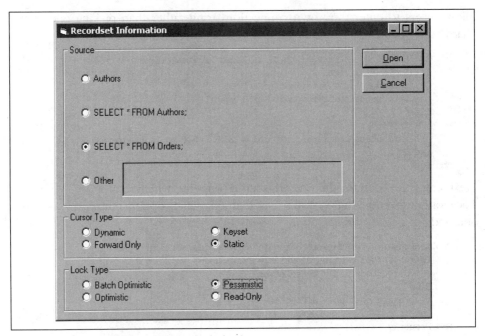

Figure B-3. The Recordset Information dialog box

three control arrays of option buttons. Add the text-box control and two command buttons, and enter the properties for each of these controls as shown in
Table B-4.

Table B-4. The Recordset Information Dialog Box Control Settings

Control	Property	Value
Frame	Caption	Source
Option Button	Name	optSource
	Index	0
Option Button	Name	optSource
	Index	1
Option Button	Name	optSource
	Index	2
Option Button	Name	optSource
	Index	3
	Caption	Other
Text Box	Name	txtSource
	MultiLine	True
Frame	Caption	CursorType
Option Button	Name	optCursorType

Table B-4. The Recordset Information Dialog Box Control Settings (continued)

Control	Property	Value
	Index	0
	Caption	Dynamic
Option Button	Name	optCursorType
	Index	1
	Caption	Keyset
Option Button	Name	OptCursorType
	Index	2
	Caption	Forward Only
Option Button	Name	OptCursorType
	Index	3
	Caption	Static
Frame	Caption	Lock Type
Option Button	Name	optLockType
	Index	0
	Caption	Batch Optimistic
Option Button	Name	optLockType
	Index	1
	Caption	Pessimistic
Option Button	Name	optLockType
	Index	2
	Caption	Optimistic
Option Button	Name	optLockType
	Index	3
	Caption	Read-Only
Command Button	Name	cmdOpen
	Caption	&Open
	Default	True
Command Button	Name	cmdCancel
	Caption	&Cancel
	Cancel	True

Begin the frmRecordset code by entering in the command-button Click-event code
and the Cancel property support just as you did for the frmConnection form:

```
Option Explicit

Private m_bCanceled As Boolean

Private Sub cmdCancel_Click()
```

```
        m_bCanceled = True
        Me.Hide
    End Sub

    Private Sub cmdOpen_Click()
        m_bCanceled = False
        Me.Hide
    End Sub

    Public Property Get Canceled() As Boolean
        Canceled = m_bCanceled
    End Property
```

Use the Form_Load event to populate the Source option buttons with source-string values that can be used to open recordsets:

```
    Private Sub Form_Load()

        optSource(0).Caption = "Authors"

        optSource(1).Caption = "SELECT * FROM Authors;"

        optSource(2).Caption = "SELECT * FROM Orders;"

        optSource(0).Value = True
        optCursorType(0).Value = True
        optLockType(0).Value = True

    End Sub
```

To enable the text box when the user selects the last option button in the Source control array, enter the following code:

```
    Private Sub optSource_Click(Index As Integer)
        If (Index = 3) Then
            txtSource.Enabled = True
            txtSource.BackColor = vbWhite
        Else
            txtSource.Enabled = False
            txtSource.BackColor = &H8000000F  ' light grey
        End If
    End Sub
```

Now enter the code that returns a valid CursorTypeEnum enumeration value for the CursorType property based upon the option button that is selected by the user:

```
    Public Property Get CursorType() As ADODB.CursorTypeEnum
        If (optCursorType(0).Value = True) Then CursorType = adOpenDynamic
        If (optCursorType(1).Value = True) Then CursorType = adOpenKeyset
        If (optCursorType(2).Value = True) Then CursorType = adOpenForwardOnly
        If (optCursorType(3).Value = True) Then CursorType = adOpenStatic
    End Property
```

Do the same for the LockType property so that a valid LockTypeEnum value is returned:

```
Public Property Get LockType() As ADODB.LockTypeEnum
    If (optLockType(0).Value = True) Then LockType = adLockBatchOptimistic
    If (optLockType(1).Value = True) Then LockType = adLockPessimistic
    If (optLockType(2).Value = True) Then LockType = adLockOptimistic
    If (optLockType(3).Value = True) Then LockType = adLockReadOnly
End Property
```

Finish by entering the code for the Source property, which returns the Caption of a chosen option button unless the last one is selected, in which case the value of the Source text box is returned:

```
Public Property Get Source() As String

    If (optSource(0).Value = True) Then _
        Source = optSource(0).Caption

    If (optSource(1).Value = True) Then _
        Source = optSource(1).Caption

    If (optSource(2).Value = True) Then _
        Source = optSource(2).Caption

    If (optSource(3).Value = True) Then _
        Source = txtSource.Text


End Property
```

Now that you are done with the frmRecordset form, begin the frmCommand form, which is very similar. The frmCommand form, shown in Figure B-4, is used to allow the user to select the CommandText property used when opening a new Command object.

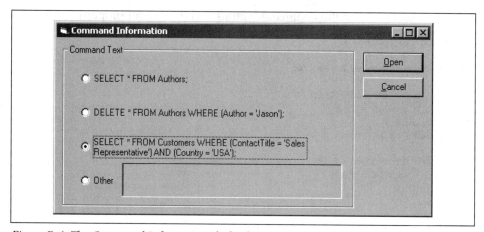

Figure B-4. The Command Information dialog box

Add a new form to your project, name it frmCommand, and set its Caption property to "Command Information". This form only has one frame and control array, as compared to the last two forms, which had at least two. Add the two command buttons, and then set all of the properties shown in Table B-5 to the values specified.

Table B-5. The Command Information Dialog Box Control Settings

Control	Property	Value
Frame	Caption	Command Text
Option Button	Name	optCommandText
	Index	0
Option Button	Name	optCommandText
	Index	1
Option Button	Name	optCommandText
	Index	2
Option Button	Name	optCommandText
	Index	3
Text Box	Name	txtCommandText
	MultiLine	True
Command Button	Name	cmdOpen
	Caption	&Open
	Default	True
Command Button	Name	cmdCancel
	Caption	&Cancel
	Cancel	True

Enter the usual code for the command buttons and the Cancel property:

```
Option Explicit

Private m_bCanceled As Boolean

Private Sub cmdCancel_Click()
    m_bCanceled = True
    Me.Hide
End Sub

Private Sub cmdOpen_Click()
    m_bCanceled = False
    Me.Hide
End Sub

Public Property Get Canceled() As Boolean
    Canceled = m_bCanceled
End Property
```

Now enter the Form_Load event procedure, which contains the code to populate
the CommandText properties on the frmCommand form:

```
Private Sub Form_Load()

    optCommandText(0).Caption = "SELECT * FROM Authors;"

    optCommandText(1).Caption = "DELETE * FROM Authors _
                            WHERE (Author = 'Jason');"

    optCommandText(2).Caption = "SELECT * " _
                    & "FROM Customers " _
                    & "WHERE (ContactTitle = 'Sales Representative') " _
                    & "AND (Country = 'USA'); "

    optCommandText(0).Value = True

End Sub
```

The following code enables the CommandText text box when the user selects the
last option button in the control array:

```
Private Sub optCommandText_Click(Index As Integer)
    If (Index = 3) Then
        txtCommandText.Enabled = True
        txtCommandText.BackColor = vbWhite
    Else
        txtCommandText.Enabled = False
        txtCommandText.BackColor = &H8000000F   ' light grey
    End If
End Sub
```

When the CommandText property is read, a CommandText string value is passed
from either the selected option button or the text box containing a user-entered
CommandText value:

```
Public Property Get CommandText() As String

    If (optCommandText(0).Value = True) Then _
        CommandText = optCommandText(0).Caption

    If (optCommandText(1).Value = True) Then _
        CommandText = optCommandText(1).Caption

    If (optCommandText(2).Value = True) Then _
        CommandText = optCommandText(2).Caption

    If (optCommandText(3).Value = True) Then _
        CommandText = txtCommandText.Text

End Property
```

Now that the frmCommand form is complete, you can move on to the last form,
the frmField form. This form allows the user to select a Field object from the

currently open Recordset or Command object. The Field form is shown in Figure B-5. Begin by adding the form to your project, changing its Name property to frmField and changing its Caption property to "Field Information."

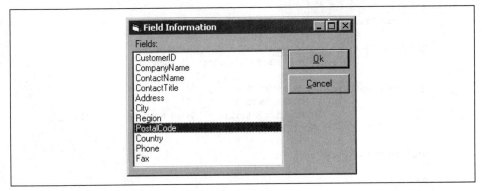

Figure B-5. The Field Information dialog box

The frmField form consists of a Label, a List View control, and two command buttons. After placing these controls onto the form, set the properties shown in Table B-6 to the values specified.

Table B-6. The Field Information Dialog Control Settings

Control	Property	Value
Label	Caption	Fields:
List Box	Name	lstFields
Command Button	Name	cmdOk
	Caption	&Ok
	Default	True
Command Button	Name	cmdCancel
	Caption	&Cancel
	Cancel	True

Enter the usual command-button and Cancel-property code—this should be familiar by now:

```
Option Explicit

Private m_bCanceled As Boolean

Private Sub cmdCancel_Click()
    m_bCanceled = True
    Me.Hide
End Sub

Private Sub cmdOk_Click()
```

```
        m_bCanceled = False
        Me.Hide
End Sub

Public Property Get Canceled() As Boolean
    Canceled = m_bCanceled
End Property
```

Enter the following code to enable the cmdOK command button only when a valid Field object is selected from the List View control:

```
Private Sub Form_Load()
    cmdOk.Enabled = False
End Sub

Private Sub lstFields_Click()
    cmdOK.Enabled = True
End Sub
```

The following code populates the List View control with a Recordset object that has been passed to it:

```
Public Property Set Recordset(rec As Recordset)

    Dim fld As Field

    For Each fld In rec.Fields
        lstFields.AddItem fld.Name
    Next fld

End Property
```

Finally, the Field property returns the name of the field that was chosen by the user from the list:

```
Public Property Get Field() As String
    Field = lstFields.List(lstFields.ListIndex)
End Property
```

C

ADO Errors

Errors are commonplace to any application. Usually, the development environment has a default exception-handling mechanism. In Visual Basic, this mechanism is the On Error statement.

All Visual Basic errors can be trapped using this mechanism, but sometimes errors occur outside of Visual Basic. In these cases, the Visual Basic exception-handling mechanism does little if any good. This is especially true with ADO where errors can occur after execution has left your Visual Basic application and has gone to the data providers.

ADO allows your Visual Basic application to deal with data-provider errors through a special object: the Error object.

Working with Errors in ADO

Two types of errors are of interest to us when using ActiveX Data Objects. The first of these types are those ADO errors that can be trapped within the development environment by using the default exception-handling mechanism. In Visual Basic, this mechanism is accessed using the On Error statement.

The second type of error are those that are reported by a data provider and that can't be trapped within the development environment. These errors are reported within the Errors collection of the Connection object. Within this collection, one or more Error objects are used to represent the individual errors that are reported by the data provider.

ADO Trappable Errors

Table C-1 lists the trappable errors related to ADO.

Table C-1. The ErrorValueEnum Enumeration

Enumeration (ADO/WFC)	Value	Description
adErrBoundToCommand (BOUNDTOCOMMAND)	3707 (&HE7B)	The ActiveConnection property of a Recordset object cannot be changed because the Recordset object's source is a Command object.
adErrCannotComplete (no ADO/WFC equivalent)	3732 (&HE94)	The server that owns the source row cannot complete the operation.
adErrCantChangeConnection (no ADO/WFC equivalent)	3748 (&HEA4)	The Connection was denied because it has different characteristics than the one already in use.
adErrCantChangeProvider (no ADO/WFC equivalent)	3220 (&HC94)	The supplied provider is different from the one already in use.
adErrCantConvertvalue (no ADO/WFC equivalent)	3724 (&HE8C)	Data value could not be converted for reasons other than sign mismatch or data overflow. For example, conversion would have truncated data.
adErrCantCreate (no ADO/WFC equivalent)	3725 (&HE8D)	Data could not be set or retrieved because the column datatype was unknown or the provider had insufficient resources to perform the operation.
adErrCatalogNotSet (no ADO/WFC equivalent)	3747 (&HEA3)	The operation requires a valid Parent-Catalog.
adErrColumnNotOnThisRow (no ADO/WFC equivalent)	3726 (&HE8E)	Column does not exist on this row.
adErrDataConversion (DATACONVERSION)	3421 (&HD5D)	A wrong datatype is being used for the operation.
adErrDataOverflow (no ADO/WFC equivalent)	3721 (&HE89)	Data value is too large to be represented by the column datatype.
adErrDelResOutOfScope (no ADO/WFC equivalent)	3738 (&HE9A)	The URL of the object to be deleted is outside the scope of the current row. Make sure the URL is inside the scope.
adErrDenyNotSupported (no ADO/WFC equivalent)	3750 (&HEA6)	The data provider does not support sharing restrictions.
adErrDenyTypeNotSupported (no ADO/WFC equivalent)	3751 (&HEA7)	The data provider does not support the requested sharing restriction type.
adErrFeatureNotAvailable (FEATURENOTAVAILABLE)	3251 (&HCB3)	The provider does not support the operation.
adErrFieldsUpdateFailed	3749 (&HEA5)	The Fields update failed.
adErrIllegalOperation (ILLEGALOPERATION)	3219 (&HC93)	The operation cannot be performed during this context.
adErrIntegrityViolation (no ADO/WFC equivalent)	3719 (&HE87)	The data value conflicts with the integrity constraints of the field.

Table C-1. The ErrorValueEnum Enumeration (continued)

Enumeration (ADO/WFC)	Value	Description
adErrInTransaction (INTRANSACTION)	3246 (&HCAE)	The operation is in the middle of a transaction and cannot close the Connection object.
adErrInvalidArgument (INVALIDARGUMENT)	3001 (&HBB9)	The argument either is not of the correct type, has a value that is not in the acceptable range, or is in conflict with another argument.
adErrInvalidConnection (INVALIDCONNECTION)	3709 (&HE7D)	The operation cannot be performed because the Connection object is closed.
adErrInvalidParamInfo (INVALIDPARAMINFO)	3708 (&HE7C)	The parameter information is not defined correctly.
adErrInvalidTransaction (no ADO/WFC equivalent)	3714 (&HE82)	The coordinating transaction is invalid or has not started.
adErrInvalidURL (no ADO/WFC equivalent)	3729 (&HE91)	The specified URL contains invalid characters. Make sure the URL is typed correctly.
adErrItemNotFound (ITEMNOTFOUND)	3265 (&HCC1)	The object requested does not exist in the ADO collection at the ordinal position or with the name provided.
adErrNoCurrentRecord (NOCURRENTRECORD)	3021 (&HBCD)	The record pointer does not point to a valid record, and one is needed for the operation.
adErrNotExecuting (NOTEXECUTING) (This seemed to be missing in 2.6)	3715	The execution could not be canceled because it was not executing.
adErrNotReentrant (NOTREENTRANT)	3710 (&HE7E)	The code within the event would cause the event to be fired again.
adErrObjectClosed (OBJECTCLOSED)	3704 (&HE78)	The object that is needed by the operation is closed.
adErrObjectInCollection (OBJECTINCOLLECTION)	3367 (&HD27)	The attempt to add the object to the collection was unsuccessful because the object is already in the collection.
adErrObjectNotSet (OBJECTNOTSET)	3420 (&HD5C)	The object does not point to a valid ADO object.
adErrObjectOpen (OBJECTOPEN)	3705 (&HE79)	The operation requires that the object is not open.
adErrOpeningFile (no ADO/WFC equivalent)	3002 (&HBBA)	The file could not be opened.
adErrOperationCancelled (OPERATIONCANCELLED)	3712 (&HE80)	An ADO operation has been canceled.
adErrOutOfSpace (no ADO/WFC equivalent)	3734 (&HE96)	The provider is unable to obtain enough storage space to complete the copy operation.

Table C-1. The ErrorValueEnum Enumeration (continued)

Enumeration (ADO/WFC)	Value	Description
adErrPermissionDenied (no ADO/WFC equivalent)	3720 (&HE88)	User does not have permission to write to the column. Check Column Privileges property.
adErrPropConflicting (no ADO/WFC equivalent)	3742 (&HE9E)	The property value was not set because it would have conflicted with an existing property.
adErrPropInvalidColumn (no ADO/WFC equivalent)	3739 (&HE9B)	The property cannot apply to the specified column.
adErrPropInvalidOption (no ADO/WFC equivalent)	3740 (&HE9C)	The specified option is invalid.
adErrPropInvalidValue (no ADO/WFC equivalent)	3741 (&HE9D)	The specified value is invalid. Make sure the value is typed correctly.
adErrPropNotAllSettable (no ADO/WFC equivalent)	3743 (&HE9F)	The property is read-only or could not be set for the particular column.
adErrPropNotSet (no ADO/WFC equivalent)	3744 (&HEA0)	The property value was not set. The value of *dwOptions* was DBPROPOPTIONS_OPTIONAL, and the property could not be set to the specified value.
adErrPropNotSettable (no ADO/WFC equivalent)	3745 (&HEA1)	The property was read-only or the consumer attempted to set values of properties in the Initialization property group after the data-source object was initialized. Consumers can set the value of a read-only property to its current value. This value is also returned if a settable column property could not be set for the particular column.
adErrPropNotSupported (no ADO/WFC equivalent)	3746 (&HEA2)	The property value was not set. The provider does not support the property.
adErrProviderFailed (no ADO/WFC equivalent)	3000 (&HBB8)	The provider failed to perform the requested operation.
adErrProviderNotFound (PROVIDERNOTFOUND)	3706 (&HE7A)	The provider could not be found.
adErrReadFile (no ADO/WFC equivalent)	3003 (&HBBB)	The file could not be read.
adErrResourceExists (no ADO/WFC equivalent)	3731 (&HE93)	The copy operation cannot be performed. The object named by destination URL already exists. Specify adCopyOverwrite to replace the object.

Table C-1. The ErrorValueEnum Enumeration (continued)

Enumeration (ADO/WFC)	Value	Description
adErrResourceLocked (no ADO/WFC equivalent)	3730 (&HE92)	The object represented by the specified URL is locked by one or more other processes. Wait until the process has finished, and attempt the operation again.
adErrResourceOutOfScope (no ADO/WFC equivalent)	3735 (&HE97)	The source or destination URL is outside the scope of the current row. Make sure the URL is inside the scope.
adErrSchemaViolation (no ADO/WFC equivalent)	3722 (&HE8A)	Data value conflicted with the datatype or constraints of the column.
adErrSignMismatch (no ADO/WFC equivalent)	3723 (&HE8B)	Conversion failed because the data value was signed and the column datatype used by the provider was unsigned.
adErrStillConnecting (STILLCONNECTING)	3713 (&HE81)	The operation cannot be executed because ADO was still connecting to the data source.
adErrStillExecuting (STILLEXECUTING)	3711 (&HE7F)	The operation cannot be executed because another command is still being executed.
adErrTreePermissionDenied (no ADO/WFC equivalent)	3728 (&HE90)	The operation is unable to access a tree or subtree due to a permissions failure.
adErrUnavailable (no ADO/WFC equivalent)	3736 (&HE98)	An operation failed to complete, and the status is unavailable.
adErrUnsafeOperation (UNSAFEOPERATION)	3716 (&HE84)	The operation is not considered safe by the environment that is currently running ADO.
adErrURLDoesNotExist (no ADO/WFC equivalent)	3727 (&HE8F)	Either the source URL or the parent of the destination URL does not exist.
adErrURLNamedRowDoesNotExist (no ADO/WFC equivalent)	3737 (&HE99)	The row named by this URL does not exist. Make sure the URL is typed correctly.
adErrVolumeNotFound (no ADO/WFC equivalent)	3733 (&HE95)	The provider is unable to locate the storage volume indicated by the URL. Make sure the URL is typed correctly.
adErrWriteFile (no ADO/WFC equivalent)	3004 (&HBBC)	The file could not be written to.
adwrnSecurityDialog (no ADO/WFC equivalent)	3717 (&HE85)	This is an internal constant only, and Microsoft asks that you do not use it.
adwrnSecurityDialogHeader (no ADO/WFC equivalent)	3718 (&HE86)	This is an internal constant only, and Microsoft asks that you do not use it.

The errors listed in Table C-1 are generated by using ADO itself rather than from an underlying problem occurring within the data provider. These are errors that are caused by using ADO improperly.

Data-Provider Errors

Errors that occur within the data provider are not easily trappable within the traditional runtime exception-handling mechanism of a development environment like those generated by ADO itself.

These errors, generated by the data provider, are visible through the Error objects within the Errors collection of the Connection object. Every time an ADO operation causes a data-provider error, the Errors collection is populated within one or more errors (and in some cases, warnings) through individual Error objects.

The Errors collection is not cleared until a new ADO operation causes a data provider error or the user manually clears the Errors collection with the Clear method. Warnings do not clear the Errors object, so it is a good idea to clear the Errors collection manually with the Clear method before calling any ADO operation that can generate warnings in order to determine whether a warning has been reported.

The Resync, UpdateBatch, and CancelBatch methods, as well as the Filter property, of the Recordset object can generate warnings. In addition, the Open method of a Connection object can also generate data-provider warnings.

Each Error object within the Errors collection can be accessed through the use of the default property of the Errors collection (Item), and the number of Error objects within the Errors collection can be obtained by using the Count property.

Each Error object has properties that access the details about the error or warning generated by a data provider:

Number
Returns a Long value representing the constant value of the error or warning.

Description
Returns a String value representing the textual description of the error or warning.

Source
Returns a String value representing the object or the application that raised the error or warning. This value can be the object's class name or programmatic identification.

SQL State
Returns a String value five characters long. This value represents the ANSI SQL standard for error codes generated by SQL data sources.

NativeError

Returns a Long value representing the native error code from the data provider. This number does not have any meaning to ADO itself, but it can be used in conjunction with the data provider to gather more information about the error or warning.

HelpFile

Returns a String value representing the name of a file, if any, that contains more information about the particular error or warning.

HelpContext

Returns a Long value representing context identification within the help file named by the HelpFile property, which contains more information about the particular error or warning.

The most common and useful properties that are used to determine a data-provider error are the first three described previously—the Number, Description, and Source properties of the Error object.

The Errors Example

To better understand how the Errors collection of the Connection object works, I have come up with an example application conveniently named the Errors Collection Example.

This example allows you to execute an operation within ADO that will (hopefully) generate an error. In addition, you can add more error-generating code to the example to further investigate the usage of error handling within ADO.

The first form within the Errors Collection Example asks the user what type of error he would like to generate, as shown in Figure C-1.

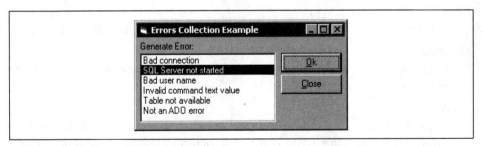

Figure C-1. The Errors Collection Example form

After the user selects an error from the list and presses the Ok button, the operation that generates the error or errors is attempted, and with any luck, the ADO Error(s) form is displayed detailing each error, as shown in Figure C-2.

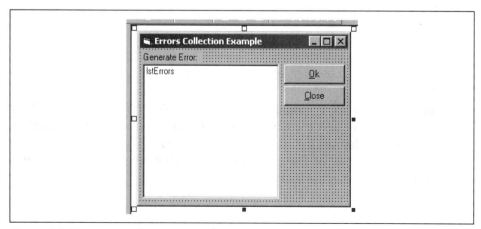

Figure C-2. The ADO Error(s) form

To begin this example, create a new project within Visual Basic, and be sure to set a reference to the Microsoft ActiveX Data Objects *xx* Library, where *xx* represents the version of ADO that you have on your machine (1.0, 1.5, 2.0, 2.1). Name the project ErrorsCollectionExample.

The Main Form

Once your new project is created, change the name of Form1 to frmErrorsCollectionExample, and add a label, a list box, and two command buttons, as shown in Figure C-3.

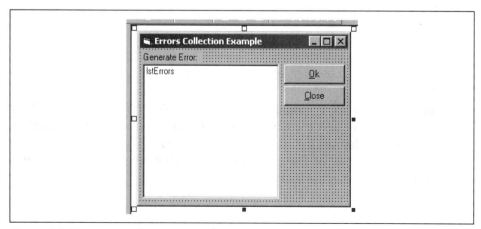

Figure C-3. The Errors Collection Example form in Design mode

Once the controls have been placed on the form, set the values of the properties listed in Table C-2.

Table C-2. The Errors Collection Form Control Settings

Control	Property	Value
Form	Caption	Errors Collection Example
Label	Caption	Generate Error:
List Box	Name	LstErrors
Command Button	Name	cmdOk
	Caption	&Ok
Command Button	Name	cmdClose
	Caption	&Close

Begin entering the following code. This is a list of constant values that represent each error the user can generate. If you want to add additional errors to the list, create a new constant for it here:

```
Option Explicit

Private Const BAD_CONNECTION_ERROR = 1
Private Const SQL_SERVER_NOT_STARTED_ERROR = 2
Private Const BAD_USER_NAME_ERROR = 3
Private Const INVALID_COMMANDTEXT_VALUE_ERROR = 4
Private Const TABLE_NOT_AVAILABLE_ERROR = 5
Private Const NOT_AN_ADO_ERROR = 6
```

Now add the code for the Command buttons. The Close button unloads the form, but the Ok button calls the GenerateError method with the constant representing the error selected. You will see later that each item in the list box has its ItemData property to set the constant value of its corresponding error:

```
Private Sub cmdClose_Click()
    Unload Me
End Sub

Private Sub cmdOk_Click()
    GenerateError lstErrors.ItemData(lstErrors.ListIndex)
End Sub
```

Enter the following code to populate the list box with the errors that have been predefined. As you can see, the Form_Load event calls the PopulateErrors method, which in turn calls the AddToErrorList method for each possible error that can be generated. A description of the error and the constant representing the error is used for each item within the list box.

If you want to add additional errors to the list, enter another call to the AddTo-ErrorList method within the PopulateErrors method for each:

```
Private Sub Form_Load()
    PopulateErrors
End Sub

Private Sub PopulateErrors()

    AddToErrorList "Bad connection", BAD_CONNECTION_ERROR
    AddToErrorList "SQL Server not started", SQL_SERVER_NOT_STARTED_ERROR
    AddToErrorList "Bad user name", BAD_USER_NAME_ERROR
    AddToErrorList "Invalid command text value", INVALID_COMMANDTEXT_VALUE_ERROR
    AddToErrorList "Table not available", TABLE_NOT_AVAILABLE_ERROR
    AddToErrorList "Not an ADO error", NOT_AN_ADO_ERROR
    lstErrors.ListIndex = 0

End Sub

Private Sub AddToErrorList(sError As String, _
                           lErrorIndex As Long)

    lstErrors.AddItem sError
    lstErrors.ItemData(lstErrors.ListCount - 1) = lErrorIndex

End Sub
```

The GenerateError method generates the error that was chosen by the user. Again, if you have added additional errors to the list, add another Case statement to generate the error that you want:

```
Private Sub GenerateError(lErrorIndex As Long)
On Error GoTo ERR_GenerateError:

    Dim con As ADODB.Connection

    Set con = New ADODB.Connection

    Select Case (lErrorIndex)

        Case BAD_CONNECTION_ERROR:
            con.Open "Bad Connection"

        Case SQL_SERVER_NOT_STARTED_ERROR:
            MsgBox "Make sure that the SQL Server service is not started.", _
                vbInformation + vbOKOnly, _
                "Information"
            con.Open "DSN=NorthwindDSN"

        Case BAD_USER_NAME_ERROR:
            MsgBox "Make sure that the SQL Server service is started.", _
                vbInformation + vbOKOnly, _
                "Information"
            con.Open "DSN=NorthwindDSN", "INVALID USER"
```

```
        Case INVALID_COMMANDTEXT_VALUE_ERROR:
            con.Open "DSN=BiblioDSN"
            con.Execute "INVALID COMMANDTEXT VALUE"

        Case TABLE_NOT_AVAILABLE_ERROR:
            con.Open "DSN=BiblioDSN"
            con.Execute "MISSINGTABLE", _
                        , _
                        adCmdTable

        Case NOT_AN_ADO_ERROR:
            con.Execute "SELECT * FROM Authors;"

    End Select

    Set con = Nothing

Exit Sub

ERR_GenerateError:

    If (Not frmDisplayADOError.IsAnADORelatedError(Err, con.Errors)) Then

        MsgBox Err.Number & ": " & Err.Description, _
               vbExclamation + vbOKOnly, _
               "General Error"

    Else
        Resume Next
    End If

End Sub
```

Notice that in the previous GenerateError method, the Visual Basic exception handling mechanism, On Error, is used to trap a Visual Basic runtime error. If one is
generated, the method IsAnADORelatedError of the frmDisplayADOError form is
called with the Visual Basic runtime-error information to determine whether it is
an ADO-related error.

You will soon see that if it is in fact an ADO-related error, the error is handled
through the frmDisplayADOError form, but if it is not, the value **FALSE** is returned
so that the GenerateError method can display its own error message.

The ADO Error(s) Form

Begin creating the ADO Error(s) form as shown in Figure C-4. Create a list box
control within one frame and a number of controls within another. This second
frame should contain eight labels and eight text boxes. In addition, add a Command button to the bottom of the form as shown in order to unload the form from
memory.

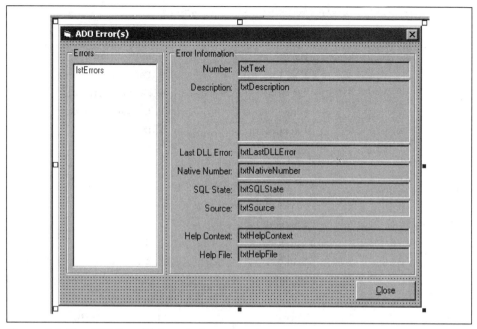

Figure C-4. The ADO Error(s) form in Design mode

Once you have placed all of the controls on the form, you can enter the values for the properties shown in Table C-3.

Table C-3. The ADO Error(s) Form Control Settings

Control	Property	Value
Form	Name	frmDisplayADOError
	Caption	ADO Error(s)
Frame	Caption	Errors
List Box	Name	lstErrors
Label	Caption	Number:
Text Box	Name	txtText
	BackColor	Button Face
	Enabled	False
Label	Caption	Description:
Text Box	Name	txtDescription
	MultiLine	1-True
	BackColor	Button Face
	Enabled	False
Label	Caption	Last DLL Error:
Text Box	Name	txtLastDLLError

Table C-3. The ADO Error(s) Form Control Settings (continued)

Control	Property	Value
	BackColor	Button Face
	Enabled	False
Label	Caption	Native Number:
Text Box	Name	txtNativeNumber
	BackColor	Button Face
	Enabled	False
Label	Caption	SQL State:
Text Box	Name	txtSQLState
	BackColor	Button Face
	Enabled	False
Label	Caption	Source:
Text Box	Name	txtSource
	BackColor	Button Face
	Enabled	False
Label	Caption	Help Context:
Text Box	Name	txtHelpContext
	BackColor	Button Face
	Enabled	False
Label	Caption	Help File:
Text Box	Name	txtHelpFile
	BackColor	Button Face
	Enabled	False
Command Button	Name	cmdClose
	Caption	&Close

Begin by entering the following code into the General Declarations section of the frmDisplayADOError form. The type TVBAError, shown next, is used to hold the information from a Visual Basic runtime error as you will soon see:

```
Option Explicit

Private Type TVBAError
    Number As Long
    Description As String
    LastDllError As Long
    Source As String
    HelpContext As Long
    HelpFile As String
End Type
```

```
Private m_oVBAError As TVBAError
Private m_oADOErrors As ADODB.Errors

Private Const VBA_ERROR = 1
Private Const ADO_ERROR = 2
```

Add the following code to close the form:

```
Private Sub cmdClose_Click()
    Unload Me
End Sub
```

The following function, AddErrorToList, adds a single error—either a Visual Basic runtime error or an ADO data-provider error—to the list box shown on the form:

```
Private Function AddErrorToList(lErrorNumber As Long, _
                     lErrorType As Long)

    Dim sErrorType As String

    Select Case (lErrorType)
        Case VBA_ERROR: sErrorType = "(VBA)"
        Case ADO_ERROR: sErrorType = "(ADO)"
    End Select

    lstErrors.AddItem CStr(lErrorNumber) & " " & sErrorType
    lstErrors.ItemData(lstErrors.ListCount - 1) = lErrorType

End Function
```

The following method, IsAnADORelatedError, is the method that was called by the frmErrorsCollectionExample form to display the errors if they related to an ADO operation or return **False** if they didn't. In the conditional shown later, if the ADO Errors collection passed to the method has any Error objects in it, then the errors are ADO-related.

With the **Else** portion of the conditional, the Visual Basic runtime error that was trapped in the frmErrorsCollectionExample is copied into the TVBAError type that was declared earlier. It is important to note whether this information has to be copied, because the ErrObject object can be cleared without warning by Visual Basic itself.

Once the Visual Basic error is copied, it is added to the list via the AddErrorToList method call. The same is done for each Error object within the Errors collection passed to the method:

```
Public Function IsAnADORelatedError(oVBAError As VBA.ErrObject, _
                        oADOErrors As ADODB.Errors) As Boolean

    Dim oADOError As ADODB.Error

    If (oADOErrors.Count = 0) Then
```

```
        IsAnADORelatedError = False
        Unload Me

    Else

        m_oVBAError.Number = oVBAError.Number
        m_oVBAError.Description = oVBAError.Description
        m_oVBAError.LastDllError = oVBAError.LastDllError
        m_oVBAError.Source = oVBAError.Source
        m_oVBAError.HelpContext = oVBAError.HelpContext
        m_oVBAError.HelpFile = oVBAError.HelpFile

        AddErrorToList m_oVBAError.Number, VBA_ERROR

        Set m_oADOErrors = oADOErrors

        For Each oADOError In m_oADOErrors
            AddErrorToList oADOError.Number, ADO_ERROR
        Next oADOError

        lstErrors.ListIndex = 0

        IsAnADORelatedError = True
        Me.Show

    End If

End Function
```

When a new error is selected from the list box on the form, the lstErrors_Click event is raised. Enter the code for this event as shown in the next code. Notice that for each type of error, there is different information. The Visual Basic error does not have a NativeNumber or SQLState property, but it does have a Last-DLLError property that the ADO Error object does not:

```
Private Sub lstErrors_Click()

    Dim lIndex As Long

    lIndex = lstErrors.ListIndex

    Select Case (lstErrors.ItemData(lIndex))

    Case VBA_ERROR:

        With m_oVBAError
            txtNumber.Text = .Number
            txtDescription.Text = .Description
            txtLastDLLError = .LastDllError
            txtNativeNumber = ""
            txtSQLState = ""
            txtSource = .Source
            txtHelpContext.Text = .HelpContext
            txtHelpFile.Text = .HelpFile & ""
```

```
            End With

        Case ADO_ERROR:

            With m_oADOErrors(lIndex - 1)
                txtNumber.Text = .Number
                txtDescription.Text = .Description
                txtLastDLLError = ""
                txtNativeNumber = .NativeError
                txtSQLState = .SQLState
                txtSource = .Source
                txtHelpContext.Text = .HelpContext
                txtHelpFile.Text = .HelpFile & ""
            End With

    End Select

End Sub
```

Once you have entered all of the code, your Errors Collection Example is ready to go. Simply run it, and generate all the errors you want.

D

The ADO Data Control

The ADO Data Control is the third in a line of controls that are used to easily create a connection to a database. The first of these three was the intrinsic Data Control that utilized DAO technology. The next in line was the Remote Data Control that used the RDO technology. What would a data-access technology be without the familiar VCR button–style interface that was called the data control?

The ADO Data Control allows for an easy way to connect to a data source. Once that connection is made, it can be easily bound to data-aware controls such as the DBList and DBCombo controls found in the Microsoft Data Bound List Controls component.

The ADO Data Control Property Pages

The ADO Data Control is very easy to configure by means of its Property Pages, which are accessible through the Custom property shown in the controls property list.

The first page of the ADO Data Control Property Pages allows you to select a source of connection in one of three ways. This tab is shown in Figure D-1.

The first way to specify a source of connection is by specifying a Data Link File. A Data Link file is a file that contains the Connection-string information used to establish a connection to a data source. We will look into how to create Data Link Files in the next section of this chapter.

The second way to select a source of the database connection is by specifying a Data Source Name. To create a new DSN you can use the ODBC Data Source Administrator, which can be found in the Control Box or by pressing the New button located to the right of the Combo Box.

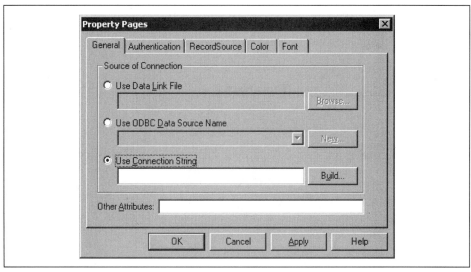

Figure D-1. The General tab of the ADO Data Control Property Pages

The third way to select a source of the database connection is to specify a Connection-string value. If you would like to, you can create a connection string by using the Build button. Creating connection-string values is also covered in the next section of this chapter.

Once you have specified the correct connection information for a data source, you can use the next tab of the Property Pages dialog box, the Authentication tab, to enter a username and password. This is shown in Figure D-2.

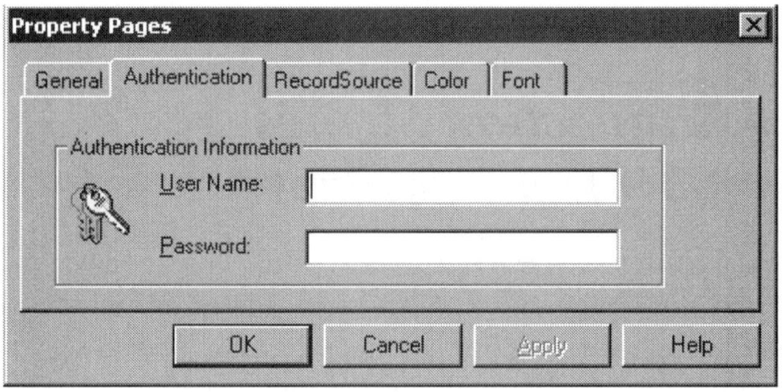

Figure D-2. The Authentication tab of the ADO Data Control Property Pages

The third tab, the RecordSource tab, allows you to specify the information necessary to create a recordset from the data source specified. This tab is shown in Figure D-3.

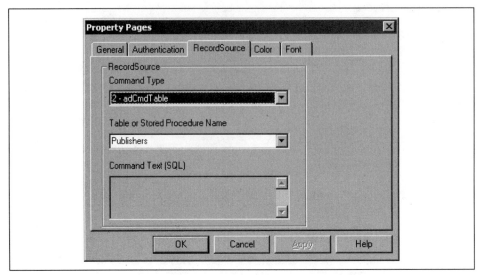

Figure D-3. The RecordSource tab of the ADO Data Control Property Pages

The RecordSource tab of the Property Pages dialog box allows you to specify the CommandType property of the recordset that is going to be created internally by the ADO Data Control.

If you specify that the CommandType is either adCmdTable or adCmdStoredProc, then you can select a Table or Stored Procedure Name from the drop-down list provided. If you specify that the CommandType is either adCmdUnknown or adCmdText, you can enter in a CommandText value in the section provided.

The last two tabs of the ADO Data Control's Property Pages dialog box are used for setting the physical characteristics of the data control, the Color and Font.

Creating Connection Strings with the ADO Data Control

One of the best features of the ADO Data Control is its ability to create connection strings. From the beginning of ADO (somewhere around Version 1.5), connection strings have been a daunting and tedious task. The ADO Data Control has given us a wizard to guide us through these rough waters.

Data Link Properties Dialog Box

The Data Link Properties dialog box is a wizard that allows you to create ADO connection strings. To access the Data Link Properties dialog box, press the Build button for the Connection-string property in either the first tab of the Property Pages dialog box (Figure D-1) or the Property Pages dialog box that is shown when you go into the Connection String property dialog box (Figure D-4). Incidentally, the first tab of the Property Pages dialog box is identical to the property dialog box of the Connection String dialog box.

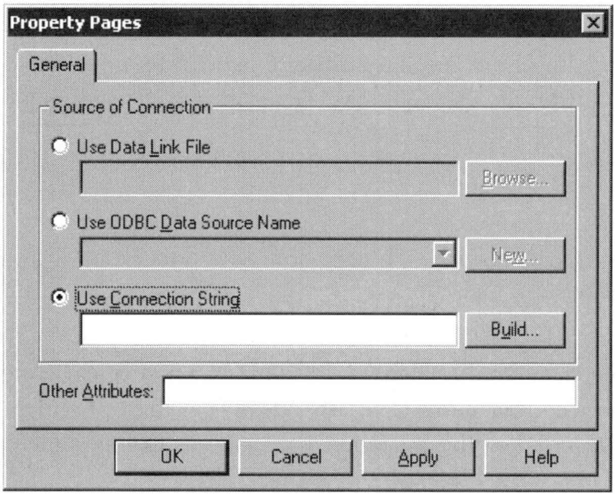

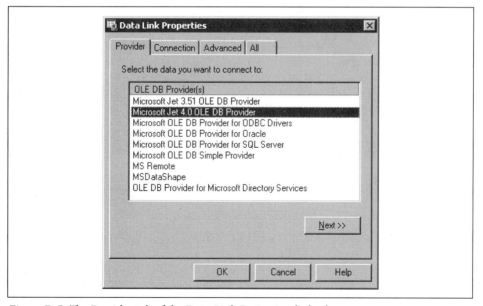

Figure D-4. The Connection String Property dialog box

Entering provider information

Afteryou press the Build button, the Data Link Properties dialog box will appear as shown in Figure D-5.

Figure D-5. The Provider tab of the Data Link Properties dialog box

The first tab of the Data Link Properties dialog box is the Provider tab, which allows the user to select an installed Data Provider from a list of available data providers.

Entering connection information

The second tab in the Data Link Properties is dependent upon the provider chosen in the first tab. Currently, there are four types of data providers included with the Microsoft Data Access Components:

- Jet
- ODBC
- SQL Server
- Oracle

For each of the providers shown here, there is a specific Connection tab with unique property combinations that are used by that provider. For all other providers not included in the Microsoft Data Access Components, a generic Connection tab is used.

The Jet providers. The Connection tab of the Data Link Properties dialog box for Jet connections is shown in Figure D-6.

Figure D-6. The Connection tab of the Data Link Properties dialog box for Jet providers

Within this dialog box you can select an Access database, the username and password and a few settings regarding the password itself.

The first option, Blank Password, will place a blank password in the connection string. The second option, Allow saving password, will place the password in the connection string unmasked and unencrypted.

To test the connection after you have made the proper settings, click the Test Connection button. If the connection was made successfully, you should see the message box shown in Figure D-7.

Figure D-7. The Test Connection Succeeded message box

If you don't see the Test Connection Succeeded dialog box, check the properties that you have entered for an error.

The ODBC provider. The Connection tab of the Data Link Properties dialog box for ODBC connections is shown in Figure D-8.

The first step in specifying the connection information for ODBC connections is to enter either a data source name (DSN) or an ODBC connection string. If you want to build an ODBC connection string, you can click the Build button for the Connection-string property. This will allow you to create either a File DSN (DSN-less connection string) or a Machine DSN (DSN-based connection string).

The second step allows you to enter a username and password. You can also indicate if the password should be blank in the connection string (the Blank password option) or if the password should be saved in the connection string (the Allow saving password option), which will neither mask or encrypt the password.

Finally, you can choose which database to use for the connection under the Initial Catalog property.

Once you have completed this information, test the connection with the Test Connection button.

The SQL Server providers. The Connection tab of the Data Link Properties dialog box for SQL Server connections is shown in Figure D-9.

The first step in specifying the connection information for SQL Server connections is entering the server name from which the database resides.

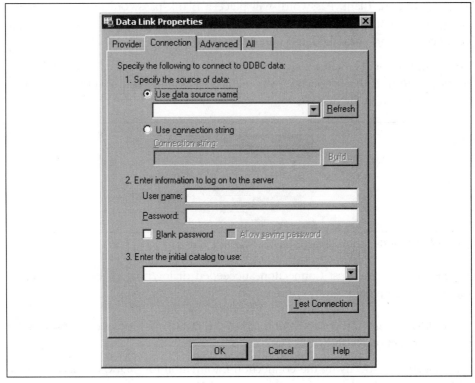

Figure D-8. The Connection tab of the Data Link Properties dialog box for the ODBC provider

Next, you can choose to use the Windows NT integrated-security option if your OLE DB provider supports an authentication service and you have permission in the data source to use that authentication service. If you choose not to use the Windows NT integrated security, you can enter a username and password manually. In addition, you can specify that the password is blank in the connection string or the password is saved in the connection string (although it is not masked or encrypted).

Finally, select the database to use that is on the server specified. You can either select a database from a list, or if you have SQL Server 7.0, you can attach a SQL-database file as a database name and enter the name of the single-file database file.

Once you are done setting up the connection specifications, you can test the connection with the Test Connection button.

The Oracle providers. The Connection tab of the Data Link Properties dialog box for Oracle connections is shown in Figure D-10.

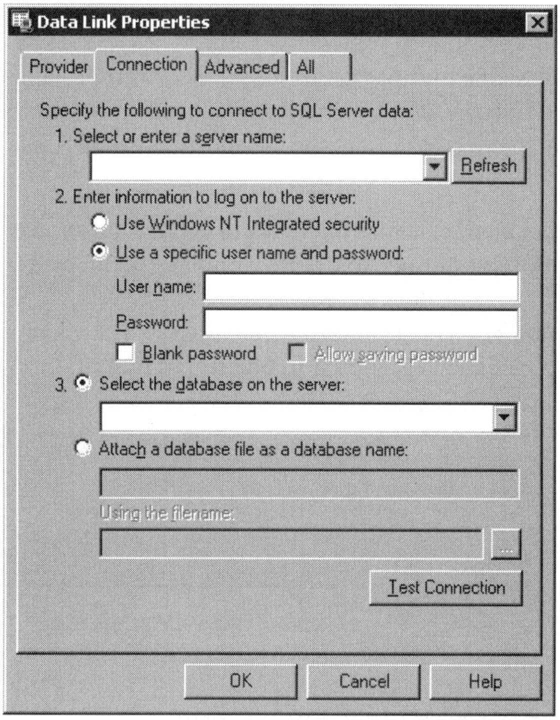

Figure D-9. The Connection tab of the Data Link Properties dialog box for SQL Server providers

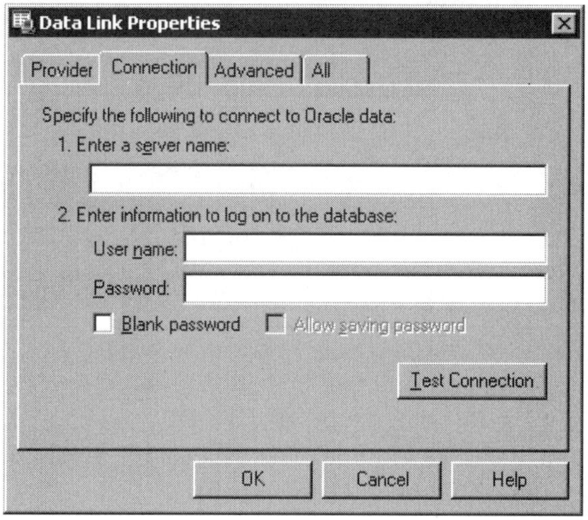

Figure D-10. The Connection tab of the Data Link Properties dialog box for Oracle providers

When specifying Oracle connection information, first enter the name of the server on which the Oracle database resides.

Next, enter the username and password to be used when establishing the connection. In addition, you can specify to include a blank password in the connection string or to save the password in the connection string unmasked and unencrypted.

Once you have specified all of the Oracle connection information, you can test the connection with the Test Connection button on the bottom of this tab.

Other OLE DB providers. The Connection tab of the Data Link Properties dialog box for all other connections is shown in Figure D-11.

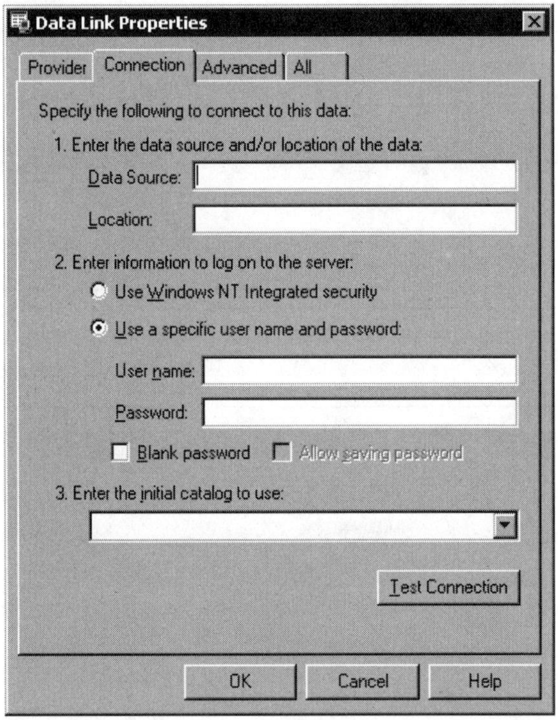

Figure D-11. The Connection tab of the Data Link Properties dialog box for other providers

When connecting with any other type of OLE DB provider, the first step is to specify the data source and its location. The data source would usually be a server name, and the location would be a database name.

Next, choose to use either Windows NT integrated security or to enter a username and password manually.

If you choose to use the Windows NT integrated-security option, you must be sure that the OLE DB provider that you are using supports an authentication service, and you must have permission to use that authentication service in the data source that you are choosing.

If you choose to enter a username and password manually, you can also specify to have a blank password entered in the connection string or, if you have a password, have it saved to the connection string although it will be done so unmasked and unencrypted.

The final step on this tab would be to identify the initial catalog that the connection will use. This means that you need to enter the database that you want to access.

Once you are done with all of this information, you can test the connection by using the Test Connection button.

Entering advanced information

The third tab of the Data Link Properties dialog box is shown in Figure D-12. This tab is used to set the advanced properties of a data-source connection: the impersonation level, the protection level, the connection timeout, and the access permissions.

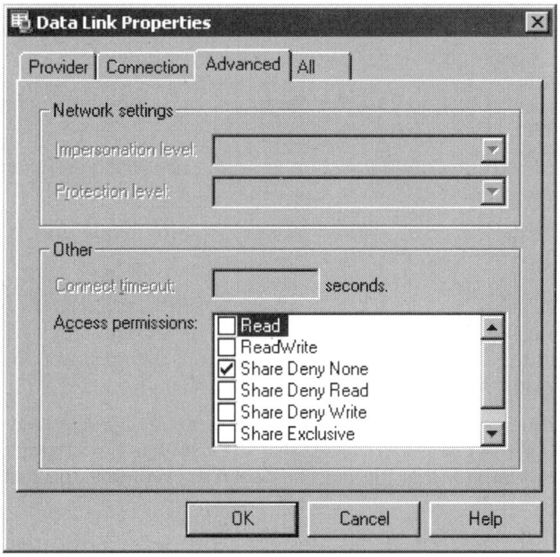

Figure D-12. The Advanced tab of the Data Link Properties dialog box

Impersonation level. The impersonation level only applies to network connections that are not RPC (Remote Procedure Call) connections. This property indicates what level of impersonation the server can use when it is impersonating the client. The value of the impersonation-level property can be set to any of the values shown in Table D-1.

Table D-1. Impersonation Level Settings

Value	Description
Anonymous	Indicates that the server cannot get identification information about the client and, therefore, cannot impersonate it.
Identify	Indicates that the server can identify the client, allowing it to impersonate it. However, it cannot access system objects as the client.
Impersonate	Indicates that the server can impersonate the client's security context.
Delegate	Indicates that not only can the server impersonate the client's security context, but it can also make calls to other servers on behalf of the client.

Protection level. The protection level also only applies to network connections that are not RPC connections. This property represents the level of protection of the data that is sent across the network, between the client and the server. The value of the protection-level property can be set to any of the values shown in Table D-2.

Table D-2. Protection Level Settings

Value	Description
None	Indicates that no authentication of data is done between the client and the server.
Connect	Indicates that authentication is done only when the client connects with the server.
Call	Indicates that authentication is done at the beginning of each request to the server from the client.
Pkt	Indicates that authentication is done on all data received by the client.
Pkt Integrity	Indicates that authentication is done on all data received by the client and that the client checks to ensure that the date has not changed during the transmission.
Pkt Privacy	Indicates that authentication is done on all data received by the client, that the client checks to ensure that the data has not changed during the transmission, and that the data has been encrypted to protect its privacy.

Connection timeout. The connection-timeout property indicates, in seconds, the time that the OLD DB provider is to wait for initialization of the connection to complete.

If the connection-timeout value causes the connection to actually timeout, an error is raised, and the attempt to create a connection is canceled.

Access permissions. The access permissions of a connection can be one or more of the values shown in Table D-3.

Table D-3. Access-Permission Settings

Value	Description
Read	Indicates that the connection is read-only.
Write	Indicates that the connection is write-only.
ReadWrite	Indicates that the connection is both read- and write-enabled.
Share Deny None	Indicates that the connection cannot deny read or write access to other connections.
Share Deny Read	Indicates that the connection prevents read access to other connections.
Share Deny Write	Indicates that the connection prevents write access to other connections.
Share Exclusive	Indicates that the connection prevents other connections from read and write access.

Reviewing all of the Data Link information

The last tab of the Data Link Properties dialog box is the All tab, which shows all of the providers' initialization properties and their set values. Figure D-13 shows the All tab of the Data Link Properties dialog box.

The properties shown in this tab will vary from provider to provider. You can alter individual values by selecting a property in the list and by clicking on the Edit Value button.

Once you are done setting these properties, simply click the OK button to finish. Depending on where you invoked the Data Link Properties dialog box, you should see a created connection string. If you are not using the ADO Data Control and you are coding by hand, you can cut this connection string and paste it into your application.

Data Link Files

Microsoft allows you to save connection string information into a file called a Data Link File. This file has the .UDL extension.

To create a Data Link File, first press the Browse button for the Data Link File property in either the first tab of the Property Pages dialog box (Figure D-1) or the Property Pages dialog box that is shown when you go into the Connection String property dialog box (Figure D-4). Once you have pressed the Browse button on one of these dialog boxes, you are presented with Select Data Link File dialog box as shown in Figure D-14.

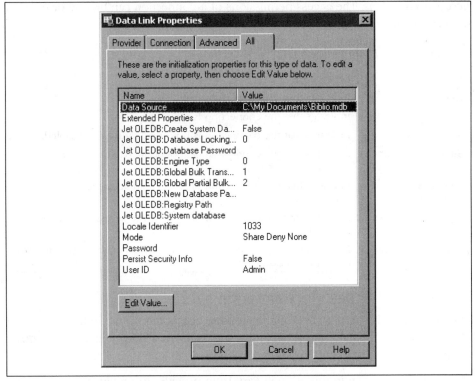

Figure D-13. The All tab of the Data Link Properties dialog box

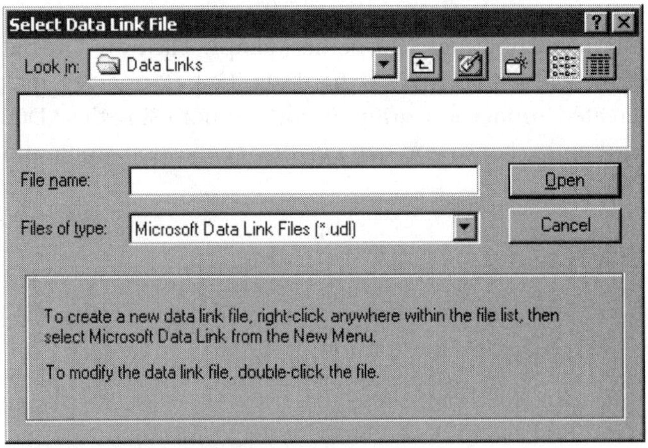

Figure D-14. Selecting a Data Link File

This dialog box will direct you to the *Program Files\Common Files\System\ OLE DB\Data Links* directory, which will contain a list of the currently installed Data Link Files on your computer. Chances are if you are reading this section, the list will be empty.

The dialog box also instructs you on how to create a new Data Link File by clicking the right mouse button anywhere within the file list of the dialog box.

Once you perform the right-click on the mouse and select New from the pop-up menu, you should be presented with a menu that looks like that shown in Figure D-15. Choose the Microsoft Data Link from this cascading pop-up menu.

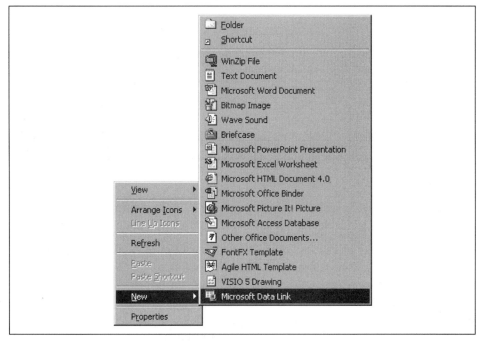

Figure D-15. The Microsoft Data Link menu

This will add a new file to the current directory shown in the dialog box with the name "New Microsoft Data Link.UDL". You can rename this file if you like.

Double click on the file, as the dialog box instructs, or right click on the file and chose Properties from the menu to modify its contents. Once you have double-clicked on this file, you should see the now familiar Data Link Properties dialog box shown in Figure D-5. Begin creating your connection string. It will be saved to your Data Link File when you close this dialog box.

The ADO Data Control Example

Lets take a look at the ADO Data Control with an example. We will be using the ADO Data Control to bind text-box controls to the Publishers table of the *Biblio.mdb* Access database file. Figure D-16 shows the ADO Data Control Example during runtime.

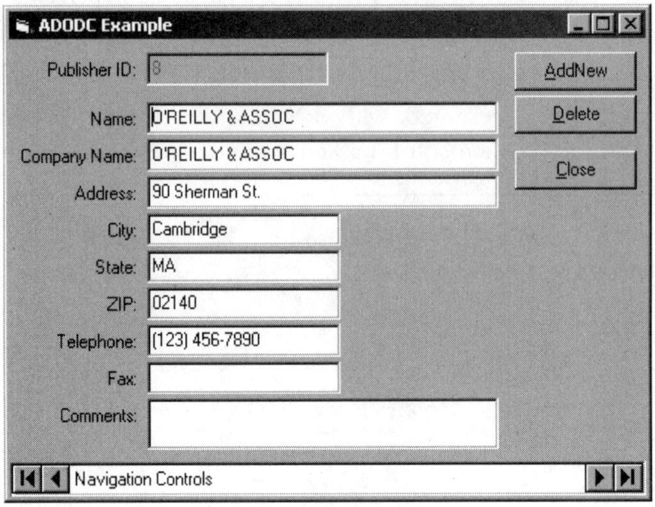

Figure D-16. The ADO Data Control Example

To begin, place the controls shown in Figure D-17 onto a form. This includes an ADO Data Control, ten labels, ten text boxes, and three command buttons.

Begin by setting the properties for the ADO Data Control. You can use the steps outlined earlier to create a Data Link File that points to the *Biblio.mdb* database file. After you have created a Data Link File, you can use the Custom property of the ADO Data Control to point to that Data Link File through the first tab of the dialog box, the General tab (shown in Figure D-1). Then switch to the Record-Source tab (shown in Figure D-3) to set the CommandType property to adCmd-Table and the Table property to Publishers.

Now you are ready to set the rest of the properties as specified in Table D-4.

Notice that the two properties that are being selected for all of the text boxes are DataField and DataSource. First choose the DataSource property for the text box from the drop-down list. There should only be one valid ADO Data Control listed since it is the only one on your form. Because all of the ten text boxes should have the same value for the DataSource property, you can set them all at once by multiselecting all of the text boxes before setting the DataSource property.

Once the DataSource property is set for a given text box, the list box for the DataField property will contain all of the valid Field names within the Recordset specified by the ADO Data Control. Choose the appropriate Field name for the text box you are setting.

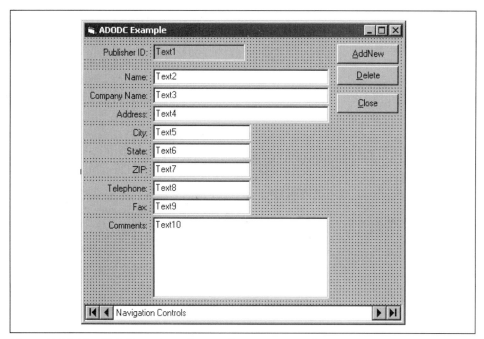

Figure D-17. The ADO Data Control Example in Design mode

Table D-4. The ADO Data Control Example Control Settings

Control	Property	Value
Form	Name	FrmADODCExample
ADO Data Control	Name	adcPublishers
Label	Caption	Publisher ID:
Text Box	BackColor	'Button Face
	DataField	"PubID"
	DataSource	"adcPublishers"
	Enabled	0 'False
Label	Caption	Name:
Text Box	DataField	"Name"
	DataSource	"adcPublishers"
Label	Caption	Company Name:
Text Box	DataField	"Company Name"
	DataSource	"adcPublishers"
Label	Caption	Address:
Text Box	DataField	"Address"
	DataSource	"adcPublishers"
Label	Caption	City:

Table D-4. The ADO Data Control Example Control Settings (continued)

Control	Property	Value
Text Box	DataField	"City"
	DataSource	"adcPublishers"
Label	Caption	State:
Text Box	DataField	"State"
	DataSource	"adcPublishers"
Label	Caption	ZIP:
Text Box	DataField	"Zip"
	DataSource	"adcPublishers"
Label	Caption	Telephone:
Text Box	DataField	"Telephone"
	DataSource	"adcPublishers"
Label	Caption	Fax:
Text Box	DataField	"Fax"
	DataSource	"adcPublishers"
Label	Caption	Comments:
Text Box	DataField	"Comments"
	DataSource	"adcPublishers"
	MultiLine	-1 'True
Command Button	Name	cmdAddNew
	Caption	&AddNew
Command Button	Name	cmdDelete
	Caption	&Delete
Command Button	Name	cmdClose
	Caption	Close

The point of the ADO Data Control is minimal coding. When the application is run as it is right now, the recordset will be created by the ADO Data Control, and the text boxes will be populated with the information bound to the data control. When the navigation buttons on the ADO Data Control are used, the record displayed through the ten text boxes will change.

To make things a little more interesting, we are going to add the ability to add and delete records from the recordset in a neat and efficient manner, but first, let's get the closing code out of the way:

```
Private Sub cmdClose_Click()
    Unload Me
End Sub
```

The easiest of the two new methods is adding a new record. Accessing the Recordset object of the ADO Data Control directly, as shown in the following code, can do this:

```
Private Sub cmdAddNew_Click()
    adcPublishers.Recordset.AddNew
    txtName.SetFocus
End Sub
```

After entering this code, try running the application. When you press the AddNew button, the record is cleared, and the cursor is placed in the Name text box waiting for you to add the record information. As you know with the AddNew method, the record is not saved until the record pointer changes location or the Update method is called. In this example, we are relying on the user to change the record pointer by using one of the navigation controls of the ADO Data Control.

To code the functionality to delete a record, enter the cmdDelete_Click event shown in the following code:

```
Private Sub cmdDelete_Click()
On Error GoTo ERR_cmdDelete_Click:

    adcPublishers.Recordset.Delete
    adcPublishers.Recordset.MovePrevious
    If (adcPublishers.Recordset.BOF) Then _
        adcPublishers.Recordset.MoveFirst

Exit Sub

ERR_cmdDelete_Click:
    Select Case (Err.Number)
        Case -2147217842: ' canceled by user
        Case Else:
            MsgBox "Error #" & Err.Number & ": " & Err.Description, _
                   vbExclamation + vbOKOnly, _
                   "Error"
    End Select
End Sub
```

For a moment, ignore the code labeled by **ERR_cmdDelete_Click**.

When the user clicks the Delete button on our example form, this method calls the Delete method of the Recordset object belonging to the ADO Data Control. As with the AddNew method, the change does not take place until the record pointer is moved. This is then done with the call to MovePrevious (and the call to Move-First if the MovePrevious call moved the record pointer before the first record—this will occur if the user deletes the first record in the recordset).

Too often users delete things they don't mean to. Even more often users expect to be asked if they are sure they want to go ahead with their instructions. Our example should cater to this.

Because the ADO Data Control exposes the Recordset object, it also exposes the Recordset's events. Of interest to us is the WillChangeRecord event, which we can use to trap the deletion of the current record, as shown in the following code:

```
Private Sub adcPublishers_WillChangeRecord( _
                            ByVal adReason As ADODB.EventReasonEnum, _
                            ByVal cRecords As Long, _
                            adStatus As ADODB.EventStatusEnum, _
                            ByVal pRecordset As ADODB.Recordset)

    Dim lResponse As Long

    If (adReason = adRsnDelete) Then
        lResponse = MsgBox("Are you sure that you want to delete " _
                        & "the current record?", _
                        vbQuestion + vbYesNo, _
                        "Delete")

        If (lResponse = vbNo) Then adStatus = adStatusCancel
    End If

End Sub
```

In the adcPublishers_WillChangeRecord event shown previously, if the record is being deleted (adReason is equal to adRsnDelete), then the user is asked if they are sure they want to proceed with this action. If the user responds No, then the adStatus flag is set to adStatusCancel.

At this point, we are referred back to the code in the cmdDelete_Click event:

```
ERR_cmdDelete_Click:
    Select Case (Err.Number)
        Case -2147217842: ' canceled by user
        Case Else:
            MsgBox "Error #" & Err.Number & ": " & Err.Description, _
                    vbExclamation + vbOKOnly, _
                    "Error"
    End Select
End Sub
```

Once ADO attempts to move the record pointer, directly after the Delete method call, the WillChangeRecord event is fired. When the user answers No to cancel the deletion, an error is raised in the calling method (cmdDelete_Click) and is trapped in the code shown previously.

If the error number is equal to −2147217842, it is an indication that the user canceled the method (by changing the adStatus flag to adStatusCancel in the WillChangeRecord event), as well as an indicator to continue without stopping.

As an added safety measure, since we are trapping errors, we added the Case Else: statement to display any other errors that may have occurred in this method. If we hadn't added this statement, errors could go unnoticed.

Although this is an extremely basic example of how you can use the ADO Data Control, it proves that using the ADO Data Control is extremely basic to implement. In addition, it should be noted that additional code would still need to be implemented in order to perform other "basic" requirements of any application, such as validation of field data and additional error handling.

E

Enumeration Tables

This appendix contains an alphabetical list of the Enumerations used by the members of ADO objects and collections.

Next to each enumeration name is a list of the versions of ADO that contained the particular enumeration. For each enumeration, there is a description, a table, and in some cases a "See Also" section with a list of related ADO objects, collections, methods, properties, events, and enumerations.

In each enumeration table, the first column, "Enumeration (ADO/WFC)," contains the enumeration constant for both ADO and WFC (Java). The middle column displays the numeric value for the enumeration constant, and the last column contains the description.

ADCPROP_ASYNCTHREADPRIORITY_ENUM Enumeration (Versions 2.0, 2.1, 2.5, 2.6)

The ADCPROP_ASYNCTHREADPRIORITY_ENUM enumeration sets the execution priority of an asynchronous thread receiving data. This enumeration value is used within the Recordset dynamic property, Background Thread Priority.

Table E-1. The ADCPROP_ASYNCTHREADPRIORITY_ENUM Enumeration

Enumeration (ADO/WFC)	Value	Description
adPriorityAboveNormal (ABOVENORMAL)	4	The priority is set between normal and highest.
adPriorityBelowNormal (BELOWNORMAL)	2	The priority is set between lowest and normal.
adPriorityHighest (HIGHEST)	5	The priority is set to the highest possible setting.

Table E-1. The ADCPROP_ASYNCTHREADPRIORITY_ENUM Enumeration (continued)

Enumeration (ADO/WFC)	Value	Description
adPriorityLowest (LOWEST)	1	The priority is set to the lowest possible setting.
adPriorityNormal (NORMAL)	3	The priority is set to the normal setting.

ADO/WFC

The ADCPROP_ASYNCTHREADPRIORITY_ENUM enumeration is part of the com.ms.wfc.data package, and the constant values are preceded with AdoEnums.AdcPropAsyncThreadPriority.

ADCPROP_AUTORECALC_ENUM Enumeration   (Versions 2.1, 2.5, 2.6)

The ADCPROP_AUTORECALC_ENUM enumeration dictates whether, within a hierarchical recordset, the MSDataShape provider recalculates the aggregate and calculated columns. This enumeration value is used within the Recordset dynamic property, Auto Recalc.

Table E-2. The ADCPROP_AUTORECALC_ENUM Enumeration

Enumeration	Value	Description
adRecalcAlways	1	Default. Indicates that values are recalculated whenever the MSDataShape provider can determine that data used for calculated columns have changed.
adRecalcUpFront	0	Indicates that the calculation is done only when building the hierarchical recordset.

ADO/WFC

The ADCPROP_AUTORECALC_ENUM enumeration does not have ADO/WFC constants.

ADCPROP_UPDATECRITERIA_ENUM Enumeration   (Versions 2.0, 2.1, 2.5, 2.6)

The ADCPROP_UPDATECRITERIA_ENUM enumeration indicates which fields dictate conflicts during optimistic updates. This enumeration value is used within the Recordset dynamic property, Update Criteria.

Table E-3. The ADCPROP_UPDATECRITERIA_ENUM Enumeration

Enumeration (ADO/WFC)	Value	Description
adCriteriaAllCols (ALLCOLS)	1	If any column of the data-source row has been changed, a conflict is detected.
adCriteriaKey (KEY)	0	If the key column of the data-source row has changed (the row has been deleted), a conflict is detected.
adCriteriaTimeStamp (TIMESTAMP)	3	If the timestamp of the data-source row has been changed (the row has been accessed after the Recordset was obtained), a conflict is detected.

Table E-3. The ADCPROP_UPDATECRITERIA_ENUM Enumeration (continued)

Enumeration (ADO/ WFC)	Value	Description
adCriteriaUpdCols (UPDCOLS)	2	If any columns of the data-source row that correspond to the updated fields in the Recordset object have changed, a conflict is detected.

ADO/WFC

The ADCPROP_UPDATECRITERIA_ENUM enumeration is part of the com.ms.wfc.data package and the constant values are preceded with AdoEnums.AdcPropUpdateCriteria.

ADCPROP_UPDATERESYNC_ENUM Enumeration   (Versions 2.5, 2.6)

The ADCPROP_UPDATERESYNC_ENUM enumeration specifies whether calling the Update-Batch method automatically calls the Resync method afterwards—including some additional options. This enumeration value is used within the Recordset dynamic property, Update Resync.

Table E-4. The ADCPROP_UPDATERESYNC_ENUM Enumeration

Enumeration	Value	Description
adResyncAll	15	Indicates that the Resync method is called, but with the combined values of the other ADCPROP_ UPDATERESYNC_ENUM enumeration values.
adResyncAutoIncrement	1	Default. Indicates that the new value for columns that are automatically updated by the data source are retrieved if possible. This would include any automatic row-ID values or auto-number datatypes.
adResyncConflicts	2	Indicates that the Resync method is called for all rows for which an update or delete failed because of a conflict.
adResyncInserts	8	Indicates that the Resync method is called for all successfully inserted rows.
adResyncNone	0	Indicates that the Resync method is not invoked.
adResyncUpdates	4	Indicates that the Resync method is invoked for all successfully updated rows.

ADO/WFC

The ADCPROP_UPDATERESYNC_ENUM enumeration does not have ADO/WFC constants.

See Also

Recordset.Resync Method

AffectEnum Enumeration   (Versions 2.0, 2.1, 2.5, 2.6)

The AffectEnum enumeration indicates which records are affected by an invoked operation.

Table E-5. The AffectEnum Enumeration

Enumeration (ADO/ WFC)	Value	Description
adAffectAll (ALL)	3	Indicates that all records will be affected by the operation if there is no Filter applied or if a Filter is set to a member of the FilterGroupEnum enumeration or an array of bookmarks. If the Filter property is set to a String value, then the operation will affect only those rows that are visible within the current chapter.
adAffectAllChapters (ALLCHAPTERS)	4	Indicates that all records in all sibling chapters of the Recordset object will be affected by the operation. This includes those records not visible with an applied filter.
adAffectCurrent (CURRENT)	1	Indicates that only the current row will be affected by the operation.
adAffectGroup (GROUP)	2	Indicates that all records, which satisfy the current Filter if it is set to a member of the FilterGroupEnum enumeration or an array of bookmarks, will be affected.

Note

The adAffectAll enumeration value does not appear in the Object Browser.

ADO/WFC

The AffectEnum enumeration is part of the com.ms.wfc.data package, and the constant values are preceded with AdoEnums.Affect.

See Also

FilterGroupEnum Enumeration, Recordset.CancelBatch Method, Recordset.Delete Method, Recordset.Resync Method, Recordset.UpdateBatch Method, Recordset.Filter Property, Filter-GroupEnum Enumeration

BookmarkEnum Enumeration   (Versions 2.0, 2.1, 2.5, 2.6)

The BookmarkEnum enumeration specifies a bookmark that indicates where an operation is to begin.

Table E-6. The BookmarkEnum Enumeration

Enumeration (ADO/ WFC)	Value	Description
adBookmarkCurrent (CURRENT)	0	Indicates that the operation will start at the current record.
adBookmarkFirst (FIRST)	1	Indicates that the operation will start at the first record.
adBookmarkLast (LAST)	2	Indicates that the operation will start at the last record.

ADO/WFC

The BookmarkEnum enumeration is part of the com.ms.wfc.data package, and the constant values are preceded with AdoEnums.Bookmark.

See Also

Recordset.GetRows Method, Recordset.Move Method

CommandTypeEnum Enumeration   (Versions 2.0, 2.1, 2.5, 2.6)

The CommandTypeEnum enumeration indicates how a command argument should be interpreted.

Table E-7. CommandTypeEnum Enumeration Values

Enumeration (ADO/ WFC)	Value	Description
adCmdFile (FILE)	256 (&H100)	Indicates that the CommandText property should be evaluated as a name of a file that contains a persisted recordset.
adCmdStoredProc (STOREDPROC)	4	Indicates that the CommandText property should be evaluated as a stored-procedure name.
adCmdTable (TABLE)	2	Indicates that the CommandText property should be evaluated as a table name. This table name will be converted to a SQL statement by ADO to return all of its columns.
adCmdTableDirect (TABLEDIRECT)	512 (&H200)	Indicates that the CommandText property should be evaluated as a table name.
adCmdText (TEXT)	1	Default. Indicates that the CommandText property should be evaluated as a SQL statement or a data provider–specific command (including a stream).
adCmdUnknown (UNKNOWN)	8	Indicates that the type of the CommandText property is not specified.

ADO/WFC

The CommandTypeEnum enumeration is part of the com.ms.wfc.data package, and the constant values are preceded with AdoEnums.CommandType.

See Also

Command.CommandStream Property, Command.CommandType Property, Command. Execute Method, Connection.Execute Method, Recordset.Open Method, Recordset.Seek Method

CompareEnum Enumeration   (Versions 2.0, 2.1, 2.5, 2.6)

The CompareEnum enumeration indicates how two bookmarks compare.

Table E-8. The CompareEnum Enumeration

Enumeration (ADO/WFC)	Value	Description
adCompareEqual (EQUAL)	1	Indicates that the two bookmarks are equivalent.
adCompareGreaterThan (GREATERTHAN)	2	Indicates that the first bookmark is located after the second bookmark.
adCompareLessThan (LESSTHAN)	0	Indicates that the second bookmark is located after the first bookmark.
adCompareNotComparable (NOTCOMPARABLE)	4	Indicates that the two bookmarks cannot be compared.
adCompareNotEqual (NOTEQUAL)	3	Indicates that the two bookmarks are not equal and not ordered.

ADO/WFC

The CompareEnum enumeration is part of the com.ms.wfc.data package, and the constant values are preceded with AdoEnums.Compare.

See Also

Recordset.CompareBookmarks Method

ConnectModeEnum Enumeration   (Versions 2.0, 2.1, 2.5, 2.6)

The ConnectModeEnum enumeration indicates the available permissions for modifying data in a Connection object, opening data in a Record object, or specifying values within a Record or Stream object.

Table E-9. The ConnectModeEnum Enumeration

Enumeration (ADO/WFC)	Value	Description
adModeRead (READ)	1	Indicates that the data has read-only privileges.
adModeReadWrite (READWRITE)	3	Indicates that the data has both read and write privileges.

Table E-9. The ConnectModeEnum Enumeration (continued)

Enumeration (ADO/WFC)	Value	Description
`adModeRecursive` (no ADO/WFC equivalent)	4194304 (&H400000)	Used with `adModeShareDenyNone`, `adModeShareDenyWrite`, and `adModeShareDenyRead` to extend sharing restrictions to all children records of the current record. This value has no effect if the current record has no children and causes an error if it is used with `adModeShareDenyNone` alone.
`adModeShareDenyNone` (`SHAREDENYNONE`)	16 (&H10)	Prevents other users from opening the connection with any permissions.
`adModeShareDenyRead` (`SHAREDENYREAD`)	4	Prevents other users from opening the connection with read permissions.
`adModeShareDenyWrite` (`SHAREDENYWRITE`)	8	Prevents other users from opening the connection with write permissions.
`adModeShareExclusive` (`SHAREEXCLUSIVE`)	12	Prevents other users from opening the connection with read and write permissions.
`adModeUnknown` (`UNKNOWN`)	0	Default. Indicates that the permissions have not yet been set or that they cannot be determined by ADO.
`adModeWrite` (`WRITE`)	2	Indicates that the data has write-only privileges.

ADO/WFC

The ConnectModeEnum enumeration is part of the com.ms.wfc.data package, and the constant values are preceded with AdoEnums.ConnectMode.

See Also

Connection.Open Method, Record.Mode Property, Record.Open Method, Stream.Mode Property, Stream.Open Method

ConnectOptionEnum Enumeration (Versions 2.0, 2.1, 2.5, 2.6)

The ConnectOptionEnum enumeration specifies whether a connection to a data source is opened synchronously or asynchronously.

Table E-10. The ConnectOptionEnum Enumeration

Enumeration (ADO/WFC)	Value	Description
`adAsyncConnect` (`ASYNCCONNECT`)	16 (&H10)	Indicates that the connection will be opened asynchronously.
`adConnectUnspecified` (`CONNECTUNSPECIFIED`)	−1	Default. Indicates that the connection will be opened synchronously.

ADO/WFC

The ConnectOptionEnum enumeration is part of the com.ms.wfc.data package, and the constant values are preceded with AdoEnums.ConnectOption.

See Also

Connection.ConnectComplete Event, Connection.Open Method

ConnectPromptEnum Enumeration   (Versions 2.0, 2.1, 2.5, 2.6)

The ConnectPromptEnum enumeration indicates whether the user is prompted to enter missing parameters when opening connection. This enumeration value is used within the Connection dynamic property, Prompt.

Table E-11. The ConnectPrompt Enumeration

Enumeration (ADO/WFC)	Value	Description
adPromptAlways (ALWAYS)	1	Indicates that the user is always prompted for parameter information.
adPromptComlete (COMPLETE)	2	Indicates that the user is prompted for additionally required parameters.
adPromptComleteRequired (COMPLETEREQUIRED)	3	Indicates that the user is prompted for parameters that are required, but optional parameters are not allowed.
adPromptNever (NEVER)	4	Indicates that the user is never prompted for parameter information.

ADO/WFC

The ConnectPromptEnum enumeration is part of the com.ms.wfc.data package, and the constant values are preceded with AdoEnums.ConnectPrompt.

CopyRecordOptionsEnum Enumeration   (Versions 2.5, 2.6)

The CopyRecordOptionsEnum enumeration indicates the behavior of the CopyRecord method.

Table E-12. The CopyRecordOptionsEnum Enumeration

Enumeration	Value	Description
adCopyAllowEmulation	4	Indicates that the CopyRecord method will attempt to simulate the copy using the downloaded and uploaded operations if the method fails due to the Destination being on a different server or being serviced by a different provider than the Source.

Table E-12. The CopyRecordOptionsEnum Enumeration (continued)

Enumeration	Value	Description
adCopyNonRecursive	2	Indicates that the CopyRecord method copies only the current directory and its subdirectories.
adCopyOverWrite	1	Indicates that the CopyRecord method will overwrite the file or directory specified as the Destination, if it already exists.
adCopyUnspecified	-1 (&HFFFFFFFF)	Default. Indicates that the CopyRecord method will copy all of the subdirectories and files of the current directory and that it will not overwrite existing files and directories if they already exist.

ADO/WFC

The ADCPROP_UPDATERESYNC_ENUM enumeration does not have ADO/WFC constants.

See Also

Record.CopyRecord Method

CursorLocationEnum Enumeration (Versions 2.0, 2.1, 2.5, 2.6)

The CursorLocationEnum enumeration specifies the location of the cursor service.

Table E-13. The CursorLocationEnum Enumeration

Enumeration (ADO/WFC)	Value	Description
adUseClient (CLIENT)	3	Indicates that the cursor service is located on the client machine.
adUseServer (SERVER)	2	Indicates that the cursor service is located on the server machine.

ADO/WFC

The CursorLocationEnum enumeration is part of the com.ms.wfc.data package, and the constant values are preceded with AdoEnums.CursorLocation.

See Also

Connection.CursorLocation Property, Recordset.CursorLocation Property

CursorOptionEnum Enumeration   (Versions 2.0, 2.1, 2.5, 2.6)

The CursorOptionEnum enumeration indicates for which functionality the Supports method is testing.

Table E-14. The CursorOption Enumeration

Enumeration (ADO/WFC)	Value	Description
adAddNew (ADDNEW)	16778240 (&H10004000)	Indicates that the AddNew method is supported.
adApproxPosition (APPROXPOSITION)	16384 (&H4000)	Indicates that the AbsolutePosition and Abso-lutePage properties are supported.
adBookmark (BOOKMARK)	8192 (&H2000)	Indicates that the Bookmark property is sup-ported.
adDelete (DELETE)	16779264 (&H1000800)	Indicates that the Delete method is supported.
adFind (FIND)	524288 (&H80000)	Indicates that the Find method is supported.
adHoldRecords (HOLDRECORDS)	256 (&H100)	Indicates that the Recordset can retrieve more records or change the position of the record pointer without committing all pending changes.
adIndex (INDEX)	8388608 (&H800000)	Indicates that the Index property is supported.
adMovePrevious (MOVEPREVIOUS)	512 (&H200)	Indicates that the MoveFirst, MovePrevious, Move, and GetRows methods can be used to move the record pointer backwards without the use of bookmarks.
adNotify (NOTIFY)	262144 (&H40000)	Indicates that the data provider supports notifica-tions and in turn indicates that Recordset events are supported.
adResync (RESYNC)	131072 (&H20000)	Indicates that the Resync method is supported.
adSeek (SEEK)	4194303 (&H400000)	Indicates that the Seek method is supported.
adUpdate (UPDATE)	16809984 (&H1008000)	Indicates that the Update method is supported.
adUpdateBatch (UPDATEBATCH)	65536 (&H10000)	Indicates that the UpdateBatch and the Cancel-Batch methods are supported.

ADO/WFC

The CursorOptionEnum enumeration is part of the com.ms.wfc.data package, and the constant values are preceded with AdoEnums.CursorOption.

See Also

See Also

Recordset.AbsolutePage Property, Recordset.AbsolutePosition Property, Recordset.AddNew Method, Recordset.Bookmark Property, Recordset.CancelBatch Method, Recordset.Delete Method, Recordset.Find Method, Recordset GetRows Method, Recordset.Index Property, Recordset.Move Method, Recordset.MoveFirst Method, Recordset.MovePrevious Method, Recrodset.Seek Method, Recordset.Supports Method, Recordset.Update Method, Recordset.UpdateBatch Method

CursorTypeEnum Enumeration   (Versions 2.0, 2.1, 2.5, 2.6)

The CursorTypeEnum enumeration indicates the type of cursor to be used with the Recordset object.

Table E-15. The CursorTypeEnum Enumeration

Enumeration (ADO/ WFC)	Value	Description
adOpenDynamic (DYNAMIC)	2	Indicates a dynamic cursor for the recordset. The recordset allows the application to see new records, edited records, and deletions by other users.
adOpenForwardOnly (FORWARDONLY)	0	Default. Indicates a forward-only cursor for the recordset. The recordset does not report added, edited, or deleted records by other users. Think of this cursor as a snapshot of the recordset. This is the fastest type of cursor and is the default setting.
adOpenKeyset (KEYSET)	1	Indicates a keyset cursor for the recordset. The recordset allows the application to see changes in records made by other users. It also denies access to deleted records, but it does not allow you to see records that have been added by other users.
adOpenStatic (STATIC)	3	Indicates a static cursor for the recordset. The recordset does not allow the application to see any changes in the recordset at all. This cursor is only surpassed in speed only by the forward-only cursor.

ADO/WFC

ADO/WFC

The CursorTypeEnum enumeration is part of the com.ms.wfc.data package, and the constant values are preceded with AdoEnums.CursorType.

See Also

See Also

Recordset.CursorType Property, Recordset.Open Method

DataTypeEnum Enumeration   (Versions 2.0, 2.1, 2.5, 2.6)

The DataTypeEnum enumeration indicates the datatype of the particular parameter, field, or property.

Table E-16. DataTypeEnum Enumeration Values

Enumeration (ADO/ WFC)	Value	Description
adArray (ARRAY)	8192 (&H2000)	Indicates an array of values. This value is always combined with another DataTypeEnum enumeration value.
adBigInt (BIGINT)	20 (&H14)	Indicates an 8-byte signed integer.
adBinary (BINARY)	128 (&H80)	Indicates a binary value.
adBoolean (BOOLEAN)	11	Indicates a Boolean value (True or False).
adBSTR (BSTR)	8	Indicates a null-terminated character Unicode string.
adChapter (CHAPTER)	136 (&H88)	Indicates a 4-byte Chapter recordset (for hierarchical recordsets).
adChar (CHAR)	129 (&H81)	Indicates a String value.
adCurrency (CURRENCY)	6	Indicates a currency value that is an 8-byte signed integer with a scale factor of 10,000.
adDate (DATE)	7	Indicates a Date value stored as a Double, where the whole part is the number of days since December 30, 1899, and the fraction represents the time of day.
adDBDate (DBDATE)	133 (H&85)	Indicates a date value in the form of *yyyymmdd*.
adDBTime (DBTIME)	134 (&H86)	Indicates a time value in the form of *hhmmss*.
adDBTimeStamp (DBTIMESTAMP)	135 (&H87)	Indicates a date/time stamp in the form of *yyyymmddhhmmss*, including a fraction in billionths.
adDecimal (DECIMAL)	14	Indicates an exact numeric value with a fixed-precision and scale factor.
adDouble (DOUBLE)	5	Indicates a double-precision floating-point number.
adEmpty (EMPTY)	0	Indicates that no value is specified.
adError (ERROR)	10	Indicates a 32-byte error code.
adFileTime (FILETIME)	64 (&H40)	Indicates a file's time with a 64-bit value that represents the number of 100-nanosecond intervals since January 1, 1601.

Table E-16. DataTypeEnum Enumeration Values (continued)

Enumeration (ADO/ WFC)	Value	Description
adGUID (GUID)	72 (&H48)	Indicates a globally unique identifier.
adIDispatch (IDISPATCH)	9	Indicates a pointer to an IDispatch interface on an OLE object.
adInteger (INTEGER)	3	Indicates a 4-byte signed integer.
adIUnknown (IUNKNOWN)	13	Indicates a pointer to an IUknown interface on an OLE object.
adLongVarBinary (LONGVARBINARY)	205 (&HCD)	Indicates a long binary value only for a Parameter object.
adLongVarChar (LONGVARCHAR)	201 (&HC9)	Indicates a long String value only for a Parameter object.
adLongVarWChar (LONGVARWCHAR)	203 (&HCB)	Indicates a long null-terminated string value only for a Parameter object.
adNumeric (NUMERIC)	131 (&H83)	Indicates an exact numeric value with a fixed-precision and scale factor.
adPropVariant (PROPVARIANT)	138 (&H8A)	Indicates an automation PROPVARIANT.
adSingle (SINGLE)	4	Indicates a single-precision floating-point number.
adSmallInt (SMALLINT)	2	Indicates a 2-byte signed integer.
adTinyInt (TINYINT)	16 (&H10)	Indicates a 1-byte signed integer.
adUnsignedBigInt (UNSIGNEDBIGINT)	21 (&H15)	Indicates an 8-byte unsigned integer.
adUnsignedInt (UNSIGNEDINT)	19 (&H13)	Indicates a 4-byte unsigned integer.
adUnsignedSmallInt (UNSIGNEDSMALLINT)	18 (&H12)	Indicates a 2-byte unsigned integer.
adUnsignedTinyInt (UNSIGNEDTINYINT)	17 (&H11)	Indicates a 1-byte unsigned integer.
adUserDefined (USERDEFINED)	132 (&H84)	Indicates a user-defined variable.
adVarBinary (VARBINARY)	204 (&HCC)	Indicates a binary value only for a Parameter object.
adVarChar (VARCHAR)	200 (&HC8)	Indicates a string value only for a Parameter object.
adVariant (VARIANT)	12	Indicates an OLE Automation Variant.

Table E-16. DataTypeEnum Enumeration Values (continued)

Enumeration (ADO/WFC)	Value	Description
adVarNumeric (VARNUMERIC)	139 (&H8B)	Indicates a numeric value only for a Parameter object.
adVarWChar (VARWCHAR)	202 (&HCA)	Indicates a null-terminated UNICODE character string only for a Parameter object.
adWChar (WCHAR)	130 (&H82)	Indicates a null-terminated UNICODE character string.

ADO/WFC

The DataTypeEnum enumeration is part of the com.ms.wfc.data package, and the constant values are preceded with AdoEnums.DataType.

See Also

Command.CreateParameter Method, Field.Type Property, Fields.Append Method, Parameter. Type Property, Property.Type Property

---

EditModeEnum Enumeration

(Versions 2.0, 2.1, 2.5, 2.6)

The EditModeEnum enumeration indicates the current edit status of a record.

Table E-17. The EditMode Enumeration

Enumeration (ADO/WFC)	Value	Description
adEditAdd (ADD)	2	Indicates that the AddNew method has been called and the new record currently contains values that have not yet been saved.
adEditDelete (DELETE)	4	Indicates that the current record has been marked for deletion but has not yet been deleted in the database.
adEditInProgress (INPROGRESS)	1	Indicates that there is currently no editing being done on the given record.
adEditNone (NONE)	0	Indicates that there are currently values in the given record that have not yet been saved.

ADO/WFC

The EditModeEnum enumeration is part of the com.ms.wfc.data package, and the constant values are preceded with AdoEnums.EditMode.

See Also

Recordset.AddNew Method, Recordset.EditMode Property

ErrorValueEnum Enumeration   (Versions 2.0, 2.1, 2.5, 2.6)

The ErrorValueEnum enumeration contains the constants for ADO runtime errors.

Table E-18. The ErrorValueEnum Enumeration Values

Enumeration (ADO/WFC)	Value	Description
adErrBoundToCommand (BOUNDTOCOMMAND)	3707 (&HE7B)	The ActiveConnection property of a Recordset object cannot be changed because the Recordset object's source is a Command object.
adErrCannotComplete (no ADO/WFC equivalent)	3732 (&HE94)	The server that owns the source row cannot complete the operation.
adErrCantChangeConnection (no ADO/WFC equivalent)	3748 (&HEA4)	The Connection was denied because it has different characteristics than the one already in use.
adErrCantChangeProvider (no ADO/WFC equivalent)	3220 (&HC94)	The supplied provider is different from the one already in use.
adErrCantConvertvalue (no ADO/WFC equivalent)	3724 (&HE8C)	Data value could not be converted for reasons other than sign mismatch or data overflow. For example, conversion would have truncated data.
adErrCantCreate (no ADO/WFC equivalent)	3725 (&HE8D)	Data could not be set or retrieved because the column datatype was unknown or the provider had insufficient resources to perform the operation.
adErrCatalogNotSet (no ADO/WFC equivalent)	3747 (&HEA3)	The operation requires a valid Parent-Catalog.
adErrColumnNotOnThisRow (no ADO/WFC equivalent)	3726 (&HE8E)	Column does not exist on this row.
adErrDataConversion (DATACONVERSION)	3421 (&HD5D)	A wrong datatype is being used for the operation.
adErrDataOverflow (no ADO/WFC equivalent)	3721 (&HE89)	Data value is too large to be represented by the column datatype.
adErrDelResOutOfScope (no ADO/WFC equivalent)	3738 (&HE9A)	The URL of the object to be deleted is outside the scope of the current row. Make sure the URL is inside the scope.
adErrDenyNotSupported (no ADO/WFC equivalent)	3750 (&HEA6)	The data provider does not support sharing restrictions.
adErrDenyTypeNotSupported (no ADO/WFC equivalent)	3751 (&HEA7)	The data provider does not support the requested sharing-restriction type.
adErrFeatureNotAvailable (FEATURENOTAVAILABLE)	3251 (&HCB3)	The provider does not support the operation.
adErrFieldsUpdateFailed	3749 (&HEA5)	The Fields update failed.

Table E-18. The ErrorValueEnum Enumeration Values (continued)

Enumeration (ADO/WFC)	Value	Description
adErrIllegalOperation (ILLEGALOPERATION)	3219 (&HC93)	The operation cannot be performed during this context.
adErrIntegrityViolation (no ADO/WFC equivalent)	3719 (&HE87)	The data value conflicts with the integrity constraints of the field.
adErrInTransaction (INTRANSACTION)	3246 (&HCAE)	The operation is in the middle of a transaction and cannot close the Connection object.
adErrInvalidArgument (INVALIDARGUMENT)	3001 (&HBB9)	The argument either is not of the correct type, has a value that is not in the acceptable range, or is in conflict with another argument.
adErrInvalidConnection (INVALIDCONNECTION)	3709 (&HE7D)	The operation cannot be performed because the Connection object is closed.
adErrInvalidParamInfo (INVALIDPARAMINFO)	3708 (&HE7C)	The parameter information is not defined correctly.
adErrInvalidTransaction (no ADO/WFC equivalent)	3714 (&HE82)	The coordinating transaction is invalid or has not started.
adErrInvalidURL (no ADO/WFC equivalent)	3729 (&HE91)	The specified URL contains invalid characters. Make sure the URL is typed correctly.
adErrItemNotFound (ITEMNOTFOUND)	3265 (&HCC1)	The object requested does not exist in the ADO collection at the ordinal position or with the name provided.
adErrNoCurrentRecord (NOCURRENTRECORD)	3021 (&HBCD)	The record pointer does not point to a valid record, and one is needed for the operation.
adErrNotExecuting (NOTEXECUTING) (This seemed to be missing in 2.6)	3715	The execution could not be canceled because it was not executing.
adErrNotReentrant (NOTREENTRANT)	3710 (&HE7E)	The code within the event would cause the event to be fired again.
adErrObjectClosed (OBJECTCLOSED)	3704 (&HE78)	The object that is needed by the operation is closed.
adErrObjectInCollection (OBJECTINCOLLECTION)	3367 (&HD27)	The attempt to add the object to the collection was unsuccessful because the object is already in the collection.
adErrObjectNotSet (OBJECTNOTSET)	3420 (&HD5C)	The object does not point to a valid ADO object.
adErrObjectOpen (OBJECTOPEN)	3705 (&HE79)	The operation requires that the object is not open.
adErrOpeningFile (no ADO/WFC equivalent)	3002 (&HBBA)	The file could not be opened.

Table E-18. The ErrorValueEnum Enumeration Values (continued)

Enumeration (ADO/WFC)	Value	Description
adErrOperationCancelled (OPERATIONCANCELLED)	3712 (&HE80)	An ADO operation has been canceled.
adErrOutOfSpace (no ADO/WFC equivalent)	3734 (&HE96)	The provider is unable to obtain enough storage space to complete the copy operation.
adErrPermissionDenied (no ADO/WFC equivalent)	3720 (&HE88)	The user does not have permission to write to the column. Check Column Privileges property.
adErrPropConflicting (no ADO/WFC equivalent)	3742 (&HE9E)	The property value was not set because it would have conflicted with an existing property.
adErrPropInvalidColumn (no ADO/WFC equivalent)	3739 (&HE9B)	The property cannot apply to the specified column.
adErrPropInvalidOption (no ADO/WFC equivalent)	3740 (&HE9C)	The specified option is invalid.
adErrPropInvalidValue (no ADO/WFC equivalent)	3741 (&HE9D)	The specified value is invalid. Make sure the value is typed correctly.
adErrPropNotAllSettable (no ADO/WFC equivalent)	3743 (&HE9F)	The property is read-only or could not be set for the particular column.
adErrPropNotSet (no ADO/WFC equivalent)	3744 (&HEA0)	The property value was not set. The value of *dwOptions* was DBPROPOPTIONS_OPTIONAL, and the property could not be set to the specified value.
adErrPropNotSettable (no ADO/WFC equivalent)	3745 (&HEA1)	The property is read-only or the consumer attempted to set values of properties in the Initialization property group after the data-source object was initialized. Consumers can set the value of a read-only property to its current value. This value is also returned if a settable column property could not be set for the particular column.
adErrPropNotSupported (no ADO/WFC equivalent)	3746 (&HEA2)	The property value was not set. The provider does not support the property.
adErrProviderFailed (no ADO/WFC equivalent)	3000 (&HBB8)	The provider failed to perform the requested operation.
adErrProviderNotFound (PROVIDERNOTFOUND)	3706 (&HE7A)	The provider could not be found.
adErrReadFile (no ADO/WFC equivalent)	3003 (&HBBB)	The file could not be read.
adErrResourceExists (no ADO/WFC equivalent)	3731 (&HE93)	The copy operation cannot be performed. The object named by destination URL already exists. Specify adCopyOverwrite to replace the object.

Table E-18. The ErrorValueEnum Enumeration Values (continued)

Enumeration (ADO/WFC)	Value	Description
adErrResourceLocked (no ADO/WFC equivalent)	3730 (&HE92)	The object represented by the specified URL is locked by one or more other processes. Wait until the process has finished, and attempt the operation again.
adErrResourceOutOfScope (no ADO/WFC equivalent)	3735 (&HE97)	The source or destination URL is outside the scope of the current row. Make sure the URL is inside the scope.
adErrSchemaViolation (no ADO/WFC equivalent)	3722 (&HE8A)	The data value conflicts with the datatype or constraints of the column.
adErrSignMismatch (no ADO/WFC equivalent)	3723 (&HE8B)	The conversion failed because the data value was signed and the column datatype used by the provider was unsigned.
adErrStillConnecting (STILLCONNECTING)	3713 (&HE81)	The operation cannot be executed because ADO was still connecting to the data source.
adErrStillExecuting (STILLEXECUTING)	3711 (&HE7F)	The operation cannot be executed because another command is still being executed.
adErrTreePermissionDenied (no ADO/WFC equivalent)	3728 (&HE90)	The operation is unable to access a tree or sub-tree due to a permissions failure.
adErrUnavailable (no ADO/WFC equivalent)	3736 (&HE98)	An operation failed to complete, and the status is unavailable.
adErrUnsafeOperation (UNSAFEOPERATION)	3716 (&HE84)	The operation is not considered safe by the environment that is currently running ADO.
adErrURLDoesNotExist (no ADO/WFC equivalent)	3727 (&HE8F)	Either the source URL or the parent of the destination URL does not exist.
adErrURLNamedRowDoesNotExist (no ADO/WFC equivalent)	3737 (&HE99)	The row named by this URL does not exist. Make sure the URL is typed correctly.
adErrVolumeNotFound (no ADO/WFC equivalent)	3733 (&HE95)	The provider is unable to locate the storage volume indicated by the URL. Make sure the URL is typed correctly.
adErrWriteFile (no ADO/WFC equivalent)	3004 (&HBBC)	The file could not be written to.
adwrnSecurityDialog (no ADO/WFC equivalent)	3717 (&HE85)	This is an internal constant only, and Microsoft asks that you do not use it.
adwrnSecurityDialogHeader (no ADO/WFC equivalent)	3718 (&HE86)	This is an internal constant only, and Microsoft asks that you do not use it.

ADO/WFC

The ErrorValueEnum enumeration is part of the com.ms.wfc.data package, and the constant values are preceded with AdoEnums.ErrorValue.

See Also

Error.Number Property

EventReasonEnum   (Versions 2.0, 2.1, 2.5, 2.6)

The EventReasonEnum enumeration indicates why a given event was fired.

Table E-19. The EventReasonEnum Enumeration

Enumeration (ADO/WFC)	Value	Description
adRsnAddNew (ADDNEW)	1	Indicates that a new record has been added by an operation.
adRsnClose (CLOSE)	9	Indicates that the Recordset object has been closed by an operation.
adRsnDelete (DELETE)	2	Indicates that a record has been deleted by an operation.
adRsnFirstChange (FIRSTCHANGE)	11	Indicates that the first change to a record has been made by an operation.
adRsnMove (MOVE)	10	Indicates that the record pointer has moved within the Recordset object by an operation.
adRsnMoveFirst (MOVEFIRST)	12	Indicates that the record pointer has been moved to the first record of the Recordset object by an operation.
adRsnMoveLast (MOVELAST)	15	Indicates that the record pointer has been moved to the last record of the Recordset object by an operation.
adRsnMoveNext (MOVENEXT)	13	Indicates that the record pointer has moved to the next record in the Recordset object by an operation.
adRsnMovePrevious (MOVEPREVIOUS)	14	Indicates that the record pointer has moved to the previous record in the Recordset object by an operation.
adRsnRequery (REQUERY)	7	Indicates that an operation has required the Recordset object.
adRsnResynch (RESYNCH)	8	Indicates that an operation has resynchronized the Recordset object.
adRsnUndoAddNew (UNDOADDNEW)	5	Indicates that a newly added record has been reversed by an operation.
adRsnUndoDelete (UNDODELETE)	6	Indicates that a deleted record has been reversed by an operation.

Table E-19. *The EventReasonEnum Enumeration (continued)*

Enumeration (ADO/WFC)	Value	Description
adRsnUndoUpdate (UNDOUPDATE)	4	Indicates that an update has been reversed by an operation.
adRsnUpdate (UPDATE)	3	Indicates that an operation has updated an existing record within the Recordset object.

ADO/WFC

The EventReasonEnum enumeration is part of the com.ms.wfc.data package, and the constant values are preceded with AdoEnums.EventReason.

See Also

Recordset.MoveComplete Event, Recordset.RecordChangeComplete Event, Recordset.RecordsetChangeComplete Event, Recordset.WillChangeRecord Event, Recordset WillChangeRecordset Event, Recordset.WillMove Event

EventStatusEnum Enumeration (Versions 2.0, 2.1, 2.5, 2.6)

The EventStatusEnum enumeration specifies the current status of an executed event.

Table E-20. *The EventStatusEnum Enumeration*

Enumeration (ADO/WFC)	Value	Description
adStatusCancel (CANCEL)	4	Indicates that the application is requesting the cancelation of the operation that has caused the current event to occur.
adStatusCantDeny (CANTDENY)	3	Indicates that the operation that has caused the current event to occur cannot be canceled.
adStatusErrorsOccurred (ERRORSOCCURRED)	2	Indicates that the operation that has caused this event to occur did not complete successfully.
adStatusOK (OK)	1	Indicates that the operation that has caused this event to occur completed successfully.
adStatusUnwantedEvent (UNWANTEDEVENT)	5	Indicates that the application no longer wishes to receive subsequent notifications of the event that has been fired.

ADO/WFC

The EventStatusEnum enumeration is part of the com.ms.wfc.data package, and the constant values are preceded with AdoEnums.EventStatus.

See Also

Connection.BeginTransComplete Event, Connection.CommitTransComplete Event, Connection.ConnectComplete Event, Connection.Disconnect Event, Connection.ExecuteComplete

Event, Connection.InfoMessage Event, Connection.RollbackTransComplete Event, Connection.WillConnect Event, Connection.WillExecute Event, Recordset.EndOfRecordset Event, Recordset.FetchComplete Event, Recordset.FetchProgress Event, Recordset.FieldChangeComplete Event, Recordset.MoveComplete Event, Recordset.RecordChangeComplete Event, Recordset.RecordsetChangeComplete Event, Recordset.WillChangeField Event, Recordset.WillChangeRecord Event, Recordset.WillChangeRecordset Event, Recordset.WillMove Event

ExecuteOptionEnum Enumeration   (Versions 2.0, 2.1, 2.5, 2.6)

The ExecuteOptionEnum enumeration indicates how a data provider should execute a command.

Table E-21. The ExecuteOptionEnum Enumeration

Enumeration (ADO/WFC)	Value	Description
adAsyncExecute (ASYNCEXECUTE)	16 (&H10)	Instructs ADO to execute the command asynchronously.
adAsyncFetch (ASYNCFETCH)	32 (&H20)	Instructs ADO to fetch the records returned from this command asynchronously after the initial number of rows (indicated by the CacheSize property) are returned.
adAsyncFetchNonBlocking (ASYNCFETCHNONBLOCKING)	64 (&H40)	Instructs ADO to never block the main thread while executing. If the row that is requested has not been read, it is automatically moved to the end of the file.
adExecuteNoRecords (NORECORDS)	128 (&H80)	Instructs ADO that the CommandText property does not return rows and, if it does, to discard them. This value is always combined with adCmdText or adCmdStoredProc of the CommandTypeEnum enumeration.
adExecuteStream (no ADO/WFC equivalent)	1024 (&H400)	Indicates that the returned object of the Command object's Execute method will be a Stream object. This value is invalid for all other uses.

ADO/WFC

The ExecuteOptionEnum enumeration is part of the com.ms.wfc.data package, and the constant values are preceded with AdoEnums.ExecuteOption.

See Also

Command.Execute Method, Connection.Execute Method, Recordset.Open Method, Recordset.Requery Method

FieldAttributesEnum Enumeration   (Versions 2.0, 2.1, 2.5, 2.6)

The FieldAttributesEnum enumeration indicates attributes of a field.

Table E-22. The FieldAttributesEnum Enumeration

Enumeration (ADO/WFC)	Value	Description
adFldCacheDeferred (CACHEDEFERRED)	4096 (&H1000)	Indicates that the ADO caches the value of this field, and any future attempts to read this value will be read from the cache.
adFldFixed (FIXED)	16 (&H10)	Indicates that the field's value is of fixed length.
adFldIsChapter (no ADO/WFC equivalent)	8192 (&H2000)	Indicates that the field specifies a chapter value, which in turn contains a child record-set.
adFldIsCollection (no ADO/WFC equivalent)	262144 (&H40000)	Indicates that the field is a collection of other resources such as a folder, directory, etc.
adFldIsDefaultStream (no ADO/WFC equivalent)	131072 (&H20000)	Indicates that the field contains the default Stream object for the record.
adFldIsNullable (ISNULLABLE)	32 (&H20)	Indicates that the field accepts Null values.
adFldIsRowURL (no ADO/WFC equivalent)	65536 (&H10000)	Indicates that the field contains the URL that names the resource from the data store.
adFldKeyColumn (no ADO/WFC equivalent)	32768 (&H8000)	Indicates that the field belongs to a key within its table.
adFldLong (LONG)	128 (&H80)	Indicates that the field's value is a long binary field. This also indicates that you may use the AppendChunk and GetChunk methods on this field.
adFldMayBeNull (MAYBENULL)	64 (&H40)	Indicates that this field may have Null values that you can read.
adFldMayDefer (MAYDEFER)	2	Indicates that this field's value is not retrieved from the current record until it is explicitly requested.
adFldNegativeScale (NEGATIVESCALE)	16384 (&H4000)	Indicates that the field is based upon a negative scale.
adFldRowID (ROWID)	256 (&H100)	Indicates that this field contains a record identifier.
adFldRowVersion (ROWVERSION)	512 (&H200)	Indicates that this field contains a time or date stamp to track changes.
adFldUnknownUpdatable (UNKNOWNUPDATABLE)	8	Indicates that the data provider cannot determine whether you can write to this field.
adFldUpdatable (UPDATABLE)	4	Indicates that you can write to this field.

ADO/WFC

The FieldAttributeEnum enumeration is part of the com.ms.wfc.data package, and the constant values are preceded with AdoEnums.FieldAttribute.

See Also

Fields.Append Method, Field.Attributes Property

FieldEnum Enumeration   (Versions 2.5, 2.6)

The FieldEnum enumeration indicates the special fields referenced in a Record object's Fields collection.

Table E-23. The FieldEnum Enumeration

Enumeration	Value	Description
adDefaultStream	−1 (&HFFFFFFFF)	Indicates that the field contains the default Stream object for the Record object.
adRecordURL	−2 (&HFFFFFFFE)	Indicates that the field contains the absolute URL of the current Record object.

ADO/WFC

The FieldEnum enumeration does not have ADO/WFC constants.

FieldStatusEnum Enumeration   (Versions 2.5, 2.6)

The FieldStatusEnum specifies the status of the current field.

Table E-24. The FieldStatusEnum Enumeration

Enumeration	Value	Description
adFieldAlreadyExists	26 (&H1A)	Indicates that the field already exists.
adFieldBadStatus	12	Indicates that an invalid status value was sent from ADO to the OLE DB provider.
adFieldCannotComplete	20 (&H14)	Indicates that the server of the URL specified by Source could not complete the operation.
adFieldCannotDeleteSource	23 (&H17)	Indicates that during a move, a tree or subtree was moved to a new location, but the source could not be deleted.
adFieldCantConvertValue	2	Indicates that the field cannot be persisted or retrieved without losing some data.
adFieldCantCreate	7	Indicates that the field cannot be added because a limitation has been reached.

Table E-24. The FieldStatusEnum Enumeration (continued)

Enumeration	Value	Description
adFieldDataOverflow	6	Indicates that the data returned from the provider has overflowed the datatype that is used to store it.
adFieldDefault	13	Indicates that the default value for the field was used.
adFieldDoesNotExist	16 (&H10)	Indicates that the field does not exist.
adFieldIgnore	15	Indicates that the field was skipped when setting data values in the source.
adFieldIntegrityViolation	10	Indicates that the field is a calculated field and cannot be directly modified.
adFieldInvalidURL	17 (&H11)	Indicates that the URL specifying the data source contains invalid characters.
adFieldIsNull	3	Indicates that the data provider returned a Null value for the value of the field.
adFieldOK	0	Default. Indicates that the field was successfully added or deleted.
adFieldOutOfSpace	22 (&H16)	Indicates that the data provider cannot obtain enough space to perform the move or copy.
adFieldPendingChange	262144 (&H40000)	Indicates that a change is pending for the field.
adFieldPendingDelete	131072 (&H20000)	Indicates that the field has been marked for deletion.
adFieldPendingInsert	65536 (&H10000)	Indicates that the field has been marked to be added to the Fields collection after the Update method is called.
adFieldPendingUnknown	524288 (&H80000)	Indicates that the data provider cannot determine what operation has caused the status of the field to be updated.
adFieldPendingUnknownDelete	1048576 (&H100000)	Indicates that the data provider cannot determine what operation has caused the status of the field to be updated, but it will be removed from the Fields collection after a call to the Update method.
adFieldPermissionDenied	9	Indicates that the field cannot be modified because it is read-only.
adFieldReadOnly	24 (&H18)	Indicates that the field is read-only.
adResourceExists	19 (&H13)	Indicates that the data provider was unable to perform the specified operation because the resulting resource already exists.

Table E-24. The FieldStatusEnum Enumeration (continued)

Enumeration	Value	Description
adFieldRsouceLocked	18 (&H12)	Indicates that the resource specified is locked by another process and the data provider is unable to perform the operation specified.
adFieldResourceOutOfScope	25 (&H19)	Indicates that a URL value specified is outside the scope of the current record.
adFieldSchemaViolation	11	Indicates that a schema constraint for the field has been violated by the value.
adFieldSignMismatch	5	Indicates that the data returned by the data provider is unsigned because the datatype for the ADO field will not accept signed data.
adFieldTruncated	4	Indicates that the data has been truncated (in the case of variable-length data).
adFieldUnavailable	8	Indicates that the data provider cannot determine the value from the data source.
adFieldVolumnNotFound	21 (&H15)	Indicates that the storage volume indicated by the URL cannot be found.

ADO/WFC

The FieldStatusEnum enumeration does not have ADO/WFC constants.

See Also

Field.Status Property

FilterGroupEnum Enumeration   (Versions 2.0, 2.1, 2.5, 2.6)

The FilterGroupEnum enumeration specifies which groups of records are to be filtered out of the Recordset object.

Table E-25. The FilterGroupEnum Enumeration

Enumeration (ADO/WFC)	Value	Description
adFilterAffectedRecords (AFFECTEDRECORDS)	2	Filters the recordset so that you can see only records affected by the last Delete, Resync, UpdateBatch, or CancelBatch method call.
adFilterConflictingRecords (CONFLICTINGRECORDS)	5	Filters the recordset to include only those records that failed the last batch update.

Table E-25. The FilterGroupEnum Enumeration (continued)

Enumeration (ADO/WFC)	Value	Description
`adFilterFetchedRecords` (`FETCHEDRECORDS`)	3	Filters the recordset so that you can see only records from the last fetch from the database—only the records in the current cache.
`adFilterNone` (`NONE`)	0	Tells the Filter property to remove any current filter and restore the recordset to its original state, showing all records. If you set the Filter property to an empty string (""), it is the same as setting it to the `adFilterNone` value.
`adFilterPendingRecords` (`PENDINGRECORDS`)	1	Used when in batch update mode. Filters the recordset so that you can see only the records that have since changed but have not yet been sent to the data provider to be saved.

ADO/WFC

The FilterGroupEnum enumeration is part of the com.ms.wfc.data package, and the constant values are preceded with AdoEnums.FilterGroup.

See Also

AffectEnum Enumeration, Recordset.Filter Property

GetRowsOptionEnum Enumeration   (Versions 2.0, 2.1, 2.5, 2.6)

The GetRowsOptionEnum enumeration indicates how many records are to be retrieved from the Recordset object.

Table E-26. The GetRowsOptionEnum Enumeration

Enumeration (ADO/WFC)	Value	Description
`adGetRowsRest` (`REST`)	−1 (`&HFFFFFFFF`)	Indicates that the rest of the rows are to be retrieved from the Recordset object.

ADO/WFC

The GetRowsOptionEnum enumeration is part of the com.ms.wfc.data package, and the constant values are preceded with AdoEnums.GetRowsOption.

See Also

Recordset.GetRows Method

IsolationLevelEnum Enumeration   (Versions 2.0, 2.1, 2.5, 2.6)

The IsolationLevelEnum enumeration indicates the level of transaction isolation for the Connection object.

Table E-27. The IsolationLevelEnum Enumeration

Enumeration (ADO/WFC)	Value	Description
adXactBrowse (BROWSE) adXactReadUnCommitted (READUNCOMMITTED)	256 (&H100)	Indicates that you can view uncommitted values within other transactions.
adXactChaos (CHAOS)	16 (&H10)	Indicates that you cannot change values that are pending from higher-level transactions.
adXactCursorStability (CURSORSTABILITY) adXactReadCommitted (READCOMMITTED)	4096 (&H1000)	Indicates that you cannot view uncommitted values within other transactions.
adXactIsolated (ISOLATED) adXactSerializable (SERIALIZABLE)	1048576 (&H100000)	Indicates that each transaction is conducted in complete isolation of other transactions.
adXactRepeatableRead (REPEATABLEREAD)	65536 (&10000)	Indicates that you cannot view uncommitted values within other transactions, but by requerying, you can see new recordsets.
adXactUnspecified (UNSPECIFIED)	-1 (&HFFFFFFFF)	Returned if the data provider is using a level of isolation that cannot be determined.

ADO/WFC

The IsolationLevelEnum enumeration is part of the com.ms.wfc.data package, and the constant values are preceded with AdoEnums.IsolationLevel.

See Also

Connection.IsolationLevel Property

LineSeparatorEnum Enumeration   (Versions 2.5, 2.6)

The LineSeparatorEnum enumeration indicates the character(s) used as line separators for text in Stream objects.

Table E-28. The LineSeparator Enumeration

Enumeration	Value	Description
adCR	13	Carriage return.
adCRLF	−1 (&HFFFFFFFF)	Default. Carriage return and line feed.
adLF	10	Line feed.

ADO/WFC

The LineSeparatorEnum enumeration does not have ADO/WFC constants.

See Also

Stream.LineSeparator Property, Stream.SkipLine Method

LockTypeEnum Enumeration   (Versions 2.0, 2.1, 2.5, 2.6)

The LockTypeEnum enumeration specifies the lock to use on records while they are being edited.

Table E-29. The LockTypeEnum Enumeration

Enumeration (ADO/WFC)	Value	Description
adLockBatchOptimistic (BATCHOPTIMISTIC)	4	Required for batch update mode. Should be used only by a keyset or static cursor.
adLockOptimistic (OPTIMISTIC)	3	Indicates that the record is locked once the Update method has been called.
adLockPessimistic (PESSIMISTIC)	2	Indicates that the record is locked once editing has begun.
adLockReadOnly (READONLY)	1	Default. Indicates that the data is read-only.

ADO/WFC

The LockTypeEnum enumeration is part of the com.ms.wfc.data package, and the constant values are preceded with AdoEnums.IsolationLevel.

See Also

Connection.WillExecute Event, Recordset.Clone Method, Recordset.LockType Property, Recordset.Open Method

MarshalOptionsEnum Enumeration   (Versions 2.0, 2.1, 2.5, 2.6)

The MarshalOptionsEnum enumeration indicates which records should be returned to the server.

Table E-30. The MarshallOptionsEnum Enumeration

Enumeration (ADO/WFC)	Value	Description
adMarshalAll (ALL)	0	Default. Returns all of the records to the server.
adMarshalModifiedOnly (MODIFIED)	1	Returns only those records that have been modified to the server.

ADO/WFC

The MarshalOptionsEnum enumeration is part of the com.ms.wfc.data package, and the constant values are preceded with AdoEnums.MarshallOptions.

See Also

Recordset.MarshalOptions Property

MoveRecordOptionsEnum Enumeration   (Versions 2.5, 2.6)

The MoveRecordOptionsEnum enumeration indicates the behavior of the MoveRecord method.

Table E-31. The MoveRecordOptionsEnum Enumeration

Enumeration	Value	Description
adMoveAllowEmulation	4	Indicates that the data provider will attempt to simulate the move.
adMoveDontUpdateLinks	2	Indicates that the MoveRecord method will not update the hypertext links.
adMoveOverWrite	1	Indicates that the MoveRecord method will overwrite the destination if it already exists.
adMoveUnspecified	−1 (&HFFFFFFFF)	Default. Indicates that the MoveRecord method will fail if the destination already exists and that all hypertext links will be updated.

ADO/WFC

The MoveRecordOptionsEnum enumeration does not have ADO/WFC constants.

See Also

Record.MoveRecord Method

ObjectStateEnum Enumeration   (Versions 2.0, 2.1, 2.5, 2.6)

The ObjectStateEnum enumeration provides a status of the current object.

Table E-32. The ObjectStateEnum Enumeration

Enumeration (ADO/ WFC)	Value	Description
adStateClosed (CLOSED)	0	Default. Indicates that the current object is closed.
adStateConnecting (CONNECTING)	2	Indicates that the current object is connecting to the data source.
adStateExecuting (EXECUTING)	4	Indicates that the current object is executing a command.
adStateFetching (FETCHING)	8	Indicates that the current object is fetching rows from the data source.
adStateOpen (OPEN)	1	Indicates that the current object is open.

ADO/WFC

The ObjectStateEnum enumeration is part of the com.ms.wfc.data package, and the constant values are preceded with AdoEnums.ObjectState.

See Also

Command.State Property, Connection.State Property, Record.State Property, Recordset.State Property, Stream.State Property

ParameterAttributesEnum Enumeration   (Versions 2.0, 2.1, 2.5, 2.6)

The ParameterAttributesEnum enumeration specifies the attributes of a Parameter object.

Table E-33. The ParameterArgumentsEnum Enumeration

Enumeration (ADO/ WFC)	Value	Description
adParamLong (LONG)	128 (&H80)	Indicates that the current parameter can accept long binary-data values.
adParamNullable (NULLABLE)	64 (&H40)	Indicates that the current parameter can accept Null values.
adParamSigned (SIGNED)	16 (&H10)	Indicates that the current parameter can accept signed values.

ADO/WFC

The ParameterAttributesEnum enumeration is part of the com.ms.wfc.data package, and the constant values are preceded with AdoEnums.ParameterAttributes.

See Also

Parameter.Attributes Property

ParameterDirectionEnum Enumeration   (Versions 2.0, 2.1, 2.5, 2.6)

The ParameterDirectionEnum enumeration indicates whether the parameter receives information, returns information, both receives and returns information, or if it is a return value of a stored procedure.

Table E-34. The ParameterDirectionEnum Enumeration

Enumeration (ADO/WFC)	Value	Description
adParamInput (INPUT)	1	Default. Input parameter only.
adParamInputOutput (INPUTOUTPUT)	3	Both an input and output parameter.
adParamOutput (OUTPUT)	2	Output parameter only.
adParamReturnValue (RETURNVALUE)	4	A return value from a command.
adParamUnknown (UNKNOWN)	0	Unknown parameter type.

ADO/WFC

The ParameterDirectionEnum enumeration is part of the com.ms.wfc.data package, and the constant values are preceded with AdoEnums.ParameterDirection.

See Also

Command.CreateParameter Method, Parameter.Direction Property

PersistFormatEnum Enumeration   (Versions 2.0, 2.1, 2.5, 2.6)

The PersistFormatEnum enumeration indicates in which format a Recordset object will be persisted.

Table E-35. The PersistFormatEnum Enumeration

Enumeration (ADO/WFC)	Value	Description
AdPersistADTG (ADTG)	0	Indicates that the Recordset object will be saved in the Microsoft Advanced Data TableGram (ADTG) format.
AdPersistXML (XML)	1	Indicates that the Recordset object will be saved in the Extensible Markup Language (XML) format.

ADO/WFC

The PersistFormatEnum enumeration is part of the com.ms.wfc.data package, and the constant values are preceded with AdoEnums.PersistFormat.

See Also

Recordset.Save Method

PositionEnum Enumeration

(Versions 2.0, 2.1, 2.5, 2.6)

The PositionEnum enumeration specifies the current position of the record pointer within a Recordset object.

Table E-36. The PositionEnum Enumeration

Enumeration (ADO/WFC)	Value	Description
adPosBOF (BOF)	−2 (&HFFFFFFFE)	Indicates that the record pointer is immediately before the first record in the Recordset object.
adPosEOF (EOF)	−3 (&HFFFFFFFD)	Indicates that the record pointer is immediately after the last record in the Recordset object.
adPosUnknown (UNKNOWN)	−1 (&HFFFFFFFF)	Indicates that the Recordset is empty, the position is unknown, or the data provider cannot determine the current position.

ADO/WFC

The PositionEnum enumeration is part of the com.ms.wfc.data package, and the constant values are preceded with AdoEnums.Position.

See Also

Recordset.AbsolutePage Property, Recordset.AbsolutePosition Property

PropertyAttributesEnum Enumeration

(Versions 2.0, 2.1, 2.5, 2.6)

The PropertyAttributesEnum enumeration specifies the attributes of a Property object.

Table E-37. The PropertyAttributesEnum Enumeration

Enumeration (ADO/WFC)	Value	Description
adPropNotSupported (NOTSUPPORTED)	0	Indicates that the current property is not supported by the data provider.
adPropOptional (OPTIONAL)	2	Indicates that the current property does not have to receive a value before the data source can be initialized.
adPropRead (READ)	512 (&H200)	Indicates that the property can be read.
adPropRequired (REQUIRED)	1	Indicates that the current property must receive a value before the data source can be initialized.
adPropWrite (WRITE)	1024 (&H400)	Indicates that the current property object can be set.

ADO/WFC

The PropertyAttributesEnum enumeration is part of the com.ms.wfc.data package, and the constant values are preceded with AdoEnums.PropertyAttributes.

See Also

Property.Attributes Property

RecordCreateOptionsEnum Enumeration   (Versions 2.5, 2.6)

The RecordCreateOptionsEnum enumeration indicates whether the new record should be created or an existing record should be opened when using the Open method of the Record object.

Table E-38. The RecordCreateOptionsEnum Enumeration

Enumeration	Value	Description
adCreateCollection	8192 (&H2000)	Indicates that a new record is to be created. If one already exists, a runtime error is generated unless if this value is combined with adOpenIfExists or adCreateOverwrite.
adCreateNonCollection	0	Indicates that a simple record (type adSimpleRecord) will be created.
adCreateOverwrite	67108864 (&H4000000)	Indicates that a new record is to be created if one does not already exists, or, if it does exist, that it will be overwritten.
adCreateStructDoc	–2147483648 (&H80000000)	Indicates that a structured document (type adStructDoc) will be created.
adFailIfNotExists	–1 (&HFFFFFFFF)	Default. Indicates that a runtime error will be generated if the record specified does not already exist.
adOpenIfExists	33554432 (&H2000000)	Indicates that the record specified will be opened only if it exists.

ADO/WFC

The RecordCreateOptionsEnum enumeration does not have ADO/WFC constants.

See Also

Record.Open Method

RecordOpenOptionsEnum Enumeration   (Versions 2.5, 2.6)

The RecordOpenOptionsEnum enumeration indicates options for opening a Record object.

Table E-39. The RecordOpenOptionsEnum Enumeration

Enumeration	Value	Description
adDelayFetchFields	32768 (&H8000)	Indicates that the provider need only retrieve the fields when they are accessed, rather than in advance.
adDelayFetchStream	16384 (&H4000)	Indicates that the provider need only retrieve the default stream when it is accessed, rather than in advance.
adOpenAsync	4096 (&1000)	Indicates that the Record object should be opened asynchronously.
adOpenExecuteCommand	65536 (&H10000)	Indicates that the Source field of the Record object contains a command that should be executed.
adOpenOutput	8388608 (&H800000)	Indicates that if the source of the Record object points to an executable script, then the Record object contains the results of the executed script.
adOpenRecordUnspecified	−1 (&HFFFFFFFF)	Default. Indicates that no special options are specified.

ADO/WFC

The RecordOpenOptionsEnum enumeration does not have ADO/WFC constants.

See Also

Record.Open Method

RecordStatusEnum Enumeration   (Versions 2.0, 2.1, 2.6, 2.6)

The RecordStatusEnum enumeration indicates the status of a record within a Recordset object with regards to bulk operations such as batch updates.

Table E-40. The RecordStatusEnum Enumeration

Enumeration (ADO/WFC)	Value	Description
adRecCanceled (CANCELED)	256 (&H100)	Indicates that the record has not been saved because the operation was canceled.
adRecCantRelease (CANTRELEASE)	1024 (&H400)	Indicates that the new record has not been saved because of record locks.

Table E-40. The RecordStatusEnum Enumeration (continued)

Enumeration (ADO/WFC)	Value	Description
adRecConcurrencyViolation (CONCURRENCYVIOLATION)	2048 (&H800)	Indicates that the record has not been saved because optimistic concurrency (the assumption that collisions between data rarely occur, and therefore the row is left unlocked until update or deletion) was in use.
adRecDBDeleted (DBDELETED)	262144 (&H40000)	Indicates that the record has already been deleted from the data source.
adRecDeleted (DELETED)	4	Indicates that the record has been deleted.
adRecIntegrityViolation (INTEGRITYVIOLATION)	4096 (&H1000)	Indicates that the record had not been saved because the user violated integrity constraints.
adRecInvalid (INVALID)	16 (&H10)	Indicates that the bookmark of the record is bad and therefore that record was not saved.
adRecMaxChangesExceeded (MAXCHANGESEXCEEDED)	8192 (&H2000)	Indicates that the record has not been saved because there were too many pending changes.
adRecModified (MODIFIED)	2	Indicates that the record has been modified.
adRecMultipleChanges (MULTIPLECHANGES)	64 (&H40)	Indicates that the record has not been saved because it would have affected multiple records.
adRecNew (NEW)	1	Indicates that the record is new.
adRecObjectOpen (OBJECTOPEN)	16384 (&H4000)	Indicates that the record has not been saved because of a conflict with an open storage object.
adRecOK (OK)	0	Indicates that the record was successfully updated.
adRecOutOfMemory (OUTOFMEMORY)	32768 (&H8000)	Indicates that the record has not been saved because the computer has run out of memory.
adRecPendingChanges (PENDINGCHANGES)	128 (&H80)	Indicates that the record has not been saved because it refers to a pending insert.
adRecPermissionDenied (PERMISSIONDENIED)	65536 (&H10000)	Indicates that the record has not been saved because the user has insufficient permissions.
adRecSchemaViolation (SCHEMAVIOLATION)	131072 (&H20000)	Indicates that the record has not been saved because it violated the structure of its underlying database.
adRecUnmodified (UNMODIFIED)	8	Indicates that the record has not been modified.

ADO/WFC

The RecordStatusEnum enumeration is part of the com.ms.wfc.data package, and the constant values are preceded with AdoEnums.RecordStatus.

See Also

Recordset.Status Property

RecordTypeEnum Enumeration (Versions 2.5, 2.6)

The RecordTypeEnum enumeration indicates the type of the current Record object.

Table E-41. The RecordTypeEnum Enumeration

Enumeration	Value	Description
adCollectionRecord	1	Indicates the current record is a collection (containing child nodes).
adSimpleRecord	0	Indicates the current record is a simple record (not containing child nodes).
adStructDoc	2	Indicates the current record is a COM structured document.

ADO/WFC

The RecordTypeEnum enumeration does not have ADO/WFC constants.

See Also

Record.RecordType Property

ResyncEnum Enumeration (Versions 2.0, 2.1, 2.5, 2.6)

The ResyncEnum enumeration indicates whether underlying data is overwritten and if pending updates are lost when the Resync method is called.

Table E-42. The ResyncEnum Enumeration

Enumeration (ADO/WFC)	Value	Description
adResyncAllValues (ALLVALUES)	2	Default. Indicates that a call to the Resync method overwrites data and cancels pending updates.
adResyncUnderlyingValues (UNDERLYINGVALUES)	1	Indicates that a call to the Resync method does not overwrite data and that pending updates are not canceled.

ADO/WFC

The ResyncEnum enumeration is part of the com.ms.wfc.data package, and the constant values are preceded with AdoEnums.Resync.

See Also

Recordset.Resync Method, Fields.Resync Method

SaveOptionsEnum Enumeration   (Versions 2.1, 2.5, 2.6)

The SaveOptionsEnum enumeration indicates whether a file should be created or over-written when saving a Stream object.

Table E-43. The SaveOptionsEnum Enumeration

Enumeration	Value	Description
adSaveCreateNotExist	1	Default. Indicates that a new file will be created if it does not already exist when using the SaveToFile method.
adSaveCreateOverWrite	2	Indicates that if the file exists, it will be overwritten when using the SaveToFile method.

ADO/WFC

The SaveOptionsEnum enumeration does not have ADO/WFC constants.

See Also

Stream.SaveToFile Method

SchemaEnum Enumeration   (Versions 2.0, 2.1, 2.5, 2.6)

The SchemaEnum enumeration indicates the type of schema information that is returned from the OpenSchema method of the Connection object.

Table E-44. The SchemaEnum Enumeration

Enumeration (ADO/WFC)	Value	Description
adSchemaAsserts (ASSERTS)	0	Returns assertions for a catalog of a user. Constraint columns include: • CONSTRAINT_CATALOG • CONSTRAINT_SCHEMA • CONSTRAINT_NAME
adSchemaCatalogs (CATALOGS)	1	Returns the physical arguments associated with catalogs accessible from the data source. Constraint columns include: • CATALOG_NAME

Table E-44. The SchemaEnum Enumeration (continued)

Enumeration (ADO/WFC)	Value	Description
adSchemaCharacterSets (CHARACTERSETS)	2	Returns the available character sets for a catalog of a user. Constraint columns include: • CHARACTER_SET_CATALOG • CHARACTER_SET_SCHEMA • CHARACTER_SET_NAME
adSchemaCheckConstraints (CHECKCONTRAINTS)	5	Returns the check constraints for a catalog of a user. Constraint columns include: • CONSTRAINT_CATALOG • CONSTRAINT_SCHEMA • CONSTRAINT_NAME
adSchemaCollations (COLLATIONS)	3	Returns the character collations for a catalog of a user. Constraint columns include: • COLLATION_CATALOG • COLLATION_SCHEMA • COLLATION_NAME
adSchemaColumnPrivileges (COLUMNPRIVILEGES)	13	Returns privileges for columns of tables in a catalog of—or granted by—a user. Constraint columns include: • TABLE_CATALOG • TABLE_SCHEMA • TABLE_NAME • COLUMN_NAME • GRANTOR • GRANTEE
adSchemaColumns (COLUMNS)	4	Returns columns of tables and views for a catalog of a user. Constraint columns include: • TABLE_CATALOG • TABLE_SCHEMA • TABLE_NAME • COLUMN_NAME
adSchemaColumnsDomainUsage (COLUMNSDOMAINUSAGE)	11	Returns columns of a catalog dependent on a domain for a catalog for a user. Constraint columns include: • DOMAIN_CATALOG • DOMAIN_SCHEMA • DOMAIN_NAME • COLUMN_NAME

Table E-44. The SchemaEnum Enumeration (continued)

Enumeration (ADO/WFC)	Value	Description
adSchemaConstraintColumnUsage (CONSTRAINTCOLUMNUSAGE)	6	Returns the columns used by referential constraints, unique constraints, check constraints, and assertions for a catalog of a user. Constraint columns include: • TABLE_CATALOG • TABLE_SCHEMA • TABLE_NAME • COLUMN_NAME
adSchemaConstraintTableUsage (CONSTRAINTTABLEUSAGE)	7	Returns the tables that are used by referential constraints, unique constraints, check constraints, and assertions for a catalog of a user. Constraint columns include: • TABLE_CATALOG • TABLE_SCHEMA • TABLE_NAME
adSchemaCubes (CUBES)	32 (&H20)	Returns information about the available cubes in a schema (or catalog for providers that do not support schemas). Constraint columns include: • CATALOG_NAME • SCHEMA_NAME • CUBE_NAME
adSchemaDBInfoKeywords (DBINFOKEYWORDS)	30 (&H1E)	Returns a list of keywords that are specific to the provider. There are no constraint columns for this schema.
adSchemaDBInfoLiterals (DBINFOLITERALS)	31 (&H1F)	Returns a list of literals for text commands that are specific to the provider. There are no constraint columns for this schema.
adSchemaDimensions (DIMENSIONS)	33 (&H21)	Returns one row of information for each dimension of a cube. Constraint columns include: • CATALOG_NAME • SCHEMA_NAME • CUBE_NAME • DIMENSION_NAME • DIMENSION_UNIQUE_NAME

Table E-44. The SchemaEnum Enumeration (continued)

Enumeration (ADO/WFC)	Value	Description
adSchemaForieignKeys (FOREIGNKEYS)	27 (&H1B)	Returns foreign key columns for a catalog of a user. Constraint columns include: • PK_TABLE_CATALOG • PK_TABLE_SCHEMA • PK_TABLE_NAME • FK_TABLE_CATALOG • FK_TABLE_SCHEMA • FK_TABLE_NAME
adSchemaHierarchies (HIERARCHIES)	34 (&H22)	Returns information about the hierarchies available in a dimension. Constraint columns include: • CATALOG_NAME • SCHEMA_NAME • CUBE_NAME • DIMENSION_UNIQUE_NAME • HIERARCHY_NAME • HIERARCHY_UNIQUE_NAME
adSchemaIndexes (INDEXES)	12	Returns the indexes for a catalog of a user. Constraint columns include: • TABLE_CATALOG • TABLE_SCHEMA • INDEX_NAME • TYPE • TABLE_NAME
adSchemaKeyColumnUsage (KEYCOLUMNUSAGE)	8	Returns the columns for a catalog that are constrained as keys for a user. Constraint columns include: • CONSTRAINT_CATALOG • CONSTRAINT_SCHEMA • CONSTRAINT_NAME • TABLE_CATALOG • TABLE_SCHEMA • TABLE_NAME • COLUMN_NAME

Table E-44. The SchemaEnum Enumeration (continued)

Enumeration (ADO/WFC)	Value	Description
adSchemaLevels (LEVELS)	35 (&H23)	Returns the information regarding the levels in a dimension. Constraint columns include: • CATALOG_NAME • SCHEMA_NAME • CUBE_NAME • DIMENSION_UNIQUE_NAME • HIERARCHY_UNIQUE_NAME • LEVEL_NAME • LEVEL_UNIQUE_NAME
adSchemaMeasures (MEASURES)	36 (&H24)	Returns information about the levels available in a dimension. Constraint columns include: • CATALOG_NAME • SCHEMA_NAME • CUBE_NAME • DIMENSION_UNIQUE_NAME • HIERARCHY_UNIQUE_NAME • LEVEL_NAME • LEVEL_UNIQUE_NAME
adSchemaMembers (MEMBERS)	38 (&H26)	Returns information about the available measures. Constraint columns include: • CATALOG_NAME • SCHEMA_NAME • CUBE_NAME • DIMENSION_UNIQUE_NAME • HIERARCHY_UNIQUE_NAME • LEVEL_UNIQUE_NAME • LEVEL_NUMBER • MEMBER_NAME • MEMBER_UNIQUE_NAME • MEMBER_CAPTION • MEMBER_TYPE • An OLAP Tree Operator
adSchemaPrimaryKeys (PRIMARYKEYS)	28 (&H1C)	Returns the primary key columns defined for a catalog of a user. Constraint columns include: • PK_TABLE_CATALOG • PK_TABLE_SCHEMA • PK_TABLE_NAME

Table E-44. The SchemaEnum Enumeration (continued)

Enumeration (ADO/WFC)	Value	Description
adSchemaProcedureColumns (PROCEDURECOLUMNS)	29 (H1D)	Returns information about the columns of rowsets returned by procedures. Constraint columns include: • PROCEDURE_CATALOG • PROCEDURE_SCHEMA • PROCEDURE_NAME • COLUMN_NAME
adSchemaProcedureParameters (PROCEDUREPARAMETERS)	26 (&H1A)	Returns the tables on which viewed tables, for a catalog of a user, are dependent. Constraint columns include: • PROCEDURE_CATALOG • PROCEDURE_SCHEMA • PROCEDURE_NAME • PARAMETER_NAME
adSchemaProcedures (PROCEDURES)	16 (&H10)	Returns the procedures for a catalog owned by a user. Constraint columns include: • PROCEDURE_CATALOG • PROCEDURE_SCHEMA • PROCEDURE_NAME • PROCEDURE_TYPE
adSchemaProperties (PROPERTIES)	37 (&H25)	For each level of the dimension, returns information about the available properties. Constraint columns include: • CATALOG_NAME • SCHEMA_NAME • CUBE_NAME • DIMENSION_UNIQUE_NAME • HIERARCHY_UNIQUE_NAME • LEVEL_UNIQUE_NAME • MEMBER_UNIQUE_NAME • PROPERTY_TYPE • PROPERTY_NAME
adSchemaProviderSpecific (PROVIDERSPECIFIC)	-1 (&HFFFF FFFF)	Used if the data provider has defined its own nonstandard schema queries. Constraint columns are provider specific.
adSchemaProviderTypes (PROVIDERTYPES)	22 (&H16)	Returns the base datatypes supported by the data provider. Constraint columns include: • DATA_TYPE • BEST_MATCH

Table E-44. The SchemaEnum Enumeration (continued)

Enumeration (ADO/WFC)	Value	Description
adSchemaReferentialConstraints (REFERENTIALCONTRAINTS)	9	Returns the referential constraints for a catalog, owned by a user. Constraint columns include: • CONSTRAINT_CATALOG • CONSTRAINT_SCHEMA • CONSTRAINT_NAME
adSchemaSchemata (SCHEMATA)	17 (&H11)	Returns the schemas owned by a user. Constraint columns include: • CATALOG_NAME • SCHEMA_NAME • SCHEMA_OWNER
adSchemaSQLLanguages (SQLLANGUAGES)	18 (&H12)	Returns the conformance levels, options, and dialects supported by the SQL-implementation processing data for a catalog. There are no defined constraint columns for this schema.
adSchemaStatistics (STATISTICS)	19 (&H13)	Returns the statistics defined in the catalog that are owned by a user. Constraint columns include: • TABLE_CATALOG • TABLE_SCHEMA • TABLE_NAME
adSchemaTableConstraints (TABLECONSTRAINTS)	10	Returns the table constraints for a catalog that are owned by a user. Constraint columns include: • CONSTRAINT_CATALOG • CONSTRAINT_SCHEMA • CONSTRAINT_NAME • TABLE_CATALOG • TABLE_SCHEMA • TABLE_NAME • CONSTRAINT_TYPE
adSchemaTablePrivelages (TABLEPRIVILEGES)	14	Returns the privileges on tables for a catalog that are available or granted by a user. Constraint columns include: • TABLE_CATALOG • TABLE_SCHEMA • TABLE_NAME • GRANTOR • GRANTEE

Table E-44. The SchemaEnum Enumeration (continued)

Enumeration (ADO/WFC)	Value	Description
adSchemaTables (TABLES)	20 (&14)	Returns the tables and views for a catalog of a user. Constraint columns include: • TABLE_CATALOG • TABLE_SCHEMA • TABLE_NAME • TABLE_TYPE
adSchemaTranslations (TRANSLATIONS)	21 (&15)	Returns the character translations defined for a catalog of a user. Constraint columns include: • TRANSLATION_CATALOG • TRANSLATION_SCHEMA • TRANSLATION_NAME
adSchemaTrustees (TRUSTEES)	39 (&H27)	Returns information about trustees. There are no defined constraint columns for this schema.
adSchemaUsagePrivileges (USAGEPRIVILEGES)	15	Returns the usage privileges on objects for a catalog that are available or granted by a user. Constraint columns include: • OBJECT_CATALOG • OBJECT_SCHEMA • OBJECT_NAME • OBJECT_TYPE • GRANTOR • GRANTEE
adSchemaViewColumnUsage (VIEWCOLUMNUSAGE)	24 (&H18)	Returns the columns on which viewed tables, for a catalog and owned by a user, are dependent. Constraint columns include: • VIEW_CATALOG • VIEW_SCHEMA • VIEW_NAME
adSchemaViews (VIEWS)	23 (&H17)	Returns the views for a catalog of a user. Constraint columns include: • TABLE_CATALOG • TABLE_SCHEMA • TABLE_NAME

Table E-44. The SchemaEnum Enumeration (continued)

Enumeration (ADO/WFC)	Value	Description
adSchemaViewTableUsage (VIEWTABLEUSAGE)	25 (&H19)	Returns the tables on which viewed tables—for a catalog and owned by a user—are dependent. Constraint columns include: • VIEW_CATALOG • VIEW_SCHEMA • VIEW_NAME
adSchemaPrimaryKeys (PRIMARYKEYS)	28 (&H1C)	Returns the primary key columns defined for a catalog of a user. Constraint columns include: • PK_TABLE_CATALOG • PK_TABLE_SCHEMA • PK_TABLE_NAME

ADO/WFC

The SchemaEnum enumeration is part of the com.ms.wfc.data package, and the constant values are preceded with AdoEnums.Schema.

See Also

Connection.OpenSchema Method

SearchDirectionEnum Enumeration   (Versions 2.0, 2.1, 2.5, 2.6)

The SearchDirectionEnum enumeration indicates in which direction the Find method of the Recordset object is to look.

Table E-45. The SearchDirectionEnum Enumeration

Enumeration (ADO/WFC)	Value	Description
adSearchBackward (BACKWARD)	-1 (&HFFFFFFFF)	Indicates that the Find method will search backwards until either a match is found or the BOF marker is reached.
adSearchForward (FORWARD)	1	Indicates that the Find method will search forward until either a match is found or the EOF marker is reached.

ADO/WFC

The SearchDirectionEnum enumeration is part of the com.ms.wfc.data package, and the constant values are preceded with AdoEnums.SearchDirection.

See Also

Recordset.Find Method

SeekEnum Enumeration

(Versions 2.1, 2.5, 2.6)

The SeekEnum enumeration indicates the type of Seek to perform.

Table E-46. The SeekEnum Enumeration

Enumeration (ADO/WFC)	Value	Description
adSeekAfter (AFTER)	8	Indicates that the Seek will occur just after where a match with KeyValues would have occurred.
adSeekAfterEQ (AFTEREQ)	4	Indicates that the Seek will occur where a key equals KeyValues or just after where a match would have occurred.
adSeekBefore (BEFORE)	32 (&H20)	Indicates that the Seek will occur just before where a match with KeyValues would have occurred.
adSeekBeforeEQ (BEFOREEQ)	16 (&H10)	Indicates that the Seek will occur where a key equals KeyValues or just before where a match would have occurred.
adSeekFirstEQ (FIRSTEQ)	1	Indicates that the Seek will occur to the first key equal to KeyValues.
adSeekLastEQ (LASTEQ)	2	Indicates that the Seek will occur to the last key equal to KeyValues.

ADO/WFC

The SeekEnum enumeration is part of the com.ms.wfc.data package, and the constant values are preceded with AdoEnums.Seek.

See Also

Recordset.Seek Method

StreamOpenOptionsEnum Enumeration

(Versions 2.5, 2.6)

The StreamOpenOptionsEnum enumeration specifies options for opening a Stream object.

Table E-47. The StreamOpenOptionsEnum Enumeration

Enumeration	Value	Description
adOpenStreamAsync	1	Indicates that the Stream will be opened asynchronously.
adOpenStreamFromRecord	4	Indicates that the contents of the Source parameter to the Open method contain an already open Record object.
adOpenStreamUnspecified	-1 (&HFFFFFFFF)	Default. Indicates that no special options are selected.

ADO/WFC

The StreamOpenOptionsEnum enumeration does not have ADO/WFC constants.

See Also

Stream.Open Method

StreamReadEnum Enumeration   (Versions 2.5, 2.6)

The StreamReadEnum enumeration indicates whether one line or the entire Stream should be read.

Table E-48. The StreamReadEnum Enumeration

Enumeration	Value	Description
adReadAll	-1 (&HFFFFFFFF)	Default. Indicates that the entire Stream is to be read.
adReadLine	-2 (&HFFFFFFFE)	Indicates that the next line is to be read in from the Stream.

ADO/WFC

The StreamReadEnum enumeration does not have ADO/WFC constants.

See Also

Stream.Read Method, Stream.ReadText Method

StreamTypeEnum Enumeration   (Versions 2.5, 2.6)

The StreamTypeEnum enumeration indicates what type of data is stored in a Stream object.

Table E-49. The StreamTypeEnum Enumeration

Enumeration	Value	Description
adTypeBinary	1	Indicates that the Stream contains binary data.
adTypeText	2	Indicates that the Stream contains textual data.

ADO/WFC

The StreamTypeEnum enumeration does not have ADO/WFC constants.

See Also

Stream.Type Property

StreamWriteEnum Enumeration (Versions 2.5, 2.6)

The StreamWriteEnum enumeration indicates whether a line separator is appending to a String written to a Stream object.

Table E-50. The StreamWriteEnum Enumeration

Enumeration	Value	Description
adWriteChar	0	Default. Indicates that the specified text string is written to the Stream object.
adWriteLine	1	Indicates that the specified text string followed by a line separator will be written to the Stream object.

ADO/WFC

The StreamWriteEnum enumeration does not have ADO/WFC constants.

See Also

Stream.WriteText Method

StringFormatEnum Enumeration (Versions 2.0, 2.1, 2.5, 2.6)

The StringFormatEnum enumeration indicates the format of a recordset when retrieving it as a string value.

Table E-51. The StringFormatEnum Enumeration

Enumeration (ADO/WFC)	Value	Description
adClipString (CLIPSTRING)	2	Indicates that when importing a Recordset as a String value, rows are delimited by RowDelimiter, columns by Column-Delimiter, and NULL value by NullExpr.

ADO/WFC

The StringFormatEnum enumeration is part of the com.ms.wfc.data package, and the constant values are preceded with AdoEnums.StringFormat.

See Also

Recordset.GetString Method

XactAttributeEnum Enumeration   (Versions 2.0, 2.1, 2.5, 2.6)

The XactAttributeEnum enumeration indicates the transaction attributes of a Connection object.

Table E-52. The XactAttributeEnum Enumeration

Enumeration (ADO/WFC)	Value	Description
adXactAbortRetaining (ABORTRETAINING)	262144 (&H40000)	Indicates that by calling the RollbackTrans method, ADO will start a new transaction automatically.
adXactCommitRetaining (COMMITRETAINING)	131072 (&H20000)	Indicates that by calling the CommitTrans method, ADO will start a new transaction automatically.

ADO/WFC

The XactAttributeEnum enumeration is part of the com.ms.wfc.data package, and the constant values are preceded with AdoEnums.IsolationLevel.

See Also

Connection.Attributes Property

Index

We'd like to hear your suggestions for improving our indexes. Send email to *index@oreilly.com.*

About the Author

Jason T. Roff is the author of three database-development books, including *ADO: ActiveX Data Objects*. He specializes in Visual Basic, ASP, and SQL Server development and architecture, and has experience working with C++ and Assembly on everything ranging from a Commodore to a Unix box. Jason graduated from the University of Albany with a degree in computer science with applied mathematics. Currently, he manages local and offsite development teams to create web- and Windows-based applications.

Colophon

Our look is the result of reader comments, our own experimentation, and feedback from distribution channels. Distinctive covers complement our distinctive approach to technical topics, breathing personality and life into potentially dry subjects.

The bird on the cover of *ADO: ActiveX Data Objects* is an ivory-billed woodpecker (*Campephilus principalis*). Considered extinct by many naturalists and ornithologists (the last confirmed sighting was in the 1950s), the "ivory-bill" was never abundant in its habitat, the southeastern United States and Cuba. With glossy black plumage, white markings, and a red tufted crest (males only), the ivory-bill looks extremely similar to the pileated woodpecker, with whom it also shared its habitat. The similarities between the two birds has been the cause of much trouble, as eager amateurs add to unconfirmed sighting reports of the ivory-bill when they have probably spotted the pileated woodpecker. This is especially troublesome for naturalists who hold out hope that the ivory-bill may still exist in the far reaches of Louisiana forests or in Cuba. In the early 1990s, many nature and birding groups spent considerable amounts of money mounting search efforts for the ivory-bill.

As do all woodpeckers, the ivory-bill has a chisel-like bill and a long, hard-tipped, sticky tongue; the first for drilling and scaling bark, the latter for retrieving beetles and grubs on which to feed. Retrieving food in this manner, however, is not what creates the drumming sound that many associate with woodpeckers. Rather, woodpeckers drum when reinforcing their claim to a territory, creating the loudest drum possible by striking the tops of dead, hollow trees.

Important differences between the closely linked ivory-billed and pileated woodpeckers include their bills (the ivory-bill's was, well, ivory, while the pileated woodpecker's bill is gray), their sizes (the ivory-bill was the largest of all North

American woodpeckers), and their calls (the ivory-bill's was a "toot"; the pileated's is a "kuk"). In 1987, Dr. Jerome A. Jackson of Florida Gulf University caught the ivory-bill's distinctive call on eighteen minutes of tape in Louisiana, adding to the excitement created by various unconfirmed sightings. The most recent and credulous sighting occurred in 1999, when graduate student David Kulivan sighted a pair of what were supposedly ivory-bills in southeastern Louisiana.

While The Nature Conservancy declared the ivory-bill extinct in 1994, the U.S. Fish and Wildlife Service has not yet added it to its extinction list. The reason for its near or possible extinction: logging of the old-growth forests in which it lived.

Jeffrey Holcomb and Sarah Jane Shangraw were the production editors for *ADO: ActiveX Data Objects*. Jeffrey Holcomb copyedited the text. Linley Dolby, Matt Hutchinson, and Claire Cloutier provided quality control. Pamela Murray, Sarah Jane Shangraw, and Joe Wizda wrote the index. Sarah Jane Shangraw did page composition.

Hanna Dyer designed the cover of this book, based on a series design by Edie Freedman. The cover image is a 19th-century engraving from the Dover Pictorial Archive. Erica Corwell produced the cover layout with QuarkXPress 4.1 using Adobe's ITC Garamond font.

Melanie Wang designed the interior layout based on a series design by Nancy Priest. Anne-Marie Vaduva converted the files from Microsoft Word to FrameMaker 5.5.6 using tools created by Mike Sierra. The text and heading fonts are ITC Garamond Light and Garamond Book; the code font is Constant Willison. The illustrations that appear in the book were produced by Robert Romano and Jessamyn Read using Macromedia FreeHand 9 and Adobe Photoshop 6. This colophon was written by Jeffrey Holcomb.

Whenever possible, our books use a durable and flexible lay-flat binding. If the page count exceeds this binding's limit, perfect binding is used.

More Titles from O'Reilly

In a Nutshell Quick References

VB & VBA in a Nutshell: The Language

By Paul Lomax
1st Edition October 1998
656 pages, ISBN 1-56592-358-8

For Visual Basic and VBA programmers, this book boils down the essentials of the VB and VBA languages into a single volume, including undocumented and little documented areas essential to everyday programming. The convenient alphabetical reference to all functions, procedures, statements, and keywords allows VB and VBA programmers to use this book both as a standard reference guide to the language and as a tool for troubleshooting and identifying programming problems.

Windows 2000 Administration in a Nutshell

By Mitch Tulloch
1st Edition February 2001
798 pages, ISBN 1-56592-713-3

Anyone who installs Windows 2000, creates a user, or adds a printer is a 2000 system administrator. This book covers all the important day-to-day administrative tasks, and includes the tools for performing each task in an alphabetical reference for easy look-up. What's the same and what's different between Windows 2000 and Windows NT? Has the GUI or the networking architecture changed, and if so, how? This book will help you bridge the gap between Windows NT and Windows 2000.

Web Design in a Nutshell

By Jennifer Niederst
1st Edition November 1998
580 pages, ISBN 1-56592-515-7

Web Design in a Nutshell contains the nitty-gritty on everything you need to know to design Web pages. Written by veteran Web designer Jennifer Niederst, this book provides quick access to the wide range of technologies and techniques from which Web designers and authors must draw. Topics include understanding the Web environment, HTML, graphics, multimedia and interactivity, and emerging technologies.

VBScript in a Nutshell

By Paul Lomax, Matt Childs, & Ron Petrusha
1st Edition May 2000
508 pages, ISBN 1-56592-720-6

Whether you're using VBScript to create client-side scripts, ASP applications, WSH scripts, or programmable Outlook forms, *VBScript in a Nutshell* is the only book you'll need by your side – a complete and easy-to-use language reference.

MCSD in a Nutshell: The Visual Basic Exams

By James Foxall, MCSD
1st Edition October 2000
632 pages, ISBN 1-56592-752-4

Programmers tend to be specialists – they often do the same kind of programming over and over. The MCSD exam is targeted at technical generalists – developers familiar with a broad array of Microsoft technologies and development approaches. With its comprehensive overview of core technology areas, *MCSD in a Nutshell* is the perfect study guide and resource to help developers master the technologies that are less familiar to them.

Visual Basic Controls in a Nutshell

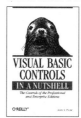

By Evan S. Dictor
1st Edition July 1999
762 pages, ISBN 1-56592-294-8

This quick reference covers one of the crucial elements of Visual Basic: its controls, and their numerous properties, events, and methods. It provides a step-by-step list of procedures for using each major control and contains a detailed reference to all properties, methods, and events. Written by an experienced Visual Basic programmer, it helps to make painless what can sometimes be an arduous job of programming Visual Basic.

O'REILLY®

TO ORDER: **800-998-9938** • *order@oreilly.com* • *http://www.oreilly.com/*
OUR PRODUCTS ARE AVAILABLE AT A BOOKSTORE OR SOFTWARE STORE NEAR YOU.
FOR INFORMATION: **800-998-9938** • **707-829-0515** • *info@oreilly.com*

Visual Basic Programming

Visual Basic Shell Programming

By J. P. Hamilton
1st Edition July 2000
392 pages, ISBN 1-56592-670-6

Visual Basic Shell Programming ventures where none have gone before by showing how to develop shell extensions that more closely integrate an application with the Windows shell, while at the same time providing an advanced tutorial-style treatment of COM programming with Visual Basic. Each major type of shell extension gets attention, including customized context menu handlers, per instance icons, and customized property sheets.

Access Database Design & Programming, 2nd Edition

By Steven Roman
2nd Edition July 1999
432 pages, ISBN 1-56592-626-9

This second edition of the bestselling *Access Database Design & Programming* covers Access' new VBA Integrated Development Environment used by Word, Excel, and PowerPoint; the VBA language itself; Microsoft's latest data access technology, Active Data Objects (ADO); plus Open Database Connectivity (ODBC).

Writing Word Macros

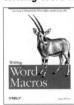

By Steven Roman
2nd Edition October 1999
410 pages, ISBN 1-56592-725-7

This no-nonsense book delves into VBA programming and tells how you can use VBA to automate all the tedious, repetitive jobs you never thought you could do in Microsoft Word. It takes the reader step-by-step through writing VBA macros and programs.

COM+ Programming with Visual Basic

By Jose Mojica
1st Edition June 2001
364 pages, ISBN 1-56592-840-7

There's simply no other documentation available for much of what's in *COM+ Programming with Visual Basic*; this book draws from the author's wide experience as a COM+ developer and instructor. The first part delivers information that's indispensable for creating robust, efficient, high-performance COM+ applications. The second focuses on incorporating individual COM+ services, like transaction support, security, and asynchronous operations, into applications.

Win32 API Programming with Visual Basic

By Steve Roman
1st Edition November 1999
534 pages, Includes CD-ROM
ISBN 1-56592-631-5

This book provides the missing documentation for VB programmers who want to harness the power of accessing the Win32 API within Visual Basic. It shows how to create powerful and unique applications without needing a background in Visual C++ or Win32 API programming.

CDO & MAPI Programming with Visual Basic

By Dave Grundgeiger
1st Edition October 2000
384 pages, ISBN 1-56592-665-X

CDO and MAPI Programming with Visual Basic dives deep into Microsoft's Collaboration Data Objects (CDO) and the Messaging Application Programming Interface (MAPI), then moves into succinct explanations of the types of useful messaging applications that can be written in Visual Basic.

Visual Basic Programming

ASP in a Nutshell, 2nd Edition

By A. Keyton Weissinger
2nd Edition July 2000
492 pages, ISBN 1-56592-843-1

ASP in a Nutshell, 2nd Edition, provides
the high-quality reference documentation
that web application developers really need
to create effective Active Server Pages. It
focuses on how features are used in a real
application and highlights little-known or
undocumented features.

Developing ASP Components, 2nd Edition

By Shelley Powers
2nd Edition March 2001
832 pages, ISBN 1-56592-750-8

Microsoft's Active Server Pages
(ASP) continue to grow in popularity
with web developers – especially as web
applications replace web pages. *Developing
ASP Components, 2nd Edition*, provides
developers with the information and real
world examples they need to create custom ASP components.

Subclassing & Hooking with Visual Basic

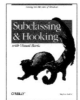

By Stephen Teilbet
1st Edition June 2001
704 pages, ISBN 0-596-00118-5

Subclassing and the Windows hooking
mechanism ("hooks") allow developers
to manipulate, modify, or even discard
messages bound for other objects within the
operating system, in the process changing the
way in which the system behaves. This book
opens up a wealth of possibilities to the Visual Basic developer –
possibilities that ordinarily are completely unavailable, or at least
not easy to implement.

How to stay in touch with O'Reilly

1. Visit Our Award-Winning Web Site

http://www.oreilly.com/

★ "Top 100 Sites on the Web" —*PC Magazine*
★ "Top 5% Web sites" —*Point Communications*
★ "3-Star site" —*The McKinley Group*

Our web site contains a library of comprehensive product information (including book excerpts and tables of contents), downloadable software, background articles, interviews with technology leaders, links to relevant sites, book cover art, and more. File us in your Bookmarks or Hotlist!

2. Join Our Email Mailing Lists

New Product Releases
To receive automatic email with brief descriptions of all new O'Reilly products as they are released, send email to:
ora-news-subscribe@lists.oreilly.com
Put the following information in the first line of your message (*not* in the Subject field):
subscribe ora-news

O'Reilly Events
If you'd also like us to send information about trade show events, special promotions, and other O'Reilly events, send email to:
ora-news-subscribe@lists.oreilly.com
Put the following information in the first line of your message (*not* in the Subject field):
subscribe ora-events

3. Get Examples from Our Books via FTP

There are two ways to access an archive of example files from our books:

Regular FTP
- ftp to:
  ftp.oreilly.com
  (login: anonymous
  password: your email address)
- Point your web browser to:
  ftp://ftp.oreilly.com/

FTPMAIL
- Send an email message to:
  ftpmail@online.oreilly.com
  (Write "help" in the message body)

4. Contact Us via Email

order@oreilly.com
To place a book or software order online. Good for North American and international customers.

subscriptions@oreilly.com
To place an order for any of our newsletters or periodicals.

books@oreilly.com
General questions about any of our books.

software@oreilly.com
For general questions and product information about our software. Check out O'Reilly Software Online at **http://software.oreilly.com/** for software and technical support information. Registered O'Reilly software users send your questions to: **website-support@oreilly.com**

cs@oreilly.com
For answers to problems regarding your order or our products.

booktech@oreilly.com
For book content technical questions or corrections.

proposals@oreilly.com
To submit new book or software proposals to our editors and product managers.

international@oreilly.com
For information about our international distributors or translation queries. For a list of our distributors outside of North America check out:
http://www.oreilly.com/distributors.html

5. Work with Us

Check out our website for current employment opportunites:
http://jobs.oreilly.com/

O'Reilly & Associates, Inc.
101 Morris Street, Sebastopol, CA 95472 USA
TEL   707-829-0515 or 800-998-9938
          (6am to 5pm PST)
FAX   707-829-0104

Titles from O'Reilly

International Distributors

http://international.oreilly.com/distributors.html

UK, EUROPE, MIDDLE EAST AND AFRICA (EXCEPT FRANCE, GERMANY, AUSTRIA, SWITZERLAND, LUXEMBOURG, AND LIECHTENSTEIN)

INQUIRIES

O'Reilly UK Limited
4 Castle Street
Farnham
Surrey, GU9 7HS
United Kingdom
Telephone: 44-1252-711776
Fax: 44-1252-734211
Email: information@oreilly.co.uk

ORDERS

Wiley Distribution Services Ltd.
1 Oldlands Way
Bognor Regis
West Sussex PO22 9SA
United Kingdom
Telephone: 44-1243-843294
UK Freephone: 0800-243207
Fax: 44-1243-843302 (Europe/EU orders)
or 44-1243-843274 (Middle East/Africa)
Email: cs-books@wiley.co.uk

FRANCE

INQUIRIES & ORDERS

Éditions O'Reilly
18 rue Séguier
75006 Paris, France
Tel: 1-40-51-71-89
Fax: 1-40-51-72-26
Email: france@oreilly.fr

GERMANY, SWITZERLAND, AUSTRIA, LUXEMBOURG, AND LIECHTENSTEIN

INQUIRIES & ORDERS

O'Reilly Verlag
Balthasarstr. 81
D-50670 Köln, Germany
Telephone: 49-221-973160-91
Fax: 49-221-973160-8
Email: anfragen@oreilly.de (inquiries)
Email: order@oreilly.de (orders)

CANADA (FRENCH LANGUAGE BOOKS)

Les Éditions Flammarion ltée
375, Avenue Laurier Ouest
Montréal (Québec) H2V 2K3
Tel: 00-1-514-277-8807
Fax: 00-1-514-278-2085
Email: info@flammarion.qc.ca

HONG KONG

City Discount Subscription Service, Ltd.
Unit A, 6th Floor, Yan's Tower
27 Wong Chuk Hang Road
Aberdeen, Hong Kong
Tel: 852-2580-3539
Fax: 852-2580-6463
Email: citydis@ppn.com.hk

KOREA

Hanbit Media, Inc.
Chungmu Bldg. 210
Yonnam-dong 568-33
Mapo-gu
Seoul, Korea
Tel: 822-325-0397
Fax: 822-325-9697
Email: hant93@chollian.dacom.co.kr

PHILIPPINES

Global Publishing
G/F Benavides Garden
1186 Benavides Street
Manila, Philippines
Tel: 632-254-8949/632-252-2582
Fax: 632-734-5060/632-252-2733
Email: globalp@pacific.net.ph

TAIWAN

O'Reilly Taiwan
1st Floor, No. 21, Lane 295
Section 1, Fu-Shing South Road
Taipei, 106 Taiwan
Tel: 886-2-27099669
Fax: 886-2-27038802
Email: mori@oreilly.com

INDIA

Shroff Publishers & Distributors Pvt. Ltd.
12, "Roseland", 2nd Floor
180, Waterfield Road, Bandra (West)
Mumbai 400 050
Tel: 91-22-641-1800/643-9910
Fax: 91-22-643-2422
Email: spd@vsnl.com

CHINA

O'Reilly Beijing
SIGMA Building, Suite B809
No. 49 Zhichun Road
Haidian District
Beijing, China PR 100080
Tel: 86-10-8809-7475
Fax: 86-10-8809-7463
Email: beijing@oreilly.com

JAPAN

O'Reilly Japan, Inc.
Yotsuya Y's Building
7 Banch 6, Honshio-cho
Shinjuku-ku
Tokyo 160-0003 Japan
Tel: 81-3-3356-5227
Fax: 81-3-3356-5261
Email: japan@oreilly.com

SINGAPORE, INDONESIA, MALAYSIA AND THAILAND

TransQuest Publishers Pte Ltd
30 Old Toh Tuck Road #05-02
Sembawang Kimtrans Logistics Centre
Singapore 597654
Tel: 65-4623112
Fax: 65-4625761
Email: wendiw@transquest.com.sg

ALL OTHER ASIAN COUNTRIES

O'Reilly & Associates, Inc.
101 Morris Street
Sebastopol, CA 95472 USA
Tel: 707-829-0515
Fax: 707-829-0104
Email: order@oreilly.com

AUSTRALIA

Woodslane Pty., Ltd.
7/5 Vuko Place
Warriewood NSW 2102
Australia
Tel: 61-2-9970-5111
Fax: 61-2-9970-5002
Email: info@woodslane.com.au

NEW ZEALAND

Woodslane New Zealand, Ltd.
21 Cooks Street (P.O. Box 575)
Waganui, New Zealand
Tel: 64-6-347-6543
Fax: 64-6-345-4840
Email: info@woodslane.com.au

ARGENTINA

Distribuidora Cuspide
Suipacha 764
1008 Buenos Aires
Argentina
Phone: 5411-4322-8868
Fax: 5411-4322-3456
Email: libros@cuspide.com

O'REILLY®

TO ORDER: **800-998-9938** • **order@oreilly.com** • **http://www.oreilly.com/**
OUR PRODUCTS ARE AVAILABLE AT A BOOKSTORE OR SOFTWARE STORE NEAR YOU.
FOR INFORMATION: **800-998-9938** • **707-829-0515** • **info@oreilly.com**